AF607968

POETRY ON STAGE: THE THEATRE OF THE ITALIAN NEO-AVANT-GARDE

UNIVERSITY OF TORONTO PRESS
Toronto Buffalo London

Toronto Buffalo London
utorontopress.com

ISBN 978-1-4875-0666-7 (cloth)
ISBN 978-1-4875-3463-9 (EPUB)
ISBN 978-1-4875-3461-5 (PDF)

Toronto Italian Studies

Library and Archives Canada Cataloguing in Publication

Title: Poetry on stage: The theatre of the Italian neo-avant-garde / Gianluca Rizzo.
Names: Rizzo, Gianluca, author.
Description: Includes bibliographical references and index.
Identifiers: Canadiana (print) 20200207997 | Canadiana (ebook) 20200208004 | ISBN 9781487506667 (hardcover) | ISBN 9781487534639 (EPUB) | ISBN 9781487534615 (PDF)
Subjects: LCSH: Experimental drama, Italian – History and criticism. | LCSH: Italian drama – 20th Century – History and criticism.
Classification: LCC PQ4145.R59 2020 | DDC 852/.9140911–dc23

This book has been published with the assistance of Colby College.

University of Toronto Press acknowledges the financial assistance to its publishing program of the Canada Council for the Arts and the Ontario Arts Council, an agency of the Government of Ontario.

Funded by the Government of Canada | Financé par le gouvernement du Canada | Canada

Contents

Acknowledgments

I have been working on this book, in one way or another, for over a decade. The journey began with a phone call by friend and mentor Prof. Luigi Ballerini, who said, "Why don't you go visit Elio and Cetta Pagliarani in Rome, look through their papers: Elio's plays have never been collected and it is time someone did it." The trip opened my eyes to a research topic that has occupied my professional life for many years. Needless to say, I am very grateful for Luigi's relentless guidance and Elio and Cetta's warm hospitality.

Many individuals and institutions have supported my efforts. I would like to acknowledge the Centro Manoscritti at the Università di Pavia, its director and staff, and in particular Dr Nicoletta Trotta for aiding my research over multiple visits. The Istituto per il Teatro e il Melodramma of the Fondazione Cini in Venice preserves the library of Luigi Squarzina, whose holdings were crucial in advancing my work. The Office of the Provost and Dean of Faculty at Colby College and the Humanities Division have shown me continued and generous support in the form of research fellowships and grants that have allowed me to travel through Italy, speak to some of the protagonists of the events reconstructed here, and collect precious materials. The publication of this volume has been in part funded by the Office of the Provost and Dean of Faculty.

Among the colleagues and friends who have cheered me on through this long journey, I would like to acknowledge especially Beppe Cavatorta and Federica Santini, who have proved to be the ideal support group: they listened, encouraged, prodded, and consoled, depending on the moods and circumstances; I feel very fortunate to have them as my partners and travelling companions during our many intellectual adventures. I am also grateful to Stefano Colangelo, for the many conversations regarding poetry and its practitioners, and all the good suggestions he has given me over the years. Federico Milone has been an exceptional guide to Alfredo Giuliani's papers, and I thank him for sharing with me some of his wonderful discoveries. Dominic Siracusa has spent countless hours poring over the manuscript: I don't think I would have finished writing it if it hadn't been for his selfless, unremitting resolve to straighten my crooked English. I am also grateful to Rainer J. Hanshe, who helped me prepare the manuscript for submission. Valentina Valentini, Pippo Di Marca, Giuliano Scabia, and the late Nanni Balestrini, the four interviewees who agreed to meet and speak with me on several occasions, and who so graciously donated their time, also deserve a special mention: their words, memories, and insights have lent vitality to my topic.

Finally, I would like to thank my family in Italy and here in the United States, and in particular Sophie Park, my wife, for being the one fixed star by which I steer my course.

Note on Terminology

In this volume, I often use the terms *Neoavanguardia*, "neo-avant-garde," Gruppo 63, *Novissimi*, "experimental poetry," *poesia di ricerca* (research poetry), *poesia sperimentale* (experimental poetry), etcetera, almost interchangeably. Clearly, they are not: each one of them carries distinct implications and can be employed to highlight important distinctions in the chronology, aesthetics, and poetics of the complex history of Italian literature in the second half of the twentieth century. I have conflated all of them because the subject matter treated herein is immense, and because at this first level of generality the distinctions between the aforementioned terms are not relevant. I look forward to a time when the preparatory work on the role played by theatre in the evolution of the aesthetic thinking of the Neoavanguardia will be completed and we can begin to discuss how different components (the various currents and groups within the movement) have implemented different strategies in using theatre to reimagine literature. Until then, the advantages offered for the ease of writing and reading by the availability of so many terms seem to me to outnumber the potential misunderstandings they might generate.

POETRY ON STAGE: THE THEATRE OF THE ITALIAN NEO-AVANT-GARDE

Introduction

An Anecdote

I began researching this book in the summer of 2007, when I visited Elio Pagliarani and Cetta Petrollo. The plan was to go through Pagliarani's archive looking for plays (some of which had already been published) and collect all of them (including those that had never left his desk) in a single volume.[1] I spent a week with Pagliarani and Petrollo, between their places in Rome and Bocchignano, and by the end of my stay we had developed a harmonious routine, which included the morning ceremony of newspapers. After breakfast, we would walk to the newsstand to buy the national ones, which we would read for an hour or so, passing them between us; then, before I got to work on the archive, we would chat a bit. Pagliarani would encourage me to ask him questions; something that, I later learned, was absolutely unprecedented for this inveterate curmudgeon. It was during one of these discussions that I brought up the subject of the Second World War: I wanted to know how it had affected him and his family. He told me a couple of anecdotes that are now included in his memoir, *Pro-memoria a Liarosa*.[2] Then I asked him about Giovanna Bemporad: I had just read a few letters the two had exchanged, and I was curious about their relationship over the years. Pagliarani answered with a long story, which involved himself, Bemporad, the Germans, Venice, and poetry – a story that didn't make it into his memoir[3] and that I would like to recount here, because it says something about the connection between poetry and life, and how theatre (or live performance) has something to do with the continuation of both. Were we to exaggerate a bit, we could consider it a sort of origin myth for the journey on which we are about to embark with this book, almost a cosmogony (although I am sure Pagliarani would not have approved of such a pretentious preamble to his tale, as he was always suspicious of any form of abstraction and all vague mysticisms).

It was the spring of 1945, in May, and Pagliarani decided to enrol in the University of Padua, in the Facoltà of Political Science. The railway between Rimini and Padua had been destroyed during a bombing, but the trains were still running between Venice and Padua. Pagliarani managed to get a ride in a car going to Venice; then he would take the train to Padua. On the way there, the car was stopped countless times at roadblocks set up by the Allied forces and by the Partisan brigades. As a result, it was almost dark by the time they reached Venice: the next train to Padua would not leave till the following day. Stranded in Venice, and not knowing what to do with himself, Pagliarani went looking for a café and ran into Giovanna Bemporad. The two hadn't seen each other in a while and started chatting. First, they sat down at one of the café tables, but then closing time came and they had to leave. Because of the curfew, they couldn't leave through the front door: they climbed a wall and disappeared into the night, walking the back alleys until they finally reached the Lido, the beach. Bemporad, (here Pagliarani paused) had a prodigious memory for verse: she knew the classics by heart, and she could recite them in a few different languages. Deep in conversation, the two came upon an Italian patrol; they were in violation of curfew, and they were taken to the local police station, so that they could be identified and cleared. The process took the rest of the night, and the two found themselves once again free and on the streets early the next morning. They decided to go back to a café in Piazza St Lucia, to regroup and wait for the first train to Padua. There, Giovanna Bemporad told Pagliarani this was not the first time she had been caught by a patrol while out at night, after curfew. A few weeks earlier, under German occupation, she was taking a stroll, alone, when she ran into a German patrol. They arrested her. She was in real trouble: the penalty for breaking curfew was summary execution. They had another man with them, whom they had just caught. They took the two of them to a secluded side street, and they tied the man to a pole. A firing squad was formed and the man was shot dead. They removed the corpse, took Giovanna by the arm, and tied her to the same pole: she was going to be executed. Pagliarani paused to check my reaction. I must have looked rapt enough, and he immediately continued, with that scruffy voice of his. "Here," he said, "is where she had a stroke of genius: she began declaiming Goethe, in German. The soldiers were taken aback, they started looking around and at each other: none of them had the courage to shoot that young woman, who was declaiming poetry they could understand, in their own language. The leader of the patrol untied her, and they let her go." This was the end of the story. Pagliarani looked at me in search of a reaction and, for once, I knew exactly what to say, or, at least, I thought I did: "So, Elio, poetry really saves lives!" He shook his head a bit and, with an extra scruffy voice, as if he was reading one of his verses, exclaimed, "Poetry *in German* saves lives!"

For a number of years, I told this story at the beginning of my "Introduction to Poetry" classes. I find it to be very rich and productive, symbolic of a number of things, a great teaching tool. It was also a fine piece of storytelling, especially given the tale within the tale, Bemporad recounting the previous incident like a Scheherazade who had escaped her fate, and the perfect rhyme between the two sets of events, the first and second captures in the dead of night. Here, in the context of this volume, I think we could look at this anecdote as a way of showing, via hyperbole, how the performance of poetry, in certain situations, can be and has been a matter of life and death. And this, I have come to realize after studying these issues for more than a decade, happens more often than one would think.

A Few Preliminary Considerations

The best way to begin this journey is, perhaps, by acknowledging the complexity of the task at hand: I intend to approach the variegated galaxy of the Neoavanguardia from the unusual perspective of focusing on their theatre work. I will argue that the theatre was the physical and ideal place many writers used as an incubator for their stylistic and linguistic experiments, a means through which they could establish direct contact with their audience and verify the solutions they were devising to the many practical and theoretical problems raised by their stances in politics and poetics.

Not many attempts have been made in this direction over the years, and perhaps for good reason: the sheer scope of the investigation is such that anyone would feel discouraged about undertaking it. And yet, I believe, a better understanding of the "experimental" or "research" poetry written in the second half of the twentieth century (from the Novissimi to Gruppo 93) requires that we include theatre in the picture, with its theoretical debates and controversies, its ground-breaking performances and protagonists, its connections with the world of literature and the polemics that surrounded them.

The time frame we will consider goes from 1961 – when the Novissimi anthology was first published, and thus the Neoavanguardia was born – to, roughly, the summer of 1979, when the Festival Internazionale dei Poeti of Castelporziano, Rome, marked the symbolic and almost ritualistic end of experiments that had pushed contemporary poetry onto the stage. Some of the plays we will discuss might have been written and performed after 1979, but their origins and motivations are squarely rooted in those two decades, and especially in the 1960s.

There is a great amount of work that needs to be done; in this first phase, I attempted to frame the main issues, seek a preliminary answer to some of the most burning questions, and offer a few practical examples of the way theatre has influenced poetry by looking at the texts put forth by a few of the most prolific and representative voices among the Neoavanguardia. As I am writing this, I am reminded of a page from Lucio Vetri's monograph *Letteratura e caos*. I will copy it here below, as a talisman and a source of comfort to those who will decide to join in the efforts:

> Ci sono e sono di certo possibili molti modi di accostare un fenomeno letterario e culturale (non meno, del resto, che di altra natura): è il fenomeno stesso ad autorizzare di per sé, nella sua costitutiva complessità, una pluralità di letture, e anzi a pretendere – più ancora e meglio ancora – d'essere guardato proprio in tutta la sua composita interezza, perciò sotto vari aspetti e da diverse angolazioni: a pretendere, insomma, un'analisi a più livelli e un procedimento interdisciplinare di lettura. Ben s'intende, tuttavia, come un'indagine di tal fatta, che richiede innumerevoli specifiche competenze, non possa condursi ad opera d'un singolo ricercatore, ma necessiti piuttosto, e per forza, d'un ben congegnato lavoro d'équipe. Ove una maniera d'indagine così impostata non sia praticabile, altro non resta che la meditata e consapevole scelta d'un approccio particolare: *consapevole*, nel senso che alla necessaria adozione d'un approccio particolare, quale che esso sia, deve sempre accompagnarsi, per l'appunto, la consapevolezza dei suoi inevitabili limiti; e *meditata*, giacché – pur nella parzialità che tutti li caratterizza e pur essendo tutti legittimi nei loro limiti – non tutti gli approcci figurano parimenti produttivi, fertili: non tutti, non tutti nella stessa misura, garantiscono una lettura *comprensiva* del fenomeno oggetto di studio. Non v'è dubbio, per esempio, che una forte riduzione delle possibilità di conoscenza comporti il procedere all'indagine del fenomeno muovendo da significati prestabiliti, o forzandolo entro rigidi schemi interpretativi, o facendone soltanto un pretesto per la trattazione di questioni d'ordine generalissimo o particolarissimo che, seppure concernono il fenomeno, tuttavia non ne toccano che un singolo aspetto, come tale dunque non assolutizzabile né, a rigore, ben intendibile se considerato isolatamente dagli altri aspetti che, tra loro strettamente connessi, concorrono a configurare il fenomeno.[4]

> [There are many possible ways to approach a literary and cultural phenomenon (not unlike what happens with those of a different nature): it is the phenomenon itself that authorizes, in its intrinsic complexity, a plurality of readings. In fact, it demands – to put it more precisely – to be examined in all of its composite totality, and thus in all of its various aspects and from different perspectives: it demands, in brief, a multi-level analysis and an interdisciplinary reading. Clearly, a similar analysis, which requires countless specialized knowledge, cannot be performed by a single researcher, but rather calls for well-coordinated teamwork. If a manner of investigation thus fashioned were not possible, the only choice left is the pondered and deliberate selection of a particular approach: *deliberate*, in the sense that whenever a particular approach has to be taken with any given issue, it must be aware of its inevitable limitations; *pondered*, because although every particular approach is equally partial and equally legitimate, not all of them are equally productive and fruitful: not all of them guarantee an equally comprehensive survey of the phenomenon that is the object of study. There is no doubt, for instance, that a significant reduction of the possibilities for knowledge is the result of an investigation of a phenomenon that moves from pre-established meanings, or that forces it within strict interpretive categories, or that reduces it to a pretext for debating overly general or overly specific issues that, although implied by the phenomenon, do not exhaust its significance and cannot be understood correctly in isolation from the other factors that contribute to the configuration of the phenomenon.]

Without access to an *équipe* of colleagues willing to aid my research, I found myself quoting from a wide variety of available sources: monographs, journal articles, biographies, newspaper accounts, and personal testimonies. In spite of all that, there are still some lacunae, a few elements are still missing, more time could have been dedicated to some of the themes that are only outlined here, and more attention should have been given to writers only mentioned in passing.

Yet, a first step had to be taken, a first monograph published, so that a conversation could begin. I will be grateful to anyone who points out the improvements and additions this volume needs: I will add them to the many I am already painfully aware of, and I shall strive to address them in the next conference paper, article, and book, hoping that others will take this as an opportunity to come forward and participate in the fun (work).

As for the "reduction of the possibilities for knowledge" mentioned by Vetri, I think we are here facing the opposite case: by focusing on this one aspect of the Neoavanguardia, an aspect that is generally overlooked and underestimated, we will bring to light a number of crucial issues that would remain, otherwise, out of reach and out of focus, thus allowing this phenomenon to emerge with an additional dimension, coming a step closer to understanding it *iuxta propria principia,* so to speak. Before closing this brief introduction, I will offer an overview of each chapter, so that readers may follow the general argument more easily, and direct their interests accordingly.

The Structure of This Volume

In the first chapter, I tried to provide an overview of the main issues implicated by the exchanges between poetry and theatre that took place in Italy in the 1960s and 1970s, without separating the discussion on theory and poetics from the practice of textual analysis. Thus, after sketching the linguistic and aesthetic problems at hand, I verified their actual presence in the works of authors who were active in both poetry and theatre. The first half of the chapter is dedicated to showing the relevance of theatre for the poetry of the Neoavanguardia in general. Then, taking Pagliarani's poetry as an exemplary case, I demonstrate how theatre and poetry are intertwined in the practical writing and fruition of the texts. The rest of the chapter is devoted to outlining a definition and the main characteristics of the theatre of the neo-avant-garde through the analysis of a few particularly useful documents I uncovered while researching Pagliarani's *Tutto il teatro.* At the end, I discuss a few of Giuliani's documents (some previously published, others unpublished) that explain his particular approach to theatre and put it in dialogue with that of his fellow Neoavanguardia writers, in particular Sanguineti, Balestrini, and Porta.

Chapter 2 reconstructs the cultural climate that saw the birth of the Nuovo Teatro movement from the *cantine romane* to the Convegno di Ivrea. The key figures of this flourishing of creativity are analysed and their careers summarized, from the end of the 1950s to the early 1970s. The connections with the work and the lives of the poets of Gruppo 63, and the Neoavanguardia more in general, are highlighted. The intellectual climate and the theoretical debate around theatre are also reconstructed, especially through the controversies between those who wanted to revolutionize the theatre through a radical renovation of its language (Bene, Ricci, Quartucci's early works); those who wanted to enact a series of progressive changes in society using the theatre as a means of propaganda (Bajini); those who wanted to extend the reach of theatre to some parts of the Italian population that had been historically denied access to it (Scabia, Quartucci's *Camion*); and those who remained anchored to a more traditional understanding of the role of the author within the theatrical troupe (Pasolini and the Teatro del Porcospino).

In chapter 3, after discussing the vicissitudes of the poets and the *teatranti* between the end of the 1950s and the mid-1970s, we will take a step back, and consider the convergence between theatre and poetry from a more theoretical perspective, placing it in the wider context of the *Novecento*. Goldmann's concept of "homology" will be introduced, and we will verify its applicability to our topic by squaring it with Gasparini's idea of poetry as "body-voice." In this new context we will be able to read it as just the latest instalment of a trend that, in poetry, had tried to reconcile the written word with its breath. Artaud, Zumthor, and Olson will be relied on to shore up this theory and give it concreteness. Barthes and Derrida, on the other hand, will be used to describe the changing status of the text (and the very idea of textuality) within Italian experimental literature and theatre. Giuliano Scabia's approach to a decentralized, radically inclusive, and "spoken" theatre will be shown to be exemplary, yet outside the field of investigation for this monograph. On the other hand, Antonio Porta's deployment of the voice within his verses and his openness toward the tools and opportunities offered by the theatre will be shown to be an ideal example of how to incorporate the possibilities offered by the body-voice. Finally, we will look at the 1979 Festival Internazionale dei Poeti as the final act of this long and complicated relationship between theatre and poetry: on the beach at Castelporziano, as we will show, the poetry of the "corpo-voce" finds its ritual end in a Dionysian celebration of minestrone and the power of the audience.

In chapter 4, I identify Pagliarani's reasons for including theatre in his writing process. Moving from a close analysis of the "manifesto minimo" he published on the occasion of the first performance of Compagnia Teatro dei Novissimi, in 1965, I reconstruct the complex relationship between his theatre and his poetry, where the first is a way of "testing" and "verifying" the efficacy of the latter. I draw a connection between Pagliarani's process and Scabia's: a very unconventional pairing that is justified by the attention both poets dedicated to the relationship with their audience. I summarize the main traits of Pagliarani's theatre, and I demonstrate how they can also be observed in his poems. I show how Giordano Bruno could be considered one of the ancestors of Pagliarani's theatre, and I finally offer a few reflections on the endings of his plays: as with his poems, they, too, avoid a logical and univocal conclusion, preferring irony and polysemy. While chapter 1 focuses on Pagliarani's poetry to highlight the theatrical traits it displays, this chapter closes the circle, so to speak, by examining his plays, and their relationship with his poetics.

Chapter 5 explores the connections between the plays written by Pagliarani, Celli, and Sanguineti. First, we discuss a few theoretical writings by Giuliani (some of them previously unpublished), which will help us further clarify how the poet saw a substantial continuity between the writing of verse and the writing of (and for) the stage, both in his own literary output as well as that of his fellow Neoavanguardisti. Then we analyse *Donkeyskin*, a rewriting of Perrault's classic fable by Giuliani and Pagliarani. The archival find of preparatory drafts of this play allows us a glimpse of the creative process followed by the two authors and helps us focus on the conceptual knot around which the play revolves: the nexus between money, sex, and excrement. The same themes can be found in Giuliani's *travestimento* of Jarry's *Ubu* plays, a text he prepared for the RAI (Radio Audizioni Italiane – the national Italian broadcasting channel). It illuminates the neo-avant-garde's debt to this forgotten ancestor, something that has so far escaped the attention of critics and commentators. After a brief overview of two other plays by Giuliani, we concentrate on Pagliarani's and Celli's rewritings of Goethe's *Faust*: the two poets, independently of each other, revisited this canonical text, infusing it with their concerns about the risks that recent scientific discoveries (genetic manipulation and atomic energy) pose to our society.

To round out this volume, I thought it a good idea to include the voices of those who have been studying this phenomenon for many years, or who have lived it directly. Valentina Valentini is a professor in the Department of History of Art and Performing Arts at the Università La Sapienza in Rome. In her interview we discuss some of the key themes of this book, including the roles that Brecht and the Living Theatre had in inspiring the renovation of the Italian stage carried out by Nuovo Teatro. Pippo Di Marca is both a protagonist and a chronicler of those experimental times: he was in the thick of it, so to speak, as he was operating his own Roman *cantina*, the Meta-Teatro, but has also endeavoured to preserve the memory of the people, places, and plays that made Nuovo Teatro by writing a crucial book, entitled *Sotto la tenda dell'avanguardia*, which is repeatedly quoted in the pages that follow. Nanni Balestrini and Giuliano Scabia are recurring characters in this volume: it is invaluable, I think, to hear what they have to say about those years, what their recollections are, and how useful they consider the lessons learned half a century ago to be in our own time. In order to preserve the tone, the inflections, the hesitations of these protagonists' voices, I tried to edit our interviews as little as possible, translating them in as colloquial a language as intelligibility would permit. Ultimately, this was also a way of allowing the reader a direct glimpse of the reality and history I laboured to reconstruct throughout this monograph.

1 Why the Theatre? The Role of the Stage in the Theoretical Debate Surrounding the Poetry and Poetics of the Neo-Avant-Garde[1]

"attivare l'inerzia della carne è già protesta …"

– Elio Pagliarani

1.1 A Bitter *aperitivo*

By now, the story of how it all began has been told many, many times. Between 3 and 8 October 1963, during the Settimana Internazionale della Nuova Musica, thirty-four writers (most of them from northern Italy) descended on Palermo ("the wagon-lit avant-garde," as Umberto Eco dubbed it) and, at the Hotel Zagarella, engaged in meetings, public debates, performances, and readings of their works in progress: it was the beginning of Gruppo 63, and the official introduction of the Neoavanguardia to the cultural life of the nation.

After all these years, however, the risk of submitting to superficial nostalgia is always lurking. A good antidote, the best form of insurance against all facile enthusiasms, can be found, I believe, in the popular press, in the way it saw and described the artists present in Palermo, their speeches, talks, and plays. During one of my research trips to the Centro Manoscritti in Pavia,[2] while searching through the papers of Germano Lombardi, I came across a juicy article, published by a periodical called *Successo* ("Success") in November 1963, and thus mere weeks after the "incontro di Palermo" (Palermo meeting), as it is often referred to by specialist publications. The name of the author, unfortunately, does not appear in the clipping. Here are some of its crucial passages, which I'd like to offer as a bitter *aperitivo* to the large meal I have laid out in the rest of the volume, in the hope that it will stimulate readers' palates and get their gastric juices flowing:

> **"LA SPEDIZIONE DEI '63' CONTRO I NIPOTINI DEL GATTOPARDO."**
>
> **A Palermo si è svolto il primo convegno della letteratura italiana di avanguardia che, sotto l'etichetta di "*Gruppo 63*," ha riunito più di trenta fra giovani poeti, romanzieri e critici.**
>
> Un ubriaco scamiciato che bestemmia in dialetto padovano contro la miseria, le corna, il governo, barcollando al centro del palcoscenico; sullo sfondo, a destra una balia che imbocca col cucchiaio un giovanotto travestito da lattante e issato su di un gigantesco seggiolone verde; a sinistra un signore azzimato che tenta continuamente di telefonare a un numero sempre occupato. "Quartetto su un motivo padovano" è il titolo della *pièce*, durata dieci minuti, scritta da Germano Lombardi e rappresentata la sera del 3 ottobre alla Sala Scarlatti di Palermo nel corso della serata dedicata al teatro degli scrittori del "*Gruppo 63*."[3]
>
> **["THE EXPEDITION OF THE '63' AGAINST THE LEOPARD'S GRANDCHILDREN"**
>
> **Palermo hosted the first meeting of avant-garde Italian literature, which, under the banner of "*Gruppo 63*," gathered more than thirty young poets, novelists, and critics.**
>
> A shirtless drunkard curses, in Paduan dialect, the government and his misfortunes as a penniless cuckold, staggering in the middle of the stage; in the background, on the right, there is a wet-nurse who's using a little spoon to feed a young man dressed like an infant, perched on a giant, green high chair; on the left, a thin gentleman is on the phone, he keeps dialling a number, finding it always busy. "Quartet on a Paduan motif" is the title of this ten-minute piece written by Germano Lombardi and performed on the 3rd of October, in Palermo's Sala Scarlatti, during an evening devoted to the theatre of the "*Gruppo 63*" writers.]

The article opens with a description of the performance at the Sala Scarlatti, and thus with a first confirmation of the importance of theatre for Gruppo 63, their theoretical investigations, as well as their public image and media presence. The journalist names the theatre companies involved, and their directors, and notes how the plays by Lombardi and Giuliani were the ones preferred by the audience. Then his attention shifts to audience members, producing an extraordinary description of the local "authorities" and their welcoming of Gruppo 63 to the city's social club, with liveried servants and candelabra. Particularly juicy is the bit describing the programmed (or, one could say, threatened) happening, with the public burning of a copy of Tomasi di Lampedusa's novel *The Leopard*:

> Nelle ultime file della platea sedevano, leggermente preoccupati i promotori dell'impresa: gli assessori della regione siciliana e i dirigenti dell'azienda del turismo: volgevano di tanto in tanto nervosamente lo sguardo verso i rappresentanti dell'*élite* palermitana, gli Alliata, i Lanza, i Paternò. Questi, anche se considerati tuttora nobili "gattopardiani," hanno reagito al modo giusto, secondo le aspettative dell'avanguardia: sono passati infatti attraverso i due strati, prima dell'irritazione e poi della curiosità. Alle due di notte il lunghissimo spettacolo era finalmente terminato, gli autori erano stanchi, gli attori sfiniti, ma il barone Francesco Agnello, dinamico organizzatore della settegiorni musico-letteraria, ha invitato Edoardo Sanguineti, Alberto Arbasino e Umberto Eco, le punte di diamante dell'*équipe* letteraria degli scrittori d'avanguardia, a palazzo Trabia, sede del Circolo dell'Unione, il più chiuso e aristocratico di Palermo. Qui, davanti a una tavola illuminata da candele e servita da camerieri in polpe, si è avuto un attimo di *suspence* quando la voce di un "novissimo" ha proposto per la sera seguente un "happening" nel *foyer* del Teatro Massimo, durante l'intervallo del più importante concerto del Festival: punto culminante sarebbe stato il rogo di una copia del "Gattopardo." Il gelo si è però sciolto alla domanda di un'avvenente signora che chiedeva con candore cosa fosse l'"happening." Il poeta Nanni Balestrini si è allora impegnato in una esauriente spiegazione, illustrando come l'"happening," che trae le sue origini dai beatnik americani, sia un avvenimento non preordinato che assume il valore di opera d'arte.[4]
>
> [The organizers were sitting in the back row, looking slightly worried: the officials of the Sicilian regional government and the directors of the tourist agency were in attendance: every now and then they would nervously turn their gaze to the representatives of Palermo's élite, the Alliata, Lanza, and Paternò. Although they are still considered as "leopard" nobles, they reacted well, according to the expectations of the avant-garde: they went through two different phases, first irritation, then curiosity. At two in the morning the long show was finally over, the authors were tired, the actors exhausted, but Baron Francesco Agnello, the dynamic organizer of the week-long musical and literary event, invited Edoardo Sanguineti, Alberto Arbasino, and Umberto Eco, the leaders of the literary *équipe* of avant-garde writers, to the Circolo dell'Unione, in palazzo Trabia, the most exclusive and aristocratic club of Palermo. There, at a dinner table lit by candles, served by waiters in livery, there was a moment of *suspense* when one of the "Novissimi" proposed, for the following night, a "happening"

> to be held in the foyer of Teatro Massimo, during the intermission of the most important concert of the Festival: the climax was going to be the burning of a copy of the *Leopard*. The embarrassment was overcome when a pretty lady candidly asked to know what a "happening" was. Poet Nanni Balestrini promptly launched into a comprehensive explanation, relating how the "happening," which started with the American beatniks, is a loosely planned event that is considered a work of art.]

The following description of the actual proceedings is quite perplexing, and begins to cast some doubt on the credibility of the narrator and the verisimilitude of the events he recounts; in fact, one can't help but suspect that the chronicler has resorted, perhaps more often than he should have, to his vivid imagination, in order to enhance some of the events he witnessed. The atmosphere of final examination he describes, with Guglielmi, Barilli, and Filippini cast as professors and evaluating committee, clashes with other reports we have of those days, all of which stress the open collegiality and frankness of the discussion, where everyone was treated as an equal and their work judged exclusively on its merits. Furthermore, the comment about Carla Vasio is quite inappropriate, and rather depressing:

> Le giornate dei congressisti erano organizzate secondo un ritmo frenetico: nonostante le ore piccole causate dagli spettacoli musicali e teatrali della sera, ogni mattina i partecipanti si sedevano intorno a una lunga tavola allestita nel night-club dell'albergo e a turno leggevano poesie, brani di romanzo o di lavori teatrali, che venivano poi discussi collettivamente. Ci sono stati momenti emozionanti, l'atmosfera era quella degli esami di maturità, i professori della commissione erano di volta in volta Angelo Guglielmi, Renato Barilli, o Enrico Filippini. C'erano i primi della classe, che sono passati ad ali spiegate, come il poeta Elio Pagliarani, avvantaggiato anche da una dizione da primo attore, o come Francesco Leonetti, che ha presentato un brano del suo nuovo romanzo, da tutti lodato; mentre nessuno si aspettava di vedere uscire così malconcio Massimo Ferretti, vincitore quest'anno di un premio Viareggio, accusato da Sanguineti di "stile da complesso di inferiorità." Buon successo ha riportato la poetessa Amelia Rosselli, e così anche l'altra componente femminile del gruppo, la romana Carla Vasio, la cui piattaforma elettorale è stata costituita, oltre che dai meriti letterari, anche dalla galanteria di Paolo Milano.[5]

> [The participants of the conference kept a hectic schedule: in spite of the late nights at concerts and performances, every morning they sat around a large table prepared in the hotel's night club and took turns reading poems, passages from novels or plays, and then discussing them as a group. There

were a few exciting moments, and the atmosphere was like that of a final examination, with Angelo Guglielmi, Renato Barilli, and Enrico Filippini as professors and evaluating committee. Some performed admirably, passing with flying colours, like, for instance, Elio Pagliarani, who took advantage of his theatrical style of declamation, or Francesco Leonetti, who presented a passage from his latest novel, which was universally praised; on the other hand, none could have foreseen the treatment reserved for Massimo Ferretti, winner of this year's Viareggio prize, whom Sanguineti accused of employing a "style with an inferiority complex." Poet Amelia Rosselli was very well received, not unlike the other female member of the group, the Roman Carla Vasio, whose electoral consensus was based, in addition to her literary merits, on the gallantry of Paolo Milano.]

The next episode, involving the writers of the Palermo School, sounds equally apocryphal: Giuliani had written the introduction to the volume published by Feltrinelli (the "Milanese publishing house" mentioned in the article), where the very name "Palermo School" had been devised for the first time. In that essay, Giuliani had praised the work of his Sicilian colleagues, and it is therefore very difficult to imagine why any of them would utter such nonsense at the conference.[6] Again, one must suspect that the creative imagination of the journalist has provided some embellishment to the facts he had observed. Furthermore, a complete mystery surrounds the identity of the additional three writers who would have joined Perriera, Di Marco, and Testa in their public display of disdain.[7]

> La sorpresa maggiore è stata però offerta da tre giovani autori siciliani, recentemente pubblicati da una Casa editrice milanese in un libro collettivo dal titolo "La scuola di Palermo"; si sono presentati al convegno con aria battagliera e hanno dichiarato: "Prima eravamo in tre, adesso siamo in sei, l'anno venturo saremo ancora di più e vi batteremo tutti."[8]
>
> [The greatest surprise, however, was seeing three Sicilian authors, whose works were recently released by a Milanese publishing house in a collective volume entitled "La scuola di Palermo" ("The Palermo School"); they arrived at the conference with a combative air and promptly declared: "We used to be just three, now we are six, next year we will be even more, and we will beat you all."]

Moving toward the conclusion, we encounter another, truly remarkable, image: Alberto Moravia, restlessly wandering the grounds of Hotel Zagarella, like a soul in purgatory, nervously monitoring the activities of his young rivals. Once more, the reporter's fantasy has added some coloration to the truth. However, it is the closing paragraph where the general tone of innuendo reaches its most ludicrous point: Luciano Anceschi is cast as an ominous ringleader, acting in the shadows, smiling a strange and indefinable smile, which feels almost like a vague threat. The article closes on him, climbing the steps leading to an airplane that is about to leave, a disquieting smile still on his lips:

> Alle due le riunioni avevano termine, ma proseguivano ai tavoli del ristorante con nuove energie, provocate spesso dall'apparizione di Alberto Moravia che si aggirava per la Conca d'Oro attentissimo alle mosse dei giovani rivali. Soprattutto durante le conferenze pubbliche del pomeriggio che il "*Gruppo 63*" aveva organizzato nella sala del Conservatorio, Moravia si è generosamente buttato nella mischia delle discussioni, impegnandosi in una lotta disperata con avversari incalzanti e ferratissimi. E un maligno aveva messo in circolazione la voce che fosse stato inviato in avanscoperta dagli scrittori della "vecchia guardia," decisi a organizzare l'anno venturo un loro festival a Ferrara, in un famoso giardino … Luciano Anceschi, l'eminenza grigia di questo possibile "nuovo corso" della letteratura italiana, l'unico critico più anziano a cui i giovani si sentano legati, ne era evidentemente convinto, e aveva uno strano sorriso dietro i rotondi occhiali da professore universitario, mentre a Punta Raisi saliva sull'aereo che lasciava l'isola dove le avanguardie sono di casa.[9]

> [At two the meetings were suspended, only to continue, with renewed energy, at the restaurant tables, often stirred by the apparition of Alberto Moravia, who was wandering the Conca d'Oro [Golden Plain, on the outskirts of Palermo], paying close attention to the moves of his young rivals. Especially during the public conferences of the afternoon, which "*Gruppo 63*" had organized in the rooms of the Conservatorio, Moravia valiantly joined the discussions, engaging in a desperate fight with relentless and very knowledgeable adversaries. A malignant gossiper had spread the rumour that he had been sent ahead by the writers of the "old guard," who wanted to organize a Festival of their own for the following year, in a famous garden in Ferrara … Luciano Anceschi, the *éminence grise* behind this possible "new deal" of Italian literature, the only elder critic that the younger generation respects, was clearly optimistic, and was wearing a strange smile behind his round professorial glasses as, in Punta Raisi, he was boarding the flight leaving the island where the avant-garde feels right at home.]

1.2 A Knot of Theoretical and Practical Issues

When reading this article, in spite of all its faults – one cannot condemn enough the sexism of certain passages, hence the bitter taste of this *aperitivo* – the scholar of contemporary poetry cannot help but feel a pang of nostalgia. It is, on the one hand, a longing for a time when the vicissitudes of literature and its practitioners found their way into the pages of popular magazines, especially in the face of today's complete indifference, apart from the occasional commotion over the latest literary "discovery."

On the other hand, it seems almost incredible that there had been a time, not so long ago, when literature still seemed to have a shot at changing the world. Although, as it turned out, the impact of Gruppo 63 on contemporary Italian society was, ultimately, rather limited, for a brief moment they stood as living proof that it could be done, that the written and spoken word still possessed that ancient magic, the *poiesis*, the ability to create something out of nothing. Granted, these writers' handle on reality was mediated by language, and they claimed to influence the former only through a manipulation of the latter; yet, that was as good an outcome as there had been, at least in Italy, since futurism.

John Picchione, in his fundamental monograph on the neo-avant-garde, a point of reference for any English-speaking reader interested in these issues, used an ecological metaphor to describe the workings of this mechanism:

> It can be submitted that, for the neo-avant-garde, literature behaves like an ecosystem. Like any other environment, it is affected by all sorts of pollutants and waste. Worn-out and rotting materials are dumped daily into its territory, making it sterile and unproductive. As the literary word reaches a state of obsolescence and tumescence, it is turned into a reified and alienating presence, its power of communication and imagination inevitably lost. The linguistic otherness pursued by *Neoavanguardia* represents an attempt to revitalize the word by revolting against any sign of decay both within literature's environment and within that larger environment of communication, namely language as a social system. Ultimately, … dislodging atrophied and conventional forms of writing meant abandoning ossified and alienated forms of thought. In exposing the negativity of an alienated human existence, the new avant-garde recognized literature's liberating function.[10]

Picchione then continues, saying that the poets and writers of Neoavanguardia had given up the hope of influencing life in a significant and revolutionary manner, but did not resign themselves to an idea of literature as completely self-referential and entirely separate from the world and other manifestations of culture.

The study of exactly how they attempted to affect reality – that is, to exert a political and social influence on their contemporaries – as well as the extent to which they succeeded, has been carried out by several scholars over the past decades, and has yielded excellent results.[11] However, there is one aspect that has yet to receive full attention: the use of theatre in finding and implementing the main rhetorical and linguistic techniques deployed by these authors in their works: theatre was both a physical and an ideal space in which they found solutions to the practical dead ends and theoretical impasses that hindered their path toward the new and reformed national literature they were trying to create.

There are many reasons why criticism has not taken on this aspect of the neo-avant-garde: 1) the texts written by these authors for the theatre are, for the most part, not readily available, as they were published by small presses and in limited print runs, or in the pages of journals and magazines (if they were published at all); 2) while poetry has always been at the centre of the theoretical and aesthetic debates, and while a whole meeting of Gruppo 63 (the third one, held in 1965) was dedicated to discussing the novel, the literary neo-avant-garde did not engage in a systematic reflection on the theatre;[12] 3) even when any plays were published and made available, they were only faint traces, the first stage of a preparatory work for the shows, and as such they are not representative of the final products and certainly do not give an accurate idea of what the audience experienced;[13] 4) finally, there has always been a strong permeability between poetry and drama, a fruitful exchange that allowed for a wide circulation of entire texts, short passages, and characters that were recycled and recast, thus complicating the task of the critic and the literary historian. In spite of all these reasons, it will become increasingly clear how understanding the symbiosis between poetry and theatre is crucial for appreciating the efforts made by the Neoavanguardia to engage the society contemporaneous to their time.

Although we have been speaking of Gruppo 63 and the neo-avant-garde as a cohesive whole, and even if there are some general trends uniting its different members, it would be incorrect to assume that they were in total agreement upon everything. In fact, disagreement was a distinctive trait of every one of the group's gatherings; in the introduction to the anthology that collected the works presented at the first meeting in Palermo, Balestrini and Giuliani observe that, "The following year, back in Palermo, we discussed the novel with renewed and fruitful controversy. Eco kept saying that, at that point, internal dissent had become our 'statutory sport.'"[14]

In particular, when it comes to the issue of whether literature had any chance of influencing reality – or even if there was any possible contact between the two – different members of Gruppo 63 and the neo-avant-garde held different opinions. Once again, we will follow Picchione, who identifies the group's two different camps:

> The *Neoavanguardia* cannot be defined as a movement with a unified program expressed in the form of manifestos or shared theoretical

> principles. It experiences irreconcilable internal conflicts that are explored as a split between two main blocs: one is tied to the project of modernity, the other to postmodern aesthetic postures. The first identifies literature's formal ruptures with a subversive social and ideological function. The second, considering literature as an integral part of the culture industry of late capitalism, embodies the belief that there exist no pragmatic possibilities of antagonism – through aesthetic discourses – to the specific socio-political conditions of our times.[15]

This distinction is crucial to our discussion: the *modernists* still tried to make contact with the world, and thus turned to the theatre as a source of inspiration for specific techniques, and as a place where experiments could be carried out. The *postmodernists*, in general, didn't show much interest in the theatre, and even when they did, they displayed a very traditional, almost reactionary, approach to the way in which their texts would interact with the actors, directors, and stage.

In spite of this fundamental difference, there was still plenty of common ground between the various camps of the Neoavanguardia, especially when it came to identifying the problems that had to be faced and overcome (the solutions, naturally, were a different matter altogether). Here is a quotation from Giuliani's second preface to the Novissimi anthology:

> Con tutte le premesse negative che facevamo nostre, e con tutte le contraddizioni e immaturità delle nostre poesie, mostravamo un positivo tratto in comune ... l'accorgimento che la disorganizzazione, il "caos," è un problema strutturale. E tutte le nostre preoccupazioni e idiosincrasie "tecniche," mostravano un particolare tipo di "impegno" troppo spesso eluso nel dopoguerra italiano. Il fatto che non proponessimo una poesia "ideologica" era accuratamente calcolato: mostrando che non si può fare poesia pensando nella direzione della poesia se non come tecnica, lasciavamo aperte all'ideologia, o, come dice Sanguineti, al linguaggio-ideologia, tutte le strade. E proprio su questo punto, che a qualcuno pare dolente, e che a me sembra pacifico, bisogna aggiungere che non proponevamo neppure una "poetica" univoca.[16]

> [Despite all the negative premises that we adopted, and with all the contradictions and the immaturity of our poems, we showed a positive common trait ... the realization that disorganization, "chaos," is a structural problem. And all of our preoccupations and "technical" idiosyncrasies revealed a particular kind of "engagement" that was too often overlooked in post-World War II Italy. The fact that we did not advocate for an "ideological" poetry was the result of a deliberate calculation: showing that the only way of producing poetry was to think of it in terms of technique,

> we were opening up to ideology or, as Sanguineti put it, to the language-ideology, all kinds of possibilities. And precisely on this issue, which some consider controversial, but that I take as self-evident, we must add that we did not advocate for a single, univocal form of "poetics," either.]

What brought together the different members of the Novissimi first, and the Neoavanguardia later, was not a series of stylistic traits, nor a homogeneous poetics; rather, it was an uneasiness, a restlessness regarding the relationship between literature, language, and the world of society and culture. Their similarities were rooted in the questions they needed to answer, rather than in a number of solutions they wanted to implement. The ultimate goal, at least for the modernist wing, was updating the "pre-constituted meanings that writers find in the language," as Pagliarani put it,[17] in an effort to reach an audience that was moving farther away from an engaged, self-aware, and self-reflective kind of literature and toward the escapist entertainment promoted by the mainstream cultural industry. By communicating the political engagement of their author, the works of the Novissimi and the Neoavanguardia were meant to cause a positive change within Italian society. This entire strategy, it must be stressed, was pursued exclusively through the manipulation of language. Here is, once again, Picchione:

> Setting aside the various blocs and conflicting positions that distinguished the theoretical positions of the group, it can safely be claimed that the aesthetic orientation of the neo-avant-garde rests on the premise that in literature reality occurs first and foremost in the form of linguistic modalities. It is in this postulate that the specificity of literature resides. Indeed, the identification of literature ... with the exploration of language bears far-reaching effects on both the formal organization of the text and the role of the reader. Although the neo-avant-garde problematized deeply the possibility of literature to produce a direct impact on praxis (to subvert social and economic conditions by providing the necessary ground for a revolution within the context of late capitalism) it did not abandon the transgressive traits of all avant-garde movements.[18]

If there was to be any change, the Novissimi and the modernist wing of the Neoavanguardia believed it could be facilitated by literature only through a careful use of style, and by highlighting all the traces that traditional institutions (but also habit, capitalism, history, etc.) had left within the fabric of literature's language. Making their readers aware of the existence of such traces, and of their influence on their everyday life, was the beginning of the only change that was possible to achieve through the written word.

The passage from Giuliani's introduction quoted above is also useful in that it enumerates the many problems that are entangled and part of effecting change through literature; here is a first list of the main three components of this complicated theoretical knot: 1) the *impegno* (that is to say, political engagement); 2) linguistic and stylistic experimentalism; 3) a rejection of an "ideological" literature, that is, a form of writing that acritically embraces the current stylistic conventions to communicate a propagandistic set of ideas and contents.

In trying to reconcile these three demanding principles, the writers of the Neoavanguardia resorted to two rhetorical macro-strategies: 1) a "reduction of the I," formulated by Giuliani in the first preface to the Novissimi anthology; and 2) the research and practice of an anti-mimetic form of literary realism. We will speak more about both strategies when we demonstrate how theatre helped the poets of Gruppo 63 overcome the impasse they found themselves in. For now, we will turn once again to Picchione, and his explanation of the role that "the reduction of the I" played within the Novissimi's poetics:

> Giuliani identifies the "reduction of the I" ... as an essential feature of the poetry produced by the *Novissimi*. Following the premise of the phenomenological method, he advocates a return to things as a way to advance a consciousness uncluttered with beliefs and presuppositions. The phenomenological reduction (*epochè*) proposes the suspension of all pre-constituted ideologies (beliefs placed in abeyance as a matter of method) in order to gain access to a pre-conceptual experience of the world (being-in-the-world implies that we experience the world *before* we can come to know it). The phenomenological bracketing of subjectivity does not simply express the rejection of traditional lyrical and sentimental poetry. The "I" (the empirical self) is bracketed inasmuch as it is considered the result of an alienated subjectivity, divorced from a genuine life of experience. The centrality of the I and the author is supplanted by the centrality of language and of the other – an assemblage of pre-existing linguistic fragments and voices of characters that speak through that of the poet.[19]

According to this perspective, a "reduction of the I" is a tool that works on two parallel tracks: that of politics (and, thus, of *impegno*), and that of linguistic experimentation. This second aspect of the neo-avant-garde is rendered even more pressing by the technological revolution that had overturned the Italian mass media, as a result of the introduction of television and, consequently, the creation of a unified national spoken language. In fact, at the end of the Second World War, for the first time since the Romans, Italians saw a common tongue emerge across the peninsula: this was clearly a momentous opportunity, and one not to be wasted. Unfortunately, commerce, capital, and the injudicious use of radio and television were transforming this new idiom into yet another instrument of inequality, exploitation, and imperialism. Everybody agreed, literature had to do something to combat this disease. The discussion of what exactly had to be done lasted for a couple of decades and proved to be of extreme interest (even beyond its relevance to Italian matters). The most interesting solutions stemmed, as mentioned above, from one radical idea: the invasiveness of the "lyrical I" in poetry had to be contrasted.[20]

Equally important and rife with consequences was the discussion regarding realism, which Italian intellectuals were occupied with for the best part of the 1950s and 1960s (especially if we include the theoretical debate surrounding neo-realism in cinema). In fact, many looked at realism as the place where a compromise between the sometimes-contradictory demands of linguistic experimentalism and political engagement could be found. But how, exactly, does the "tyranny of the I" relate to the problem of language and thus to the issue of politics? What did a search for an anti-mimetic form of realism have to do with this already complex issue? And, finally, in what way did the theatre provide a viable solution to untangle this theoretical knot? All of these questions will be addressed shortly.

When it comes to the issue of *impegno*, we cannot overstate its pervasiveness within contemporary Italian culture, especially among leftist intellectuals. Following the end of the Second World War and after enduring two decades of cultural isolationism as a result of fascist rule, Italian society was undergoing massive transformations that caused artists and writers to feel perplexed and concerned (to say the least). Internal migration was displacing workers from the countryside to the city's factories, from the rural south to the industrialized north. The introduction of television and the improvements to the transportation infrastructure threatened regional identities. Consumerism was slowly replacing traditional values and eroding the strength of local communities. All these issues had been addressed by neo-realism, which endorsed a *politica culturale* based on gradual and sustained reforms, a stance that was essentially in line with the policies advocated by the Italian Communist party (at least for a while). On the level of artistic research, neo-realism often employed a narrative style that relied on a compassionate identification with the plight of the poor and oppressed within Italian society as a rhetorical strategy to advocate for change. The Neoavanguardia took a rather different, more nuanced position. Some within it would advocate for a revolutionary approach, and saw their artistic endeavours as preparatory to a political revolution. Others took their role as limited to the realm of art, and while sympathizing with radical political views, did not perceive their work as artists as being subservient to a specific political mission. Finally, more moderate intellectuals were close to the official Communist party line. Most of the Neoavanguardisti, however, espoused a markedly "experimental" style, where identification was replaced with critical distance and mimetic realism with an exploration of the limits and cultural implications of the various artistic forms.[21]

Theatre played an important role in structuring this controversy; using a selection of contemporary sources, we will highlight how important it was for the writers of the neo-avant-garde (not just as a side project, but rather as a cornerstone of their artistic vision), and how well-known their theatrical experiments were to contemporary readers and audiences.

1.3 Contemporary Press Coverage

Let us begin with an article by Luigi Gozzi published in the first issue of *Marcatrè: Notiziario di cultura contemporanea*, in November 1963, entitled "Teatro: *Gruppo 63* a Palermo." The journal, which started its life in Genoa, moved to Milan after issue five, and from its very beginning was clearly aligned with the positions of the Neoavanguardia (in fact, Eco, Sanguineti, and Dorfles were among the founding members). The Palermo meeting had just taken place the previous month: this was one of the first opportunities to take stock of the situation and try to clarify exactly what had happened. Consequently, the first issue of *Marcatrè* gave considerable attention to the event, opening with two articles on this topic: the first was a long reportage on the discussions that took place at Hotel Zagarella; the second, written by Gozzi, focused exclusively on the theatre. Here is Gozzi's opening paragraph:

> Un primo risultato positivo ottenuto a Palermo durante la IV Settimana della Nuova Musica e il convegno degli scrittori del Gruppo '63, lo si può rilevare dalla sola lettura del programma: uno spettacolo "Teatro Gruppo '63" composto da diversi testi di giovani scrittori e affidato per la messa in scena al Centro Teatrale di Bologna e all'Act di Roma, una conferenza-dibattito tenuta da me e da Giuseppe Bartolucci. Si è avuto insomma il coraggio, per usare parole grosse, di inserire nel complesso di manifestazioni che si proponevano come prodotte da una situazione di punta avanzata (di avanguardia), sia per quanto riguarda la musica che per quanto riguarda la letteratura (in misura minore erano presenti anche

le arti figurative), anche il teatro la cui posizione arretrata in Italia, su tutti i piani, da quello organizzativo al suo significato come presenza culturale, non credo possa essere messa in discussione da nessuno.[22]

[A first positive result gained in Palermo during the Fourth Week of Nuova Musica and the conference of writers of Gruppo 63 can be observed just by looking at the program: a show entitled "Teatro Gruppo '63," which comprised various scripts by young writers and was staged by the Centro Teatrale of Bologna and the Act of Rome, as well as a public talk led by Giuseppe Bartolucci and myself. To put it boldly, we've had the guts to introduce – in the context of a festival that was clearly marked as belonging to the most advanced research (avant-garde) in the fields of music and literature (visual arts were not as well represented) – the theatre, whose backward position in Italy, on all levels, from its organization to its meaning and its cultural relevance, is certainly indisputable.]

In addition to marking the importance of the inclusion of theatre within the art forms represented and discussed at the meeting in Palermo, it is important to note how this presence wasn't limited to a theoretical debate but included a proper performance that involved some of the experimental theatrical companies active in Italy at that point, which dramatized scripts by the writers in attendance.[23]

In the rest of his article, Gozzi took some time to define what the new theatre he was advocating should look like. We will quote the relevant passage below, and, at this point, we will keep the commentary to a minimum: there will be plenty of opportunities to illustrate these ideas in the next chapter. It is important, however, that we stress the lucidity and the foresight displayed by Gozzi and some of the key members of Gruppo 63 and the Neoavanguardia, who were capable, from the very start, of identifying the crucial elements of the debate, articulating them clearly, pointing them out to their fellow artists, and formulating sophisticated strategies to overcome the difficulties and exploit the possibilities that the situation presented.

Soffermiamoci un momento su questo "elemento" della messa in scena: si può dire che tutta la regia moderna, sicuramente da Stanislavskij in avanti abbia sottoposto la recitazione (così come la presentava la tradizione tardoromantica) a un netto processo di stilizzazione, con l'intenzione cioè di verificare un modello prestabilito forzando e i mezzi dell'attore (le sue disponibilità) e i materiali del testo drammatico. Ora, senza dimenticare il valore di un processo di stilizzazione, come capace di "informare" e di creare una (o più) prospettive drammatiche, è certo che teorie e pratiche più recenti (relativamente) tendono ad attribuire all'oggetto scenico (per esempio all'attore con tutti i suoi mezzi e le sue possibilità) una significanza più diretta, quasi il valore di una "testimonianza scenica." Esigenza che è senza dubbio già presente in Meyerhold, in tutta la scena francese da Artaud in avanti (in una sua particolare accezione) e che trova una sua teorizzazione (una tra le possibili) nella pratica della messa in scena brechtiana. Resta da dire come una organizzazione (un abbozzo di organizzazione) dello spettacolo, in questo senso, collochi in una posizione nuova e interessantissima il testo, il quale viene sollecitato non già (o non solo) nella sua strutturazione ma anche, e più, nella sua qualità di "materiale scenico" …; e nella mia relazione mi sono sforzato di segnalare e di esemplificare quei casi, già noti e recenti, nei quali il testo drammatico, che, si direbbe, viene a collocarsi come un vero e proprio "sistema di notazione," si muove in questa direzione, o quanto meno presenta elementi assimilabili come esemplari di una tale prospettiva.[24]

[Let us pause for a moment on this "element" of the staging process: one could argue that all modern directing, certainly from Stanislavski onward, subjected acting (as it was passed down by the late romantic tradition) to a process of stylization, that is to say an attempt to verify a pre-established model stretching to their limit both the actors' expressive means (and their potential) and the materials offered by the script. Now, without discounting the importance of the stylization process in "shaping" and creating various dramatic perspectives, it is certain that more recent theories and practices have given the scenic object (for instance the actors, with all their expressive means and possibilities) a more direct significance, and almost the value of a "stage testimony." This is something that can already be seen in Meyerhold as well as all French theatre, beginning with Artaud (in a certain sense) and that found one of its possible theorizations with Brecht's staging practices. Finally, it should be pointed out how a new way of organizing the show (or, at least, the beginning of a new way of organizing the show) places the script in a new and very interesting position, utilizing it not only for the structure it offers to the performance but also as a source of "stage materials" …; in my talk I tried to mention and enumerate those cases (the more famous ones as well as the more recent) in which the script is used as a "notation system," thus moving in this direction, displaying elements that prove this new perspective.]

Gozzi acutely concentrates his attention on three key elements, each of which we will see as a returning refrain in the next chapter: 1) he mentions the names that will be at the centre of the *New Theatre*'s theoretical debate (Artaud, Brecht, and later on in the text, but not in this quotation, Beckett); 2) he clearly highlights the new tasks assigned to actors and directors, according to which the former must concentrate on their bodies, their resources, and the possibilities offered by their physical presence before the audience, while the latter is no longer the sole author of the show, but should rather coordinate the creative efforts of each contributor; 3) he points out that the script can be seen as one of the many components of the spectacle; thus, it is not considered as a binding contract with the author but rather as the starting point of a conversation between the director, actors, and the writer (dramaturg).

Forty years later, during a conference in Bologna (8–11 May 2003) entitled "Il Gruppo 63 quarant'anni dopo," Gozzi, along with most of the artists who were present at that first meeting in Palermo, was able to reflect on that experience. It is interesting to compare what he had to say then with the original comments just quoted. First, here is his recollection of the circumstances surrounding the show:

> In un giorno della primavera, credo, del '63 mi interpellò Nanni Balestrini e mi disse se volevo mettere in scena qualche breve pièce teatrale perché si stava preparando il convegno del Gruppo 63. Così nacque la cosa … a Palermo, a settembre, ottobre forse, non ho dati e mi ricordo male, andò in scena uno spettacolo in cui furono presentati undici … testi … Io feci la regia dei primi tre sicuramente, e degli ultimi quattro … Per quanto i testi degli autori fossero piuttosto brevi, lo spettacolo, faticosissimo (perché faceva anche un caldo spaventoso), durò, mi pare, più di tre ore. Fu un tentativo, lo dico in tutta onestà, anche mancato. A distanza di quarant'anni non è agevole dirlo ma io non ne sono, non ne fui e nella memoria non ne sono tuttora soddisfatto. È probabilmente un fatto personale, non interessa a nessuno a tanta distanza di tempo.[25]

> [One day, in the spring of 1963, I think, Nanni Balestrini contacted me and asked me if I wanted to stage a few small pieces that they were preparing for the conference of Gruppo 63. That is how it began … in Palermo, in September, or maybe it was October, I don't have all the details and I don't really remember, the show was performed and eleven different scripts … were presented. I directed the first three and the last four … Although the scripts were rather short, the show, which was exhausting (also because it was frightfully hot), lasted, I think, more than three hours. It was a somewhat failed attempt, I say it in all honesty. After forty years, it is not easy for me to say it, but I am not, I wasn't and still am not, in my memory, pleased with it. It is probably a personal issue, that doesn't interest anyone else, now that so much time has gone by.]

The candour shown by Gozzi in this statement is quite impressive: in spite of the celebrations that surround him in that fortieth anniversary since the first meeting of Gruppo 63, he is still not satisfied with his work. As he moves on to consider the quality of the texts submitted by the authors, however, his judgment becomes more lenient:

> Però a ripensare a questi testi posso dire che nonostante la loro brevità e quindi la complessiva impossibilità di instaurare una qualche convenzione scenica, a rileggerli, dicevo, vi si potrebbero trovare spunti e forme di notevole interesse, aggiornamenti a impianti drammaturgici allora poco consueti. Naturalmente era arrivato Beckett, come naturalmente il più diffuso brechtismo, oppure erano presenti interessanti scomposizioni sceniche e contemporaneità di azioni che avrebbero avuto, e secondo me hanno ancora senso e possono essere reinventati; senza dire, naturalmente, della qualità linguistica, la lingua di "battuta," dei suoi impasti, di un diffuso senso e gusto del paradosso che davano a quei testi una notevole estraneità e distanza dalla contemporanea drammaturgia italiana.[26]

> [And yet, thinking back to these texts I can say that in spite of their brevity, and thus in spite of the overall impossibility of establishing any stage conventions, reading them again, as I was saying, one could find a number of suggestions and very interesting forms, updates to dramaturgic conventions that were rather uncommon back then. Naturally, we had Beckett, and Brechtism was quite widespread, and there were also interesting scenic fragmentations and simultaneous actions that made a lot of sense, and could still be reinvented today; to say nothing, of course, of their linguistic quality, their language tailored to the "lines," based on pastiche, their fondness and taste for paradox, all elements that set those texts apart from the contemporary Italian dramaturgy.]

It is truly remarkable to notice the continuity that emerges from a comparison of this assessment with the evaluation expressed forty years earlier. The points of reference in the international context have remained the same, and also similar is the focus on the linguistic qualities of the texts, in terms of their ability to turn into action, to inspire the physicality of the actor, to become "lines." Gozzi makes one last point that is very important and that will become very useful to think of when we speak about Sanguineti and the position of his theatre within the context of Neoavanguardia:

> Era il teatro di regia, che dominava, e che ha dominato a lungo. Perciò non deve stupire che quello che stava accadendo e che accadrà di lì a poco nel teatro italiano riguarderà molto poco la drammaturgia ma invece la regia, il complessivo mettere in scena. Il nuovo teatro, che io considero abbastanza affine al Gruppo 63, quel nuovo teatro che si incontrerà pochi anni dopo

a Ivrea, incentrerà tutto il suo interesse e la sua ricerca sul rinnovamento scenico, ignorando e anzi spesso rifiutando la drammaturgia.[27]

[It was the *teatro di regia* (director's theatre) that dominated for a long time. Thus, it is not surprising that what was happening at the time and what would have happened later on in the Italian theatre had very little to do with dramaturgy and instead focused on directing, on the staging. The new theatre, which I consider rather similar to Gruppo 63, that new theatre that would meet a few years later in Ivrea, based all its energy and its research on the renovation of the stage, ignoring and often even rejecting all dramaturgy.]

The distinction between a theatre based on dramaturgy – and thus on the work of staging a play according to a traditional division of labour, and to a traditional process (with a director who is ultimately in charge of all artistic decisions) – and a theatre based on staging – and thus on the interaction and collaboration of all the professionals involved in the creative process as equals, and an attention given to the physicality and the presence of actors over the words they pronounce on stage – is of crucial importance.[28]

However, as already mentioned, we will postpone a thorough discussion of these issues to the next chapter. Continuing our overview of contemporary testimonies about the presence of theatre within the activities of Gruppo 63, we will consider the following extract from an article by Vito Pandolfi, published in *Il punto* (26 December 1964). The opportunity was offered by a program organized by Enrico Filippini for German television: a performance of *Povera Juliet* ("Poor Juliet") by Alfredo Giuliani and *Traumdeutung* ("Dream Interpretation") by Edoardo Sanguineti, with Toti Scialoja's scenography. The initial project had also included a one-act by Filippini, entitled *Gioco con la scimmia* ("Game with a Monkey"), but,

La complicazione dei casi ha finito col sacrificare l'atto di Filippini. Già da quindici giorni, durante le prove, lo si stava amputando. Era divenuto sempre più esile, finché nelle tempeste che inevitabilmente precedono le prime e particolarmente quelle all'insegna della mancanza di mezzi, non è stato reciso brutalmente d'un sol colpo, e sostituito da colloqui tipo "tavola rotonda" in merito al gruppo e all'iniziativa, che potevano apparire superflui, ma che hanno rivelato, attraverso gli interventi di Sanguineti e Scialoia [*sic*], non solo il perché dello spettacolo, ma anche le ragioni dell'evidente tendenza del gruppo alla raffigurazione scenica. Edoardo Sanguineti e Nanni Balestrini (che rappresentava il gruppo, pur non presentandosi come autore teatrale) si sono fatti portavoce di una esigenza diffusa: quella di comunicare direttamente con il pubblico (e in definitiva non c'è mezzo più idoneo idealmente della scena, tanto più che consente una utile intesa con l'arte figurativa e con la musica).[29]

[A number of complications ended up causing Filippini's act to be cut. Over the last two weeks of rehearsal, it had been progressively shortened. It had become thinner and thinner, until the storm that inevitably precedes all first performances, especially those marked by a lack of funds, took it away in one swoop, replacing it with a "round table" on the group and their initiatives; this is something that might have seemed superfluous, but that actually turned out to be very important, giving Sanguineti and Scialoia [*sic*] a chance to explain not only the reasons behind that show, but also the draw they felt for the stage. Edoardo Sanguineti and Nanni Balestrini (who intervened as a representative of the group, although none of his plays were being performed) voiced what they considered a shared need: communicating directly with the audience (and, after all, there is no better means than the stage, which offers the additional advantage of bringing together also music and the visual arts).]

Theatre is, thus, a "shared need" among the members of Gruppo 63, for it is the best way to interact with, on the one hand, the audience (without any technological mediation, be it the written page, the silver screen, or the cathode ray tube), and, on the other hand, with other fellow artists, both within and outside the field of literature. After all, for many of the participants of that first meeting in Palermo, their memory of that theatre performance had turned out to be the most vivid and surprising.

Piero Dallamano, for instance, in the pages of *Paese Sera*,[30] writes about the evening of 3 October at Sala Scarlatti:

Nella rassegna palermitana delle musiche di avanguardia il teatro è entrato di prepotenza, con qualche titolo di legittimità. Ed è forse una facile previsione che assegna, per il futuro, al teatro il boccone più grosso di queste settimane internazionali della "Musica nuova": si accorgeranno i musicisti di aver covato nel loro nido l'uovo di cuculo. Sia come sia, la serata dedicata a ben undici atti unici, di poeti e scrittori che occasionalmente si sono rivolti al teatro di avanguardia, ha sollevato una curiosità, nel pubblico, quale i concerti più stravaganti non possono avere. Va da sé che in un pranzo di undici portate, tutte di nuova confezione, azzardate secondo un ricettario che mescola la paprica alla panna, c'è da uscirne con lo stomaco sconvolto. Qualcuno però ha fatto centro.[31]

[Theatre has become an integral part of the festival of avant-garde music in Palermo, and not without any legitimacy. And, perhaps, this is a facile prediction, but we think that theatre will become, in the future, the most important part of these international weeks of "New music": will the musicians realize they have welcomed the cuckoo's egg in their own nest? In any event, the evening devoted to as many as eleven one-act plays, by the writers and poets who, for this occasion, have turned to the avant-garde theatre, has been appreciated by the audience more than any of the other extravagant concerts. It goes without saying that after a dinner of eleven courses, all dished out for the first time, and composed according to a recipe book that brought together paprika and whipped cream, one's stomach is rather upset. And yet, some of them have centred the target.]

The confidence with which Dallamano predicts the good fortune of this experimental theatre is quite remarkable: in fact, the plays are the only thing he talks about in the whole article; there is no mention of the readings of poems and novels, nor does he report on the public debates and lectures that had animated the conference at the Hotel Zagarella.

If this review is, all in all, quite positive, apart from the reservations about some of the exotic ingredients and the unusual pairings, many other journalists made quite harsh critiques of the proceedings of the first Gruppo 63 meeting, so much so that Piero Buttitta, showing a great degree of humour and self-irony, built a wonderful article by piecing together the juiciest ones. The fruits of his labour were later included in an anthology of texts by the *Gruppo* members. Here is a brief sample:

Per Beppe Fazio dell'"Ora" (4–5 ottobre 1963) è rimasto, tra gli altri, questo interrogativo, dopo aver assistito allo spettacolo teatrale organizzato dai partecipanti all'"Incontro":

"In realtà certe volte viene da chiedersi se molti di questi giovani autori teatrali non ritengano che per fare dell'avanguardia basti sostituire alle parole che strappavano l'applauso nel drammone borghese perché ritenute cariche di *pathos* – come *madre, ideale, patria* – la parola *culo*, per esempio; se, addirittura, non trasportino sinceramente quel vecchio retorico pathos in queste parole da loro usate non soltanto per *choccare* gli ingenui." [32]

[According to Beppe Fazio, journalist with the *Ora* (4–5 October 1963), upon viewing the theatrical performance organized by the participants to the "meeting," there remained, among others, the following unanswered question:

"Actually, at times, one wonders if many of these young playwrights believe that, in order to be avant-garde, all that is needed is substituting

> one of those words that used to win the audience's applause, when used in bourgeois dramas, because of their *pathos* content – words like *mother, ideal, fatherland* – with the word *arse,* for instance; perhaps, they might be honestly attempting to transport that old-fashioned pathos into these words, which they use to shock the naïve."]

The many articles we have quoted serve to prove how theatre was considered a central activity of Gruppo 63, and not a mere side note to the more important work that was being done regarding poetry and the novel (as many critics who later examined these issues seem to believe). Both the protagonists of those events, as well as the occasional witnesses, saw them as a crucial part of the process of reform of the national artistic and literary landscape that had begun some time before. This renewal process – as is clearly visible, although as if through a filigree, in this last passage – was squarely based in language and, from there, extended its influence to every other aspect of "bourgeois drama." Now that we have established this important fact, it is time to return to the questions posed in the previous section.

1.4 Poetry and the Stage

How did theatre help the Neoavanguardia to untangle the theoretical knot we have described? Here are, in brief, at least four different ways:

1. Theatre helped with the "reduction of the I," for it encouraged polyphony, and often implied the simultaneous presence of many different characters on stage, thus making it mandatory for the writer to weave together various voices, each with a different personality, accent, and outlook on the world. As a consequence, the author had to resort to a larger number of rhetorical resources and could not focus solely on lyricism.
2. Theatre helped to reach the audience more directly. During a performance, the spectators are right there, in front of the writers, provided they decide to participate in the event. They can verify the points of strength and weakness of their works, the effectiveness of their stylistic choices. Additionally, theatre requires a different effort: on stage the actors *speak* the words, and the audience *listens* to them. The oral dimension of language becomes a strong influence on the rhetorical strategies that are employed, and this is particularly meaningful, and rife with consequences for Italian,

which has traditionally been a written and literary language; the writer is thus forced to face the multitude of dialects and regional varieties commonly used by the audience.

3. The ritual component implicit in the theatre, predicated on the physical presence of the actors, allows the writer to introduce more radical experiments, making them more easily digested by the audience. The language employed can be shredded to the point of becoming an unrecognizable collection of fragments, which can be made to clash and become contaminated by a multitude of different influences. Yet, most of the work implicit in such an experiment would fall on the actor, whose body can supply a number of nonverbal clues capable of keeping open the channels of communication with the spectators. In addition to such a ritual, there are also the possibilities offered by mime, dance, choruses, controlled and altered movements, and so on.
4. Finally, theatre promotes the circulation of texts, stories, characters, languages, humour, and breaths (as Pagliarani would put it). In drama as well as in comedy, the script is a textual trace that yearns to transform itself and take on new form.[33] The author must collaborate with a number of other professional artists (actors, director, costume designer, scenographer, etc.) as well as the audience, whose reactions modify the result of the performance, making each one unique and impossible to replicate. And this, it should be pointed out incidentally, is yet another way in which theatre can help with the "reduction of the I."

These considerations, which are given here in synthetic form, can not only be inferred *ex post*, through a critical survey of the available texts and documents but are actually expressed very clearly in the writings of the protagonists of those years, as we will see shortly. But let us proceed methodically: how, exactly, does the "tyranny of the I" relate to the problem of language, realism, and thus to the issue of politics? And in what way did the theatre (as we suggested earlier) provide a viable solution to this problem? We will dedicate the next section of this chapter to the latter question, looking at Pagliarani's poetry, for it is exemplary of a certain way of employing the tools of theatre to solve this dilemma. He, however, was not the only one who considered it a useful resource.

Many Italian writers, beginning in the second half of the 1950s, had been voicing their frustration with a form of populist naturalism that had pervaded the country's literary scene since the end of the Second World War. In his essay "Il midollo del leone" ("The Lion's Bone Marrow"), Calvino expressed the need for a form of concrete engagement alternative to the vague and generalist approach he saw in some of his colleagues:

> Noi crediamo che l'impegno politico, il parteggiare, il compromettersi sia, ancor più che dovere, necessità naturale dello scrittore d'oggi, e prima ancora che dello scrittore, dell'uomo moderno ... Ma non ci riconosciamo certo nel volontarismo espressionistico che inturgida le vene e il linguaggio di una spinta al lirismo irrazionale, quasi di una mistica comunione con le forze collettive.[34]

> [We believe that political engagement, partisanship, and commitment are more than a duty, they are necessities for today's writers; in fact, they are necessary not only to writers, but to all human beings ... However, we don't identify with the expressionistic volunteerism that swells one's veins and pushes language toward irrational lyricism, an almost mystical communion with the collective forces of society.]

Note Calvino's strong criticism of "irrational lyricism" and "mystical communion," both of which he saw as a widespread attitude in the works of his colleagues. In that same essay, Calvino writes, "We said that an emotional relationship with reality doesn't interest us; we're not interested in the emotions, the nostalgia, the pious screens, the misleading solutions to today's difficulties ..."[35]

Although the form this proposed engagement (*impegno*) would have to take was still rather unclear, Calvino, along with the more sensible artists of the time, pushed for a solution that would go beyond mere sentimental commentary; he envisioned a form of engagement predicated on the rational level, articulated according to logical (not emotive) forms. The personalization of issues, their oversimplification, the excessive appeal to the pathos of the audience, rather than to their logos, were rhetorical devices condemned by history and ill-suited to make a real impact on contemporary society.

An approach that was too rigorous and rational, however, risked alienating the audience's sympathies: many of the artists who heeded Calvino's plea were later accused of empty formalism, intellectualism, and so on. The path to a new, reformed, engaged, national literature would prove riddled with difficulties. And yet the solution Calvino suggested in that same essay, dated 1955, is strikingly similar to the one proposed by Giuliani in his introduction to the Novissimi anthology. As Calvino wrote,

> Ritornare a una più calma considerazione del posto delle idee e della ragione nell'opera creativa vorrà dire la fine d'una situazione per cui l'io

dello scrittore è sentito come una specie di maledizione, di condanna. E questo avverrà forse solo il giorno in cui l'intellettuale si accetterà come tale, si sentirà integrato nella società, parte funzionale d'essa, senza più dover sfuggirsi o sfuggirla, camuffarsi o castigarsi.[36]

[A return to a more relaxed appreciation of the role that ideas and reason play within the creative work will put an end to those circumstances that cause the writer to perceive his own "I" as a curse, as a kind of punishment. And perhaps this will happen the day the intellectual will accept himself for what he is, he will feel part of society, one of its integral components, and will stop feeling the need to hide from himself or from society, to disguise and punish himself.]

While Giuliani wrote,

Due aspetti delle nostre poesie vorrei far notare particolarmente: una reale "riduzione dell'io," quale produttore di significati, e una corrispondente versificazione, priva di edonismo, libera da quella ambizione pseudo-rituale che è propria della ormai degradata versificazione sillabica e dei suoi moderni camuffamenti.[37]

[I would like to highlight two different aspects of our poems: a true "reduction of the I," understood as the producer of meaning, and a corresponding way of composing verse that is devoid of hedonism, free from the pseudo-ritual ambitions that are typical of the worn-out syllabic tradition and of its modern disguises.]

In Calvino's words, the subjectivity of the author becomes an impediment to the work, a hurdle that must be overcome in order to give meaning to the words. The condition he posits as the only possible scenario under which the writer's "I" can return to play a central role and be used as an organizing principle for the work of art seems so unlikely that it closely resembles an *adynaton*, an impossibility. In a society that has elevated alienation to the organizing principle of its work force, an intellectual will never feel at home with himself or his function. Thus, the writer's "I" cannot be used as the unifying principle underlying the work of art.[38] If we continue reading Giuliani's introduction to the Novissimi anthology, we find the following:

Quanto alla riduzione dell'io, bisogna intendersi. Anche qui, soprattutto qui, l'artefatta polemica sui "contenuti" non reca alcuna schiarita. Troppo frequentemente, nelle poesie che vorrebbero essere le più aliene dall'intimismo, l'io si nasconde con orgoglio e pervicacia dietro una presunzione di oggettività.

> Le apparenze, come di solito, ingannano. In realtà – e ciò spiega perché diamo importanza a un certo orientamento metrico – il *tono* non solo fa la musica del discorso, ma ne determina l'operatività, il significato. Così la riduzione dell'io dipende più dalla fantasia linguistica che dalla scelta ideologica.[39]
>
> [When it comes to the reduction of the I, we must be clear. Here too, actually, especially here, the artificial controversy about "content" doesn't help. All too often, those poems that are presented as the furthest away from intimism, contain a proud and stubborn "I," hidden behind a screen of objectivity. As usual, appearances are misleading. In reality – and this explains why we prefer a certain type of metre – the *tone* not only creates the music for the discourse, but it also determines its performance, its meaning.]

And here lies the crucial connection between the issue of lyricism and that of politics. The hypertrophic presence of the author's "I" runs deeper than the manifest content of a given work. It is not an issue of genre, either. No matter what the "content" or the "ideology" professed by a text, what really matters is its style, the linguistic choices that shaped it. For that is the true mandate of literature, its area of influence, its fundamental expertise. By reflecting critically on this dimension of the work, without being distracted by the "I" of the author, literature can give its contribution to the advancement of society. But why the fixation with language? Wouldn't a rose by any other name smell as sweet? Giuliani provides us with a rationale for a negative answer in that same introduction:

> Poiché tutta la lingua tende oggi a divenire merce, non si può prendere per dati né una parola né una forma grammaticale né un solo sintagma ... La passione di "parlare in versi" urta, da un lato, contro l'odierno avvolgente consumo e sfruttamento commerciale cui la lingua è sottoposta; dall'altro contro il suo codice letterario, che conserva l'inerzia delle cose e istituisce l'*abuso di consuetudine* (il fittizio "è così") nella visione dei rapporti umani.[40]
>
> [Since all of language today tends to become merchandise, one can't consider words, grammatical structures or syntagms as stable ... The passion for "speaking in verse" clashes on the one hand with the all-encompassing consumerism and commercial exploitation language undergoes in everyday life; on the other hand, it clashes with the literary code, which is governed by the inertia of forms and promotes the *abuse of the routine* (the fictitious "that's the way it is") in the approach to human relationships.]

And this is the duplicitous way in which a consumerist society progressively empties language of meaning, while at the same time destroying all the mechanisms through which literature (and poetry in particular) can counter this process of exponential degeneration.

Guglielmi and Pagliarani also share this same view of poetry's mission. In the introduction to their own anthology, *Manuale di poesia sperimentale*, they write,

> La nostra ipotesi di lavoro è che la mediazione tra poesia e cultura sia rappresentata dall'istituto linguistico ... Di fatto la lingua che noi normalmente usiamo è largamente ideologica (nell'accezione marxiana), carica piuttosto di qualità che di significati. In un siffatto tipo di processo ideologico, il nome non indica la cosa (più precisamente il referente), ma è strumento del suo travestimento o della sua mistificazione operata dal nostro modo sociale di essere, dai nostri interessi, passioni, ecc.[41]
>
> [Our working hypothesis is that the mediation between poetry and culture happens through the linguistic construct ... The language we normally use is highly ideological (in the Marxist sense), charged with qualities, rather than meanings. In such an ideological process, the name doesn't stand for the thing (technically, the referent), but is an instrument of its disguise, of its mystification performed by our social way of being together, by our interests, passions, etcetera.]

Thus, uniting all the different threads of our argument, we could say that the problem of literature's political engagement can be resolved only through a radical reduction of the pervasiveness of lyricism. Such a reduction shouldn't be practised just at a superficial level: it's not a matter of genre (e.g., lyrical poems) or ideology (e.g., bourgeois individualism) but a much more fundamental problem. In order to obtain a true "reduction of the I," the work of the writer must be concentrated on style, and more specifically on language.

Thus, the political problem is ultimately, as far as literature is concerned, a linguistic problem, which must be solved not at the individual level but rather collectively. The audience must be included in the discussion and in the formulation of a solution (or of a possible set of solutions) alongside the writers. Once again, we have a confirmation that the kind of literature capable of doing all this is not an escapist, lyrical one, but rather, as Pagliarani would call it, an epic literature. The relationship with the audience, the connection between author and reader, producer and consumer of the artistic product, becomes crucial for the success of the whole operation.

In fact, if we look at the discussion regarding the definition of this new approach to literature, and whether it should be called avant-garde, or experimental, we'll find an interesting definition by Pagliarani, who, arguing in favour of an avant-garde nomenclature, stated that,

> Nei movimenti di avanguardia abbiamo di diverso, *in più*, ... la critica della funzione dell'operatore e del rapporto operatore-consumatore a tutti i livelli possibili; che viene quindi a rappresentare, secondo questo discorso, l'elemento specifico caratterizzante dei movimenti d'avanguardia rispetto agli altri movimenti artistico-letterari.[42]

> [In the avant-garde movements we have a different element, an *extra one*, ..., that is the criticism of the function of the cultural operator and of the relationship operator-consumer on all possible levels; this difference becomes, according to this argumentation, the characterizing element of the avant-garde movements that differentiates them from other artistic and literary movements.]

An unchecked, rampant form of capitalism and a widespread consumerism aren't the only two factors that contribute to the hollowing out of language. Tradition has a strong impact, too, especially when it comes to those codified forms of artistic expression. Pagliarani called them the "worn-out institutions," and Giuliani also mentioned them in his famous introduction:

> Perché siamo tanto preoccupati del lessico, della sintassi, del metro e via dicendo? Perché se conveniamo che, in quanto "contemporanea," la poesia agisce direttamente sulla vitalità del lettore, allora ciò che conta in primo luogo è la sua efficacia linguistica. Ciò che la poesia *fa* è precisamente il suo "contenuto": se, poniamo, fa sospirare o annoia, la sua verità è, definitivamente, il sospiro o il tedio del lettore. E nei periodi di crisi il *modo di fare* coincide quasi interamente col *significato*.[43]

> [Why are we so concerned with lexicon, syntax, metre, and so on? Because, if we agree that, since it is "contemporary," poetry directly impacts the reader's vitality, then what matters most is its degree of linguistic efficacy. What poetry *does* constitutes its "content": if, let's say, it makes you sigh or it bores you, its ultimate truth is the reader's sigh and boredom. In times of crisis the *way of doing* coincides almost exactly with *meaning*.]

Given the necessity of involving the audience and reminding them of the great untapped potential inherent in language and available to everyone to enjoy, what really matters, in this new and experimental type of art, is not the final product but rather the process. If, in fact, the ultimate solution to the linguistic problem has to be a truly collective one, it cannot come from the intellectual class but has to arise from the bottom up, from the audience itself.

This is the reason why writers shouldn't concern themselves too much with providing a perfect specimen of language; instead they should devise efficient and replicable processes for the creation of meaning. Such processes can then be shared with the audience, who can, in turn, adopt them to create their own language, one that is now truly collective, without sacrificing its critical dimension. As Pagliarani, in his article titled "Per una definizione dell'avanguardia," wrote,

> Molti fra i più impegnati dell'avanguardia … ritengono … che la finalità e/o funzione dell'arte sia quella dell'*opposizione* … Ma qui preme far rilevare che l'opposizione è una *modalità* e non una finalità. Osserviamo intanto, brevemente, come si è realizzata e si realizza l'opposizione. Prima di tutto, negando l'esistenza di luoghi poetici privilegiati, temi, contenuti, atteggiamenti, individuati all'origine dell'espressione, cioè nel linguaggio: negando quindi l'esistenza di un linguaggio poetico privilegiato. Allargando l'orizzonte, … la negazione si è specificata come contestazione. Contestazione dei significati, dei significati precostituiti, che lo scrittore trova nella lingua … Contestazione dei significati precostituiti e usurati della *langue*, e *progettazione* di nuovi significati. Progettazione e non fondazione di nuovi significati, perché la fondazione di nuovi significati relativamente alla lingua è opera della collettività, della società nella storia: chiedere allo scrittore di fondare nuovi significati immediatamente validi per tutti, significa incorrere in un certo tipo di idealismo nel quale cade spesso, per esempio, il vecchio e il nuovo Sartre. Progettare il nuovo, perché non basta negare …[44]

> [Many of the most engaged intellectuals of the avant-garde … believe … that the final goal and/or purpose of art is *opposition* … But here it is important to note how opposition is a *modality* not a finality. Let's first briefly observe how opposition is and was practised. First of all, one must deny the existence of privileged poetic places, themes, subjects, approaches, as they can be found at the origin of expression, that is, inside language: that is to say, one must deny the existence of a privileged poetic language. Looking at the big picture, … the negation is better specified as protest. A protest against received meanings, the ones that are completely worn out and belong to the *langue*, and the *planning* of new meanings. I speak of planning new meanings, and not of creating them, because the creation of new meanings, when it comes to language, should be left to the community, society in history: to ask a writer to create new meanings

would inevitably lead to a form of idealism, as in the case of the old and new works by Sartre. It's a matter of planning the new, because negation is not enough …]

The clarity with which he was able to identify the problem is truly remarkable. Any writer who would attempt to provide a ready-made solution to the issue of language and style would inevitably slip into idealism. The experimentation must go on, then, and the audience must be invited to take part and contribute to the final product.

If we use this description of the ideal process of creation and fruition of the literary text, it becomes easy to see why theatre appeared as the ideal place for this sort of experimentation, and how its tools became very popular among Italian writers. In fact, it offered a place where stylistic research and a direct dialogue with the public could finally coexist and be renewed night after night, show after show.

There is another aspect, as mentioned earlier, through which theatre can offer significant help, and that is in devising a brand of realism that is non-mimetic and thus can support, on the one hand, a rigorous linguistic and stylistic research, while on the other leaving a door open to the kind of *impegno* that was felt to be indispensable to many Italian intellectuals.

The discussions regarding the exact characteristics of this new kind of realism went on for most of the 1950s and 1960s, sparking one of the most interesting controversies of the *dopoguerra* (postwar period). Given the complexity of the issue, and the varied positions held by various writers, the brief answer we will articulate here must make use of a few simplifications. With Luperini, Cataldi, and Marchiani, we will say that,

In Italia la svolta si verifica a metà degli anni Cinquanta. Essa prende avvio da due riviste assai diverse fra loro: "Officina" e "Il Verri." Dalla prima si svilupperà una tendenza sperimentale ma non avanguardistica; dalla seconda nascerà la Neoavanguardia italiana. Mentre "Officina" resta interna alla cultura italiana di quegli anni, largamente dominata dal crociogramscismo e dallo storicismo, "Il Verri" si ispira invece alla fenomenologia e alle nuove scienze umane, sino allora quasi sconosciute nel nostro paese.[45]

[In Italy the turning point happened in the 1950s. It started with two very different journals: *Officina* and *Il Verri*. The first will begin a trend that was experimental but not avant-garde; from the second the Italian Neoavanguardia will be born. While *Officina* remains within the confines of the Italian culture of those years, largely dominated by Crocio-Gramscism and historicism, *Il Verri* was inspired by phenomenology and by the new human sciences, which were, until then, almost unknown in our country.]

In spite of their many differences, however, the two factions agreed on the importance of reconciling innovation and engagement, a renewal of the traditional forms and a progressive political and social agenda. The issue of realism can be traced exactly to this crux.

The writers around *Officina* (Pasolini, Roversi, Leonetti) stressed emotional investment over ideological rigour – or, to put it more fairly, their most interesting and innovative poetry stems from that tension between emotional investment and intellectual rigour. The artist's mission was to "feel" reality and its conflicts, to participate in and express it through one's subjectivity. As a consequence, the author's voice is often brought to the fore (especially by Pasolini), perhaps in an attempt to encourage a deliberate (self-aware and even critical) identification of readers with the poet. The intervention in reality, the *impegno*, is made possible mainly through a rhetorical strategy based on the use of apostrophe, declined according to its different aspects of allocution, invocation, and execration. The poet includes himself in his own texts, addresses readers directly, calling them to action, and pointing to those aspects of reality that must be changed.

This approach to writing, which relies on the strength of its pathos for its effectiveness, necessarily implies a high degree of mimesis. Reality must be presented as susceptible to investigation and objective description, so that readers may react directly, in an emotional manner, to the text that is put in front of them and that must work as a valid surrogate of the reality it was meant to represent. As a consequence, the space available for formal and linguistic experimentation is minimal. In order for a more perfect and transparent illusion to be created, the rules of genre and the literary conventions must be scrupulously respected. Furthermore, that form of worn-out lyricism, almost an original sin of Italian literature, becomes an inevitable poetic feature (the over-exhibited subjectivity mentioned above).

Thus, for the *Officina* group, political engagement is understood in terms of direct involvement, on the personal level, outside the mediation of political parties, and it hinges on a direct relationship with the reader. From the stylistic point of view, the main feature employed is a mimetic form of realism, centred on politically charged contents rather than formal research, and rhetorically predicated on pathos and on direct identification with the lyric subject inscribed in the text. This may appear as an excessively reductive summary, but a few quick quotations from the theoretical essays dating back to those years will corroborate our account. Here is a first, brief passage from an article published by Pasolini in 1966:

> In confronto mettiamo a Ginsberg, tutti i contestatari linguistici appaiono degli abatini – come un giornalista imitatore di Contini, chiama i giocatori di calcio graziosi e accademici. Tutta l'avanguardia italiana, per esempio (a parte certi arrivisti, volgari e quasi fisicamente ripugnanti) è composta di tali abatini.[46]
>
> [In comparison with, let's say, Ginsberg, all these linguistic protesters appear like little abbots – as a journalist, imitator of Contini, calls those gracious and academic soccer players. The whole Italian avant-garde, for instance (save for some vulgar, almost physically repugnant careerists), is composed of these little abbots.]

Here Pasolini does not try to hide his contempt for the opposing faction, which he gratifies with the epithets "little abbots" and "linguistic protesters."[47] Their dissent, their *impegno*, in his estimation, was limited to a "linguistic scandal." In fact, he continues, "after I am done reading an avant-garde text, what do I learn? What information did I receive from that mode of writing?" Naturally, nothing, according to Pasolini, save that it was a linguistically experimental kind of literature. "But what do I learn about *the author* of that text?" he wonders. "Ah, on this account, absolutely nothing. Or, rather, I learn only one thing: I learn that he is a *literatus*."

Thus, according to Pasolini, expressing something of the author as an individual human being is a fundamental part of poetry's job. Continuing on in the same essay, he says,

> Ciò che mi intriga – e mi intriga perché ne sono maturo – è il fatto che i due più avanzati e straordinari rappresentanti del saggismo europeo, che io conosca, ossia Goldmann e Barthes, sono ambedue ciò che noi in Italia chiameremmo dei "contenutisti" ... Ma io ero arrivato, comunque, a questo ... "contenutismo" ... come il solito ... per vie tortuose, mal definibili e includenti vicissitudini biografiche e passioni incontinenti, per un fare fatto sempre prima di essere capito. In breve: il sentire di non poter più scrivere usando la tecnica del romanzo si è trasformato subito in me, per una specie di autoterapia inconscia, nella voglia di usare un'altra tecnica, ossia quella del cinema.[48]
>
> [What intrigues me – and it intrigues me because I am ready for it – is the fact that the two most advanced representatives of European essayism I know, Goldmann and Barthes, are both what here in Italy we would call "*contenutisti*" ("contentists") ... But, anyway, I had arrived at this ...

"contentism"... as usual ... through winding roads, difficult to define, and through meandering biographic vicissitudes, incontinent passions, thanks to a practice that precedes understanding. In short: the feeling that it was impossible to write using the form of the novel had turned, as far as I am concerned, into a sort of unconscious self-therapy, in the desire to use a different technique, that of cinema.]

Thus, to the synthetic description outlined above, one must add "contentism" to the characteristics of realism according to *Officina*, at least in Pasolini's opinion. The solution to the problem of *impegno* in literature and to the stylistic renovation must be sought, it would seem, in cinema.[49] Then Pasolini goes on to write,

> Perché ho fatto tutto questo stravagante discorso? Perché mi ci è voluto il cinema per capire una cosa enormemente semplice, ma che nessun letterato sa. Che la realtà si esprime da sola; e che la letteratura non è altro che un mezzo per mettere in condizione la realtà di esprimersi da sola *quando non è fisicamente presente.* Cioè la poesia non è che una evocazione, e ciò che conta è la realtà evocata che parla da sola al lettore, come ha parlato da sola all'autore.[50]
>
> [Why did I make this extravagant digression? Because only after encountering cinema was I able to understand something enormously simple but that no writer knows. That reality expresses itself by itself; and that literature is nothing but a means to put reality in the condition of expressing itself by itself *when it is not physically present.* That is, poetry is nothing more than an evocation, and what matters is the reality that is evoked and speaks on its own, as it did with the author.]

Here he finally makes explicit the fundamental assumption behind mimetic realism: reality is seen as something objective, stable, perfectly knowable, and that can be univocally represented. The work of the artist is, thus, that of imitating as accurately as possible that reality which is given objectively, exploiting the tools of the trade in such a way that they remain invisible to the reader, so that the final result may appear as neutral, natural, sharing the same objectivity that is postulated to belong to reality. From this perspective, the preference given to cinema over literature can be easily understood: it is much easier to create an impression of complete transparency through the use of moving images on a silver screen than through printed words on a page.[51]

Fortunately, the vast majority of Italian writers did not give up the pen to embrace the camera but rather tried to reconcile the need for a stylistic reform of literature with the need for political engagement. Let us turn, for a moment, to Sanguineti, who, regarding the supposed neutrality of reality and its representation, in an interview with Ferdinando Camon, stated that

> Il linguaggio non può darmi la realtà nella sua immediatezza, o come neutralità …, ma significa creare artificiosamente un certo prodotto convenzionale, culturale, storico, che mi rinvia alla realtà ma che nello stesso tempo forma un certo organismo, caratterizzato ideologicamente dalla sua stessa struttura. Il linguaggio naturalistico era un filtro verso la realtà; il linguaggio naturalistico, che finge che non ci sia praticamente divario fra ciò che è detto e le cose come sono, in realtà è, lo sappiamo, un certo modo di organizzare ideologicamente la realtà, di filtrarla, in un sistema culturale, in una mitologia, per usare il mio termine, in cui questi elementi ambiscono a presentarsi al massimo grado neutri ed innocenti.[52]
>
> [Language cannot give me reality in its immediacy, or as a neutrality …, but it can artificially create a certain conventional, cultural, historical product that points to reality and at the same time gives shape to a certain organism, which is ideologically marked by its very structure. Naturalistic language was a filter on reality; naturalistic language, which acts as if there were practically no distinction between what is said and things as they are in reality is, as we all know, a certain way of organizing reality according to a given ideology, filtering it, a cultural system, a mythology, to use my own term, within which these elements aspire to present themselves as neutral and innocent to the utmost degree.]

Sanguineti not only indicates the impossibility of a naturalistic representation of reality, deeming it an illusion; he goes on to demonstrate how such an idea is actually a dangerous ideological weapon:

> Ora, l'aspirazione a creare un linguaggio neutro, a offrire una neutralità di percezione del reale, è l'aspirazione borghese massima proprio perché nell'orizzonte borghese non c'è più realmente storia ma è ormai soltanto natura; il linguaggio della borghesia si presenta come il linguaggio naturale dell'uomo allo stesso modo che l'esperienza dell'uomo borghese si presenta come l'esperienza naturale dell'uomo. Il capitalismo è la forma immortale verso cui tendeva la storia dell'umanità, e ora essa, finalmente pacificata, guarda il mondo così com'è, una volta per tutte.[53]
>
> [Now, the aspiration to create a neutral language, to offer a neutral perception of reality, is the highest bourgeois aspiration, especially because, from a bourgeois perspective, there is no more real history left, but only nature; the language of the bourgeoisie presents itself as

the natural language of man in much the same way as the experience of the bourgeois man presents itself as the natural experience of mankind. Capitalism is an immortal form toward which the totality of the history of humanity was headed; now that it has reached it, finally at peace, men can look at the world as it really is, once and for all.]

In a similar manner, the issue of *impegno* cannot be resolved, according to Sanguineti and the group of *Il Verri*, at the level of individual, emotional, pathetic involvement. And it is precisely from the role played by poets and their subjectivity that the criticism of Novissimi takes its start. One must only remember the oft-quoted introduction by Giuliani that condemned the hypertrophy of the lyrical I and advocated its reduction. The role of intellectuals requires the most stringent rigour possible, since their mission consists in providing those tools indispensable for the subordinate classes to acquire full awareness of themselves and of the condition of exploitation in which they live, and to reclaim their rights.

Literary experiments, then, must be adjusted accordingly and, instead of concentrating on reality (the contents Pasolini emphasizes in his writings), they should focus on the rhetorical instruments that the dominating class wields to perpetuate its hegemonic position. The critical attention of the neo-avant-garde is thus pointed to the ideology of language (the interference or, better yet, the osmosis between ideology and language), and to the rhetoric of the discourse of power. Their formal experiments are not merely aimed at creating linguistic scandal but are intended to dismantle those rhetorical and linguistic instruments that enable this control and alienation and that allow them to be perpetrated and spread within society.

For all these reasons, the kind of realism that is suggested by *Il Verri* is anti-mimetic: it doesn't try to portray the expressive means it uses as natural and neutral. It is a kind of realism concerned with the rhetorical level of language (so as to denounce the interferences between language and power) rather than with the referential one. In that same interview with Camon, Sanguineti continues as follows:

Diciamo allora che nessuno più di me ha dimostrato di essere estraneo alle posizioni del "realismo socialista"; ma nessuno più di me rimane legato al fatto che un'estetica del realismo, con una sua chiara fondazione ideologica, e politica, è comunque il problema *a partire dal quale* si pone in generale ogni problema estetico, oggi. Il realismo non sarà allora quello, ingenuo, che si è foggiato quel nome e si è configurato come "realismo socialista" all'epoca dello stalinismo; ma che il problema rimanga quello di una capacità minore o maggiore, da parte di questa o quella posizione letteraria, e ideologica di abbracciare un'autentica realtà e di non mistificarla nella sua espressione

> artistica questo, mi pare, è fuori di dubbio. Che io sia dunque fautore di una poetica del realismo, rimane vero, non sarà ripeto, l'ingenuo "realismo socialista" che poi per me è davvero un momento regressivo nel senso di nostalgie borghesi e, peggio, piccolo-borghesi.[54]
>
> [Let us say, then, that nobody has been shown to be extraneous to the positions of "socialist realism" more than I; but nobody is more convinced than I that an aesthetic of realism, with a clear ideological and political foundation, is the problem *from which anyone must begin* in order to articulate any other aesthetic problem. Naturally, realism will not be, then, that naïve style that had been called "socialist realism" and flourished at the time of Stalinism; and yet, it is crystal clear that the problem remains whether this or that literary trend is capable of offering an image of reality that can embrace its authenticity without mystifying it in its artistic expression. Thus, it is true that I am the supporter of a realist poetics; however, I repeat, mine is not a naïve "socialist realism," which should be considered as a truly regressive movement, riddled with bourgeois or, better, petit-bourgeois nostalgia.]

Therefore, according to the *Il Verri* group, political engagement requires a high degree of intellectual and ideological rigour, often expressed through an anti-mimetic form of realism, anchored on the plane of *logos*, and aimed at the dismantling of those linguistic weapons meant for control and alienation. Pursuing this kind of realism leads inevitably to a radical reform of the linguistic institutions that capitalism and the bourgeoisie use to perpetrate their dominant position.

Even though this way of framing the problematic knot of engagement-experimentalism-realism seems much more coherent than the one offered by *Officina*, the issue of the relationship with the audience still remains unresolved. Finally, we have reached the core of the matter: the "linguistic protesters" of *Verri* attempted to reconcile the need for a rigorous political engagement with some formal research capable of expressing the complexity of reality (both inside and outside language, which is, naturally, itself a part of reality, an object among objects), as well as the risks and complications that any attempt at representation implies. Such a formal experimentation makes for a difficult relationship with the audience: it would be much easier if writers tried to reach them on the emotional level, using rhetorical tools that they can recognize as traditional and therefore familiar. The risk is that of appearing elitist, removed from everyday reality precisely when trying to portray its complexities as well as possible. Intellectual rigour often demands the use of a highly specialized terminology, which reinforces such communication problems. It is easy to see how quickly this situation can turn paradoxical: on the one hand, the writers of the Neoavanguardia want to impact reality through a direct influence on their audience; on the other hand, an excess of intellectual rigour impedes their effectiveness and might even result in a completely adverse outcome. Theatre is the only way out of this catch-22.

1.5 The Example of Pagliarani

The discussion we have just outlined above is crucial to Italian culture in those years (the 1960s and early 1970s). However, it is also very relevant today, for it tackles the fundamental issue of the role literature plays within our society, and the practical ways in which literature can reach its audience. Within this discussion, we find many different positions but very little agreement. And this is what is truly fascinating about this debate: the sheer number of solutions that have been proposed from the theoretical point of view. But even more astonishing is the variety of practical, temporary strategies that were devised.

Although there was no agreement within the group, it doesn't mean that there was no common ground. In fact, the most interesting modes of research converged in many ways. We saw the two examples of the "reduction of the I" and the harsh criticism of a more conventional form of lyricism. The use of theatre and its tools is another one of the areas in which different lines of research overlapped. In this regard, we can quote Testa, who, in the introduction to his own anthological reconstruction of the Italian poetry of the second half of the twentieth century, writes,

> Questo decisivo passaggio nella storia della nostra poesia concretamente si realizza modificando gli equilibri della tradizionale situazione lirica e della sua immobilità fonologica e centripeta ... Si tratta, in sintesi, di modalità ascrivibili al tipo del racconto e, soprattutto, del dramma, spesso in interazione. Schemi drammatici sono nei libri di Sereni e Caproni, innervano scene e monologhi in Giudici (e Raboni), dettano la presenza di plurime voci (interiori e no) ne *La Beltà* di Zanzotto, suggeriscono il dantesco articolarsi degli scontri tra l'io e i suoi interlocutori in *Nel magma* di Luzi.[55]

> [This decisive transition in the history of our poetry was concretely realized by transforming the traditional standing of lyricism, and its phonological and centripetal immobility ... In short, it is an issue of the shape the narrative or (more importantly) the drama took, often interacting with each other. We find theatrical modes in the works of Sereni and Caproni, theatrical scenes and monologues in Giudici (and Raboni), various voices (interior or otherwise) in Zanzotto's *Beltà*, a Dantesque clash of the "I" and its interlocutors in Luzi's *Nel magma*.]

The survey of texts Testa mentions must be left for another time. What matters here is to register once more the fact that many different authors were experiencing the same stylistic restlessness, and that an interesting selection of them, across groups, schools, and cliques, looked to the theatre as a source of inspiration.

It's also important to highlight again how this observation is not something that has become available only *a posteriori*, after the fact, and with the benefit of temporal distance. In fact, Pagliarani displayed his usual lucidity when, in 1967, he observed,

> Sembra chiaro che il teatro, almeno quello inteso alla maniera di Artaud, è lo strumento più adatto a superare linguisticamente la crisi della parola (e il romanzo quello meno adatto, perché ha meno possibilità strutturali di contestarla, straniarla, stravolgerla, senza con ciò stesso precludersi troppo spesso linguaggio, comunicazione; laddove il verso risulta già relativamente più autonomo, e più capace di auto straniamento).[56]

> [It seems clear that the theatre, at least the kind of theatre Artaud envisioned, is the instrument best suited to linguistically overcome the crisis of the word (and the novel is the least suited, for it possesses fewer structural possibilities to protest this crisis, to estrange it, to turn it upside down, without rendering language and communication impossible; on the other hand, verse is already more independent, and more capable of estranging itself).]

Pagliarani's choice of the theatre is a deliberate one, intended to overcome the shortcomings he had previously identified in contemporary literature. In addition to being the place for formal and linguistic experimentation, the theatre is identified by Pagliarani as the ideal place where author and audience can meet face to face, where exchange and criticism can happen freely, where the new language, a truly collective one, can be created. In an article devoted to syntax and genres, he writes,

> S'intende, ovviamente, che la sperimentazione plurilinguistica ha come intrinseco finalismo l'espressione monolinguistica; ma con la nostra tradizione letteraria ce ne vorrà del tempo per risciacquare i panni in Arno! Tempo che si potrà mettere a frutto magari anche seguendo l'indicazione di Eliot sulla forza sociale che acquista la poesia quando è proposta in forma teatrale (forza che rompe le stratificazioni del pubblico); ma forse l'unico modo per accelerare i lavori è che ci sia proprio necessità oggettiva di scrivere tragedie ... Per il *genre* "dramma in versi" direi che ora gli strumenti li abbiamo.[57]

> [Naturally, it is understood that plurilinguistic experimentation is intrinsically intended to eventually lead to a monolinguistic expression; however, given

our literary tradition, washing our clothes in the Arno will take quite a while! Perhaps we could use that time to follow Eliot's suggestion regarding the strength poetry acquires when it is couched in a theatrical form (capable of breaking up the audience's stratifications); but perhaps the only way of speeding up the process is that of being forced to face the objective necessity of writing tragedies … I'd say that now we have all the proper tools for the *genre* of "drama in verse."]

Pagliarani often looked to Eliot for his ideas on multilinguism and theatre.[58] We will note in passing that what Pagliarani calls here "drama in verse" he elsewhere describes as "poemetto narrativo, con la sua brava terza persona, che si occupasse di vicende contemporanee che non mi riguardassero troppo direttamente," – that is, a "narrative poem, told in the third person, which deals with contemporary events that didn't involve me too directly" – and the two could very well be the same thing. In fact, their most important characteristic is that of working toward the creation of a monolinguistic code out of plurilinguistic experimentation: that shared creative process between consumers and producers we have been talking about. The theatre, as Pagliarani puts it, is capable of breaking up the stratifications of the audience – that is, it is capable of creating, for the short time of the show, a cohesive group of people that is not differentiated by class and thus one that can aid in the effort to create that new monolinguism in a critical, non-hegemonic way.

The approach to theatre happens in two different ways: on the one hand many writers begin composing texts especially for the theatre, and for representation through actors, productions, and so on. On the other hand, certain forms and tools of the theatre are adopted and appropriated by poetry. Pagliarani, as well as some of his fellow travellers, pursued both avenues.[59] Over the next few pages, however, we will look only at the influence theatre has had on his poetry. In chapters 4 and 5 we will spend more time analysing his plays.

What do we mean when we say "forms and tools of the theatre"? First of all, we can identify in Pagliarani's poetry a strong presence of orality, understood as the simulation of a co-presence of speaker and audience.[60] In this regard, as Testa, in the already quoted introduction to his anthology, notes,

> Se ci limitiamo, per il momento, a registrare dati grammaticali o superindividuali … è agevole vedere come i termini, fraseologie e costrutti morfosintattici di stampo parlato siano ora assunti nella scrittura poetica con un grado di ospitalità di cui è difficile trovare l'eguale in passato … Ne *Gli strumenti umani* (1965) Sereni ricorre ad un'impaginazione discorsiva in cui i tratti parlati (scorciature, dislocazioni, termini informali), hanno,

a differenza dei libri precedenti, un ruolo decisivo nella resa, vibratile e nervosa, della sua insoddisfazione per il tempo avuto in sorte. Il *Congedo del viaggiatore cerimonioso* (1965) di Caproni s'impianta su una divagante recitazione, fitta di moduli colloquiali e scandita dal mutare di toni e inflessioni della voce in rapporto al profilo del personaggio in scena. Emblematico il caso di *Nel magma* (1963) di Luzi, un autore che sin qui si era sempre tenuto lontano dalla frequentazione del registro parlato della lingua. Nella raccolta del '63 si opta invece per una discorsività quasi prosastica (con termini alla moda e parole del quotidiano) ritenuta necessaria a pedinare la "chiacchiera" del mondo e il frantumarsi delle esperienze di chi lo abita.[61]

[If, for the time being, we limit ourselves to the consideration of the grammatical and super-individual elements, we can easily see how the terms, phrases, and morpho-syntactic constructs based on spoken language are now warmly welcomed by poetic writing, as never before … In *Gli strumenti umani* ["The Human Instruments"] (1965) Sereni employs a discursive layout in which the spoken elements (contractions, dislocations, informal expressions) have a decisive role in portraying his dissatisfaction with the time in which he lived, in the most vivid and nervous of ways. Caproni's *Congedo del viaggiatore cerimonioso* ["Farewell of the Ceremonious Traveller"] (1965) is predicated on a digressive type of recitation, filled with colloquial expressions and marked by the changes in tone and inflection of the voice in relation to the character presented on stage. Particularly representative is the case of Luzi's *Nel magma* ["In the Magma"] (1963). Up until now, this author had kept away from the spoken register of language. In his 1963 collection, instead, he chooses a form of discourse that is almost prose (including fashionable words and terms taken from everyday life). He considers this necessary in order to keep up with the world's "chatter" and the fragmentation of the experiences of those who live in it.]

If this is what happens with the less openly experimental poets of those years, we can imagine that the phenomenon is even more pronounced when it comes to the members of the neo-avant-garde:

Anche la maggiore avanguardia persegue ora un inedito rapporto con l'italiano d'uso. Muovendo dall'esigenza di ampliare al massimo il vocabolario poetico, Pagliarani, con *La ragazza Carla* (1960), contamina registri differenti e ripropone sulla pagina un repertorio vastissimo di costrutti del parlato, inteso come un'organica realtà da cui nulla va estromesso. Sanguineti abbandona il genere informale del monologo praticato in *Laborintus* e ricerca, in *Purgatorio de l'Inferno* (terzo tempo di *Triperuno* del 1964), una nuova grammaticalità della dizione a cui

> partecipano, da vere protagoniste, formule oralizzanti (come le ripetizioni pronominali o le dislocazioni) destinate a divenire in seguito sigle caratteristiche della sua scrittura.[62]
>
> [Even the most important part of the avant-garde movement is now pursuing an unprecedented relationship with spoken Italian. Motivated by the necessity of expanding his poetic vocabulary, Pagliarani, with *La ragazza Carla* (1960), mixes different registers and taps into a vast repertoire of spoken constructs, understanding them as part of an organic reality from which nothing is excluded. Sanguineti abandons his informal style, the monologue he developed for *Laborintus*, and, in *Purgatorio dell'Inferno* (the third part of *Triperuno*, 1964), he searches for a new form of grammar of diction that will include as its main component formulas taken from oral language (like pronominal repetitions or dislocations), which would later become the trademark of his style.]

The use of a more demotic variety of language can be read in at least three different ways. On the one hand, it is a reaction to the excessive codification caused by more than six centuries of almost exclusive written use. Since a common, spoken variety of Italian had become available, it was only natural for poets to appropriate and experiment with it. At the same time, it also constitutes a means of protest (as Pagliarani defined it) against the idea that there is a privileged place, code, or subject matter for poetry. Finally, it is a way of simulating the presence of speakers and audience within the same space. The shift of the linguistic code toward a spoken register allows producers and consumers to come together, to interact. However, this interaction would not be based on an emotional, pathetic level (as we saw in the traditional forms of lyricism) but rather on the rational level of the logos, of discourse and language.

Such a development involves not only the more determined experimenters (like Pagliarani and Sanguineti) but also more conservative voices like those of Sereni, Luzi, and Caproni. The latter's *Congedo del viaggiatore cerimonioso* ("Farewell of the Ceremonious Traveller") is a particularly remarkable example: it approximates with astounding vividness the close quarters of a train compartment and the conversations that can be heard there and on the platform of a station, and is at the same time mundane and charged with existential overtones.

Furthermore, we must not forget the prosodic dimension of this newfound orality. We saw how Giuliani, in his introduction, connects these two aspects as fundamental elements that unite the works of the different poets collected in the Novissimi anthology: the reduction of the I and a new form of versification. The most traditional forms of lyricism also have a distinctive rhythm (see, for instance, certain poems of Pasolini's in *Le ceneri di Gramsci* ["The Ashes of Gramsci"]); in much the same way, orality has its own rhythm, its distinctive metre, which changes from author to author but can be effectively epitomized by Pagliarani's *"verso a fisarmonica spalancata"* (open accordion verse). In this regard, as Luigi Ballerini observes,

> Il verso sgorgante e mulinante di Pagliarani ha le sue molteplici radici nella nenia, nella filastrocca, nella fabulazione popolare, nella recita ingenua (in famiglia, o dei guitti in teatri improvvisati), nella lettura collettiva del giornale, nel comizio all'angolo della strada, o della discussione scalmanata a opera di sfaccendati riuniti in roccolo.[63]

> [Pagliarani's overflowing and swirling verse has its many roots in lullabies, nursery rhymes, folk tales, playful acting (either within the family, or by jesters in makeshift theatres), in the collective reading of newspapers, in the political rally on the street corner, or in the loud discussions of idle bystanders gathered in circles.]

In fact, Pagliarani is a master of exploiting the communicative and expressive potential of a number of rhetorical devices habitually employed in everyday conversations by all kinds of speakers. He elevates them to the level of sophisticated tools, capable of manipulating not only the structure of the verse but also the entire narrative of his *romanzi in versi*.[64] In his by now familiar introduction, Giuliani made a similar observation:

> Così l'atteggiamento sentimentale e quello letterario di Pagliarani perfettamente coincidono in uno stile "umile" e saldo, che sembra terra terra e invece tocca un'esemplare drammaticità, sorda di fatica, frantumata in tante prove di coraggio e delusione, com'è il tempo del suo raccontare … Schietto, non vorrebbe mai parlare in prima persona: se vuol dire qualcosa, inventa un personaggio (magari un certo poeta che somiglia a Pagliarani) oppure un "coro" come spesso nella *Ragazza Carla*: si faccia caso a quei recitativi che nel poemetto spezzano continuamente l'andatura da ballata popolare e giuocano d'equilibrio con quel tanto di lirismo che egli si lascia estrarre solo in questo modo indiretto.[65]

> [Thus, Pagliarani's emotional and literary attitudes coincide perfectly in a "humble" and sound style, which seems unsophisticated and instead reaches an exemplary dramatic dimension, consumed by fatigue, fragmented into a number of acts of courage and disappointments, just like the time of his narration … Pagliarani is exceptionally frank, and there is so much he would

> never say in the first person: if he wants to say something, he invents a character (maybe a certain poet who resembles Pagliarani) or a "chorus," as found in *La ragazza Carla*: see for instance those recitatives that continually break the popular ballad rhythm of the poem and carefully incorporate the small amounts of lyricism he allows himself only in an indirect way.]

We're particularly interested in Giuliani's intuition regarding the use Pagliarani makes of masks and dramatis personae. Whenever forced to say something about himself, he would create a character and lend to that fictitious construct the thoughts and impressions he wanted to express. In a sense, this is the simplest and most direct way of employing theatre to break free of the "tyranny of the I." The interesting element resides in Pagliarani's choice of fictional characters: they are always very different from him, and, in their mouths, his words and feelings become distorted and estranged, often acquiring a completely new meaning and losing all that *conseguente bagaglio* (resulting baggage) which pity for oneself inevitably brings. The idea that masks can be used to reduce the excessive presence of the author within the poetic text is also noted by Testa, who in his introduction writes,

> L'insistenza su modalità narrative e teatrali, accomunate dalla categoria del personaggio (vero cardine compositivo della poesia del periodo), sottopone l'antico schema del lirismo ad una sorta di dilatazione su più registri e movenze; la quale è, a sua volta, connessa alla messa in questione delle pretese assolutistiche di una soggettività chiusa in se stessa (un aspetto, questo, su cui quasi tutti, anche se con obiettivi diversi, polemicamente insistono: da Porta a Caproni).[66]

> [The insistence on theatrical and narrative modalities, linked by the use of fictional characters (the true focal point of the poetry of the time), subjects the old formula of lyricism to a sort of dilation over different registers and tones; and this, in turn, is connected to the criticism of the absolute demands advanced by a self-absorbed subjectivity (this is an aspect that everyone, from Porta to Caproni, agrees on, even though their final goals remain very different).]

If Testa calls them characters, we prefer to consider them masks worn by the author's subject, but the textual phenomenon is indeed the same; and this is a trait shared by almost everyone, although in different ways, and for different purposes. In an article published in *Quindici*, Fausto Curi reviewed *Lezione di fisica e Fecaloro* ("Physics Lesson and Fecaloro"), then recently published by Feltrinelli. After framing the problem of the new poetry as inescapably linked to the problem of readership – "Chi legge i libri di poesia? E che senso ha, oggi, leggere un libro di poesia?" (Who reads poetry? And what does it mean, today, to read a book of poems?) – and providing a definition of poetry that is rooted in language and begins with the experience of those who seek poetry to obtain something that cannot be gained by consuming any other cultural form – "Di fronte alla storia mistificata in infinite parole, leggere un libro di poesia è esperire nella lingua la verità mitica della storia" (Faced with a history that has been mystified through endless words, reading a book of verse is experiencing through language the mythical truth of history) – Curi turns to Pagliarani's verses (*Lezione di fisica e Fecaloro*'s, in particular), and their way of engaging the reader by adopting some of the stylistic means and the rhetorical postures of the theatre:

> Quella conversazione accidentata e intermittente che costituisce il modulo fondamentale di quasi tutti i testi di Pagliarani potrebbe, in prima istanza, autorizzare l'ipotesi di una poesia, appunto, come conversazione, realizzata transfunzionando in istituzione stilistica la fortissima inclinazione al dialogo. In una prospettiva esegetica globale non si tarda però ad accertare il carattere semplificante e riduttivo di tale ipotesi. Per Pagliarani, infatti, la poesia non è solo il risarcimento linguistico dell'alienazione, ma è il luogo dove tale risarcimento si compie ricostituendo la figura dell'alterità.[67]

> [That uneven and episodic conversation which is the fundamental module of almost all of Pagliarani's texts could, at first, authorize the hypothesis of a poetry that is actually a conversation, achieved by transforming into a stylistic institute its strong inclination toward dialogue. Upon taking a global interpretative look, however, such a hypothesis will be quickly shown to be a rather reductive simplification. In fact, according to Pagliarani, poetry is not only the compensation for linguistic alienation but rather the place where such compensation can be achieved through a reconstitution of the "other."]

The first consideration from which Curi moves his analysis is the peculiar style of Pagliarani's syntax, predicated on anacoluthon, aposiopesis, and the frequent interjection of extraneous voices and discourses that constantly interrupt the main linguistic thread, bearing all the marks of a spontaneous conversation carried out in realistic, lifelike conditions. As Curi points out, the main objective of this style is not mimesis: it is not simply trying to reproduce a dialogue in the way it might naturally occur within society. Rather, it is a very ingenious way of re-creating the "other," an interlocutor who does not need to be made explicit but is instead constantly implied in the unravelling of the text. In addition to contrasting that "tyranny of the I" we often spoke of, such a technique is, at its core, theatrical:

> Ora, si sa, fra tutte le forme artistiche il teatro è, per eccellenza, quella dove l'alterità linguistica si attua con le maggiori possibilità dialettiche: vi è una dialettica di partiture dialogiche e di connessioni gestuali e – strettamente congiunta con l'altra nel circuito linguistico che insieme istituiscono – una dialettica di parola-gesto e di pubblico. Di esse, la seconda non è estranea a Pagliarani, nella misura in cui la sua poesia presuppone degli spettatori e implica, non sempre felicemente, uno spazio acustico di dizione-ascoltazione, e nella misura in cui i versi sono circondati da una sorta di alone sonoro, a volte un po' greve, la parola è segnata come da una dilatazione fonica e contiene una più o meno intensa carica di gestualità. Si tratta, comunque, di una dialettica per forza di cose limitatamente fruibile da un poeta, per il quale una poesia come teatro è assai meglio attuabile nel gioco delle interrelazioni testuali. Prevalentemente in questo senso sembra muoversi Pagliarani.[68]

> [Now, as we all know, out of all artistic forms of expression, theatre is the one that can best exploit the dialectic possibilities of a linguistic "other": there is a dialectic of dialogic scores and gestural connections – internal to language – and a dialectic between the word-gesture and the audience. Out of these two, the latter is not irrelevant to Pagliarani's writing, in so far as it postulates the presence of spectators and implies, not always in a satisfactory manner, an acoustic space of declamation-listening. His verses are surrounded by a sound halo, at times a bit heavy, and his words are marked by a sort of phonic dilation that contains a varying degree of gestural energy. However, this is a kind of dialectic that, for practical reasons, a poet can experience only in a limited capacity, especially since, for him, poetry in the form of theatre can be more easily pursued at the level of textual interrelations. Pagliarani seems to be moving primarily in this direction.]

This second half of Curi's reflection is not as intuitively accessible as the first. He argues that we shouldn't take the theatrical and dialogic qualities of Pagliarani's verse at face value and presuppose an immediate transformation of those different voices and discourses in as many different characters. That, he argues, would be an oversimplification. If it is true that the poet's words are marked by a residue of the spoken language – an "oral" coloration that implies the presence of an audience to which the poem is directed – the real theatrical dimension is to be found in the way Pagliarani makes different texts interact, argue, clash, and collide, so that a different and more nuanced understanding of reality can manifest itself through the cracks and the sparks generated by this friction.

To conclude his essay, Curi turns to Derrida's reflections on Artaud, and his "cure" for the "malady" afflicting the "West":

> Quale sia questa "malattia," si sa bene. È la verbalità, l'unidimensionalità del linguaggio, le parole senza il corpo fisico dei gesti, mortificate nella loro condizione di scrittura, di cose dette una volta per sempre, e dunque non più vive. ... Col suo ostinato rifiuto di un teatro come "poesia," paradossalmente Artaud fornisce un fondamentale ausilio a una poesia come teatro. Distanziando le edonistiche, evasive e – esse sì, davvero – mistiche soluzioni grafiche cui oggi ricorre, nella gran parte dei casi, la poesia visiva, la sua idea di una "matérialisation visuelle et plastique de la parole," di una parola da usare "dans un sens concret et spatial," da manipolare "comme un object solide et qui ébranle des choses" (cf *Théâtre oriental et théâtre occidental*) può offrire fertili stimoli all'impazienza della poesia di travalicare sia la propria verbalità sia le frontiere del libro per istituirsi come progetto di comportamento in uno spazio fisico virtuale.[69]
>
> [What this "malady" is, we all know. It is verbosity, the unidimensionality of language, words without the physical body of gestures, mortified in their condition of writing, of things said once and for all, and thus no longer alive ... Paradoxically, with his stubborn rejection of theatre as "poetry," Artaud provides a fundamental aid to the constitution of poetry as theatre. Distancing itself from the hedonistic, evasive, and mystical graphic solutions to which, in the majority of cases, visual poetry resorts, his idea of a "*matérialisation visuelle et plastique de la parole*," of a word to be used "*dans un sens concret et spatial*," to be manipulated "*comme un object solide et qui ébranle des choses*" (see *Théâtre oriental et théâtre occidental*), he can offer fertile stimuli to poetry's eagerness to trespass its own verbosity as well as the boundaries of the book, and assert itself as a behavioural project in a virtual physical space.]

In this quotation, Curi stresses the importance of Artaud for the culture of the Neoavanguardia and the theatrical debate in Italy, in the fields of both literature and theatre.[70] He also expresses a very critical position in regard to the experiments that many artists were making in the field of *poesia visiva* (visual poetry).[71] Recently, there has been a resurgence of interest in Gruppo 70's work, and we can only hope that this will lead to more detailed studies and further publications.[72] The final part of the quotation, however, restates the importance of the theatre as a physical and ideal space in which language can reinvent itself, adding a gestural, "behavioural" dimension that is impossible to achieve within the confines of the written page.

In the last paragraph of his essay, Curi highlights once more the importance of the stage as a laboratory for linguistic experimentation:

> Occorre non dimenticare, d'altro canto, al di là di ogni paradigma, che per chi la lingua è, in essenza e primariamente, comunicazione anche nell'adempimento della funzione poetica, il teatro in quanto luogo di confronto linguistico (luogo, cioè, dove la lingua si costituisce come alterità e tensione dialogica) è per eccellenza il genere che consente allo scrittore di sperimentare immediatamente lo scrivere *pratico*, e dunque di patire fino in fondo l'alienazione della parola ma anche di misurarci con le possibilità attive della parola.[73]
>
> [On the other hand, we must not forget that, regardless of the paradigm, for those who consider communication to be language's primary essence (even when it is used in a poetic function), the theatre – considered as the place for linguistic confrontation (that is, the place where language can manifest itself as "otherness" and dialogic tension) – is the genre where a writer can best and immediately experience a *practical* writing, and thus where he can suffer the alienation of the word in all its strength, while at the same time experimenting with its active possibilities.]

In other words, the theatre, given its oral dimension and the inevitable interaction between stage and stalls, becomes a place where all the shortcomings of "spoken Italian" become most apparent, and it is also, quite logically, the place where a solution to this linguistic "alienation" should begin, and where language can be experienced according to its gestural, "active" potential, rather than in the reified, ossified form of the written sign.

It is time to move to a direct analysis of the texts, so that we may verify the various claims and observations we have been noting regarding the issues of engagement, realism, and language. As we mentioned, the solution to all three passes through a reduction of the lyrical "I." The final objective is to provide the audience with a method to independently elaborate a new linguistic code that is truly collective, shared, and critical: a linguistic code capable of "planning new meanings," as Pagliarani put it. From the theoretical discussion and the poetic experiments of the time, we can see how theatre has been identified as one of the privileged places in which such methods could be effectively elaborated and then shared with the audience. Theatre offered not only a shared space in which the producers and consumers of poetry could physically meet but also certain rhetorical and linguistic tools that could be exported to other fields and exploited in order to obtain similar results. So far, critics have identified two of these tools: an emphasis on orality (understood in its different dimensions: lexical, grammatical, rhetorical, and prosodic) and the use of masks, capable of reducing the overbearance of the "I."

Let us begin by quoting a passage from *La ragazza Carla*,[74] the first of Pagliarani's *romanzi in versi*:

un istinto battagliero
          li condusse a passare per il parco
e fu peggio, che un silenzio
gli cadde addosso e Carla aveva freddo
e Piero zitto e lei anche nel parco di dicembre
                    Chi sarà questo Ravizza?
chiese Piero, e pentito si nascose
le mani in tasca, che gli davan noia.
Poi uscirono, che zone luminose, allora
qui a Milano,
          a Carla assorta e lieve
Piero prese a dire:
          Marcia,
                    quest'anno,
                              il campionato,
                                        che è un piacere.[75]

[a bold instinct
          led them through the park
and it got worse, when a silence
fell over them and Carla felt cold
and Piero kept quiet and so did she in the park in December
                              Who is this Ravizza guy?
Piero asked, instantly regretting it and hiding his hands
in his pockets, since they bothered him.
Then they emerged, what bright areas there were then,
here in Milan,
                              to Carla delicate and lost in thought
Piero began to say:
          The soccer season's
                    pretty exciting
                              this year
                                        don't you think?]

In this depiction of a walk through a park, we can see some of Pagliarani's most recognizable stylistic traits. First of all, we observe the common use of aposiopesis, which simulates the rhythm and the sentence structure of the spoken language. The pauses and awkwardness of the conversation between the two young lovers is mirrored by the shifting of subjects, and by sentences that constantly change their trajectories. The last few lines of this passage provide a great example of that "verso a fisarmonica" (accordion verse) we have been talking about. The breath of the verse is extended and parsed by the sliding arrangement of the words on the page. This creates an effect of suspension during the reading, which, in this case, is used to amplify the silence surrounding this innocent remark by the young man, inexperienced in the fine art of wooing women. The result is an ironic and yet delicate portrait of two young people trying to negotiate their way into adulthood. Radically different is the spirit of the following stanza, taken from *La ballata di Rudi*,[76] although the stylistic techniques are almost identical:

Uno che compra una millequattro e mette il motore a metano
e la notte anzi la mattina presto fa il giro dei night per caricare
quelli che non hanno macchina, e di giorno gira attorno agli ospedali perché
    negli ospedali succede
che chi porta un malato con un taxi e dentro lo fanno aspettare parecchio
gli può far comodo una macchina quando esce con la coscienza a posto questo
    con il millequattro
a metano è un tassista clandestino.[77]

[One buys a Fiat 1400 and puts in a propane engine
and at night actually early morning goes around nightclubs to pick up
those who don't have a car, and during the day drives around hospitals since at
    the hospital
those who took a sick guy by taxi and they keep them waiting a lot
they can use a car when they get out with a clean conscience this one with a Fiat
    1400
with a propane engine is an illegal cabbie.]

The opening "uno che" is then utilized again and again in the remainder of the poem (and elsewhere in the same collection), and is clearly derived from a spoken register. In much the same way, the whole syntactical structure, based on the predominance of parataxis, is designed to simulate impromptu speech, organized according to the principle of accumulation rather than meticulous planning. And yet, the rhythm and the organization of the verse are carefully arranged to enhance the overall impression of colloquialism.

Similar examples are present in Pagliarani's entire poetic output, from the first experiments of *Cronache* (1954), all the way to the *Epigrammi* (2001). The same can be said regarding his use of masks, although there has been a clear evolution over the years. In fact, we can move from the choruses of *La ragazza Carla* to the cases of impersonation found in the *Epigrammi*, where the words and not only the personas of Savonarola and Martin Luther are appropriated for the poet's purposes. Here we'll provide a brief example of both. From the *Ragazza Carla*, here is the famous Cavalcantian chorus that concludes the *poemetto*:

Quanto di morte noi circonda e quanto
tocca mutarne in vita per esistere
è diamante sul vetro, svolgimento
concreto d'uomo in storia che resiste
solo vivo scarnendosi al suo tempo
quando ristagna il ritmo e quando investe
lo stesso corpo umano a mutamento.[78]

[*How much of death surrounds us and how much*
of it must we turn into life to exist
is diamond on glass, the concrete unfolding
of a man in history enduring
alone alive unfleshing when it's his time
when the rhythm stagnates and when it bestirs
the human body to transformation.]

If we compare this passage with the one we previously quoted from the *Ragazza Carla*, the contrast between their two styles would prompt one to consider them the work of different authors. While the former passage was based on parataxis and a simple lexicon, this one possesses a rather complex syntactical structure, and employs words such as "mutare," "scarnire," and "ristagnare," which don't belong to the same low register.

While the earlier verses dealt with a delightful scene of quotidian life, this one comments upon the tragic, existential truths of the human condition. They are so different that one is prompted to ask which one more closely reflects the poet's point of view. Naturally, it is impossible to decide such an issue, and that is precisely the objective Pagliarani is trying to achieve. By using a series of masks, he can disguise his point of view and let the audience decide for themselves, in that aforementioned spirit of collaboration.

This way of using the theatrical device of masks would evolve over the course of the poet's career into a more radical approach. Let us look, for example, at *Epigramma* VII:

Molti si pascono di certe figure e cerimonie, e sono nelli monumenti
cioè nelle spurcizie delli peccati,

e sonvi stati quattro dì.
Il primo dì è il peccato della cogitazione.
Il secondo della lingua. Il terzo delle opere.
Il quarto della consuetudine.
Tu sei marcio.[79]

[Many of those who feed on certain figures and ceremonies, and they become monuments,
that is, they exist in the filth of sin,
and they remained there four days.
The first day is the sin of thinking.
The second, the sin of language. The third, that of works.
The fourth, of habit.
You are rotten.]

For this exercise Pagliarani wears not only Savonarola's mask, but also his words, transforming them from the inside out, and using them to comment upon his contemporary reality. The poem begins with a rather vague and distant comment on people's hypocrisy, then moves on to analyse their sins, and the way in which they evolve. Finally, in a dramatic twist that reminds us of Baudelaire's "Au Lecteur" from the *Fleurs du mal*,[80] Pagliarani turns directly to the audience, accusing them of being rotten. The direct address to the reader implies the sharing of the same space between producer and consumer of the artistic product, and constitutes yet another confirmation of the observations we have been accumulating so far.

The process Pagliarani followed in the composition is explained in his note to the text:

Qui ho trascritto, scandito, sottolineato (o saccheggiato: certo talvolta, una o due volte distolto bruscamente dal contesto) brani delle Prediche di Frate Hieronymo da Ferrara, segnatamente quelle *Sopra Ezechiel*. Non che fra le poesie vere e proprie di padre Geronimo manchi l'attualità … ma, come è evidente a chiunque abbia anche soltanto sfogliato *Poesie* e *Prediche* di Savonarola, l'impatto linguistico originale e la tensione liricodrammatica stanno quasi esclusivamente nelle *Prediche* … Ne ho rimessi in luce ben pochi frammenti, alcuni forse ridotti a brandelli (e uno, ma soltanto uno, è del tutto apocrifo). Per me non si è trattato soltanto di un esercizio: e mi auguro che ciò risulti alla lettura.[81]

[Here I have transcribed, parsed, underlined (or sacked: true, once or twice I've torn them out of context) passages from the *Sermons* by Friar Hieronymo from Ferrara, in particular those from *On Ezekiel*. It is not that

> one cannot find urgency in father Geronimo's poetic output ..., but as everyone can easily see just by browsing through the *Poems* and *Sermons* by Savonarola, the original linguistic innovations and the lyrical and dramatic tension are contained almost exclusively in the *Sermons* ... I have dug out only a few fragments, some of them I perhaps reduced to shreds (and one, just one of them, is completely apocryphal). To me this wasn't just an exercise: and I hope that this will be clear to the reader.]

Pagliarani speaks of parsing, underlining, and "sacking" the original texts. On one occasion, however, he admits to having interpolated it with an apocryphal fragment. The curious reader can peruse Bernardini's essay[82] and learn exactly which fragment that is. However, for those who approach this collection for the first time, it is impossible to determine to what extent Savonarola's words have been manipulated, and which words don't belong to him at all. This uncertainty casts a peculiar light on the whole collection, leaving the reader to guess, opening the road to a legitimate overinterpretation[83] of the text. The impossibility of distinguishing between the words of the poet and those of his characters is yet another example of that use of masks we are illustrating.

Up to this point, we have been expanding on the critical work done by ourselves and others on Pagliarani's poetry. We will now discuss a few more characteristics of his output that, so far, have eluded the critical gaze, and that we find particularly interesting in discussing the ways in which the poet utilized the theatre to address issues of engagement and experimentalism.

The passage just quoted, in fact, provides an additional clue to the way in which Pagliarani is capable of involving the audience in his writings. At the end of that *epigramma*, he turns directly to the readers, addressing them with the colloquial *tu* and accusing them of being rotten. Now, as we just remarked, this *coup de théâtre* is not a new one, and it is in line with the tradition of epigrams, in which Italians are skilled practitioners. Especially popular, everywhere in the peninsula, is the polemical epigram. One must think only of Pasquino in Rome and the genre of *pasquinate*[84] to appreciate the importance this genre has for Italian letters. The apostrophe, that *tu* directed to the reader, is a rhetorical device very common in epigrams. What is new here is that the addresser of such an apostrophe is not entirely clear, and thus the addressee becomes equally blurry. Who is rotten? Who is calling whom rotten? The ambiguity creates a situation in which nobody can reasonably be considered safe from the criticism. Thus, both producer and consumer, poet and audience, coexist within the same critical space.

However, we must remember that such coexistence is not exclusively metaphoric. For many of Pagliarani's compositions, we know that he routinely tested his work in progress on live audiences, in order to fine tune and "verify," as he put it,[85] their efficacy. In this passage from "Cronistoria minima" ("Essential Chronicle"), he explains the process he followed in writing "La ragazza Carla":

> Il poemetto lo terminai il giorno di Ferragosto del 1957. Potrei dire di averlo scritto *en plein air* perché man mano che lo scrivevo me lo recitavo ad alta voce, misurando il verso "secondo l'orecchio," e più ancora perché ne leggevo via via dei brani ad alcuni amici, sempre ad alta voce, anche per strada o meglio nei parchi, più spesso in trattoria, anche in vere e proprie osterie ...[86]
>
> [I finished the *poemetto* on 15 August 1957. One could say that I wrote it *en plein air* because as I was writing it, I was reciting it out loud to myself, measuring the verse "by ear," and even more importantly, I would read ample passages to my friends, always out loud, even on the street, but better in the park, or more often at the *trattoria*, or even in bars ...]

The declamation, the enunciation of the verses, the public performance of the spoken word, and the consequent presence of the audience are routinely included in the structure of his poems, reflected by a number of markers left within the text. The most interesting among them is what Marin, in his *On Representation*,[87] called the "delegate figure." Here, we do not have the time to explore in depth this line of research, which promises to be very productive. In fact, although devised for the analysis of visual texts, Marin's ideas can be fruitfully applied to poetry.

He identified three types of meta-figures, used by the artist to negotiate the reception his work will receive: they constitute the textual strategy the painter hoped would influence the meaning viewers might attach to the visual text they would find in front of them. As Marin explains,

> In fact, a much more specific strategy of iconic signs is evoked in a way immanent to the representation, a strategy that is set up by the "learned" painter, but that he does not make completely explicit; he simply uses it to set the "interpretative undertaking" in motion. He actually supplies the recipient with the first principles of a possible interpretation; he sets up a "representational trap," a "dummy receiver"; he models and modalizes his receiver.[88]

He identifies three such meta-figures, and all of them can be found in Pagliarani's poems as well. The first one he calls the "commentator":

> The figure called the "commentator" is thus indeed the figure of articulation between the structure of reception and the structure of content: it is in a way a meta-figure of the reception of representation in representation itself. It is *part of the content represented;* it represents *the reception of that content;* it presents *the relation between the content represented and the structure of reception of that content: it figures the interpretation of the representation,* it figures the signifying potential of the representation.[89]

This commentator would single out parts of the representation and offer instructions on how to interpret it. We can identify it with Pagliarani's chorus, which we remarked on earlier when we spoke of masks. Very much like the commentators described by Marin in the analysis of Dunkirk's tapestries,[90] this chorus points the reader's attention to certain aspects of the narrative and indicates a possible modality in which it could be interpreted.

The second of Marin's meta-figures is the one that constitutes the audience as such. He doesn't provide a clear label to designate it, but he describes it as characterized by a human figure looking directly at the viewer from inside the painting. It signals the artificial nature of the representation and, at the same time, transforms it into a message intended for a specific audience, the very audience that is being stared at by that figure. If we translate this into Pagliarani's works, taking the epigram we analysed as an example, we could say that the voice that turned to the audience and called them "rotten" would be a perfect candidate for this role.

Finally, there is a third meta-figure, which Marin calls the "delegate figure":

> This third figure is not merely incidental: indeed we shall find him off and on in modern pictorial representation as the delegate figure, in the representation, of the receiver-viewer of the representation, a representation of the "representation-reception."[91]

This is the most interesting and subtle of all the figures explored so far. It is a model of the viewer-receiver of the message, contained in the message itself. This odd textual construct occupies a hybrid position, halfway inside and halfway outside the representation. It is part of the fictional universe created by the artist but at the same time constitutes a stand-in for the audience, in order to include them in the work itself. In Pagliarani's poems, especially in those with a strong narrative component, they are usually silent witnesses to the actions and the speeches of the main characters. The main voices of the composition interact with them and react to their silence. A good example, in *La ragazza Carla*, is the railway bridge. Although it is an inanimate object, it is the only possible witness to Carla's solitude and estrangement from the world in the first part of this *romanzo in versi*. In this regard, the incipit is particularly poignant:

> Di là dal ponte della ferrovia
> una trasversa di viale Ripamonti
> c'è la casa di Carla, di sua madre, e di Angelo e Nerina.
> Il ponte sta lì buono e sotto passano
> treni carri vagoni frenatori e mandrie dei macelli
> e sopra passa il tram, la filovia di fianco, la gente che cammina
> i camion della frutta di Romagna.[92]
>
> [Over beyond the railway bridge
> a side-street off viale Ripamonti
> there lives Carla, and her mother, and Angelo and Nerina.
> The bridge is simply there and below it
> trains trucks freight-cars pass brakemen and cattle for the slaughterhouse
> and up above the tram goes by, the trolley lines alongside, people walking
> the fruit trucks from Romagna.]

The "ponte della ferrovia" is at the same time the witness of all the activities in the neighbourhood (and, by extension, in the city), and also the liminal space where everything intersects (very much like the delegate figure), the outside border of things, as Carla sees them, and the threshold between the two sides of the page: the inside, where the characters are, and the outside, where author and audience live.

A similar function is performed by the "pelato di ferro," the mysterious passenger of the unlicensed taxi, in this section of the *Ballata di Rudi*:

> Hai visto viene il momento buono quel pelato che mette soggezione
> andrà a Abano per fare i fanghi per quindici mattine mi ha chiesto se lo porto
> che facciamo un forfé gli ho detto calcoli i chilometri censettanta andata e
> censettanta di ritorno
> e la mia mezza giornata perché lui si fa due ore di massaggi
> ma le ore sono sei del mio lavoro ha detto centomila
> glien'ho chieste centocinquanta ha detto centoventi più la mancia

gli ho detto che ci metteremo d'accordo …
                    Cristo, non parla mai
che dica mai una parola fortuna che m'addormento le due ore che l'aspetto
davanti all'albergo delle terme.[93]

[You see finally an opportunity that bald man the intimidating one,
is going to Abano's spa for the mud treatment for fifteen mornings he asked
    me to drive him
we'll do a flat rate I told him look at the mileage a hundred each way
and a half-day pay for me since he gets a two-hour massage
but that comes to six hours of work for me he said a hundred thousand liras
I asked for one fifty he said one twenty plus the tip
I told him we'll come to an agreement …
                    Jesus, he never talks
never says a word good thing I fall asleep the two hours I wait for him
in front of the spa's hotel.]

The negotiations between the taxi driver, whose endless chatter fills this entire section of the poem, and the mysterious character could be construed as a figure of the linguistic negotiations between the poet and his audience. This risky guess is only partially motivated by the remarks that close this passage, that complaint about the customer's silence, which is very similar to that of the absent audience. Once again, this liminal figure is at the same time inside and outside the page.

We move now to the final point I would like to raise. In addition to the oral dimension, the masks, and the inclusion of the audience through proxies and delegates within the narrative structure, there is one last way in which Pagliarani exploits the resources of the theatre. We mentioned before how one of the most appealing aspects of drama is that it is an endless process, a performative act that requires repetition and infinite variations in order to function. As such, it constitutes a perfect model of avant-garde art, which, according to Pagliarani's own definition, is focused on the criticism of the relationship between the producer and the consumer of the work, and is deeply rooted in opposition, which he understands as a modality, a process.

Both these aspects of the theatre (the process valued over the incidental result, and the repetition) are adopted by Pagliarani in his own poems, and he translates them into a spectacularization of the process of signification, which is the process of assigning meaning to sounds. Here we will provide only two examples, but this is a device that can be identified elsewhere in Pagliarani, and more generally in a great number of experimental writers. The first example is taken from *La merce esclusa* ("The

Excluded Merchandise"), and it shows how, beginning from trivial premises (a simple mathematical problem), through a mere recombination of the linguistic materials, one can create wondrous and surreal results:

> Problema: un ragazzo vede conigli e polli in un cortile Conta
> 18 teste e 56 zampe
> quanti polli e conigli ci sono nel cortile?
> Si consideri una specie di animale
> a sei zampe e due teste: il conigliopollo; ci sono nel cortile 56 zampe: 6 zampe = 9 coniglipolli
> Nove coniglipolli che necessitano di 9 x 2, 18 teste
> Restano dunque 18 – 18, 0 teste nel cortile.[94]

> [Problem: a kid sees rabbits and chickens in a barnyard He counts
> 18 heads and 56 paws
> how many chickens and rabbits are there in the barnyard?
> You might consider an animal species
> with six paws and two heads: the chickenrabbits; in the barnyard there are 56 paws: 6 paws = 9 chickenrabbits
> Nine chickenrabbits that necessitate 9 x 2, 18 heads
> Thus the remainder is 18 – 18, 0 heads in the barnyard.]

One does not need to be a specialist, an experimenter, or an expert, to try producing new meanings and to criticize existing ones. Using the work of schoolchildren, Pagliarani shows how it is possible to subvert reality (that is, the superstructure devised by the capital, not the "real" reality) through the manipulation of the signs we use to name and indicate it. A "conigliopollo" can be as easy to create as (and definitely more fun than) a war disguised as a peace operation, or a fundamental right redefined as an issue of charity. Furthermore, once the "conigliopollo" is born, its logical counterpart, the "coniglio spollato," cannot be too far behind. In other words, the critique of the linguistic code and its progressive perversion by capital and the hegemonic power is too important to be left to poets and writers alone. The necessary tools are available to everybody, even to children. Pagliarani is showing a possible direction, and whether to follow, adopt, or refuse it is the job of his audience.

A similar ludic and didascalic intent can be found in the variations of "proviamo ancora col rosso":

> proviamo ancora col corpo: corpo, un cerchio intorno, poi corpo su corpo: avessimo, Nandi
> sul corpo un viluppo di corpi un punto sette punti del corpo se avessero
> la macchia a cavallo del corpo, che segna il triangolo mobile macchia su corpi

costretti nel viluppo dei corpi, che segue ai bordi il triangolo, deborda oltre il corpo
nel tempo, si sparge sul tempo del corpo, sul corpo scavato dal tempo fin dentro il midollo dell'osso
tempo del corpo nell'intreccio del plesso, avendo, Nandi, corpo e fiato del corpo nel corso del tempo
nel fiato del vento, corpo nel corpo, fiore del corpo sul gambo del corpo nel bosco
del corpo sulla spiaggia dei corpi dove il vento odora solo di corpo
troppo corpo Nandi o troppe parole sul corpo o un corpo sgomento dal corpo?
proviamo ancora col corpo: corpo, perché cerchio? nessun cerchio intorno, corpo su corpo
c'è un cerchio: corpo, corpo[95]

[let's try again with the body: body, a circle around it, then body on body: if we had, Nandi
on the body a tangle of bodies a point seven points of the body if they had
a stain straddling the body, that marks the triangle mobile stain on bodies
forced in the tangle of bodies, that follows the border of the angle, overflowing the bodies
in time, it spreads over the time of the body, over the body hollowed by time down to the marrow of the bone
time of the body in the entwined plexus, having, Nandi, body and body's breath in the course of time
in the breath of wind, body within body, flower of the body on the stem of the body in the forest
of the body on the beach of the bodies where the wind smells only of body
too much body Nandi or too many words about the body or a body dismayed by the body?
let's try again with the body, why circle? No circle around it, body on body
there is a circle: body, body.]

In addition to the criticism implicit in the cyclical substitution of the words "rosso," "corpo," and "lingua," we would like to draw attention to the phonetic experimentation contained in these verses. The potentially limitless variations are intended to show a method through which everyday linguistic materials can be charged with meaning, then repeated and manipulated until that meaning is completely gone and all that is left is pure sound, pure phonetic stimuli.[96] In his memoir, Pagliarani wrote about this poem,

quando uscì nel 1970 su *Nuova Corrente* quel brano della *Ballata di Rudi* intitolato "Proviamo ancora" (col rosso), brano di componimento destinato alla lettura ad alta voce per un pubblico il più ampio possibile, brano quindi con pochi ma chiarissimi concetti composto soprattutto di *flatus vocis* e di ritmo (il concetto essendo praticamente unico, cioè "troppo rosso Nandi o troppe parole di rosso o un rosso sgomento dal rosso?"), non se ne accorse nessuno né su rivistine qualsiasi né tantomeno su quotidiani di sinistra. Soltanto Pasolini lo segnalò nella sua rubrica sul settimanale "Tempo"; il giudizio non era favorevole: definiva, come un'accusa, "poundiano" il brano in questione ma a me fece piacere ugualmente, non se n'era accorto nessun altro, ma Pasolini sì e mi bastava.[97]

[when, in 1970, that passage of *Ballata di Rudi* entitled "Proviamo ancora" (col rosso) ["'Let's Try Again' (with red)"] was published in *Nuova Corrente*, no one noticed it, neither the small literary journals nor the left-leaning newspapers. It was a text intended to be read out loud, before an audience, and thus it used few but very clear concepts and was made up mostly of *flatus vocis* and rhythm (in fact it contained only one concept, that is "too much red, Nandi, or too many words about red or a red dismay about red?"). Pasolini was the only one who mentioned it, in his column in *Tempo*, and his review was not favourable: he defined it as "Poundian," as if that was an accusation. I was pleased with that review: nobody had noticed it, but Pasolini did, and that was enough.]

The reference to Pound seems to be particularly interesting and productive, especially considering that Pasolini intended it as a note of demerit. The beginning of the creative process underpinning this kind of composition can be found in the body, in the physical presence of the author, of his voice, and in the closeness to the audience. It then expands in waves, invests the whole of reality, and then contracts once again, returning to the author, allowing another cycle to begin.

Each of the techniques that we have identified in Pagliarani's works is part of a process, a methodology that can be repeated with any sort of linguistic materials. They constitute his way of avoiding the pitfall of idealism, which is always ready to swallow all those writers who don't limit themselves to showing a method of creating new meanings but actually try to provide them for their readers. Pagliarani stays clear of it, stressing the cyclical, repetitive nature of his composition techniques: it is the process that matters, not the product.[98]

1.6 Sanguineti and the Theatre of the Neoavanguardia

In addition to the various references we have been collecting and discussing in the previous pages, there have been a few occasions (in fact, many) when the writers of the Neoavanguardia have spoken explicitly about theatre and its relationship with their poetry. In this section of the chapter, we shall leaf through the most interesting ones, noting the most representative positions of some of the protagonists of those years.

The attentive reader will notice two conspicuous absences: Elio Pagliarani and Edoardo Sanguineti. While Pagliarani's theoretical writings will be discussed in detail in chapters 4 and 5 (and have, at least in part, already been referenced in the previous pages), Sanguineti's views on the relationship between stage and verse will be only briefly addressed here. His vast production of scripts, theatrical reductions, and "travestimenti" (disguises), however, will not be considered part of the scope of this investigation. The reason for this exclusion is duplicitous: on the one hand, out of all the plays written by Neoavanguardia authors, his are the only ones[99] that have received any real circulation or attention during the poet's lifetime and after his death.[100]

On the other hand, although Sanguineti, like other Neoavanguardisti, saw the theatre as an important tool to help with the "reduction of the I," the way in which he used it throughout his career does not reflect how his colleagues used it. Giuliani, as we will see shortly, thought of it as the place to express the full potential of his "dialogic pastiches"; Pagliarani considered it as a lab in which the efficacy of his poetry could be tested and "verified"; Balestrini inscribed it in his strategy of opposition and revitalization of language exhausted by daily use and the targeted distortions of power and the mass media. Sanguineti, instead, embraced the role theatre could have in promoting a better appreciation of the oral dimension of linguistic signs; however, his ideas about "linguistic gesture" and the "theatre of word," as we will see, show that he did not identify theatre as a crucial tool in the reform of the linguistic and stylistic institutions of poetry, as Pagliarani and Giuliani did.

But let us take a step back and begin by looking at the similarities between Sanguineti and his fellow avant-garde poets: they all thought theatre could help reduce the "tyranny of the I." In a very useful interview with Maria Dolores Di Pesce, first published in the journal *Parol* and now available online, Sanguineti makes this point very clear:

> Cioè, chi scrive per il teatro affida a una o a molte voci, a uno o molti personaggi, quello che viene detto e agito sulla scena, e a un certo punto finisce per credere davvero ad una sorta di passaggio della parola a una figura immaginaria, davvero ad un altro, che parla al suo posto. Insomma il poeta è ancora tutto sommato come il narratore, un "io" che racconta, e questo io può essere molto fittizio molto simulato, può cancellarsi, (la poetica dei Novissimi nacque proprio dall'idea di deprimere il ruolo dell'io) ma nel teatro questo ruolo, in qualche modo, si cancella davvero. In scena è un personaggio, e il personaggio non è l'autore. Può essere anche

un portavoce dell'autore, come spesso si verifica, ma nella maggior parte dei casi, e alcuni casi teatralmente davvero efficaci, è proprio qualcuno che parla in qualche modo per conto proprio. Allora si ha l'impressione di scrivere come scriverebbe un medium, o di scrivere, è il caso di dirlo, proprio in "maschera," in "travestimento."[101]

[Those who write for the theatre entrust what they want to say to one or more characters, one or more voices, and at a certain point they begin to believe in a sort of transference of their words to an imaginary figure, truly an "other," who speaks in their stead. In fact, the poet is, after all, still similar to a narrator, an "I" that tells a tale, and this "I" can be very fictitious, very virtual, it can be erased (the poetics of the Novissimi was born precisely from the idea of diminishing the role of the I), but in theatre its role, in some way, is truly erased. There is the character on stage, not the author. It may be that he speaks for the author, as sometimes happens, but in the majority of cases, especially during one of those truly effective theatrical moments, he is really someone else who speaks of his own accord. Thus one has the impression he is writing like a medium would, or as if wearing a "mask," or a "disguise."]

This is a position, as we mentioned, entirely in line with that of the other Gruppo 63 members. Unlike the other *Gruppo* poets, however, Sanguineti did not use theatre to navigate the various issues of poetics we have been discussing (linguistic experimentation, engagement, relationship with the audience). Whenever he approached the stage, he did so not as a poet but rather assuming the much humbler role of dramaturg, a *paroliere*, sharing with the troupe his trained ear of *literatus* to enhance the spectacle's chances of success.

Consequently, his writing was always subservient to the needs of the show and the company but, at the same time, was produced not as a "material" to be changed, adapted, or modified by the troupe, a mere starting point for a conversation (like most of the texts penned by other Neoavanguardisti). On the contrary, his plays are offered as complete, stable, finalized creations that then await the work of actors and director but also pre-exist the encounter with them. And this, as we will see in the next chapter, is a crucial distinction that sets them apart from the commonly accepted practices of the Nuovo Teatro.

Additionally, Sanguineti never exploited the resources offered by the stage as the training field in which rhetorical and stylistic solutions could be devised and experimented upon (as, for instance, Pagliarani did). This is not to say that his approach was inferior to that of the other Neoavanguardia writers – or that the results he achieved are not as interesting. In fact, the opposite is probably true, especially if one judges according to the popularity of the final results, both the spectacles and the books that those shows generated.

We can find a clear confirmation of these statements in the already quoted interview with Di Pesce, when Sanguineti speaks of his idea of "travestimento" (disguise):

> Da un lato il "travestimento" è, come dire, un genere teatrale specifico. Si lavora su un materiale che, in qualche modo, preesiste, che può essere un testo già teatrale o un testo non teatrale, e viene elaborato in vista di una particolare messa in scena. Allora, in questo caso, il lavoro è molto vicino a quello che si potrebbe definire proprio del "drammaturgo," nel senso che la parola ha, per esempio, nel teatro fuori di Italia, soprattutto in Germania … In una cultura, poniamo come quella tedesca, la figura del "dramaturg" è una figura diversa dall'autore e diversa dal regista. È colui che progetta le modalità della realizzazione scenica, e poi, lavorando sul canovaccio o sul copione dato dall'autore, sul testo letterario, diciamo così lo gira, dopo averlo in qualche modo elaborato e ripensato, al regista che lo realizza, poi, con gli attori. In fondo il lavoro di travestimento è un lavoro di drammaturgia, ecco, in questo senso.[102]
>
> [On the one hand the "travestimento" is, so to speak, a specific theatrical genre. The work is done on materials that, in one way or another, already existed: it can be a theatrical or non-theatrical text that is rearranged in view of a particular performance. In this case, then, the work is very similar to that of the "dramaturg," in the sense that this word has, for instance, in the theatre outside of Italy, in Germany especially … In a cultural context such as the German one, for instance, the role of the "dramaturg" is very different from that of the author and that of the director. He is the one who plans the modes of scenic representation; then, after he has worked on the "canovaccio" or on the script produced by the author – the literary text, so to speak —, after having rethought and re-elaborated it, he hands it over to the director, who stages it with the actors. After all, the work of "travestimento" is a dramaturgic one, in the sense just described.]

Working as a "dramaturg" rather than as an "author" opened a number of creative possibilities but also drew a clear distinction between Sanguineti's poetic writing and the kind of writing he intended for the stage. While the first was completely free from audience constraints and did not presuppose a particular space or environment in which it would be experienced, the latter was almost always targeted to a specific theatre, festival, director, or group of actors. And this is, again, another crucial difference from the procedural approach adopted by other poets.

> La prima cosa di teatro che ho scritto fu nel '59, *K*: l'ho composto quasi per caso e per il gusto di assaggiare la dimensione teatrale. Non avevo nessuna prospettiva di possibilità rappresentative concrete. Dopo, invece, ho lavorato per il teatro proprio seguendo le occasioni accettabili: perché si può abbastanza, secondo me, immaginare la scrittura di una poesia indipendentemente da qualsiasi destinazione immediata, può rimanere nel cassetto; già mi pare più difficile per il romanzo; ma per il teatro direi che è impossibile. Il teatro mi interessa direi come uscita, fra l'altro dalla solitudine della scrittura. La cosa che più mi appassiona è quest'idea di collaborazione lavorativa e, quindi, come si dice del cucire un abito, scrivere un testo addosso a uno spazio, a un corpo di attore, a una voce: è questo che mi attrae del teatro.[103]
>
> [The first text I wrote for the stage was *K*, in 1959: I composed it almost by chance, and for the sake of experiencing the theatrical dimension. I didn't have any real prospect of ever seeing it performed. After that, instead, I worked for the theatre following the concrete occasions that presented themselves: in my opinion, in fact, one can easily imagine a poem independent of any immediate destination, it can be kept in one's drawer; something like that is already more difficult when it comes to a novel; as for the theatre, I think it would be impossible. Theatre interests me, I would say, as an escape, among other things, from the loneliness of writing. The thing I find most engaging is the idea of working in collaboration and, thus, as one says about clothing, of tailoring a text to a specific space, to the body of an actor, to a voice: this is what draws me to the theatre.]

The general observations we made on how the Neoavanguardia used theatre might still apply to *K* and *Traumdeutung*.[104] After all, these texts were the earliest dramatic experiments attempted by Sanguineti, and were performed in conjunction with other scripts, written by other Gruppo 63 members. Starting with Sanguineti's rewriting of Ariosto's *Orlando* for Ronconi, however, things took quite a different turn, as his techniques of "travestimento" began to take shape and dominate his stage productions. This last quotation also confirms what we were saying regarding the theatre as a strategy to aid the "reduction of the I," and it is further proof that Sanguineti accepted with enthusiasm the role of dramaturg and the collaboration with other professionals involved in the production of a show.

As we mentioned, Sanguineti was keenly interested in the oral dimension of language (inevitable with a theatrical performance), which is a trait he shared with other poets of the neo-avant-garde. On the one hand, this interest manifested itself in his work as a *librettista* and his collaborations with many avant-garde musicians.[105] On the other hand, it motivated an approach to the stage Sanguineti called *teatro di parola* (theatre of the word), based on *gesto linguistico* (linguistic gesture), which drew attention to the physical presence of language by concentrating all the action of the characters in the words they spoke on stage:

> Legato all'idea di un teatro di parola, e perciò nemico di ogni didascalia (e amico di un linguaggio che suscita e decide, da solo, lo spazio teatrale, e la scena e il gesto), dovevo, prima o poi, scrivere una cosa come *Traumdeutung*, che porta questa idea al limite, e pertanto, ovviamente, la rovescia.[106]
>
> [Bound, as I was, to the idea of a theatre of the word, and therefore an enemy of any stage direction (and friend of a language that inspires and decides, by itself, the stage space, the scenography, and the gesture), I had to write, sooner or later, something like *Traumdeutung*, which pushed this idea to the limit and, thus, obviously, turned it upside down.]

After quoting this passage in his essay dedicated to Sanguineti's theatre, Moroni comments that, "Here Sanguineti is outlining the idea of *gesto linguistico* (linguistic gesture), understood as the constitutive element of a *teatro di parola* (theatre of the word): a performance that relies exclusively on the power of the word in the dramaturgic text."[107] This aesthetic position sets Sanguineti apart from the other poets of Gruppo 63, who strove to use the physical presence of the actor's body as an expressive resource to further the connection with the audience and support their linguistic experimentation (an aspect that was also important for the authors and directors of the Nuovo Teatro). The only dimension that Sanguineti seemed to care about, instead, was the voice.

Di Pesce, in the already quoted interview, asked Sanguineti directly about the relationship between his writings for the theatre and his poetry:

> Credo che il rapporto sia abbastanza stretto, nel senso che anche quando scrivevo poesie, le pensavo sempre molto destinate ad una voce che le eseguisse. Questo non significa pensare in termini teatrali, ma pensare comunque ad un primato della comunicazione orale su quella visiva scritta che è quella da noi dominante … perché l'idea di comunicazione vocale era molto forte, oserei dire che persino … nella scrittura romanzesca pensavo sempre in qualche modo ad una presenza della voce, e la presenza della voce è di per sé una presenza corporea, che implica almeno a livello immaginativo, se non a livello di fatto, una realtà anche gestuale. La voce è corpo.[108]

[I believe that the relationship is a rather close one, in the sense that even when I wrote poems, I always thought of them as destined to be declaimed by a voice. This doesn't mean that I was thinking in theatrical terms, but it still assigns a primary role to oral communication over the visual and written dimension, which is the dominating one in our culture ... because the idea of vocal communication was very strong, I dare say that even ... when writing for a novel I always thought, in one way or another, about the presence of the voice, and the presence of the voice is in itself a bodily presence, which implies, at least at an imaginative level, if not on a factual one, a gestural reality. The voice is body.]

Sanguineti's approach to theatre was rather varied and nuanced. In his writings, he interwove many different kinds of texts, depending upon the occasion and on the show he was producing, appropriating, rewriting, or "disguising." All of these activities fell under a theoretical umbrella whose principal aim was reactivating tradition and bringing about an Artaudian literature of cruelty.[109] In spite of this variety, however, it is evident how language was always at the centre of his theatrical operations. While the other Gruppo 63 experimenters were using theatre to add something to their language and their poetry (the breath, the body, the presence, the ritual, etc.), Sanguineti instead believed that his poetry and his language could actually renovate theatre: here lies the source of his radical difference from the other experiments discussed in this monograph.

For the most part, Sanguineti's highly complex and original path has already been explored by many critics. What their accounts lack is an organic attempt to reconcile all these different threads as well as the various observations and already formulated and published analyses into a coherent theory, but this certainly goes beyond the intentions of this volume.

1.7 A "Manifesto minimo" for a Teatro dei Novissimi

In trying to identify the characteristics of the *teatro della neoavanguardia*, among the many documents that we could choose to quote from, none is more clear and succinct than a brochure I uncovered as I was researching Pagliarani's papers, in preparation for the edition of his collected plays.[110] It was the playbill for a show that took place at Teatro Parioli, in Rome, on 3 June 1965, where the Compagnia Teatro dei Novissimi, directed by Piero Panza and with scenes by Toti Scialoja, staged texts by three of the Novissimi (Giuliani, Balestrini, and Pagliarani), as well as a one-act play by Giordano Falzoni, a rather interesting artist, painter, director, and dramatist who was very active in the 1960s and 1970s and whose connection with Novissimi and Gruppo 63 would warrant a study of its own.[111] In 1965, Rizzoli published a selection of his plays; on the back cover of that volume is a very interesting biographical note, from which we learn that the group ACT, mentioned at the beginning of the chapter as one of the two theatre companies that had staged the theatrical evening at the first meeting of Gruppo 63, in Palermo, had been born when Falzoni, Ken Dewey, Carmen Scarpitta, and John Coe met, in the spring of 1963, in Rome.[112]

Returning to the playbill, we find it contains a series of short reflections by the authors and directors in which they explain the reasons that made them choose the theatre. I believe we can learn a great deal from a close analysis of this precious document.[113] Let us begin, then, with the introductory note, a general declaration of intentions that is not signed but that, judging from the style and the ideas expressed within it, can reasonably be attributed to Giuliani's pen:

> Quando continuità vuol dire vergogna, noia, e insieme un modo di girare alla larga e mantenersi ai margini, frantumazione è un modo di libertà, se non di rivolta. In questo senso il *collage* dei poeti "novissimi" è un modo di risalire di colpo al centro scheggiato di una situazione, un modo di troncare e riprendere un discorso – tante volte finché cominci ad avere un senso … Se non un teatro della crudeltà questo Teatro dei Novissimi sia almeno un teatro dello stupore. Lo stupore di chi si risveglia e si ritrova comicamente legato mani e piedi. Forse un teatro di inermi, o meglio un teatro di servi che si stupiscono, con breve sbalordimento, di essere tali. Non c'è bisogno di scomodare il mitico teatro dei Zanni italiani, né le diavolerie esorcizzanti della Commedia dell'Arte. Questa necessità di frantumazione, di dissociazione, di *non-sense*, di assurdo, di gratuito, è certamente una tecnica di scandaglio verso un ignoto se stesso, ma prende anche significato dalla minorazione perpetua, dalla frustrazione e deformità in cui ci stiamo accorgendo di essere costretti, fin dalla nascita, a vivere. Il Teatro dei Novissimi non può non esprimere – persino suo malgrado – la nausea e il terrore di tale situazione adulterata, con i soli modi a portata di mano: i gesti sconnessi, scimmieschi, di chi si sorprende allo specchio nell'atto di una azione degradante, e con un soprassalto schizofrenico non può trattenersi, in quella penombra, di cacciar fuori la lingua a se stesso. Nella penombra, o meglio nell'ombra, di troppe false istituzioni.[114]
>
> [When continuity means shame, boredom, and also a way of keeping the distance and staying at the margins, fragmentation is a mode of freedom, if not of open revolt. In this sense the *collage* of the Novissimi poets is a way of regaining, in one jump, the splintered centre of a situation, a

way of cutting off and restarting a conversation – many times, until it starts making sense … If not a theatre of cruelty, this Teatro dei Novissimi should be at least a theatre of amazement. The amazement of those who wake up and find themselves comically tied, hands and feet. Perhaps it is a theatre of the harmless, or, better, a theatre of servants that are amazed, almost stunned, by their condition. There is no need to bring into the conversation the mythical theatre of Zanni, or the Commedia dell'Arte's diableries. The necessity of fragmentation, dissociation, non-sense, absurdity, gratuitousness, is certainly a technique for probing the depth of an unknown self, but draws its meaning from the perpetual sense of being in the minority, the frustration and deformity in which we are realizing we are forced to live, since our birth. The Teatro dei Novissimi can only express – sometimes in spite of itself – the nausea and the terror for such an adulterated situation with the only tools it has at hand: the disconnected, monkey-like gestures of those who catch themselves in the mirror while performing a degrading action and, with a schizophrenic startle, cannot help but stick their tongue out at themselves. In the twilight or, better, in the shadows of too many false institutions.]

From the start, we can see some of the themes we already encountered when speaking of poetry and the way language can be reformed and restored to a more useful and expressive form. The first observation deals with collage, and the power that this technique has in the eyes of most of the Neoavanguardia. The reasons for this fascination can be traced back to Benjamin and his reflections on allegory and contemporary mass media society.[115]

Giuliani, like Balestrini, Pagliarani, and many other poets and writers, used collage as a way of freeing language from the encrustations deposited through centuries of use and verbal sloppiness. When texts are broken up in random sections and reassembled according to a semi-stochastic method, both authors and readers can be surprised by the associations and unusual combinations that suddenly become possible. Additionally, the interpretation of such unprecedented pairings can become the grounds on which author and reader collaborate on an equal footing to determine the meaning of a text, for neither has the authority to impose their personal interpretation over the other countless possible ones that exist.

The "shame," the "boredom," the sense of entrapment inspired in this passage by "continuity" are also to be read as signs of impatience with the impositions placed on language (on literature, its genres, its formulas) by habit and all the other forces of society, which try to direct the speakers and writers to perpetuate the same old solutions and traditional forms rather than devising new, innovative ones. The fastest, safest way of breaking with such constrictions is to destroy "continuity," embracing the freedom of the "fragment," restarting the conversation as many times as needed, "until it starts making sense."

Finally, the image at the end of the passage, of someone intent on a compromising activity who catches himself in his reflection in a mirror, is a reference to Eliot and his poem "Portrait of a Lady," as well as a nod to "schizomorfismo" (schizomorphism), one of the key stylistic traits of Novissimi, presented by Giuliani in his first introduction to the 1961 anthology.[116]

Continuing with the document, and before we get into the theoretical reflections of the individual authors, we will turn to the text – the longest in the whole playbill – submitted by the director Piero Panza, and the scenographer Toti Scialoja. They start with a quotation from Bergson:

> Gesti sono le attitudini, i movimenti, e perfino le parole attraverso cui una condizione psichica si manifesta senza calcolo, senza ragione, per puro effetto di una specie di prurito interiore. Ogni azione è voluta, e in tutti i casi cosciente; il gesto è irresistibile e automatico (Bergson).[117]

> [Gestures are the attitudes, the movements, and even the words through which a psychic condition manifests itself without any specific agenda, any reason, as the mere consequence of a sort of interior itch. All actions are intentional, and in all cases, deliberate; gestures are irresistible and automatic (Bergson).]

It is very telling that, from the start, they intend to draw a distinction between action and gesture, expressing a strong preference for the latter. If we keep in mind what we have read about collage in the introductory text, it is as if the Teatro dei Novissimi wanted to establish a connection between the modes of signification of collages and that of gestures: they are both automatic, ruled by chance rather than by deliberate will, and, because of their nature and these very characteristics, are particularly revealing and liberating. The next paragraph confirms this impression:

> Un teatro di gesti irresistibili, elementari. Sulla scena una serie di gesti puri, vissuti e consumati in quanto tali. Essi possono coincidere con i gesti naturali, e forse ne sono l'essenza o l'esaltazione, ma seguono sempre delle proprie leggi e solo in questo modo arrivano direttamente ad essere giusti. Questi gesti non vogliono "rappresentare," ma significano. Il contrario esatto di ogni pantomima, cioè di ogni passività naturalistica.[118]

> [A theatre of irresistible, elementary gestures. On stage a series of pure gestures, lived and consumed as such. They may coincide with natural gestures, and maybe they are their essence and magnification, but they always follow their own laws and only through this path they become right. These gestures are not meant to "represent," but rather to signify. The exact opposite of all pantomimes, that is of all naturalistic passivity.]

Gestures are a direct manifestation of the inner workings of the body and mind; as such, they relate to the world outside the stage in a very particular manner: they are not a way of narrating or representing reality, for this is how pantomime uses them; rather, they are indexes (to use Peirce's categories)[119] of what lies on the inside of the character who performs them. In other words, they are not to be taken as a substitute for a specific meaning, the way a word, exhausted and worn out through daily use, signifies an object. Instead, they are direct emanations of a meaning that, while not limited to them, nor completely expressed by them, still presupposes them. Conversely, these very gestures contribute to the definition of the meaning that had generated them. They are indeed at the core of the new theatre proposed by the director and scenographer:

> Il Teatro dei Novissimi vuol fondarsi sul calcolo di questo "non calcolo," sulla ragione di questa "non ragione." Risuscitando un "esser presente" che è insieme del giuoco e della magia. Muovendosi entro una liberatoria, ilare, espostissima convenzione. Allora tra parola e gesto, sulla scena, non c'è interdipendenza strumentale o didascalica, ma si stabilisce una attrazione reciproca, un fenomeno di risonanza che si diffonde all'infinito. La parola del testo (la conoscenza) diviene gesto attraverso la voce fisica dell'attore. La voce, come uno specchio crudele e inconfondibile del corpo, è la grande rivelatrice. Il riaffiorare così, in ogni parola, di un senso più vero, corrisponde al rinascere dal nulla (o meglio da un oscuro centro) del gesto.[120]

> [The Teatro dei Novissimi wants to be founded on the agenda of this "non-agenda," on the reasons of this "non-reason." It wants to resuscitate a "being present" that belongs at the same time to the dimension of games and magic. It wants to traverse a liberating, exhilarating, transparent convention. Thus, on stage, there isn't an instrumental, didascalic interdependence between words and gestures but rather a reciprocal attraction, a phenomenon of resonance that extends to infinity. The words of the text (knowledge) become gestures through the physical voice of the actor. The voice, like a cruel and unmistakable mirror of the body, is the

> great revealer. In this way, the surfacing of a proper meaning in each word corresponds to the rebirth of the gesture from nothingness (or, better, from an obscure core).]

The new relationship that the Teatro dei Novissimi intends to establish between gestures and meaning on the one hand and gestures and reality on the other is here further explored. It is not to be seen as didascalic, with one element used to better explain and illustrate the other. Rather, it is a rule of attraction: there is a similar, "obscure core" from which both gesture and meaning emanate, and by juxtaposing one to the other, the Novissimi intend to shed a little more light on that mystery. At the same time, Panza and Scialoja insist on the importance of the actor and his physical presence for this "game" to work, for the "magic" to actually happen. The next paragraph addresses the role of scenography:

> La pittura, sulla scena, può raggiungere una intenzionalità che addensa e apre a ventaglio, attorno al gesto, ogni possibile piega dello spazio, e lo rende patibile come una respirazione. Infatti lo spazio scenico è una superficie sensibile contro cui il gesto deve schiacciarsi e dilatarsi per divenire ritmo visivo.[121]

> [Paintings on stage can reach an intentionality that concentrates and opens around gestures, as if they were a fan, all possible folds of space, making it possible to experience it through pathos, as if it were a form of breathing. In fact, scenic space is a sensitive surface against which all gestures must press and expand, in order to become a visual rhythm.]

Once again, we find an insistence on breathing, which is directly connected to pathos and the possibility of experiencing the performance, the words and gestures, not as a simplistic representation (a one-to-one correspondence between the actions on stage and those in the real world), but rather as a more complex, ritualized, and somewhat mystical relation predicated on sympathy and the convergence of pathos. This rhythmical breathing that pervades language and gestures extends to include images as well, which must pulsate in unison with the other elements on stage. In the last part of their text, Scialoja and Panza seem to impart a direction to this rhythmical movement:

> Questo Teatro è dunque il tentativo di partire da gesti semplici in rapporto a un oggetto. Ad esempio: avvoltolare una benda di garza, la corsa dei quattro cantoni, aprire un pacco di carta, passarsi di mano in mano un

bicchiere colmo d'acqua. Partire da questi moti essenziali per risalire al tempo fluente del dramma, al fiato della *suspense*, vuol dire sperimentare il senso del ritmo come un processo e un percorso che conduca dal visibile all'invisibile. Il gesto, come necessità – e fatalità – dell'atto semplice, scandisce, sulla scena, il vero tempo dell'uomo.[122]

[This Teatro is thus an attempt to begin from simple gestures in relation to an object. For instance: spooling a cloth bandage, playing puss-in-the-corner, opening a parcel, passing around a glass full of water. Starting from these essential movements and retracing the flowing time of drama, all the way to the breath of *suspense*, means experimenting with the meaning of rhythm as a process and a path that leads from the visible to the invisible. The gesture, taken as the necessity – and the inevitability – of the simple act, marks, on stage, the true beat of man.]

This final paragraph assigns an almost metaphysical dimension to breath, making it the measuring unit of all that happens on stage. One is reminded in particular of Charles Olson's essay on projective verse, published by the author for the first time in issue 3 of *Poetry New York*, and translated into Italian by Aldo Tagliaferri in 1961, when it appeared in the first issue of the new series of *Il Verri*.[123] The most interesting aspect, however, is the insistence on the procedural nature of these experiments: they are to be viewed not as completed, finished products, but rather as a series of attempts, all part of a journey "that leads from visible to invisible," and thus, receive their meaning from practice, their very repetition: their significance does not precede their performance; on the contrary, it depends on it.

The next section of the document is dedicated to Giuliani; here are his thoughts on the text he was presenting that evening:

Per me un pezzo di teatro è come una tavola di Rorschach; o una serie dialogica casuale (stocastica) in cui ogni battuta suggerisce uno schema di avvenimento. La poesia moderna, da Rimbaud in poi, ha sempre in qualche modo adoperato le correnti sintattiche e semantiche rivelate dalla tecnica del collage e del rebus. L'ideogramma e il collage emergono direttamente con Apollinaire e il futurismo e prendono stabilmente luogo nella paratassi sostituendo la funzione un tempo primaria della metafora. Il teatro, appunto, non è una metafora del reale, ma una funzione immaginaria: è il linguaggio in forma d'azione, il linguaggio come gesto che fissa e libera.[124]

[To me, a *pièce* is like a Rorschach table; or a random (stochastic) dialogic series in which every line suggests the structure of an event. Modern poetry, from Rimbaud onward, has always somehow employed the syntactic and semantic currents revealed by the technique of collage and rebus. The ideogram and the collage emerge directly with Apollinaire and futurism, and gain a permanent position in parataxis by taking over the function that once belonged to the metaphor. Theatre, thus, is not a metaphor of reality, but an imaginary function: it is language in the form of action, language as a gesture that fixates and liberates.]

Giuliani reformulates some of the observations we have already summarized, and in particular the importance of chance as a strategy to activate the creative contribution of the reader in the definition of the text's meaning and to overcome the ossified rhetorical structures found in language. Very important is his rooting of this strategy in tradition: he reconnects it to Apollinaire and futurism, highlighting the visual current that runs throughout modernist poetry (one cannot help but think of Pound in connection to the mention of ideograms). Very original is the definition given of theatre: seeing it as the place where language turns into action means that the whole body of the actor (not just the breath) is used as a resource to aid expression and linguistic experimentation.

Nel 1962–63 mi dedicai per qualche tempo al collage. Non avevo un programma ben definito. Ero stupito e divertito dalle inedite possibilità semantiche dei brani di giornale (titoli, occhielli, sottotitoli, manchettes pubblicitarie, tutti luoghi dove la "condensazione" del discorso e le vivide necessità dell'informazione agiscono ferocemente e spesso oltre l'intenzione del giornalista): ritagliando e rincollando, quei brani di lingua usata e spesso forzosa mi si componevano e ricomponevano quali "pezzetti percettivi"; nell'operazione del collage la dicibilità, sia pure sconnessa, slabbrata e priva della profonda costrizione del sogno, si riapriva enormemente: potevo saggiare i quanti di frustrazione e la carica di rivolta, l'umanità e la beffa che si potevano immettere nel mondo linguistico meno "poetico" che conosciamo. Andando avanti nella ricerca (e nel gioco che questo tipo di esperimento comportava, almeno quale misura cauzionale) anche frasi e brani ricavati dallo stesso contesto dei giornali cominciarono ad affermare una loro strana vitalità. Richiami di cronaca, spunti di aneddoti, piccoli o grandi simboli impreveduti: nel trascrivere il testo degli ultimi collages fatti nei primi mesi del '63 mi accorsi che non erano che *impasti dialogici*. È di qui che comincia il mio *spazio teatrale*. Di qui è nata *Povera Juliet*. Aggiungo che il finale della pièce, dal momento in cui entra in scena il bambino, è la trascrizione di un sogno.[125]

[In 1962–63 I turned for a while to collage. I didn't have a well-defined program. I was surprised and amused by the unsuspected semantic

> possibilities of those newspaper clippings (titles, headings, captions, advertisement strips, all those places where "condensation" of speech and the lively needs of communication act ferociously and sometimes surpass the intentions of the journalist): after cutting and pasting, those passages of worn out and often stiff language would become "perceptive pieces"; through the operation of collage, the area of that which can be said (although in a fragmented, uneven way, that did not have the deep constraints of dreams) was greatly enlarged: I could experience the quanta of frustration and the charge of rebellion, the humanity and the mockery that could be poured into the least "poetic" part of the linguistic world. Carrying on the research (and the game that this kind of experiment implied, at least as a form of cautionary measure) even sentences and passages taken from the same context of newspapers began to assert their own strange vitality. Bits of news, beginnings of anecdotes, unforeseen symbols, big and small: in transcribing the texts of the last collages composed in the first months of 1963 I realized that they were nothing but *dialogic pastiches*. This is where my *theatrical space* begins. This is where *Poor Juliet* was born. I will add that the end of the *pièce*, from the moment the baby takes to the stage, comes from the transcription of a dream.]

Here Giuliani offers a detailed description of his method for the composition of collages. The indication I find most revealing, however, is his reference to "condensation" as the most attractive characteristic of the source materials (newspaper headlines, advertisements, etc.) he selects for his composition. When speaking of condensation in relation to poetry, one cannot help but think of Ezra Pound, and his *ABC of Reading*, a work that Giuliani was certainly familiar with, and which he quoted from in his famous essay on versification, appended to the Novissimi anthology.[126] Here is the relevant passage:

> "Great literature is simply language charged with meaning to the utmost possible degree."
>
> *Dichten = condensare.*
>
> I begin with poetry because it is the most concentrated form of verbal expression. Basil Bunting, fumbling with a German-Italian dictionary, found that this idea of poetry as concentration is almost as old as the German language. "Dichten" is the German verb corresponding to the noun "Dichtung" meaning poetry, and the lexicographer has rendered it by the Italian verb "to condense."[127]

This is also consistent with the previous mention of the "ideogram" function within modernist poetry, from its futurist inception (as Giuliani reconstructs it). In fact, Pound argued, the ideogram is the most condensed form of linguistic expression; hence his fascination with the Chinese language and Fenollosa's theories.[128] Giuliani had expressed a similar general understanding of how poetry works in his introduction to the Novissimi, where he famously began the essay with the sentence: "scopo della 'vera contemporanea poesia' … è di accrescere la vitalità": that is, "the goal of 'true contemporary poetry' … is increasing vitality." And one could argue that this maxim is congruent with Pound's exhortation to charge language with meaning "to the utmost degree."

Returning to Giuliani's statement in the playbill – after praising collage once more for its ability to rejuvenate language, the poet observes that this technique can also serve another important purpose: enlarging the number of things that are "speakable" in poetry. Since the time of Pascoli, a constant trend in the Italian lyric has pushed for the "allargamento semantico," that is, a "semantic widening" of the poetic lexicon. Each generation has provided its contribution in achieving this goal; however, the use of collage introduced by Giuliani quickens the process considerably, bringing an unprecedented number of realities and referential contexts within the reach of poetry.

The last notation addresses the creation of "dialogic pastiches," which is an undifferentiated mass of linguistic materials that, while containing multiple overlapping voices, does not specify the characters to whom they belong, or the situation within which they are uttered. As such, these "pastiches" can activate the creative process in the actors and directors, as well as the spectators; hence, the formation of that "theatrical space" mentioned by Giuliani.

We can now move on to Balestrini's declaration of poetics, one that approaches the issue of theatre and literature in a rather oblique way. Here it is:

> Non posso non voglio non devo dire il teatro delle scarpe. E i personaggi vengono incontro con i loro malintesi i loro manifesti le loro maglie i loro mariti. Poi vanno via un momento e tornano subito. Tutti sapranno cosa è successo intanto. Si dicono delle altre cose ancora. Poi vanno via un momento e tornano subito. Ma quelle scarpe non se le tolgono mai. Invece. Quale parco? quale palcoscenico? quale viale? quale sole? quale passeggiata? quale riflessione? quale orologio? quale zio? quale barba? e via di questo passo. Un passo dopo l'altro. Ma. Senza tutte quelle scarpe. O le carpe. O le arpe. Pausa. Perché tanto non si possono cambiare i caratteri e non ne vale la pena. Perché la società è malata in pericolo povera ma noi la salveremo. Col teatro e coi teatri. E allora tutti saranno contenti e potranno finalmente concedersi le loro giuste improvvisazioni. Bisogna fare qualcosa. Non c'è tempo da perdere. Il tempo stringe. Improvvisiamo. Il primo che capita è il Gabbiano che si divide in due parti. Le parole che l'attore pronuncia sul

palcoscenico. Le parole che non vanno pronunciate. Mai. Tra parentesi. Per fretta malafede o disattenzione qui l'uso delle due parti risulta invertito.[129]

[I cannot, should not, and do not want to say the theatre of shoes. And the characters come forward with their misunderstandings, their manifestos, their weavings and their wives. Then they leave for a moment and come back immediately. In the meanwhile, everyone knows what has just happened. Even more things are said. Then they leave for a moment and come back immediately. But they never take off those shoes. Instead. What park? what stage? what avenue? what sun? what walk? what reflection? what watch? what uncle? what beard? and so on, like that. One step at a time. But. Without all those shoes. Or the hoes. Or the os. Pause. For, after all, characters do not change and it is not even worth it. For society is sick and in danger, poor thing, but we will save it. With theatre and the theatres. And then all will be happy and will finally be able to afford their rightful improvisations. Something must be done. There is no time to waste. Time is running out. Let us improvise. The first to show up is the Seagull that splits in two parts. The words that the actor speaks on stage. The words that are not to be spoken. Ever. In parenthesis. Because of haste, bad faith, or distraction, here the use of the two halves is inverted.]

Why a theatre of shoes? Could this be a reference to Samuel Beckett's *Waiting for Godot*, a play that was very popular with the Italian neo-avant-garde, both on and off stage?[130] Perhaps; but there was also, as in Giuliani, the need to escape the traditional syntactical organization of the text, united with the ludic dimension of the artistic endeavour, the non-sense, and the endless possibilities of collage and the stochastic combination of words and sentences.

Another aspect that must be highlighted is the sense of urgency that seems to emanate from the whole paragraph, a desire to act, to address contemporary reality without lingering too much on the level of literary theories. In this way, I believe, we could read Balestrini's call for improvisation: a style of performance that, while rigorously planned, is capable of accommodating the spontaneous vitality and creative energy of everyone involved (not only the author, but also the actors, the director, the scenographer, and the spectators).

We can shed some additional light on Balestrini's cryptic remarks by considering the text he presented that evening; the title was *Improvvisazione* (the actors: Sabina De Guida, Deborah Hayes, Paola Megas, Wilma Piergentili, Grazia Volpi; scenes and costumes by Toti Scialoja), as we know from the playbill,[131] and it was published in 1967 by the journal *Grammatica*, in a monographic issue dedicated to the theatre.[132]

It is a montage of the stage directions taken from Anton Chekhov's *Seagull*. The park, the stage, the avenue, the sun, and all the other objects mentioned in the paragraph quoted above belong to those stage directions. This also explains the last portion, where Balestrini mentions a split between the words spoken by the actors on stage and those that are never to be spoken: clearly the former are the actual lines, while the latter are the stage directions. The reason for this inversion is rather puzzling: it doesn't seem to be predicated on aesthetics but rather on quite external circumstances ("because of haste, bad faith, or distraction"). However, one can't help but suspect another instance of misdirection, a technique often employed by Balestrini, who baulks and jibs whenever he is forced to provide a detailed account of his poetics. This is a strategic choice, for whenever one pauses to elaborate a coherent poetics, he exposes himself to the risk of being captured and assimilated, "normalized" by the forces that operate within language and society to neutralize any possibility of opposition.

If we return to Balestrini's short essay "Linguaggio e opposizione" ("Language and Opposition"), which is included in the Novissimi anthology, we read:

> Oggi … il muro contro il quale scagliamo la nostra opera rifiuta l'urto, molle e cedevole si schiude senza resistere ai colpi – ma per invischiarli e assorbirli, e spesso ottiene di trattenerli e di incorporarli … È in un'epoca tanto inedita, imprevedibile e contraddittoria che la poesia … non dovrà tentare di imprigionare, ma di seguire le cose, dovrà evitare di fossilizzarsi nei dogmi, ed essere invece ambigua e assurda, aperta a una pluralità di significati e aliena dalle conclusioni …[133]

> [Today … the wall against which we hurl our works rejects the impact, soft and yielding, it opens without resisting the blows – but rather entangles and absorbs them, often managing to retain and incorporate them … In such an unprecedented, unpredictable, and contradictory age, poetry … should not attempt to imprison things, but it should move with them, it should avoid fixating on dogmas, and instead it should be ambiguous and absurd, open to a plurality of meanings and extraneous to conclusions …]

And thus, instead of stating the reasons that led to the choice of Chekhov's *Seagull* and its stage directions, he deflects the issue: in place of a declaration of poetics, Balestrini provides yet another chance for the audience to help build the meaning of the spectacle.

Before we move on to the second and last of the documents we will use as our primary sources in establishing the poetics of the *teatro della neoavanguardia*,[134] I would like to open a parenthesis and briefly transcribe (and translate) a page I ran across while researching Alfredo Giuliani's papers at the Centro Manoscritti in Pavia:

> Molte poesie dei Novissimi contenevano o suggerivano una tensione dialogica o una giustapposizione di piani diversi di discorso, tali da esprimere chiaramente l'impulso di questi scrittori verso una comunicazione di tipo teatrale. Negli anni più recenti fa dunque naturale che i Novissimi e gli scrittori giovani a loro più affini si mettessero a scrivere direttamente per il teatro. Se comune convinzione di questi scrittori è che il testo (e pertanto un rinnovamento del linguaggio) è il primo fondamento del teatro, diverse sono le vie che ciascuno segue. Balestrini e Sanguineti concepiscono un teatro di parola nel quale l'evento teatrale è piuttosto raccontato che rappresentato; al contrario, Giuliani concepisce un teatro nel quale ogni battuta è un'azione proposta al regista e agli attori (questi sono infatti invitati a cercare nel testo le proprie battute e inventare così la loro storia); all'altro limite, Filippini sembra proporsi un teatro in cui le parole non contano nulla, ma servono da stimolo all'esecuzione di atti scenici; altri, come Lombardi e Manganelli, utilizzano una forma genericamente tradizionale investendola di ironia e di intenzioni catastrofiche; Pagliarani, infine, pensa di innestare insieme teatro epico (nel senso quasi didattico di Brecht) e assurdità semantica conservando un fondo naturalistico all'intrecciarsi di diversi livelli di significato.[135]
>
> [Many poems of the Novissimi contained or suggested a dialogic tension or a juxtaposition of different levels of discourse, such that they clearly expressed these writers' impulse toward a communication of a theatrical kind. In more recent years, it is therefore natural that the Novissimi, and the younger writers who share a taste similar to theirs, started to write directly for the theatre. While they all agree that the text (and therefore a renovation of language) is the first foundation of theatre, they all follow different paths. Balestrini and Sanguineti pursue a "teatro di parola" [theatre of the word] in which the theatrical event is narrated rather than performed; contrarily, Giuliani is building a theatre in which every line is an action proposed to the director and the actors (they are invited to find their own lines from inside the text, thus creating their own story); on the other end of the spectrum, Filippini seems to pursue a theatre in which words have absolutely no importance, but serve as the stimuli for the performance of scenic acts; others, like Lombardi and Manganelli, employ a generically traditional form, casting on it a strong irony with catastrophic intentions; finally, Pagliarani tries to reconcile epic theatre (almost in the same didactic sense as Brecht's) and semantic absurdity

while preserving a realistic background against which he interweaves various levels of meaning.]

This is a remarkable document, for several reasons: first of all, it establishes a continuity between poetry and theatre. The kind of writing operating in the two venues is different and yet homologous: it springs from the same necessity and it attempts to address the same rhetorical, pragmatic, and sociological problems of the two art forms, using similar tools that are, however, shaped and fine-tuned to reflect the two specific sets of languages, environments, and operators (and this has been my contention throughout the chapter).

Second, the hierarchy it establishes between the script and the other elements of the stage performance reveals a crucial divide that separated the authors of Gruppo 63 from the dramaturgs, directors, and actors of Nuovo Teatro. We will discuss this issue in more detail in chapter 3; it will suffice here to say that while Giuliani seems to think that the most important part of the theatrical spectacle is the script (the words pronounced by the actors on stage), the *teatranti* of the New Theatre considered it just one of the many, equally significant, components that come together to form the "specifico teatrale" that is theatre's particular linguistic code, the complex system of signs through which it communicates. All attempts at collaboration between the literary Neoavanguardia and Nuovo Teatro that went beyond the occasional performance, would eventually fail due to this basic, irremediable misunderstanding.

Thirdly, and finally, Giuliani sketches a quick taxonomy of the various paths followed by the different authors in their approach to theatre. It is particularly interesting that he lumps together Balestrini and Sanguineti, while creating a different category for himself.[136] A quick perusal of the texts will point out, on the one hand, how different Sanguineti and Balestrini's plays are, while, on the other hand, it shows the similarities between Giuliani's collages and Balestrini's compositions.

Here is the beginning of *K*, by Sanguineti:

K Femminile?
J Femminile. Una sensibilità femminile.
K Pathicus, insomma.
J Ah, ecco, ecco, pathicus.
K Concluda, Gustav.
J Concludere? Mi spiego, anzi: qui muliebria patitur.

K Muliebria? Ah, muliebria! Si spiega, si spiega: Weibliches.
J-K Das Ewig-Weibliche.
K Ah, che ti venga, Gustav, un canchero![137]

[K Female?
J Female. A feminine sensibility.
K Pathicus, then.
J Ah, yes, yes, pathicus.
K Conclude, Gustav.
J Conclude? I'll explain myself, actually: qui muliebria patitur.
K Muliebria? Ah, muliebria! Right, right: Weibliches.
J-K Das Ewig-Weibliche.
K Ah, damn you, Gustav!]

Here is the beginning of Giuliani's *Povera Juliet*:

— Penose irritazioni/come può una ragazza
— se l'ha fatto apposta
— sarebbe entrare nella pelle
— nel paese dell'odio scacciamo persone d'amore
— povera Juliet, Frank morto dopo un sorso
— ma sai che poi svanisce
— è la flussione particolarmente intensa delle regole elementari
— la prescrizione è contenuta nel prodotto
(*Un attore imita il nitrito di un cavallo*).[138]

[— Painful irritations/how can a girl
— if it was deliberate
— it would be like piercing the skin
— in the land of hate we banish people of love
— poor Juliet, Frank dead after one sip
— but then you know it vanishes
— it is the particularly intense fluxion of elementary rules
— the prescription is included in the product
(*An actor imitates the neigh of a horse*)]

And here are the first few lines of Balestrini's *Improvvisazione*:

— una parte del parco che sta nella proprietà
— un largo viale (che dalla parte opposta al pubblico conduce in fondo al parco verso il lago) è sbarrato da un palcoscenico improvvisato per uno spettacolo in famiglia in modo che la vista del lago è nascosta.

— a destra e a sinistra del palcoscenico degli arbusti
— alcune sedie e un tavolinetto
— sul palcoscenico con il sipario abbassato insieme ad altri operai
— di ritorno da una passeggiata entrano da sinistra.[139]

[— a part of the park that is inside the property
— a wide avenue (which on the side opposite to the audience leads to the back of the park) is blocked by a makeshift stage erected for a family show in such a way that the view of the lake is hidden.
— bushes on the left and on the right of the stage
— a few chairs and a small table
— on the stage the curtain down together with other workers
— back from a walk they enter from the left]

Naturally, it is very difficult to assess the differences between these shows if we base our observations solely on the scripts (the delivery of the actors, their stage actions, the lights, the scenography, the sounds could have been in radical opposition to the words that have been published and thus preserved). However, even without any additional indications, there are certain characteristics that are undeniable, clearly defined, and immediately apparent.

For instance, we can openly see how Sanguineti's general approach is much more traditional: he provides a brief, introductory stage direction informing us that the two characters are in a café, in Prague, in 1922. These indications can be very useful in guessing the meaning of the many vague references peppered throughout the dialogue. The characters, although designated by mere initials, are two well-differentiated men, who appear to maintain their individuality throughout the play. An additional note, appended to the second edition of the play, further explains that K is short for Franz Kafka, while J is Gustav Janouch. Even without this clarification, however, all the hints and oblique references included would make guessing the identities of the two quite easy.

The progression of the conversation is rather laborious: here Sanguineti concentrates the efforts of his experimentalism. The terms used for communicating seem to be in constant need of redefinition, one misunderstanding leading to another, in spite of the countless attempts at specifying the meaning. Multilingualism is another strong trait, present even in the small passage quoted above (consider the Latin and German interjections).

Giuliani's *Povera Juliet* is also introduced with a brief stage direction: we are told that there are at least two men and two women on stage, and a baby in the final scene. The setting is a generic living room, with a number of ordinary objects (including a stationary bike). The last few sentences, however, are particularly telling:

> La distribuzione delle battute sarà convenuta tra il regista e gli attori; i personaggi commentano oscuri avvenimenti della vita di Juliet che via via viene "formata" attraverso il dialogo e infine prende posto in scena.[140]
>
> [The distribution of lines will be decided by the director and actors; the characters are commenting on the obscure events in the life of Juliet, who is gradually "shaped" through the dialogue and finally takes her place on stage.]

The main element of innovation is the fact that Giuliani does not pre-assign the lines, but leaves a creative space for the actors and directors, who are invited to assemble their own characters by piecing together the provided words. It is, therefore, conceivable that there will be an endless series of Juliets, "shaped" in different productions, by different theatre companies, performing for different audiences.

The dramaturgic mechanism of this play is much more abstract than the one employed by Sanguineti; additionally, if we look at the progression of the lines, we will see how the paratactic strategy hinges on the surprise effects obtained through linguistic collage and its non-sequiturs. We move from "painful irritations" to a "prescription" included in the package of a given product, and throughout this parade of trivial topics, every now and then, there are disturbing references to dark events ("Frank dead after one sip"). Equally disquieting is hearing a character imitating a horse's neigh: the extra-linguistic resources of the actors are deployed to amplify the writing's expressive potential.

As for Balestrini's *Improvvisazione*, we have already mentioned how it is composed of the stage directions from Chekhov's *Seagull*. Being, as it is, entirely made up of those directions, it doesn't contain any of its own: it is a conceptual and abstract work. Who are the characters who speak these lines/directions? How many of them are on stage at the same time? What tone do they use when they speak? Is it realistic, mimetic? If so, what is the situation and the subtext they imply? If they are not mimetic, how do they utter these words?

The author offers no indication; it is the job of the actors and director, it would seem, to provide the context, perhaps deriving it from the lines of the original *Seagull* that in Balestrini's version, however, go unspoken. And how will the spectator react to this bizarre text, especially since it is very unlikely anyone in the stalls will be able to recognize Chekhov's original play? Balestrini does not seem too interested in providing answers; his entire operation is an attempt to probe the limits of dramaturgy, surrendering to the theatrical troupe complete control for the planning of the performance.

As we have seen, then, there are a number of similarities between these three texts:[141] each of them is predicated on the properties of verbal collage and depends on it for its functioning. The intensity with which these tools are deployed, however, is different from one to the next, going from a minimum of intensity in Sanguineti's *K* to a maximum in Balestrini's *Invocazione*. Giuliani's *Povera Juliet* seems to be a compromise, where the author has imposed a direction and a progression on the quasi-random dialogic pastiche, while leaving the actors and director a wide margin of interpretation.

1.8 *Il Verri*'s *inchiesta* "Sul teatro"

Issue 25 of *Il Verri*, published in December 1967, was almost entirely dedicated to the theme "Teatro come evento" ("Theatre as Event"). It contained articles by Luciano Anceschi, Luigi Gozzi, and Cesare Sughi as well as translations of essays by Charles Marowitz, Peter Brook, and Artaud's "Il teatro e la cultura," which would later be reprinted by Einaudi as the preface to the volume *Il teatro e il suo doppio*.[142] A section entitled "Sul teatro" ("On Theatre") collected the answers given by "poets, novelists, and essayists" to a few questions asked by the editorial board. A brief introduction specified that this was not "un'inchiesta formale" (a formal investigation), but that, nonetheless, "the statements that [had] been sent in" were not entirely devoid of interest, and "paint[ed] a rather vast and varied picture, rich with implications and issues to which it [would] be necessary to return." The "inchiesta" was answered by the following authors: Alberto Arbasino, Giordano Falzoni, Enrico Filippini, Augusto Frassinetti, Alfredo Giuliani, Alberto Gozzi, Germano Lombardi, Giorgio Manganelli, and Antonio Porta. We will offer a brief overview of Giuliani's and Porta's submissions.

Giuliani titled his text "La poesia a teatro" ("Poetry on Stage"), and began his observations by drawing a direct connection between current experiments and the "serate futuriste" (futurist evenings), which he considered "le origini dei duri colpi inferti alla 'dizione' della poesia e al suo stravolgersi in rappresentazione" (the origins of the hard blows imparted to "declamations" of poetry and its radical change into performance). Then, Giuliani reaffirmed the close relationship that had been established between theatre and poetry:

> Ogni volta che il teatro vuole distruggersi e reinventarsi, bene o male ricorre alla poesia e magari s'illude doppiamente, ma deve farlo; e quando la poesia vuole rompere la costrizione della pagina scritta aspira naturalmente allo spazio scenico.[143]
>
> [Every time that theatre wants to destroy and reinvent itself, for better or worse, it resorts to poetry, and perhaps this is a double illusion, but it is the only way; and when poetry wants to break the constrictions of the written page it naturally aspires to the space of the stage.]

The co-dependency of theatre and poetry in matters of experimentalism, a connection we have been emphasizing throughout this chapter, couldn't have been stated in clearer terms. But Giuliani continues, specifying what each of the two art forms can gain by this contamination:

> Ciò che dovrebbero avere in comune poesia e teatro è dunque la possibilità di rivelarsi vicendevolmente le proprie virtualità, fino al punto che esse appaiano trasmutabili. Linguaggio che "agisce," la poesia è fatta della stessa sostanza del teatro, azione che "parla" ...[144]
>
> [What poetry and theatre have in common is, therefore, the possibility of revealing to each other their own virtualities, to the point that they might appear transmutable. A language that "acts," poetry is made of the same substance as theatre, an action that "speaks" ...]

Theatre and poetry stand in front of each other as linguistic mirror-images; they can even be interchangeable, provided that each one is ready to attempt the work usually performed by the other. And it is precisely from this temporary reversal that new energies can be created and both forms of art can be reformed and revitalized. Poetry is a kind of theatre *in absentia*, one could argue, a virtual theatre, in which all the actors, the scenes, and even the audience have been internalized in the mental space of the author's language. In much the same way, theatre can be a virtual poetry, where the same rhetorical mechanisms it uses (metaphor and metonymy) can be exploited as building blocks of dramatic situations: scenes that are built not on mimesis or the psychology of the characters but rather on the machinations of phonetics and the free associations coming from prosody as well as etymology. But how can poetry be performed on stage? As Giuliani theorizes,

> la poesia contemporanea con la sua dialogicità interna, spesso addirittura strutturale e portante l'intero significato, con la sua discontinuità immaginativa, la sua esattezza nella scomposizione, col suo giustapporre toni e ordini del discorso, è meno che mai comunicabile nei modi della vecchia dizione e appare inadatta a lasciarsi cogliere veramente dalla sola lettura interiore.[145]
>
> [contemporary poetry, with its internal dialogic quality – something that is often even a structural element, crucial for its whole meaning – with its discontinuity of the imagination, its precision in dismantling, its juxtaposition of tones and levels of discourse, can no longer be communicated according to old modes of diction and cannot be adequately captured by an interior reading alone.]

The first step is defining what poetry on stage is not and cannot look like. Clearly, it cannot be limited to the declamation of verse by an actor: the dialogic elements that have been built into it would prevent any attempt in this direction. At the same time, it cannot be a mere "interior reading," that is, a reading that is done exclusively in the mind of the audience. What is the solution? Here is a first possibility:

> Se la poesia a teatro non può offrirsi che come lettura "esteriore," il pubblico che la guarda entra nell'occhio del teatro e acquista una parola che forse silenziosamente, nel suo "foro," non avrebbe pronunciato. Per ottenere questa possibilità di accrescimento percettivo la poesia deve lasciare ai mezzi propri del teatro l'iniziativa dell'interpretazione. La prima volta che ho avuto occasione di vedere realizzata l'ipotesi che finora ho tentato di argomentare, fu a Palermo nell'ottobre del '63 e per merito di Ken Dewey nella messa in scena della poesia di Pagliarani *Lezione di fisica* e della mia *Povera Juliet* ... E per finire con gli esempi, si spiega come la parte più originale e convincente dello spettacolo diretto da Toti Scialoja e Piero Panza, a Roma, nel giugno del '65, risultasse la poesia di Pagliarani *La merce esclusa*: la non-teatralità del testo aveva agito evidentemente quale sfida all'immaginazione e all'invenzione di una lettura teatrale. La poesia non fu manomessa, ma isolata in tutti i suoi sintagmi, ognuno dei quali, talvolta con opportune iterazioni, trovò un equivalente scenico-visivo e fu inserito in una ritmica di movimenti e figure che riproduceva a suo modo la metrica della pagina scritta.[146]
>
> [If poetry on stage cannot be offered in any other way than that of an "exterior" reading, then the audience that watches the performance acquires the eye of the theatre, and may access a word that perhaps couldn't

> have been pronounced in the silence of its usual forum. In order to acquire this possibility of a perceptive increase, poetry has to allow theatre to use its proper means of interpretation. The first time I was able to see the hypothesis that I have been describing brought to fruition was in Palermo, in October of 1963, when Ken Dewey staged the poem *Lezione di fisica*, by Pagliarani, and my *Povera Juliet* … And to offer one last example, this also explains why the most successful part of the show directed by Toti Scialoja and Piero Panza in Rome, in June 1965, was the poem by Pagliarani entitled *La merce esclusa*: the non-theatricality of the text had functioned as a clear challenge to the imagination and invention of a theatrical reading. The poem was not disrupted, but each of its syntagma was isolated and then sometimes through the necessary iterations was transformed into its scenic-visual equivalent and woven into a rhythm of movements and figures that reproduced, in their own way, the written verse's metre.]

In order to express the potential for innovation and reform that poetry contains, it must be represented on stage by exploiting the means of expression that belong to the theatre and are specific to its language. The advantages go beyond mere enjoyment: if done correctly, by watching poetry being performed on stage, the audience "can acquire the eye of the theatre," can learn some of the techniques that belong to the theatre and apply them to other poems, drawing more meaning from their relationship with poetry and amplifying the efficacy of the linguistic and stylistic tools embedded in the verses. If the objective of the Neoavanguardia was that of influencing reality by manipulating language, then the theatre becomes the natural conduit through which this process can be conveyed from the poets to the audience.

Giuliani offers a practical example: Pagliarani's *La merce esclusa* ("The Excluded Merchandise"), as it was staged during the show of June 1965, the very same show whose playbill we have just discussed and analysed. The rhythms and movements of Pagliarani's verses are translated by Panza and Scialoja into the rhythms and movements of the actors on stage; the text is modified, edited, and repeated accordingly, to allow for this transformation.

> La poesia a teatro non può essere indossata come una maschera, ma se mai va rivelata dalla doppia nudità, animale e spirituale, dell'attore; e piuttosto smascherata che comunicata … Ora, il teatro può giungere a sprigionare tutti gli elementi extraverbali, ossia tutti i segni visivi sonori emotivi in qualsiasi modo referenziali, che la forma del contatto verbale riesce a suggerire; ma non può farlo come si trattasse d'una traduzione

> o trasposizione da un sistema di segni a un altro: deve muovere dal contenuto linguistico della poesia tale e quale, tenendo conto che lì le categorie grammaticali, sintattiche e morfologiche, gli aspetti fonici e i procedimenti costruttivi con cui tutto ciò è posto in contrasto o in relazione … hanno "un elevato tenore semantico."[147]
>
> [Poetry on stage cannot be worn like a mask, but should rather be revealed in the double animal and spiritual nudity of the actor; it must be unmasked, rather than communicated … Now, the theatre can unleash all the extra-verbal elements, that is, all the visual, auditory, and emotional signs, with a strong referential value, that a verbal encounter can suggest; but it cannot do it as if it was a matter of translating or transposing from one system of signs to another: it has to move the linguistic content of the poem such as it is, keeping in mind that the grammatical, syntactical, and morphological categories, the phonetic elements and the constructive procedures through which all of these factors relate to each other … have "a high semantic tenor."]

Here, once more, Giuliani stresses the central role entrusted to actors and their bodies, unmasked and exhibited in their "animal and spiritual nudity." It is not a matter of mimesis – of rendering every single word of the poem by finding a corresponding theatrical element. Rather, the poem must be translated into the new language of theatre: stripped down to its components and rebuilt in the new code, exploiting the expressive means that are specific to theatre.

> Oggi, avendo in mente pochi fatti, alcuni testi, e l'idea molto tentatrice di poter ristabilire un rapporto funzionale tra la poesia e la scena, tra poesia e pubblico, sono disposto a credere che lo "spettatore di poesia," se esiste, possa aiutare lo stesso autore a leggere meglio in quello che è costretto a scrivere.[148]
>
> [Today, keeping in mind a few facts, a few texts and the idea, which is really tempting, of being able to establish a functional relation between poetry and the stage, between poetry and audience, I am open to believing that "the spectators of poetry," if they exist, can help the authors themselves in reading better that which they are forced to write.]

Giuliani dedicates a final reflection to the role of the audience: if something such as "poetry spectators" exist, then they can be an invaluable resource for the author, who can draw on their presence, their "breath," to give more energy and vitality to his words; as a result, the poems will be much stronger after they have been performed than they were when the poet first wrote them. And this is, in essence, the "functional relation between poetry and the stage" envisioned by the poets of Gruppo 63 (in particular, by Pagliarani, Giuliani, and Balestrini).

As we mentioned, Giuliani was not the only one to submit his answers to the *inchiesta*. Among the more interesting contributions was that of Antonio Porta. As in the case of Sanguineti, his idea of theatre is very different from that of Giuliani, Pagliarani, and Balestrini, and we will discuss it briefly, but in some detail, later on, in chapter 3. It is particularly heartening to note a renewed interest in his theatrical works, an interest that, we may hope,will lead to a critical and collected edition of his plays.[149]

Porta begins by outlining a brief history of "poetry that tries to escape from the book," a trend that first appeared at the turn of the last century, "the moment of crisis for the traditional relationships of space and time." Porta states that, if we look exclusively at collage as the main tool capable of articulating the problem of "the space of poetry," the scope of the possibilities is inevitably reduced.

Instead, he traces the roots of this new outlook to the introduction in Western culture of the "hypothesis of relativity." The radical shift in scientific discourse led, over time, to a change in aesthetic categories and artistic sensibilities. Another revolution was the one caused in psychology by the work of Sigmund Freud, work that had enormous repercussions throughout European culture of the time.

> La relativizzazione dei concetti di tempo e di spazio continuamente sperimentata anche nella cosiddetta "patologia mentale," produce, dunque, quella "fuga" dal contesto tradizionale che, continuando il discorso cominciato come descrizione particolare (collages), va integrata con due precisazioni: a) ricerca di un *nuovo spazio sintattico*; b) integrazione della nuova sintassi con un *sistema di combinatorietà intrusiva*. È chiaro che il nuovo spazio sintattico può essere costruito e contemporaneamente consumato, sia all'interno di una metrica rigorosamente accentuativa, sia allargando la pagina in tutti i modi pensabili. In egual misura la combinatorietà può essere utilizzata sia a livello "visuale" che all'interno della pagina, sempre integrandosi con una sintassi mobile.[150]

> [The revitalization of the concepts of time and space continually experienced also in "mental illness" thus causes that "escape" from the traditional context that, to continue what we said regarding individual

> descriptions (collages), must be supplemented by two clarifications: a) the search for a *new syntactical space*; b) complementing the new syntax with a *system of intrusive combinations*. It is clear that the new syntactic space can be built and simultaneously consumed within a prosodic system rigorously based on stresses, as well as by expanding the page in every conceivable way. In much the same way, a system of combinations can be used both at the "visual" level and within the written page, provided it is supplemented by a mobile syntax.]

The language used by Porta is rather opaque, but one can identify a few recurring elements, also found in the theoretical writings of other Gruppo 63 members. He believes that psychology, and the work done by some of its pioneers, can be used as a system of tools in the search for stylistic and linguistic reform. In the passage just quoted, he seems to equate the effects of a deliberate use of collage with the symptoms of "mental illness."

A true "escape from the traditional context," however, cannot rely on collages alone, but must be supplemented by the creation of a "syntactical space" and a "system of intrusive combinations." Although the names devised by Porta are different, the concepts are quite familiar, for we have already encountered them in the theoretical writings of Balestrini and Giuliani. By "syntactical space" Porta means the same phenomenon Giuliani called "theatrical space" – that is, a dialogic dimension that emerges from the poem as a consequence of the different layers it contains, the various voices and discourses that have been woven together by the author.[151] Porta expands on this idea by noting that such a space can be built either by relying on the rhythm embedded within the verse (the stresses each word carries) or by a careful arrangement of the line on the written page (the "visual" element he mentions).

The "system of intrusive combinations" he evokes is very similar to Giuliani's "dialogic pastiches" and Balestrini's linguistic opposition: by bringing together words that are not commonly found together, the poet allows himself and his readers to be surprised by the expressive potential of language; the energy thus produced can be harnessed to instil a greater vitality in the poem and put it in a position to compete with the other means of communication that crowd our society. One of the goals, in fact, is to "expand the page in every conceivable way."

> Va sottolineato che questo progetto di lavoro, proposto da Balestrini, soltanto ora comincia ad acquisite il suo carattere indispensabile di ipotesi di "nuovo spazio" ... Viene quindi fatto di osservare che in questo modo

la possibilità di lettura della poesia si allarga spontaneamente fino al teatro. Ma in Italia non pare vi siano possibilità attuali di integrazione tra il "mondo del teatro," fondato sulla concezione borghese della comunicazione di "fatti" ben determinati e circoscrivibili, rinchiusi nel triangolo "soggiorno-camera da letto-giardino," e le dilatazioni inevitabili conseguenti allo "spazio della poesia." Pochi registi sono disposti a capire e, per contro, sostengono che non vi è un pubblico ricettivo. Non si accorgono che occorre fare esplodere i teatri e finalmente tentare esperimenti cominciando ad operare al solo livello "uditivo." Poi si potranno costruire dei veri teatri.[152]

[We must stress that this work plan, suggested by Balestrini, is only now beginning to gain the indispensable characteristic of being a hypothesis for a "new space" ... Thus, it must be pointed out that, in this way, the possibilities for reading poetry are spontaneously extended to include theatre. However, in Italy, the actual possibility to reconcile the "world of theatre" doesn't seem to exist – founded on the bourgeois understanding of communication based on well-established "facts," limited to the triangle "living room-bedroom-garden" —, and the inevitable dilations required by the "space of poetry." Few directors are open to understand this and, instead, argue that we lack a receptive audience. They don't realize that we must blow up the theatres and begin experimenting by focusing on the "auditory" level alone. Then we will be able to build true theatres.]

It is important to remember that this *inchiesta* was published in December of 1967, and therefore a few months after the "Convegno di Ivrea" (which gathered in June of that year), where the avant-garde artists of the Italian theatre met to discuss the current situation and a strategy for the future (as we will see in the next chapter). Porta seems to be very pessimistic regarding the state of the Italian stage, and chooses not to mention all the great experiments that were being carried out in Rome, both inside and outside the *cantine*.[153]

Generally speaking, however, his analysis is congruent with that of the professional *teatranti*: the Italian stage had to be radically reformed, "blown out," to make room for a new sensibility, promoted by new operators, and a newly found "dilation" of the "space of poetry." The solution he suggests, however, tied as it is to the "auditory level alone," reminds one of Sanguineti and his "teatro di parola" more than, say, the daring experiments carried out in those same years by Carmelo Bene and Giuliano Scabia. Even remaining within the Gruppo 63 circle, Giuliani and Balestrini, as we have just seen, had a much more radical understanding of how a new relation between poetry and the stage could be established.

All differences aside, however, there seems to be one issue on which Porta and all the fellow artists of Neoavanguardia and Nuovo Teatro seem to agree: the situation of the Italian theatre was untenable; a clear break was needed. In those years, at least on the metaphorical level, as we will see, many theatres would be "blown out" in order to make room for a few, truly new ones.

2 The Italian Stage in the 1960s

On 10 June 1967, a colourful group of actors, directors, and scenographers, hailing from different parts of Italy, descended on the sleepy town of Ivrea. There, in the space provided by the enlightened industrialist Adriano Olivetti – through the good offices of his director of marketing and cultural affairs, Renzo Zorzi – they discussed the possibility of giving birth to a Nuovo Teatro (New Theatre). The proceedings of this conference, later referred to as the Convegno di Ivrea, got off to a rocky start and turned into a complete disaster by day two of the three that had been planned.

Now that half a century has passed, one episode seems particularly meaningful, especially from our vantage point. The details are fuzzy, given the scant surviving documentation: there seem to be at least two different versions of the events, one taking place in a bar, the other in the stalls of a theatre. Perhaps both are true. For the first we turn to Lorenzo Mango:

> Nel 1967, durante il Convegno di Ivrea, primo grande momento organizzativo delle tendenze sperimentali del teatro italiano, mentre il dibattito ferveva in sala, al bar un Carmelo Bene un po' ebbro scagliava contro il muro il suo bicchiere in un accesso d'ira in difesa del primato di Marinetti contro chi stava osando in sala sbeffeggiarlo.[1]
>
> [In 1967, during the Conference of Ivrea, the first organizational meeting of the different trends of the Italian experimental theatre, as the debate was growing heated in the room, at a bar, Carmelo Bene, perhaps a bit tipsy, hurled his glass against a wall, overtaken by anger and in defence of Marinetti's primary role within Italian culture, against those who had dared ridicule him.]

And here is the alternative version (but this may just be a preamble to the bar scene) as remembered by Ettore Capriolo, who was there.

Gruppo d'Ottobre, an experimental theatrical troupe led by Sandro Bajini and composed of Nuccio Ambrosino, Massimo De Vita, and Vittorio Franceschi, was performing a piece (of their own devising) entitled *Gorizia tu sia maledetta!* ("Damn you, Gorizia!"):

> All'interno di questo spettacolo veniva detta in termini ironici la famosa poesia di Marinetti sulla guerra: *L'assedio di Adrianopoli.* Allora si alzò Carmelo, e fece la grande piazzata, dicendo che a un convegno sull'avanguardia non si poteva assolutamente tollerare questo, non si poteva assolutamente sfottere Marinetti. Non aveva tutti i torti, però se ne uscì in un modo: da quel momento la cosa degenerò, perché ci fu chi prese posizione a favore e chi prese posizione contro, con grandi risse. Lo spettacolo fu interrotto. Ci furono una serie di persone che andarono a parlare al microfono: quelli che avevano fatto lo spettacolo per difenderlo, gli altri per prendere posizione, qualcuno per cercare di mettere pace, fatto sta che lo spettacolo venne sospeso e mai più ripreso, con grande rabbia del gruppo. Chi si infuriò moltissimo fu Zorzi, che disse: "Come vi permettete di interrompere uno spettacolo, una cosa che ospito io?" e ritirò tutto il suo patrocinio, tutto il suo appoggio alla cosa.[2]

> [This performance included an ironic declamation of the famous poem on war by Marinetti: *The Siege of Adrianople.* At that point Carmelo (Bene) got up and made a big stink about it, saying that at a conference on the avant-garde such as that one, something like that could not be tolerated, no one, under any circumstance, should mock Marinetti. He had a point, but the way he reacted … from that moment on, things got out of hand: some stood up in favour, others in opposition, a riot. The performance was suspended. A number of people went on stage to speak at the microphone: the performers to defend their show, others to take sides, someone tried to act as peacemaker, but the result was that the show was interrupted and never resumed, which angered the *Gruppo.* Zorzi was furious; he said "How dare you interrupt a show, something I am hosting?" and he withdrew his support for the whole thing.]

In describing the state of the Italian experimental theatre, this anecdote is emblematic for two reasons. First, it shows that, beyond a common dissatisfaction toward the *circuiti* (circuits) of *teatri ufficiali* (official theatres) and *teatri stabili* (stable theatres), the different groups that made up this alternative theatrical scene shared little aesthetic common ground and displayed very different sensibilities as to the manner in which politics, and the issue of engagement, were to become part of their various performances. Second, many of these misunderstandings and incompatibilities could be traced back to the different attitudes the individual groups had developed toward the historical avant-gardes, the lessons that could be learned from them, and the possibility of forming a new, updated version, or a second wave, of those same avant-gardes. Furthermore, these different attitudes also determined the way in which the *teatranti* (theatre professionals) evaluated and responded to the forays into Gruppo 63 and the literary neo-avant-garde theatres. Those who, like Bene, regarded Marinetti, futurism, and the lessons learned from the early *Novecento* as a resource to be exploited had a more fair-minded reception of their contemporary experimental poets. Those who showed intolerance for the initiators and innovators of times past treated their (putative) successors with the same contempt. As Visone observes:

> Viene, così, alla luce, e si estende a tutti gli artisti presenti, il contrasto, già emerso, tra Bene e Bajini, riguardo alla concezione del rinnovamento teatrale, che, per alcuni, doveva avvenire attraverso una rivoluzione dei "modi," mentre per altri attraverso una rivoluzione "dei fini." Ad emergere è così una nuova dimensione politica del teatro, che rinnega i contenutismi ideologici, sostenendo, all'inverso, la politicità di una rivoluzione tutta linguistica.[3]

> [The divide that had just surfaced between Bene and Bajini, in regard to the renovation of theatre, came to light and was made manifest to all the artists who were present. According to some, this goal had to be pursued through a revolution of the "means," while others advocated for a transformation of the "ends." What was emerging was a new political dimension of theatre that rejected ideological subject matter, embracing, on the other hand, the political value of a strictly linguistic revolution.]

At its core, the Nuovo Teatro was attempting a complete reform of the language of theatre; such a radical change was intended to affect both the words pronounced by the actors on stage (and thus the texts prepared by the authors) and, more importantly, the artistic means that are specific to theatre (that is to say, scenography, staging, costumes, lighting, but also the actors' voices and gestures, the relationship between audience and performers, the organization of space on and off stage, and the very nature of the ritual and the spectacle of theatrical representation). It is this attempt at a sweeping reform that the Nuovo Teatro and Neoavanguardia have in common.

However, before discussing further the overlapping areas between poetical and theatrical research (a topic we reserve for the next chapter), it will be useful to look at some of the key theatre experimenters of those years, offering a brief summary of their main contributions to the evolution of stage performance and the progressive renovation of its language, while, at the same time, highlighting the connections each of them had with the Gruppo 63 members and the literary neo-avant-garde.

Let us, therefore, take a step back and retrace the different paths through which the most representative and interesting reformers of the Italian stage arrived at the Ivrea conference. We will look at each of them separately, beginning with Carmelo Bene.

2.1 Carmelo Bene

At the end of the 1950s, as Italy was beginning to experience that rapid period of growth later referred to as the "economic miracle," while the first signs of an incipient Nuovo Teatro could be detected, the national theatre seemed to have reached a period of uncertainty, if not decline. The intellectuals and artists who had contributed to restarting Italian theatre after the Second World War (Giorgio Strehler, Luigi Squarzina, and Gianfranco de Bosio, to name only a few), were now safely installed at the helm of different *teatri stabili*. From this somewhat institutional position, they were less likely to take aesthetic risks, and while their shows maintained a consistently high level of quality, they did not actively promote innovation and experimentation. At the same time, the first signs of a looming economic crisis began to appear: ticket sales plummeted (by 50 per cent in the ten years between 1950 and 1960); ticket prices doubled in that same decade; and half of the national ticket sales were concentrated in the cities of Rome and Milan.[4] Such a dramatic drop in attendance led directors and administrators to focus on the most immediate commercial and organizational concerns, leaving aside every other artistic and cultural consideration. The solutions that were developed to increase attendance included the search for "great spectacles," as well as the normalization and streamlining of all productions. The search for new forms of theatre, better suited to attracting the audience's attention and captivating their favour, was never really a part of the conversation. In an attempt to describe this situation, and to expose its causes, in an imaginary interview in the magazine *Sipario*, renowned critic Franco Quadri asked some of his fellow Italians why they had decided to stop going to the theatre:

> Chi dirà di vivere in una città dove le compagnie non sostano più da venti o trenta anni. Chi dirà di non aver mai visto una sala teatrale. Chi dirà che il biglietto costa troppo. Chi dirà che lo smettere di lavorare alle sette

non gli consente di essere al teatro per le nove. Chi dirà che gli spettacoli terminano troppo tardi. Chi dirà che a teatro ci si diverte raramente. Chi dirà che la TV è più varia e più comoda. Chi dirà che non gli permette quella scelta che il cinema invece gli concede. Chi dirà che a teatro si rappresentano lavori troppo oscuri, troppo difficili. Chi dirà che nulla vale un bel "Carosello" o un bel "Campanile sera." Chi dirà che l'attore Tizio non si può più ascoltarlo, dato che nel recitare sempre allo stesso modo rende una parte uguale all'altra. Chi dirà che a lui piacciono, soprattutto, le commedie comiche, ma non le commedie baggiane o tragiche, e che a teatro le commedie comiche non ci sono più, e che se ci sono si tratta di scemenze o di malinconie o di simbolismi non sempre decifrabili.[5]

[Some will say they live in a city where theatre companies haven't stopped by in twenty or thirty years. Some will say they have never seen the inside of a theatre. Some will say tickets are too expensive. Some will say that finishing work at seven, they can't be at the theatre by nine. Some will say that shows end too late. Some will say that you don't always enjoy yourself at the theatre. Some will say that TV offers more variety and is more comfortable. Some will say that cinemas offer more choices than the theatre. Some will say that the plays are too obscure, too difficult. Some will say that nothing's better than a good "Carosello" or a good "Campanile Sera."[6] Some will say that actor so-and-so is unbearable, and that you can't tell apart one role from another, since he acts the same in each of them. Some will say that, most of all, they like comedies, not the stupid or tragic plays, but comedies aren't performed at the theatre anymore, if they put on any comedies at all, they are either silly ones, or melancholic ones, or filled with so many symbols you can never fully understand them.]

Quadri used this long and imagined litany of complaints to call attention to one of the key underlying causes of the decline in popularity of the Italian theatre: the audience did not see themselves reflected on stage. There was a considerable distance between the language, the situations, and the messages conveyed by the *teatri stabili* and the lives of regular people.

In part, as we will see, it was a linguistic difference that kept people from attending the theatre: the actors did not speak like the people in the streets. Incidentally, this also explains the enduring popularity of the dialect theatre, and in particular that of Edoardo de Filippo,[7] who managed to devise a relatable, understandable (if regionally marked) spoken variety of Italian that resonated as true and authentic with audiences; in addition, he discussed current themes and issues that contemporary spectators could easily empathize with.

On the other hand, the disconnect audiences felt was also due to an aesthetic issue: the traditional forms of the bourgeois theatre (its organization of the performance space and time, its narrative, its characters, etc.) were incapable of captivating a changing audience, whose media diets had recently expanded to include television and an ever-increasing number of films, coming from the cinematic traditions and markets of both Europe and the United States, which had previously (during the fascist era) been unavailable, as a result of national censorship and protectionist policies. These circumstances created the conditions for a number of theatrical experiments that operated outside of, as an alternative to, and at the margins of the "official theatre." Exemplary in this regard is the case of Carmelo Bene, whose meteoric appearance on the Italian stage was impossible to ignore, even for the stiffest, most reactionary, and most closed-minded critics.[8]

In 1959, after quitting the Accademia Drammatica of Rome without graduating, Carmelo Bene joined the actors of the *compagnia* "I Liberi" and, in October of that year, debuted in a staging of Camus's *Caligula*, directed by Alberto Ruggiero. Soon after, he set out on his own, bringing to the stage a wide variety of plays and adaptations: *Spettacolo Majakovskij* (1960); *Pinocchio* and *Amleto* (1961); *Cristo '63* (shut down by censors after just a few performances); *Edoardo II* and *I Polacchi (Ubu roi)* (1963); and Wilde's *Salomè* (1964).

As Marco De Marinis points out, all the main characteristics of Bene's theatre can be easily discerned even in these early works:[9] 1) a "deformed" and markedly "physical" style of acting: the voice is never used realistically or mimetically, but, rather, in an expressionistic way that includes screams, whispers, babbling, yelps, and so on; similarly, the movements of the body are never "natural" but always excessive, repetitive, syncopated; 2) an undeniable penchant for exhibitionism and scandal, both on and off the stage; 3) a passion for ridiculing and subverting all theatrical conventions; 4) a predilection for *pastiche*, contaminations, and an unconventional synthesis of different texts, sometimes separated by a significant distance of time and space. Above all, Bene's theatre was centred on himself (not in a subjective or biographical sense, but rather on his body and voice, understood as an "actorial machine"), on the persona of actor-author he kept building and dismantling over the years, so much so that one of his most successful performances, *Nostra Signora dei Turchi* ("Our Lady of the Turks" – first a novel [1966], then a play [in 1966 and 1973], and finally a movie [1968]), is a strange mixture of autobiography and mythical invention. In this sense, his theatre has been, since its beginnings, radically against all representation, presenting itself as a place where traditional texts and acting techniques can be dissected, analysed, deconstructed, and rebuilt.

In 1962, Bene took his research a step further, abandoning traditional theatrical spaces and starting his own Teatro Laboratorio in Trastevere, thus establishing the first of the Roman *cantine* in piazza San Cosimato. It was in the basement of a building, adjacent to a restaurant. It wasn't a very large space, but Bene had finally all the freedom he required. Here he created and performed eight different shows in just over six months, filling the roles of actor, director, author, and impresario, while making a name for himself in the process.

The critics were divided as to the use he made of the texts and language of the theatre. His contemporary colleagues approached the classics mostly in two ways: either they attempted a philological reading, trying to faithfully reconstruct the conditions under which the very first audiences experienced the plays; or they adapted the texts to current conditions, updating their settings, language, and general atmosphere to make them more "natural" and relatable.

Needless to say, Bene despised both choices; his engagement with the classics was predicated on the "betrayal" of the letter of the text, in an attempt to render more vivid and apparent their deep, core meanings, and thereby liberate them from the centuries of critical platitudes that had encrusted their surfaces. He rewrote these works, cutting what he judged to be unnecessary, interpolating passages by other authors that were intertextually, sometimes convolutedly, connected to them, turning quotation and manipulation into stylistic as well as theatrical devices.

Paradoxically, this very modern, avant-garde contempt for a conventionally chronological vision of history was derived from a traditional acting practice, something Visone calls the "model of the great Italian actor":[10]

> In questo senso, allora, l'artista (Bene) ritorna al modello del grande attore all'italiana, ignorando l'intero sistema registico; tuttavia, dà vita ad un metodo interpretativo originale, in quanto nega alla radice l'arte stessa da cui discende. In altre parole, l'artista pugliese assimila la tradizione del grande attore per negarne la sua essenza intima e per mostrare in scena l'impossibilità di rappresentare. Egli si presenta come il creatore unico della scena, un attore *artifex* che assoggetta a sé tutti gli elementi scenici. Nell'epoca moderna, però, l'attore *artifex* fa ormai i conti con l'impossibilità di rappresentare, pertanto suo intento è quello di annientare tutti i fattori che costituiscono lo spettacolo di rappresentazione (il testo, il regista, l'attore).[11]
>
> [In this sense, the artist (Bene) returns to the model of the great Italian actor, ignoring the entire system of directors; however, he still manages

to create an original interpretive method, for he negates at its core the very art from which he derives inspiration. In other words, the Pugliese artist assimilates the tradition of the great actor only to negate its intimate essence and show on stage the impossibility of representation. He presents himself as the only creator, as an actor *artifex*, who dominates all the elements of the scene. Yet, in modern times, the actor *artifex* must come to terms with the impossibility of representation, and thus his attention turns to destroying all the factors of which the spectacle of representation is composed (the text, the director, the actor).]

On stage, Bene gave an exquisitely, if cruelly, parodic version of the gilded tradition from which he drew inspiration. He claimed as his own all the tools of the trade, and dramatized on stage the impossibility of putting them to any use. Seen from this perspective, his work on the text – his obsessive erasing, inserting, and interpolating, and the use of continuous interruptions – made perfect sense. As did his incessant manipulation of language (his inarticulate sounds, his whispers and cries) and his manipulation of his own body (his stiff, repetitive, and deliberately ineffective movements).

All these elements are well represented in his *Amleto* ("Hamlet"), which debuted in 1962, in that same Teatro Laboratorio *cantina* in Trastevere, and which he later took to the Festival dei due mondi in Spoleto. Bene devised his own translation and adaptation of Shakespeare's text, often cobbling together bits and pieces from other versions of the Hamlet story from different time periods, emphasizing an ironic dissonance of tones and styles. The plot and the scenes were taken apart and reassembled, sometimes cross-cut, in a simultaneous montage, with lines belonging to different characters jumbled together. The stage was organized prospectively, and divided into three levels, each containing a different set of characters.

Another version of Bene's *Amleto*, entitled *Basta con un "Vi amo" mi ero quasi promesso. Amleto o le conseguenze della pietà filiale* ("Enough, with Just One 'I Love You' I Had Almost Promised. Hamlet or the Consequences of Filial Piety," 1965), incorporated Jules Laforgue's book and emphasized a parodic perspective, while a third and final production, which dates to 1967 and is entitled *Amleto o le conseguenze della pietà filiale da Laforgue secondo Carmelo Bene* ("Hamlet or the Consequences of Filial Piety by Laforgue According to Carmelo Bene"), relied even more on Laforgue's writings.[12]

Bene would continue to follow his path of research and would eventually receive positive attention from many contemporary intellectuals, including Gilles Deleuze,[13] who wrote insightful essays on him and his theatre and film work. His radically different, extremely personal theatrical language, however, isolated him from the rest of his colleagues and from most of the critics, who were not quite sure what to make of him, or how to classify and interpret his performances. As we saw with the Convegno di Ivrea incident, however, Bene was very well aware of the avant-garde tradition to which he belonged, had an acute critical understanding of the forces at play in the great battle for the reform of the Italian theatre, and was not shy when voicing his displeasure with less talented and less sophisticated colleagues. He also managed to build strong friendships with those *teatranti* who were more open to the aesthetic reform he was pursuing, even though they had set off on routes different from his own.

This very short description of Bene's early career does not do justice to his importance in the evolution of Italian theatre nor to the many interesting and stimulating connections between his experimentation and that of the literary neo-avant-garde. His approaches to theatre, performance, text, authorship, and staging have served as a source of inspiration for countless artists both in Italy and in Europe; in spite of his importance, however, little is being done to honour and study his legacy, perhaps also because we lack a competent English translation of his plays.[14]

2.2 Mario Ricci

Another somewhat isolated (although he was friends with many poets and artists) and yet crucial experimenter of those early years, Mario Ricci, began his career as a painter and sculptor, coming from a very different background than Carmelo Bene, or any other protagonist of this first season of Italian avant-garde theatre. His research focused on the material aspects of the theatre, and from there he elaborated a more encompassing reform of its representational strategies. Here is how he reconstructs his beginnings:

> Nel quadro generale e, sfortunatamente, generalizzato, della ricerca e sperimentazione di nuove formule per il rinnovamento del linguaggio teatrale, il lavoro da me sin qui svolto si pone decisamente in quella zona comunemente definite "tecnica." Rinnovamento del linguaggio teatrale attraverso nuove tecniche formalmente estranee ad ogni presunto o reale rinnovamento contenutistico, significante, ecc … Questa scelta unica nel suo genere in Italia oggi …, oltre che da singolari esperienze e da considerazioni che andavo maturando … mi si è, in un certo senso, imposta assistendo a uno spettacolo di "teatro meccanico" che Harry

> Kramer presentava al "Marionetteatern" di Stoccolma, dove ho lavorato in epoche diverse sotto la direzione di Michael Meschke per circa due anni (1960–61, 1961–62).[15]
>
> [In the general and, unfortunately, generalized landscape of research and experimentation of new forms for the renovation of theatre's language, the work I have done so far belongs to the area commonly known as "technical." A renewal of theatre's language through new techniques, formally extraneous to any renewal based on content, on the signifier, etc. ... This choice, unique in Italy, has come to me from a performance of "mechanical theatre," organized by Harry Kramer at the "Marionetteatern" of Stockholm, where I worked on and off, under director Michael Meschke, for almost two years (1960–61, and 1961–62).]

Ricci, and all his critics, attributed great importance to his experiences in Sweden. Those were his formative years, and much of what he would later accomplish can be traced back to that time. What is also remarkable is the clarity with which he is able to identify the most innovative aspects of his theatre and his determination in highlighting its "technical" nature, claiming this shift as a crucial decision in his career.

As we have seen with Bene and the writers of the literary neo-avant-garde, the driving force behind Ricci's experiments is the compelling need to reform the traditional theatre so that it can respond to the changing times and the demands of new audiences. And here, too, this renewal begins with a focus on the specific language of this art form, an experimentation with the ways in which it communicates, an exploration of its basic components. While Bene was dismantling them by working from the inside, Ricci tried to rebuild them from scratch, starting from a bare stage and, progressively, adding more elements.

Here is how Ricci describes the first, all-important show at the Marionetteatern of Stockholm that was to have such a lasting effect on him:

> Questa parte dello spettacolo era realizzata con tre di queste sculture sistemate una al centro e due ai lati del piccolo palcoscenico, ricavato all'interno di quello esistente, che misurava non più di tre metri e cinquanta per un metro di profondità e il cui boccascena era alto non più di un metro e venti. Le sculture, grandi in giusta proporzione con il palcoscenico, erano in alcune parti vivamente colorate e, appena appena astratte, si lasciavano volentieri confondere con mezzi meccanici realmente esistenti. Sorrette da una brillantissima colonna sonora ... e sapientemente regolate, alternavano i propri movimenti con strani periodi di stasi seguendo un

> ritmo piatto poi, mano a mano, caotico, confuso, e sorprendentemente in ascesa; comunque di grande effetto.[16]
>
> [This part of the show consisted of three of these sculptures, one placed at the centre, the other two at each side of a small stage, carved out of the already existing one, measuring a bit more than ten feet in length, three feet deep, whose proscenium was about four feet high. The sculptures, proportional to the stage, were in part brightly coloured and just a bit abstract: they could easily be mistaken for real machines. Sustained by a brilliant soundtrack … and carefully manipulated, they alternated their movements with strange periods of rest, following a flat rhythm at first, then, little by little, the movement became more chaotic, confused, reaching a surprising climax; the whole thing was very impressive.]

The music is described quickly, almost in passing, while the visual aspects of this show are noted in great detail: the dimensions of the stage, the positioning of the sculptures, and so on. One could argue that Ricci dedicated the first few years of his career to elaborating lessons learned from Kramer, using them as a starting point for his own understanding of a theatre he wanted to create. Between 1962, when he debuted his first show in the Roman house of art critic Nello Ponente,[17] and 1966, when the next phase of his production began, he created four different shows: *Movimento numero uno per marionetta sola* ("Movement Number One for Lone Puppet," 1962), *Spettacolo di tre pezzi* ("Show in Three Pieces," January 1964), *Movimento per marionetta sola numero 2* ("Movement for Lone Puppet Number 2," December 1964), *Movimento uno e due* ("Movements One and Two," 1965).

Here is his description of one of the "pieces" included in his *Spettacolo di tre pezzi*:

> Iniziava con il canto del gallo ripetuto tre volte, poi, dall'alto, alternativamente, calavano in scena sette tubi di diametro e altezza diversi che si disponevano sul palcoscenico non secondo uno schema stabilito, ma secondo i nostri umori di ogni sera … Dopo alcune semplici evoluzioni di questi tubi ne calavano in scena altri quattro, però a gomito, e il gioco si ripeteva. Per ultimo calavano ventisette sezioni di tubi di uguale diametro (due centimetri) ma di differente altezza (fra i sedici e i diciotto centimetri) e tutti fissati con dei fili a un supporto mobile. La differente altezza faceva sì che, cambiando il parallelismo del supporto rispetto al piano del palcoscenico i tubi cambiassero immediatamente la loro posizione, e quindi la composizione ottenuta … Il susseguirsi di queste "azioni visive" era provocato, o solo accompagnato, dal sonoro (jazz, rumori, voci inarticolate …) e dalle luci di scena.[18]

[It began with a rooster crowing three times, then, from above, one after another, seven pipes of differing length and diameter were lowered down and placed on the stage not according to a pre-ordained scheme, but depending upon the fancy of each evening … After a few simple movements, four more pipes were lowered onto the stage, only those ones that were bent, and the game would start all over again. Finally, twenty-seven sections of pipe equal in diameter (three quarters of an inch) but of different lengths (between six and seven inches) were lowered down, hanging by strings attached to a movable support. When modifying the angle of the support in respect to the floor, the different heights allowed the pipes to immediately change their position, thus transforming the whole composition … The switch from one of these "visual actions" to the next was triggered, or simply accompanied, by a soundtrack (jazz, noises, inarticulate voices …) and by stage lights.]

It is easy to imagine the bafflement of audience and critics when faced with Ricci's very abstract, minimalist theatre. Nothing like that had been shown on the Italian stage before (with the exclusion, naturally, of futurist theatre, of which I'll speak presently). The first positive reactions did not come from Ricci's colleagues or professional theatre critics but rather from the world of visual arts and literature. Yet, some of the more open-minded *addetti ai lavori* quickly came around and recognized Ricci's importance and contribution to the renewal of the Italian stage. Here is Bartolucci, singling out three main characteristics of his theatre:

Immagine – movimento – spazio: sono le tre nozioni attorno a cui Mario Ricci lavora da diversi anni: con un'anticipazione e con una precisazione di ordine formale delle quali soltanto oggi ci rendiamo perfettamente conto; oggi che su quelle nozioni si comincia ad imbastire un discorso meno sprovveduto e meno affrettato, l'immagine non essendo più quella plastica del teatro tradizionale, il movimento applicandosi al di là dello sviluppo dell'azione drammaturgica tout court, lo spazio risultando una combinazione di immagini-movimento con apporti di luci e colori. È davvero incredibile come la cultura teatrale italiana abbia ignorato e disprezzato tutta questa zona di ricerche teatrali, se non sapessimo che a suo tempo furono coltivate dai futuristi, Balla in particolare, e subito catalogate tra le non citabili e le non perseguibili sperimentalmente e criticamente, con quel vuoto di effettiva ricerca che ne venne.[19]

[Image – movement – space: these are the three notions around which Mario Ricci has been labouring for the past few years: with a foresight and a formal exactness that has become apparent only today; and now those same notions have become part of a more rigorous, more poised debate.

> The image is not the plastic image of traditional theatre; the movement goes beyond the development of dramaturgical actions; the space is the result of a combination of images and movements enhanced by lights and colours. It would be truly unbelievable that the Italian theatrical culture has ignored and disparaged this whole area of research if we didn't remember that it was first explored by the futurists, and Balla in particular, and immediately catalogued as unquotable, experimentally and critically impossible to pursue; and this attitude caused a void of actual research.]

Bartolucci focuses on the basics, showing how Ricci's experimentation sought to reconstruct Italian theatre from the ground up. Very telling is the reference to futurism: once again, the experiments carried out by the first wave of the avant-garde serve as an inspiration to the younger artists; at the same time, they also offer a frame of reference for a new generation of critics who are trying to understand, contextualize, and provide an informed appreciation of the works they are seeing. Much of the misunderstanding between these new experimenters and their critics can be traced back to the latter's prejudice against futurism, a prejudice that is derived from political and ideological considerations.[20]

In reflecting on his own approach to theatre, Ricci often focuses on the audience. One of the main objectives of his experiments, it would seem, is to gauge their reactions and incorporate the knowledge thus gained into successive versions of that same performance and, eventually, into other shows. The inclusion of the audience and their feedback in the creative process, as we saw in the previous chapter, is one of the defining traits of the avant-garde, a trait that was particularly important for the Gruppo 63 poets and writers.

However, audiences don't always react the way an artist would prefer. Here Ricci is speaking, again, about his *Spettacolo di tre pezzi* ("Show in Three Pieces"), expressing dissatisfaction with certain ingrained interpretive habits of the viewers:

> Ovviamente, per spettacoli come quello realizzato con i vecchi tubi di stufa, alla prima lettura, cioè alla "lettura di reazione," quella che poi a me interessava, ne seguiva una seconda. Il pubblico dava cioè la "sua" personalissima interpretazione di quanto aveva visto, collocandolo in diverse aree di suo esclusivo dominio. Ognuno inventava la sua storiella. Storielle piacevoli, alcune divertenti; ma il più delle volte idiote e caratterizzate da una mancanza di immaginazione portentosa ... Questo non era esattamente quello che volevo; e poi quelle storielle non mi interessavano. Il mio interesse finiva prima delle loro storielle, cioè al punto in cui era riuscito a stabilire un

contatto sicuro con materiali, così come usati, originali, non significanti se non quello che visivamente rappresentavano.[21]

[Naturally, for shows like the one made from old stovepipes, the first reading, that is, the "reactive reading," the one that really interested me, was followed by a second reading. Audiences would give their "own" very personal interpretation of what they had seen, providing for it a very specific context. Everyone invented their own little story. Pleasant stories, some even funny; but most of the time they were idiotic and revealed a staggering lack of imagination ... That was not exactly what I had in mind; and, after all, I wasn't interested in their little stories. My interest stopped before their little stories started, at the point where I managed to establish a stable connection with the materials, the way they were used, for what they were, in their originality, meaning nothing else but what they physically represented.]

The narrative expectations of the audience are perhaps one of the most resilient aspects of traditional theatre;[22] certainly, one of the hardest to reform, given the limited and indirect influence artists (authors, actors, scenographers, etc.) have on the audience. From this perspective, the convergence between a new generation of *teatranti* and a new generation of critics becomes even more important: it is a precious tool for educating the public and managing their expectations, effectively creating the conditions for the birth and establishment of a new theatre in Italy.

In addition to his revolutionary approach to the substance of the theatrical spectacle, which he re-created from scratch, starting from very basic but never simplistic elements, Ricci attempted to also reshape the space in which these shows were offered, the physical place where audiences and artists gathered for the performance. We have already mentioned how Carmelo Bene had moved out of the *circuito ufficiale* of theatres and started his own Teatro Laboratorio in a basement in Trastevere. Bene insisted, however, that this choice was dictated merely by practical concerns: to him, the *cantina* was just a space that happened to be available, a space he could afford; and he often insisted that he never "theorized the *cantine*" and never entertained "the aspiration to become an arthritic hero," for "basements (which are only good for catching rheumatisms) and the theatre of catacomb martyrs" never interested him.[23]

The opposite is true for Ricci: in his case, the choice of a *cantina* was a crucial part of the systematic renewal of the established practices of Italian theatre that he had initiated. As early as December 1964, he had inaugurated in Rome his Teatro Club Orsoline 15, a room that measured twenty-six by eighteen feet, with a small stage, eighteen by eighteen feet, on one end and enough benches to accommodate twenty or thirty people in the audience.[24] In Ricci's eyes, the opening of Teatro Club Orsoline was such an important event that he traced the birth of Nuovo Teatro to this moment.[25] As he retells the story of how his theatre evolved over the years, he assigns it a prominent place within the national landscape:

> Ottobre del 1964 prendo in affitto una vecchia stalla ripulita in vicolo delle Orsoline e, aiutato da alcuni "volenterosi" (come si dice), tra i quali attivissima mia moglie Gabriella Toppani, lo trasformo in un teatro club. Questa operazione, nel suo genere, è la prima in Italia e destinata ad avere incredibili ripercussioni, se si considera che oggi di teatrini-club in Italia ve ne sono almeno una trentina.[26]

> [October 1964, I rent out an old, repurposed stable in Vicolo delle Orsoline and – helped by a few "willing and able" (as they say) people, first among them my wife, Gabriella Toppani – I turned it into a theatre club. This solution, completely unprecedented, was destined to have an incredible influence, especially considering that at this point in Italy there are at least thirty different theatre clubs in existence.]

In the next paragraph of this same document, Ricci also claims to have taken a prominent role in questioning the existing theatrical conventions, elaborating a new "language" that would better fit the changed space and audience:

> Il ragionamento che mi spinge a questa operazione è semplicissimo: impossibile tentare la strada dell'altro teatro! Ma questo ragionamento vuol dire non solo rifiuto della struttura, diciamo così, politico-sociale, ma anche soprattutto, di quella specificatamente teatrale nel senso dei "linguaggi" (parolaccia!).[27]

> [The reasoning that prompted that solution was very simple: it was impossible to pursue the other theatre! But this reasoning does not only imply the rejection of the socio-political structure of the theatre, so to speak, but also, and most importantly, the more specifically theatrical aspects, that is to say its "language" (what an ugly word!).]

If we combine the two elements, the reform of language and the reform of the location, the definition of these early experiments as a "new theatre" will appear more realistic and the role played by Ricci is perhaps even more crucial. He was among the first intellectuals to examine the stage with new eyes and to introduce a radically different organization of its space and its contents. The *cantina* becomes both a metaphor of the new aesthetic sensibility and an engine that propels further experimentation and innovation. The new theatrical language that emerges must take into account the logistical limitations of the environment that bred it, the modest economic means it can dispose of, and the type of audience it can attract: fewer people, mostly intellectuals who already know the director and appreciate his work.[28]

In 1966 Ricci staged three new plays: *Salomè*, *Sacrificio Edilizio* ("Building Sacrifice"), and *Viaggi di Gulliver* ("Gulliver's Travels"), introducing, for the first time, human actors and projected films as part of his growing theatrical language. Not everyone was pleased with his choice: Bartolucci, for instance, argued that, in *Salomè*, the director "simply wanted to tell a well-defined story," thus committing a "small betrayal" of his own beliefs.[29]

From our vantage point, it is safe to say that, in spite of Bartolucci's contemporary perplexities, Ricci's theatrical new language was undergoing a reasonable evolutionary process, becoming more and more complex as time went by. Therefore, the reintroduction of the human element is not only understandable but, in a sense, almost unavoidable, especially if we consider that actors, at least in this first phase, are not the privileged inhabitants of the theatrical space but rather mere objects, whose movements and actions are no more important than those of the rest of the props.

A similar, natural progression can be seen in Ricci's early inclusion of projected images, including both photographs and films. Starting with *Viaggi di Gulliver*, cinema would become a widely used component of his performances:

> Il cinema da me regolarmente utilizzato all'interno di uno spettacolo teatrale deve essere considerato, innanzitutto funzionale, nel senso che do a questo "cinema" valore di elemento spettacolare alla pari di una luce, d'un colore, d'un attore.[30]
>
> [Cinema, which I regularly employed in my plays, must be considered as a prominently functional element, that is to say that I give to this "cinema" the same value as the one pertaining to a light, a colour, an actor.]

Each element on Ricci's stage has equal importance, be it a human being or an image projected on a screen, a body, or any other object. In fact, the interaction between the different elements coexisting on stage is often at the core of his theatrical machines: their assembly, disassembly, and slow mutations are the central focus of the action, and replace plot, characters, and a mimetic representation of reality. In this context, Ricci theorizes a "four-dimensional cinema":

> Riflessioni che si potrebbero così condensare ..., "cinema a quattro dimensioni," in cui le prime tre dimensioni sono rappresentate dal particolare schermo-palcoscenico e cioè la sua altezza, larghezza e profondità e la quarta dal particolare movimento che viene a crearsi all'interno di esso tenendo presente la "capacità" di sommarsi dei movimenti intrinseci nella pellicola girata appositamente e quelli del materiale scenico vero e proprio, cioè attori e oggetti in movimento.[31]
>
> [Reflections that could be thus synthesized ... as "four-dimensional cinema," in which the first three dimensions are given by the particular screen-stage, its height, length, and depth, while the fourth is given by the particular movements created on it considering the "potential" for interaction between the different movements of the film, recorded specifically for the show, and the scenic materials proper: actors and moving objects.]

Ricci takes full advantage of this "four-dimensional cinema" for the first time in his 1967 show *Illuminazione* ("Illumination"), a visual translation of a text collage by Nanni Balestrini. Ricci remembers that experience as "the most spectacular piece: the most brilliant." The show included three eight-millimetre projectors that showed simultaneously three different films specifically created for that purpose. One projected on a rotating mirrored kaleidoscope, placed above the centre of the stage, while the other two were projected onto eight prisms with a triangular base, anchored to the stage but capable of revolving, with one side covered by mirrors, and the other two simply painted white. When the images were projected onto the mirrors, they would be reflected back onto the audience, involving the viewers.

As for the script, Ricci considered *Illuminazione* "truly a non-text." It was composed of two halves: the stage directions of Chekhov's *The Cherry Orchard*, and the instructions of a booklet on physical exercises to be performed at home. The two scripts had been read and recorded by the actors. The tape offered the plot for their movements on stage. The same actors were also the protagonists of the short film projected, augmenting the general effect of a fun-house's hall of mirrors.[32]

One of the main reasons why Ricci was proud of this show is that none of its elements assume a primary importance; instead, all work simultaneously to disorient the audience and help dissipate and deflect those expectations for a mimetic, narrative, and psychological theatre he was trying to reform. For these purposes, Balestrini's text is ideal, being completely devoid of any characters or narrative arc. The fragmentation of language routinely employed by Balestrini and his use of quasi-stochastic methods of composition work perfectly well with Ricci's theatrical machines. To the textual layer, one must add the movements of the actors, which, although being contiguous to the instructions offered by the text, are not directly caused by them. And a final level of complication and abstraction is added by the use of projection. In this regard, Sinisi observes that,

> Le immagini filmiche non aggiungono elementi narrativi all'accadimento scenico, ma sezionano il lavoro con ingrandimenti di particolari, messa a fuoco di oggetti e dettagli anatomici con il rigore analitico di un esperimento *in vitro* ... la scomposizione del testo trova corrispondenza immediata nella frantumazione dell'immagine affidata a filmati e diapositive proiettati su due schermi mobili ... dando luogo ad un gioco illusionistico di lucidi inganni che asseconda la perdita di senso e di orientamento con un tracciato labirintico di sembianze mutevoli.[33]
>
> [The images don't add narrative elements to the events on stage, but rather divide the work using enlargements of small details, close-ups of objects and anatomical details that show a rigorous level of analysis, as if they were experiments *in vitro* ... the disassembling of the text is reflected by the images fragmented through films that have been projected onto two movable screens ... thus generating an illusion of lucid deceptions that emphasizes the loss of meaning and direction through the labyrinthine traces of shifting appearances.]

This was not the only direct contact Ricci had with Gruppo 63. The fact that he began his career in the visual arts made him always open to a series of collaborations with other artists and writers. Before working with Balestrini, he had performed Giuliani and Pagliarani's *Pelle d'asino* in 1965. Here is his recollection of that show:

> *Pelle d'asino* di Pagliarani e Giuliani, esponenti di spicco della associazione Gruppo 63 ... *Pelle d'asino* rispetto alla mia produzione di quel periodo, così tesa verso l'elaborazione d'un linguaggio teatrale affatto originale, forse a causa d'un eccessivo rispetto per il testo scritto non rappresenta motivi di novità. Uno spettacolo piacevole del quale ho un modesto ricordo.[34]
>
> [*Pelle d'asino* ("Donkeyskin") by Pagliarani and Giuliani, two of the most important *Gruppo 63* members ... In comparison to my other plays of the time, which were trying to achieve a rather original theatrical language,

> perhaps because of an excess of respect for the written text, *Pelle d'asino* does not show many innovative traits. A pleasant show that wasn't particularly memorable.]

We will have an opportunity to speak more about this text later on,[35] but I think it would be useful here to qualify Ricci's assessment of this experience. He points to "an excess of respect for the written text" as the main cause for its lack of success – unlike Balestrini's *Illuminazione, Pelle d'asino* tells a story, with distinguishable characters and a plot: all the outward signs of experimentation are muted, given in a subtler, more restrained fashion. What is truly interesting in this piece is its investigation of the relationship between the subconscious, love, sex, and the economy, and the fact that it does all that through the rewriting of a traditional fairy tale. The means used by Pagliarani and Giuliani to conduct such an investigation are rooted not in language but rather in myth, and this element complicated the staging process, forcing Ricci to make compromises and move his theatrical research in a direction with which he was not completely comfortable. However, it seems ungenerous to characterize it as a near failure: it is rather the sign of a basic misunderstanding. In spite of being headed in the same direction, theatre and literature were taking very different paths, and only rarely, and exceptionally, has a play been able to reconcile the two.[36] Balestrini's text offered a lot more freedom to Ricci, who used it to achieve one of the best shows in the first phase of his career. The kind of experiments that Pagliarani and Giuliani were attempting with *Pelle d'asino*, however, did not match well the environment created by Ricci. Maurizio Fagiolo, a contemporary critic, seems to confirm Ricci's recollection of the performance when he writes that this work "belongs to a more conventional repertory."[37]

2.3 Carlo Quartucci

While Bene began with the existentialism of Camus's *Caligula* and then moved on to his own very personal brand of experimentation, based on an "expressive baroque passion,"[38] and while Ricci focused on the basic elements of theatrical language, Carlo Quartucci started with Samuel Beckett's "theatre of the absurd," which he reinterpreted in a radically original way. However, in spite of their different approaches, all three shared the same goal: "to erase the traditional language of theatre and reinvent a new grammar composed of concrete signs, strictly belonging to the stage."[39]

Quartucci's first performance debuted in 1959, the same year as Bene's. It was a production of *Waiting for Godot*, a play to which he returned for a second time in 1964. The previous year, he had also staged *Endgame* using his very own company, called *Teatro Studio*. The relationship with the Irish playwright was predicated on radical freedom and independence. Quartucci used Beckett's dramaturgy and characters as a starting point, as "raw materials" from which he extracted an "abstract, geometrical, and coldly formalized" acting style. The theatre he was trying to build was going to experiment with "a non-psychological, non-narrative, and non-realistic use of words, gestures, and scenography, considering all of them as autonomous means of expression and communication."[40]

While Ricci had begun with a bare stage, subsequently adding a few sparse elements through which he would tell his abstract stories, Quartucci's approach was based on a progressive stripping away of the materials offered by Beckett: he eliminated what he considered unnecessary, deleting and erasing all indications of continuity in time and space, character and story[41] – all the mimetic devices that are conventionally meant to bring the stage closer to the real world. His objective was that of creating an empty space, a free and liberated stage within which a new theatre could be born. To do this, a new grammar and a new language were urgently needed.

The choice of Beckett as the starting point for this process, however, was not immune to controversy. In fact, some openly doubted that any real change could come from looking to a body of texts that had already been accepted by the "establishment" as modern classics. Bartolucci, at least at first,[42] was among the doubtful, although he later changed his mind after having experienced Quartucci's subsequent work. As Bartolucci noted, in a volume that collected a number of essays on the New Theatre entitled *La scrittura scenica*,

> Così un incontro di questo tipo, tra una scrittura drammaturgica in un certo senso già classica, e identificabile oggettivamente e storicamente per successive sperimentazioni, e una scrittura scenica che tende a superare questa oggettività e questa storicità, mediante il contributo di una visione gestico-fonetica di essa, partendo dall'interno della scrittura drammaturgica stessa, ed ampliandosi via via per apporti di vita e di scena, diventa improvvisamente ... un incontro sostanzialmente innovatore, non soltanto ai fini di una ricerca scenica del Quartucci ma anche ai fini di una resa scenica di Beckett ...[43]

> [Thus, an encounter of this kind, between a theatrical writing that is already, in a sense, a classic (objectively, historically identifiable through subsequent experiments), and a stage writing that tries to go beyond this

objectivity and historicity by expressing it in a gestural and phonetic way, beginning from the very core of that same theatrical writing, but expanding it little by little, with the addition of bits of life and stage, suddenly becomes ... an eminently innovative encounter, not only for what concerns Quartucci's research, but also for the stage performance of Beckett ...]

Here Bartolucci also makes an interesting distinction between Beckett's "scrittura drammaturgica" and Quartucci's "scrittura scenica" (we have translated the first as "theatrical writing" and the second as "stage writing"). In Bartolucci's critical vocabulary this is no inconsequential difference. Beckett is still thinking of theatre in the traditional sense: a space in which the distinction between audience and actors, stage and stalls, is clearly marked. The role of the script that is to be performed every night in the same exact way is also very stable and well defined.

Quartucci's "scrittura scenica," on the other hand, implies a radically new understanding of the actors' work, their role as co-creators of the text, and the theatre as a space where audience and *teatranti* are participating in an event that is not simply a performance. The script is seen as the platform from which actors and director can launch their exploration of the theatre's space and language. The characters are mere aggregates of gestural traits, so much so that Quartucci writes of their gestural, sonic, and spatial relationships as follows:

rapporti gestici (le complementarietà di Vladimiro-Estragone da una parte, Pozzo-Lucky dall'altra, risolte in complementarietà figurative: Vladimiro una linea che avvolge il corpo di Estragone tendente ad atteggiarsi come massa, e legame di forze fisiche in continuo contrasto tra Pozzo e Lucky), rapporti sonori (i personaggi cambiano voce tenendo conto di compensi e scompensi ritmici) e rapporti spaziali (scenografia non indicativa di ambienti, ma vocativa di zone mentali, l'unico luogo rappresentante l'esistenza.)[44]

[gestural relationships (the complementarity of Vladimir-Estragon on the one hand and Pozzo-Lucky on the other, expressed through a complementarity of figures: Vladimir is a line that wraps around Estragon's body who, in turn, tends to act as a solid mass; Pozzo and Lucky are a knot of physical forces in continuous contrast), the sound relationships (the characters change their voices according to a series of rhythmic compensations and decompensations), and space relations (the scenography does not suggest an environment, but rather evokes a mental zone, the only place where existence is represented.)]

Thus, when working on *Waiting for Godot*, on a first layer, based on Beckett's "theatrical writing," Quartucci superimposes another layer of "stage writing" through which he seeks to highlight, and take advantage of, all the non-verbal elements of human communication that are usually not contemplated in a script prepared by a traditional author. In fact, when it comes to this aspect, Beckett's writing is still rather conventional. It doesn't make use of (save for a few exceptions) the actors' bodies, their voices, their physical presence in front of the spectators. The work demanded by theatre is not limited to actors, director, and troupe. The audience must be involved, too. Quartucci tasks it with bringing together these two different layers of the performance; this is a highly emotional job, for it must reconcile the raw expressions of grief, anger, rage, desperation, and so on, conveyed by the actors through sounds and gestures, with the rational, linguistic signs they articulate.

As mentioned above, in 1963, Quartucci was performing Beckett's *Endgame* at the Teatro Quirino, in Rome, as part of the "Pomeriggi del Quattro," an experimental space created by Franco Enriquez. Luigi Squarzina, who at the time was the director of the Teatro di Genova, was in attendance one afternoon and was greatly impressed by the show, so much so that he invited the whole company of *Teatro Studio* to move to Genova.

Naturally, Quartucci accepted: this was the first collaboration between the "official" theatre and Nuovo Teatro. The relationship between these two entities was not always easy, and didn't last very long, but it was very important, for it confirmed certain intuitions Quartucci had had, chief among them that a reform of the theatre also had to involve a reform of the physical space where performances took place:

> La concezione architettonica delle sale da spettacolo è determinante ai fini delle scelte del pubblico, e di conseguenza del repertorio; è stata anzi la matrice prima del linguaggio "medio" adottato, l'unico in grado di soddisfare i bisogni, sempre troppo limitati, del pubblico borghese. Di più, la stessa collocazione topografica delle sale da spettacolo, poste sempre ed indiscutibilmente nelle zone "centrali" (addirittura nei "centri storici") delle città qualifica inequivocabilmente il beneficiario dell'attività teatrale. Questi quattro elementi (edificio, sua collocazione topografica, pubblico e linguaggio) coesistono inscindibilmente quasi in un unico guscio, tanto che sarebbe impensabile apportare delle variazioni anche ad uno di essi senza provocare squilibri d'ogni genere.[45]
>
> [The architecture of performance spaces is crucial in determining the choice of the audience, and thus the repertory; in fact, it is the first cause

> of this "median" language that has been adopted, the only one capable of satisfying the all-too-limited needs of a bourgeois audience. Furthermore, the very topographical placement of these performance spaces, always and inevitably located at the "city centre" (if not in the very "historical downtown"), unequivocally determines the intended beneficiary of the theatre's activity. These four elements (building, topographical location, audience, and language) coexist and are impossible to separate, as if contained in one single shell, so much so that it would be unthinkable to change one of them without compromising the general balance.]

The move to Genoa, whose Teatro was architecturally and topographically unsuited for the kind of language and audiences he sought, made Quartucci restless, although he was not quite ready to move just yet. He still needed time to perfect his personal stage writing, capable of appealing to and actively involving the spectators, whom he considered as a "listening community ... a dialectically active partner."[46] This may appear as a contradiction: on the one hand, Quartucci was developing a more abstract and experimental language; on the other, he was trying to reach a larger audience. In fact, this is the very same contradiction (or tension) in which the poets and writers of the neo-avant-garde found themselves, as discussed in the previous chapter.

In 1965, which, as we have seen, turned out to be a crucial year for the Nuovo Teatro, Quartucci, who at that point was still collaborating with the Teatro stabile of Genoa, prepared a new show with the Compagnia del Teatro Universitario di Genova entitled *Cartoteca*, basing it on a script by the Polish author Tadeusz Różewicz. The troupe was composed entirely of students. The piece revolved around the memories of a protagonist whom we see on his deathbed. The loose dramatic structure allowed Quartucci to insert within the preordained narrative a number of elements taken from current events, such as the war in Vietnam, the peace protests around the world, as well as other national and international news elements. The audience was invited to participate directly in the performance by reacting to the topics that were presented on stage. Quartucci exploited the compositional freedom offered by Różewicz's text to create room for his student-actors to express themselves. The rehearsal in preparation of the performance was equally unorthodox: the director would ask his troupe to create complete chaos for thirty minutes; then he would assign each of them themes and subjects that changed every day. The aim was to get the students used to quickly switching from one character to the next, since each actor was required to play ten or fifteen of them. The students' participation in the show, their ability to improvise and manage the "chaos," determined every night the different development of the performance. "I enjoyed seeing it change every night, depending upon the students' participation," Quartucci stated, for "the actor must be a continuous geography, within which one can change without ever settling on anything."[47]

For the first time, at least for Quartucci, the performance of the actors and the audience was structurally intertwined: the text was just a trace, a starting point, and each evening the show changed with the different news items, the actors' improvisations, and the spectators' reactions. So much so, in fact, that one could replace the term "performance" with "event," which marked a great victory for Quartucci and his creative vision, bringing him one step closer to a full realization of his artistic objectives.

Soon after the debut of this show, Quartucci and his troupe left Genoa to try a radically new experiment. A few months later they were just outside of Rome, at Prima Porta. There, they organized the Festival di Prima Porta, the first ever in Italy dedicated to the theatre of Samuel Beckett: usually, similar summer festivals would perform classical works, but this one was unique in that it focused entirely on the Irish playwright. The plays offered were *Aspettando Godot* (*Waiting for Godot*), *Finale di partita* (*Endgame*), and *Atto senza parole II* (*Act without Words II*). In each, Quartucci continued to experiment with his signature approach to Beckett's dramaturgical materials. Audience and actors gathered out in the open, around a circular wooden stage set in the Roman countryside, a location that was in fact quite difficult to reach. Evening after evening, Quartucci's new approach to theatre captured people's imagination and encountered popular success. He continued to develop his original vision, reserving more space for the creative contribution of the actors, who were encouraged to improvise and add to the show they were bringing to life.

However, greater inclusion came at a cost: it required a longer rehearsal time, so that every individual involved in the process could coordinate their efforts and present a final product that was fully matured and well-rounded. To address the complicated logistics while remaining within the limits of an extremely meagre budget, Quartucci decided to settle on the banks of the river Tiber, setting up a camp that, judging from the surviving testimonies, reminded most of its visitors of a bucolic and somewhat idyllic bohemian caravan. Reading Quartucci's memories of those times, we learn of morning fishing expeditions to provide food for lunch, followed by conferences and workshops with the actors on the most disparate subjects, from the *Informale* movement in the visual arts to Stockhausen's experimental music: all part of a conscious attempt to break away from the conventional gestures of everyday life and bring about a new form of physical expression. The results were remarkable. Here is a contemporary review of the Festival di Prima Porta by critic Alberto Perrini:

> Truccature stupende, costumi fantastici: angosciose apparizioni notturne d'incubo, maschere spettrali, o bambole di paglia dal viso cadaverico, burattini gonfi, cenciosi, dipinti a mano in modo che sembrino creature strinate dal fulmine o affogate nel latte zuccherato. Clownismo fatto di vocette, urli e sospiri, timbri, intonazioni, impostazioni, ritmi e modulazioni assurdi. Aspri, taglienti, laceranti o morbidi, acquosi, incubati e cavernosi; guizzare di pesci metallici, rimbalzare di biglie sul vetro, gracidare di rane, squittii, boati, lamenti, frustrate, risa, schiaffi e cachinni.[48]

> [Wonderful makeup, fantastic costumes: nightmarish, sorrowful night apparitions, spectral masks, or straw puppets with faces like corpses, bloated rag dolls painted by hand to resemble creatures burned by lighting or drowned in sugary milk. Clowneries made of thin voices, cries and sighs, timbre, intonation, posturing, rhythms, and absurd modulations. Harsh, cutting, wrenching or soft, watery, incubating, cavernous; a jumping of metallic fish, a bouncing of marbles over glass, a croaking of frogs, squeaks, roars, wailings, whippings, laughter, slaps, giggles.]

Note how the bulk of Perrini's impressions gravitate around location and staging: by now, Quartucci's Beckett had become a familiar feature. What really attracted the audience's attention during these new performances was the novelty of finding themselves *en plein air*, at night, in the countryside, in parts of Rome's suburbs they didn't quite know, surprised by the somewhat otherworldly experience the actors had worked so hard to conjure. The other crucial element that remained deeply ingrained in the spectators' imagination was the sound. It wasn't composed merely of words; there was an additional, complex layer of non-verbal communication that served as a means to reach the audience in an unprecedented way, casting a surreal, oneiric light on the whole performance.

The peculiar circumstances that surrounded the show (the living arrangements of the troupe, the darkness, the countryside, the difficulties in reaching the theatrical space, etc.), reactivated a ritual dimension that had mostly been lost to bourgeois theatre, creating a sense of belonging that united actors and audiences. This experience reinforced Quartucci's intuition that the future of Italian theatre would be found outside of conventional places, far from the historical centres, and could be brought to fruition only through a strict collaboration between authors, actors, and spectators.

Additionally, the experience of this festival, although never repeated, made possible the encounter with Scabia and thus was crucial for the next chapter in Quartucci's career. The two began work on the groundbreaking show *Zip Lap Lip Vap Mam Crep Scap Plip Trip Scrap e la Grande Mam* (from here on, simply *Zip*), which we will discuss in the next section.

Finally, as the Festival di Prima Porta was still in full swing, toward the end of the summer of 1965, Quartucci and his troupe began preparations for a show that would have included three one-act plays by writers belonging to Gruppo 63, to be performed that September at the third annual meeting of the group, held, once again, in Palermo. The plays were: *Furfanti* ("Scoundrels") by Gaetano Testa, *Gioco con la scimmia* ("Game with Monkey") by Enrico Filippini, and *I Sigari di Jupiter* ("Jupiter's Cigars") by Germano Lombardi.

2.4 Giuliano Scabia

Scabia first approached the world of theatre through contemporary music, the same Musica Nuova whose festival, in 1963, in Palermo, hosted the first Gruppo 63 gathering. His encounter with Luigi Nono was a crucial event that set him on the path he would follow for the rest of his career. He met the composer during a performance of his *Intolleranza 1960* ("Intolerance 1960"), his first ground-breaking experimental opera, which included electronic recordings of natural sounds and noises, as well as Vedova's original sceneries and projections, and a *lanterna magicka* (scenographic machine) by Joseph Svodoba.[49]

Scabia was to write the libretto for Nono's next experimental opera, *La fabbrica illuminata* ("The Illuminated Factory"). In it, Nono once again combined his experimental style of composition with his political engagement, authoring a stern condemnation of the working conditions inside the modern factory. For this project, he recorded the sounds of steel manufacturing at the Italsider Mill in Genoa. Scabia's text focused on the health and safety risks to which all the workers were exposed: the toxic fumes, the blinding lights, and the frequent accidents. The finished opera proved to be a powerful political statement, as well as a remarkable document of a new aesthetic sensibility, open to the contemporary world and its contradictory realities.

In the spring of 1965, Scabia wrote *All'improvviso* ("Suddenly"),[50] his first theatrical script and a text in which, for the very first time, he sought to elaborate and put forth his vision for an acentric theatre. The performance is divided into several actions that include characters, animals, puppets, a chorus, and projections. The stage directions and actors' lines are only slightly differentiated, and many times the words predisposed by the author deteriorate into sounds, lullabies, and mere phonetic utterances. In this very early phase, Scabia tried to include in his performances the whole space of the theatre, abolishing the distinction between stage and stalls, and employing a number of different techniques (including projections and sound recordings) to ensure that the audience would have an immersive experience.[51] As he states in the notes he includes in the published version of *All'improvviso,*

> *All'improvviso* è stato scritto nel febbraio–marzo 1965, prima di (*Zip*). Ne contiene in qualche modo i principali problemi che si possono riassumere in: 1) uso di tutto il teatro; 2) uso straniato e ironico degli oggetti; 3) uso dell'attore come *oggetto* animato, e quindi come fatto plastico-visivo oltre che sonoro; 4) introduzione di parti puramente fonetiche; 5) uso del palcoscenico come luogo di visione "relativo," alla stregua di un video percorribile in profondità.[52]

> [*All'improvviso* was written from February to March 1965, before (*Zip*). In a sense, it addresses the same key issues, which can be summarized thus: 1) the use of the whole theatre; 2) an estranged and ironic use of objects; 3) the use of actors as animated *objects*, and therefore as plastic-visual (in addition to sound) entities; 4) the introduction of purely phonetic parts; 5) the use of the stage as a place for "relative" vision, as if it were a video with a depth that can be traversed.]

This last item on the list is especially interesting: Scabia wanted to highlight the visual component of his theatre, putting it on the same level as the aural, in order to reduce the importance that has been traditionally given to the words pronounced by the actors, often to the detriment of every other element involved in the performance. The same point is better clarified in another theoretical article, published around the same time as this note:

> Oggi, mutata l'idea dello spazio teatrale, bisogna andare verso una scrittura completa e alla scrittura prospettica (la parola come punto focale dello spettacolo) va sostituita una scrittura anch'essa acentrica in cui non ci sia un elemento privilegiato. In un certo senso si tratta di approntare delle partiture teatrali non limitate alla scrittura del dialogo, inventando lo spazio già in sede del testo. In tal modo non ci saranno più battute e didascalie ... ma tutto: dialoghi, descrizione di luce, di tono, di gesti, di movimenti, farà parte del testo e della scena.[53]

[Now that the idea of theatrical space has changed, we need to move toward a complete writing, and the perspective writing (wherein the word is the central focus of the show) must be replaced with a kind of writing that is itself acentric, wherein no element is predominant. In a sense, it is a matter of creating theatrical scores that are not limited to the dialogue, where the space is invented as early as the script is written. In that case, there would be no more need for lines and stage directions … but everything: dialogues, light descriptions, the tone, the gestures, will be a part of the text and of the scene.]

This melding together, on an equal plane, of all the elements that constitute the performance can be experienced (at least virtually) by looking at the pages of Scabia's published plays. Most of the traditional conventions used to organize the script (chief among them being the distinction between stage directions and characters' lines) are dropped, resulting in a very evocative, sometimes poetic form of stage writing. However, we must not forget that one of the key objectives pursued in these scripts is the reshaping of the theatre space, so that the audience, the author, and the actors may find themselves on the same level, all of them active participants in the theatrical event that unfolds all around them.

Scabia's is an experimentation that begins with the organization of the space within the "box" of the theatrical space, and that seeks to attribute equal importance to every element it contains. This egalitarian approach is reflected in the role assigned to the actors, scenographer, author, and every other participant in the show: each of them contributes equally to the performance. Clearly, there is a convergence with Quartucci's ideas: they both want to involve the actors and audience in a much more substantial and meaningful way. Thus, a collaboration between the two seemed like the natural next step. The perfect opportunity, as mentioned above, presented itself with *Zip*, a show directed by Quartucci and written by Scabia.

Here are Scabia's initial plans and intentions – the way in which he envisioned the final product of this collaboration:

far vivere, partendo da un testo verificato continuamente sulla scena,[54] dieci maschere contemporanee: dieci forme capaci di racchiudere ognuna più tipi. Non maschere fisse, come nella commedia dell'arte, bensì maschere mobili, aperte, in continua crescita nel gesto, nel costume, nella voce, nel significato, durante tutto lo spettacolo.[55]

[bring back to life, beginning with a text that is continuously verified on stage, ten contemporary masks: ten shapes, capable of expressing multiple types each. Not fixed masks, like in the Commedia dell'Arte, but rather movable masks, open and in constant growth with their gestures, their costumes, their voice, their meaning, throughout the show.]

Each element of this first aspirational description reveals the new importance given to the actors, the degree of freedom assigned to them, and the space carved out so that their creative process may assert itself. In fact, Scabia and Quartucci sought to work toward a performance that didn't require a script, a show that is the result of a close collaboration between author, director, actor, and scenographer. The performance derives from a rehearsal period during which the whole troupe explores a theme, a situation, an image. From the repeated interactions and subsequent discussions of every member of the company would emerge, almost organically, the finished product.

As mentioned above, the time to work on this show came as the Festival Samuel Beckett at Prima Porta was winding down. In that pastoral setting, the two men embarked on this new experiment:

> Quartucci mi parla dell'idea di mettere in scena clowns, dai nomi strani di Zlip [*sic*], Crap, Plop ecc. Comincio a pensarci. Ho pronta una scena, ancora semiformale, che ho leggermente ripulito e stretto, il dialogo finale tra Lip e Lap, prima della finta fucilazione. Partiamo di là. I personaggi per ora sono contrassegnati con A e B. Un po' per volta mi si fa strada l'immagine di un inizio scenico. Il grande uovo. Far nascere i personaggi sulla scena. Caratterizzarli poco a poco, nel gesto, nel suono, nel movimento, nella lingua. Seguirli dalla nascita a una prima definizione aperta: creare delle maschere in evoluzione, persone con molti tipi dentro … Deve trattarsi di un gioco scenico. Bisogna far entrare lo spettatore dentro il gioco fantastico.[56]

> [Quartucci tells me about an idea of putting on stage a few clowns with strange names such as Zlip [*sic*], Crap, Plop, etc. I start thinking about it. I have a scene ready, still half-formalized, which I had cleaned up and tightened, the final dialogue between Lip and Lap, before the fake execution by firing squad. We take it from there. The characters, for now, are designated as A and B. Little by little I begin to envision a theatrical beginning. The great egg. Have the characters be born on stage. Making them more and more concrete little by little, using gestures, sounds, movement, language. Follow them from their birth to a first open characterization: creating masks in evolution, personae with many types within them … It must be a scenic game. We must have the spectators become part of this fantastical game.]

It was a very ambitious goal: Scabia wanted to do something that had never really been accomplished before in Italy. Unfortunately, the conditions were not entirely ideal: they didn't have much time to rehearse (just twenty-three days),[57] but at least they received "institutional" support from the official theatre – the Festival di Venezia (organized by Venice Biennale) and the Stabile di Genova had agreed to produce *Zip* to the tune of 3 million 400 thousand liras (an extremely low budget for such a complex project).[58]

The relationship between the Teatro Stabile di Genova and Quartucci had not always been easy. In fact, just at the end of the previous season, Quartucci had decided to leave Genoa and set off on his own, organizing the very successful Festival di Prima Porta (as we already mentioned). This made the support of the Stabile di Genova and the Biennale all the more meaningful. It was a sign that the "establishment" was beginning to notice their younger colleagues and took their experiments seriously. But what did these institutions receive for their money?

The show was divided into two acts; at the beginning of the first, the characters were "born" on stage, out of a gigantic egg, and appeared still wrapped in shipping paper. At first, the ten characters were just generic clowns, without distinct personalities. Little by little, through repeated interactions with each other, with the environment, and with the Grande Mam, a sort of robotic presence symbolizing the then contemporary consumer society, each mask turned into an individual, displaying original characteristics. The space of the performance was extended to the whole theatre, through the use of a system of platforms and gangways. The costumes and the scenography (by Emanuele Luzzati) were reminiscent of the historical avant-gardes, futurism and Dada in particular, and employed collages and juxtapositions of varied and sometimes incongruous materials and images. After familiarizing themselves with their environment, the masks began to employ language, starting from basic phonemes and sounds, and progressively moved into the use of complete words and sentences. In the second act, the free use of gestures, mime, sounds, and expression was replaced by a more conventional, more realistic style of communication.

The show immediately divided audience and critics, some of whom took the opportunity to denigrate not only Scabia's and Quartucci's work but also the attempts at a radical reformation that had been put forth by the whole theatrical neo-avant-garde of the Nuovo Teatro, so much so that De Marinis spoke of a "regolamento di conti con l'avanguardia," that is, a "settling of scores with the avant-garde."[59] In his opinion, the main issue with the new style of rehearsing adopted by Scabia and Quartucci was that it had been carried out too hurriedly; it had the potential of revolutionizing the Italian stage, but the actors had not been given enough time to adjust to the new kind of work that was required of them. Many of them, in fact, did not really grasp the implications of their new role, and even resented the author and the director for interfering with their usual methods.

Some critics didn't like the progression between the first and second act; they especially didn't appreciate how the language and gestures became increasingly normalized during the last part of the show. Some lamented the absence of a clear script. Others criticized the style of recitation, which emphasized physical rather than linguistic elements. And, finally, many had misgivings regarding Scabia's key idea of an acentric theatre.[60] The discussions around *Zip* grew into a full-blown controversy, with critics taking sides for and against. In response to this situation, Quartucci and Scabia attempted to clarify their intentions by publishing a small manifesto in *Sipario* entitled "Per un'avanguardia italiana" ("For an Italian Avant-garde"). In it, they laid out the three key aspects of their theatre. The first one, not surprisingly, was space:

> In *Zip* si recita in un teatro trasformato tutto in palcoscenico. Naturalmente per noi si tratta di un punto d'arrivo e insieme di partenza. È questa un'esperienza già in parte teorizzata o attuata in passato (Mejerchold-Artaud), che oggi va ripresa, portata avanti, approfondita. Si tratta di immergere lo spettatore *anche fisicamente* nello spettacolo, coinvolgendolo nei rapporti che si creano fra attore e attore, battuta e battuta, suono e suono che gli passano sopra e lo attraversano.[61]

> [In *Zip* the whole theatre has been turned into a stage on which we act. Naturally, for us, this is both a point of arrival and a point of departure. It is an experiment that had already been theorized and partially actualized in the past (Meyerhold-Artaud), but it is something that, we feel, today must be revived, continued, explored in more depth. It is a matter of immersing, *even physically*, the spectators inside the show, involving them in the relationships that are established between actor and actor, line and line, sound and sound, all elements that fly above and through them.]

The strategy Quartucci and Scabia chose in defending the solutions they devised for their show was rather interesting: they pointed at two fundamental figures from the recent past of European theatre who, however, were still not very well known in Italy (especially Artaud, whose works were translated into Italian only in June of 1965, in the journal *Sipario*). The two *teatranti* aimed at creating a precedent for their ideas, and then appealed to that external authority to justify their practices. Additionally, they rendered explicit the ultimate objective they were trying to achieve: building an immersive experience for the spectator.

In pursuing this goal, the type of relationship that the actors established with both the characters and the audience was crucial. This is the second key point in their manifesto:

> Gli attori hanno partecipato abbastanza attivamente, fin dall'inizio delle prove, alla costruzione scenica di *Zip*. Attraverso lunghe discussioni, addirittura mediante la ricerca in comune della battuta adatta, o con suggerimenti per il taglio delle scene. Si è raggiunta così una recitazione analizzata, cosciente di sé, che tiene a distanza la maschera e lo spettatore, pur coinvolgendolo fisicamente e intellettualmente. Si tratta di avvicinare e allontanare continuamente dall'attore e dallo spettatore il personaggio e lo spettacolo, in modo da avere insieme la partecipazione razionale e la partecipazione fisica e affettiva dello spettatore e dell'attore.[62]

> [The actors participated quite actively, since the very beginning of rehearsal, in the scenic construction of *Zip*. Through long discussions, even by looking together for the right line, or through suggestions on how to cut the individual scenes. Thus, we have reached a style of acting that is examined, aware of itself, capable of keeping the mask and the spectators at a distance, while, at the same time, involving them both physically and intellectually. It is a matter of constantly pushing the actors and the spectators away from the characters and the show, so as to elicit at the same time the physical and emotional participation of the spectators and actors.]

Quartucci and Scabia doubled down on their commitment to include the actors in the creative process, advertising it as a central point of strength of their dramaturgy. And yet, it was not an end in itself, but rather a means for producing a very specific effect on the viewer: only through this direct and deliberate participation of the actor could an almost impossible task be accomplished; that is, only through this style of acting could the author appeal to both the emotional and the intellectual aspects of the audience and compel them to participate in the performance. On the one hand, there was a consistent effort to problematize representation and avoid a passive reception on the part of the spectator. Alternatively, by appealing to the physicality of the interpreters, the author could speak more directly to his audience, attempting to involve them at an emotional level that did not involve logic or rational thought.

A final point of clarification addressed the relationship with the historical avant-garde:

> Nella tradizione della cosiddetta *avanguardia* del Novecento vediamo una immensa riserva di soluzioni, di tecniche, di sperimentazioni, di risultati meravigliosi e di fallimenti desolanti: un patrimonio da cui bisogna attingere, di cui bisogna servirsi … Non si è saputo vedere quanto di nuovo, a livello del linguaggio e della coscienza di un senso della storia, si veniva scoprendo attraverso e mediante l'avanguardia. Naturalmente servirci di una tradizione non vuol dire ripeterla. Oggi non crediamo né utile né necessario partire da zero, perché nella situazione in cui ci troviamo è possibile essere tanto più precisi quanto più si è coscienti delle esperienze che sono già state iniziate e portate avanti.[63]
>
> [In the tradition of the so-called *avant-garde* of the Novecento we see an immense reserve of solutions, techniques, experiments, wonderful results and distressing failures; a patrimony that must be exploited, on which we must be able to build … Some don't want to see how much innovation, on the level of language and in creating an awareness of a sense of history, has been gained through and thanks to the avant-garde. Naturally, the fact that we want to use a tradition does not mean we intend to repeat it. Today, we believe that starting from scratch is neither useful nor necessary: given our current situation, the more we are aware of the experiences that have already been attempted and carried out, the more effective we can be.]

Here Quartucci and Scabia are clearly addressing their detractors and their accusation of being mere imitators of experiments already introduced by futurism and the other avant-garde movements of the first half of the Novecento. Not only would it be wasteful, the two *teatranti* argue, to disregard the vast amount of experience accumulated by these predecessors, but it would actually be irresponsible to act as if such experiences had never happened. The Italian New Theatre could not ignore their contributions if it wanted to join the level of sophistication that was common among its more up-to-date and cosmopolitan European counterparts.

In closing this section, it is important to reiterate some of the reasons why *Zip* remains a key text for the Nuovo Teatro,[64] in spite of the play's actual performance history and the controversy that it generated. In the young tradition of Italian New Theatre, *Zip* was the very first text to be written from scratch, specifically for the purpose of being performed on stage, implementing every element of the "scrittura scenica." Until this moment, the pioneers of research had each relied on texts that already existed, and came from a different language (and literature): Camus and then Shakespeare for Bene, Samuel Beckett for Quartucci, while Ricci's early shows did away with verbal language altogether.

The production of *Zip* was the first collaboration between a Teatro stabile and an avant-garde group (and, unfortunately, it also marked the first in a long line of somewhat failed attempts and missed opportunities). It also prompted an important debate between critics in favour of the recent experiments and those who opposed them. Finally, and perhaps most importantly, it was the first time an organic collaboration of actors, director, author, and scenographer was attempted; if nothing else, it showed that it was possible to shorten the distance separating the writing and the stage. Additionally, it highlighted all the difficulties, resistances, and prejudices implicit in this attempt, not only by the critics and the audience, but also by each of the professionals involved in it.

2.5 After 1965

By now it has become rather obvious that 1965 was a crucial year in the history of the Nuovo Teatro; this is true for the innovative shows that debuted, and the many changes that came to pass on the national stage. However, there are at least three more reasons why it can be considered a turning point for the events we have been reconstructing: 1) the quick establishment of a circuit of *cantine* in Rome;[65] 2) the progressive sedimentation of a *Nuova Critica*, which was instrumental in making the Nuovo Teatro available to and approachable by a wider audience; and 3) the radical changes in the career trajectories of Quartucci and Scabia. We will briefly address each reason.

Even though Carmelo Bene had technically established the first *cantina* in 1964, with his Teatro Laboratorio, he never viewed that space as particularly significant: it was just a container for his shows, where he could experiment with a higher degree of freedom. In December 1965, Ricci had opened his Club Orsoline 15, inaugurating the season of Roman *cantine*.[66]

In June 1965, Antonio Calenda acquired the space that would later become Teatro dei 101, located on via Euclide Torba, 26. The first performance dates to 1966, and was entitled *Direzione Memorie* ("Direction Memories"). The script was by Corrado Augias; Giuseppe Bartolucci, in a review he published soon after the opening, pointed out its affinities with the dramaturgy of Beckett and Genet, praising the show as useful in the process of bringing the Italian theatre to the same level as the European one.[67] The following two shows, which debuted in

December 1966, were Apollinaire's *Mammelle di Tiresia* (*The Breasts of Tiresias*, 1903), and Picasso's *Il desiderio preso per la coda* (*Desire Caught by the Tail*). These two texts connected the contemporary experiments of the Nuovo Teatro with the avant-garde movements of the beginning of the Novecento, thus sending a clear signal to critics and audiences: Calenda and the Teatro dei 101 troupe were drawing from those early European experiments in their attempt to reform contemporary Italian theatre. The next shows scheduled and performed at the 101 were Fernando Arrabal's *Il labirinto* (*The Labyrinth*) and Harold Pinter's *Un leggero malessere* (*A Slight Ache*).

In 1961, while Bene was establishing himself in a Trastevere basement, Claudio Remondi tried to open a new theatre in a *cantina* in that same neighbourhood, in Vicolo del Leopardo, and wanted to call it Teatro del Leopardo. However, he couldn't secure the necessary permits, for the building was deemed unsafe by local authorities. He tried a second time a few years later, and on 13 April 1966, in Monteverde Nuovo, a suburb of Rome, he finally succeeded in opening his theatre, which he named Teatro del Leopardo, as a tribute to that first, failed attempt. It was the first *cantina* outside the historical downtown, and critics lauded Remondi's courage and his intention to involve an audience that had been routinely neglected by the official theatre. The first season opened with two one-act plays by Sławomir Mrożek: *In alto mare* (*Out at Sea*) and *Karol*. The direction was credited to a collective composed of Remondi and some of the other company members. From reading contemporary reviews, it is not clear what exactly happened on stage, but many critics pointed out connections between these plays and Quartucci's style of direction, with a geometrical, mechanical, puppet-like way of managing the space and the actors' movements. All in all, the reactions were mixed: in general, they were appreciative of the intentions expressed by the show but formulated a few doubts as to the execution and delivery of the performance. A worse reception was given to the next show prepared by the group, Remondi's *Prima del falò* ("Before the Bonfire"). Once again, the source of inspiration and the model were Beckett and the theatre of the absurd, seen through Quartucci's reinterpretation. Critics pointed out how Remondi's contribution to this tradition failed to question some of the basic, material assumptions of traditional, bourgeois theatre, and therefore, they argued, he fell short of the objectives he had set out to accomplish.[68]

In 1966, Franco Molè debuted his first show, *Settanta volte sette* ("Seventy Times Seven"), together with Leo de Berardinis, in a space called all'Armadio, on Via La Spezia, a room that also doubled as the local chapter of the PCI (the Italian Communist Party). The script was by

Molè, and the show was particularly praised by the New Critics for its acentric approach to writing, to use Scabia's own terminology. Achille Mango identified the show's ties with Beckett and the theatre of the absurd, but also with the emerging experiments of the Living Theatre: the actions on stage did not seem to evolve according to a narrative logic but rather followed the physical and gestural abilities of the actors.[69] This was a crucial sign of the renewal that was being pursued by Molè and his troupe: script and stage actions were put at the same level, and thus considered equally important; and this was, in essence, the most revolutionary novelty introduced and championed by the Nuovo Teatro.

After this first experience, Franco Molè opened his own, independent space on Via Fonte dell'Olio, just behind the Basilica of St Maria in Trastevere, calling it Alla Ringhiera. The first performances were held in January 1967: a script by Molè, entitled *Concerto Grosso per Brugh* ("Brugh's Concerto Grosso"). The plot is rather simple and somewhat Kafkaesque: an oboe player is forbidden to perform, challenges the authorities, and is jailed. The actors staged the dialogues between the protagonist, his assistant, and their tormentors in a surreal, anti-mimetic style, breaking down the lines into their composing syllables, chanting, and moving their bodies in ways that contradicted the words they uttered. The show received mixed reviews: critics appreciated the attempt to innovate the style of performing but considered the director's approach contrived and somewhat forced.[70]

In May of 1966, in a deconsecrated church on Via Belsiana, Paolo Bonacelli and Carlotta Barilli inaugurated the first show of the Compagnia del Porcospino. In its first phase, however, the group and the space were not yet called by this name. After the first performances – of Martin Walser's play *La scappatella* ("The Escapade"), directed by Roberto Guicciardini – the company was dissolved, and the two founders opened their doors to a group of writers and intellectuals that would become the new Compagnia. Among the new members were Alberto Moravia, Dacia Maraini, Enzo Siciliano, Ernesto Colli, and Carlo Montagna. The name was chosen by Moravia. The collaboration lasted for two seasons and produced performances of plays written or translated by some of the company's writers. *Il guerriero, l'amazzone, lo spirito della poesia nel verso immortale del Foscolo* ("The Warrior, the Amazon, the Spirit of Poetry in Foscolo's Immortal Verse") by Carlo Emilio Gadda, directed by Sandro Rossi, which opened in February 1967, was the show that enjoyed the widest critical success. The warrior of the title is Napoleon; the amazon, Luigia Pallavicini, the countess in whose honour, on the occasion of her falling off a horse, Ugo Foscolo wrote an ode. Napoleon famously fell off a horse, too, during the battle on the

Arcole Bridge. These two equestrian accidents are the starting point of a spirited discussion between a professor who is also a critic, and a lawyer who is also an anarchist. The main attraction of the show is Gadda's language, which the actors and director managed to deliver to their audience in all of its sparkling vitality.

Beginning in 1967, critics frequented with more continuity the *cantine romane*, writing about the shows that were performed there, and effectively putting the Nuovo Teatro and its protagonists on the national (and international) map; among them some of the more active were the already mentioned Giuseppe Bartolucci and Franco Quadri. On the other hand, a cohort of more conservative critics offered conflicting views, repeatedly attacking these new experiments, thus creating, from the perspective of theatregoers, a very confusing environment: "the evaluation of the shows performed in the *cantine* is often contradictory …; based on antithetical motivations, critics either praise them or deny that they have any value."[71]

Beginning in the early 1960s, Giuseppe Bartolucci had championed the cause of a radical renovation of the Italian theatre, chronicling the first experiments of the Nuovo Teatro and its early pioneers. Valentina Valentini, who edited a selection of Bartolucci's writings, thus summarizes, in her introduction, the critic's approach to his work:

> La sua battaglia come intellettuale impegnato, già a partire dai primi anni sessanta è il "rinnovamento del teatro italiano" che va affrontato sia da una rilettura della sua storia (nel senso di riappropriarsi della modernità di Pirandello e dell'eredità futurista in senso contemporaneo) sia con l'energica affermazione delle esperienze nazionali e internazionali che incarnano il *nuovo*: il Living, Carmelo Bene, Genet, la giovane regia europea e non ultimo con uno svecchiamento della critica … Bartolucci ritrova infatti, nel teatro di Pirandello, D'Annunzio, nei manifesti futuristi, come nella pratica della regia critica del secondo dopoguerra (Strehler, Squarzina, Visconti), quei tratti di antinaturalismo e antillusionismo che sono i prerequisiti della scrittura scenica di cui spia sintomatica è l'uso della didascalia.[72]
>
> [His battle as an engaged intellectual begins in the early 1960s, and is waged for a "renewal of Italian theatre" which must be pursued through a re-reading of its history (meaning that one must learn to appreciate from a contemporary perspective Pirandello's modernity and the legacy of futurism) and through an energetic appreciation of those national and international experiments that bring about the *new*: The Living Theatre, Carmelo Bene, Genet, the young European directors, as well as

a generational change in criticism ... In fact, Bartolucci identifies in the theatre of Pirandello, D'Annunzio, and in futurist manifestos, as well as in the critical style of directing after World War II (Strehler, Squarzina, Visconti), those traits of anti-naturalism and anti-illusionism that are the prerequisites of a stage writing whose clearest symptom is the use of stage directions.]

Stressing the connection between the historical avant-gardes and the most recent innovators is one of Bartolucci's greatest contributions to the discussion surrounding Nuovo Teatro. In addition to reconstructing its "prehistory," he acted as a strong supporter of the experiments that were being carried out both nationally and internationally, and he initiated a process aimed at reforming and updating the language of dramatic criticism, focusing on the "material" aspects of the shows and reducing the importance that was traditionally given to the words spoken by the actors, and to their interpretation.

Bartolucci pursued these goals by tirelessly exercising his criticism in the pages of many journals and magazines. In particular, he promoted two crucial investigations, both in *Sipario*: the first had to do with the role played in Italy by *teatri stabili*; the second assessed the state of theatrical criticism. The first investigation highlighted how a lack of generational renewal in the direction of those institutions stifled innovation and caused Italian theatre to lag behind, relegating it to a rearguard position when compared to the rest of Europe (Peter Brook, The Living Theatre, Grotowski).[73] Consequently, the *teatri stabili* saw a decline in the size of their audience, for they failed to reflect the changes in the audience's taste and sensibility.

Issues 251, 252, and 254 of *Sipario* included a three-part investigation entitled "Situazione della critica" ("The Situation of Criticism"): Bartolucci asked some of the most influential critics (as well as the emerging ones) to define the state of their trade, and the gap that seemed to separate the world of criticism from the world of the stage. In a key essay entitled "Per un diverso linguaggio critico"[74] ("For a Different Critical Language"), he laid out his idea of criticism, pointing his attention to "seeing" the show according to the "right" parameters. That is, a focus on a technical analysis of the material elements, capable of clearly explaining its "stage writing," the complex interaction of every factor that concurs to shape the audience's experience, without privileging the literary text, the plot, or the psychology of the characters, as was usually the case in much of the criticism published in newspapers and specialized journals. The aim of this new way of writing was to make the audience aware of the more technical aspects of the show, so as to encourage a better understanding and appreciation of the way author, director, actors, lights, sounds, and so on, contributed to its success. The role of the critic would be that of an intermediary, someone who kept one eye on developments in the theatre world (both nationally and internationally), and the other on societal changes as well as the transformations happening in other arts.

Bartolucci was hardly alone in establishing the *Nuova Critica*. Next to him, one must at least mention Corrado Augias, Ettore Capriolo, Edoardo Fadini, and Franco Quadri, who joined him in laying the groundwork and then organized the Convegno di Ivrea in 1967. Bartolucci, Fadini, and Capriolo also founded the journal *Teatro*, a prominent arena for discussing the changes in Italian theatre. Quadri, on the other hand, became the editor-in-chief of *Sipario* in 1962, and used his influence to shed light on the emerging new theatre that could be experienced in the *cantine romane*.

The *Sessantotto* (1968) was a year of radical transformation throughout Europe, and in all fields of artistic research, and the theatre of the *cantine romane* was no exception: many existing theatres closed down, while many new ones opened up, although they were moved by a rather different set of aspirations. Carmelo Bene's theatre, now called Del Divino Amore, ceased all activities, while Bene focused, for the next five years, on cinema. Club Orsoline, Teatro 101, Teatro del Leopardo, and Teatro del Porcospino all closed down. Calenda and his troupe were invited to join Piccolo Teatro in Milan, and seized this opportunity to free themselves from the constant financial preoccupations that had marked their experience until then. Ricci, in 1967, had closed down his Club Orsoline but had joined with Molè for his two latest shows, *Illuminazione* and *Edgar Allan Poe* (1967). In 1968, he opened a new space, which he called Abaco. Finally, Remondi, besieged by creditors, was forced to sell his Teatro del Leopardo in 1968. The only venue capable of weathering the storm was Molè's Alla Ringhiera, although it was mainly used for the promotion of visual artists.

The theatre Beat 72 deserves one last mention. Although it was not, technically, a *cantina* (because of its physical location, at least partially above ground, and because of its internal organization), it played a crucial role in the cultural scene of the late 1960s and early 1970s. It was founded in 1966 by Ulisse Benedetti, who was later joined by Simone Carella, and it was different from the other *cantine* in that it was open to the work and experiments of many different groups. Its stage welcomed shows by Carmelo Bene, as well as Memè Perlini, Giuliano Vasilicò, Pippo Di Marca, Claudio Remondi, and Riccardo Caporosso, just to mention a few. It wasn't the expression of a single creative group but rather a space "curated" by Benedetti and Fulvio Servadei and frequented by some of the most influential intellectuals of the time. However, following the very interesting story of Beat 72 would lead us well into the 1970s, and therefore it must be left for another occasion.

2.6 The Evolution of Quartucci's and Scabia's Theatre

We have had several opportunities to remark upon how important 1965 was in the careers of some of the protagonists of Nuovo Teatro; this is particularly true in the case of Quartucci and Scabia, whose research took an even more radical turn.

Quartucci had experimented first with a very abstract, almost geometrical style of performance when directing Samuel Beckett's plays. Then, especially with *Zip* and in his collaboration with Scabia, he had attempted a more systematic dismantling of the separation between the stage and the stalls. He was trying to reach out to an audience that had been excluded from traditional theatre, because of its location, its level of education, or a number of other socio-cultural factors. These spectators did not have many preconceived expectations regarding the performance, considering their previous exposure to other traditional shows, and therefore posed very particular challenges while, at the very same time, offering unique opportunities. This was going to be Quartucci's chosen audience.

After that seminal show with Scabia, he and his Compagnia di Ripresa returned to working with the Teatro Stabile di Genova for the 1965–6 season. There they performed their *Zip* again, attracting the attention of young audiences, especially the Centro Universitario Teatrale (CUT) students. The shows would often be followed by a debate between the actors and students regarding the techniques and working methods employed on stage.

Meanwhile, the collaboration with the Stabile was going increasingly badly, finally reaching a breaking point: Quartucci felt isolated from the main, "official" part of the *Teatro*.[75] After breaking off on his own once again, in 1966, he introduced his latest show, *Libere stanze* ("Free Rooms"), written by Roberto Lerici, who was a key author in the second half of the 1960s. Closely associated with Carmelo Bene, who performed on stage in many of his scripts, Lerici was also the founder of the influential journal *Marcatrè* and one of the organizers of the Convegno di Ivrea. The performances received mixed reviews from critics, as was to be expected. It was another confirmation that the sharp divide between the Nuova Critica, favourable to the experiments of the Nuovo Teatro, and the older generation of critics, hostile to the younger artists, was still in place. This time, however, Quartucci publicly expressed his impatience toward those critics who defined his work as avant-garde. He resented them for applying a label to him that would have pushed away precisely the kind of audience he was so keenly trying to attract. He feared that being perceived as "avant-garde" would have made him and his experiments look elitist, out of touch, and therefore not suited for the common man.

Perhaps also because of such concerns, he assembled a very different show that same year, *Il giornale a pista centrale* ("The Centre Ring Newspaper"), which included actors, puppets, marionettes, and projected images. It was based on a collage of texts by Garcia Lorca, Brecht, Calvino, and Rabelais. Quartucci used this disparate collection of source materials and techniques to speak about current events, a topic that was sure to engage the interest of his audience. The performance revolved around a staging device made of wooden panels and screens that could be moved and rearranged and on which images were projected; there were also a number of boxes used by the actors as a stage in the main part of the show.

The following piece, which he created in collaboration with Roberto Lerici, was entitled *Majakovskij & C. alla Rivoluzione d'Ottobre* (Mayakovsky & Co. at the October Revolution); it debuted in 1967, toured all over Italy, and was very well received by audiences everywhere. The tradition of cubo-futurism, so important for the aesthetic of the Russian revolution, was popularized by Quartucci and his actors, who used the opportunity to further refine their practice of including the spectators in their performances.

Finally, in July 1971, the director went even a step further in his experiments when he bought an old Lancia Esatau, a large truck that he painted white and started calling *Camion*. For the next four years, Quartucci would tour the outskirts of Italian cities, as well as the countryside and all those areas that were isolated and considered marginal by contemporary Italian culture. There, his *Camion* would make a stop with the intention of building a show that included the audience as an active participant. He developed a modus operandi according to which various materials (stories, testimonies, people, travels, characters) were "loaded" on *Camion* and then "unloaded," that is, distributed and diffused throughout the journey of this theatrical vehicle.

This experiment took to an extreme some of the trends we observed in Quartucci from the very beginning: he went beyond the theatre as an institutional place located in the central areas and managed to bring it to all those who were willing to engage with it, in a truly democratic, acentric atmosphere of collaboration and co-ownership. The performance was no longer a spectacle that divided the people involved into performers and spectators with a clear demarcation between them, but rather an event in which everyone was, potentially, an equal participant and there was no proscenium.

After the experience of *Zip*, Scabia participated in the proceedings of the Convegno di Ivrea and was one of the artists who signed the resulting document (more on this later). In 1968, he introduced a new show, entitled *Interventi per la visita alla prova dell'isola purpurea* ("Interventions for the Visit to the Rehearsal of the Purple Island"). The original script, by Mikhail Bulgakov, dealt with the theme of censorship. Scabia, who at the time was translating it into Italian, decided to adapt it for the stage by making a few additions of his own: between Bulgakov's words he interpolated a number of statements, lines, and sentences taken from public speeches and press releases by Strehler and Grassi, the two directors of the Piccolo Teatro, the very institution that was hosting the show. Needless to say, the two directors did not appreciate being mocked by Scabia, and terminated their relation with the young *teatrante*, even going so far, it would seem, as to physically remove him from the premises.[76]

The following year, Scabia met the Comunità Teatrale dell'Emilia Romagna, a group of young actors with whom he soon began collaborating, continuing his experiments of acentric writing and his collaborative approach to theatre. Beginning in 1969, he inaugurated what he called a "teatro a partecipazione" (theatre of participation), whose first concrete initiative was the "azioni di decentramento" (decentralizing actions), performed in Turin, in collaboration with its Teatro Stabile, in November 1969 and April 1970. The idea was to reach out to the suburbs of the city, to its inhabitants, and involve them in an experiment of collective theatre, with spaces for political debate as well as laboratories and workshops. Scabia engaged different institutions as financers, and tried to include the local populations, remaining always independent and often in conflict with the very offices that commissioned the works he was performing. Through these highly original forms of collaboration/conflict that mediated between different marginal places and central public institutions, Scabia produced a great number of shows well into the 1970s, and therefore beyond the limits of this brief historical reconstruction. He joined the faculty at the University of Bologna, where he continued to engage his students in the production of plays and "actions" that centred on the students' experience of the dramaturgical process, focusing on local institutions, schools, festivals, and gathering places (something he termed his "Wondering Theatre"). In all of these different experiences he managed to reconcile improvisation and rigorous planning, capturing, with an artistic sensibility, the spontaneous contributions coming from his team of collaborators, always adapting to the different situations and circumstances, exploiting phonetic experiments, the visual writings of the neo-avant-gardes, but also the multilinguism of Italy's dialects and peasant roots.[77]

2.7 Brecht and "Brechtismo"

Brecht's influence on the Italian theatre (something that has often been mentioned herein) can be traced back to France, and, more specifically, to the debut, on 29 June 1954, at the Théâtre Sarah-Bernhardt, of his *Mutter Courage*, performed by the Berliner Ensemble. This show captured the imagination of many French intellectuals, who saw it as the solution to the problem of how to reconcile political engagement with an experimental style, while at the same time ensuring the direct involvement and participation of the audience:[78]

> We must … highlight how utterly surprised we were when faced with *Mutter Courage*, by the Berliner Ensemble: like any great work, Brecht's is a radical criticism of the evils that preceded it: in any case, we are deeply *educated* by *Mutter Courage*: this performance has spared us years of research. This education comes with a special joy: we have seen how this profound criticism built that very theatre, free from alienation, which we had ideally postulated and which, suddenly, appeared in front of us, in its adult and already perfected form.[79]

Mother Courage showed that it was possible to practice a politically "militant" theatre, capable of articulating a clear and radical criticism of bourgeois society, without using its ideological categories and, what was also crucial, without the preachy, sermonizing posture that often alienated audiences. The vital criticism was delivered directly, through an organic and effective combination of script, acting, and staging techniques.

From then on, Roland Barthes and Bernard Dort, who were frequent contributors to the journal *Théâtre Populaire*,[80] would frame what was going to be called the debate around *brechtisme*, pointing the public's attention to the anti-Aristotelian characteristics of Brecht's dramaturgy, as well as its opposition to the literary tradition that had influenced the French stage up to that point.[81] In the eyes of the two French critics, Brecht became the quintessential example of what could be achieved by an engaged intellectual capable of wielding his chosen means of expression as a weapon in the struggle against bourgeois aesthetics, conveying revolutionary political ideas.

Between 1962 and 1963, Brecht's works were finally translated into Italian,[82] and the debate around his theatre began around 1963; in 1964, a series of articles written by Squarzina and Bartolucci[83] aimed at placing his contribution in the Italian context, connecting it with some precedents in our own history (once again, the historical avant-gardes) as well as some of the latest developments, both domestically and abroad (the Nuovo Teatro on the one hand, and Peter Brook and the Living Theatre on the other).

Bartolucci lamented that, in Italy, there hadn't been a semiotic approach to Brecht's work, the kind promoted, instead, by Roland Barthes in France; this omission led to many bad imitations of his plays and techniques, rather than to the radical renovation of the institution that had happened in France and was hoped for on this side of the Alps. In part, observed Bartolucci, this was also the responsibility of the dramaturg's heirs, who prevented his main works from being performed in Italy, favouring instead the diffusion of minor ones.[84] In fact, The Berliner Ensemble would visit Italy (Venice) only in 1966, introducing *L'Opera da tre soldi* (*The Threepenny Opera*), *La resistibile ascesa di Arturo Ui* (*The Resistible Rise of Arturo Ui*), and *Coriolano* (*Coriolanus*).[85]

In the meantime, from the point of view of performances, Brecht's presence in Italy had been strictly tied to the activity of Giorgio Strehler and the Piccolo Teatro in Milan, which he directed. This activity culminated, in the 1962–3 season, with the debut of the *Life of Galileo*, a record-breaking show of immense popularity, hailed by critics as both the confirmation of Strehler's mastery of Brecht's message and theatrical techniques and the beginning of a "sazietà brechtiana"[86] (Brechtian satiety), as Bartolucci put it, that would mark a switch away from Brecht and toward Artaud.[87]

2.8 Artaud and the Living Theatre

The fortunes of Artaud and his ideas on theatre in the Italian theoretical debate (as well as the imaginations of theatregoers) are intrinsically linked to those of the Living Theatre. On 13 and 14 June 1961, the Teatro Club in Rome (founded by Gerardo Guerrieri and Anne d'Arbeloff) invited the American troupe to perform two shows: *The Connection*, by Jack Gelber, and *Many Loves*, by William Carlos Williams. This first visit attracted the enthusiastic attention of specialists but was not really noticed by larger audiences. The journals *Sipario* and *Il Dramma* published glowing reviews, and even an interview with Judith Malina, but the rest of the country hardly took notice.[88]

The professionals of the Italian stage certainly had an appetite for the kind of reform and research that the group was experimenting with. Therefore, it is not surprising that, in 1964, *Sipario* began publishing a series of articles on different foreign theatre troupes that were inspired, either directly or indirectly, by Artaud's theories; in some cases, they didn't have any direct contact with the ideas of the French writer, but their performing practices displayed enough similarities with them, and were therefore subsumed under that same area of experience. Some of the names more frequently mentioned were Peter Brook, Charles Marowitz, and, naturally, the Living Theatre.[89]

In 1965, the American company visited Italy for a second time, staying for a longer tour that included performances of *Mysteries and Small Pieces*, *The Brig*, and *Frankenstein*. This time they received more attention from the national audience, especially for their participation in the Biennale in Venice, where they performed on 26 and 27 September. The critics were split in their assessment of these shows: some, like Enrico Bassano, invoked the intervention of a psychiatrist;[90] other more open-minded witnesses, such as Bartolucci (but also Quadri, Fadini, and Capriolo), praised the Living Theatre for the quality, freshness, and originality of their research.[91]

In 1965, *Sipario* published a number of excerpts from Artaud's works, translating them for the first time into Italian. Particularly significant is issue 230, released in June, which included "Primo manifesto della crudeltà" ("The First Manifesto of Cruelty"), "Il teatro e la peste" ("The Theatre and the Plague"), a short biography of Artaud, and one of his plays, dating back to 1935, *I Cenci* (*The Cenci*).[92] Two months later, *Sipario* dedicated another double issue to Artaud, which included an anthology of some of the plays that had an important role in defining the French dramatist's ideas on cruelty.[93]

In 1966, as part of the XIV Festival Universitario di Parma, the first Italian conference on Artaud was convened; among the speakers and participants were Luigi Gozzi, Charles Marowitz, Piero Panza, and Jacques Derrida.[94] In his talk, later published as the preface to the Italian edition of Artaud's *Il teatro e il suo doppio*,[95] Derrida laid out some of the defining characteristics of the theatre of cruelty:

> È senza dubbio estraneo al teatro della crudeltà: 1. Qualsiasi teatro non sacrale. 2. Qualsiasi teatro astratto che escluda qualche cosa nella totalità dell'arte, dunque della vita e delle sue risorse di significazione: danza, musica, volume, profondità, plastica, immagine visiva, sonora, fonica, ecc. 3. Qualsiasi teatro che dia un primato alla parola, o piuttosto al verbo. 4. Qualsiasi teatro della distanziazione (della) non partecipazione degli spettatori all'atto creatore. 5. Qualsiasi teatro non politico. La festa deve essere un atto politico e non la trasmissione più o meno eloquente,

> pedagogica, educata di un concetto o di una visione politico-morale del mondo. 6. Qualsiasi teatro ideologico, qualsiasi teatro di cultura, qualsiasi teatro di comunicazione, di interpretazione, che cerchi di trasmettere un contenuto, di diffondere un messaggio (quale che ne sia la natura: politica, religiosa, psicologica, metafisica, ecc.), che dia da leggere a un uditorio il senso di un discorso, che non si esaurisca completamente con l'atto e col tempo presente della scena, che non si confonda con essa, che possa essere ripetuto senza di essa.[96]
>
> [The theatre of cruelty certainly isn't: 1. Any theatre that is not sacral. 2. Any abstract theatre that excludes any part of the totality of art, and thus of life and its resources for signification: dance, music, volume, depth, plastic, as well as visual, sound, phonic images. 3. Any theatre that puts words, or better, verbs first. 4. Any theatre of distancing, which lacks the spectators' participation in the creative act. 5. Any theatre that is not political. The feast must be a political act and not a more or less eloquent, pedagogical, polite transmission of a concept or a political and moral vision of the world. 6. Any ideological theatre, any cultural theatre, any theatre of communication, of interpretation, that tries to convey content, to spread a message (whatever its nature may be: political, religious, psychological, metaphysical, etc.), any theatre that makes the audience read the meaning of a speech, that is not entirely contained in the act and in the present tense of the stage, that doesn't become one with it, that can be repeated without it.]

It is important to note how this is a negative definition. It is very clear what this new theatre, which Derrida wants to trace back to Artaud, doesn't want to do. It is not exactly easy to extrapolate from this description what, in the positive, a theatre of cruelty would prescribe. Certainly, the essays, plays, and documents made available by *Sipario* helped to clarify the nature of Artaud's intentions. However, in the absence of a more transparent definition, the theatre of cruelty was closely identified with the experiments of the Living Theatre, at least in Italy. The company had contributed to exposing a sense of uneasiness and dissatisfaction with the traditional theatre that had begun to manifest itself (as we have been noting) since at least 1959. In particular, the Italian *teatranti* responded to their work on the manipulation of language, as well as the voice and the body of actors and spectators. We return once more to the three basic elements we have been discussing all along: the relationship between stage and stalls, that between director and script, and, finally, the role of the actor.[97] In particular, the prominence given by the Living Theatre to the body of the actors over the words pronounced on stage resonated profoundly with the Italian practitioners.

2.9 The Convegno di Ivrea

The Convegno per un Nuovo Teatro took place between the ninth and twelfth of June 1967 in Ivrea, and it was a crucial event in the history of the renovation of the Italian stage and, in a sense, the official consecration of a number of young authors, directors, and actors. The Convegno also marked the end of the illusion that the very different components of the Nuovo Teatro could be reconciled into a coherent movement, with a common agenda and a shared plan to implement it.[98]

Before moving forward, let us try to review what did actually happen: in November 1966, in the pages of *Sipario*, Quadri and twenty-four of his colleagues (most of the critics, actors, and directors mentioned in the previous pages) issued a sort of manifesto entitled "Per un convegno sul nuovo teatro" ("For a Conference on New Theatre"), a document that was intended to frame a discussion among the *addetti ai lavori* and prepare the ground for a more in-depth and, it was hoped, productive conversation. We will highlight a few of its main points, quoting it directly. One first element offered for consideration, clearly expressed in the following passage, is the dissatisfaction with the current circumstances and the need for linguistic reform:

> Sono mancati d'altra parte il ricambio e l'aggiornamento delle tecniche di recitazione, l'analisi e l'applicazione di rinnovati materiali di linguaggio, gestici e plastici, mentre lo stesso innegabile affinamento della regia ha finito per risolversi in un estenuato perfezionismo di sterile applicazione, contro ogni possibilità di rinnovamento dei quadri.[99]
>
> [On the one hand, there hasn't been a renewal of acting techniques, or the analysis and use of updated linguistic, gestural, and plastic materials; on the other, the increasingly refined quality of the direction has turned into an exhausted and sterile perfectionism, incapable of incorporating a rejuvenation of the workforce.]

To this declaration of discontent with the state of the art of acting and its practitioners, the signatories of the manifesto add a declaration of intolerance toward the critics, who, in their opinion, had not carried out their duties in a satisfactory manner:

> La critica drammatica istituzionale, dal suo canto, invece di svolgere una funzione di provocazione e di stimolo su questa situazione generale, ha contribuito al mantenimento dello stato di fatto e si è troppo facilmente

> allineata alle posizioni ufficiali, ancorando linguaggio e metodi a modalità ormai superate con una rinuncia di fatto al suo compito primo di ricerca e di interpretazione.[100]
>
> [The institutional theatre criticism, instead of performing its function, encouraging and stimulating this general situation, helped maintain the status quo, and aligned itself too readily with the positions of the establishment, anchoring its language and methods to an outmoded style, thus renouncing its primary task of research and interpretation.]

Since this very first programmatic stage, the organizers of the conference were well aware of how diverse the group they were about to gather was, and tried, in a way, to set the expectations at a realistic level; it was not a matter of agreeing on everything, they seemed to argue, but a matter of coming together around some key issues, so as to find strength in numbers:

> Per la diversità dei metodi e dell'ispirazione che improntano l'attività in cui siamo impegnati, noi non ci poniamo come gruppo almeno nel senso in cui questa parola ha caratterizzato passate esperienze nella vita letteraria e teatrale. Al di sopra di ogni diversità pensiamo però di poter individuare una sufficiente forza di coesione nel trovarci comunque di fronte a problemi di lavoro fondamentalmente analoghi.[101]
>
> [Given the variety of methods and inspirations that inform our activities, we cannot present ourselves as a group, at least not in the sense that this word has had for previous experiences in the life of our theatre and literature. Beyond every difference, however, we think we can identify a strong enough bond that comes from sharing a number of analogous working problems.]

One of the key differences among the varied group of *teatranti* who had been summoned to Ivrea was their attitude toward the reforms that they were demanding. As De Marinis points out, some shared a "prospettiva rivoluzionaria" (revolutionary perspective), while others were more keen on a "strategia riformista" (reformist strategy): the first wanted to pursue an "absolute and global opposition" to the traditions and institutions of the Italian stage; the latter sought to create an independent space for themselves where they would be free to experiment with new forms and a new language, but without burning all bridges with the establishment.[102] Confirmation of De Marinis's impression can easily be found in the manifesto. On the one hand, the signatories declared that all they wanted was a seat at the table:

> Non c'è nuova strada nel teatro come in ogni altra attività della scienza e dell'arte che non implichi di necessità estesi margini di errore. Noi li rivendichiamo. Non vogliamo dar vita a un teatro clandestino per pochi iniziati, né rimanere esclusi dalle possibilità offerte dalle organizzazioni di pubblico alle quali riteniamo di avere diritto; rifiutiamo però un'attività ufficialmente definita come sperimentale, ma costretta ad allinearsi alle posizioni dominanti.[103]
>
> [All new roads, in the theatre as well as any other art or science, must allow, as a necessity, for a wide margin of error. We claim that margin for ourselves. We do not want to inaugurate a clandestine theatre, meant for a few initiates, nor do we want to be excluded from the possibilities offered by the organizations of the audience to which we believe we are entitled; however, we reject an activity that has been officially sanctioned as experimental, but is then forced to conform with the dominant positions.]

Conversely, however, one can also find startlingly radical statements in the manifesto, such as the following: "Theatre must be allowed to reach the absolute and complete dissent."[104]

With so many and such deep differences among the participants, it is not surprising that the proceedings of the conference turned out to be as tumultuous as they did. In the end, the alliance that would be forged was an entirely pragmatic compromise, meant to carve out some visibility and some space to manoeuvre within the "official" national theatre, something that De Marinis called "a 'cartel' of theatre people whose only common characteristic is a shared enemy."[105]

That is why Quadri and the other *teatranti* didn't call attention to their differences in matters of aesthetics and politics in the preparatory manifesto. The document, as we showed, was not concerned with the definition of the new theatre as a coherent entity, organized around a common platform. Rather, the whole issue was quickly bypassed in order to focus on the common problem of access, and the shared enemies (critics and gatekeepers of the official theatre).

In accordance with their pragmatic approach, Quadri and the other conveners prepared another document entitled "Elementi di discussione del Convegno per un Nuovo Teatro" ("Discussion Points for the Conference on the New Theatre").[106] Their intention was to establish a direction and shape the debate around some key issues. As it turned out, they were unsuccessful in doing so, but the document they prepared proves that they had a very clear understanding of the situation and the Italian theatrical landscape, for they identified all the various points we have been discussing when describing the pioneers of the Nuovo Teatro. The themes offered for consideration were: 1) "theatre-laboratory"; 2) "new scenic materials"; and 3) "how to reach a new audience through new organizational strategies." Here are three quotations from that document that will briefly illustrate these discussion points. By "theatre-laboratory" Bartolucci, Quadri, Fadini, and Capriolo mean a theatre that

> deve porsi programmaticamente come struttura aperta, sia sul piano del linguaggio sia su quello dei mezzi e degli strumenti scenici … L'elaborazione delle tematiche popolari presuppone un lavoro di gruppo in quanto richiede una partecipazione del pubblico in senso rivoluzionario. Il lavoro di gruppo è già una prefigurazione di questo nuovo rapporto tra pubblico e teatro … La forza contestativa di un teatro di laboratorio presuppone, appunto, la fusione tra una tematica popolare rivoluzionaria e l'uso di mezzi scenici nuovi che la debbono esprimere e, inoltre, il reciproco condizionamento dell'una nei riguardi degli altri.[107]

> [must be approached programmatically as an open structure, both on the level of language and on that of the means and tools of the stage … The implementation of populist themes presupposes a group effort in that it requires the participation of the audience in a revolutionary sense. The group effort is already a first manifestation of that new relationship between the audience and the theatre … The strength of the dissent that can be expressed through a laboratory theatre demands that a populist revolutionary theme be joined to the use of new scenic means capable of expressing it and, moreover, the reciprocal influence of one over the other.]

As for the renewal of the scenic materials, they wrote,

> La collettivizzazione del fatto teatrale e la radicalizzazione dei contenuti nei confronti della realtà contemporanea comportano un tipo di scrittura scenica unitaria nella quale i vari elementi che contribuiscono alla sua attuazione (scrittura drammaturgica, regia, interpretazione, scenografia, musica, luci, spazio scenico e architettura) sono da ricomporre in un insieme di base, i cui elementi temporalmente concomitanti e senza alcuna preminenza l'uno nell'altro, sono: a) gesto; b) oggetto; c) scrittura drammaturgica; d) suono (fonetica e sonorizzazione); e) spazio scenico (come luogo teatrale e come rapporto platea-palcoscenico).[108]

[The collectivization of the theatrical event and the radicalization of its contents in relation to the contemporary context imply a kind of unifying *scrittura scenica* [stage writing] in which all the different elements that are crucial for its implementation (*scrittura drammaturgica* [theatrical writing], direction, acting, scenography, music, lights, scenic space and architecture) are put together in such a way that they may form a coherent whole, with none of them taking a preponderant role over the others; these elements are: a) gestures; b) objects; c) *scrittura drammaturgica*; d) sound (phonetics and sound effects); and e) scenic space (understood as a theatrical place and as the relationship between the stage and the stalls).]

Once again, we see the distinction between a "scrittura drammaturgica" – which here we take to mean the writing of the script for a play – and a "scrittura scenica" – which, instead, indicates the weaving together of the different linguistic codes of the theatre to achieve a unified, final aesthetic result. The critics then proceed to analyse each of these elements in detail. The uniform importance given to every different component of the performance is, by now, a recurring and very familiar theme. And so is the stress on gestures as well as the non-verbal aspects of human communication.

Finally, here are their thoughts on how to reach a wider audience:

Questi fatti impongono, quindi, da un lato, una radicale riforma di struttura nei teatri a gestione pubblica, con conseguente arretramento, in ordine di importanza, del concetto di "teatro come servizio pubblico" in favore di un più vasto e profondo interesse per un'effettiva penetrazione del teatro nel corpo sociale. Dall'altro, la necessità di collegarsi con quei nuovi canali di diffusione e distribuzione che siano più intimamente legati alle varie forme di vita associativa così come essa si sviluppa all'interno degli ambienti culturali più diversi (dalla fabbrica alla scuola).[109]

[These considerations mandate, on the one hand, a radical reform of publicly run theatres, through the progressive abandonment of the idea of "theatre as a public service," and its replacement with a deeper and more general concern with the actual penetration of the theatre within the social context. Alternatively, it is imperative that we access those new distribution channels that are more intimately connected with the various places of social interaction that are specific to the different cultural environments (from factories to schools).]

A detailed account of the proceedings of each individual day of the Convegno can be read in Visone.[110] What must be emphasized is the fact that, from the very beginning, the participants resisted every effort made by the organizers to lead a traditional discussion. In spite of all the preparatory work done, very few points of the original program were actually addressed. The format of "conferenza-spettacolo" (conference-performance) which, at least in theory, should have served as a way of sharing with one's fellow *teatranti* the preliminary results of one's research, soon devolved into a series of "conferenze-discussione" (conference-discussions), during which people mixed, in a chaotic and often antagonistic and unproductive fashion, different topics that were supposed to be reserved for separate days and different panels. Many participants to the Convegno objected to the very basic organizing principles that the conveners had identified in order to give shape and direction to the debate, and demanded a free space where they could talk in a less structured way.[111]

In spite of all the disagreements, the chaotic nature of the conference, and the anarchic spirit that animated many of its protagonists, there were at least three things that all the participants had in common. We will list them here, providing short quotations from contemporary sources when appropriate: 1) The political mission (the "engagement") of the theatre that they all wanted to create. Part of the "utopia" envisioned by these artists involved a closer relationship with the audience and a better understanding of its needs. In order to achieve that, a direct intervention within the body of society was needed, an intervention based on "popular themes in which the relationship with reality is rendered in a problematic way, free from a moralistic attitude," as Guido Boursier put it; the ultimate goal would be to lead the audience to gain "an awareness of the crucial moments of contemporary history that may cause them to question the political and social system."[112]

2) Everyone agreed that the Nuovo Teatro could assert itself, or even just survive, only outside the official circuit of *teatri stabili* – hence the "cartel" mentioned by De Marinis. 3) The relationship that each group and each author/director had with the historical avant-gardes determined the way in which they pursued the common objectives of aesthetic reform and political "engagement": those who learned their lessons, who appreciated the technical and linguistic solutions they devised, experimented in a more radical fashion with language, and, politically, were not aligned according to party lines; on the other hand, those who despised the historical avant-gardes thought of the technical and linguistic issues as secondary, and focused on a more explicit, propagandistic way of using their art for political purposes.

At the beginning of this chapter, we discussed the episode involving Carmelo Bene, Sandro Bajini, and Marinetti's legacy. Another example of this deep divide among the *teatranti* of the Nuovo Teatro can be found in Eugenio Barba's reception at the Convegno. On 10 June, he was scheduled to give a demonstration about the way in which his group worked in their studio, as well as to perform a few scenes from their *Ornitofilene* (1965). We should point out how, at this point in time, the world of Italian theatre was just beginning to discover the emphasis on the body of the actor and its physical resources. The prevailing opinion was that, while good physical shape was desirable, it wasn't actually crucial for the quality of the spectacle. Barba, on the other hand, based his whole stage approach on the work actors did on their own bodies, shaping them to gain greater control of their untapped potential.

Faced with the unusual exercises and routines Barba demanded of his actors, many of the Italian *teatranti* reacted with irony and mockery, missing the whole point of the presentation. Mario Ricci and Leo de Berardinis, for instance, openly made fun of him and his troupe. Here is Ricci's recollection of the episode:

> All'Unione Culturale di Torino, da Fadini, c'era Barba che doveva fare una dimostrazione delle sue tecniche: mi ricordo che c'erano con lui degli attori di questo centro in Danimarca. Il povero Barba a forza di stare all'estero parlava l'italiano abbastanza male, e cominciò a presentare: "Faremo prova di nostro esercizio, ragazzi debbono saltare, uno girare con corda, altri ragazzi devono saltare quando la corda arriva presso di loro" ... "Certo quando ragazzo sbaglia salto prende frustata sulla gamba!" E purtroppo al primo giro sbagliarono il salto e presero una frustata![113]

> [At the Unione Culturale, in Turin, at Fadini's, there was Barba, who was scheduled to give a demonstration of his techniques: I remember that he had brought along a few actors from his centre in Denmark. Poor Barba had spent so much time abroad that his Italian was quite rusty, and he started to explain: "We will show example of our exercise, guys have to jump, one swings rope, others must jump when rope reaches them" ... "Naturally, when guy makes mistake he gets whipped on leg!" And unfortunately, at the first try, they made a mistake and got whipped!]

And here is how Leo de Berardinis remembers it:

> A Ivrea c'era anche Barba, e siamo morti dalle risate quando faceva vedere l'addestramento degli attori con la frusta in mano. Ricordo che c'eravamo io, Carmelo, Mario, e c'era De Bosio che faceva finta di prendere appunti![114]

> [In Ivrea there was also Barba, and we almost died from laughter when we saw the way he had trained his actors, with a whip in his hand. I remember

Carmelo, Mario, and I were there, and also De Bosio, who was pretending he was taking notes the whole time!]

The antics of these unruly spectators were not lost on Barba, who, instead, proved to be the more mature artist and to have a better sense of the big picture. In fact, twenty years later, in a letter he sent to Quadri on the occasion of a new conference organized to celebrate that first one in Ivrea, in 1967, Barba wonders if "the solidarity, the reciprocal respect, the affection" could have "been reconciled with the intransigence," for this is, at its core, "the problem of the relationship among people who follow different paths, some of which will never cross, but who also cannot remain alone, in a hostile environment, in spite of the acceptance or success that, every now and then, the various forms of theatre may enjoy."[115]

On 11 June, in Ivrea, the scheduled theme for discussion was the language of theatre; unfortunately, it turned into another opportunity to verify how little each of the participants had in common. Their research agendas, it turned out, were completely different, and the directions of their inquiries could not be reconciled. That day, one of the planned shows was Leo de Berardinis's and Perla Peragallo's *La faticosa messa in scena dell'Amleto di Shakespeare* ("The Difficult Staging of Shakespeare's Hamlet"). In a rare display of unity, everybody showed genuine appreciation for the performance. They mostly liked the mixture of moving images projected on the screens and live action on stage.

In his reinterpretation of Shakespeare's tragedy, de Berardinis focused on the archetypical relationship that ties Hamlet, his mother, and his uncle together by introducing a number of enigmatic mummies that were projected on the screens, and thus updating with a contemporary, modern twist the traditional, meta-theatric dimension of Shakespeare's drama.

Next up was Bajini, with his *Gorizia, tu sia maledetta*, the show whose rough treatment of Marinetti provoked Carmelo Bene's strong reaction.[116] In addition to their differences regarding crucial aesthetic issues, it seems that the two genuinely disliked each other. From a transcript of the proceedings, we learn that Bajini would refer to Bene as the "fellow with a flowery jacket," and he advocated for the use of theatre as a means of "political propaganda":

È ancora tutto da verificare che il Teatro così concepito possa ottenere dei risultati concreti e possa realizzare un'efficace propaganda politica. Tuttavia deve tentare: il teatro deve essere comizio, senza avere paura di denunciarsi come tale. … Il teatro non deve perseguire l'arte, perché l'arte o non esiste o viene esercitata da un numero eccessivo di artisti. Il Teatro sarà tanto più valido quanto più sarà politico e fazioso. E quanto

> più bassa sarà la dose di fantasie e giochi che conterrà … In che modo sarà realizzata la propaganda scenica? Ma è evidente. Con una serie di parole d'ordine, di slogan e specie nella maniera più antiartistica possibile. L'attore, naturalmente, dovrà recitare nella maniera più convenzionale e accademica con la voce perfettamente impostata degli annunciatori della Radio. Ecco, io dico che questo, e soltanto questo deve essere il Teatro.[117]
>
> [The jury is still out on whether the Theatre can achieve any practical results and enact effective political propaganda. And yet, it must try: the theatre must turn into a political rally, without any fear of being identified as such … The theatre must not pursue art, for art either doesn't exist or is practised by too many artists. The Theatre is all the more meaningful the more it is political and biased. The fewer the fantasies and the games, the better … What shape will this scenic propaganda take? It is very clear. It will adopt a series of catch-phrases, slogans, especially the most anti-artistic ones. Naturally, actors will perform in the most conventional and academic ways, with the same poised voice as radio broadcasters. There, I say that this, and only this, is what the Theatre must be.]

Bajini's derisive tone highlights the distance between his positions and Bene's: he saw theatre as an aesthetically neutral battlefield on which he was going to wage his war for a radical reform (perhaps even a revolution) within Italian society; Bene had no intention of actively intervening in any political struggle. Rather, he was interested in an anthropological revolution that invested the human experience as a whole and at whose centre was the theatre as a means of investigation and public, collective research. While Bajini was intent on inciting a political revolution, Bene wanted to practice a linguistic one. Their positions can be generalized to describe the contemporary Italian landscape: some sought a linguistic revolution, a rethinking of the way in which theatre was done; others wanted to exploit theatre for their political aims and were therefore not interested in reforming its linguistic institutions (in fact, they opposed any serious attempt aimed in that direction). Another way of articulating this fundamental difference is by concentrating on "scrittura scenica" (stage writing): those in favour of it attempted a reform of the language of theatre; in this category we find Bene, Quartucci, Ricci, and de Berardinis. Bajini and those who "remained focused on the central role of political content within theatre," instead, had no interest in practising the new stage writing.[118]

What had begun as a promising opportunity to bring together all the diverse agents of change within the Italian theatre, shaping a common platform for the renewal of the contemporary theatre, led to a very disappointing final result: the formation of that "cartel" (to use De Marinis's expression) among the different groups, with the intention of forging a theatrical circuit alternative to that of the *teatri stabili*. And even this small and diminutive achievement would not last very long: the underlying differences that separated each of the various players within the Nuovo Teatro would soon make even this form of collaboration impossible. Here is Bartolucci's overview of the results at the end of the convegno:

> Essendo mancata la discussione sul linguaggio critico, essendo mancata la discussione sulla scrittura scenica, essendo mancate le testimonianze critiche, improvvisamente il discorso si è rovesciato sull'attività pratica, che a noi interessava alla fine – doveva essere infatti l'argomento di discussione di questa mattina –, ed è accaduto che i vari gruppi si siano scontrati sulle tendenze, si siano scontrati sul modo di fare, sul procedimento, e, naturalmente, il fatto di vedersi in viso per la prima volta, il fatto di operare in maniera diversa, ha acceso gli animi. ... I problemi restano: restano per il gruppo di Bajini, per quello di Carmelo Bene, per il gruppo di Quartucci, per Bussotti. Si è persa un'occasione di confronto e di lavoro che speriamo di non dover abbandonare ... questo tipo di collaborazione ...[119]
>
> [Since there has been no discussion on the critical language, ... on stage writing, ... and since there has been no critical assessment, suddenly the discussion turned to the practical activities, which we wanted to engage last – in fact, it was supposed to be the topic for this morning – and it turned out that the various groups clashed around the trends, the ways of acting, the procedures, and, naturally, the fact that they were meeting each other for the first time, coupled with the differences in their methodologies, have sparked the controversy ... The problems stay: they are there for Bajini's group, for Carmelo Bene's, and for Quartucci's and Bussotti's. We missed an opportunity for dialogue and working together, and we hope we won't have to give up ... this kind of collaboration ...]

From this moment on, the different paths of experimentation within the Nuovo Teatro (as well as those few attempts made to unite the aesthetic research in poetry and theatre) began to diverge hopelessly, becoming more and more diversified, and the perspective of reconciling them, or even rendering them compatible, seemed increasingly improbable. Some kept exploring the new territories that their personal research had opened up to them within either the theatre or poetry. Others, like Scabia, found a very personal way of merging their writing and performing, involving audiences and readers in the process. There were also those who, by their own admission, failed in their encounter with the stage but still contributed a great deal to the theoretical discussion and the cultural life of the nation (we will see Pasolini's example shortly).

However, the brief moment of convergence was irrevocably over. Some of the poets of the neo-avant-garde would continue to write for the theatre, but they would do so according to their own ideas and standards – ideas and standards that were radically different from those set for themselves by the *teatranti*. In the next chapter, we will discuss in more detail how these theoretical stances converged, intersected, and finally diverged.

2.10 Pasolini and the "Teatro di Parola"

The survey of the young, experimental Italian theatre that we have outlined above would not be complete without at least a brief mention of Pasolini's manifesto and his short-lived experiments with the theatre. His "Manifesto per un nuovo teatro," published in the 1968 January–March issue of the journal *Nuovi Argomenti* (and, therefore, mere months after the Convegno di Ivrea), generated a bit of controversy and was almost unanimously rejected by the Italian practitioners of the theatre. Before making the few observations we believe are necessary, let us provide a quick overview of the manifesto's contents and its relevance within the discussions of those years.

Pasolini's manifesto begins with a radical (and somewhat vague) challenge to the status quo ("Theatre should be what theatre is not") and then proceeds to advocate for a "Teatro di Parola" (Theatre of the Word) aimed at the "bourgeoisie's advanced groups," whom he considered the only segment of the Italian population that could be realistically reached through theatre. He then criticizes on the one hand what he called the "Teatro della Chiacchiera" (Theatre of Chit-chat) for being too traditional and academic; on the other hand, he also disliked the "Teatro del Gesto o Urlo" (Theatre of Gesture or Scream). Pasolini's "Teatro di Parola" is described as a place for "debate, exchange of ideas, literary and political struggle." Intellectuals would participate in it and, given their "direct relationship" with the working class, the latter would also be involved, even if only indirectly.[120] It is important to highlight at least two different issues:[121]

1) The criticism that Pasolini formulated against contemporary practitioners of the art. He attacked, rather violently, both parties: the avant-garde that was trying to reform the Italian institutions of theatre

(which he gratifies with the nickname "theatre of the gesture and the scream"), as well as the more conservative, established world of *teatri stabili* (which he defined, unflatteringly, as the "theatre of chit-chat"). With Pasolini having thus made enemies on both sides, it is not surprising that his manifesto encountered an almost universal disapproval and was promptly rejected by nearly everyone upon its publication.[122]

One might be tempted to verify whether the theoretical positions expressed by Pasolini in this manifesto were actualized in the plays he published around the same time. However, such an exercise would not be advisable, for at least two reasons: Pasolini thought of his theatre experiments as quite unsuccessful, and soon turned to cinema, with the remarkable results we all know and admire. In this regard, it may be worthwhile to quote a letter he sent to Andrea Zanzotto just a few months before the publication of the manifesto, in which he defines *Orgia*, one of his plays, as

> [un'esperienza] sbagliata per colpa mia, perché ho tentato, appunto, di raggiungere con il teatro quel famoso decentramento che scavalcasse gli obblighi, ovvero le direzioni obbligate della cultura di massa. Ma per questo bisognerebbe decidere di dedicarsi al teatro, come dei pionieri, per tutta la vita, oppure è meglio rinunciare. Io l'ho fatto, ma solo parzialmente, con un'esperienza incompleta, riuscita a metà.[123]

> [a flawed (experience), and it was all my fault, because I tried, through theatre, to attain that famous decentring capable of overcoming the duties (and the obligatory paths) of mass culture. But, in order to achieve that, one would have to dedicate himself to theatre for his entire life, like a pioneer, or else it is better to give up. I did that, but only in part, and with an incomplete experience, only half-finished.]

Thus, it wouldn't seem that he really valued his own experiments. However, more importantly, it is the contradiction at the centre of the manifesto (between the refusal of the status quo and the inability to articulate a viable alternative) that constitutes its most remarkable and stimulating characteristic. As Valentini writes, "Actually, Pasolini's 'theatrical vocation' does not correspond to a clearly definable theoretical position; in fact, it is its contradiction that marks his ideas regarding theatre."[124]

2) The second aspect of the manifesto worth highlighting is its stress on the importance of spoken Italian and, in general, the attention it gives to the oral dimension of language. In 1964, when he published (in the journal *Rinascita*) an article entitled "Nuove questioni linguistiche,"

Pasolini had initiated an interesting and useful discussion on what he called the "italiano tecnologico" (technological Italian) – that is, the new linguistic *koine* created, across the peninsula, by internal migration (from the countryside to the factories of the city) and by the introduction of television. The manifesto for the theatre adds to that discussion the element of oral communication, rejecting the unnatural and fake language of bureaucratic Italian that was slowly replacing the colourful and stratified multilinguism that had served as an endless reservoir of energy and inspiration for writers, directors, and actors alike.[125]

It is on these grounds, on the realization of the importance of the spoken word and the physical presence of the actor's (and the poet's) body on stage, that theatre and poetry met and, for a little while, walked the same path. The *teatranti* learned how seductive the sounds of language can be, and how to exploit the long fugues of signifiers and interpretations that could be triggered by a deliberate use of poetic language; the *poeti* learned the power of breath, and how to share a space with the audience in such a way as to allow "an exchange of breaths," as Pagliarani put it.[126] The next chapter will focus more specifically on this overlapping area, investigating poetry from a theoretical perspective that considers it the interplay between the presence and the absence of the voice.

3 A Few Theoretical Notes on Breath and Text: Antonio Porta and Giuliano Scabia

While in the previous two chapters, we looked separately at experimental theatre and poetry, only sporadically drawing the necessary connections between the two, here we will take a step back, and look at both art forms in the wider context of European culture, focusing on the long-term aesthetic processes that, ostensibly, have been pushing the written page and the stage toward each other.[1]

3.1 An Ambivalent Relation

In spite of the general trend noted above, a profound ambivalence characterized the relationship between the Nuovo Teatro and the literary Neoavanguardia: depending upon the artist and the circumstances, one could describe it either as a mutually beneficial exchange or as a long series of miscommunications and misunderstandings. Valentina Valentini, for instance, argues that Gruppo 63 played a crucial role in starting the process that led to the radical reform of the traditional stylistic institutions of the Italian theatre:

> Il Gruppo 63 segna per noi l'avvio di un processo critico, teorico, estetico e pragmatico che coinvolge lo statuto del teatro e le sue pratiche, in rapporto alle tendenze neoavanguardistiche del cinema, della letteratura, delle arti visive e della musica … Rispetto ai letterati della scena ufficiale, il Gruppo 63 segnava invece una controtendenza, proprio perché … tendeva a concepire il testo letterario come una mera traccia materiale, sia grafica che sonora da manipolare e non da eseguire da parte dell'attore e del regista.[2]

> [Gruppo 63 marks the beginning of a critical, theoretical, aesthetic, and pragmatic process that involves the status of theatre and its practice,

in relation to the avant-gardist tendencies in cinema, literature, visual arts, and music ... Unlike the authors of the official theatre, Gruppo 63 ... understood the literary text as a mere material trace, both visual and auditory, that actors and director could manipulate rather than just follow.]

At the same time, however, it is not uncommon to hear some of the *teatranti* who belonged to the experimental environment surrounding Nuovo Teatro downplay the influence of the Gruppo 63 writers, sometimes even expressing rather harsh judgments of them. Here, for instance, is what actor and director Rino Sudano had to say on this subject:

Ci hanno proposto questa messinscena di tre pezzi, abbiamo vomitato, ma li abbiamo messi in scena lo stesso. Il nostro rapporto con il Gruppo 63 è finito lì. In quel momento ci era molto chiaro che le avanguardie erano proprio nostri nemici. Il termine avanguardia non ci interessava minimamente. Non ci riconoscevamo parte di un clima, di una situazione, di un movimento di qualcosa. Perché non c'era, in realtà non c'era ...[3]

[Gruppo 63 reached out to us, but it was a failure. They proposed us these three pieces: we vomited, but we still staged them. Our relationship with Gruppo 63 ended there. In that moment, it became clear to us that the avant-gardes were really our enemies. The term avant-garde did not interest us in the least. We didn't see ourselves as part of a climate, of a situation, of any kind of movement. Because there was none, in reality, there was none ...]

Sudano is referring to a show presented during the Festival di Palermo, in 1965, that included three one-act plays, by Gaetano Testa (*Furfanti*, "Scoundrels"), Enrico Filippini (*Gioco con la scimmia*, "Game with Monkey"), and Germano Lombardi (*I sigari di Jupiter*, "Jupiter's Cigars"). Clearly, there is a sense of deep mistrust, almost contempt, toward the neo-avant-garde, which is perceived as too abstract, too invested in aesthetic debate, and too distant from the daily practice of the arts.[4]

Conversely, many authors of the neo-avant-garde often misunderstood or misrepresented to what degree they could reform theatre, and the role the stage could play in their own writing (at least when it came to the ways in which their writing could be performed on stage). In an essay already mentioned in chapter 1, Giuliani writes that many of the poems of the Novissimi contained what he called a "dialogic tension" and thus intrinsically displayed a "communication of a theatrical kind." Then he specifies that while these authors took different paths in their research, "they all agree that the text (and therefore a renovation of language) is the first foundation of theatre."[5] Depending on how one decides to interpret the word "text," this can be construed as either a progressive position (if we include in the definition of "text" the work done by director, scenographer, actors, etc., to stage the script created by the author), or it can be seen as a very conservative, even reactionary position (if by "text" we mean just the script created by the author), a position usually held by those writers who didn't have direct, first-hand knowledge of how a dramatic performance comes to life. Hence the reservations and ambivalence toward the Neoavanguardia voiced by some of the actors and playwrights of the Nuovo Teatro: the contemporary experiments in the field of dramaturgy were moving toward an increased focus on the expressive potential of actors and the resources offered by their bodies, and away from the traditional performance of a script.

In a different article, entitled "Teatro nudo," Giuliani confirms his theoretical stance on this issue, but also introduces a new element that further complicates matters. After recalling the path that had led him to the stage, he gives a thorough explanation of his method for composing collages,[6] and finally moves on to define how, in his opinion, "theatrical language is all there is to theatre":

> Dirò, con una *lapalissade*, che per me il linguaggio teatrale è tutto il teatro. Tendo all'eliminazione delle zeppe, le riduco al minimo. Le battute sono tutta l'azione e se c'è, nei miei bravi testi, un'ambizione è precisamente quella che il lettore (o l'ipotetico regista) "sentano" immediatamente (fuori da ogni convenzione di distribuzione delle parti) la presenza dello spazio teatrale. Un teatro senza personaggi? Un teatro senza storia? Non esattamente: i personaggi vanno a cercarsi le battute nella partitura, e così inventano la loro storia. Ciò che deve esserci nel teatro è il dramma, e la Battuta deve contenere in sé tutto: gesto, personaggio (uno dei tanti possibili), configurazione dello spazio teatrale (non necessariamente un fatto).[7]

> [I will utter a *lapalissade* by saying that, for me, theatrical language is all there is to theatre. I usually eliminate all fillers; I reduce them to a minimum. The lines are all the action and if there is, in my little texts, any ambition, it is that the reader (or a hypothetical director) will "feel" immediately (outside any conventions of explicitly assigned parts) the presence of a theatrical space. A theatre without characters? A theatre without plot? Not quite: the characters look for their lines within the score, and that's how they invent their plot. What must be there, in theatre, is drama, and the Lines have to contain everything within themselves: gestures, characters (one of the many possible ones), configurations of theatrical space (not necessarily a fact).]

The ambiguity, the contradiction, we have been defining in the past few pages, is clearly displayed in the passage just quoted. On the one hand, Giuliani feels that the most important aspect of the theatrical performance is spoken language; and by language, he doesn't seem to mean the complex system of signs that combines all the various elements of the dramatic representation (movements, lights, scenography, etc.), but rather just the script, the words that the actors will be pronouncing during the performance. On the other hand, however, he leaves the actors and the director completely free to allocate the words he has predisposed in any manner they see fit, encouraging them to carve out their own dramatic creation from the raw materials he has provided (he calls them "partitura," as if the script were a musical score). This contradictory stance, which is not unique to Giuliani but is actually rather common among experimental writers, is the source of every misunderstanding and conflict between poets and *teatranti* and, at the same time, the reason why the possibility of collaboration between the two art forms seemed so enticing.

3.2 Reasons for Convergence and Divergence

Although we have established the existence of an ambiguous relationship between the literary Neoavanguardia and the Nuovo Teatro, we still haven't explained the reasons behind it, the circumstances that led the two groups of artists to share (sometimes enthusiastically, at other times reluctantly) a common path of experimentation, at least for a brief period. The answer to this relatively simple question will prove to be rather complicated. A good starting point for our analysis can be found in contemporary aesthetic theories, and in particular those proposed by some of the most influential intellectuals of the time: Lucien Goldmann, Roland Barthes, and Jacques Derrida. Let us begin with Goldmann's idea of "homology," as it directly concerns the relationship between different art forms and can therefore help us explain how and why theatre and poetry came to be so closely intertwined.

In 1966, Bompiani published the Italian translation of Goldmann's monograph *Pour une sociologie du roman* (1964), which had already been circulating in the original French edition for a few years. Here is how Barilli summarizes the influence of this book on the Italian intellectual climate:

> Sul piano teorico, ... il concetto di omologia stabiliva quell'unità d'azione tra ideologia e linguaggio che Sanguineti si limitava a postulare, in modi più fideistici che razionalmente articolati; e bastava a dimostrarlo il fatto

> stesso di ricorrere al termine invecchiato, e perfino improprio, dal punto di vista marxiano, di ideologia. Invece Goldmann superava il tradizionale privilegio attribuito alla "struttura," sempre da parte del pensiero marxiano, portato a identificarla col sistema dei mezzi di produzione e del relativo controllo da parte di una classe sociale, rispetto a una "sovrastruttura," consistente nelle attività artistiche e scientifiche di superficie, di cui invano ci si affrettava a dichiarare l'importanza e la "relativa" autonomia. Un rapporto così impostato faceva di quelle seconde, irrimediabilmente, un prodotto derivato, dipendente, posto in subordine. Invece Goldmann aveva il coraggio di sancire "la pari dignità," l'equipollenza dei due momenti, la loro convergenza in un'unità e identità di funzionamento.[8]
>
> [On the theoretical level, the concept of homology established a unity of action between ideology and language, which Sanguineti had already postulated in a more fideistic rather than rational manner; to prove this last point, it is enough to look at the term he used: ideology, an older and even improper term, from a Marxist point of view. Instead, Goldmann had gone beyond the traditional privilege attributed to "structure" by Marxist thought, which identified it with the system of the means of production, and the relative control exercised over it by a given social class. This "structure" was traditionally accompanied by a "superstructure" that consisted of all artistic and scientific activities. Although confined to the surface, the "superstructure" was quickly, and not convincingly, declared as important as the "structure," and "relatively" autonomous. A relationship such as the one described inevitably made "superstructure" a secondary product, a dependent one, of lesser importance. Instead, Goldmann had the courage to declare the "equal dignity," the identical power of the two, and their convergence in one, singular functioning unit.]

Goldmann postulated the existence of a necessary connection between economic and sociological structures on the one hand, and the artistic manifestations of a given historical period on the other. Furthermore, he argued that both "structures" should be considered as operating on an equal footing, both responsible in shaping the reality experienced by common citizens in their daily lives. According to this understanding, it is not surprising, then, that a similar set of demands and expectations was placed on both theatre and poetry, which then converged toward a common ground, predicated on the importance of the voice and the physical presence of the actor and poet. Many intellectuals belonging to the Neoavanguardia and the Nuovo Teatro viewed their contemporary society through this lens, and thus approached their work and assessed its significance in accordance with these theories. To be clear, I am not arguing that there was a direct dependence, a deterministic relation, between Goldmann's concept of homology and the convergence of poetry and theatre. I am simply suggesting that it can help us understand and contextualize some of the choices and theoretical statements made by the poets, dramatists, and writers of the time.

In fact, there were several other forces that pushed the two art forms toward each other (and others that kept them apart). Let us first enumerate them, in as simple and clear a manner as possible. Theatre and poetry converged because of: 1) a generational turnover after the Second World War, especially in connection with the long-term effects of fascism and its cultural isolationism; 2) the necessities dictated by *impegno*, political engagement, which took different forms and different aims but which was a central concern for the artists of the *dopoguerra* and the economic boom; 3) following from the two reasons just mentioned, the need for reforming the linguistic and stylistic institutions inherited from tradition, that is, a the need for a radical reform of the linguistic code ("*lo specifico*," to use the nomenclature of the time) of the two art forms, and especially of language, which played a crucial role in both theatre and, naturally, poetry.

To these three reasons, we can add two more, which worked in both directions, sometimes bringing together poetry and theatre, sometimes pushing them apart: 4) the changing status of the "text," which was no longer understood as a stable, "closed," finished product, given once and for all but which instead became an "open" collaboration between artist and audience (not an object of interpretation and aesthetic contemplation, but rather a process, which demanded the intervention of the reader/spectator); and 5) a widespread desire, among artists, to cross the borders between disciplines, forcing their craft to incorporate tools, spaces, rhetorical devices, and forms that traditionally belonged to a different art.

Finally, there is at least one other factor that drove a wedge between poets and *teatranti*: 6) the traditional power struggle between author, director, and actors over the control of the final product, the performance that results from the collaboration between these figures of the trade. In fact, between 1963 and 1965, the specialized press widely discussed the issue of why Italian writers were not interested in the theatre. In May 1965, the journal *Sipario* issued an *inchiesta* (inquiry), to which a number of authors (including Italo Calvino, Carlo Cassola, Umberto Eco, Eugenio Montale, and Alberto Moravia) replied that the fracture between the two worlds was due to the lack, in Italy, of a bourgeois class and a common spoken language. As Alberto Arbasino stated, "The very idea that one of my scripts could be examined, or subjected to the observations of one of our actors, or one of our directors, is enough to fill one's soul with such a profound horror that one is prompted to take extreme measures: never leave the narrative or essay genres."[9] Valentini paints a very similar picture when she notes that "[t]he hostility must be attributed to the unavoidable attrition between stage and text, which the Italian writers – not only the official ones – are not inclined to resolve, opening the written text to the oral dimensions of the theatrical space, to the actor, to the vision of the director."[10]

In spite of this traditional distrust, the world of poetry and that of theatre have devised different ways of interacting over the past century; De Marinis, in his *Visioni della scena*, offers a few categories that can help us bring some order to this complicated issue:

> Soprattutto nel Novecento, i rapporti tra teatro e poesia si sono sviluppati bene al di là della rappresentazione di testi drammatici in versi, cioè del "teatro di poesia" in senso tradizionale e stretto … Cerchiamo di vedere, allora, molto schematicamente quanti tipi di rapporti e di operazioni possono essere compresi dentro questo campo che il titolo "teatro e poesia" delimita …: a) il teatro basato su testi drammatici in versi; b) le opere per il teatro, non necessariamente in versi, composte da poeti; c) i testi drammatici e/o gli spettacoli incentrati su figure di poeti; d) l'utilizzazione scenica di testi poetici non-drammatici, da recital di poesie a vere e proprie drammaturgie basate su materiali di poesia; e) il teatro basato su di una utilizzazione "poetica" di mezzi scenici: dallo spazio all'attore, allo stesso linguaggio verbale.[11]
>
> [In the Novecento especially, the relationship between theatre and poetry has gone far beyond the staging of plays in verse, that is, beyond the "theatre of poetry" in a traditional and strict sense. Let us try to see, then, very briefly, how many kinds of operations can be subsumed within this field we can entitle "theatre and poetry," …: a) a theatre based on plays in verse; b) works for the theatre that, while not necessarily written in verse, were composed by poets; c) plays and/or shows centred on the figure of a poet; d) the use on stage of non-dramatic poetic texts, from the declamation of poems to a more traditional dramaturgy based on poetic materials; e) a theatre based on a poetic use of stage means: from the space to the actors, and also verbal language itself.]

With so many different ways of understanding the interaction between theatre and poetry, it is no wonder that there were misunderstandings between the artists involved, especially when they belonged to different communities, each of which focused on a different art form. The texts on which we will concentrate in the last part of this volume belong to the categories "b" and "d," although a number of very interesting experiments carried out by Nuovo Teatro, and homologous to the ones attempted in literature, belonged to category "e."

3.3 The Words of "corpo-voce": Oral versus Written

In spite of their clear usefulness, De Marinis's categories might actually obfuscate another trend that runs throughout the Novecento and that brought together theatre and poetry, focusing on the way Western culture approaches the author's voice – the relationship between orality and the written (or recorded) word. Francesca Gasparini dedicates a groundbreaking monograph precisely to this issue: *Poesia come corpo-voce* ("Poetry as Body-Voice"). We shall quote a number of crucial passages from Gasparini's text that can help us advance our understanding. Her key contention is that, when discussing the dynamics between poetry and theatre, we should look beyond the mere recitation of poems before an audience; rather, she argues, a certain strain of modern poetry contains a number of stylistic marks, embedded deep inside the verse, that engage the oral dimension of language, bestowing a performative aspiration (a desire to be "acted") on the poetic word.

The reverse is also true; that is, actors and directors have often used the tools of poetry and written language (metaphor, metonymy, the seduction of phonetics and etymology, etc.) as rhetorical devices to shape their dramatic actions and escape the traditional bonds of the characters' psychology and the conventional use of space, time, and the principle of causality in ordering their plots (we already showed some examples in chapter 2, when discussing Pagliarani's poetry). This is, more specifically, what we meant above when we included "a widespread desire of crossing the borders between disciplines" as one of the elements that contributed to uniting theatre and poetry.

The same principle, however, can work in the opposite direction, pushing the two apart, especially in those cases when the tools and rhetorical strategies (but also texts, situations, and characters) devised in one sphere are mechanically transferred to the other, without the necessary adjustments required by the linguistic code specific to each art form. But let us turn to Gasparini, for a very productive way of posing the issue of how oral and written sensibilities can interact:

> Per comprendere a pieno lo spessore di questa ipotesi occorre porre l'attenzione su uno snodo focale: la sostituzione dell'antitesi tra oralità e scrittura con la dialettica tra vocalità e gestualità, cioè tra una coppia di

> termini che non si oppongono più ma si compenetrano e procedono per sovrapposizioni, e intersezioni, lungo una linea di demarcazione fluida. E è proprio così, conquistando questa prospettiva, che poesia e teatro si fanno più vicini, quasi si confondono, e la loro relazione si fa necessitata, vicendevolmente illuminante.[12]
>
> [To fully understand the relevance of this hypothesis one must focus the attention on a crucial switch: the substitution of the antithesis writing versus orality, with a dialectic relation between vocality and gesturality, that is, between a pair of terms that are no longer diametrically opposed but rather permeate each other, through frequent overlapping and intersecting, along a fluid borderline. And it is precisely by conquering this perspective that poetry and theatre become closer, almost uniting, while their relationship becomes a necessary, mutually illuminating one.]

The hypothesis Gasparini mentions at the beginning of the quotation postulates that there is, in the poetic landscape of the Novecento, a distinct brand of poetry, which she calls the *corpo-voce* (body-voice), and it depends entirely upon the "crucial switch" she describes. Once the line that separates the oral language from the written one becomes fluid, provisional, or temporary, the implications of the word also change: the dynamic between presence and absence, which is at the core of the fascination with poetic language, acquires a new layer. Poetry can draw energy from the absence of the body, the breath that gives life to the inert signs on the page; theatre can voice the silent memory of a past trapped in paper, immutable and incomplete. In this regard, Paul Zumthor, in one of his volumes on this subject, writes:

> Infatti, quale che sia la potenza espressiva e simbolica dello sguardo, il registro del visibile è sprovvisto di questo spessore concreto della voce, dell'attività del soffio, dell'urgenza del respiro. Manca ad esso questa capacità della parola, di rilanciare senza sosta il gioco del desiderio con un oggetto assente e tuttavia presente nel suono delle parole.[13]
>
> [In fact, no matter how great the expressive and symbolic power of the gaze, the visual register lacks the concrete level the voice has: the activity and the urgency of the breath. It lacks the ability of the word to incessantly renovate the game of desire for an absent object that is made present by the sound of words.]

Therefore, our goal should be not so much that of establishing where poetry and theatre have met over the second half of the Novecento but that of focusing on the long-term process that has led poets and writers to recuperate the oral elements of language and include them in their writings. Gasparini expresses this ambiguity very convincingly:

> Si delinea una sorta di storia della prassi poetico-teatrale o teatrale-poetica in cui si mostra che il vero rapporto tra poesia e teatro non si costruisce sul piano dell'interpretazione e della rappresentazione. Si costruisce sul piano dello scavo della lingua, della lotta con la lingua, della fascinazione/dissacrazione della parola, della ricerca di stati alterati di coscienza, della disarticolazione delle forme teatrali convenzionali, della ridefinizione dei concetti di teatro e poesia, della sperimentazione e decostruzione sul corpo e sulla voce, del tentativo di fondazione di una ritualità straniata, del miraggio di un'azione corporea e scritturale che parli un linguaggio extra-quotidiano, plurale, sacrificale.[14]

> [We can build a history of the praxis of this poetry-theatre, or theatre-poetry, which can demonstrate how the true relationship between poetry and theatre is not predicated on the level of interpretation and representation. It is built, instead, on the level of the research on language, the fight with language, the fascination/desecration of the word, the research into altered states of consciousness, the disarticulation of conventional theatrical forms, the redefinition of the ideas of theatre and poetry, the experimentation (with) and deconstruction of body and voice, the attempt to found an estranged reality, the mirage of a bodily and scriptural action that speaks an extra-quotidian, plural, sacrificial language.]

This passage is very dense and, in fact, it contains all the elements that Gasparini explores in the rest of her volume. What matters most for our purposes is the energy with which she stresses how, from the perspective of the linguistic experimenter, the distinction between theatre and poetry is an entirely external and arbitrary one. The various attempts that have been made in the Novecento to change and update language so that it could still be a useful artistic tool, have led writers and artists on a journey in time to retrace the original and auroral state of linguistic production. That mythical beginning was, inevitably, an oral one, in which language existed as a modulation of the breath, an entirely physical, tactile, kinetic endeavour. Therefore, the link between poetry and theatre is not an external, accidental, unnecessary occurrence but rather the inevitable result of this journey of linguistic reform.

One of the first artists to make this theoretical (and aesthetic) breakthrough was Antonin Artaud; it is not surprising, then, that his influence is crucial not only for the development of contemporary theatre, but also for literature. Here is how Gasparini summarizes his contribution:

> Ma il punto in cui Artaud tocca un passaggio niente affatto scontato del rapporto tra teatro e poesia è quello in cui spiega cosa la poesia sia in grado di offrire al teatro in vista della sua trasformazione: si tratta delle "... sue capacità di *espansione oltre le singole parole, di sviluppo nello spazio, di azione dissociata e vibratoria sulla sensibilità,*" perché la poesia provoca trance con la forza stessa della sua materia forgiata alle origini del linguaggio. Andare lì, sui bordi di quel magma da cui sono nati insieme e la parola ritmico-incantatoria e il movimento corporeo regolato significa riscoprire l'essenza di entrambi e farla finita con le rigidità del linguaggio articolato e del gesto illustrativo.[15]

> [But the point where Artaud says something remarkably original regarding the relationship between theatre and poetry is when he explains what poetry is capable of offering theatre, in view of its transformation: "... its ability to *expand beyond the individual words, to develop into space, to produce actions that are detached and resonate with sensibility,*" for poetry induces a trance with the same strength contained in its matter, which was forged at the origins of language. Going there, at the edge of that magma from which were born, at the same time, the rhythmic enchanting word and the regimented movement of the body, means to rediscover the essence of both, putting a stop to the rigidity of articulated speech and illustrative gesture.]

The terminology used by Gasparini is influenced by Artaud's visionary style; and yet, she is absolutely right in pointing to the connection between poetry, theatre, and the primordial stage of language's development as the most productive link established by the Neoavanguardia, the only one truly capable of enacting both real change and a radical renovation of both art forms. She brings to the forefront poetry's ability to evoke an ideal space that predates natural languages as we know them, where the rhythmic movements of the body and the free modulations of the voice possess an endless potential for communication and expression. By putting everyday language in contact with this primitive, mythical state, poetry can help reform theatre; by providing a ritualistic space that gathers, physically, audience and performers, theatre can restore the incantation of breath to the words of poetry.

Although it lacks this breath, the written verse possesses a number of phonetic and rhetorical elements, commonly found in oral language, that remain dormant, waiting for a voice. This "oral poetry" is, at the same time, dependent on the original, primeval language (for certain basic features) and completely free from its limitations. At the root of both, there is a purely auditory practice that usually results in singing, and that privileges timbre and rhythm over semantics. Some of the written poems retain this oral dimension, so much so that, in scanning them with our eyes, we cannot resist the temptation to read them aloud. In this perspective, then, the poet is someone who possesses a voice, while his verses contain a desire for the reader's breath.

The other crucial connection Gasparini highlights is the one between poetry and dance, between the modulations of the voice and "regimented movement." In this regard, as Zumthor writes,

> La maggior parte di questi procedimenti (della poesia orale) comportano, nella loro realizzazione, determinate regole foniche: la manipolazione dell'elemento linguistico contribuisce a provocare o a rafforzare la rima, l'allitterazione, gli echi sonori di ogni sorta, o, più in generale, mette in risalto la scansione di ritmi ... Simili giochi, quando toccano una certa densità, influiscono sulla formazione del senso. In casi estremi, la frase, e le stesse parole, si annullano in concatenazioni prive di significato codificato, riducendosi a pure suggestioni sonore ... I due (o tre) ultimi gradi di questa scala (di alterazioni) non si distinguono dal vocalizzo, che si è creduto connesso alla danza.[16]
>
> [The majority of these procedures (of oral poetry) imply, for their realization, precise phonic rules: the manipulation of the linguistic element contributes to a strengthening of rhymes, alliterations, sound echoes of all kinds, and, more generally, they highlight the beat of the rhythm. Similar games, when they reach a certain intensity, influence the formation of meaning. In extreme cases, sentences, and the words themselves, dissipate into long chains devoid of codified meaning, becoming pure sound. The last two (or three) rungs of this ladder (of alterations) are indistinct from vocalization, long believed to be connected to dance.]

And Gasparini comments on this very passage as follows:

> Insomma, la poesia conserva in quei valori ritmici e sonori che la identificano, in quella lotta tra linguaggio e libertà fonica, il suo rivelarsi compiutamente come azione del piede (i versi della metrica greca si misurano in piedi) che è cadenza nel movimento e suono nel battito (il suono di piedi che battono la terra) cioè come danza.[17]
>
> [Overall, through those rhythmic and sound values that characterize it, and that fight between language and phonetic freedom, poetry reveals itself as an action of the foot (verses, in ancient Greek, were measured

> in feet), that is, a cadence in the movement and a sound in the beat (the sound of feet that strike the ground), as in a dance.]

Although, at first glance, the connection between oral poetry and dance could seem far-fetched, a closer examination will reveal that the two have an intuitive, or rather, physiological connection, due to the way humans experience rhythm as a modulation of breath, in itself a form of "regimented movement." Once this connection becomes clear, it will be almost impossible to ignore it in the context of contemporary poetry. We could, first, refer to Ezra Pound, and his *ABC of Reading*, which was so influential among the Neoavanguardia poets.[18] Let us look, for instance, at the following passage:

> The author's conviction on this day of New Year is that music begins to atrophy when it departs too far from dance; that poetry begins to atrophy when it gets too far from music; but this must not be taken as implying that all good music is dance music or all poetry lyric. Bach and Mozart are never too far from physical movement. *Nunc est bibendum / Nunc pede libero / pulsanda tellus*.[19]

Pound takes Horace's famous exhortation as the ideal epigraph and emblem for his approach to the study of poetry. By building a link between it, music, and dance, he is trying to achieve two main results: on the one hand, he is striving for the rigour and pragmatism required to gain proficiency in those two other arts. That is, he is advocating for a practical approach to the study of poetry: pupils learn as they compose verses, using the masters as a source of inspiration and an inexhaustible repertoire of technical solutions. On the other hand, the program he institutes for his students presupposes an understanding of poetry as a mode of action within the world, and not just a mere speculative, inward-looking pursuit. Poetry, he seems to suggest, cannot exist in isolation, in silence, but requires the collegiality of an audience, the presence of music, and a resonance chamber, a space within which it can vibrate. And it is easy to see how a poetry so conceived cannot be too far removed from either music or dance.

Another connection[20] that immediately comes to mind is with Pagliarani's poem, "Dittico della merce":

> L'arte anche a me pare di poco conto
>   ma è il nostro affare
>   e il nostro daffare al momento
>   è saltare è saltare è saltare
>   se no sulla coda ci mettono il sale

Non dire anche tu che l'arte non c'entra col tempo
quando è uno dei modi del tempo
di essere, quando sono di più i modi di non essere del tempo.[21]

[To me, too, art seems of little consequence
but it is our business
and our occupation at the moment
is jumping is jumping is jumping
or they'll put salt on our tails
Don't say that art has nothing to do with time
when it is one of the ways of time's
being, when the ways for time's not being are even more.]

This very same passage is the starting point for a remarkable journey through Pagliarani's poetics, described by Luigi Ballerini in one of his early essays. In looking at the poet's use of a rhetorical technique similar to the *assemblage* employed in the visual arts, the critic highlights a number of stylistic elements that mark Pagliarani's language as belonging to a grotesque variety that exaggerates certain traits found in "natural" speech. In these verses, Ballerini identifies a mechanism similar to that described by Gasparini, according to which the words on the page manifest their desire to be read aloud, to be turned into breath:

> Ma quel che va sottolineato qui è che, al di là, o prima di tutto questo, la funzione di un brano come quello citato, è altra rispetto a quelle più o meno razionalizzabili. E, la si trova nella forza con cui persuade a farsi leggere e rileggere, cioè nella volontà di farsi oggetto verbale di un rito svolgibile su di un piano mimetico in continuo divenire, sul piano, infine, dove il ritmo non descrive la materia ma è già il doppio dell'energia.[22]

> [What needs to be underscored here is that, before or beyond everything else, the function of the passage we just quoted cannot be appreciated on a rational level. Rather, it demands to be read and reread, it desires to become a verbal object through a ritual that can unfold on an ever-changing mimetic plane, where rhythm doesn't function as a description of matter, but rather as a double of energy.]

Here Ballerini speaks of energy. Later on, he will refer to the function of the poet as similar to that of the shaman. We return to the idea, expressed by Gasparini in the passage quoted earlier, of that mystical and mythical substratum of poetry that emerges in every period of crisis and whenever there is a need for a serious reform of its linguistic medium. It is precisely at this point that the ritual dimension of linguistic *poiesis* becomes strictly connected to rhythmic movement (dance) and requires the presence of an audience. As Ballerini, in that same essay, notes,

> Siamo già ricorsi in queste righe all'immagine del poeta sciamano e abbiamo parlato delle sue operazioni come esempi di magia. Di magia bianca dobbiamo aggiungere, nel caso ce ne fosse bisogno, cioè di un rituale che non può darsi senza l'attiva e fiduciosa partecipazione della tribù la quale esprime così una forma, sia pur elementare, di interferenza gestaltica.[23]
>
> [We have already resorted, in this article, to the image of the poet-shaman, and we have spoken of its operations as examples of magic. It is white magic, we must add, in case it was necessary, that is, a ritual that cannot happen without the active and eager participation of the tribe, which thus expresses an elementary form of interference with the *Gestalt*.]

The ritual magic enacted by the ancestral poet-shaman is reproduced, recast by Pagliarani inside his verse, exploiting the rhythmic resources of spoken language, thus building that solid connection we have mentioned between poetry, music, and dance:

> È a questo punto che possiamo ritirare fuori lo stilema del continuo saltare e rivisitarlo alla luce delle affermazioni bretoniane; e cioè, in pratica, dire così: che Pagliarani nello scrivere segue una traccia (leggi: si sforza [o finge] di aderire a un'analisi) poi l'abbandona e via dicendo, riuscendo alla fine non certo a fissare la forma di un certo contenuto, ma a inventare invece una danza.[24]
>
> [It is at this point that we can return to that stylistic feature, that continuous jumping, and reconsider it in light of Breton's statements; that is, we can say: in his writing, Pagliarani follows a trace (by which I mean: he tries [or pretends] to subscribe to a given analysis), then he abandons it, and so on and so forth; what he manages to do in the end is certainly not to fix a given content in a definitive shape, but rather to create a dance.]

We have been insisting on the "oral," "gestural,"[25] and "physical" elements displayed by the writings of the Neoavanguardia, pointing out the importance of breath, rhythm, and even dance. It is important to stress that these factors are not dependent on the performance of the written text but are instead properties of the language they are written in. Here is Gasparini, on this very important issue:

> Ma vorrei fare un'ultima considerazione. Mi preme mettere in evidenza ancora una volta come gli aspetti interni alla natura della poesia che ho

definito come *corporei* (cioè la tensione della poesia verso la significazione, la fascinazione del puro gioco ritmico sonoro, e addirittura la glossolalia) e che certo si manifestano con chiara evidenza in quelle tipologie poetiche che fanno programmaticamente uso di tali possibilità insite nella materia della poesia quali strumenti compositivi ed espressivi o che programmaticamente prevedono come parte stessa del loro farsi un intento esecutivo reale; dicevo tali aspetti non necessitano della performance per la loro esistenza ma sono compresi, e risultano vitali, nella materia verbale stessa della poesia.[26]

[It is important to highlight that the internal aspects of poetry which I have defined as *corporeal* (that is, the tension within poetry toward signification, the fascination for the purely rhythmic, sound play, and even glossolalia) – and that are clearly present in those kinds of poetry that use them deliberately as expressive and communicative tools, or that programmatically postulate their actual performance – don't have to be performed in order to exist, but are included (and in fact are crucial to) poetry's verbal materials.]

That is to say that these "oral" features exist regardless of whether the verses are declaimed aloud on stage, turned into a full-fledged dramatic performance, silently pronounced internally by readers, or simply scanned visually.

There is also another poet, artist, and theorist, whose essays and ideas on poetry and "breath" have exercised a great influence on the Italian avant-garde culture: Charles Olson. His groundbreaking article "On Projective Verse" was first translated and published by *Il Verri* in 1961.[27] Giuliani refers to it in his essay on versification, which was appended to the Novissimi anthology.[28] A brief quotation will suffice to establish the strong connection between Olson's theories and those expressed in the previous pages:

If I hammer, if I recall in, and keep calling in, the breath, the breathing as distinguished from the hearing, it is for cause, it is to insist upon a part that breath plays in verse which (due, I think, to the smothering of the power of the line by too set a concept of foot) has not been sufficiently observed or practiced, but which has to be if verse is to advance to its proper force and place in the day, now, and ahead. I take it that PROJECTIVE VERSE teaches, is, this lesson, that that verse will only do in which a poet manages to register both the acquisitions of his ear *and* the pressures of his breath.[29]

Olson insists on the importance of the breath of the poet throughout this essay, making it the very measure of the poem's rhythm:

> And together, these two, the syllable *and* the line, they make up the poem, they make that thing, the – what shall we call it, the Boss of all, the "Single Intelligence." And the line comes (I swear it) from the breath, from the breathing of the man who writes, the moment that he writes, and thus is, it is here that, the daily work, the WORK, gets in, for only he, the man who writes, can declare, at every moment, the line its metric and its ending – where its breathing, shall come to, termination.[30]

Throughout his theoretical reflections, Olson devoted continuous attention to the stage and the dramatic dimension of verse. In particular, in an article entitled "Notes on Language and Theater," he offers a quick overview of the history of theatre (including its pre-Aeschylean phase) as he is trying to identify a few basic, primordial typologies of dramatic actions: what he calls "the rhabdians," "the comedians," and "the saturos." Of these three, he believes the "rhabdian" is due to make a comeback:

> the theater, as we call theater, will soon be once more *rhabdian*, plots gone, gab gone, all the rest of the baggage of means, stripped down, these "recitations" now going on in public hall a sign, but Dylan Thomas more, the hunger of people merely to hang their ears out and hear, not any longer the jigging of their eyes, all that "luxury," Schubert seats etc. [31]

In addition to confirming that long-term trend of *corpo-voce* poetry identified by Gasparini, this passage, with its "*rhabdian*" mode of doing theatre, prefigures one of the ways in which the Neoavanguardia would later bring poetry to the stage: a stripped-down "recitation" in which all the spectacular, psychological, and narrative elements of conventional dramatic representation have been eliminated. Olson concludes the essay on an unusual note, as he reconnects it to that almost mystic function poetry takes on when it appears conjoined with theatre and a ritualistic, rhythmic dance:

> What the *saturos* travestied or represented on the hinter side, was all that is now dubbed ancient or hidden knowledge. But which was, I'm convinced from the evidence, a danced (or crawled) sung (or with ratchets, loud as thunder) witnessed (everybody in it) THEATER PEFORMANCE. Call it that. At which point I buck off. For cause. I had thought this mystery was priest-business, but I know now that "priests" go with a contrary system,

> with exactly the system which intervenes between a man and his path, and which intervened, historically, the moment when the secular overtook what wasn't, in the first place, "religious," in fact, when movement and thought (language as one) were split. Theater is language, that unit more than it is all the other things it is.[32]

This characterization of "ancient knowledge" as "danced, sung, witnessed" is very similar to the definition of poetry we have been piecing together in this chapter. Olson calls this ancestral form of communication "language as one," and indicates the theatre as its preferred habitat. Thus, we keep seeing, in different theorists of the *Novecento* (from Artaud to Olson and Bene), hailing from different countries, and expressed in different languages, the same ideas on theatre and poetry, repeated in slightly different ways.

Among the list of reasons for the convergence of theatre and poetry we compiled earlier, we included the need many artists felt to cross the boundaries between art forms and disciplines. In fact, in addition to the contamination between poetry and theatre, which, as we have seen, was very common, many experimented by connecting poetry and the visual arts. Balestrini, Giuliani, Porta, and many others produced visual poems as part of their artistic output. Intuitively, one would be led to think that this kind of experimentation followed a different path from the one that brought poetry toward theatre. In reality, they all belong to the same sensibility, which can be traced back to the preponderant importance assigned to rhythm and breath. Here is Gasparini's take on this issue:

> Anche il lavorio grafico visuale (tutto il filone della poesia grafica, che usa ad esempio gli strumenti della stampa per arricchire la composizione poetica di un livello di fruizione aggiuntivo, collegato alla vista), all'apparenza predisposto a percorrere una via poetica alternativa (opposta) a quella orale-vocale-sonora, in realtà non è altro che un ulteriore forma grazie alla quale lo statuto fonico-corporeo della poesia riemerge e si ribella alla soppressione.[33]

> [Also, the graphic visual work (the whole strain of graphic poetry, which uses, for instance, the tools of print to enrich the poetic text with an additional level of fruition, connected to sight), apparently geared to walk down a poetic path that is alternative (if not opposed) to the oral-vocal-sound one, in reality is nothing but an additional form through which the sonic-corporeal state of poetry re-emerges and rebels against its suppression.]

Olson had reached the same conclusion in his already quoted essay on "Projective Verse," where he points to the typewriter as the technological tool that can help restore, via visual means, a sense of the poet's breath to the written text:

> What we have suffered from, is manuscript, press, the removal of words from its producer and its reproducer, the voice, a removal by one, by two removes from its place of origin *and* its destination. For the breath has a double meaning which Latin had not yet lost. The irony is, from the machine has come one gain not yet sufficiently observed or used, but which leads directly on toward projective verse and its consequences. It is the advantage of the typewriter that, due to its rigidity in space precisions, it can, for a poet, indicate exactly the breath, the pauses, the suspensions even of syllables, the juxtapositions even of parts of phrases, which he intends. For the first time the poet has the stave and the bar a musician has had. For the first time he can, without the conventional rhyme and metre, record the listening he has done to his own speech and by that one act indicate how he would want any reader, silently or otherwise, to voice his work.[34]

For a full discussion of the implications of such a rich passage, we refer the reader to monographs by Spatola and Ballerini, where the relationship between visual and traditional poetry is addressed.[35] Returning to our main topic, we have often pointed out[36] the importance, for the Neoavanguardia as well as the Nuovo Teatro, of involving their audience directly in the artistic process. The newfound, and newly emphasized, element of orality helped their efforts in this regard. A stress on the oral dimension of language implies a simulation of the co-presence of speaker and listener: for oral communication to take place, the author and the reader must be in the same space, and thus one can postulate the more direct involvement of each, and, potentially, the possibility of the audience to "speak back," to contribute actively to the communicative exchange. But there is also a deeper, more intimate effect, explained by Zumthor in the following passage:

> Il gesto, la voce dell'interprete stimolano nell'ascoltatore una risposta della voce e del gesto, mimetica e, in conseguenza di costruzioni convenzionali, ritardata o addirittura repressa ... La componente fondamentale della "ricezione" è quindi l'azione di un ascoltatore, che ricrea a suo proprio uso, e secondo le sue proprie configurazioni interiori, l'universo significante che gli è trasmesso. Le impronte che imprime in lui questa ri-creazione appartengono alla sua vita intima, e non appaiono necessariamente e immediatamente al di fuori.[37]

> [The gesture, the voice of the performer, stimulate in the audience a response of the voice and gesture, a mimetic and, as a consequence of

conventional constructs, a delayed or even a repressed one ... The crucial component of "reception" is therefore the action of a listener that recreates, for his own purposes, and according to his inner configurations, the universe of signification that has been transmitted to him. The marks impressed on him by this re-creation belong to his own inner life, and do not necessarily or immediately show on the outside.]

Whenever oral communication occurs, the listener undertakes a more active role in re-creating the "universe of signification" transmitted by the performer. The immediacy of such contact, thanks to the mediation of the "grain" of the voice and the gesture, has a strong evocative effect that stimulates the audience's "inner life." As a consequence, a number of elements that belong to the deep "inner configuration" of the spectator come to the forefront of his attention, become clear and apparent to him, even if he doesn't "immediately show [it] on the outside."

Gasparini uses this same passage from Zumthor to reiterate the connection between music, poetry, and dance:

> Nel suo saggio *Cultura orale e civiltà della scrittura,* Havelock spiega come la struttura metrico-ritmica della poesia, che si manifesta nelle vere e proprie azioni corporee messe in atto dai polmoni, dalla laringe, dalla lingua e dai denti, si trasmetta poi a ondate fino a arrivare a compenetrare tutti i livelli di quel mondo che è l'azione poetica (essa comprende oltre il corpo dell'esecutore anche lo strumento che eventualmente lo accompagna e il pubblico che lo vede-ascolta). ... allo stesso modo anche i movimenti del corpo nella sua globalità, quelli più evidenti del poeta-esecutore e quelli quasi impercettibili del pubblico, cioè la danza, non sono altro che poesia estesa al corpo. Ecco dunque quel corto circuito tra musica e poesia, tra danza e poesia: non una banale giustapposizione, ma un rispecchiamento dei ritmi corporei.[38]

> [In his essay *Prologue to Greek Literacy,* Havelock explains how the metric-rhythmic structure of poetry, which reveals itself in the very physical actions performed by the lungs, larynx, tongue, and teeth, is then transmitted in waves and permeates all levels of the complex world of poetic actions (which include, in addition to the body of the performer, also the instrument that may or may not accompany him and the audience in attendance) ... in this way the overall movements of the body, the more apparent ones of the poet-performer as well as the subtler ones of the audience, that is the dance, are nothing but poetry conveyed through the body. Here is, thus, that short circuit between music and poetry, between dance and poetry: it is not simply a trivial juxtaposition, but a mirroring of corporeal rhythms.]

If we bring together and systematize all the considerations and theoretical insights mentioned in these last pages, it is easy to see how the convergence between theatre and poetry was not merely a superficial phenomenon resulting from the experimental climate of the artistic world of the 1960s but rather the result of a long-term aesthetic change, certainly parallel to the socio-economic conditions, as Lucien Goldmann argued, that pervaded the entire European poetic landscape, influencing, to various degrees, the most representative writers and intellectuals. However, this was not the only trend causing a rapid transformation of the literary scene.

3.4 The Changing Status of the Text

Among the reasons listed in section 3.2 for the convergence of theatre and poetry was the radical change in the status of the text, a change that modified the rhetorical strategies and the communicative tactics of many European artists in the second half of the *Novecento*. It is worth specifying that, when we speak of "text," we don't have only literature in mind, but in fact all forms of art. Any given product of human communication can be considered a text: a symphony, a painting, even an automobile or a building, for all of them are the manifestation of a human will to communicate through an organized set of signs and bear the marks of the ideas used by different cultures in ordering the world, making sense of it, of their place within it, and within society. In this regard, Roland Barthes wrote:

> Semiology aims to take in any system of signs, whatever their substance and limits; images, gestures, musical sounds, objects, and the complex associations of all of these, which form the content of ritual, convention or public entertainment: these constitute, if not *languages*, at least systems of signification.[39]

The increase in popularity of semiology and semiotics brought more attention to the fundamental issues connected to the transmission of meaning and the communication of emotions through the various linguistic codes humans use in their cultures. In Italy the theories surrounding the "open work" of art, formulated by Umberto Eco, were at the centre of many discussions within the Neoavanguardia as well as between it and its detractors (and also the more conservative critics).

Eco begins his treatise, entitled *Opera aperta* (*The Open Work*), first published in 1962, by studying experimental, post-Weberian music, which he came into contact with through his job at RAI and his friendship with renowned composer Luciano Berio. After the first chapter, Eco applies a similar idea of "openness" in compositional techniques to the literary text. This new way of understanding artistic creation brings very important consequences. First of all, the text is seen as a "lazy machine" that requires the cognitive investment of the audience to operate properly. The communication that is thus established is a process of cooperation between addresser and addressee. This is an aspect that particularly appealed to the Italian culture of the time, which was striving to include readers and spectators as active participators in artists' work. The second main implication, strictly connected to the one just expressed, is of a political nature, and is perfectly summarized by Picchione in his monograph:

> Discussing Brecht, in particular his *Galileo*, Eco concludes that in this case the poetics of openness becomes "an instrument of revolutionary pedagogics" ... Undoubtedly, Eco's notion of *openness* (the emphasis on the collaborative relationship between composer, performer, and listener, or between author and reader) and the cultural orientation it displays are very much aligned with the politics of the *Novissimi*, in particular as defined by Giuliani in his introduction to the anthology.[40]

As mentioned, the issue of *impegno* was among the driving factors causing a radical renovation of Italian literature (and, more in general, of all art forms). But Eco wasn't the only intellectual who re-examined the traditional understanding of text and communication. The discussion on this issue was also heavily influenced by a number of French theorists, with Roland Barthes and Jacques Derrida being the most popular and well-known.

Barthes's series of brief essays, later collected in the volume *Mythologies*,[41] increased the number of human artifacts that could be considered as texts, and such texts were thus eligible for cultural analysis. Suddenly, soap boxes, children's toys, margarine ads, and the latest model Citroen could be included in a discourse that investigated long-term cultural trends, discussed the rhetorical strategies deployed by political power, and attempted to build the tools and resources necessary to contrast them.

On the other hand, in his plan to shake the very foundations of Western metaphysics, Derrida used writing, the text, and the opposition between the written and the oral as a starting point for his asystematic treatise. He returned time and again to the opposition between presence and absence, speech, silence, and the "repression" of silence. The volume *Of Grammatology*, published in 1967, is crucial for understanding his thinking. As the title reveals, the book is about a new science (which Derrida himself posits to be, in all likelihood, impossible) centred on writing: etymologically, in fact, *gramme-logy* conveys the somewhat paradoxical idea of speaking about writing. The philosopher embraces the paradox, but has no intention of solving it; on the contrary, as Arthur Bradley writes:

> For Derrida ... grammatology is the site of a problem rather than a solution and it raises a whole series of large questions – about writing, about speech, about the nature of science and even of truth itself – that will be the main subject of his work.[42]

And this, according to Derrida, constitutes an even better reason to pursue this line of study (and, incidentally, can explain the tortuous and opaque path taken by his prose). At its centre is a radical criticism of Western metaphysics and its foundational concept of "presence," something that he calls the "metaphysics of presence":

> If western philosophy has developed in many different directions over the last 2,500 years, what all these movements have in common is an attempt to posit a full or pure "presence" as the supreme value by which all reality can be judged. From the spatial presence of something we can see, hear, or touch, through the temporal presence of the "here and now" in which we live, up to and including the *absence* of some presence that has been lost (such as an Edenic state of nature) or which may be achieved in the future (such as the return of God), western thought consistently comes to the same conclusion: *what is most real, true, or important is what is most present*.[43]

The connection with the *corpo-voce* strain of contemporary poetry we have been describing in this chapter is clear and immediately evident. Derrida's sceptical attitude toward this "metaphysics of presence" can, on the one hand, help explain that duplicity and ambiguity we recorded at the beginning of this chapter. On the other hand, it casts an interesting light on the efforts made by poets to include some elements of the theatre (the "presence" of the voice, the body, the actor, etc.) in their poetry, while at the same time remaining stubbornly, squarely planted within their own art form, based on writing and on a celebration of the "absence" (of the voice, of the addressee, of the "thing," which is substituted by the word, etc.).

In fact, Derrida's investigation, which revolved around the opposition between writing and speaking, favours the former as a place where the paradoxes and repression ("the history of silence") used to mask logocentrism[44] (what lies at the core of Western metaphysics) could be more readily experienced. It is perhaps ironic, or maybe just a confirmation of the power of these deep-seated cultural assumptions, that his works spread and became popular precisely at a time when there was a renewed interest, across North America and Europe, in the voice and the power of the physical presence of actors and poets.

The research on various issues surrounding the text carried out by Eco, Barthes, and even Derrida, with his radical criticism, shows how lively and multi-faceted the aesthetic sensibility of the time was. Artists and philosophers were experiencing a peculiar cultural climate in which change, an epochal sort of change, seemed to be imminent and inevitable, opening the door to an entirely new system of artistic expression. In retrospect, from our vantage point, we know that this was not the case, that a wave of restoration would soon have swept through Italy, leading to a call to order and a fall back on more moderate, even conservative, positions. Those among the artists of the time who were more lucid and astute warned others against this excess of enthusiasm, and the unrealistic desire for a completely new sense of art; they tried to argue for a dialectical understanding of the process through which the avant-garde worked within society, emphasizing how the opposition (to traditional values and traditional genres and formulae) was one of the phases of this dialectic, an integral part of the process but not an end in itself (see, for instance, Sanguineti's description of the dynamics between *mercato* and *museo*,[45] and Pagliarani's idea of "opposition" as a modality, and not an end, of the avant-garde).[46]

Another way of framing this tension is using Eco's distinction between "*movimenti d'avanguardia*" (avant-garde movements) and "*letteratura sperimentale*" (experimental literature), a distinction that builds on Renato Poggioli's invaluable analysis.[47] Eco stresses the distance separating an experimental sensibility – which he describes as interested in the individual work of art, produced within a dialectical and intertextual relationship with tradition and the past – and an avant-garde approach – inclined to disregard the "opera" (work) in favour of a poetics, and more interested in provoking the aesthetic, political, and social status quo than in building a viable alternative.[48]

This ambiguity, this tension between the value attributed to the individual work and to the larger experimentation within the boundary of the art form, or within the Italian society of the time, also speaks to the changing status of the written word. In the midst of all this ferment, theatre behaved as a catalyst for all the uneasiness and restlessness that surrounded the artistic text, perhaps because of the traditional conflict between authors and directors, one of those "aporie costitutive del teatro di poesia" (constitutive aporias of poetry's theatre), as

De Marinis called them,[49] that was mentioned earlier. Here is, to close this section, one last quotation from Gasparini, which is also a warning we must keep in mind as we take stock of the situation:

> La battaglia stessa della moderna teatrologia contro il testocentrismo negli studi teatrali ha forse contribuito al pregiudizio metodologico nei confronti della parola poetica a teatro, del suo senso e del suo valore nel contesto della riforma del teatro stesso.[50]
>
> [The battle of modern theatrology against the text-centrism in theatre studies has perhaps contributed to the methodological prejudice against the poetic word on stage, its meaning, and its value in the context of the reform of theatre itself.]

The progressive abandonment of a traditional idea of script as the basis of dramatic performances is one of the few points on which most of the experimenters of the Nuovo Teatro agreed, and it was generally connected to the ideas of "cruelty" formulated by Artaud.

In an article published in the journal *Antropologia e Teatro*, Fabio Acca describes this trend in the following terms:

> Tra il 1965 e il 1967, l'aggressività attribuita alla "comunicazione crudele" del teatro di Artaud rappresenta un elemento di fascinazione troppo forte per non essere assunto dalla comunità teatrale dell'epoca come linea guida per un teatro alla ricerca di una chiave esclusiva attraverso cui rendersi riconoscibile. La centralità attribuita alla drammaturgia del corpo nello spazio, la qualità fisica, violentemente corporea della composizione teatrale e il progressivo ridimensionamento e riqualificazione dello statuto verbale nella creazione scenica sono sicuramente alla base della nascita del Nuovo Teatro.[51]
>
> [Between 1965 and 1967, the aggressiveness attributed to the "cruel communication" of Artaud's theatre constitutes a strong element of fascination that was taken by the theatrical community of the time as a guiding principle for a theatre that sought a distinctive element through which it could be easily identified. The central role attributed to the dramaturgy of the body inside the space, the physical, violently corporeal quality of the theatrical composition, and the progressive reduction and requalification of the verbal component within the scenic creation are certainly at the core of the birth of the Nuovo Teatro.]

The starting point of this revolution in the hierarchy between the various elements of the theatrical spectacle can be found in Artaud, but soon spread to most of the experimental and avant-garde theatre troupes that operated in Italy. A similar switch happened in the world of criticism, where the aesthetic standards used to interpret and evaluate the shows reflected this new-found sensibility. Here is Acca, again:

> Anche le nozioni di "scrittura scenica" e "corporeità," coniate in quegli anni da Giuseppe Bartolucci, sono figlie di una trasversalità neanche troppo velatamente artaudiana. La frantumazione progressiva della centralità della parola, lo spostamento del fuoco creativo nel circuito del gesto e del corpo nello spazio, la concertazione attoriale dei segni scenici in chiave antinaturalistica e antipsicologica, il ruolo di testimonianza attiva dello spettatore sono tutti segnali di possibili declinazioni artaudiane, modellate sulle figure che più richiamano, nell'immaginario teatrale del tempo, l'attuazione del teatro della crudeltà ...[52]
>
> [The notions of "stage writing" and "corporality," created in those years by Giuseppe Bartolucci, are also the product of a perspective that is clearly inspired by Artaud. The progressive destruction of the central role assigned to the word, the shift of the creative focus toward the realm of gestures and the body in space, the concentration of the actor's scenic signs in an anti-naturalist and anti-psychological direction, the role of active witness assigned to spectators, are all indicators of Artaud's influence, and are designed to recall, in the contemporary theatrical imagination, the practice of a theatre of cruelty ...]

As the theatre was becoming increasingly less tied to a script that needed to be performed night after night, so poetry was experimenting with glossolalia, onomatopoeia, vocalizations, and all non-linguistic aspects of verbal communication. As we will see, in a few cases this led to the creation of unprecedented, groundbreaking work. At other times, especially when there was a mismatch between authors and performers, or when the writers were not willing to relinquish control over their words, the collaboration became impossible.

3.5 Giuliano Scabia: An Extreme, Exemplary Path

In focusing on two of the most important long-term trends that shaped the European literary world throughout the 1960s and 1970s (the oral dimension of poetry and the changing status of the text), we have also taken a few steps toward a better definition of our field of investigation. As we have seen, our main interest is not the Nuovo Teatro, for there are already a number of publications (although none of them has been translated into English) that address it (and its history and evolution).

Nor are we investigating the different paths that stemmed from poetry and reached out to other art forms, giving birth to visual poetry, sound poetry, video poetry, and so forth. Rather, we are interested in the grey area between the poetic text and the stage: that peculiar incarnation of the *corpo-voce* that emerged at the border between the experiments of theatre and those of poetry, through which some of the writers of the Neoavanguardia and Gruppo 63 were trying to overcome the impossible situation in which they found themselves, resorting to a reappropriation of the "breath" in all its manifestations (textual, performative, spectacular) to move their research forward.

When it comes to defining the time period for our research, things get even more complicated, given the diversity in the paths followed by the various writers over their career. On the one hand, there was an indubitable moment, at the very beginning of Gruppo 63, when theatre and poetry truly walked on parallel paths, and the exchanges were frequent and, for the most part, fruitful. In spite of the writers' differences and misunderstandings, there was a genuine desire to collaborate and enrich one another's research, to reflect on one's own art using the others' as a mirror, capable of providing a new point of view and an inspiration to do things differently. This phase, generally speaking, lasted from 1963 to, approximately, 1967, when, at the Convegno di Ivrea, the Nuovo Teatro constituted itself as an entity, at least in the eyes of the national press. Although it failed to unite the experimental components of Italian theatre, the Convegno gave an opportunity to the various companies, dramaturgs, and directors to verify their relative distance from one another, and to appreciate the deep theoretical divide that separated their respective poetics.[53] After the Convegno, the different components of the Nuovo Teatro decided it was impossible to constitute themselves in a coherent group, not even following the loose model of Gruppo 63, whose statutory sport, according to Eco, was disagreement.[54]

A second phase, a sort of prolonged twilight, followed the disbanding of Gruppo 63 with the closure of *Quindici*, in 1969, and the wave of *rappel a l'ordre* that invested Italian literature in the mid-1970s.[55] This long "decline" lasted until 1979: over this decade, the collaboration between theatre and poetry continued only in a few, isolated cases. However, in this same period, several institutions, especially municipal governments of bigger and smaller cities, organized a number of poetry festivals, principally during the summer time, where the performance of poetry on stage was not an uncommon occurrence. And so, we come to what some[56] have dubbed the "battle of Castelporziano," the first Festival Internazionale dei Poeti, which can be considered the extreme, posthumous instalment of this phenomenon. We will discuss the implications of this event in a few pages, in the last section of this chapter.

Eugenio Barba, looking at the issue from the point of view of the stage, often spoke of a "superamento dell'involucro teatrale"[57] (going beyond the shell of theatre) when describing the direction his research (with the Odin Teatret) had taken in the 1960s and 1970s. With this expression, he meant "the liberation of the actor and the spectator from the logic of representation/interpretation."[58] In chapter 1, we observed a similar trend that ran through poetry, and that we could define as the attempt to "go beyond the shell of verse."

By calling attention to these two tendencies in theatre and poetry, we were able to identify an overlap between the two artistic fields, within which we observed the manifestation of a peculiar form of poetry-theatre. Now that this new area of study has been defined, however, we must face a terminological problem, to which is connected a more important aesthetic issue. Choosing to call this "grey area" poetry-theatre or theatre-poetry, or pointing at the attempts to go beyond the "shells" of theatre or verse, has meaningful implications, as it establishes an ideal starting point (and a direction) for this movement: from the inside of the shell of theatre to the outside, presumably toward poetry, or vice versa, if we start from within poetry.

This way of looking at things excludes the possibility of permanently inhabiting the ambiguous space that exists between the two shells, thus beginning a truly innovative way of making art that is located outside of disciplinary boundaries and that can involve the audience in unprecedented ways.[59] Although many discussed and hoped for the advent of such a mixed art form, none of the poets who will be discussed in the last portion of this volume ever truly went "beyond the shell of verse," and with good cause: being "in between" carried the risk of being ignored by fellow artists operating in either of the two traditional disciplines; it made it difficult to secure commissions, spaces, audiences, and funds. In fact, such a synthesis is not what this study intends to focus on; here we intend to concentrate on the efforts that came from poets who looked to the theatre as a source of inspiration and renewal. However, it is important to recognize that at least one person, Giuliano Scabia, did take this path seriously, and pursued it all the way, going beyond the two *involucri* and establishing this new art. Here is how De Marinis characterizes Scabia's career:[60]

> Le tappe principali del "viaggio" teatrale di Scabia (dalla scrittura "d'avanguardia" di *Zip* alle azioni di decentramento nei quartieri di Torino, alle azioni "a partecipazione" con i bambini e con la gente) costituiscono

infatti altrettanti momenti di una progressiva radicalizzazione della ricerca, nella direzione (che è la stessa di tutto un ampio versante della sperimentazione contemporanea) di una sempre maggiore *dilatazione della scrittura e della pratica teatrali.*[61]

[The main stages of Scabia's theatrical "journey" (from the "avant-garde" writing of *Zip* to the decentring actions in Turin's neighbourhoods, and the "participation" actions with children and regular people) mark the different moments of a progressive radicalization of his research, in the direction (the same as a whole group of contemporary experimenters) of an ever-increasing *dilatation of writing and theatrical practice.*]

De Marinis calls this a "dilatation of writing and theatrical practice," but it is the same process we described as "going beyond the shell of theatre and verse." Scabia was one of the few writers who truly ventured into that "no-man's land" in between literature and theatre and made it his home, exploring it, and exploiting its potential for involving the audience and, thus, being actively engaged on the political level. In the introduction to one of his earlier books, *Teatro nello spazio degli scontri* ("Theatre in the Space of Confrontations"), he writes, under the heading "Scrittura" ("Writing"),

L'ipotesi mia, da un certo momento in poi, è stata quella di "fare scrittura" attraverso un modo nuovo di fare teatro. La strada che ho cercato di percorrere è pertanto anche una strada della scrittura. Scrivere teatro può avvenire a priori (il testo scritto prima della pratica scenica), o a posteriori (gli schemi vuoti riempiti di azioni). Uno schema vuoto ..., può essere riempito in molti modi, abbastanza casuali. Ma si tratta pur sempre di un'azione su traccia, in cui sono dati alcuni passaggi fissi. In tal modo l'azione teatrale aperta assume una sua struttura narrativa (un principio e una fine, una scansione, una metrica temporale e spaziale), una sua dinamica scenica. Ed è tutto questo che diventa insieme pratica e scrittura, identità totale ... D'altra parte il rapporto tra linguaggio (teatrale) e lingua del tempo (e in particolare, oggi, con la koinè linguistica che si va formando nei quartieri delle grandi metropoli) costituisce la pratica reale del teatro. Nella ricerca di questo rapporto sta il fulcro della ricerca teatrale.[62]

[My hypothesis, from a certain moment onward, was that of "practising writing" through a new way of practising theatre. The path I tried to take is, thus, one of the paths of writing. Writing theatre can be *a priori* (the text is written before the performance on stage), or *a posteriori* (the empty charts filled by actions). An empty schema ..., can be filled in many different ways, leaving things up to chance. However, it is still an action based on an outline, which requires certain fixed moments. This way, the open theatrical action can acquire its narrative structure (a beginning and an end, a rhythm, a temporal and spatial metre), its own scenic dynamic. And all of this becomes, at the same time, practice and writing, one inseparable unit … In fact, the relationship between (theatrical) language and the language of the times (in particular, today, the linguistic *koine* that is taking shape in the neighbourhoods of the large metropolises) constitutes the real practice of theatre. The search for this relationship is the real core of theatre's research.]

This quotation contains all the elements of Scabia's poetics, the most important of which is the identity between "writing" and "action." In several places, he claims the complete equivalence between the two: neither is seen as playing a privileged role in the creative process. The writing of "empty schemas," later to be "filled" by the "actions" and "improvisations" of the professional actors – as well as the reactions of the audience – is all part of this new, "dilatated," as De Marinis put it, form of writing. The publication of a volume that follows, chronicles, and discusses the experiences acquired through this "practice of writing" is an additional step, an added level of writing that, although useful and interesting, must remain separate and distinct from the new creative procedure established by Scabia.

Bringing to the extreme this understanding of theatrical writing leads, inevitably, to an aporia, which De Marinis describes in the following terms:

[Una] contraddizione oggettiva instauratasi in una scrittura che, mentre, da un lato, continua tutto sommato a essere prodotta secondo le regole drammaturgiche tradizionali (testo scritto *a priori* e individualmente, struttura compatta e rigorosa), dall'altro ambisce, nella sua stessa fase progettuale, a un'apertura sempre maggiore …; apertura che, evidentemente, essa non può sopportare oltre un certo limite senza con ciò mettere radicalmente in discussione i suoi stessi caratteri costitutivi, arrivando a negarsi in quanto tale. Al di là di questo limite, la scrittura drammaturgica deve trasformarsi necessariamente in qualcosa di profondamente diverso, che possiamo chiamare ugualmente "scrittura" … ma non ha più niente a che vedere con il *playwriting* tradizionale.[63]

[[An] objective contradiction that took shape within a writing that, while on the one hand continues to be produced according to the traditional dramaturgic rules (text written *a priori* and individually, with a compact

> and rigorous structure), on the other hand aspires, starting from its planning stage, to an ever-increasing opening …; an opening that it clearly cannot endure beyond a certain limit without questioning, in a radical manner, its very own constitutive characteristics, and thus negating its own existence. In order to cross this limit, the theatrical writing must transform into something profoundly different, something we can still call "writing" … but that has nothing to do with traditional playwriting.]

Once again, we come to that undetermined space that separates poetry and theatre, planned performance and spontaneous event, the rigours of the written text and the endless possibilities offered by the oral utterance, the expressive potential of the word and that of the gesture. One final note regarding language: in the last portion of the quotation from *Teatro nello spazio degli scontri*, Scabia highlights the importance of facing the changes in contemporary Italian society and their impact on the way in which common people experienced "standard" speech in their everyday lives. We mentioned the great transformation brought about by the "economic miracle"; not only were the mass media increasingly more present in the quotidian experience of more citizens, but the internal migration caused by the high demand for unskilled labour in the factories of the north also put many people in touch with the way other fellow Italians spoke in other parts of the peninsula. Traces of this new sensibility can be seen in the neo-realist movies of the *dopoguerra*, as well as in Pasolini's novels and films. Scabia wants to tap into the vitality of this new linguistic *koine*, without stigmatizing it or casting it in a paternalistic light; rather, he intends to exploit its potential for innovating the traditional theatrical forms and connecting with a new kind of audience.

This is true not only for texts, stories, and characters that are born for the stage but also for other more narrative works. In fact, even when writing novels (see *Nane Oca*,[64] for instance), he still preserves the grain of his voice, the rhetorical strategies, the "breath" that pervades his participative shows. *Nane Oca*, with its repetitions, its fascination with rhythm and sounds, its insistence on the carnal joys of life and the flesh of its fairy-like characters, is a witness to the irrepressible oral nature of Scabia's inspiration. Here is Gasparini:

> la poesia (è) presenza viva, atto che si esplica nel corpo stesso di chi la genera, *performance* che si compie con gli strumenti che le sono propri (linguaggio, prosodia, sonorità, metafora, ritmo) nel momento stesso della sua produzione, teatro che si dà sempre anche senza palcoscenico, senza voce, senza spettatori, perché incorpora le prerogative nella sua

> stessa materia. Mi sembra che Giuliano Scabia, da poeta che riflette sul proprio fare, chiarisca molto bene nel testo *Il tremito* questo statuto della poesia.[65]
>
> [poetry (is) a live presence, an act that takes place in the very body of those who create it, a performance that is carried out with its specific tools (language, prosody, sound, metaphor, rhythm), in the very moment of its production, a theatre that is always devoid of a stage, without a voice, an audience, for it incorporates those prerogatives in its own material existence. It appears clear to me that Giuliano Scabia, as a poet who is reflecting on his own activities, addresses, in his poem entitled "Il tremito" ("The Tremble") this way of understanding poetry.]

Gasparini brings the issue back to the body of the poet, one of the few places where the demands of theatre and those of poetry can be adequately satisfied. She quotes from Scabia's poem, as follows:

> … quando viene il tremito della poesia …
> quando nelle rocce della mente si apre una fessura
> e la vivenza profonda della lingua si scatena in terremoti che parlano nel corpo – il corpo
> trema e ha febbre – si infebbra —
> fervore/tremore che porta in altro luogo:
> luogo che è il futuro della lingua e del corpo,
> in germoglio, sbocciato dentro la *presenza*.
> …
> L'esperimento è sempre con lei, lingua,
> paterna e materna,
> combattimento con lei, avventura con lei,
> per cercarla e trovarla nel soffio del corpo voce[66]
>
> [… when the tremble of poetry comes …
> when in the rocks of the mind a crack opens up
> and the deep life of language is unleashed in earthquakes that speak of the body – the body
> trembles and shows a fever – becomes feverish —
> fervour-trembling that leads elsewhere:
> a place that is the future of language and body,
> budding, sprouting inside the *presence*.
> …
> She, language, is always the experiment
> father and mother tongue,

struggle against her, adventure with her,
seeking and finding her in the breath of the body-voice.]

Scabia's brand of experimentation takes him on a radically original path, far from the practices followed by other contemporary poets. As a consequence, he will be considered, by his peers, a *teatrante*, even though his research led to the formulation of precisely the ideal that many of them claimed as their own goal. In spite of the great fascination this path exercises, Scabia will remain a "theoretical limit," on the other side of a border we don't intend to cross.

3.6 Antonio Porta's Hungry Verse

Someone who, instead, remained on this side of that limit, perhaps also because of his premature death, was Antonio Porta, who explored, throughout his literary output, the boundary between theatre and poetry, the written and the spoken word. Thus, it seems fitting to pause here and reflect on his journey – one that was, at the same time, highly personal and truly representative of the tensions, contradictions, and restlessness that animated his fellow Novissimi and Neoavanguardisti.

We could begin from a rather plain and agreeable observation: Porta's writings are hungry, with an all-encompassing, pervasive, pantagruelic sort of hunger.[67] On more than one occasion, Porta himself explicitly linked writing and the need to feed oneself; let's take, for instance, the first of the many introductory notes that accompany the poems included in *Nel fare poesia*, the poet's auto-anthology, first published in 1985, where we read:

> Oscillando tra menzogna e verità, tra folgorazione realistica e ombra mitica, il linguaggio del sogno si giustifica con la sua stessa esistenza; non si può non sognare. Il linguaggio della poesia corrisponde a una necessità analoga: non si può non esprimersi, non si può non mangiare … Il paradosso sta nel fatto che (la poesia) ci nutre con domande più che con risposte.[68]

> [Fluctuating between lies and truth, between realistic epiphany and mythical shadows, the language of dreams finds its justification within its own existence; we cannot help but dream. The language of poetry responds to a similar necessity: we cannot help but express ourselves, we cannot help but eat … The paradox is that (poetry) nourishes us with questions rather than answers.]

Singing, naming, narrating, and writing are all, according to Porta, equally essential human needs, as much as eating. In the paragraph we just quoted, he could have written "we cannot help but breathe" just as easily, but he chose to say "eat," and, as we will see, the choice is not inconsequential. But what is Porta's poetry hungry for? In the preface that introduces his translation of Plautus's *Persa*, he writes, "Every poet, every writer or critic ... is an 'eater of languages.' I am an omnivore, not only when it comes to food, but also for languages, from that of sports to that of comedy, from that of science to that of poetry."[69] Thus, Porta is hungry for different kinds of language; his verses, as we will see in a moment, keep a more varied diet.

Although both sources we just quoted date back to 1985, it's important to clarify that the trait we just observed, the assimilation of writing and feeding, is not limited to a phase of Porta's literary output but is actually a common thread that runs through his whole career. In fact, we can observe it as early as 1960, in the poem entitled "Dialogo con Herz" ("Dialogue with Herz"), included in the Novissimi anthology.

Let us consider especially lines 5 to 7: "squittivo, / di notte, e brucavo le foglie, di cavolo / e di tabacco. D'inverno consumai le riserve" (I squealed / in the night, and chewed on leaves, of cabbage / and tobacco. That winter I used up the reserves)[70] From the very first stanza of this poem we hear about hunger and penury. Two lines down, we read: "La lepre muore / di freddo, di fame, di vecchiaia o fucilata" (The hare dies / of cold, hunger, old age or shot down), and thus the very word "hunger" is mentioned, and portrayed as an imminent risk in the life of the animal. Besides hares, this poem contains also birds, whose dietary needs are rather easily satisfied since, as we learn, "Basta agli uccelli, spesso, un forte / vento notturno" (Often, for birds, a strong night wind / is enough), where it is not explicitly stated that the birds subsist on mere wind, but the implication that this is the case is certainly there.

Hunger is not limited to animals; even gutters suffer from it, in a startling objectivization and antiphrastic attribution of an appetite to inanimate objects: "verremo risucchiati da una grondaia in un giorno / di pioggia, emblema di violenze" (we're going to be sucked down a drain on a rainy / day, an emblem of fury). Although it is usually water that runs down the gutters, one of the voices of the dialogue that animates this poem is worried that they will be swallowed by it to satisfy a paradoxical and violent impulse. In addition to animals and objects, Porta's plants also are hungry: "Toccare le radici / e leccare sostanze nutritive" (To lick the roots / and taste the nourishing substances). Finally, all these different forms of craving are summarized by one of the two voices, in what amounts to the longest streak of uninterrupted speech within the whole poem: "Scivolo nuotando fra alghe pericolose"

(I slip swimming through dangerous seaweed), perhaps a reference to the journey through the gutters mentioned earlier: "Affondo / in fitte vegetazioni, ricoperto / di formiche e di foglie" (I sink / in thick vegetation, I fill up / with ants and leaves), where we find again the plants, with the addition of insects: "Mastico piume" (I chew feathers), and, finally, here are also the birds.

It is worth underscoring one last element, clearly marked by the title of this poem: its dialogic, and therefore intrinsically theatrical, dimension. In the corresponding note from *Nel fare poesia*, Porta speaks about a "real dialogue between two friends," and even the setting for the performance is clearly stated twice: a "terrace" that is mentioned in the second and in the last stanza. The structure of this dialogue, with its ever-shifting conversation, constitutes a model for the theatrical texts Porta would write in this period, and, especially, for *Stark* (1967) and *Si tratta di larve* (*It's Some Sort of Larvae*, 1968).

If we put side by side the two observations we just laid out, the hunger on the one hand and the dialogic, theatrical dimension on the other, the connection with Antonin Artaud becomes immediately apparent. The tie between Porta and Artaud has been investigated by many scholars. We could turn, for example, to Niva Lorenzini, who dedicated an essay to tracing the presence of cruelty in the poetry of the sixties, in which she discusses the introductory note that Porta wrote for Lautrèmont's complete works (*Opere complete*), published by Feltrinelli in 1968. There, Porta mentions Artaud's preface to *Theatre and Culture*, an essay dating back to 1938 and then reused as the introduction to his *Complete Works* in 1946. As Lorenzini points out, "Porta writes, almost translating [from Artaud]: 'it is certain that now literature can be justified only as long as it serves "ideas that are as urgent as hunger."'"[71] This is a way of showing that Porta read Artaud very closely and used his writing in his own critical essays. For additional confirmation, we can turn to Stefano Agosti:

> Della violenza espressiva che caratterizza, in generale, la poesia di Porta, si possono subito circoscrivere i due piani, perfettamente omologhi, di manifestazione:
>
> 1. il piano tematico, ove la violenza assume gli aspetti della ferita, del sangue e della morte, con correlate fenomenologie di azioni quali l'aggressione, la mutilazione, la fagocitazione (di animali su animali, ma anche, sia pur per metafora, di tipo cannibalico), e così via;
> 2. il piano formale, ove la violenza si manifesta nel disassestamento (nel decentramento) della sintassi, dovuto all'affollamento e addirittura

> alla congestione dei vari *realia* (termini-oggetto o immagini) vocati a instaurare la rappresentazione, e alla loro sostanziale eterogeneità.[72]

[We could quickly delineate the two, perfectly homologous levels of expressive violence within Porta's poems:

1. the thematic level, where violence takes the appearance of wounds, blood and death, with the related phenomenology of actions such as aggression, mutilation, fagocitation (of animals by other animals, but also, although metaphorically, of a cannibalistic nature), and so on;
2. the formal level, where violence is conveyed through the disarticulation (the decentralization) of syntax, through an overcrowding and a congestion of various *realia* (term-objects or images) evoked to shape the representation, and through their fundamental heterogeneity.]

From these premises, Agosti moves on to connect Porta's verse to Artaud's and his theatre of cruelty. I think it is important to emphasize two aspects mentioned here: on the one hand the "cannibalistic" elements, that is to say, metaphorically speaking, the assimilation of the same; on the other hand, there is also an interest in the gathering, the accumulation, of disparate and heterogeneous objects. To the two levels identified by Agosti, I would add a third one, an intertextual level that is halfway between cannibalism and the passion for heterogeneity, a level that explains the circulation of materials that are at the origins of Porta's writings: sometimes these are titles, sentences, lines that appear first in a collage form as a visual poem and then are reworked into a "linear" poem, and finally they might be digested into a theatrical piece only to be reformatted into a new poem. At other times, these materials come from the outside, from works by other writers, from the literary tradition (see, for instance, Shakespeare's *Hamlet,* which is transformed into "La scelta della voce").[73] In much the same way, however, they are ingested, metabolized, and reassembled. Thus, Porta's poetry doesn't contain only a cannibalism of the flesh, described at the level of the imagery; also very important is this violent and ruthless reuse of pre-existing writing and literature.[74]

If Artaud's influence is absolutely undeniable, and amply documented in the scholarship on Porta, the characteristics we have been reviewing so far lead us to include another possible ancestor, to be added alongside the inventor of the theatre of cruelty: Alfred Jarry, or, to be more precise, his most influential creation, *père* Ubu.[75] The hunger, the violence, the cannibalism (that is to say, both the threat of consuming other characters' flesh and the circulation of pre-existing materials between the various works), united with an intertextual appetite for the whole of the Western literary tradition are all constitutive elements of Jarry's theatre that reach in the Ubu plays the highest degree of concentration and emphasis within the modern canon.

Porta's writings are hardly the only ones showing Jarry's influence. In fact, if we look across the various poets of the Neoavanguardia, we will notice how Ubu and in general Jarry's attitude toward literature resurface in more than one place. One need only think of the Novissimi Pagliarani and Giuliani, and especially their *Pelle d'Asino*, or even of the first few pieces written by Sanguineti (things changed rather significantly with his *Faust*).[76] However, there are at least four other examples among the intellectuals surrounding the Novissimi that deserve a special mention: 1) one of the earliest shows staged by Carmelo Bene, in 1963, in one of those newly inaugurated *cantine romane*, was *I Polacchi* (*The Poles*), subtitled *Ubu roi*,[77] and thus Jarry was a clear inspiration for one of the most original innovators of the Italian stage; 2) Giuseppe Bartolucci, in reviewing the play by Filippini entitled *Gioco con la scimmia*, speaks of "a theatrical line from Jarry to Artaud,"[78] and thus Jarry was already considered a point of reference for the theatre of the neo-avant-garde by contemporary critics (at least the more astute ones); 3) although it is not necessarily clear that it had a direct impact on the ongoing conversations surrounding the Italian stage, Luigi Gozzi's essay "Di Jarry e del personaggio" shows a remarkable understanding of Jarry's legacy and the opportunities it opened for his fellow Neoavanguardisti;[79] 4) and finally, in 1973, Giuliani wrote a treatment of Jarry's main works for Italian radio entitled *Nostro padre Ubu*, a piece that weaves together the French author's biography (with some of its most preposterous anecdotes) and his literary production.[80]

There are many other such connections to point out, but it is time to move on to a more systematic discussion of Porta's theatre in relation to Jarry's *Ubu*. We could begin with *Stark*, published for the first time in that same issue of *Grammatica* that contained the essay by Bartolucci we just mentioned. Through a rather disjointed dialogue, filled with lateral shifts and non sequiturs, we witness the clash between two "reactionaries," designated only as 1° and 2°, and two "revolutionaries," indicated as A and B. Stark is the name of another character, a torturer who is mentioned at the beginning and end of the play. There are also common citizens involved in the exchange: M, N, and O.

The stage directions are divided into three different parts, entitled, respectively, "Gli attori" ("The actors"), "L'azione" ("The action"), and "La scenografia" ("The set"). Under "L'azione" we read: "the actors will exchange objects and products indispensable to life." And then, after a few sentences: "the action shouldn't represent just a basic economic situation but should also try to make it 'total,' starting from the daily food and all the way to a continually destroyed metaphysics of possible values."[81] From this brief note, and from the names of the two groups of characters involved, it is easy to see the predominance of the political theme (which is a characteristic in line with the driving interests of the time), and the important role attributed to physical objects, presented on stage as a way of criticizing the growing consumeristic society of the day. In fact, under the "scenografia" section of the stage directions we read, "The shadows will repeat the movements of exchange, which will happen in plain sight, a bit everywhere, using very visible objects: bananas, irons, pears, shoes, etc."[82]

In addition to this appetite for an ever-growing set of disparate things, *Stark* displays also the same level of violent imagery critics normally associate with Porta's verse. Let us consider, for instance, the following passage taken from the beginning of the play:

> 2° – Se non l'avesse vista, se non fosse impazzito, se non l'avesse chiamata, odiata disperatamente, frustata, se non l'avesse chiavata con quel pezzo di ferro, quella pannocchia di bronzo
> 1° – Se non le avesse fatto perdere quella gamba, se non le avesse strappato tutte quelle dita, in un colpo solo
> 2° – Se non si fosse messo a perdere tutta quella roba per strada, merde!, così come un vecchio incontinente, con gli sfinteri allentati
>
> [2° – If only he hadn't seen her, if he hadn't gone mad, if he hadn't called her, hated her so desperately, whipped her, if he hadn't screwed her with that piece of metal, that bronze corncob
> 1° – If only he hadn't caused her to lose that leg, if he hadn't ripped out all those fingers, in one single blow
> 2° – If only he hadn't started losing all his stuff on the street, merde!, like an old incontinent man, with loose sphincters]

In addition to mentioning even more incongruent objects ("bronze corncob"), these lines introduce an extremely dehumanizing language that reduces the body of the other to mere flesh, amorphous and inert, important only in so far as it offers a place where the violence of the dominating subject can be expressed. Also, I would like to highlight the presence of that "merde!," which I chose to interpret as a borrowing from the French.[83] I suspect this to be a direct quotation of that famous "Merdre!" with which Jarry begins his own *Ubu,* an interjection that has been renormalized by the subtraction of that extra "r" that had made it even more scandalous and upsetting when it was first pronounced in front of a Parisian audience.

As we move on to the second play written by Porta, entitled *Si tratta di larve* (*It's Some Sort of Larvae*, 1968), I would like to pause here on a short fragment from John Picchione's monograph, where he briefly connects Porta's writings with those of Jarry and is therefore the only one among recent critics, as far as I can tell, who has explicitly made this connection:

> *Si tratta di larve* è un atto unico provocatorio e sarcastico, la cui irrisione del mondo borghese da un lato si ispira alla lezione di Alfred Jarry o del teatro dadaista e, dall'altro, nella situazione al limite dell'inverosimile e dell'assurdo si richiama alle invenzioni e all'*humour noir* di un commediografo come Ionesco.[84]
>
> [*It's Some Sort of Larvae* is a provocative and sarcastic piece, whose ridicule of the bourgeois world is inspired, on the one hand, by the example of Alfred Jarry's theatre or that of the Dadaists; on the other hand, given the improbable circumstances it describes, often bordering on the absurd, it reminds one of the inventions and the *humour noir* of a playwright such as Ionesco.]

As Picchione remarks, we are in a typically bourgeois interior, with a number of characters attempting to save the appearance of civilized behaviour, while strange creatures, the larvae of the title, progressively take control of their bodies and intellectual capacities, killing the men and impregnating the women with a monstrous offspring. These larvae could be a symbol for the insidious elements (ideas, attitudes, behaviours) of the consumer society or, alternatively, they could be a representation of how bourgeois culture has traditionally seen and characterized leftist revolutionary ideas. Regardless of the interpretation we choose, it is clear that the author intends to elicit the audience's reflection by proposing an absurd situation; in the process, he takes no small pleasure in mocking his characters' words and reactions, exposing all the superficial vacuity of those strategies we all employ in our daily lives in order to cope with the absurdities that society forces us to endure.

The stage directions, once again, are very revealing; Porta notes that, "At the centre of the stage there is a couch and two or three armchairs; a tea set on a small table. Naturally, there are no other objects on the scene."[85] What grabs one's attention is that rather incongruous "naturally": given the preponderant importance of objects in the previous play, one would expect the same to be true here. Perhaps it is the bodies of the characters that are the only objects allowed here: the continuous attempts of the larvae to take control of them destroyed any remaining illusion of subjectivity, utterly objectifying them, reducing them to the state of tools, means of locomotion, incubators for the next generation of larvae. If this interpretation is true, it makes sense that there would "naturally" be no additional objects to distract the audience and dilute the message. It should be said, however, that the characters make very good use of the tea set provided by deliberately pouring several cups over each other's clothes at regular intervals, throughout the play.

Although, as we said, there are no other objects, two of the characters (the son of the host and a friend of his, designated as 1° and 2°) periodically appear on and disappear from the stage, reciting a long list of things, and limiting their utterance to the following odd and disquieting catalogues, which they repeat twice – "tree/tree/horse/horse/rocket/rocket/feet/feet/etcetera/etcetera/door/door ..."[86] – as if to say that in the absence of the concrete items, linguistic labels can be bandied about in just as incongruous a manner.

If we continue following this theme through Porta's theatrical output, we will find an interesting mention of objects also in his *La presa del potere di Ivan lo sciocco* ("The Seizure of Power by Ivan the Idiot"), a play staged for the first time in 1974 and then published as a slender volume by Einaudi that same year. A few years have gone by from *Si tratta di larve*, and a lot has changed in the meantime. However, as we will see, the key components of Porta's theatre have remained the same and, if possible, the use of the tools and strategies we have identified has become even more deliberate, open, and emphatic. The plot relates the rise to power of Ivan, whose idiocy consists in being honest, working hard, and treating his fellow human beings with love and respect. While these admirable qualities will first cause him to rise to power they will also, eventually, doom him to lose his crown and the respect of his subjects, as he proves to be no match for the compromises and injustices power always demands of those who wield it.

The play stems from the collaboration between Porta and Sergio Porro, the director of a theatrical troupe called the Teatro Artigiano di Cantù. In a very informative essay on his collaboration with Porta, Porro writes:

> Avevamo in comune (senza saperlo) una cosa: l'uso degli oggetti, io in teatro lui nei versi. Ecco perché lo spettacolo dei Maya gli era piaciuto molto, non c'era un solo momento in cui ogni attore non avesse con sé un oggetto da manovrare. E anche l'*Ivan* stava prendendo corpo alla stessa maniera: in ogni momento ogni attore aveva con sé un oggetto da

maneggiare e da mostrare "come un arto artificiale aggiunto." Ogni cosa era esibita ...[87]

[We had one thing in common (even though we didn't know it at the time): the use of objects; I in my theatre, he in his verses. This is why he had liked so much our show on the Mayans; there wasn't a single moment in which the actors didn't have an object to manipulate. And *Ivan* was following the same path: at all times each actor had an object to handle and show "as if it were an added artificial limb." Everything was displayed ...]

Porro mentions the circumstances that had brought them together: a 1973 show that investigated the relationship between peasants and priests within the Mayan culture, entitled "Il mondo poggia sul dorso di un grande caimano" ("The World Rests on the Back of a Giant Caiman"). The most remarkable part of Porro's recollection of his collaboration with Porta, however, is the focus on objects as the catalysts for the action on stage, a focus that places both squarely within the most productive avant-garde tradition of the twentieth century.

In fact, if we turn to Alfred Jarry and his plays, we will notice how they also share this same trait, as père Ubu is constantly surrounded by a variety of strange (as well as rather ordinary) objects that play a crucial role in defining him and in advancing the plot. For instance, we could mention the two "sticks" that père Ubu always carries around: the "baton à physique," which he keeps under his arm, in a rather menacing way, a symbol for nature, the sciences, and the institutions he commands in his disarticulate and anarchic folly; and the "croc à phynances," the hook with which he captures the noblemen and stuffs them through the trapdoor that leads to his dungeons, thus a symbol of the accumulation of wealth, his only discernible political program. Above all, we shouldn't forget his "pompe à merdre," with which he constantly threatens to hollow out his adversaries, turning them into yet another set of objects he can either incorporate or reject.[88]

An additional connection between Jarry and Porta can be found in the fable-like structure of their plays, which rework a number of elements and conventions taken from popular entertainment and storytelling. In fact, in the note that accompanies the Einaudi edition of the play, Porta speaks of a "theatrical structure [that] remains very close to the genre of 'mystery play.'" The reference is to those forms of popular theatre that were common throughout Europe in the Middle Ages and usually involved characters and situations taken from the scriptures but anachronistically set in the atemporal, eternal present of collective consciousness. In fact, the insistence on the popular, demotic, spontaneous forms of theatre and literature is an element that brings together most of the plays created by the Neoavanguardia, especially in an early phase (although it has significant staying power in the works by Pagliarani and Giuliani, who will resort to it throughout their career).

The adventures of Ubu are equally indebted to this same tradition, as they are clearly inspired by the puppet theatre, especially the kind that displays a childish, often scatological sense of humour. Not only do the mechanics of these performances reproduce very closely those of the puppet theatre, but also the characters Porta and Jarry create and present on stage are often frail and ethereal, as if they were marionettes whose substance was exclusively linguistic and whose strings were pulled only by an unwavering determination to expose how painfully close their existence as abstract, approximate, fictional human beings is to the social reality we all inhabit in our daily lives. In describing Ubu, Giuliani writes about a creature that can't be bothered to grow a soul but rather asserts himself as a "mechanism of allusion."[89] I think this description fits most of Porta's dramatis personae: they are all mere linguistic dummies whose purpose is to circulate words, expressions, sudden illuminations that happen upon them in a chaotic and frenetic manner. These multiple mechanisms of allusion function in many respects as the allegorical engine that moves forward the experimentation with the linguistic conventions of literature and theatre. And here I use the term "allegory" with the meaning attributed to it by Benjamin.[90]

In a particularly insightful article entitled "Poetry and the Abject: The Case of the Italian New Avant-Garde," John Picchione connects Benjamin's idea of allegory with the concept of "abject,"[91] contributing another piece of evidence to the connection we have been sketching, in more than one place in this monograph, between Alfred Jarry and the Italian Neoavanguardia. In his essay, Picchione writes that

> the abject can be traced as a thematic strategy and as a formal practice. The thematic components are displayed by the presence of atrocities, dehumanized images of existence, decay, acts of defecation and urination as emblems of our civilization. The formal components are evinced by the adoption of linguistic waste through the accumulation of heterogeneous materials collected both from oral and written messages ... The montage of the materials is carried out through the construction of syntactic dismemberments and other linguistic lacerations. Indeed, the linguistic disorder is achieved not only on a syntagmatic level, but also within words, often shredded into phonemes or assaulted by violent processes of mutilation.[92]

We can clearly hear a convergence between Picchione's observations and Agosti's approach to Porta's verses, even though, at this point in the essay, Picchione is still referring to the poetry of the Neoavanguardia in general. The same elements mentioned by Agosti and Picchione are also a crucial part of Jarry's theatre, so much so that Linda Klieger Stillman, in her monograph on the French author, highlights several times what she calls the triad "merdre, phynance, and physique."[93] The first and the last elements of this triad are congruent with the interest the neo-avant-garde displayed in all the waste and refuse of literature and poetry. This is true in at least two different ways: on the one hand, literature has traditionally focused on a very small portion of the human body and, through a process of abstraction and stylization that has lasted centuries, has striven to render these few chosen parts "worthy" of being included in poetry (think, for instance, of Laura's beautiful hair and Beatrice's eyes); all other manifestations of our bodies and our physical impulses have been systematically excluded (at times positively removed) from the realm of admissible subject matter. Thus, the revolutionary, astounding, and long-lasting effects of the "merdre" and the "physique" Jarry exhibits throughout his plays (and the neo-avant-garde's fascination with them).

On the other hand, a whole set of cultural products and by-products that were traditionally deemed unfit for verse are now deliberately included, juxtaposed with more traditional themes, words, and objects, used as a way of correcting the distortions imposed by our own bias and ideology and as an opportunity to criticize entrenched powers and established privileges in those places where it is hardest to mount a defence, where the ridicule and the derisive, sarcastic laughter of the audience has its highest potential for disruption, for bringing about radical reform and even, perhaps, revolution. And this consideration leads us to the third, central element: the role of the economy and, given its influence on society and culture, the importance of politics and engagement. While Jarry opted for a radical form of anarchist criticism, choosing to oppose directly and violently the institutions of bourgeois society, the Neoavanguardia would sometimes take a more nuanced stance. In many cases, however, and Porta is certainly one of them, Jarry provided a clear model that could be implemented, after the necessary adjustments, to the Italian circumstances of the 1960s and early 1970s.

As for the connections with Benjamin's idea of allegory, it is easy to see how the syntactic violence often noted in both Porta and Jarry can be construed as the translation into the practice of writing of that mechanism of allusion we have already mentioned several times. Going back to Picchione's essay we hear that

> The text becomes an artificial construct that simulates alienation and thus refuses to provide the reader with the false impression that the world possesses an harmonious wholeness and order. Indeed, in this respect, the neo-avant-garde is much in tune with Benjamin's concept of allegory. As opposed to the symbol ... allegory promotes the transient, the dismembered, the discontinuous accumulation of objects and events ... Allegory and the abject are two faces of the same coin.[94]

The fragments and events hoarded through this allegorical mechanism constitute the diet that nourishes Porta's verse, at the same time sustaining it and further intensifying its hunger. Here, too, the parallel with Jarry's *Ubu* seems particularly pertinent, as one has only to think of the second scene of Act One, in which the protagonist cannot wait for his guests and fellow conspirators to arrive, and begins to consume the feast *mère* Ubu has laid out;[95] later, after the success of the coup, Ubu would proceed with insatiable lust to seize all the wealth of Poland. More importantly, it is not uncommon for Ubu's appetite to turn violent, becoming a direct attack on the human body, a force that disarticulates it, displaying, at times, cannibalistic intentions. In fact, during Ubu's reign, the noblemen are stripped of their titles and possessions, and then unceremoniously "de-brained";[96] the peasants are forced to pay taxes or to suffer "torture, twisting of the neck, and decapitation";[97] even mère Ubu is not safe from this violence, as père Ubu threatens to "sharpen [his] teeth on [her] shanks."[98]

The relationship between the Ubu spouses, and thus the interaction between men and women, allows us to draw one last parallel with Porta's theatre, which constantly explores this theme. In particular, we could look at *La scelta della voce*, a play already mentioned in passing. The original title for this piece, the one under which it was first staged at the Out/Off theatre in Milan between 16 and 18 January 1979, was "Elogio del cannibalismo" ("In Praise of Cannibalism"). Since it was inspired by Shakespeare's *Hamlet*, this piece continues Porta's practice of poetic dialogue, in which the meaning of the various lines and even the personalities of the characters are in constant flux; the action is entirely concentrated in the words pronounced by the actors; the conversation progresses in an oblique, slanted manner, exploiting the phonetic surface of language as well as the deep, psychological associations elicited by certain words or images. The very beginning of the text, the first stanza, contains a set of instructions that, in a way, functions as (contradictory) stage directions:

Questa lettura deve avvenire tutta al buio,
le parole le ripeto tutte a mente, segno
la carta con l'indice e ripeto quello che ho sentito
riproduco a braccio quello che ho capito, perché
amare significa questo: mutare
la repulsione dell'amata, la repulsione dell'amato
mutare una bocca laida in un cespuglio fiorito[99]

[This reading must take place in the dark,
I repeat the words from memory, mark
the page with the index and repeat what I heard
reproduce off-hand what I understood, because
to love means this: to change
the repulsion of the loved one, man, woman
mutate a filthy mouth into a flowering bush]

The choice of darkness[100] as the place where these words are to be ideally spoken is the first of the theatrical indications contained in this poem/*pièce*, which often attracts attention to the oral and auditory dimensions of the medium of communication it aspires to engage. Love and the relationship between man and woman are also prominently displayed from the very beginning, and are presented as anchored in language. As we observed before, Porta's characters are often mere linguistic marionettes, and their modes of interaction, even (or perhaps especially) when they are of an erotic nature, are squarely based within words, which are not meant to function as substitutes for objects taken from the real world but are actually understood as instruments of change, marks of instability, and means through which reality can be transformed. This instability and unreliability of language is reflected in the second stanza, which contradicts the first, acting as its opposite, its mirror image:

Questa lettura può avvenire tutta alla luce
seguendo la carta con l'indice, seguendo
la penna che scrive per dire quello che non ho
capito, per riferire quello che non ho visto perché
amare significa questo: seguire il programma
naturale lanciarsi senza salvezza nel vuoto.[101]

[This reading may take place in the light
following on the page with the index, following
the pen writing to say that which I did not
understand, to describe what I did not see because
to love means this: to follow the natural sequence
to throw oneself without hope into the void.]

The categorical instructions of the first stanza ("this reading must take place in the dark") are replaced by a more flexible suggestion ("this reading may take place in the light"): when both opposites are presented as legitimate choices, the power of language to distinguish one object from another and that of the subject to choose among the different options are implicitly questioned. The act of "repeat[ing] words from memory" is thus related, through the parallelism between the two stanzas, to "following the pen writing," thus negating the distance separating oral cultures, which preserve their identity and values through memory, from literate cultures, which can indulge in a form of oblivion supported by writing. Similarly, love is both a force that urges one to radically transform reality and, conversely, an impulse to accept the world as it is, "follow[ing] the natural sequence."

These contradictions find their resolution in the human body, or, more precisely, in the "writing" of the human body, as it is clearly stated in section 4:

Quello che sembra opporsi non si oppone e insieme
la contraddizione resiste, è il segnale, la scrittura
scrivendosi vuole cancellarsi, la parola
vuole negarsi dicendo …
il corpo lo dimostra, la nostra storia scritta nel corpo
con tutte le dita recise cadute
in grembo alla madre
la merda che si mischia allo sperma.[102]

[What appears to oppose itself does not and together
the contradiction resists, it is the sign, the writing
writing itself wants to erase itself, the word
wants to negate itself by saying …
the body shows it, our story written in the body
with all the severed fingers fallen
into the mother's lap
shit mixing with sperm.]

This body made of words, the body of the characters on stage and of the voices that populate Porta's verses, is the place where opposites can be reconciled, the place where the writing of the pen and the reading through the eye and voice can meet. The violence of "severed fingers" and the abject of "shit mixing with sperm" are also present, reinforcing the rebellious, allegorical value of these linguistic bodies. It is from this same perspective that we should understand the startling cannibalistic acts and rituals described by Porta in section 8:

per poter continuare ti offro
gli occhi in un piatto a guardarti
servite sopra un vassoio e a farcire
le mammelle recise/a fette i prosciutti delle cosce
lambisco e nascondo in una madia per servire
poi appena sfornato col pane fragrante
me lo denudo senza vergogna per chiederti
cucita ti sei come le labbra rimango
scorticato senza entrare nel sogno quando esco[103]

[so as to continue I offer
eyes on a plate to look at you
served in a tray and stuffed
severed tits/hams of thighs in slices
I lap up and hide in a kneading trough to serve
with the fragrant freshly baked bread
I bear it without shame to ask you
you've sewn yourself like the lips I remain
flayed without entering into the dream when I leave]

The darkness invoked by Porta at the beginning of *La scelta della voce* echoes the darkness of Jarry's dungeons, where all the noblemen and the riches of Poland disappear; or the deep darkness of Ubu's belly, the "gidouille," where endless quantities of meats and victuals routinely disappear. The cannibalism advocated by Porta is a metaphoric and linguistic one, and thus it is completely congruent with Jarry's, as it is directed not only at the bodies of the characters on stage, but also at their sentences, their syntax, and the traditional literary materials that they recycle.[104]

The conclusion of *La scelta della voce* includes one last element we have highlighted repeatedly in the plays of both Porta and Jarry: the fabulistic element. Here is the beginning of the last stanza, subtitled "(Finale)":

È ritornata la calma
possiamo riposare per una notte
e un giorno e un amore per una notte e
un giorno prima di ritornare nel bosco o
dentro la Città Labirinto
dal principio ti racconto una storia
forse una fiaba per cullarti fino al momento del distacco
ancora adagiandoti sulle mie ginocchia di donna.[105]

[Once again it's all quiet
we can rest for one night
and one day and one love for one night and
one day before going back to the woods or
inside the City Labyrinth
from the beginning I'll tell you a story
perhaps a fable to lull you until it's time to leave
still laying you down on my womanly knees.]

The very word "fable" is directly included in this verse, as well as some of the typical locations of its plots (the woods, the city-labyrinth). Some of the formulaic expressions of this kind of story telling ("per una notte e un giorno") are also used. The circumstances surrounding the fruition of this genre of popular entertainment are explicitly mentioned: the fable is intended to lull the audience to sleep while they are lying down on the speaker's knees. Finally, we see how that ambiguity, that coexistence of opposites, that we have observed at the very beginning of this piece is here restated: the voice of the poet, which has throughout the duration of the text identified ambiguously with both female and male characters, finally qualifies itself explicitly as female, referencing its "womanly knees." The transformation that had been identified at the start as the essence of love, at least when it came to poetry, has finally been achieved.

Before closing this section dedicated to Porta, we need to underscore the importance of *La scelta della voce*, as this text marks a shift in the relationship between verse and stage. The need for direct contact with the audience of poetry was now a clear necessity, especially in light of the failure of the other strategies that had been attempted through the public meetings of Gruppo 63 and the experience of *Quindici*. A direct intervention of intellectuals into Italian society and politics had also been shown to be problematic and riddled with pitfalls, especially if we remember how the bloody wave of domestic terrorism had pushed many to retreat to their own personal lives; in fact, poetry in general had become a rather suspicious endeavour. *La scelta della voce* is an important witness to all these changes and can function as the perfect preamble to one of the most emblematic and yet deeply mysterious and opaque events of those years, the Festival Internazionale dei Poeti at Castelporziano. There, the deep, insatiable hunger of Porta's verses and their urgent desire to meet their audience through an oral, instantaneous, and slightly antagonistic form of communication would finally be realized; although the results would probably be nothing like what Porta or any other Neoavanguardista had imagined or hoped.

3.7 The "Battle of Castelporziano"

The practice of reading poems aloud, in front of an audience, is currently alive and well in Italy. A number of initiatives promote it, and it has been reframed, from the theoretical perspective, by the discussions initiated in the mid-1980s by Gruppo 93 on the issues of "oralità" and "oratura."[106]

There was, however, one dramatic incident that shows how relevant and poignant (but also rife with risks as well as the potential for disruption) were the efforts made by some poets to include the oral aspect of language in their work, thus inviting the participation of the audience in the creation of a poetic "event," that mythic and mystic ritual we have often referred to in the preceding pages. We are speaking, of course, of the Festival Internazionale dei Poeti, held from 28 to 30 June 1979 at Castelporziano, near Ostia, a few miles outside Rome. It was, in many ways, the culmination and undoing of the theories, attempts, and discussions that had been animating the Italian cultural scene for the previous two decades. It can be considered as one last, valiant attempt to bring together, perhaps a bit naively and without the necessary preparatory work, the poets and their audience.

Some of the most lucid members of the neo-avant-garde had foreseen the risks implicit in such an endeavour. Pagliarani, who was scheduled to read but, at least judging from the transcripts of the festival that have been passed down to us,[107] did not recite his poetry, had written an almost prophetic warning:

> Mi convinco sempre di più che il teatro, quando funziona, presuppone, e realizza, l'intervento del pubblico come elemento costitutivo dello spettacolo. I generi teatrali, da questo punto di vista, saranno due: quello

> in cui il pubblico è il protagonista dello spettacolo, e quello in cui è l'antagonista. Nel primo caso si tratterà di allestire una macchina di capacità prevalentemente liberatorie, nel secondo caso di capacità prevalentemente provocatorie; nel primo caso il pedale ideologico risulterà sommesso, nel secondo esagitato; l'uno coinvolgerà prevalentemente la ragione (ma mai solo quella) l'altro prevalentemente i sensi (ma mai solo quelli).[108]

> [I am becoming more and more convinced that theatre, when it works, presupposes (and accomplishes) the intervention of the audience as a constitutive element of the spectacle. Theatrical genres, from this point of view, will be only two: one in which the audience is the protagonist of the spectacle, and another in which it is the antagonist. In the first case, it will be a matter of devising a machine with mainly liberating capabilities; in the second case, they will have to be mainly provocative; in the first case the ideological tone will be subdued; in the second it will be exaggerated; the former will mainly address reason (but never exclusively that), the latter mainly the senses (but never exclusively those).]

It is not difficult to decide to which of these two macro-genres of spectacle the Festival di Castelporziano belonged: the audience was clearly an antagonist of the poets, who were perceived as deliberately provocative; the "ideological tone" was clearly exaggerated; and the target of the entire experience was certainly the senses. In addition, just a few days before the festival, at the beginning of June, Pagliarani had written the following observations as part of a review for *Paese Sera* of a recital of Ripellino's poems:

> Intanto, l'attuale voga nel declamare poesie in pubblico dovrebbe come minimo tenere conto che ci sono poesie adatte ad essere semplicemente lette in solitudine e in silenzio, con gli occhi, altre che ambiscono invece al grido in piazza, e altre ancora che preferiscono essere sussurrate fra pochi affini in uno spazio esiguo ... Infine, ho da molto tempo la convinzione che tranne pochissime note eccezioni (Gassman, Carmelo Bene) gli attori italiani non sappiano recitare versi nè classici nè contemporanei ...[109]

> [Meanwhile, the current fad of declaiming poems in public should at least be mindful that there are poems that lend themselves to be simply read in solitude and in silence, with one's eyes, others that require the loud cries of the piazza, and others yet that prefer to be whispered among a few associates within an intimate space ... Finally, I have been convinced for a while now that, save for a few known exceptions (Gassman, Carmelo

Bene), Italian actors don't know how to declaim poems, neither the classics nor the contemporaries ...]

In the remainder of the review, Pagliarani argued that Ripellino's verses belonged to the third and final category and were therefore not suitable for onstage declamation (unless drastically modified by the director, the actors, or whoever was in charge of planning the performance).[110] Naturally, this wasn't true in his case: his poems were explicitly made to be performed in front of an audience; and yet the crowd that had gathered at that beach outside of Ostia was no ordinary audience. Before we go any further, however, I think it is best to recall the events, as far as they can be reconstructed from the various available sources.

At the relatively tranquil and isolated beach of Castelporziano, Simone Carella, Franco Cordelli, and Ulisse Benedetti (the artists and cultural activists responsible for the Roman *cantina* Beat 72), with 35 million liras provided by Renato Nicolini (the *assessore alla cultura* of the Roman municipal government), decided to erect a large stage, right on the sand, the sea water gently lapping against the metal poles that supported it. As intended by the organizers, this precarious platform, which would partially collapse before the end of the festival, was to host some of the most influential and best-known poets from Italy, Europe, and the United States. Listed among the participants were Allen Ginsberg, William Burroughs, Amiri Baraka, Lawrence Ferlinghetti, Gregory Corso, Peter Orlowski, Anne Waldman, Ted Berrigan, Diane Di Prima, Ted Joans, Evgeni Evtuscenco, Jacqueline Risset, Osvaldo Soriano, Elio Pagliarani, Alfredo Giuliani, Antonio Porta, Corrado Costa, Amelia Rosselli, Dacia Maraini, Valentino Zeichen, Dario Bellezza, and many, many others.

However, the audience that gathered on the beach, spending there the entire three days and two nights of the festival, camping underneath the stage boards, had different plans and, from the very beginning, assumed an active role, demanding to speak at the microphone and constantly interrupting the reading of poems. The evenings took a surreal turn as a result of the intervention of a few characters who seemed more suited to a Harlequin farce than to reality (and the national press picked up on it, portraying them as living symbols of everything that was wrong with these new artistic expressions and the young generation that supported them). [111]

Perhaps the most famous of them all was the "Ragazza cioè," who kept stealing the microphone and refused to get off the stage, standing on its edge, sulking, and questioning, in a rather confused manner, the verses declaimed by the various poets. Many years after the actual events, Franco Cordelli published a strange and beautiful diary of those days, which included his musings on the festival, its participants, and the general cultural climate of the time. Here is one of his recollections of "Ragazza cioè":

> È a questo punto che una ragazzina in costume da bagno, infreddolita e tremante, forse non solo per il freddo, si è impossessata del microfono: "Cioè ... mi chiedo, cioè, se qui ci sia della comunicazione ... Ma perché non si può dicere ... Vorrei sapere a chi dite la morte se parlate di morte ... Vorrei sapere perché parlate di morte." Forse drogata forse schizoide, il suo lungo monologo è passato dai cioè ad un dialetto molto stretto incomprensibile, e anziché gelare la platea ha acceso le ultime polveri. Un ragazzo le ha strappato e lei glielo ha ripreso subito dopo il microfono di mano, e ridendo ha detto che nessuno parlava di morte, che a loro della morte non gliene fregava niente. Ma la ragazzina napoletana era destinata a rimanere – presenza funebre ed emblematica di una dissociazione tra i giovani, le istituzioni e il linguaggio leitmotiv della serata. Chiunque volesse parlare doveva con dolcezza contenderle il microfono, mentre lei continuava, sonnambula, a ripetere: cioè, devo dire una cosa. È stata la vittima sacrificale di un pubblico inebriato dalla presenza di lei nello spettacolo, ma privo, anche, di una minima pietà verso quella ragazzina sperduta e triste ...[112]
>
> [It is at this point that a young woman who was wearing a swimsuit, shaking because of the cold, but perhaps also for different reasons, took hold of the microphone: "Like ... I wonder, like, if there is any communication here ... Why can't you say ... I would like to know with whom you speak of death when you say death ... I would like to know why you speak of death." Perhaps she was on drugs, or a schizoid, her long monologue went from the "likes" to a thick dialect, which was difficult to understand, and instead of putting off the audience, it lit up their enthusiasm. A young man took the microphone from her, although she took it right back, and laughing, he said that nobody was talking about death, they didn't want anything to do with death. But the young Neapolitan lady was destined to remain right there – a funereal and emblematic presence of a dissociation between youth, institutions, and language, the leitmotiv of that evening. Anyone who wanted to speak had to delicately dispute with her the possession of the microphone, while she continued, as if sleepwalking, to repeat: "like, I have something to say." She was the sacrificial victim of an audience that was drunk with her presence in the spectacle, and yet was incapable of any kind of mercy for that young lady, so lost and sad ...]

Later on, someone wrestled the microphone away from Victor Cavallo (who, with Simone Carella, was trying to perform the duties of an emcee), and started complaining about the price of the sandwiches and beers that were being sold. He suggested that they take up a collection, buy some produce, and cook up a minestrone; sure enough, the following night the vegetable soup made its triumphal debut on the festival's stage (and the papers didn't miss the opportunity to dub it a "minestrone di poesia"). Half-way through that evening, a distraught Simone Carella snapped,

> Non vorremmo dire che il minestrone batte la poesia 1–0 perché non è il caso. Comunque le persone che stanno sulla spiaggia che vogliono sentire i poeti che erano stati invitati sono pregate di farsi sentire anche loro, di far sentire la loro voce, e di dire che c'è qualcuno che vuole sentire i poeti. Non è venuto qui soltanto per mangiare il minestrone, anche il minestrone è poesia, ma una cosa non impedisce l'altra; l'ho mangiato, l'ho mangiato, l'ho mangiato il minestrone![113]

> [I wouldn't want to say that the minestrone beat poetry 1–0, for it is really not the case. Anyway, I would ask the people who are on the beach and want to hear the poets that have been invited to make their voice heard, to say that there is someone who wants to listen to the poets. That they didn't come all the way here just to eat the minestrone, although it's true, even the minestrone is poetry, but one thing doesn't exclude the other; yes, I've eaten the minestrone, I've eaten it, I've eaten it!]

The theme of food, eating, and the communal consumption of a ritual meal is not accidental, and, in spite of the ridiculous form it assumed in the case of the minestrone, should not be taken lightly: it runs deep into that performance of the *corpo-voce* we have been describing as crucial to the poetry of the *Novecento*. On this point, Gasparini writes:

> A Castelporziano lo sbranamento rituale del corpo poetico avviene realmente in uno scatenamento dionisiaco incontrollabile, per mezzo del quale i cosiddetti spettatori furono in grado di innescare, a partire da una proposta vuota e impoverita di poesia letta, il meccanismo dinamico e incendiario della poesia come corpo-voce.[114]

> [In Castelporziano the ritual devouring of the poetic body happens for real in a Dionysian, uncontrollable excess, through which the so-called spectators were able to enact, using as a starting point the empty and

> impoverished offering of poetry read out loud, the dynamic and incendiary mechanism of poetry as a body-voice.]

Gasparini makes a clear reference to the Maenads and their ritualistic, frenzied worship of Dionysus. Clearly, the myth of Orpheus and his gruesome death are on everyone's mind. The *corpo-voce* contained in the verses pronounced by the poets, exposed to the emptiness of the stage, performed in the vacuous ritual of the mechanical reading, inserted in the hostile, antagonistic climate of the "popular fair," was systematically, if figuratively, dismembered and consumed by the audience. The violent modality in which this ritual was carried out is due to the organizers' complete lack of preparation and understanding of the theatrical machine that they were building: they had predisposed an altar and lined up an impressive number of sacrificial victims, but when it came to performing the ritual, they did not know how to proceed; thus, the crowd had to take over. What is really quite remarkable is the degree of lucid awareness displayed by some of the occasional participants in the event. See, for instance, this uninvited speaker, identified as "Bossio figlio":

> Fate bene a spernacchiare i poeti ... Soprattutto quelli sconosciuti. Fate molto bene. Anzi. Siccome chiedevate pane, chiedete pane e circensi cioè sbranateli proprio, mangiateveli perché i poeti, soprattutto quelli come mio padre sono degli stronzi, hanno passato la vita a scrivere poesie, invece, invece potevano fare politica, fare intrallazzi, giostrare salami col culo e portare qualche soldo in modo che, così, se li sbranavate, se sbranate mio padre, me li lascia questi soldi; invece così mi lascia più bianco di quello che sono. Quindi sbranateli, mangiateli questi stronzi. Mio padre ha fatto il pecoraio fino a 16 anni poi si è preso la laura per che fare? Per fare il poeta. Bello stronzo, sbranatelo, sbranateci, sbranatelo.[115]

> [You are right, you should mock the poets ... Especially those who are little known. You are right in doing so. Actually. Since you were asking for bread, ask now for bread and circuses, that is, devour them, eat them because the poets, especially those like my father, they are all assholes, they spent their lives writing poems, instead, instead they could have gotten involved with politics, gotten into shady businesses, taken salamis up their asses and brought home a little money so that, this way, if you devoured them, if you devour my father, he would leave me that money; instead, this way, he leaves me poorer than I already am. So devour them,

eat them, the assholes. My father has been a shepherd since he was 16, then he got a degree to do what? To be a poet. What an asshole, devour him, devour us, devour him.]

In his *romanzo* Franco Cordelli was also struck by these words, and offered an interpretation of the events similar to the one suggested by Gasparini. He wrote of a "popolo guerriero":

> Erano quasi tutti nudi e molti parlavano di quel piccolo "colpo di stato" fatto da quella che Franco Cordelli ha definito l'ala estremistica della manifestazione ... Il fenomeno più importante del festival è già il suo pubblico, questo evanescente pubblico che scrive e non legge, che arriva con lo zaino in spalla oppure, indifferentemente, in taxi e vuole tutto subito: vuole la poesia, vuole il poeta, vuole divorare il suo corpo di parole, vuole bruciare l'esperienza immediata. Per questo ha bisogno soprattutto di cultura orale. Saranno cinquecento e domani, forse, cinquemila. I poeti che leggeranno tra poco non potranno far altro che offrirsi indefinitamente a questo cannibalismo. La notte non dipende da loro o dai loro testi, ma da quello strano, misterioso e informe ex "popolo guerriero" che si sta radunando, silenzioso e disfatto dal caldo intorno al palco ...[116]

> [They were all naked, and many spoke of the small "coup d'état" carried out by those whom Franco Cordelli called the extremist wing of the event ... The most notable phenomenon of the festival was its audience, they write but don't read, they arrive, indifferently, carrying a backpack or dropped off by a taxi, and they want everything, right away: they want poetry, the poets, they want to devour their body of words, they want to burn the immediate experience. For this reason, they need oral culture above everything else. They must be five hundred and tomorrow they will probably be five thousand. The poets will read in a bit and the only thing they will be able to do is offer themselves to this undifferentiated cannibalism. The evening is not up to them or their texts, but rather it is up to this strange, mysterious, and shapeless people of "ex-warriors" that is gathering around the stage, silently, tired out by the heat ...]

It is worth noting that often, in this peculiar and fascinating recounting of the events that led to the Festival Internazionale dei Poeti, Cordelli speaks of himself in the third person, becoming just another one of the characters in the story he is retelling, a fiction-memoir, half-way between the chronicle and the novel of ideas. In this passage, he summarizes many of the common complaints elevated against the younger generation of artists and spectators: they write but don't read; they pretend to be poor and bohemian, but they are really well off and bourgeois; they have no patience, and so on. When describing their relationship with the poets performing on stage, however, he too speaks of "devouring the body of words" and of "cannibalism."

A better interpretation of the entire event, one that can help explain the spirit with which it was organized, and the reaction it received from the audience, is found in this passage from *Proprietà Perduta*, the last one we will quote:

> Strano a dirsi, incontrò Renato Nicolini con la sua ragazza e il figlio di lei, in viale Tiziano, ad una fermata del tram. Come un forsennato, Nicolini cominciò a lamentarsi: "Se i poeti americani piacciono, è perché accettano di parlare alla folla" (e si sentì subito, chissà perché, che Nicolini diceva "folla" e non "popolo" o "classe" o "gente," come se stesse sottolineando con la matita una riga di Benjamin). "... non cominciò Baudelaire, assassinando la poesia perché vivesse il poeta? Per questo cantano e suonano" diceva ancora Nicolini, cercando di placare la furia del "figlio di lei" stufo di aspettare il tram "non per una festa o per un rito consolatorio, ma per parlare a chi conosce solo quel linguaggio. Perché preoccuparsi di controllare la società dello spettacolo, piuttosto che svilupparla? Per paura di riconoscere la crisi, propria o del proprio ruolo? O per paura delle energie anche distruttive che il movimento reale libera? Ammetto che io stesso non avevo capito, l'anno scorso, che il disordine dell'estate era una società in movimento ... Capisci? Ti tocca capirne le leggi senza pregiudizi, bisogna piantare i gomiti sul tavolo! ..." Inutile aggiungere, credo, che tutto finì con l'arrivo del tram. Ma Nicolini, mentre si chiudevano le porte, affacciandosi come un pazzo, fece in tempo ad aggiungere: "E forse non è così che si studia oggi! Niente più tavoli, niente gomiti rinforzati delle toppe materne, niente matite!" [117]
>
> [Oddly enough, he met Renato Nicolini with his girlfriend and her son on Viale Tiziano, at a tram stop. Like a madman, Nicolini started complaining: "If the American poets are more popular it is because they are comfortable speaking to the crowd" (and you could hear right away, who knows why, that he had said "crowd" and not "people" or "class" or "masses," as if he was underlining with his pencil a line from Benjamin). "... didn't Baudelaire start by assassinating poetry so that the poet may survive? That is why they sing and play," Nicolini kept saying, trying to control the restlessness of "her son," who was tired of waiting for the tram; "it is

not a way of turning it into a fair or a consoling ritual, but an attempt to speak to those who only know that language. Why bother with controlling the society of the spectacle when you can improve on it? Because we are scared of facing the crisis, our own, or that of our role? Or because we are scared of the energy, perhaps destructive, that the movement would free? I'll admit that I hadn't understood it either, last year, that the disorders of the summer were due to a society on the move ... get it? You must understand its laws without prejudices, we must plant our elbows on the table! ..." Needless to say, everything ended with the arrival of the tram. But Nicolini, as the doors were closing, sticking his head out of the window, like a madman, had enough time to add: "Isn't that how they study these days! No more tables, no more elbows protected by maternal patches, no more pencils!"]

It is not surprising, given the general tone of the book, and the events it relates, that the conversation soon took a rather obscure and sibylline direction. Before mentioning elbows and pencils, however, Nicolini seemed to be on to something: why not exploit the society of the spectacle to bring poetry back to the centre of the cultural debate? It is certainly a legitimate question. After all, Gruppo 63 had done just that. Yet those sixteen years that had gone by had not left the world untouched; in fact, many things had changed since the Incontro di Palermo at the hotel Zagarella.

The fact is that the core of the Neoavanguardia was composed of intellectuals who taught in universities, worked in prestigious publishing houses, and wrote for RAI or a number of well-known national newspapers; and who, when they read their verses, and debated their merits, were doing so behind closed doors, among themselves, away from the general public. Their audience, whenever they addressed it, comprised either specialists, *addetti ai lavori*, or, alternatively, the nondescript "masses." But in this last case, they would entrust their writings to professional actors and directors, who would use them as the starting point for a proper theatrical performance, that is to say, a structured consumption of the *corpo-voce* they embodied. At Castelporziano, instead, a different kind of public gathered, a "crowd," as Nicolini put it, ready to engage and disrupt, unwilling to play that passive role in the communicative exchange that had been reserved for them by the poets and organizers.

The Festival Internazionale dei Poeti marked the end of an era and, at the same time, told a cautionary tale, warning of what can happen when poetry is not effectively translated into the linguistic code of the theatre but is simply exhibited on stage; when the "corpo-voce" of the verses is exposed without being properly performed, given to an audience to be consumed without the proper arrangements.

And this is, I believe, the reason why, in spite of being listed on the bill, Elio Pagliarani, who knew theatre and could read an audience, decided not to declaim his verses.

4 An Introduction to Pagliarani's Theatre

Elio Pagliarani's poetry strives to go beyond the written page – that is, it strives to be performed. Throughout his career, Pagliarani established an explicit, symbiotic relationship between poetry and theatre, so much so that, one could say, his poetic genius speaks with a dramatic accent. Thus, in order to understand his poetry, it is also necessary to discuss his plays. As Alessandra Briganti wrote,

> Il punto di forza di questa poesia è rappresentato dalla sua intrinseca natura spettacolare che allude, a sua volta, a due fondamentali principi ispiratori dell'avanguardia, costituiti, per un verso, dalla manipolazione dei generi tradizionali e, per un altro, dall'intersezione dei diversi linguaggi artistici. La recita determina una conversione, verso esiti "drammatici" e/o narrativi, della perdurante nostalgia lirica, mentre l'identificazione del gesto col linguaggio (o viceversa) apre la strada ad una esecuzione che è recita, canto, ballo, dinamismo in ogni modo. Il gesto, che rappresenta una componente essenziale dell'esecuzione di Pagliarani, almeno quanto la modulazione della voce, denuncia un rapporto, una filiazione o una matrice culturale che sembra essere sfuggita finora all'attenzione dei lettori.[1]
>
> [The strong point of this poetry is its intrinsic spectacular nature, which alludes, in turn, to two fundamental inspiring principles of the avant-garde: on the one hand, the manipulation of traditional genres and, on the other, the contamination of different artistic languages. The recitation determines the conversion of the lingering lyric nostalgia into "dramatic" and/or narrative forms, while the identification of gesture with language (and vice versa) opens the door to a performance that is declamation, song, dance, and multifaceted dynamism. The gesture, which represents an essential component in Pagliarani's performance,

> together with the modulation of the voice reveal a relationship, a genesis, a cultural framework that seem to have escaped, so far, the attention of readers.]

Recent archival discoveries[2] have shown how this desire to trespass into different artistic fields was an integral part of Pagliarani's creative process and not just an external, occasional circumstance. Speaking of *La ragazza Carla*, Pagliarani recounted on more than one occasion how he was unsure what shape it would have taken, having cast it first as a treatment for a movie and only later as the long poem we know: "Having decided to make it into a poem, inevitably, I developed the rhythm. Inevitably the plot of this book is the rhythm of a *Mitteleuropean* city right after the end of World War II."[3]

If *Carla*'s relationship with cinema has always been a known fact for the most astute critics,[4] the exchanges with the theatre have remained, for the most part, unexplored.[5] However, Pagliarani's activities as a theatre critic for *Paese Sera*, where he worked for almost two decades, were, of course, well known. In his memoir, *Promemoria a Liarosa* ("Memo for Liarosa"), he writes,

> Ho avuto l'avventura di svolgere il mio lavoro come critico teatrale in un periodo, dalla fine degli anni Settanta ai primi degli anni Ottanta, particolarmente ricco e fertile per il teatro d'avanguardia in Italia e in tutto il mondo occidentale, direi. Le prime fondamentali esperienze in questo senso furono due, quella di Carmelo Bene, di cui ho già dato un cenno molto superficiale ma significativo, spero, e quella grandemente massiccia in tutta Europa del Living Theatre ... Il gesto in primo piano divenne poi sul loro esempio un orientamento fondamentale e vincente in tutta l'avanguardia, europea e non, americana e non, basti pensare al *Principe Costante* di Grotowski, agli spettacoli di Eugenio Barba e alla spinta che ne trassero registi già formati.[6]

> [I had the good fortune of carrying out my work as a theatre critic at a time, between the end of the 1970s and the beginning of the 1980s, particularly favourable and fertile for the avant-garde theatre in Italy, as well as in the whole Western world, I think. The first two crucial experiences in this direction were those with Carmelo Bene, which I already discussed briefly but also, hopefully, in a meaningful way, and the immensely influential one, for the entire European scene, of the Living Theatre ... The prominence of the gesture became, after their example, a crucial and successful direction of research for the whole avant-garde, both in and out of Europe, in and out of the United States;

just think, for instance, of Grotowski's *The Constant Prince*, or the shows by Eugenio Barba, and the way they inspired a number of already mature directors.]

In addition to his exposure to theatre as a journalist throughout his career, Pagliarani had also written a number of plays and texts explicitly meant to be performed on stage that have been, so far, systematically ignored by literary historians and critics. This lapse can be explained, in part, by the unavailability of the texts, which, until a few years ago, were mostly confined to the pages of old specialized journals or occasional (and ephemeral) publications.[7]

In approaching Pagliarani's dramatic output, the best starting point is certainly the short manifesto he prepared for the playbill to the already mentioned show at the Parioli Theatre in Rome, held on 3 June 1965, performed by the Compagnia Teatro dei Novissimi under the direction of Piero Panza and Toti Scialoja.[8] Here it is, in its entirety:

1. Il teatro, parafrasando Eliot, è il tramite ideale, il mezzo più diretto per verificare la capacità di provocazione della poesia.
2. La crisi del personaggio è crisi di linguaggio: cominciamo da qui.
3. Cominciando, abbiamo vari linguaggi al posto dei vari personaggi.
4. I personaggi si scontrano, cioè si drammatizzano, nell'azione; i linguaggi nel significato.
5. La ripetizione si oppone frontalmente, Kierkegaard, alla reminiscenza: nonché rifiutare la malinconica blandizie del rimpianto, si fa piuttosto ossessione, trauma, lapsus, corrosione. Dicono anche che la ripetizione è l'atto col quale l'uomo prende su di sé la propria colpa. (E Artaud, e la tragedia? un'altra volta.)
6. La crisi del personaggio (esaurimento dello psicologismo eccetera) postula uno straniamento oggettivo della recitazione: dal coro alla danza al balletto, coro danza balletto brechtianamente stravolti, appunto. Il teatro verifica l'interdisciplinarietà delle arti. Lapalisse.[9]

[1. Theatre, paraphrasing Eliot, is the ideal medium, the most direct means to verify poetry's capacity of provocation.
2. The crisis of the character is a crisis of language: let us begin from here.
3. As we begin, we have various languages instead of various characters.
4. The characters clash, that is, they produce drama, through actions; languages through meaning.
5. Repetition is the direct opposite (Kierkegaard) of reminiscence: and also one must reject the melancholic enticements of regret; rather one should pursue obsession, trauma, *lapsus*, corrosion. They also say that

repetition is the act through which men take upon themselves their sins. (And Artaud, and tragedy? another time.)

6. The crisis of the character (exhaustion of psychologisms, etcetera) postulates the objective estrangement of recitation: from chorus to dance and ballet, chorus dance ballet alienated in a Brechtian way. Theatre verifies the inter-disciplinarity of the arts. Lapalisse.]

This manifesto follows three fundamental axes: 1) the relationship between theatre and poetry (addressed in the first point); 2) the central role of language, which supersedes the characters (or else, the relationship between characters and language, which emerges as a crucial theoretical knot in points 2, 3, and 4); 3) the importance of the chorus in staging this theoretical knot (points 5 and 6). We will address each of these axes separately.

4.1 Theatre as "Verification"

How did Pagliarani understand the relationship between theatre and poetry, in general and in his particular artistic experience? What does he mean when he says that theatre is "the most direct means to verify poetry's capacity of provocation?" And how should we interpret the reference to Eliot? Let us begin from this last question. Given the absence of a detailed bibliographic reference, we cannot establish with certainty which text, among the many writings Eliot dedicated to the relationship between theatre and poetry,[10] Pagliarani had in mind. Both poets, however, enthusiastically took on the challenge implicit in the creation of a theatre of poetry: in order to describe everyday life and the common speech of regular people, dramatic verse needs to acquire a ductility that is not always indispensable in poetry. The necessity of conveying one's meaning without sacrificing the rhythm and the polysemy of the verse requires a rigorous discipline and a shrewd economy of expressive means. For such reasons, theatre can work as a test field, where the efficacy of one's poetic writing in engaging the society it addresses can be verified. In the essay entitled "Poetry and Drama," Eliot expresses some ideas that may have inspired Pagliarani:

> In writing other verse, I think that one is writing, so to speak, in terms of one's own voice ... The question of communication, of what the reader will get from it, is not paramount ... But in the theatre, the problem of communication presents itself immediately. You are deliberately writing verse for other voices, not for your own, and you do not know whose voices they will be. You are aiming to write lines which will have an

> immediate effect upon an unknown and unprepared audience ... And the unknown audience cannot be expected to show any indulgence towards the poet ... He must write with an audience in view which knows nothing and cares nothing, about any previous success he may have had before he ventured into the theatre.[11]

According to Eliot, then, writing for the theatre implies upholding a different sensibility toward the audience, an additional reflection on the relationship that ties the creative process to the fruition of the final product.[12] Pagliarani was very interested in this problem, so much so that he put it at the centre of his definition of avant-garde art. In a well-known essay on this very topic, he writes,

> a mio parere i movimenti di avanguardia sono caratterizzati: 1) dalla critica consapevole dei *mezzi espressivi* in situazione; 2) dalla critica, a tutti i livelli, della *funzione* dell'operatore e del rapporto operatore-consumatore (dei quali termini, artista e pubblico sono soltanto sinonimi; ed è evidente che mutare i termini significa già aver mutato quanto meno l'angolazione, il punto di vista dell'osservazione del fenomeno); 3) dalla critica della finalità dell'opera e/o funzione dell'arte.[13]

> [in my opinion, the avant-garde movements are characterized by: 1) the deliberate criticism of *expressive means* in context; 2) the criticism, at all levels, of the *function* of the operator and of the relation operator-consumer (artist and audience are mere exemplifications of these terms; naturally, choosing one term over another implies adopting a different perspective, a different point of view from which the phenomenon is observed); 3) the criticism of the work's purposes and/or art's function.]

In the rest of the essay, Pagliarani states that traits 1) and 3) are common to every artistic movement and, in a certain sense, are the elements used by criticism to distinguish between one school and another. The attention to "the *function* of the operator and of the relation operator-consumer," instead, is the distinctive characteristic of avant-garde movements. This is, in fact, the only kind of art that constantly reflects on fruition, and the relationship with the audience, making it an integral part of the creative process. According to Pagliarani, experimental poetry finds in the theatre the ideal space to start a dialogue with the audience, who is invited to actively participate in the progressive sedimentation of the text. Thus, the poet can perform that social (critical and didascalic) function that is one of his fundamental duties. If he wants to work within society and for society, he must abandon, sometimes, his linguistic laboratory in order to share the (partial, temporary) results of his research with the general audience; theatres offer an opportunity for people to gather. This is, in brief, a first definition of its role in the "verification" of poetry.

In another theoretical essay, first published in *Nuova Corrente*, and then largely modified and reprinted as the introduction to *Fiato della spettatore* ("The Spectator's Breath"),[14] we read:

> La socialità dell'arte intesa come capacità di provocazione immediata, quando esiste, la verificheremo nel teatro, o non la verificheremo. Ma sia intesa, anche questa verifica, come *operazione*. Idest sappiamo bene che a Leopardi – che di verificare la capacità di provocazione della sua poesia, non gliene importava niente; o non ebbe tempo e/o mezzi – nell'ottocento italiano non gli sta vicino proprio nessuno, quanto a capacità di durata e durata anche di provocazione; ma la socialità dell'arte fu verificata nel melodramma.[15]
>
> [Art's social dimension, understood as its capacity for immediate provocation, whenever it exists, can be verified exclusively in the theatre. However, this verification must be understood as an *operation*. That is, we all know that Leopardi – who had no interest in verifying his poetry's capacity for provocation, or else did not have the time and/or the means to do it – has no peers in the Italian *Ottocento* when it comes to the capacity for duration and also for duration of provocation; yet, art's social dimension was verified by melodrama.]

This different formulation of the issue includes two new elements: 1) the difference between "duration" and "immediacy" in the delivery of "provocation"; 2) the "operative" dimension of the verification carried out through theatre. Both require an explanation.

When speaking of the Italian *Ottocento*, Pagliarani draws a comparison between Leopardi's poetry and melodrama. The former is unsurpassed when it comes to the "duration of provocation," while the latter stands out for its "capacity for immediate provocation." Leopardi's poetics did not include a reflection on the relationship with the audience, or on the social function of art (because "he had no interest in [it], or else, did not have the time and/or the means to do it"); his research was aimed at duration, at acquiring a capacity for provoking an intellectual or emotional reaction in the reader over the distance of centuries. Melodrama, on the other hand, was entirely focused on the relationship with the audience, and was capable of involving it, of including it in the artistic production, of educating it without being paternalistic, carrying out that didascalic function Pagliarani postulates as the undeniable duty of the art of his time.

As for the second of the two new elements identified in the new formulation, a satisfactory explanation is rather more difficult. Pagliarani seems to encapsulate in the term "operation" at least three different phenomena that must be explained separately.

First of all, "operation" is the modality through which the audience is included in the creative process. The "verification" he outlines is not a perfunctory test whose results are already known but rather a sincere opening to the reactions of the spectators (hence his insistence on "provocation"). For Pagliarani, it is important to ensure the circulation of stories, characters, languages, voices (and breaths!), so that all these elements may acquire new vitality from their encounter with the audience:

> A teatro è il fiato dello spettatore che dà fiato all'attore. Lo so per via che ogni tanto recito versi: io vario, essi variano, in funzione di chi ascolta, e *viceversa*. (E posso anche diventare bellissimo).[16]

> [On the stage, it is the breath of the spectator that gives breath to the actor. I know this because sometimes I declaim my own verses: I change, they change, depending on who's listening, and *vice versa*. (At times I can even look beautiful).]

Secondly, Pagliarani uses the theatre as a process, an operation through which he can "give a voice" to his plays as well as some of the more "dramatic" passages of his poems. Although the considerations expressed in the previous chapter, when we discussed the notion of "corpo-voce," apply to Pagliarani and his verses, we must still specify what we mean by "giving a voice." On the one hand, there are the written plays and poems, completed before the encounter with the audience, and entrusted to the printed page: they are mute, out of necessity, but they display, as noted at the beginning of this chapter, the desire to go beyond: they possess, to use Gasparini's terminology, a "corpo-voce." When they are performed on stage, they must undergo a process of translation that "voices" them: this is precisely the "verification" posited in the short manifesto. The "operation" we have been discussing is this translation, the transition from the silent page to the noisy stage, a translation that must be periodically repeated for each of the new texts that are composed and for every different performance of a given text. It is an operation that, sometimes, Pagliarani can perform on his own, looking *bellissimo* in the process (and it is impossible not to think of his declamations of the *Ragazza Carla*).[17] However, the more dramatic poems (because they have been expressly written for the stage, or for other reasons) may require the theatre (with actors, directors, scenography, choruses, ballets, etc.).

In reviewing, for *Paese Sera,* a show directed by Quartucci and entitled "Una notte al Museo del Prado e altrove," Pagliarani reflects on the best way to bring poetry on stage, insisting on the fact that, in order to "work," the texts must be radically altered and adapted to the new medium:

> tranne forse ... rari casi in cui il poeta abbia deliberatamente cercato nuovi generi, nessuna poesia è di per sè pronta alla scena teatrale: e allora preliminarmente il regista o chi adatta un testo poetico per il teatro deve fare un *lavoro specifico,* che oscillerà entro questi limiti: come minimo dovrà essere un lavoro affine a quello di chi *traduce* una poesia da una lingua a un'altra (e qui si traduce da un *linguaggio a un altro*), e come massimo il regista adoprerà il testo poetico semplicemente come un materiale, come adopera gli attori e la scena e le luci, o come avesse soltanto *un attore in più,* e sia pure il protagonista. Va bene, ammettiamo, ma cosa gli farà fare sulla scena? Inventerà il corrispettivo teatrale dei *ritmi dei significati* della poesia, delle intenzionalità poetiche, adoprerà al limite la poesia come pretesto per costruire una macchina precisa in modo che poi diventi *necessario,* indispensabile vedere lo spettacolo a teatro, per ricavare qualcosa di più e di nuovo da quella poesia. E poi è il servizio più grande che le si possa fare, a quella poesia che sembra che lo inviti a bistrattare.[18]

> [except, perhaps ..., for a few rare cases, when the poet deliberately sought new genres, no poem is automatically ready to be performed on stage: thus, before that can happen, a director or whoever will adapt the poetic text, must carry out a *specific work,* which will oscillate between these two limits: at a minimum, it must be a work similar to that done for *translating* a poem from one language to another (in this case *from one artistic code to another*); at a maximum, the director will use the poetic text as a mere material, the way he uses actors, scenography, and lights, or as if it were an extra actor, albeit the protagonist. Fine, let us agree on this, but what will it do on stage? The director will invent the theatrical version of poetry's *rhythms of meanings,* of poetic intentions; he may even decide to use poetry as a pretext to build a precise machine, provided that, after the fact, it will seem *necessary,* indispensable to see the show in order to get something new and extra out of the poem. Which, after all, is the greatest service he can render to the poem, even though it would seem he is mistreating it.]

The similarities with the New Theatre's approach to dramaturgy are undeniable. In fact, in a different article, Pagliarani even mentions a type of "scrittura scenica" that, although it does not overlap entirely with the one Bartolucci devised, closely recalls it.[19] It is the way through which the "corpo-voce" of the verses can acquire a "breath," the blueprint that needs to be followed to transform poetry into a theatrical spectacle:

> Con la dizione di scrittura scenica si indica oggi da un punto di vista interno la consapevolezza della scrittura di essere di carta, di agitarsi fra fondali di carta, con un fruscio di carta e, da un lato esterno e proiettivo, la vocazione alla piazza, allo spettacolo di piazza, l'ambizione che la carta diventi cartapesta. In questo senso, è facilmente individuabile come scrittura scenica quella del *Baldus*, dell'*Orlando furioso* e di *Gargantua et Pantagruel*: ma qui la faccenda è anche troppo liscia perché si tratta di opere nate dalla voce, prima del libro, o da un contesto precedente al libro e vicino agli stracci, e con naturale destinazione alla piazza; meno semplice sarà riscontrare quella consapevolezza e quella vocazione in opere contemporanee, ma basteranno gli esempi di Joyce e Céline per intenderci (*Finnegans Wake*, dove è questione di voci più che di parole, e *Rigadoon* proprio non sono leggibili come libro, ma come spettacolo, a un dipresso come quei libri per l'infanzia, che oggi diremmo in qualche modo pop, donde salta fuori un bosco un castello i sette nani, a ogni pagina).[20]
>
> [With the term "scrittura scenica" we indicate, from an internal perspective, the writing's awareness of being made of paper, of moving against a paper backdrop, with the rustling sound of paper; from an external and projective perspective, the term indicates the desire to reach the piazza, to become a popular spectacle, the ambition of paper to become papier-mâché. From this vantage point, it is easy to identify as "scrittura scenica" *Baldus*, *Orlando Furioso*, or *Gargantua et Pantagruel*: but here the issue is plain, for these are works born from the voice, before they became books, or from a context that predates the book and is close to the rags [of itinerant performers], with a natural predisposition for the piazza. Less simple is identifying this same awareness and aspiration in contemporary works, but Joyce and Céline's examples should suffice to prove the point (*Finnegans Wake*, where voices are more important than words, and *Rigadoon*, cannot be read as books but as spectacles, similar to those children's books that today we would call "pop-ups," where at the turning of each page the woods, a castle, or the seven dwarves would jump out).]

On the one hand, the theatre is the place to "verify" the validity of the choices made in poetry (especially when it comes to language); on the other hand, when writing poetry Pagliarani seems to be keeping an eye on the stage, giving in to the seduction of the piazza, its rags, and its papier-mâché. The stories narrated and the languages employed must undergo the recursive trauma of this conversion from one art form to another. Their survival becomes the guarantee of their value and vitality, while all the changes that intervened during the transition will serve to streamline them, strengthen them, and increase their "capacity for provocation."

> Per le esigenze pratiche da soddisfare che esistono in tutte le arti (al massimo grado in architettura, al minimo in poesia) bisogna sempre arrivare a una tecnica, una intellettualizzazione della forma, che le affronti e soddisfi; ma bisogna arrivarvi, non già partirne; perché arrivarvi è arrivare a qualcosa di proprio, un estremo adempimento formale, conseguenza ultima della fantasia; e partirne è esattamente il contrario, uniformarsi a una forma già creata, imitare, insomma, una inibizione della fantasia.[21]

> [For the practical needs that must be met in all the arts (at the highest degree in architecture, at a minimum in poetry) one must always reach a technique, an intellectualization of the form, which can address and satisfy them; but one has to reach a technique, never start from it; for reaching it is arriving at something we possess as our own, the extreme formal achievement, the ultimate accomplishment of one's imagination; starting from it, on the contrary, means complying with a form that is found already created, that is, imitating an inhibition of the imagination.]

We have finally reached the third and last meaning of the term "operation": the search for a technique must also be understood as a process, an activity in which the public is invited to join and share. It invests all dimensions of the poetic and theatrical creation: characters, situations, stories, but also languages and registers, voices and tones. If "maintaining the efficiency of language, for everyone"[22] is part of the poet's duty, then this is the ideal starting point for the "verification." It is important to remember that this is a bi-univocal process: it goes from the page to the theatre, and then back to the page. Hence, that intense circulation of texts which can be observed throughout Pagliarani's artistic career. The *Ballata di Rudi* ("Rudi's Ballad"), for instance, includes an entire section taken from *La bella addormentata* ("Sleeping Beauty"), which had been previously verified on stage. In much the same way, many of the plays end with the declamation of verses quoted directly from Pagliarini's poetry collections as well as those by other authors (we will return to this technique later in the chapter). At other times, poems that have already been published in journals or in a volume are reissued in a theatrical version (see, for instance, "La merce esclusa" and "Col semaforo rosso,"[23] which belonged, respectively, to *Lezione di fisica* ["Physics Lesson"] and *Ballata di Rudi*.)

In these cases, the comparison between the two different versions constitutes a valuable opportunity to reach a better understanding of the internal structure and working mechanisms of these texts. The dramatization of "Merce esclusa," for instance, preserves some of the indeterminate elements that characterize the poem: the voices that populate it seem to overlap continuously, mixing with one another, resulting in a complex collage of different languages and registers. A similar effect is obtained, on stage, through an intricate attribution of roles to the company's actors: often each of them is charged with performing multiple characters,[24] while the same roles can undergo radical changes in the course of the representation. At the same time, following a trend that contradicts the one just highlighted, some aspects of the setting, the environments in which these voices exist and that were hidden in the poems, are made explicit in their staging. Returning to the "Merce esclusa," for instance, the dramatic action takes place at first inside a shopping mall, and the different voices are embodied by a group of customers, clerks, and even the manager. Suddenly, halfway through the performance, everything changes: the mall turns into a hospital, the customers become patients, the clerks, nurses, and the manager a doctor.[25]

Speaking of writing a text as a process that is perpetually evolving, and of theatre as the place where poetry is tested, brings to mind the works of Giuliano Scabia. Certainly, the comparison between these two intellectuals is not a staple of literary criticism, and yet their approach to theatre is more similar than would appear at first sight. We have already mentioned Scabia's innovative "practice of writing" in the previous chapter.[26] Here I would like to stress once more the participatory dimension of this practice: both Pagliarani and Scabia see the theatre as a place where a planned linguistic action can be exposed to the reaction of an audience; after this procedure, the text can be modified, rearranged, or adapted so as to better perform its aesthetic and political function.

For example, here is how Stefano Casi describes the performance of *Scontri generali* ("General Confrontations"), according to the author's plan:

> Con *Scontri generali,* la ricerca di elaborazione drammaturgica di Scabia fa un ulteriore passo in avanti, compiendo anzi un significativo

ribaltamento, perlomeno nelle intenzioni. Questa volta la responsabilità della partecipazione collettiva alla scrittura coinvolge anche gli spettatori. Nel progetto dell'autore, le repliche dovrebbero essere in realtà altrettante rappresentazioni-laboratorio per permettergli di prendere atto delle reazioni del pubblico nella prospettiva di una continua (permanente?) revisione drammaturgica, e secondo un progetto di partecipazione collettiva in cui si coniugano riflessioni di natura estetica (la sperimentazione su nuove forme di creazione) e politica (un reale diverso coinvolgimento responsabile del popolo). Insomma, ogni pagina del testo dovrebbe essere prima discussa con gli attori e poi con gli spettatori in apposite assemblee, permettendo la rielaborazione del testo stesso in base alle discussioni: così, "il 'pubblico' sarebbe stato inserito come parte attiva nel momento della 'scrittura' (drammaturgica) e si sarebbe trovato alla fine dentro uno spettacolo alla cui costruzione aveva contribuito."[27]

[With *Scontri generali*, Scabia's research for a dramaturgic method takes another step forward, embracing, in fact, a remarkable overturning, at least in his intentions. This time the responsibility for the collective participation in writing also involves the spectators. In the author's intentions, each performance would be in reality a different representation-laboratory, which would allow him to take into account the reactions of the audience and work toward a continuous (permanent?) dramaturgic revision, according to a plan to create a collective collaboration capable of reconciling both aesthetic (the experimentation with new forms of creation) and political (a different, real, and responsible involvement of common people) reflections. In short, every page of the text should first be discussed with the actors, then with the audience, during specific assemblies, allowing the re-elaboration of the text according to the results of the discussions: thus, "the 'spectators' would become active participants to the (dramaturgic) 'writing' and would be able to see themselves in the show they helped create."]

This participatory way of understanding the writing process, as well as the space left to the audience to intervene and modify the final product, are an extreme application of that same principle we have seen advocated by Pagliarani when he described the relationship between theatre and poetry. One last quotation from De Marinis will help us further substantiate this comparison:

Scontri generali viene composto soprattutto in vista di una collaborazione attiva del pubblico, sul quale il testo si propone di agire come *test*, al fine di scatenare una serie di reazioni che dovrebbero a loro volta tradursi

> in una sua più compiuta e (temporaneamente) definitiva stesura scritta. "La stesura che viene qui pubblicata – scrive Scabia presentando l'opera su 'Sipario' – non è probabilmente quella definitiva. Ma l'esposizione di un'opera ancora *in progress* trova la sua motivazione in una scelta metodologica tesa verso un teatro capace di coinvolgere non soltanto nel momento della sua rituale celebrazione, ma già nel suo farsi. *Scontri generali* è scritto per venire ulteriormente riempito: e cioè per essere discusso e definito attraverso una serie di incontri con quello che diventerà in seguito il pubblico: un pubblico conosciuto anticipatamente e cointeressato come collaboratore." [28]
>
> [*Scontri generali* has been composed especially in view of an active collaboration with the audience, upon whom the text intends to act as a test, so as to provoke a series of reactions that, later on, will be incorporated into a more complete and (temporarily) definitive written version. "The writing published here – Scabia writes presenting his work on *Sipario* – is probably not the definitive version. Sharing a work that is still in progress finds its motivation in a methodological choice, intended to create a theatre capable of involving the audience not only in the moment of ritual celebration, but in its very creation. *Scontri generali* is written in order to be filled at a later moment: that is, to be discussed and defined through a series of meetings with those who will later become its audience, an audience that is thus already known and invested in the work as a collaborator."]

4.2 Languages and Characters

Let us return to Pagliarani's short manifesto and move on to the second of its axes: the central role played by characters and their relation to language.[29] Who are the protagonists of his theatre? How do they speak? How do their linguistic choices relate to the contemporary debate on literary language? We shall begin from the characters: browsing through the lists of *dramatis personae*, as well as the settings of these plays, we can't help but notice the preponderance of the historic and fable-like dimensions.

To the first group belong: *Il Faust di Copenaghen* ("The Faust of Copenhagen"), which weaves together the plot of Goethe's *Faust* with the discoveries made by the physicists of the Copenhagen school that eventually led to the creation of the atomic bomb;[30] *La bestia di porpora* ("The Purple Beast"), a recasting in a hagiographic and allegoric light of the life and works of Russian poet Alexander Blok;[31] and *L'impero all'asta* ("Empire for Sale"), which stages the convulsive and violent decadence of the Roman empire.[32] The second group comprises *Le sue ragioni* ("Her Reasons"),[33] which deploys the masks of Commedia dell'Arte in a modern context; *Pelle d'asino* ("Donkeyskin"); and *La bella addormentata nel bosco* ("Sleeping Beauty"),[34] the last two both rewritings of Perrault's famous fairy tales.

The protagonists of these works are alienated puppets, having the same consistency as the words they speak ("we have various languages instead of various characters," Pagliarani wrote in his manifesto). Their vicissitudes, temporarily borrowed from other texts, are mere disguises for contemporary events, and should, therefore, be interpreted as such: corruption in current politics (*L'impero all'asta*), the unstoppable arrogance of neo-liberal capitalism (*Pelle d'asino* and *La merce esclusa*), the struggle of intellectuals to influence the world in which they live and the society that surrounds them (*La bestia di porpora*, *La bella addormentata*). In this sense, we can say that the events presented function as symbols, performing a role similar to that of the *exempla* in medieval preaching. A crucial difference, however, can be found in the conclusions: while parables and edifying stories inevitably end with a moral warning, a lesson, Pagliarani's texts jib and buck as soon as they feel that the curtain begins to close, and instead of providing an admonishment, or even a conclusion to the plot, they drag their feet, using any means to avoid closure (we will return to this point soon).

What language do these characters speak? Does it, too, undergo a similar process of stylization? The language performed on stage comprises a variety of registers, coming from every stratum of society, and from various specialized fields. It ranges from scientific jargon (see *Faust*'s use of physics, or *Pelle d'asino* and *Merce esclusa*'s references to economics) to the most demotic strain of Roman dialect (in *L'impero all'asta*), including also the language of psychology, Marxist criticism, Russian symbolist lyrics (the poems by Blok contained in *Bestia di porpora*),[35] American beatnik poetry, and even some of Pagliarani's previously published verse.

The different voices and the characters that channel them (for, after all, they are simply means for the transportation of language) are completely disconnected from one another. They inhabit the same scenic space, and yet they don't interact directly, except through the constant efforts of the spectators, who are asked to build a possible meaningful exchange starting from their disjointed words. What matters is not the action: the characters don't try to intervene directly in the world: "the crisis of the character is a crisis of language," Pagliarani noted in his manifesto. The important thing is the dramatization of the process of signification, that same process that connects (temporarily) words and things. The multitude of meanings produced by the characters is intended as a warning, a call to the spectators to act, an invitation to reflect on the pitfalls of narration, rhetoric, and representation. On the one hand, we have stylized characters that move like puppets, and on the other, hyper-specialized languages engaged in a desperate competition to define the meaning of what is happening on stage.

In reviewing *Lezione di fisica* Adriano Spatola called attention precisely to the phenomena we have been describing:

> Nello spazio mentale di Pagliarani, in quello spazio mentale che sta "prima" del fare poesia, la figura del poeta tardoromantico e quella del poeta populista ... sono diventate, a forza di autocontrollo, feticci subito individuabili. E pur lavorando contro di loro, Pagliarani lavora con loro. Invece di esorcizzarli, li ha strumentalizzati, se ne serve lucidamente, sono burattini cui presta o toglie la sua voce, e che fa agire al suo posto sulla scena, per intervenire direttamente quando si tratta di riequilibrare il tono della composizione ... Altrove, invece, i ruoli si moltiplicano, si complicano, fino alla creazione di un vero e proprio spettacolo musicale: assonanze e dissonanze di voci, e metamorfosi, cedute e impennate del discorso che non ha mai un nucleo centrale intorno al quale ruotare, ma che si svolge lungo la pagina, per accumulazione, liberamente. In questo senso, *Lezione di fisica* è un "musical" assurdo, feroce, dove il linguaggio della scienza, introdotto violentemente in un contesto che a prima vista è dei più normali ..., provoca tutta una catena di azioni e reazioni linguistiche, in un'atmosfera da cerimoniale allucinato ...[36]
>
> [In Pagliarani's mental space, that mental space which exists "before" the composition of a poem, the figure of the late-romantic poet and that of the populist poet ... have become, due to sheer self-discipline, fetishes that can be immediately identified. Although he works against them, Pagliarani exploits them. Instead of exorcising them, he uses them as tools, deliberately, as if they were puppets to whom he can give a voice (and take it away); he uses them to act on stage and take his place, so as to intervene directly when it is time to balance the tone of the composition ... Elsewhere, instead, the roles multiply, become increasingly more complicated, until they turn into a musical show: assonances and dissonances of voices, metamorphosis, ups and downs in a discourse that lacks a defining central nucleus, but that unravels on the page, freely, by progressive accumulation. In this sense, *Lezione di fisica* is an absurd, savage "musical," in which the language of science, violently introduced in a context that, at first sight, might appear completely normal ..., causes a chain of linguistic actions and reactions, an atmosphere that reminds one of a hallucinated ceremony ...]

The "mental space" postulated by Spatola as preceding the writing of verses is a theatrical space, so much so that *Lezione di fisica* can be described as a musical. In part, this definition may also have been influenced by the performance organized during the first meeting of Gruppo 63,[37] which Spatola must have seen, and that Giuliani describes as follows:

> La recitazione ... fu improntata all'idea di evitare che il pubblico potesse mai accorgersi di assistere alla dizione di una poesia. L'applicazione di questa idea poggiava su un fatto molto naturale: una sera di prove, gli attori stanchi avevano smesso di *recitare* la poesia e s'erano divertiti a cantarla in pop-music, imitando o improvvisando a turno i motivi dei diversi passaggi ... A Ken non restò che dimostrare loro la legittimità di questa scelta, opinione condivisa dall'autore.[38]

> [The performance ... was carried out in such a way as to prevent the audience from realizing they were watching a declamation of poetry. The application of this idea rested on a rather natural fact: one evening, during rehearsal, the actors became tired and stopped *performing* the poems and started singing them as if they were pop songs, imitating famous tunes, or improvising different ones according to the various passages ... The only thing left for Ken (Dewey, the director) to do was convince them of the appropriateness of that choice, an opinion shared by the author himself.]

The alienation of this form of acting reflects, on the dramaturgic level, the criticism of the stylistic institutions carried out by the text; a criticism that proceeds obliquely, juxtaposing the different varieties contained within the code, showing their fundamental incompatibility, and leaving to the spectator the task of drawing the necessary conclusions. It is worth repeating what Ballerini wrote about Pagliarani's poetry:

> l'attacco di Pagliarani alle istituzioni linguistiche non è mai frontale o mirato alla loro eliminazione – nulla dovrà dirsi meno futurista, meno minimalista, della sua scrittura poetica che conosce, semmai, ampie movenze pleonastiche – ma deve piuttosto leggersi come un rifiuto categorico opposto alla dogmatica autorità con cui tali istituzioni vengono scolasticamente e classicamente imposte (quasi che regola e gioco fossero attività che si escludono reciprocamente). Grammatica sì, dunque, ma come patrimonio comune delle possibilità di produrre significati inediti non irriconoscibili, e non preventivamente occupati.[39]

> [Pagliarani's attacks on linguistic institutions are never frontal or aimed at their elimination – nothing is less futurist, less minimalist, than his poetic writing, which, if anything, employs a generous quantity of pleonasms – instead, they must be seen as the categorical rejection of the dogmatic authority with which these institutions have been scholastically and classically imposed (as if rules and games were mutually exclusive activities). Thus, grammar must be deployed as a shared patrimony of possibilities for the production of unprecedented, unrecognizable meanings, rather than predetermined ones.]

One of the main ways in which the existing "grammar" can be used creatively to enhance the communicative and expressive capabilities of the word is by emphasizing the role played by gestures. We will speak again of their importance when discussing the function of the chorus, but it is important here to take a moment to provide a better definition: what does Pagliarani mean when he speaks of "gestures" and, in particular, "linguistic gestures"? We have seen this and similar expressions used by Sanguineti, Curi, and Giuliani, as well as Panza and Scialoja.[40]

The truth of the matter is that the notion of gesture is quite hazy and confused, given that a number of different authors and traditions have converged on this point, amplifying the ambiguity and causing all sorts of misunderstandings. On the one hand, we have the reflections of Artaud and his theatre of cruelty; on the other, Bergson, quoted directly by Panza and Scialoja in the theoretical statement that accompanied their 1965 show. And we should not forget Freud, and his notion of "lapsus" and "wit," Peirce and his idea of the sign (as well as the semiotic approach to the verbal and non-verbal human forms of communication), Lacan's interpretation of Freud, and so on.

Additionally, from the documents to which we currently have access,[41] it is very difficult to reconstruct the actual performances: even in those cases in which we have the actual *copione* (script) used by the actors and director, as is the case with the *Faust di Copenaghen* (Pagliarani's copy has survived among the papers of his archive), there is very scant photographic documentation, and hardly ever any film, video, or audio recordings. With the exception of a few, more detailed reviews, we don't really know how the lines were read, or what kind of non-verbal language the actors deployed. We do know that they were trying to incorporate a number of extra-linguistic resources that belong to the body and are normally not well exploited in poetry (following the teachings of Artaud and the example of the Living Theatre).

In Pagliarani's case, for instance, when commentators pointed to the importance of his gesturality, they usually meant the way in which he marked the rhythm of what he was reading by moving his whole body, shifting on the chair, suddenly turning left and right, and using his hands the way an orchestra conductor would (he was fond of a philharmonic metaphor whenever speaking of the public declamation of poetry). And, in fact, in this particular instance, we have many recordings of him reading his verses as well as those of other poets.[42] On the other hand, the videos we have of Spatola performing his "Aviation, aviateur" and "Seduction, seducteur"[43] clearly show how he also relied heavily on his own body and its non-verbal capacity for communication. Yet, his "gestures" are entirely different from Pagliarani's.[44]

Another tool that can be used by poets to contrast the pervasive and suffocating influence of linguistic institutions is multilinguism: this has been a resource available to Italian writers since the very beginning of our national literature – in fact, from a time that precedes the existence or even the project of a unified country. Additionally, since medieval times, the mixture of various regional dialects has been a crucial weapon in the arsenal of actors, a mixture they deployed for structural reasons (having to perform in different squares one must be conversant with the different linguistic varieties spoken there) as well as political ones (Latin was the language of the church, while the ruling class modelled its speech after a literary Tuscan heavily influenced by Petrarch, an idiom that was often presented as neutral and universal, although the skilled *guitto* knew better).[45]

It may seem somewhat far-fetched to evoke linguistic issues that date back to the Renaissance and to the *questione della lingua* (the issue of language); and yet we should not forget that precisely at this time, on 26 December 1964 to be exact, a second *questione della lingua* became the focus of discussion among Italian intellectuals and writers. Pasolini, from the pages of *Rinascita,* began the polemic on what he called the "italiano tecnologico"; and a number of *literati* participated in this very illuminating discussion on the nature of the Italian language, its history, and the influence that new mass media, such as television, had in shaping it.[46]

Instead of selecting a style that mixes various codes, Pagliarani prefers to leave them separated, deploying a careful orchestration of diastratic varieties (that is, linguistic patterns belonging to different social and disciplinary environments) in competition with one another. Rather than suggesting a possible candidate for the national language, an alternative to the "italiano tecnologico" lamented by Pasolini, he insisted on a correct formulation of the problem, presenting the forces at play, and offering his help in imagining possible solutions, but never providing a definitive one: the final decision had to be left to the audience. One of the poet's roles is that of showing how remarkable and potentially fertile is the myriad of idiolects that make up standard Italian: any attempt at uniformity should be seen as dangerous and suspicious, for it doesn't necessarily lead to a more expedient communication while it always reduces the possibilities for expression.

To show how Pagliarani translates this theoretical position into practice, we can turn to the following passage from *Bestia di porpora* ("The Purple Beast"), a play composed between 1963–4 and 1968–9, published only in 2000, and never staged:

VOCE DI ALESSANDRO Non è un problema di scelte, si tratta di attendere, come la crisalide aspetta nel bozzolo, tanto lo so che mi spunteranno le ali.
VOCE DEL I DEL CORO Nei capitoli precedenti abbiamo preso in esame quelle azioni della corteccia cerebrale
VOCE DI ALESSANDRO Macchina di presagi, l'inquietudine che mi pervade è delle forme, dei colori, con cui si presenterà la certezza.
VOCE DEL I DEL CORO che possono essere designate come nozioni di avviamento al lavoro.
VOCE DI ALESSANDRO Sarà di notte o tra le nebbie? E c'è il girasole notturno seguace della luna, giraluna? Sì c'è: la bella-di-notte. Attesa di un solo colore, quasi ragno, attesa monocroma, telaragna.
VOCE DEL I DEL CORO Queste azioni che si esercitano in seguito alla formazione di un legame temporale
VOCE DI ALESSANDRO "Aspetto un grido, cerco una risposta"
VOCE DEL I DEL CORO provocano il passaggio di un organo
VOCE DI ALESSANDRO Solo un colore, ma un colore che muti.
VOCE DEL I DEL CORO dallo stato di riposto allo stato di attività.[47]

[VOICE OF ALEXANDER It's not a matter of choices, it's a matter of waiting, like the chrysalis waits in the cocoon, for I know I'll grow wings.
VOICE FROM THE CHORUS In the previous chapters we have discussed those actions in the cerebral cortex
VOICE OF ALEXANDER An omen machine, the uneasiness that fills me belongs to the shapes, the colours, through which certainty will manifest itself.
VOICE FROM THE CHORUS that can be designated as notions of work commencement
VOICE OF ALEXANDER Will it be at night, or through the mist? Is there a night sunflower, follower of the moon, a moonflower? Yes, there is: the

four o'clock flower. Wait for a single colour, almost a spider, monochromatic wait, spider web.
VOICE FROM THE CHORUS These actions, which are undertaken after the formation of a temporal link
VOICE OF ALEXANDER "I wait for a cry, I seek an answer"
VOICE FROM THE CHORUS cause an organ to switch
VOICE OF ALEXANDER Only one colour, but a colour that may change.
VOICE FROM THE CHORUS from a state of rest to one of activity.]

The characters, completely caught up in their own words, coexist on stage but do not speak to one another. Alexander voices the speech of poetry, the chorus that of science. Both seem to be quotations from different texts, alternated so as to simulate a dialogue: Alexander is reading from a book of verse, the chorus from a manual on human physiology. They both seem to be describing some form of cerebral excitement, but they do so from radically different, irreconcilable points of view.

4.3 The Function of the Chorus

This same passage lends itself to a few observations on the role played by the chorus in Pagliarani's theatre, the last of the three axes that run through his manifesto. A quick comparison with Dario Fo and his plays will help us clarify the matter. In Fo's theatre, the chorus is a representative of the audience: it expresses its point of view on the staged situations, it denounces the hypocrisy of the characters, and it exposes the intellectual laziness of common people. In this sense, Fo's chorus resembles (and its role is often taken on by) the medieval jester:

> Quindi il giullare era qualcuno che, nel Medioevo, era parte del popolo; come dice il Muratori, il giullare nasceva dal popolo e dal popolo prendeva la rabbia per ridarla ancora al popolo meditata dal grottesco, dalla "ragione," perché il popolo prendesse coscienza della propria condizione.[48]
>
> [Thus the jester was someone who, in the Middle Ages, belonged to the populace; as Muratori writes, the jester was born from the populace and took his rage from it, only to give it back after mediating it through the grotesque, through "reason," so that the populace might become aware of its conditions.]

Thus, according to Fo, the chorus is a quasi-character, the bearer of a specific moral code and point of view, capable of engaging in a dialogue with the audience without running the risk of sounding populist or condescending. In Pagliarani's theatre, the chorus plays a radically different role: it is a disruptive element inserted in the performance so as to prevent the viewer from passively identifying with the protagonists and their language. In other words, it is used as a tool for alienation, in order to problematize both the linguistic code and the scenic actions. The constant counterpoint to the characters' words, the sarcasm toward their moral pronouncements, and the oblique and sometimes obscure commentary on events are a few of the modalities through which this alienation is achieved.

If we return to the passage quoted above, we can see how the juxtaposition of the two linguistic codes (the scientific and the poetic) casts a critical light on both of them, calling into question their adherence to "reality," and preventing the viewer from an impulsive identification with the feelings described therein. It is that Brechtian "objective estrangement" that Pagliarani mentioned in his manifesto. The chorus draws attention to the artificial (representational) nature of the show the audience is watching. In this way, the linguistic code employed on stage, rather than being perceived as transparent, independent from the events narrated and the author who devised them, can be seen in all its opacity: the product of precise choices and determined ideologies, and the result of a given historical and cultural context. And this is how Pagliarani pursues those critical and didactic aims that, in his opinion, are among the duties a work of art must perform, especially in the case of avant-garde art.

Naturally, similar observations can also be made by looking at his poetry. In time, Pagliarani would yield to the dramatic bent of his genius, writing explicitly for the stage. However, as early as *La ragazza Carla*, the chorus is already a crucial element in the architecture of the poem. See, for instance, the following famous passage:

Quanto di morte noi circonda e quanto
tocca mutarne in vita per esistere
è diamante sul vetro, svolgimento
concreto d'uomo in storia che resiste
solo vivo scarnendosi al suo tempo
quando ristagna il ritmo e quando investe
lo stesso corpo umano a mutamento.
Ma non basta comprendere per dare
empito al volto e farsene diritto:

non c'è risoluzione nel conflitto
storia esistenza fuori dell'amare
altri, anche se amore importi amare
lacrime, se precipiti in errore
o bruci in folle o guasti nel convitto
la vivanda, o sradichi dal fitto
pietà di noi e orgoglio con dolore.[49]

[*How much of death surrounds us and how much*
of it must we turn into life to exist
is diamond on glass, the concrete unfolding
of man in history enduring
alone alive unfleshing when it's his time
when the rhythm stagnates and when it bestirs
the human body to transformation.
But understanding is not enough to give
substance to a face and claim it as one's own:
there's no resolution in conflict
history or existence outside of loving
others, even if love might mean bitter
tears, or falling into error or burning
out of gears or spoiling food at boarding school
or if it means uprooting from the deep
pity for us and dignity with sorrow.]

Carla's sentimental (and existential) vicissitudes are, at this point, heading toward a conclusion that, if not a real happy ending, at least bears the signs of "normalcy." But here comes the voice of the chorus, which gets the last word and recasts the entire situation in a completely new light, using a language borrowed from Cavalcanti, forcing the reader to re-evaluate the pages just read from an entirely different point of view. It relates the adventures of the eponymous protagonist to those of national literature, showing how it is possible to employ a "realist," "engaged" style without indulging in the excesses of tear-jerking populism, all too common in the less sophisticated products of neo-realism.

Returning to the theatre, we must point out how the chorus also performs a ritual function: it is the catalyst for that "repetition [that] is the direct opposite … of reminiscence" (see item five of the manifesto). In order to avoid the "melancholic enticements of regret," the chorus introduces into the text elements of "obsession, trauma, lapsus, corrosion." A confirmation of this intuition comes from another passage of the already quoted "Teatro come verifica":

> Certamente, il gesto, nella degradazione della parola e dell'azione, acquista singolare rilevanza e, in particolare, capacità rituale, anche al di fuori di un coro danza balletto veri e propri; specialmente quando l'intera rappresentazione drammatica si postula come coralità (Living Theatre). Nel qual caso, come in tanto, valido, romanzo moderno, nonché esibire i propri meccanismi, è l'opera a porsi essa stessa come protagonista, come eroe linguistico (il gesto ovviamente essendo linguaggio). Ma questa soluzione, relativamente al teatro, mentre postula un minimo di retorica, postula altresì un massimo di adesione rituale i cui limiti non sono facilmente separabili da un certo misticismo e che comunque sembra assai difficile potersi identificare con la provocazione e lo straniamento.[50]

> [Certainly, the gesture, in the degradation of the word and action, acquires a singular importance and, in particular, a ritual capacity that goes beyond a strictly defined chorus, dance, ballet; especially when the entire dramatic performance is built on the premise of chorality (see the Living Theatre). In that case, as in many of the best examples of the modern novel, in addition to exposing its internal mechanisms, the work itself is presented as the protagonist, as a linguistic hero (the gesture being, naturally, language). However, this solution, when it comes to theatre, while implicating a minimum amount of rhetoric, also requires a maximum amount of ritual participation, whose boundaries are not easily distinguished from a certain form of mysticism, which is, in turn, hardly compatible with provocation and alienation.]

The chorus is the place where gestures (action) and words (language) collide, and thus it becomes the epicentre of that crisis that invests both characters and language. The ritual (to which the chorus inextricably belongs) is the modality through which this collision can be represented on stage. If it directly invests the actors and their bodies, it can effectively influence the audience. The implicit risk of this form of ritual, Pagliarani lucidly notes, is that like all rituals it might lead to a vague and ill-defined "mysticism,"[51] which is the enemy of critical reflection and an obstacle to acquiring an acute awareness of the historical context in which artists and audience operate. As a consequence, all the work that had been performed on language could be nullified. How can dramatists and poets prevent this outcome and solve the apparent paradox, reconciling the need to maintain a critical distance with the practical advantages offered by a ritual component of the performance? The solution lies in the last fundamental tool devised by Pagliarani: the systematic dismantling of the cause-and-effect link.

4.4 *Exempla* Devoid of Moral

I have already mentioned how Pagliarani's texts resemble medieval *exempla*, and how they behave as such up until they approach their conclusion. At that point, they swerve and reject an ending resulting in a precise moral, often forgoing any logical resolution of the events narrated up to that point. This peculiar rhetorical strategy (a rhetoric of reticence, shameless and authoritarian) is a direct criticism of the cause-and-effect link, and through it Pagliarani's writing avoids the pitfalls of mysticism, opening up to provocation and alienation. In "Physics Lesson," Pagliarani directly quotes Heisenberg's uncertainty principle:[52]

> Se si vuol sapere se A è causa dell'effetto di B
> se il microggetto in sé è inconoscibile
> se l'onda di Broglie per i fisici di Copenaghen
> non è altro che l'espressione fisica della probabilità posseduta
> dalla particella di trovarsi in un luogo piuttosto che in un altro onda cioè generata
> dalla mancanza di un rigoroso nesso causale in microfisica[53]
>
> [If one wants to determine if A is the cause of effect B
> if the micro-object is unknowable in itself
> if the de Broglie wave for the Copenhagen physicists
> is nothing other than the physical expression of the probability possessed
> by the particle of finding itself in one place rather than in another a wave generated
> by the lack of a rigorous causal nexus in microphysics]

And from a theoretical point of view, a first formulation of this same idea applied to language can be found in the following passage from "Teatro come verifica":

> E l'azione va negata quando si offre come coerente manifestazione di un rapporto definito di causa e effetto, quando è intesa in sintonia con la parola; e basta … E, comunque, *quanto più decade l'azione, tanto più ha da essere attiva la parola*.[54]
>
> [And the action must be rejected when it is offered as the coherent manifestation of a definitive relation of cause and effect, when it is understood as being in harmony with the word; and that's it … And, in any case, *the more the action decays, the more the word must be active*.]

And, a few pages after that,

> E così l'azione va negata quando è esibita come coerente manifestazione di un rapporto definito di causa ed effetto, quando vuol essere intesa in pacifica sintonia con la parola. Ma non certo negazione dell'azione quando risulti: a) manifestazione della prevaricazione esercitata dagli istituti sulla parola; cioè, tolto ogni schermo, violentata ogni separatezza, della prevaricazione sull'uomo (prevalentemente teatro dell'assurdo); b) meccanismo di scomposizione di "sintagmi" costrutti correnti alienati, e/o meccanismo di esibizione della propria artificiosità – cioè, nel caso, dell'artificiosità delle strutture teatrali (prevalentemente, teatro epico).[55]
>
> [And so the action must be rejected when it is portrayed as the coherent manifestation of a definitive relation of cause and effect, when it wants to be considered in unequivocal harmony with the word. But there will be no rejection when the action will be shown as: a) the manifestation of the abuses perpetrated by the institutions of language; that is, doing away with all pretenses, violently dispatching all separations, the abuses perpetrated on man (mostly theatre of the absurd); b) a mechanism for disassembling the "syntagms," common constructs that underwent a process of alienation, and/or a mechanism for the exposure of its own artificiality – that is, in our case, the artificiality of theatrical structures (mostly epic theatre).]

Pagliarani doesn't believe that language can describe the world, or that it can influence it directly. Therefore, he finds it impossible to organize the events he narrates according to the principle of cause and effect. In his theatre, the action is focused on language, in order to revitalize it, free it from the wear and tear of tradition and control from above. A direct intervention into reality can only be achieved through politics. The task of art is that of providing the rhetorical tools necessary for that intervention. If the action were to be represented on stage as coherent and conclusive, it would become only a useless surrogate for real action or, even worse, an implicit reaffirmation of the status quo, a form of entertainment, a consolation, or mere escapism. On this issue, one can't help but be reminded of the following verse from "Physics Lesson":

> e invece non ci basta nemmeno dire no che salva solo l'anima
> ci tocca vivere il no misurarlo coinvolgerlo in azione e tentazione
> perché l'opposizione agisca da opposizione e abbia i suoi testimoni.[56]

> [and instead it's not enough just to say no which saves only the soul
> you've got to inhabit negation measure it involve it in action and temptation
> so that opposition might act like opposition and have its witnesses.]

But how does one, in the practice of writing, avoid a passive, escapist reconfirmation of the link of cause and effect? The answer can be found in another passage from the play *Purple Beast*, in which Alexander, the protagonist, seems to be speaking for the author:

> Il mio comunque è un poema ironico. Qui intendo per ironia non il dileggio, ma il procedimento di percepire contemporaneamente due fenomeni discordi o la simultanea attribuzione dello stesso fenomeno a due serie semantiche.[57]

> [In any case, mine is an ironic poem. Here I don't mean irony as in mockery, but as the process through which one can experience two discordant phenomena at the same time, or attribute the same phenomenon to two different semantic series.]

Pagliarani's entire literary output seems to be pervaded by this type of irony, a quality that can also help explain both his multilingualism and his extravagant narrative structures. In this very play, Alexander's intimate turmoil, which had occupied the first two acts, is unceremoniously abandoned to make room for a horse race, with characters that here make their first appearance.

In an article entitled "A proposito del mio Blok" ("Speaking of my Blok"), which Pagliarani published in *L'Illuminista*, he wrote,

> Il Blok invece lo terminai non ricordo se nella tarda primavera del '68 o del '69. Ero rimasto bloccato sul finale, per un paio di anni: mi mancava soltanto la scena unica del terzo e ultimo atto; e l'intuizione di parlare di tutt'altro, anzi, meglio, di rovesciare il discorso mi venne soltanto dopo una ventina o trentina di spettacoli visti e recensiti nella mia, freschissima allora, professione di critico teatrale per un quotidiano (*Paese sera*; per un periodico di prima linea, *Ragionamenti*, invece lo stesso lavoro lo stavo facendo da due anni circa), mi venne in mente cioè per essere riuscito ad acquisire una certa praticaccia nelle tecniche del mestiere, dell'efficacia dei ribaltoni all'ultimo minuto. Io fui e sono tuttora soddisfatto di aver trovato quel finale ...[58]

> [I can't remember if I finished my Blok in the late spring of '68 or '69. I had been stuck on the conclusion, for a couple of years: I was missing just

the final (and only) scene of the third act; and the intuition of switching to something else entirely, or better yet, of turning the whole discourse on its head, came to me only after having seen twenty or thirty shows, which I had reviewed in my new (back then) profession as theatre critic for a newspaper (*Paese Sera*, which was a first-tier paper; I had been doing the same job for *Ragionamenti* for the previous two years). I thought of it because I had been able to acquire a certain familiarity with the tricks of the trade, one of which is the last-minute twist. I was, and still am, very pleased with having found that finale ...]

Something very similar happens with *Il Faust di Copenaghen*, where the action is resolved into a poetry reading, with the actors declaiming verse by Pagliarani himself, as well as other key authors of the twentieth century (from the Italian and the English-speaking tradition). Even more interesting is the case of *La bella addormentata nel bosco* ("Sleeping Beauty"), whose finale is here transcribed and translated (we will discuss it in more detail in the next chapter):

MORALE DELL'AUTORE PERRAULT
Attendere un pezzetto per avere uno sposo
ricco, ben fatto, gentile, amoroso,
                    è cosa naturale.
Ma attendere cent'anni sempre dormendo è un fatto
                    del tutto eccezionale,
né più si trova donna ch'abbia un sonno siffatto ...
                    né più si trova donna ...
E DELL'AGGIUSTATORE PAGLIA
(O GUASTATORE)
Col demiurgo Fedayn, con Nelson Mandela
noi ci chiamiamo fuori
                    ce ne laviamo le mani
                              e così sia.
Ma non è soltanto per ruffianeria
Ma non è soltanto per ruffianeria
è che siamo proprio tagliati fuori
                         noi vecchia Europa,
fuori dalla fame, dal dolore, dalla memoria,
fuori dal moto rivoluzionario della storia.[59]

[MORAL BY THE AUTHOR PERRAULT
Waiting a while to have a spouse
rich, well proportioned, kind, loving,

is a natural thing.
But waiting a hundred years always sleeping is a fact
entirely exceptional,
nor is it possible any longer to find a woman with such sleep …
nor is it possible to find a woman …
AND BY THE ADJUSTER (OR DISRUPTOR)
PAGLIA
With the demiurge Fedayeen, with Nelson Mandela
we call it quits
we wash our hands of it
and so be it.
And it's not just a matter of pandering
And it's not just a matter of pandering
it's that we're truly cut off
we old Europe,
off from hunger, pain, memory,
off from the revolutionary motion of history]

The meaning of the traditional fairy tale has been radically altered. First, Perrault's moral is given in an absurd, distorted way; then, another moral is added, created by "the disruptor Paglia[rani]," displaying the signs of such brazen irrationality that it is immediately rendered useless, indefensible. However, if we remember what was said earlier regarding the importance of irony for Pagliarani, things might become a bit clearer. That Europe has been cut off from hunger, pain, and perhaps even from the revolutionary motion of history, is a statement whose validity, although problematic, can be entertained, if just for a moment, especially if we consider the times when it was uttered: it was, after all, the age of the "yuppies" and the first triumphs of neo-liberal capitalism, which had injected an eerie, joyless optimism in many Western democracies. On the other hand, stating that "old Europe" has been cut off from memory is blatantly false. If there is one thing that the "old continent" is acutely aware of, it is its long history, and the enormous pressure it exerts upon its present. If Pagliarani, as seems more than probable, understood this last statement as ironic, then the same interpretation should be extended to the entire passage: since Europe is not cut off from memory, then it is also still very much in contact with hunger, pain, and – most importantly for a left-leaning intellectual like our poet – with the "revolutionary motion of history."

Irony "saves" the moral of the story; that is to say, if literature is prevented from having a direct influence on society, irony – calling readers into action, demanding their collaboration in the determination of meaning – opens a possible margin of manoeuvre, an access point to the real world. The moral of the "disruptor," which, at first, seemed to indicate a fatalist attitude toward current events, is instead capable of transmitting a positive value: an invitation to action that can be fulfilled only outside the theatrical space, in the public arena of politics.

In addition to this brand of irony, the text exposes its artificiality (as we have seen, an important element in denouncing the opacity of art's traditional institutes) by explicitly attaching an author to the moral, and staging an open disagreement between the two declared authorities behind the text: its original creator and its later manipulator. Far from being a natural, universal, timeless maxim, the ultimate meaning of the story is presented as contingent on the opinion of a single writer. A similar strategy is deployed, in poetry, at the close of the poem "La ballata di Rudi," which shares many passages in common with *La bella addormentata nel bosco*, and whose last lines read:

> Ma dobbiamo continuare
> come se
> non avesse senso pensare
> che s'appassisca il mare[60]

> [But we have to go on
> as if
> it didn't make sense to think
> that the sea could wither]

This is not the expression of a fatalistic resignation but rather an invitation to develop the rhetorical tools indispensable to action. Luigi Ballerini has noted the rejection of closure, that systematic procrastination of an end we have been observing as a constant feature of the plays, in Pagliarani's poetry. In a remarkably insightful essay, he decides to adopt a fluvial metaphor in describing this technique:

> *Carla* si conclude, come in una foce a estuario, con lo straordinario ed enfatico congedo di sapore cavalcantiano: "Quanto di morte noi circonda e quanto," pronunziato da un coreuta del ventesimo secolo, impegnato nel difficile e tuttavia irrinunciabile compito di godere della propria pulsione di morte ... la foce di *Rudi* non è un estuario, è un delta. È una foce sparpagliata e poco importa se ciascun braccio di scorrimento delle acque si ritiene, preso da sé, un estuario. La differenza è sostanziale e comprovata dal cosiddetto regime delle acque, ricco e impetuoso nel caso dello sbocco unico di Carla, tortuoso e rallentato nel caso dello sbocco molteplice di

> Rudi: instabile, pronto tanto a insabbiarsi quanto a modificare la direzione del proprio defluire.[61]

> [*Carla* ends, like an estuary, with the extraordinary and emphatic envoy that closely resembles the style of Cavalcanti: "How much of death surrounds us and how much," uttered by a twentieth-century chorus engaged in the difficult and yet unavoidable task of enjoying its own death drive ... the end of *Rudi* is not an estuary, but rather a delta. It is a scattered ending, and it doesn't really matter if each of the various branches thinks of itself as an estuary. The difference is considerable and clearly marked by the water regime: rich and impetuous for Carla's singular outlet, tortuous and slow in Rudi's plurality of outlets: unstable, liable to both running aground and changing the direction of its flow.]

Usually, Pagliarani's plays end in a delta; their conclusions are frayed, for they reject the cause-and-effect link, as we have seen. To this end, poetry can play an important role in postponing the resolution of the plot, effectively creating a bridge, a continuity, between the various texts, which are presented not as discrete but rather as the various resurfacings of the same underground body of water. This is why both *La bella addormentata nel bosco* and *Il Faust di Copenaghen* end with a declamation of poems. On this point, it might be useful to turn to Guido Guglielmi, who writes,

> per Brecht (parlando sommariamente) si trattava di narrativizzare il dramma, far uso del racconto e delle tecniche del montaggio per distanziare l'azione, liberarla dall'apparenza di necessità (in senso naturalistico), impedire l'effetto della mimesi. Pagliarani fa l'operazione inversa: drammatizza la narrazione, porta l'interesse dalla narrazione alla narrazione che si fa, alla continua narrazione che il mondo fa di se stesso.[62]

> [according to Brecht (speaking in general terms) it was a matter of narrating the drama, using storytelling and editing techniques to push away the action, free it from the appearances of necessity (in a naturalistic sense), and prevent the mimetic effect. Pagliarani does the opposite: he dramatizes narration, he switches the focus from the narrative to the narrative that unfolds, the world's continuous narration of itself.]

If the "world's continuous narration of itself" is the focus of the representation, then the actions of the characters cannot end, they cannot come to a conclusion and are not susceptible to being explained by a moral. They must continue endlessly, be renewed at every performance, be constantly verified at each staging. Walter Pedullà also describes Pagliarani's predilection for interrupting the text before it has a chance to end:

> Jakobson definisce "afasia metonimica" questo parlare con mezze frasi che non concludono il discorso. Ebbene, Pagliarani trasforma tale "malattia del linguaggio" in salute di questa sua poesia che fa metonimia, cioè narrativa.[63]
>
> [Jakobson defined "metonymical aphasia" as this way of speaking in broken sentences that never express a complete thought. Well, Pagliarani turns this "linguistic malady" into a healthy poetry, which progresses by means of metonymies, that is to say: a narrative.]

In another, later essay, he returns to this same idea when he writes:

> Singolare metonimia quella di Pagliarani. Una metonimia malata da cui il poeta ricava tuttavia salute, secondo ribaltamento di negativo in positivo che è stata l'epidemia della controcultura degli Anni Sessanta. Per Jakobson infatti, l'afasia metonimica è la malattia del linguaggio per la quale il parlante si interrompe senza finire il discorso. Con l'afasia metonimica Pagliarani taglia la narrazione non appena essa ha dichiarato il significato di cui è inconsapevole portatrice e la riprende da un'altra prospettiva. La frattura semantica e ritmica, con tale economia linguistica, diventa la tecnica incaricata della rivelazione del senso.[64]
>
> [Pagliarani's metonymy is a rather singular one. It is a sick metonymy, from which the poet draws health, according to that reframing of negative into positive that was the epidemic of '60s counterculture. In fact, according to Jakobson, metonymical aphasia is the linguistic malady that causes speakers to break off their sentences before they finish them. With his metonymical aphasia, Pagliarani breaks off the narration as soon as it states the meaning that it unconsciously carries, only to take it on from a different perspective. This rhythmic and semantic fracture, according to this linguistic economy, becomes the technique charged with the task of revealing the meaning.]

Pedullà's reading of Pagliarani's rhetorical strategy is absolutely correct, except for one crucial detail: in order to resist the oppression and abuse exercised by the linguistic institutes promulgated by literary tradition, the interruption of the discourse must happen immediately before a determined meaning is communicated, and not after. Pagliarani's style strives for the ambiguity that comes from polysemy (the plurality of meanings contained in a single signifier), and not for the obscurity that is caused by incompleteness. The job of deciding a "moral," of determining meaning, is left to the audience. The function of the writer is that of providing the means and the opportunity for reflection. As soon as it senses the closure of the discourse (be it the moral, the definitive meaning, or the drawing of the curtain), the author's voice has the duty to break off, and make room for the spectators' voice.

5 Collaborations and Convergences: Pagliarani, Giuliani, Celli, and Sanguineti[1]

As we have seen in *La bella addormentata nel bosco* ("Sleeping Beauty"), *Il Faust di Copenaghen* ("The Faust of Copenhagen") and, in part, also in *La bestia di porpora* ("The Purple Beast"), Pagliarani often uses a pre-existing text, or a literary corpus, as a starting point for his own plays. In many cases, his plays can be considered rewritings of the texts he adopts, although from an oblique, slanted perspective, and through a rather experimental use of theatre language and conventions. He was not alone in this choice: many of the Neoavanguardia poets shared a similar approach; the first name that comes to everyone's mind is usually Sanguineti, although his *travestimenti* (disguises) are different and unique, as we will see later on in this chapter.

Another remarkable trait many shared, at least early on in the journey of the Novissimi and Gruppo 63, is a pressing desire for collaboration with the other artists and intellectuals active in Italy and the rest of Europe at the time. In chapters 1 and 2 we have seen how, at least in the first half of the 1960s, this synergy brought together writers and theatre practitioners (directors and actors). Less frequent, and yet immensely illuminating, is the cooperation between two writers on the same play. A fortunate archival discovery among the papers held at the Fondo Manoscritti of the Centro di ricerca sulla tradizione manoscritta di autori moderni e contemporanei, located at the University of Pavia, gives us the opportunity to speak in greater detail about a play written jointly by Elio Pagliarani and Alfredo Giuliani: *Pelle d'Asino* ("Donkeyskin").[2]

5.1 Giuliani and "Il teatro dei Novissimi"

Before we analyse this play, however, I want to take a step back and transcribe a brief text I found in the archives of Giuliani's papers (also held at the Fondo Manoscritti) that shows how he viewed the relevance of theatre for the experiments of the Neoavanguardia, and the differences he believed made each author's research unique. This text is preserved in three clean, typed copies, and, it would seem, was ready to be published. In spite of my efforts, however, I wasn't able to find the venue in which it was made public.[3]

Equally difficult is the task of dating this piece; the point of view it expresses, the fact that it focuses on the Novissimi, and its references to certain plays suggest the mid-1960s; perhaps it was prepared for the 1965 performance of the Compagnia Teatro dei Novissimi,[4] as it is, in fact, entitled "Il teatro dei Novissimi." In any event, this is it:

> A parte qualche tentativo (a volte anche fallito) nel genere "cabaret" e "music-hall" non esiste in Italia un repertorio di teatro moderno, non esiste una realtà teatrale allo stesso modo in cui è reale il linguaggio della poesia e del romanzo. Il teatro è una routine di "spettacoli" guidata da mestieranti (alcuni dei quali anche bravi) che non hanno alcun contatto con la letteratura d'avanguardia. E un vero e proprio "teatro d'avanguardia" non è esistito fino a ieri.[5]

> [Aside from a few attempts (often unsuccessful) in the genre of "cabaret" and "music-hall," Italy does not possess a repertory of modern theatre; a true theatrical reality does not exist, at least not in the same way it does for the language of poetry and that of the novel. Theatre is a routine of "shows" led by craftsmen (some of whom are quite good), who have no contact with avant-garde literature. A true "avant-garde theatre" did not exist, at least not until now.]

This first paragraph reflects the by now common complaint regarding the Italian stage: its backwardness when compared to the more advanced solutions that were being attempted elsewhere in Europe. In Giuliani's opinion, the fastest way to bring it up to speed is to follow the same path already travelled by poetry and the novel: the pursuit of a deliberate and ambitious linguistic experimentation. Also very interesting is the claim that "a true avant-garde theatre" did not exist in Italy: Giuliani seems to disregard here all the work that futurism had carried out on the Italian stage at the beginning of the century; although, maybe, the references to "cabaret" and "music-hall" at the beginning of the paragraph are meant to include, at least in part, those early futurist experiments. It is worth mentioning, however, that elsewhere, in an essay already quoted in chapter 1, entitled "La poesia a teatro," Giuliani had referenced futurism and Dadaism as sources of inspiration for the poets of his generation:

> Il tempo mitico, ancora così vicino, delle "serate" futuriste e cubofuturiste, e poi delle arlecchinate dada ... è lì che corre il pensiero a ritrovare le origini dei duri colpi inferti alla "dizione" della poesia e al suo stravolgersi in rappresentazione.[6]
>
> [The mythical time, still so close, of futurist and cubo-futurist "evenings," and Dada's harlequinades ... that is what comes to mind when trying to establish the origins of the hard blows dealt to poetic "diction" and its deformation into performance.]

Even though Giuliani and his colleagues do not always recognize a debt to the "historical" avant-gardes, they are well aware of the influence their example exercises on them and their importance in the history of literature and the arts. Going back to our archival find, we read:

> Il TEATRO DEI NOVISSIMI si propone di colmare questo vuoto ed è un frutto naturale dell'evoluzione del linguaggio della poesia in Italia. Quando nel 1961 apparve l'antologia dei NOVISSIMI fu subito manifesta la profonda rottura che il linguaggio di questi cinque poeti aveva aperto nel tessuto tradizionale neo-realistico e neo-crepuscolare del dopoguerra. Allo stanco filone contemplativo intimista argomentante e alla malinconica oratoria populista si opponeva ora un linguaggio altamente drammatico, ricco di "parlato," violento nella propria struttura sintattica, consapevole della propria funzione di choc nei confronti del lettore.[7]
>
> [The NOVISSIMI THEATRE intends to fill this gap, and is a natural evolution of the language of poetry in Italy. When, in 1961, the NOVISSIMI anthology was published, the language of these five poets broke cleanly and unequivocally with the neo-realistic and neo-crepuscular traditions of post-World War II literature. It replaced the then current, exhausted, intimist, contemplative style of argumentation and the populist, melancholic oratory with a highly dramatic language, enriched by people's "real speech," characterized by a violent syntactic structure, deliberate in deploying its shock value to influence the reader.]

Giuliani continues his analysis by looking at the successes that he and his Novissimi colleagues had had in renovating the language of poetry, by moving away from some of the exhausted conventions of neo-realist and neo-crepuscular (but also neo-hermetic) lyricism, and turning to the language spoken on the streets, in offices, and in schools, stressing the shock value of this choice and its "dramatic" nature. The importance of theatre for himself and his colleagues is stated even more forcefully in the next passage, the real highlight of his short essay:

> Molte poesie dei Novissimi contenevano o suggerivano una tensione dialogica e una giustapposizione di piani diversi di discorso, tali da esprimere chiaramente l'impulso di questi scrittori verso una comunicazione di tipo teatrale. Negli anni più recenti fu dunque naturale che i Novissimi e gli scrittori giovani a loro più affini si mettessero a scrivere direttamente per il teatro. Se comune convinzione di questi scrittori è che il testo (e pertanto un rinnovamento del linguaggio) è il primo fondamento del teatro, diverse sono le vie che ciascuno segue. Balestrini e Sanguineti concepiscono un teatro di parola nel quale l'evento teatrale è piuttosto raccontato che rappresentato; al contrario, Giuliani concepisce un teatro nel quale ogni battuta è un'azione proposta al regista e agli attori (questi sono infatti invitati a cercare nel testo le proprie battute e a inventare così la loro storia); all'altro limite, Filippini sembra proporsi un teatro in cui le parole non contano nulla, ma servono per stimolo all'esecuzione di atti scenici; altri, come Lombardi e Manganelli, utilizzano una forma genericamente tradizionale investendola di ironia e di intenzioni catastrofiche; Pagliarani, infine, pensa di innestare insieme teatro epico (nel senso quasi didattico di Brecht) e assurdità semantica conservando un fondo naturalistico all'intrecciarsi di diversi livelli del significato.[8]

> [Many poems of the Novissimi contained or suggested a dialogic tension and a juxtaposition of different levels of discourse such that they clearly expressed their authors' drive toward a theatrical kind of communication. In more recent years, it was thus natural that the Novissimi (and the young writers who shared a sensibility similar to theirs) have started writing directly for the theatre. Even though all of these writers share the belief that the text (and thus a renovation of language) is the fundamental pillar of theatre, they all follow different paths. Balestrini and Sanguineti envision a theatre of the word in which the theatrical event is narrated rather than performed; on the contrary, Giuliani imagines a theatre in which each line is an action suggested to actors and directors (they are, in fact, invited to find their words within the text, and make up their own stories); at the other end of the spectrum, Filippini seems to propose a theatre in which words are completely unimportant, and only serve as stimuli for the execution of stage actions; others, like Lombardi and Manganelli, utilize a

generic and somewhat traditional form of theatre, illuminated by an ironic light and catastrophic intentions; finally, Pagliarani tries to combine an epic form of theatre (almost in the didactic sense given by Brecht to this term) and semantic absurdity, while preserving a naturalistic background that underpins the different layers of meaning.]

Giuliani portrays the passage from poetry to theatre as a "natural" progression. And this is really at the core of the argument we have been building throughout this volume. Theatre, he clearly implies, was not just one of the many experiments that were being attempted but the next logical step to build on the work that had been done in poetry and make it more effective, more readily available to the audience.

This consideration is repeated and made even more explicit in the opening paragraph of "La poesia a teatro," the essay already quoted above, where we read:

> Sono ancora tra noi alcuni favolosi creatori e testimoni di quell'epoca che portò la poesia sul palcoscenico, credo, per la prima volta e precisamente con l'intenzione di fare, con la poesia, spettacolo: il nostro delizioso Palazzeschi, e Victor Sklovskij, e Jakobson e Duchamp e Max Ernst ... Si può anche ritenere che allora sia stata tutta una faccenda di rottura e di provocazione; ma le conseguenze non cessano di farsi sentire e condizionano la tradizione moderna dei rapporti tra le arti. Ogni volta che il teatro vuole distruggersi e reinventarsi, bene o male, ricorre alla poesia e magari s'illude doppiamente, ma deve farlo; e quando la poesia vuole rompere la costrizione della pagina scritta aspira naturalmente allo spazio scenico. La ragione sta in un esasperante nodo linguistico difficile da sciogliere, e che induce sempre a ritentare.[9]
>
> [Some of the fabulous creators and witnesses of when, for the first time, as far as I can tell, poetry was taken to the stage with the manifest intention of turning it into a spectacle are still with us: our wonderful Palazzeschi, and Victor Sklovskij, and Jakobson, and Duchamp and Max Ernst ... One could argue that back then it was all a matter of breaking with tradition and provoking the audience; yet, the consequences can still be felt and still influence the modern tradition of relations between art forms. Every time that theatre wants to destroy and reinvent itself, for better or worse, it resorts to poetry, and perhaps this reinvention is all a delusion, but it must be done. When poetry wants to break the limitations of the written page, it naturally aspires to the theatrical space. The reason for this can be found in an exasperating linguistic knot that is difficult to untie and prompts one to try again and again.]

We have already quoted part of this paragraph in chapter 1,[10] but it is worth revisiting these words in order to stress Giuliani's consistency in assessing the importance of theatre for poetry, and in identifying language as the crucial issue at the core of all reflections regarding aesthetics and the relation of language to the political engagement of art.

Returning to the essay we found in the Pavia archives, it is also very interesting to observe how the various authors have been grouped and arranged in different categories. Balestrini and Sanguineti are, rather surprisingly, paired together: another indication that can help date Giuliani's piece to the first half of the 1960s. The two writers would eventually develop radically different approaches to the stage, especially if one considers that the first would progressively reduce his output in this field, while the latter would intensify his efforts as a dramaturg. At an initial stage, however, if we think about Balestrini's *Improvvisazione* ("Improvisation")[11] (included in the Teatro dei Novissimi performance of 1965) and Sanguineti's *Traumdeutung* ("The Interpretation of Dreams"), the parallels between the two are undeniable. Balestrini weaves together the stage directions of Chekhov's *Seagull*, focusing the audience's attention, in a strange and hyper-verbal way, on the actions performed by the actors, actions that are constantly (and almost exclusively) spoken about. In a parallel (equally convoluted and oblique) manner, Sanguineti's play also experiments with stage directions. Here is the author's introductory note, which can help explain this curious convergence:

> Legato all'idea di un teatro di parola, e perciò nemico di ogni didascalia (e amico di un linguaggio che suscita e decide, da solo, lo spazio teatrale, e la scena, e il gesto), dovevo, prima o poi, scrivere una cosa come *Traumdeutung*, che porta questa idea al limite e pertanto, ovviamente, la rovescia. Ecco, di conseguenza, uno psicodramma, mimato da voci trattate strumentalmente, alle quali è negata ogni possibilità di dialogo. Il germe del tutto, si capisce, era in *K.* (1959), e l'indispensabile mediazione in *Passaggio* (1961–1962).[12]
>
> [Invested as I am in the idea of theatre of the word, and thus an enemy of all stage directions (and a friend of a language that evokes and determines, on its own, the theatrical space, the scene, the gesture), I was bound, sooner or later, to write something like *Traumdeutung*, a play that pushes this idea to its limit and thus, inevitably, turns it upside down. As a consequence, here is a psychodrama mimed by voices that are treated as instruments, incapable of any form of dialogue. The seed for all of this was, clearly, *K.* (1959), through the crucial mediation of *Passaggio* ["Passage"] (1961–1962).]

Thus, for both authors, the early experiments concentrated all the action of the play inside the words spoken on stage by the actors, leading to a similar atmosphere of alienated incommunicability. Returning to Giuliani's short article, as he continues listing the contributions of his colleagues, he also speaks very briefly of his own theatre, describing the strategy he adopted as being the opposite of Balestrini and Sanguineti's: we will come back to this point later, when we briefly analyse his *Povera Juliet*. Filippini's interesting career has unfortunately been completely neglected by critics for the past decades, and his plays are all but inaccessible. The remarks on Lombardi and Manganelli are also quite accurate, and, if nothing else, can serve as a reminder that these two writers also produced a number of plays that are now almost completely ignored by critics and literary historians. Finally, we get to Pagliarani, for whom Giuliani quite correctly mentions Brecht's epic theatre, tempered by an absurdist, almost surrealist imagination.

> Una particolare ed essenziale caratteristica dell'opera di questi scrittori, o almeno di molti tra essi, è che la funzione teatrale implica fin dalla concezione l'intervento del pittore e del musicista e del coreografo. Le corrispondenze tra i Novissimi e i loro amici pittori e musicisti sono anch'esse un frutto naturale della comunione di impulsi che oggi esiste in Italia tra gli artisti d'avanguardia. Il loro fine comune è di suscitare un nuovo spazio acustico e visivo nel quale il teatro possa agire o parlare senza istrionismi.[13]

> [A distinctive and crucial characteristic of the works by these authors, or at least what is common to most of them, is that the theatrical function implies, from the very inception, the collaboration with the painter, the musician, and the choreographer. The convergences between the Novissimi and their painter and musician friends are also a natural consequence of the common drive that today animates the avant-garde artists in Italy. Their shared goal is to create a new acoustic and visual space within which theatre can act or speak without being excessively histrionic.]

Giuliani concludes his brief article by highlighting the collaborative aspect of these theatrical experiments, returning us to something that we mentioned at the very beginning of this chapter, and to the *atto unico* (one-act play) *Pelle d'Asino*, written by Giuliani and Pagliarani, and published in 1964 by Scheiwiller, in its prestigious Pesce d'Oro series, with drawings by noted artist Gastone Novelli. In fact, the thirty-five-page booklet bears the subtitle "grottesco per musica" (grotesque for music), which implies also the participation of a composer, even though the version of the play that has been published and the various drafts that have survived do not include any music.[14] While this rewriting of Charles Perrault's classic tale comprised only one act, we know from a brief note by Giuliani that it was originally meant to include two more:

> Era il tempo (1963–64) che ci divertivamo da matti scrivendo in forma di commedia parodica la più piccante delle favole: *Pelle d'Asino*. Un re che rimasto vedovo vuole sposare a tutti i costi la propria figlia (un tema alla Shakespeare). Pubblicammo da Scheiwiller (nel '64) solo il primo atto ... Il secondo era bellamente concluso, ma tu [Pagliarani] lo giudicavi meno "elegante" del primo; sul terzo c'eravamo un po' inceppati; li rimandammo a data da destinarsi.[15]

> [It was a time (1963–64) when we were having a lot of fun writing in the guise of a comedic parody the spiciest of fables: *Pelle d'Asino* ("Donkeyskin"). A king becomes a widower and wants, at all costs, to marry his own daughter (a Shakespearean theme). Scheiwiller published (in '64) only the first act ... The second act was already done, but you (Pagliarani) thought it was less "elegant" than the first; we got stuck on the third; we decided to postpone work on it until further notice.]

Giuliani's papers document the writing process that the two authors followed; included in the Pavia archives are three separate files: number 1 contains a summary of the original project, consisting of two typewritten pages; number 2 contains the first of two different versions of the second act, comprising eighteen pages, some handwritten and some typed, with many corrections in pen; number 3 contains the second version of the second act, comprising fifteen typed pages, a clean copy with almost no corrections. There is no trace of the third act mentioned by Giuliani in the aforementioned letter, although it is possible that the materials left out of the *atto unico* were re-elaborated and fitted into just one additional act (more on this presently). This find constitutes a rare opportunity for the student of the neo-avant-garde theatre, as it confirms some of the trends that can be observed in other plays and provides important details on the creative process.

A first, crucial observation is that, from its very inception, the conclusion of the play appears to be its most problematic point. In fact, the general structure of the fairy tale is well-suited to host a number of disparate materials, and can even withstand the great doses of irony with which the two writers season and manipulate them. When it comes to drawing a moral for the story, however, things become more complicated, as a delicate balance must be struck between the demands of the genre – which would require a clear-cut, concise moral pronouncement – and the changed sensibility of the times, which calls for a subtler appreciation for the intricacies of the real world. This dilemma is reinforced by theoretical, practical, and even symbolic considerations, as the ending of the play is that threshold that separates theatre from everyday reality, fiction from the real world. It is therefore particularly significant that Giuliani, in what seems to be the earliest note regarding the plot, writes,

> È la storia di una dissoluzione oggettiva: le metamorfosi della fanciulla la trasformeranno realmente nonostante ciò che lei e gli altri possono credere. Vale a dire che se si crea un'abitudine, l'abito fa il Monaco e se si rifiuta di accettare un certo tipo di realtà, non si diventa monaci ma non si è nemmeno più ciò che si era prima di una data situazione. Anzi l'attrito fra l'oggettività e la negazione passiva, passiva perché Pelle d'Asino sa soltanto quello che non vuole, provocano una dissoluzione.[16]

> [It is the story of an objective dissolution: the maiden's metamorphoses will really transform her, in spite of what she and the others may believe. That means that if you create a habit, the clothes make the man, and if you refuse to accept a certain kind of reality, you may not really be turned into a man, but surely you are not what you were before a given situation. In fact, the friction between objectivity and passive negation, passive because Pelle D'Asino (Donkeyskin) only knows what she doesn't want, causes a dissolution.]

These first reflections on habits, skin, and female protagonists immediately bring to mind Pagliarani's *Ragazza Carla*, and especially this passage from the beginning of the *poemetto*:

> Chi ci è nato vicino a questi posti
> non gli passa nemmeno per la mente
> come è utile averci un'abitudine
>   Le abitudini si fanno con la pelle
>   così tutti ce l'hanno se hanno pelle
> Ma c'è il momento che l'abitudine non tiene
> chissà che cosa insiste nel circuito
>   o fa contatto
>   o prende la tangente
> allora la burrasca
>   periferica, di terra,
> il ponte se lo copre e spazza e qualcheduno
> può cascar sotto[17]

[People born around here
it never occurs to them
just how useful it is to make a habit of it
    Habits are made with the skin
    and so everyone has them if they have skin
But there comes the moment when habits don't hold
who knows what insists in the circuit
        or makes contact
            or takes off on a tangent
then the storm,
    of dirt, on the outskirts,
it covers the bridge wipes it out and someone
could fall off]

Beyond the connection with Pagliarani's *Carla*, the meaning of Giuliani's short note and its relation to the verses just quoted is rather opaque. He might have been thinking about the progressive excavation of the self, that distinctive process of alienation that invests the inhabitants of the capitalist metropolis: the long fugue of superficial habits (as so many skins that can be worn and then discarded) causes a progressive disintegration, a dissolution of the sense of self, and leaves individuals with only a negative understanding of their personality. They only know what they don't want to be, or, to use Montale's famous verses, "Codesto solo oggi possiamo dirti / ciò che non siamo, ciò che non vogliamo."[18] This feeling, however, is lowered from its original existential sphere to the everyday "habit" of angst. Matters are rendered even more interesting by the gender of the characters expressing this continued discomfort: it might be worth remembering the epigraph that opens *La ragazza Carla*:

> Un amico psichiatra mi riferisce di una giovane impiegata tanto poco allenata alle domeniche cittadine che, spesso, il sabato, si prende un sonnifero opportunamente dosato, che la faccia dormire fino al lunedì. Ha senso dedicare a quella ragazza questa *Ragazza Carla*?[19]

> [A psychiatrist friend tells me of a young secretary who is so unprepared for Sundays in the city that, often, on Saturdays, she takes sleeping pills carefully dosed to have her sleep until Monday. Does it make any sense to dedicate to that girl this *Girl Carla?*]

Once the "skin" of the superficial habits provided by an alienating job is removed, the urban landscape becomes so inhospitable that the only practical escape is the unconsciousness (and objective dissolution, to use Giuliani's expression) of a sedated sleep.

5.2 *Pelle d'Asino*, according to Perrault

Before we continue any further with the analysis, we should reflect in brief on the oldest (as far as we are concerned) version of this tale, the one collected by Charles Perrault. The plot is well known, but it is worth highlighting a few of its details. A rich and happy king is loved by his wife and beautiful daughter; additionally, his finances are continuously replenished by a magical donkey, whose droppings are made of gold. Unfortunately, the queen dies and, with her last breath, asks the king to promise he will remarry only if he can find a bride who is more beautiful and more virtuous than herself. This is where the king gets the idea of marrying his own daughter: who else in the whole realm could rightfully be considered prettier and nobler than the late queen? The princess rejects her father's incestuous advances and, counselled by her fairy godmother, asks as a condition for her assent that enchanted, impossible dresses be made for her. The king's lust is such that he manages to satisfy every request for preposterous clothing. As a last resort, the fairy godmother suggests the princess ask for the skin of the magical donkey. The king agrees. The only thing left for the princess to do is to run away, although the fairy godmother manages to have the dresses and the donkey skin delivered to her.

The young woman seeks refuge in another realm, landing a job on a farm, where she remains for a while, wearing the donkey skin and tending to the pigs and the turkeys. The prince of that kingdom, while visiting the farm, sees Donkeyskin in one of the rare moments when she is not wearing the horrid animal hide, but rather one of her fancy magical dresses, and, naturally, falls in love with her. There are still more vicissitudes, including love-sickness, a loaf of bread containing a ring, and a ball attended by all the women in the land. Finally, the prince finds Donkeyskin and recognizes her, thanks to the ring (the one contained in the loaf of bread). His parents approve of the union, and the fairy godmother appears to explain the circumstances and offer yet more advice. They send for the incestuous king who, in the meantime, has snapped out of his folly, remarried, and is more than happy to give his blessing to the young couple. The tale, like every other by Perrault, ends with a moral, whose original French reads as follows:

> Il n'est pas malaisé de voir
> Que le but de ce Conte est qu'un Enfant apprenne
> Qu'il vaut mieux s'exposer à la plus rude peine
> Que de manquer à son devoir;
> Que la Vertu peut être infortunée

Mais qu'elle est toujours couronnée;
Que contre un fol amour et ses fougueux transports
La Raison la plus forte est une faible digue,
Et qu'il n'est point de riches trésors
Dont un Amant ne soit prodigue;
Que de l'eau claire et du pain bis
Suffisent pour la nourriture
De toute jeune Créature,
Pourvu qu'elle ait de beaux habits;
Que sous le Ciel il n'est point de femelle
Qui ne s'imagine être belle,
Et qui souvent ne s'imagine encor
Que si des trois Beautés la fameuse querelle
S'était démêlée avec elle,
Elle aurait eu la pomme d'or.[20]

[It is better to endure the worst hardships than to fail in performing one's duties. Virtue might be unlucky, but in the end, it always receives its prize. Reason is of little help against mad love, nor is there any treasure too rich that a lover wouldn't be willing to sacrifice. Pure water and stale bread is enough for any young lady, provided she has beautiful dresses. All the women in the world think of themselves as beautiful, and they all believe that, had they taken part in the famous contest of the three Beauties, the golden apple would have been theirs.]

The sexism expressed by this moral is so self-evident it hardly requires comment. Rather, I would like to make a few quick observations on the tale in general, as told in this early version: 1) as can easily be noticed from the short quotation above, Perrault's text is in verse and displays a regular rhyme pattern. Giuliani and Pagliarani have kept this structural feature in their version of the story, although they have substituted loosely organized free verse for the more rigorous scheme of the original; 2) as the story unfolds, a strong connection is built between three key elements: sex, money, and excrement. This triad has remarkable implications and echoes throughout Western culture, from patristics to psychoanalysis, and the two poets exploit this feature of the tale as much as they can in their rewriting.[21]

In fact, the fascination with "the abject" is something that is common to most writers of the Neoavanguardia, as we noted when speaking of Antonio Porta's *La scelta della voce*.[22] When it comes to Pagliarani's poetry, his general distrust for traditional ideals of order, beauty, and harmony is often expressed through a deployment of anti-sublime themes and language taken specifically from the semantic area of sex, money, and excrement we just identified. In the essay quoted in the preceding chapter, Picchione offers the following illuminating remarks:

> For Pagliarani, the seductive beauty of aesthetic forms is not only compromised by their obsolescence and fossilization, but also by their consolatory and reconciling effects. Poetry, then, must be engaged in producing forms of the anti-sublime and, through them, it must protest both against its own history and that of the world.[23]

In particular, in *Fecaloro*, a poem that is contemporaneous with the writing of *Pelle d'Asino*, "the abject is adopted rather transparently as a defiance to the value system of capitalism,"[24] focusing directly on this connection between sex, money, and feces. Once again, we can turn to Picchione's analysis:

> Fundamental structures of our present civilization are associated with acts of defecation or urination to such an extent that not only our dominant socio-economic value systems (revolving around money and gold), but also the private sphere of love are related to faeces ... The corporeal waste cannot be coopted by the capitalist principles of exchange-value and profit and thus lie outside the logic of commodification.[25]

These same mechanisms identified by Picchione in *Fecaloro* will be seen at work, quite explicitly and transparently, in *Pelle d'Asino*, which, not by chance, is subtitled "grottesco" in the version published by Scheiwiller. They are even more evident in the manuscript of Act Two, which was never published but which survives in Giuliani's archive, held at the Centro Manoscritti of the University of Pavia.

5.3 *Grottesco per musica*

The version of *Pelle d'Asino* published by Giuliani and Pagliarani begins, as was the case with Perrault's story, with a king obsessed with his wealth; only here the greed for the donkey-extruded gold is justified with vague economic theories about the circulation of currency:

PRESIDENTE Effettivamente, Maestà,
la velocità di circolazione della moneta
provoca l'inflazione, l'eccesso
di circolazione ingorga
i condotti escretori dello Stato.

È stato provato
come due più due fanno quattro.[26]

[President: In fact, your Majesty,
the speed of circulation of currency
causes inflation to go up, the excess
of circulation obstructs
the excreting conduits of the State.
It has been proven
like two and two is four.]

The economy of the country is described, metaphorically, as if it were part of the digestive tract of a living organism. Rather counter-intuitively, the excessive circulation of the gold reserve, according to the president, would lead to an excessive constipation of the entire system. And this is only one of the many incongruities scattered throughout the play. Elsewhere, we find references to pop culture and consumerism, anachronistic elements that clearly do not belong to the classic setting of a fairy tale, and that cast an ironic, parodic light on the entire plot.

In spite of all the differences and interpolations added by the two poets, this version of the story also includes the untimely death of the queen and the incestuous plans of the king for replacing her. The fairy godmother plays a smaller role, as do the magical dresses the princess requests. The decision to sacrifice the auriferous donkey and turn it into leather goods leads, at the end of the act, to a series of economic and social catastrophes: strikes, stock market crashes, and so on. Here are the last few lines of the play:

(La Principessa accenna a fuggire. Improvvisamente da tutte le soglie che danno sulla scena compaiono i messaggeri; essi compaiono secondo un rapido ritmo segnato dai tentativi di uscita effettuati dalla Principessa. Ogni volta che la ragazza si getta verso un'uscita sbatte come una falena contro un messaggero che in quel momento fa il suo annuncio. I messaggeri sono grandi grossi e impettiti. Il Re si alza e trangugia una coppa di champagne a ogni annuncio)

I MESSAGGERO – Sciopero nazionale dei trasporti
II MESSAGGERO – Interrotte le comunicazioni con la capitale
III MESSAGGERO – Serrata dei grandi magazzini
IV MESSAGGERO – Lunedì nero in Borsa
...
XII MESSAGGERO – Giovedì nero in Borsa
XIII MESSAGGERO – *(urla)* Manca la chiave!

(Pausa e fissazione generale. Il Re resta col bicchiere a mezz'aria. La Fatina dà una scoppola alla Principessa che allora riesce a fuggire. Tutti restano fermi, bloccati un attimo prima che la ragazza fugga, cioè al momento della scoppola).[27]

[(The Princess tries to flee. Suddenly, through the doors opening on stage, the messengers appear; they appear according to a quick rhythm marked by the Princess's attempts to escape. Every time the girl runs toward one of the exits, she bumps, like a moth, into a messenger who makes his announcement right at that moment. The messengers are tall, big, and imposing. At each announcement, the king gets up and drinks a glass of champagne.)

First messenger	National transportation strike
Second messenger	Communications with the capital have been interrupted
Third messenger	All shopping malls have been shut down
Fourth messenger	Black Monday at the Stock Exchange
...	
Twelfth messenger	Black Thursday at the Stock Exchange
Thirteenth messenger	(*screaming*) I'm locked out!

(Pause, everybody stops. The king is frozen, glass in hand. The Fairy Godmother slaps the Princess on the head, and she manages to flee. Everyone remains still, stuck doing what they were doing before the girl fled, that is, before the slap.)]

And here we encounter again, right at the end, the same strong irony that pervaded the entire play. In addition to the anachronistic remarks already mentioned, the authors cannot help but slip in one last gag in the old tradition of slapstick comedy: the last of the thirteen messengers delivering catastrophic news to the king cannot get in through the door; he can't find his key and he's locked out. This event casts a surreal light on the entire scene, which remains frozen and suspended, giving the Princess a chance to flee only after the encouragement of the fairy godmother's "slap."

5.4 The Play's General Plan

The general plan for the play, which survived among Giuliani's papers (file number 1 of the three mentioned on page 258), clearly precedes the version discussed above. It is interesting to note how, at that first stage of the creative process, the authors were planning on no less than four acts. The first would have ended with the death of the magical donkey, and would have included more details regarding the impossible dresses requested by the princess. There were three of them: "the dress that doesn't catch fire, the dress that doesn't stain, the dress that can't be tailored (for it's ready to wear)." Only a few hints about these magical clothes survive in the published version of the play.

Act Two introduced the hereditary prince, whom Giuliani and Pagliarani described in the following terms: "The prince is a bit dumb and snobby; he is obsessed with statistics." But the prince's idiosyncrasies went beyond these harmless traits: he had a passion for young women's tears. In one of the scenes, for instance, he witnesses Donkeyskin crying, tries to console her, and ends up with some of her tears on his hands. Immediately, he drinks them with great relish. Next, the actors perform a "ballad on the taste of tears" whose lyrics, unfortunately, have been lost. The surreal and misogynist trend continued in the next scene, where the ideal measurements of a young bride's body were discussed, leading to the "ballad of the measurements" and to the end of Act Two.

Act Three was entirely dedicated to the prince, to his lovesickness, to the conversations with a psychiatrist who was trying to cure him, and then to the decision to have all the young women in the realm parade in front of him, so that he could taste their tears. In the last scene, marriage was discussed as a last resort to cure the prince's malady.

In Act Four, Donkeyskin postponed the wedding, for she was not satisfied with the prince, who was an intellectual and lacked energy. Faced with this rejection, the prince went mad and the psychiatrist explained his problems away. At this point there was another song, this time dedicated to love. The skin of the donkey began to bleed. Another ballad followed, this one about the skin. The princess decided to return to her father, while the fairy godmother remained on stage, relating the end of the story, although the document did not specify any further details.

In this first phase, the plot was completely different: the division into acts, the prince's character, even the final resolution of the plot was changed. What needs to be emphasized, however, is that even from this early moment, the references to economics and psychology are a crucial part of the play, as well as those to the money-sex-excrement nexus that we have already mentioned and that is expressed through the insertions of specialized language in the fabric of the narrated events. The task of interrupting the action and discussing these themes is often reserved to a specific set of characters, chief among them the psychiatrist. The final version of the play does away with the specialists, and the main characters directly engage in these learned (and surreal) digressions, adding to the general sense of alienated irony.

5.5 Act Two Manuscripts

The eighteen pages of the handwritten manuscript (file 2 of our short list) constitute a first version (or, at least, one of the earliest versions) of Act Two. Handwritten pages are interspersed with long typewritten passages, which have hand corrections. This document allows the scholar to identify and appreciate certain lexical and stylistic choices. The general structure of the act, however, remains substantially the same as in the clean, typewritten copy, and thus we will concentrate our attention on that version (file 3 of the list).

While Act One ended with a locked door and the unlucky princess fleeing, the second opens on a farm where the young woman has taken refuge, without revealing her identity, using the skin of the magic animal as a disguise. A group of peasant women, who speak with a strong Venetian accent, are making ricotta, and Donkeyskin is with them. An explicit parallel is drawn between donkeys and peasants through a song sung by the labourers (the kinship between donkeys and serfs is a traditional *topos* of medieval literature throughout Europe). Giuliani and Pagliarani's farmhands sing as follows:

> Dio lo vuole! Ecco il grido bugiardo
> Che ci lanciano preti e padroni:
> e a quel grido da eterni minchioni
> ci lasciamo la pelle levar.[28]
>
> [God wants it! That's the lying cry
> priests and bosses hurl at us:
> and with that cry, like eternal simpletons,
> we let them skin us alive]

As is to be expected with a play written during the 1960s, these peasants possess a clear and focused class consciousness. What is rather surprising, though, is another passage in this same song that describes how the *padroni* (the ruling class) are capable of transmuting the sweat of the workers into money, mimicking on the one hand the work of alchemists who have successfully acquired the philosopher's stone and on the other hand the inner workings of the gold-exuding donkey.

In the following scene, the prince makes his first appearance, oversees the ricotta being made, witnesses Donkeyskin's tears, and, as in the general plan, tastes them and finds them rather delicious. The nexus excrement-sweat-tears becomes increasingly more significant:

the *padroni*, it would seem, can turn into money not only the work of their employees but also their various secretions, the very product of their passions, emotions, and pains.

Later on, Donkeyskin hides in the stables, takes off the skin that had protected her from prying eyes, and remains naked. Young Topazio, one of the farm workers, sees her and tries to seduce her. Donkeyskin lectures him on the mechanics of sex, but firmly rejects any suggestion that they proceed to a more practical approach to the subject. In the next scene, she is with the prince's secretary, who is inviting her to dine with his employer. The two indulge in a long series of sexual innuendos. Once she joins the prince for supper, however, the main topics of conversation are zoophilia and other anomalous sexual practices. The link between sex and money, between market forces and sexual drives, is further explored. At one point, the prince argues: "You speak only for yourself – here it is the opposite. It's nothing but a kind of sexual paradoxia encouraged by commercial organizations." Later, he also states: "Ah, I know the pangs of a nervous system corrupted by society. The donkey is a symbol, I know that."[29]

The characters are often aware that they belong to an apologue, and they direct the audience's attention to its most significant elements. Dinner and the lovely conversation are interrupted by a town festival taking place outside the palace. The villagers have built a large bonfire and are about to burn the "old hag," according to an ancient practice, common throughout northern Italy and central Europe. The prince embarks on a long interpretation of the ritual, using a bit of Freud and a bit of Jung. From psychology, the conversation turns to law, and to an attempt to distinguish between profanity and slander. These discussions work as an aphrodisiac, and Donkeyskin seems finally willing to give in to the prince's advances. Suddenly, however, young Topazio, who was intent on chopping up the old hag, preparing it to be burned, sets the dummy aside and jumps on Donkeyskin and the prince, stabbing both to death. The curtain is drawn and the fairy godmother appears, wrapped in a large piece of cloth; speaking in a clear, slow voice, she announces: "The problem with the dead donkey is that it requires an interpretation."[30]

Not only is the fable radically modified, but the reasons for the changes are left unexplained: it is the task of the audience to make sense of them and reconnect the various themes, observations, social criticisms, and sarcastic remarks scattered throughout the play. Thinking back to the general plan, and to Giuliani's letter, which we quoted earlier, it seems likely that a third act might not have been entirely necessary. If the two authors had decided to add one, however, it would probably have taken an entirely new and different direction, leaving behind the vicissitudes of the prince, the princess, the king, and the villagers.

In fact, as we mentioned in the previous chapter, Pagliarani's plays and poems often end in similar unresolved "deltas": the interest in the actions of the characters evaporates, and something obliquely related to the events described comes into focus, through a lateral movement. In the case of *Pelle d'Asino*, as it was for *La bella addormentata nel bosco*, the unsettling nature of this rhetorical choice is rendered even more striking by the implicit comparison with Perrault's originals: while those stories ended with clearly stated morals, intended to educate an audience that was assumed to be passive and in need of moral admonishments, Pagliarani (and Giuliani, in this case) turn the tables, directing a challenge to their viewers and readers and a request for collaboration in determining the ultimate meaning of the performance, as well as its moral and political implications.

5.6 The Comparison with Giuliani's *Povera Juliet* ("Poor Juliet")

We can now try to summarize the stylistic traits that we have observed in our analysis and that remained constant throughout the creative process that led to the different versions of the text: 1) Perrault's fable was modernized through the insertion of numerous anachronisms and was rewritten to reflect the changed social and political context; 2) many different specialized languages, coming in particular from the fields of psychology, economics, and the sciences, were mixed into the fabric of the play; 3) a final moral, determined once and for all, is explicitly rejected and is replaced with an open invitation for collaboration. As we have seen, these are some of the core characteristics of the theatre of the neo-avant-garde. We have verified this statement in detail by looking at many of Pagliarani's plays. We will have the chance to return to his work one last time to discuss his *Faust di Copenaghen* (and, more generally, the rewritings of Faust's story by the Neoavanguardia) in the second half of this chapter. At this point, I would like to pause and dedicate a few pages to Alfredo Giuliani who, in addition to providing many theoretical insights into the poetry of the Novissimi and Gruppo 63, and its relation to the theatre, has also extensively practised the art of playwriting, providing us with a few interesting and useful texts, each of which is worthy of reflection and analysis.

The obvious place to start is *Povera Juliet*, one of the first plays, if not the very first, written by Giuliani, which debuted in 1963, during the first meeting of Gruppo 63 in Palermo, and was then restaged in 1965, in Rome, by the Compagnia Teatro dei Novissimi. In a theoretical essay that reflected on the work of director Ken Dewey and his idea of "action theatre," Giuliani mentions his own play, which Dewey had directed:

> La mia breve commedia può essere considerata, del resto impropriamente, una partitura informale, giacché i personaggi non sono identificati e nel contesto (tranne le battute finali) non è indicata alcuna azione scenica ... Spettatore (o lettore), regista, attori, – questa almeno è l'intenzione – devono poter sentire la presenza di uno spazio teatrale liberato, se non da tutte, da molte convenzioni comunemente accettate.[31]

> [My brief comedy can be considered, even though that is not quite correct, an informal score, for the various characters are not identified and the stage directions (with the exception of the final lines) do not indicate any action on stage ... Spectators (or readers), director, actors – at least this was the intention – should all feel the presence of a theatrical space that has been freed from many, if not exactly all, the conventions that are usually accepted.]

And then, a few pages later:

> Lo spettatore era sottoposto ad una distrazione continua e a un'attenzione altrettanto continua, ma perpetuamente delusa e ricatturata. Fu un vero attentato al testo e al teatro a cui contribuirono i movimenti degli attori, le proiezioni sul soffitto (effettuate dal pittore Perilli), i rumori.[32]

> [The spectator had to endure a continuous distraction, as well as a continuous focus that was perpetually frustrated and then recaptured. It was an explicit assault on the text and the theatre that was made possible by the movements of the actors, the images projected on the ceiling (the work of the painter Perilli), and the noises.]

The programmatic intentions Giuliani articulates in these two passages closely match the observations we made in regard to *Pelle d'Asino*, especially if we keep in mind the systematic linguistic and cognitive dissonance deployed in that play, and the antagonistic attitude toward literary and theatrical tradition as well as formal and stylistic conventions. The opening lines of *Povera Juliet* will further confirm the validity of our remarks:

> — penose irritazioni/come può una ragazza
> — se l'ha fatto apposta
> — sarebbe entrare nella pelle
> — nel paese dell'odio scacciamo persone d'amore
> — povera Juliet, Frank morto dopo un sorso
> — ma sai che poi svanisce

— è la flussione particolarmente intensa delle regole elementari
— la prescrizione è contenuta nel prodotto.[33]

[— thoughtful annoyances/how can a girl
— but he did it on purpose
— it would be like getting under the skin
— in the land of hate we banished people of love
— poor Juliet, Frank died after just one sip
— but you know that after that it vanishes
— it's the particularly intense fluxion of elementary rules
— the prescription is included with the product.]

None of these lines has been assigned to one particular character, and the progression from one to the next seems to be regulated by a poetic rather than a theatrical flow. At the beginning, there are a few vague references to some accident or misfortune, perhaps even a case of poisoning, although it might be that the title is what is responsible for priming the reader to arrive at an interpretation that is not necessarily supported by hard textual evidence, despite "Frank died after just one sip" (perhaps a new name for the old Shakespearean Romeo?) and the "prescription is included with the product" (here, too, perhaps we find a veiled reference to the famous drama: "O true apothecary! Thy drugs are quick").[34]

In the conclusion, while one of the characters is riding a stationary bike, such as those used to exercise, a boy makes his entrance (the stage directions will offer more details):

(mentre l'ospite pedala sempre più disinvolta entra il bambino e le si avvicina)
(il bambino offre all'ospite un oggetto raccattato per terra)
— signora, signora, le è caduto questo.
— ma non è mio
(il bambino offre all'ospite un'altra cosa raccattata per terra)
— allora questo
— neppure
(il bambino trae un oggetto dalla tasca)
— prenda almeno questo
(l'ospite smette di pedalare)
— ma è caduto dal cielo
— quant'è vero, mio dio
(il bambino fa girare con la mano il pedale della bicicletta)[35]

[*(while the guest pedals increasingly more at ease, the boy enters and walks up to her)*
(the boy offers to the guest an object he picked up from the floor)

— madam, madam, you dropped this.
— but that's not mine
(*the boy offers her another object collected from the floor*)
— how about this, then
— that's not mine either
(*the boy takes an object out of his pocket*)
— at least take this one
(*the guest stops pedalling*)
— but this fell from the sky
— how true, dear god
(*using his hand, the boy turns the bicycle's pedal*)]

Here we find another final twist, the same indeterminacy and openness left to the imagination and the work of the spectator that we observed in *Pelle d'Asino* and other plays by both Giuliani and Pagliarani.

5.7 The Rewriting of Jarry's *Ubu Roi*

Another work that shows many points of contact with Pagliarani's theatre, and that of the neo-avant-garde generally, is *Nostro padre Ubu* (*Our Father Ubu*),[36] a play that Giuliani wrote for the radio around 1973, and that he intended as an introduction to the life and poetic world of Alfred Jarry, as it combines the three main Ubu plays (*Ubu Rex, Ubu Cuckolded*, and *Ubu Enchained*),[37] as well as a number of other works. In a note, Giuliani states that,

> Il testo fu commissionato dalla RAI nel 1973, in occasione del centenario di Alfred Jarry. Nel montaggio ho utilizzato alcuni brani, qua e là ritoccandoli, della traduzione di C. Rugafiori e H.J. Maxwell pubblicata nel 1969 dall'Adelphi (che qui ringrazio). Altri brani, più o meno manomessi, provengono da opere di Jarry non comprese nella raccolta Adelphi, come *L'amour en visites*, da *Almanach du père Ubu*, dai Cahiers du Collège de 'Pataphysique, biografie e agiografie di Jarry. Le pagine di musica sono riprodotte dal vol. VIII delle *Œuvres Complètes d'Alfred Jarry* (Éditions du livre, Monte-Carlo et Henri Kaeser, 1948); la proprietà della musica di Claude Terrace è delle Éditions du Mercure de France.[38]

> [This text was commissioned by RAI in 1973, on the occasion of Alfred Jarry's centenary. In this montage, I used certain passages, retouching them here and there, of C. Rugafiori and H.J. Maxwell's translation, published in 1969 by Adelphi (to whom I am grateful). Other passages, more or less altered, come from works by Jarry not included in that Adelphi

> anthology, such as *L'amour en visites*, from *Almanach du père Ubu*, from the Cahiers du Collège de 'Pataphysique, as well as various biographies and hagiographies of Jarry. The music here reproduced is from vol. VIII of the *Oeuvres Complètes d'Alfred Jarry*, Éditions du livre, Monte-Carlo et Henri Kaeser, Lausanne, 1948; the copyright of Claude Terrace's music belongs to Éditions du Mercure de France.]

The unusually detailed information (especially if compared to the way Pagliarani annotated his own texts) regarding the source materials for the play contrasts with the liberty with which Giuliani treated them, introducing numerous changes, manipulations, and interpolations. The celebratory occasion contributes to casting the rebellious and unconventional author as a classic of avant-garde literature; as such, his works become good candidates for the by-now-usual treatment reserved for the masterpieces of the past: alteration, appropriation, and modernization. In addition, Giuliani decides to blur the line that separates the author from his own work by including in his version of *Ubu* the voices of a narrator and of Jarry himself, who becomes a character with the same substance as the strange marionettes generated by his own imagination.

While the neo-avant-garde theatre's debts to futurism and to Eliot have been discussed in earlier pages of this volume, a deeper analysis of this play will reveal how crucial Jarry was to shaping the role of the stage as the place where linguistic experimentation and political engagement (although in the form of preposterous, gratuitous, and yet subtly unsettling provocation) could be reconciled. It was, in fact, quite surprising to discover so many parallels between Jarry, not usually invoked by critics as one of the inspirations for the Neoavanguardia, and the plays we have been examining.

5.8 Ubu's Intertextuality

First of all, let us look at the components of this play: Giuliani credits in his note the Adelphi translation by Rugafiori and Maxwell. However, shortly after completing the play, in 1977, the same publishing house issued a new edition of the *Ubu* plays, translated by Bianca Candian and with a preface by Giuliani himself. For that occasion, he introduced *Ubu* and its origins as follows:

> Quando nel 1888 il quindicenne Alfred Jarry fu messo in collegio a Rennes, per proseguire gli studi liceali, aveva già composto un ricco repertorio infantile di commedie in prosa e in versi della più varia ispirazione scolastica e profanatoria ... È lecito immaginare che Jarry dovette essere

> felicissimo di trovare che gli interni del collegio si tramandavano da anni una leggenda farsesca, un po' scritta e un po' orale, concepita ai danni del professore di fisica Hébert, soprannominato "le P.H." (il Piacca) o Padre Eb, Ebée, Ebon, Ebance, Ebouille e altrimenti. Il povero Hébert era divenuto oggetto di una perpetua ricreazione, trasfigurato in protagonista di un'epopea eroicomica, frutto della fantasia collettiva e di un gioco spropositato e impietoso ... È probabile che già in questa fase il personaggio (col nome di Piacca o Padre Eb) abbia acquisito i tratti primigenii e gli arnesi caratteristici della propria figura: il gran pancione tubiforme detto "ventraglia," la testa piriforme, gli occhi porcini e il muso di coccodrillo, un uncino per afferrare i nobili, il bastone da fisica (simbolo della natura, della scienza e delle istituzioni), il bastone da finanza (simbolo degli onori sociali, del reddito e dell'accumulazione), nonché la *pompe à merdre*, o pompa da fogna, con la quale l'energumeno minaccia di svuotare i suoi avversari.[39]
>
> [In 1888, when Alfred Jarry, then fifteen years old, was sent to a boarding school in Rennes to continue his studies, he had already composed a rich childish repertoire of comedies in prose and verse, characterized by a most varied scholastic and profane inspiration ... It is reasonable to imagine that Jarry must have been very happy to find out that the students of the boarding school had been passing down for many years a farcical legend, in part written in part oral, created at the expense of their physics professor Hébert, nicknamed "le P.H." (the Peeaitch) or Father Eb, Ebée, Ebon, Ebance, Ebouille, among other things. Poor Hébert had become the butt of a perpetual joke, turned into the protagonist of a mock heroic saga, born of the collective imagination and a merciless, exaggerated game ... It is likely that, as early as this first phase, the character (with the name Peeaitch or Father Eb) had already acquired the original traits and distinctive attributes of his persona: the great, cylindrical belly called "gidouille," the pear-shaped head, the porcine eyes, and the crocodile muzzle, a hook to grab the noblemen, a physics stick (symbol of nature, science, and institutions), a finance stick (symbol of social status, income, and accumulation of wealth), to say nothing of the *pompe à merdre*, or sewer pump, with which the brute threatens to suck his enemies dry.

In spite of the radically different plot and characters, *Nostro padre Ubu* recalls *Pelle D'Asino* in that both plays show a high degree of intertextuality. However, while for the collaboration with Pagliarani the materials interpolated to the original tale were anachronistically drawn from multiple sources completely external to Perrault and his milieu, here Giuliani taps into Jarry's fantastic and proto-surrealist imagination in order to regale his audience with a layered and nuanced portrait of the French writer. In fact, a marked intertextual dimension is not at all extraneous to Jarry's original play; many critics have observed how it is actually one of the key characteristics of *Ubu* as well as other works of his. Giuliani himself points this out in the already quoted preface:

> Ma la pantagruelica vitalità intestinale di Ubu non tollera antagonismi, egli divora tutto e ha la più abominevole frenesia di restituire tutto alla notte (che può essere il buco di una botola o l'abisso delle sue tasche), come dire al sempiterno ciclo parossistico della sua insaziabile "ventraglia."[40]

> [But Ubu's pantagruelic intestinal vitality doesn't tolerate antagonisms; he devours everything and cultivates the most abominable lust to give everything back to the night (which can become the opening of a trapdoor or the abyss of his own pockets), which is the same as to say the eternal, exasperated cycle of his insatiable "gidouille."]

As with every enemy he encounters, all the money he can lay his hands on, all the food that is put before him, so Ubu is endlessly incorporating quotations, echoes, and references coming from the most disparate sources. He is a black hole into which inevitably disappear all the fragments of language, thought, and culture that happen to venture too close to the gaping chasm that occupies his core. Equally uncontainable is his presence throughout Jarry's oeuvre. As Linda Klieger Stillman observes in her monograph *Alfred Jarry*,

> The "Ubu phenomenon" offers a particularly apt example of intertextuality in Jarry's works. A comprehensive interpretation of the character depends upon an understanding of Ubu, not only as the gross and lunatic panjandrum of the *Ubu* plays, but also as a cauldron of complex aesthetic and philosophical passions. Ubu appears in seven important and diverse texts, indicating the consequence of Ubu in Jarry's literary universe. *L'art et la science* ("Art and Science"), published in 1893, constitutes Ubu's official début. Unpublished versions of *Ubu roi* ("King Ubu") and *Ubu cornu* ("Ubu Cuckolded") existed, of course, with different titles, ever since the physics class of Monsieur Hébert inspired certain schoolboys to invent Ubu's ancestors. Between the ages of twelve and fifteen (1885–88), Jarry composed several plays and poems, collectively titled (between 1897 and 1898, by the adult Jarry) *Ontogénie* ("Ontogenesis"). Themes and images anticipate the *Ubu* texts. In *Les Antliaclastes* and *Bidasse et Compagnie,* for example, the scatological theme is paramount. The nascent character type, monolithic and overbearing, dominates. The adolescent Jarry already

> favored symbolic objects and machines—especially the sewage pump. His fondness for puns, neologisms, anagrammatic names, and use of archaic vocabulary was developing. All of these early works exhibit the style of the "*potache*," the impertinent and keen-witted schoolboy, clearly marking them as predecessors to the *Ubu* saga.[41]

The creation of Ubu as a character spills over several texts, and looms large over the imaginary landscape of Jarry's creative world. At the same time, he marks the place where different layers of meaning, different impressions, coming from various moments of the author's life, progressively accrete and stratify, to form the strange and excessive pear-shaped personage. To this endogenous intertextuality springing from the many versions and rewritings of Ubu's adventures one must add the numerous influences, sources, and texts from which Jarry derives his narrative. All of them, however, are smoothed out, like pebbles in a riverbed: they are reworked by the author's peculiar linguistic sensibility and his scatological humour, and are displayed throughout the play like so many wrecks lined up on the shore after a monstrous storm. As Giuliani notes in his preface,

> Difatti, la personalità (di Ubu) è una figurazione grottesca e demonicamente ambigua dell'universalità, un'astrazione che agisce con impassibile dileggio delle rimozioni. "Lo swedenborghiano dottor Misés," disse Jarry presentando Ubu Re "ha paragonato in maniera eccellente le opere rudimentali alle più perfezionate e gli esseri embrionali ai più sviluppati, in quanto ai primi difettano tutti gli accidenti, protuberanze e qualità, il che conferisce loro la forma sferica o pressappoco, com'è il caso dell'ovulo e del signor Ubu, e ai secondi si aggiungono tanti particolari personalizzanti ch'essi acquistano ugualmente la forma sferica, in virtù di questo assioma, che il corpo più levigato è quello che presenta il maggior numero di asperità. Ecco perché sarete liberi di vedere nel signor Ubu le molteplici allusioni che vorrete, o un semplice fantoccio, o la deformazione a cui uno studiantello ha sottoposto uno dei suoi professori, il quale rappresentava per lui tutto il grottesco che mai fosse stato."[42]

> [In fact, (Ubu's) personality is a grotesque, demonically ambiguous representation of universality, an abstraction that acts with the stone-faced mockery of repression. "Dr. Misés, a follower of Swedenborg," Jarry said introducing *Ubu rex*, "has beautifully compared the most rudimentary works to the most sophisticated ones, and embryonic beings to the most developed, for the former lack all accidents, protuberances, and qualities – which causes them to have a spherical, or

> nearly spherical, shape, as is the case for the egg and for mister Ubu —, the latter display so many personalizing details that they equally reach a spherical form, as a consequence of this axiom: the smoothest body is that which possesses the highest quantity of asperities. This is why you will be free to see in mister Ubu all the various allusions you desire, or a simple dummy, or the deformation to which a schoolboy has subjected one of his professors, who, in his opinion, represented everything grotesque that ever existed."]

Ubu can absorb and neutralize any number of symbolic and allegorical interpretations without being weighed down in the least by their demands on him and his behaviour. He can become an encyclopedia of all the evils in modern life and, at the same time, because of his rebellious and anarchist energy, express the best hope for overcoming those same evils.

5.9 Ubu's Language: Interpretations and Puppets

Regarding the language used by Jarry in his plays, we can easily see a convergence with the experimental research carried out by Giuliani as well as the rest of the Neoavanguardia. As Klieger Stillman notes in her monograph,

> The linguistic world of Ubu could be said to "disarticulate" language. Ambiguity, puns, neologisms, clichés, and words used for their morphophonetic rather than semantic content characterize that world. Ubu's instinctual, anarchic nature is translated by an aggressive discourse that constitutes a revolt against traditional usages of language. On phonetic, lexical, and syntactic levels, deviations from the norm abound. Words, for Jarry, function as "crossroads" and as "polyhedra": the speech on the living *polyèdres* cultivated and studied by Achras in *Ubu Cuckolded* serves as a commentary on the operation of signs in this specific literary universe. The many-sided solids not only give birth to infinite offspring but are capable of revolting against Achras who must use physical force to keep them well behaved.[43]

The parallelisms between Jarry's *Ubu* and Giuliani and Pagliarani's *Pelle d'Asino* continue if we look at the themes woven together by the two plays. While *Pelle d'Asino* was built around the connection between money, sex, and excrement, Ubu insists on "merdre," "phynance," and "physique." The first two of these terms have been deformed in that expressionistic fashion we have just observed. In particular, "merdre," the first word pronounced on stage by the inaugural Ubu play, *Ubu rex*, becomes a symbol capable of concentrating all of Jarry's explosive anarchist rebellion. Once again, we can turn to Klieger Stillman for elucidation:

> A lexical triad— *merdre, phynance,* and *physique*—underpins the *Ubu* plays. *"Merdre,"* the first word uttered in *King Ubu* (and the cause of scandal at its premiere), is a defiant child-like projectile hurled at the disdained order of the adult world. Ubu deifies excrement, singing hymns to his *merdre-pump.* The addition of the "r" resulted in the creation of a talisman, a magical word that opens into a legendary universe. It is the word shouted by Ubu to signal his political coup. Written in capital letters, it symbolizes Ubu's egocentric and vulgar nature. A simple word suddenly became charged with mythic significance: *merdre* is not merely a play on words. As the most privileged entry in Ubu's lexicon, *merdre* is happily applied to people and objects in his universe, which really only exists in relation to Ubu himself: he addresses his officer as *"garçon de ma merdre"* and his wife as *"Madame de ma merdre."* Enamored of his *pompe à merdre* in *Ubu Cuckolded,* he informs his world with overflowing, obscene matter ... *Merdre,* initially a symbol of destruction, acquires a philosophical and conceptual value. Jarry, like the alchemists he admired, transmuted matter, making even of feces an extraordinary symbol of the union of opposites.[44]

The connection with *Pelle d'Asino* and its own sex-money-excrement triad is absolutely undeniable, so much so that one wonders if Giuliani and Pagliarani were reading Jarry while composing their play. One last element, crucial to the success of the Ubu mythology with the neo-avant-garde, is the fact that, from the play's first inception, the main characters are presented as marionettes. In fact, the first performances of the *Ubu* plays that took place in the Théâtre de Phynance, a fictional institution invented by Jarry and his schoolmate Charles Morin, were puppet shows. Giuliani opens his preface insisting on this feature:

> Il nostro Re Ubu, anzi Padre Ubu, è notoriamente un burattino. Il suo più prossimo antenato è il famosissimo Guignol, e il suo maggior titolo di gloria è di essersi accaparrato con una violenta intrusione un posto di riguardo tra i miti del teatro moderno senza tradire mai la propria natura burattinesca. I greci chiamavano il burattino *neuròspastos*, "mosso per mezzo di nervi, di funicelle": la parola è mirabilmente funzionale, dato che per vocazione questa creatura insofferente d'anima non è affatto un personaggio con un destino, ma un meccanismo d'allusione. Non appena compare sulla scena, il burattino s'impone subito come fosse l'autore di se stesso. Sembrando il

suo comportamento verbale e le sue azioni dipendere esclusivamente dai "nervi," la sua personalità risulta illusoriamente semplice e sorprendente come il pensiero più esatto. In un articolo pubblicato da *La Revue blanche* il 1° (gennaio 1897), poche settimane dopo la rappresentazione di *Ubu Re*, Alfred Jarry … notava con fredda aggressività: "non c'è da stupirsi che il pubblico sia rimasto sbalordito alla vista del suo ignobile doppio." Gli "ubucoli" avevano protestato perché Ubu pronunciava idiozie invece che battute di spirito. Ma Jarry aveva facile guoco nel dimostrare che le idiozie sono più profonde. Il burattino ha la testa di legno, e questa è la sua trasmentale, immensa superiorità. In più, i suoi gesti non patiscono i limiti della volgarità umana, sono meccanici e infinitamente liberi di fissare l'impersonalità del tipo.[45]

[As everyone knows, our King Ubu, or rather Father Ubu, is a puppet. His closest ancestor is the famous Guignol, while his main claim to fame is having succeeded in securing for himself, through a violent intrusion, a place of honour among the myths of modern theatre without betraying his puppet nature. The Greeks called puppets *neuròspatos*, "moved by means of nerves, wires": the word is remarkably functional, since, by vocation, this soulless creature is not a character with a destiny, but rather a mechanism of allusion. As soon as he appears on stage, the puppet immediately asserts himself as his own author. Since his verbal behaviour and his actions seem to depend exclusively on "nerves," his personality comes across as deceptively simple and as surprising as the most abstract of thoughts. In an article published in *La Revue blanche* on the first of January 1897, after the performance of *Ubu Rex*, Alfred Jarry … noted with cold aggressiveness: "it is not surprising that the audience was shocked when faced with their vile double." The "*ubucoles*" protested because Ubu uttered idiotic statements instead of witty remarks. It is easy for Jarry to prove how idiocy is a lot deeper than wit. The puppet has a wooden head, and this is his immense, trans-mental superiority. Plus, his gestures are not constrained by the limitations of human vulgarity; they are mechanical and infinitely free to express the impersonality of the model.]

Once more, we get a taste of Jarry's uncanny ability to create paradoxes and permeate his whole text with the disquieting ambiguity that they generate. Many other authors who belonged to the "historical" avant-garde would share his interest in puppets; in fact, the Neoavanguardia theatre, as we have seen with the works of Ricci in chapter 1, for instance, would have been impossible without the use of this versatile tool, capable simultaneously of abstraction and introspection. As Klieger Stillman observes,

> To a large degree, Jarry's interest in marionettes derives from a desire to be rid of theatrical conventions, and above all the actor whom Jarry considered to always betray the poet. "Only marionettes, of which one is master, sovereign, and Creator,... translate our thoughts passively and in a rudimentary way." He preferred a symbolic rapport with the "real" world and rejected a naturalist copying of it. The décor as well as the acting of King Ubu conforms to the goals of condensation, simplification, and stylization: to that end, against an unchanging background a well-dressed character would enter, as in the puppet theater, in order to hang up a placard indicating the scene's location ... Ubu, of course, never changes his costume. He indicates superficial changes in his condition by means of an accumulation of heteroclite props: stick, stakes, broom, crown, handcuffs, ball and chains, valise, umbrella, and so forth. The tangible leads directly to "irreality." The acting must therefore be simple, synthetic, and evocative; the décor symbolic, dynamic, and synchronic, the material extension of the psyche. Finally, the *mise en scène*, borrowing from the puppet theater, but deformed to suit Jarry's personal obsessions, verges on the metaphysical. Like Ubu, oaf and vampire, it is a tragicomic model of alienation.[46]

Reality is approached by means of abstraction and symbolic substitution, rather than through a mimetic process aimed at disguising representation as a transparent and objective process. Giuliani shared the same uneasiness with Ubu's ability to turn the most concrete and even vile aspects of reality into subtle, alienating traces of a hidden, perhaps transcendental reality. In one last quotation from his preface, he writes,

> Il genio di Jarry è profeticamente ammiccante. La scrittura energica, lucida, dirompente del burattinaio scansa con cura ogni simbolismo esoterico e trascendentale, e affida la funzione simbolica agli oggetti più triviali, la dinamica teatrale ai sussulti farseschi più corrivi e sbrigativi. Lo spirito studentesco della ricreazione, che semplifica il mondo con l'arbitrio creativo, è rispettato. Eppure, ... che cos'è che sarebbe questa buffonata? L'infamia ilaro-tragica di Ubu mette addosso un sospetto metafisico, apocalittico. Chi è questo tiranno libertario, che non si pone mai il problema di se stesso, che non fa alcuna distinzione tra intelligenza e stupidità, tra catastrofe e sopravvivenza, tra regno e esilio, tra libertà e schiavitù? ... Per Jarry esoterico il cranio è un carcere, e soltanto attraverso la decomposizione del cervello si ritorna nella notte dei tempi a sognare il Paradiso. Come si sa, la patafisica inventata da Jarry è la "scienza delle soluzioni immaginarie," e il burattino la porta a spasso con perfetta e ignara improntitudine. Questa ingorda doppiezza (scienza dissimulata e totale incoscienza) garantisce Ubu dall'impatto con le "soluzioni" reali

> … La logica di Ubu, per quanto atrocemente terrestre, è commensurabile soltanto alla poesia, la cui imbecillità è sacra come la folgore.[47]

> [Jarry's genius is prophetically allusive. The energetic, lucid, explosive writings of this puppet master carefully dodge any esoteric and transcendental symbolism, entrusting the symbolic function to the most trivial objects, and the theatrical dynamics to the most farcical and facile gasps. The recess-like schoolboy spirit, which simplifies the world through arbitrary creativity, is upheld. And yet, … what is this buffoonery all about? Ubu's mock-tragic infamy instils a sort of metaphysical, apocalyptic suspicion. Who is this libertarian tyrant, who never seems to question himself, who makes no distinction between intelligence and stupidity, catastrophe and survival, reign and exile, freedom and slavery? … According to Jarry's esotericism, the skull is a prison, and only through decomposition can the brain return to the night of time, to dreaming of Paradise. As we all know, pataphysics, invented by Jarry, is the "science of imaginary solutions," and the puppet parades it around with perfect and unaware impudence. This greedy duplicity (a dissimulated science united with a complete recklessness) protects Ubu from the impact of real "solutions." … Ubu's logic, although atrociously terrestrial, is commensurable only to poetry, whose idiocy is sacred, like the thunderbolt.]

Luigi Gozzi, another important protagonist of Gruppo 63 and the Neoavanguardia, has spent much time pondering Jarry's works and probing the true essence of Ubu; he dedicated to this subject an illuminating essay entitled "Di Jarry e del personaggio," published in the same monographic issue of *Il Verri*, completely devoted to theatre, that also collected the already mentioned article by Giuliani, "La poesia a teatro." Regarding the importance of puppets, Gozzi observed that,

> Su questo si è molto disputato: non tanto, voglio dire, sulle qualità "burattinesche" dell'Ubu quanto sulla incongruenza e l'assurdità di un teatro che pretendeva attraverso il "burattinesco" di ridarci l'immagine dell'uomo, facendo ricorso alla maschera, alla finzione, all'evasione pura e semplice. Anche Ubu si cala nei panni del "pantin" (è da sottolineare in questo senso la presenza importantissima dei suoi tre "palotins": Giron, Pile, Cotice), si fa Guignol proprio per esagerare al limite la sua virtualità."[48]

> [On this issue there has been much discussion: not so much, I mean, on the "puppet-like" qualities of Ubu, but rather on the incongruity and absurdity of a theatre that, ostensibly, intended to give us back the image of man through the "puppet," resorting to masks, fictions, pure and simple escapism. Ubu

also wears the appearance of a "*pantin*" (to this purpose, it must be stressed, the presence of his three "*palotins*," Giron, Pile, and Cotice, is crucial), he becomes Guignol to exaggerate as much as possible his virtuality!]

Like Giuliani and Klieger Stillman, Gozzi also ventures to offer an interpretation of Ubu's ambiguous identity, and along with many other insightful observations, he writes that,

> Ubu è personaggio in quanto luogo di attributi, polo capace di attirare su di sé una molteplicità discorde di qualità fittizie e subito consumabili; ciò è molto lontano da qualsiasi criterio di rispecchiamento e di credibilità, caso mai si tratta di un processo in cui sia credibilità che rispecchiamento appaiono decisamente posti nella loro dimensione assoluta, e in tutta la loro ambiguità ... Attraverso la sua qualifica di protagonista incoerente Ubu afferma una chiave di lettura importantissima che è quella del principio strutturale presenza-assenza.[49]

> [Ubu is a character only insofar as he is a locus of attributes, a pole capable of attracting to himself a cacophony of fictional qualities that can be immediately consumed; this is very far from any criterion of mirroring and credibility; if anything his is a process in which credibility and mirroring are posited in their absolute dimension, in all of their ambiguity ... Through his qualifications as incoherent protagonist, Ubu affirms a very important interpretive principle, that is the structural principle of presence-absence.]

By "mirroring" and "credibility" Gozzi, I believe, refers to the same paradoxical stance observed by Klieger Stillman and Giuliani – that is, the rejection of mimesis and the creation of a symbolist and abstract form of communication. Furthermore, Gozzi identifies with great clarity the very same principle that, as we saw in chapter 3, is at the core of poetry brought to the stage: the dynamic between presence and absence, the presence of the voice in the muted pages of the book, and the way in which this absence can be exploited for the purposes of poetic expression.

5.10 Jarry's Reception in Italy

It is not surprising that a sophisticated and intelligent protagonist of the national cultural debate such as Gozzi was so keenly attuned to the rediscovery of Jarry, his works, and his contribution to the advancement of avant-garde art. One might wonder, however, how the general public viewed this revival. Once more, we can turn to the holdings of Giuliani's archives to find two newspaper clippings that preserved contemporary reviews – one by Alfredo Cattabiani in *La Stampa*, and another by Giovanni Bogliolo in *Il Tempo* – of Giuliani's *Nostro padre Ubu*, as well as the Adelphi edition of Jarry, for which he had written the preface.

In his review, Bogliolo begins by lamenting the inclusion of the French writer among the modern classics before his works had been adequately "deciphered":

> Per Jarry, l'annessione ufficiale alle storie letterarie e la consacrazione nelle collane di classici sono arrivate prima di una convincente decifrazione della sua opera, sulla scia di quella perentoria imposizione di gusti e di putative paternità letterarie che hanno sistematicamente praticato le avanguardie nel nostro secolo.[50]
>
> [In Jarry's case the official inclusion in literary history and his consecration among the classics happened before a convincing deciphering of his works, as a result of that peremptory imposition of taste and putative literary paternities that the avant-garde movements have always practised in our century.]

In Bogliolo's mind, it would seem, the popularity acquired by Jarry among intellectuals is the product of an arbitrary imposition, rather than the result of a genuine interest in the writer's style, ideas, and works. Furthermore, he implies that this is just the latest abuse perpetrated by the avant-gardes on the general public.[51] He goes on to disparage the French writer and his readers, calling them "initiates" who "reject as sacrilege any unbiased process of critical assessment"[52] of his works. In conclusion, he exhumes the old criticism, eternally levelled by detractors against the avant-gardes: their oeuvre might have been useful to destroy the most dated conventions of traditional art, but they haven't produced anything worth experiencing, nothing that will last. In his own words,

> Nessuno potrà mai disconoscere a Jarry di avere – con Ubu e con Faustroll, col Théâtre des Phynances e con la Patafisica – reso inutilizzabile la tradizione e la stessa inveterata concezione della letteratura, ma sono stati altri a fondare su quelle rovine nuove e più vitali ipotesi di lavoro letterario.[53]
>
> [No one can ever dispute the fact that Jarry – with *Ubu*, *Faustroll*, the Théâtre des Phynances, and pataphysics – has rendered unusable tradition and the most inveterate ideas regarding literature, but others have the merit of having built, on those ruins, new and more vital hypotheses for literary work.]

We are left in the dark as to the identities of these more vital builders who have rescued the *Novecento* from its ruins, but at least we are regaled with a prophecy: "when the scores of our century are settled," Bogliolo closes his article, "it will be clear how Father Ubu has had a host of nieces and nephews even more numerous and unmanageable than those of the often-reviled Father Bresciani."[54] Looking from our vantage point, now that the "new" century is well under way, Bogliolo's prediction seems rather gratuitous, especially his comparison with Antonio Bresciani, who, as we all know, was the object of a famous *stroncatura* (harsh criticism) by De Sanctis:[55] "Father Bresciani is a man of little intelligence and of vulgar temperament, without gall, without spirit, one of those men cut of so rough a cloth that the well-meaning will pity him and say: 'he is a good man!'"[56]

Not all journalists, however, extended such a cold welcome to Jarry and the fruit of his literary labours. As Alfredo Cattabiani observed with surprising acumen and conciseness in an article published in *La Stampa* on 10 February 1978,

> *Ubu* squarcia i veli delle regole e delle convenienze e disegna nel contempo una grottesca e piumata metafora del Potere totalitario, celebrando ironicamente il Terrore – filiazione dell'uomo completamente libero nella sua soggettività, illimitata e incontrollata, sovrano assoluto dopo la morte degli dei – alla luce del pensiero "patafisico universale," che sonnecchia in ogni uomo, ma è pronto a svegliarsi, ad apparire come un fantasma a lungo inconsciamente evocato, col suo riso sgangherato e provocatore che vanifica le apparenze, ponendoci di fronte all'intollerabile, all'assurdo, alla rivelazione ultima dell'esistenza.[57]
>
> [*Ubu* tears through all rules and niceties while creating a grotesque and ornate metaphor of totalitarian power, ironically celebrating Terror – the product of a man completely free in his own unlimited and uncontrolled subjectivity, crowned the absolute monarch after the death of the gods – from the perspective of "universal pataphysical" thought, something that lies dormant in every man, yet is ready to awake, to appear like a ghost that for a long time, unconsciously, we have tried to evoke, with its rickety and provoking laughter that nullifies appearances, forcing us to face the intolerable, the absurd, the ultimate revelation of existence.]

The idea that not everyone in Italy was sneering at Jarry's works is rather comforting. In fact, reading the following passage, where Cattabiani connects the dots for his readers, linking this great pioneer of theatre to the more recent experiments of Artaud (and his followers), is almost enough to restore one's hope in cultural journalism:

> Le sue (di Jarry) commedie bruciarono, al loro apparire, naturalismo, simbolismo, psicologismo, saltando al di là, o al di qua (dipende dai punti di vista) del teatro Borghese per riproporre, e Artaud non poteva non farne tesoro, un teatro viscerale, sanguigno, aggressivo, paradossale nel suo grottesco parossismo, dove come in un balletto di mostri, le vicende si dipanano a un ritmo accelerato, accumulando episodi in una sequenza frenetica, fra canti, lazzi, capriole, spargimento di sangue, resurrezioni assurde, da Grand Guignol stravolto in una smorfia grottesca.[58]

> [From the very start, (Jarry's) comedies burn naturalism, symbolism, psychologism, jumping beyond the Bourgeois theatre in order to restore – Artaud would then build on this – a visceral, sanguine, aggressive theatre, paradoxical in its grotesque paroxysm, where, as in a monstrous dance, the events unravel at an accelerated rhythm, accumulating episodes in a frantic sequence, among songs, jokes, somersaults, blood-shedding, absurd resurrections, like a Grand Guignol twisted by a grotesque grimace.]

It is time, however, to return to Giuliani's theatre, and his version of *Padre Ubu*. Rereading the play after so many years, one is struck above all by its determination to bring back into the discourse of the Neoavanguardia Jarry and his incredible, preposterous, endlessly lively works. In addition to doing that, *Nostro padre Ubu* also displays a number of traits that we, in part, noticed in other plays written by members of the neo-avant-garde, and that can be summarized as follows: 1) the starting point is constituted of a corpus of texts, containing a number of characters and situations, which are then disassembled and remounted in a completely new shape: it is another rewriting of a classic (although, in this case, a modern, avant-garde classic); 2) it brings to the forefront an aspect of the avant-garde that is often forgotten, when it is not used as an argument to demonstrate the supposedly vacuous and superficial nature of its aesthetic stance: the programmatically amateurish approach to performance, which stems from its experimental nature and economy of means when it comes to costumes, settings, make-up, and acting techniques; 3) in part, connected to this last point is the avant-garde predilection for marionettes and the working mechanisms of puppet theatre; 4) finally, and most importantly, as noticed by Cattabiani, this theatre is a form of *travestimento letterario*, as it combines different works together, manipulates and rewrites them, and mixes the vicissitudes of authors and fictional characters in one layered narrative: "Jarry was not only the greatest inspiration and founder of grotesque and surrealist contemporary theatre, but rather the mythical uncle of the Great Game of *Travestimento*, revisited by the generations that came after 1968."[59]

How exactly is a *travestimento* different from a rewriting? There are two main distinctions: 1) in *travestimenti*, the original author of the piece (or a character who strongly and explicitly represents his point of view) is usually included in the play. If we look, for instance, at *Pelle d'Asino* as a contrastive example, Perrault is not present in the published version of the play, nor in any of its various versions that survive in the archives. In *Nostro padre Ubu*, however, Jarry figures as one of the protagonists, and some of the most famous anecdotes of his life are included in the narrative. Also, 2) in the case of *travestimenti*, the re-elaboration of the original text is carried out with a specific theatrical company, or with a precise venue in mind. The writer acts as a dramaturg, according to the definition of this term as given in chapter 1.[60] Rewritings, instead, don't take into account any practical concerns relating to the staging process and, in fact, rarely lead to an actual performance. Giuliani created a few *travestimenti*, most of them intended for radio and television. Pagliarani, on the other hand, never really wrote a *travestimento*, although he included quite a few "masks" in his later verse collections.[61]

The only Neoavanguardista who practiced *travestimenti* throughout his career was Sanguineti, who, for the reasons already outlined in chapter 1, is not included in the scope of this monograph. We will, however, mention him once more later on in this chapter, when we investigate the reworking of Goethe's *Faust* by Giorgio Celli and Elio Pagliarani.

5.11 Seneca, Nero, and the Land Surveyor K.

Giuliani used the *travestimento* again in two other plays he wrote and collected in the same volume as *Nostro padre Ubu*, under the title *Tre recite su commissione* ("Three Occasional Performances"):[62] *Un dibattito mai avvenuto. Seneca e Nerone* ("A Debate That Never Took Place. Seneca and Nero"), and *L'ultimo colloquio dell'Agrimensore K* ("The Last Conversation of Land Surveyor K.").

Seneca and Nero is subtitled "*scritto per la televisione (dipartimento scuola e educazione)*" and is, in this respect, very similar to *Padre Ubu*: both of them are dramatic texts meant for different media (radio for the first, television for the second) and are intended as "educational" introductions to the literary works of giants from the past. This time, Giuliani returns to Seneca's version of the tragedy *Oedipus* and uses it as a starting point and repertoire of symbols and situations in order to talk about the historical relationship between Nero and Seneca. The result is the creation of two sets of overlapping characters – Nero-Oedipus and Seneca-Creon – whom Giuliani exploits to discuss contemporary Italian society as well as the timeless machinations (and seductions and pitfalls) of power. A video monitor showing snippets of the play is used as a way of directly quoting Seneca's original work. Beyond the reflections on the nature of political power, the play is interesting for us because it displays the same mingling of historical figures and fictional ones, and in particular the relationship between authors and their own literary creations (Seneca-Oedipus-Creon). In the introductory note we read:

> Nerone – *Sulla trentina, una floridezza sciupata, piuttosto pingue, di statura media … Il suo gusto di recitare (mistificazione che lo diverte) non esclude momenti di verità, sempre riverberata nella sua immaginazione.*
> Seneca – *Di circa settant'anni, asciutto e robusto, più alto di Nerone … È tragico; più che dissimulatore, è spiritualmente ambiguo …*
> Moderatore*: Molto discreto, dopo le parole di presentazione si limiterà ad ascoltare i due protagonisti.*
> Scena*: Un comune studio televisivo, tavolinetto, poltrone per gli ospiti, sobrio. Da un lato uno schermo Eidofor che servirà per rievocare la scena finale dell'Edipo di Seneca.*[63]

> [Nero – *Around thirty years old, florid but weary, rather portly, average height. … His predilection for acting (a mystification that amuses him) does not exclude moments of truth, always filtered through his imagination.*
> Seneca – *About seventy years old, lean and strong, taller than Nero … He is tragic; rather than a dissembler, he is spiritually ambiguous …*
> Moderator*: Very discreet, after his introductory remarks he will just listen to the two protagonists.*
> Scene*: A common television studio, a small table, chairs for the guests, sober. On one side there is an Eidophor screen that will be used to display the final scene from Seneca's* Oedipus.]

In addition to the performance screened on the monitor, Nero and Seneca will often quote from tragedies written by the latter. Half-way through the play, the finances of the empire, and the philosophical implications of some of Nero's choices, are brought to the fore:

> Nerone (al moderatore) – Vedi, nei suoi discorsi la moneta diventa una condizione metafisica: la ricchezza, la povertà. Parliamo seriamente. Nel

> 64 feci la più divertente riforma monetaria della storia romana. Decisi che da una libbra d'oro si sarebbero ricavati 45 aurei, anziché 40, e da una libbra d'argento 96 denari, anziché 84. Toglievo a ogni moneta pochi centesimi di grammo: 40 all'aureo, 45 al denario … Dando un certo vantaggio al denario, che era la moneta dei ceti piccoli e medi, incrementavo la circolazione, favorivo l'economia monetaria contro l'economia parassitica dei senatori e cavalieri. Non pochi che accumulano, ma molti che scambiano: questo era il mio principio economico.[64]
>
> [Nero (to the moderator) – You see, he always talks about money as if it were a metaphysical condition: wealth, poverty. Let's be serious. In 64 I enacted the most entertaining of monetary reforms in Roman history. I decided that 1 pound of gold would yield 45 aurei, rather than 40, and 1 pound of silver 96 denarii, instead of 84. I was subtracting a few 100ths of a gram from each coin: 40 from the aureus and 45 from the denarius … Giving a small advantage to the denarius, which was the coin of the middle and lower classes, I would increase circulation, favouring the monetary economy over the parasitic economy of senators and equites. More trading and less stockpiling: that was my economic principle.]

As we saw in *Pelle d'Asino* and *Padre Ubu*, the issues relating to economics and politics are treated as crucial. Rather different, in this respect, is *L'ultimo colloquio dell'Agrimensore K.*, which, however, displays a similar mingling of authors, fictional personae, and settings. Here, the main character is defined by the stage directions as "the protagonist of Franz Kafka's *The Castle*." In this play, the connection between authors and fictional characters is made even more explicit: from Kafka to K., and from Giuliani himself to A., which is probably the initial for Author (or Alfredo), and who is described in the notes as "the voluntary keeper of scattered documents." The relation between power, memory, and literature, which had already been investigated in *Nero and Seneca*, is also a major theme here. Giuliani seems to explicitly reflect on the role that the intellectual plays in perpetuating the injustice that pervades the social order, a complicity that is built on inaction as well as action:

> K: – … Se ti si permette di tenere un archivio, vuol dire che non sei del tutto estraneo all'autorità; anzi, anche tu fai parte del sistema di controllo. Come puoi negarlo?
>
> A: – Parlando assolutamente, non posso negare o affermare una cosa simile. Se presumessi che l'autorità, senza darmene la prova, si serve di me, questo non cambierebbe molto la mia condizione. Per quanto mi tocca,

> io sono semplicemente un custode volontario di documenti dispersi. Un custode, te lo ripeto, critico non un funzionario.[65]

> [K: – … If they allow you to keep an archive, it means that you are not completely separated from the authorities; in fact, you must be part of the control system. How can you deny that?
> A: – Speaking in absolute terms, I cannot deny or confirm something like that. If I thought that the authorities, without giving me any signs, were using me, that fact would not change my condition much. As far as I am concerned, I am simply a voluntary keeper of scattered documents. A critical keeper, as I have already said; not an officer.]

It seems particularly appropriate that Giuliani, while writing for some of the mass media that, over the course of the *Novecento,* have often been used by political power to consolidate consensus among the population, introduces such a sobering reflection on the responsibilities of intellectuals and their role within the republic. As is the case with most of the Neoavanguardia, however, the positing of the problem is not followed by a prescriptive solution; rather, the issue is left open for the audience to discuss. The play, instead, is closed by an ironic shift in tone; A., who has the last word, concludes the pièce by saying: "Now go, and bundle up, it's snowing. Goodbye!"[66]

Before leaving Giuliani's plays to shift to Pagliarani's, I would like to speak one last time of *Nostro padre Ubu,* and in particular of one of its characters, Dr Faustroll, who, originally, was the protagonist of another of Jarry's works: *Exploits & Opinions of Dr Faustroll, Pataphysician,* published only posthumously. Faustroll can be considered the incarnation of the various traits we have been identifying as crucial to Giuliani's theatre: intertextuality, linguistic experimentalism, and *travestimento letterario.* In this case, we have the superimposing of three different personae, Jarry, Ubu, and Faustroll:

> Dopo queste esperienze Jarry e il Padre Ubu si trasformarono nel dottor Faustroll, scienziato patafisico che nacque nel 1898 all'età di sessantatré anni, conservando tale età per tutta la vita … Faustroll navigò per Parigi su un canotto anfibio di sua invenzione, a forma di colabrodo allungato, inaffondabile, munito di remo da marciapiedi e di ventose a molla, e la cui chiglia, scorrendo su rotelle isometriche d'acciaio, era in grado di fendere le onde piatte della terraferma e di scivolare tra l'aridità delle case e il luccichio delle vetrine … compiute queste esplorazioni e scoperte, il dottor Faustroll scomparve nell'etere patafisico, e il Padre Ubu e Jarry ripresero le loro tradizionali sembianze …[67]

> [After these experiences, Jarry and Father Ubu turned into Dr Faustroll, pataphysic scientist who was born in 1898 at the age of sixty-three, and remained that same age for the rest of his life ... Faustroll sailed through Paris on an amphibious boat of his own invention, shaped like an elongated strainer, unsinkable, which carried a sidewalk oar and a set of spring-loaded suction cups; its keel, sliding on isometric steel wheels, was capable of slicing through the flat waves of dryland, and of slipping through the aridity of houses and the sparkle of shop windows ... After accomplishing all these explorations and discoveries, Dr Faustroll disappeared in the pataphysic ether, while Father Ubu and Jarry went back to their usual appearances ...]

Things become even more interesting if we investigate a little more closely the origins of the name "Faustroll"; in one of the excellent notes appended by Simon Watson Taylor to his edition of the *Exploits & Opinions of Dr Faustroll, Pataphysician*, we read:

> As Roger Shattuck points out in the section he devotes to "Alfred Jarry: Poet and 'Pataphysician'" in his *The Banquet Years* ..., the name of the hero, Faustroll, may be taken to be a combination of the words Faust and Troll (a goblin or imp). In 1896 Jarry appeared as one of the trolls in Lugné-Poe's production of *Peer Gynt* (the Scandinavian Faust!) at the Théâtre de l'Oeuvre. Jarry's intention was perhaps to imply that his (autobiographical) hero was the "imp of science."[68]

Therefore, the identification between Jarry and Faustroll is not as arbitrary as might seem at a first glance. Even more useful, for our own purposes, is the connection that Watson Taylor establishes with Faust, for the next part of this chapter will be dedicated to the rewritings of Goethe's masterpiece.

5.12 The Rewriting of *Faust* by Pagliarani and Celli

We will be analysing two rewritings of Goethe's play, completed by Giorgio Celli and Elio Pagliarani in 1975 and 1984, respectively: *Le tentazioni del professor Faust* and the already mentioned *Il Faust di Copenaghen*.[69] Both experiments are the vehicles of a reflection that impacts not only language but also the dramaturgic conventions that they employ, as well as the social and political dimension of the institutions they so ruthlessly criticize. Although these two plays were performed and published after the formal disbandment of Gruppo 63, the experimental spirit that animates them is the same as the one that moved those intellectuals who first convened in Palermo in 1963: some of them, like

Pagliarani and Celli, kept to the course set on that first occasion; others, unfortunately, were seduced by the sirens of a more escapist, mainstream literature.

Before moving forward, however, it will be best to spend a few words on the curious convergence between these two authors on Goethe's drama: why did both Celli and Pagliarani, completely independently of one another (although roughly at the same time), decide to rewrite *Faust*? This question becomes even more interesting if we remember that Sanguineti wrote his own *travestimento*, which was performed and published in 1985.[70] In an essay devoted to this last version of *Faust*, Niva Lorenzini, in a paragraph we quote in its entirety, explains the main reasons for the neo-avant-garde's fascination with this play:

> Il *Faust* di Goethe non l'ostacola certo quella disposizione al gioco, al *puzzle* testuale e strutturale, predisposto com'è, sin dall'inizio, alla frammentazione: lo stesso autore ne autorizzava infatti, intenzionalmente e polemicamente, una chiave di lettura che proprio a un sistema di frammenti rinvia, quando nel *Prologo in Teatro* steso nel 1798 (da accostarsi alla Dedica del '97 e al *Prologo in Cielo*, scritti tutti dopo anni di interruzione) accennava, per bocca del Direttore ("Direktor") in dialogo col Poeta teatrale ("Dichter") e col Comico ("Lustige Person"), all'opportunità di blandire i gusti del pubblico, offrendoglielo a pezzi, il dramma ... e infarcendolo, stipandolo, di materiale eterogeneo. Una decisa presa di posizione, la sua, contro un'idea di opera armonica scritta da "veri poeti" in bilico tra tormento e estasi, a favore di un contenitore, straordinario intruglio ("der beste Trank") in cui si riversi, desublimato, il "romanzo" della vita. Un' "opera mondo,"per dirla con Franco Moretti, difficilmente classificabile (tragedia? Testo lirico? Saggio filosofico?). Di sicuro anche un'opera contesta di digressioni e fratture, priva di continuità, specie nella fase avanzata del secondo *Faust*, polifonica e monologante, disarmonica ed eterogenea. Un beverone, qualcuno ha detto, triviale e tragico, frammentario e aperto alle contaminazioni: quelle del *Puppenspiel*, intanto, il teatro delle marionette che aveva rielaborato in proprio il dramma popolare, e che Goethe conosceva bene.[71]
>
> [Goethe's *Faust* certainly does not hinder an inclination for games as well as textual and structural puzzles, for it is predisposed, from the very start, toward fragmentation: in fact, its author allowed, explicitly and polemically, an interpretation that relies on a system of fragments. In the *Prologue for the Theatre*, written in 1789 (which must be paired with the *Dedication* of '97, and the *Prologue in Heaven*, all of which were written after years of hiatus), he argues, through the Director ("Direktor"), engaged in a conversation with the theatrical Poet ("Dichter") and the Comedian ("Lustige Person"), in favour of blandishing the audience by offering them the drama a piece

at a time ... seasoning and stuffing it with heterogeneous materials. His was a strong argument against the idea that a work should be harmonious, written by "true poets" balancing sorrow and ecstasy; instead, he proposed a container filled with an extraordinary concoction ("der beste Trank") that mixed together the "novel" of life, devoid of any idealization. A "world-work," to use Franco Moretti's words, that is difficult to categorize (tragedy? lyrical poem? philosophical essay?). Certainly, it is a work marked by digressions and fractures, lacking continuity, especially in the latter part of the second *Faust*, which is polyphonic and monologizing, disharmonic and heterogeneous. A cocktail, some have said, that is trivial and tragic, fragmentary and open to contaminations: those of *Puppenspiel*, first and foremost, the puppet theatre that had appropriated the form of popular drama and which Goethe knew well.]

The interest in popular forms of entertainment is a trait that brings together all the authors of the Neoavanguardia and – given the comments made regarding Porta, Giuliani, and their ties to Jarry – it is worth pausing briefly on the relationship that Faust's legend entertains, as Lorenzini points out at the end of this quotation, with the theatre of *puppenspiel*. In fact, if several stylistic traits adopted by Goethe remind some of the puppet theatre, others lament his lack of familiarity with that tradition. For instance, as Heinrich Heine at first observes in the preface to his little known *Der Doktor Faust*, which bears the descriptive subtitle *Ein Tanzpoem*,

Puppet-masters, who flourished in Elizabethan England, were swift to seize on any play which proved to be a popular success, and Marlowe's masterpiece was speedily transformed to fit the puppet-market. Thus bowdlerized, it traveled through the length and breadth of Europe till, at last, larded with good earthy German jokes, it reached the market stalls of my country. Here it greatly entertained the lower strata of the populace, at the same time inflaming the imagination of our mighty Goethe. For it was from the puppet version of the legend that our poet took the shape and form of his own masterpiece.[72]

This is the origin of that connection between Goethe's *Faust* and the *puppenspiel* we mentioned. However, in the longer and splendidly erudite letter included in that same booklet and addressed to Lumley, the director of her Royal Majesty's Theatre, the very institution that had commissioned the play, Heine explains,

You will have observed that I am not afraid to judge the second part of Goethe's *Faust* sternly, even harshly. Exception must be made for the

> manner in which he treats the episode of Helena ... for once the poet has remained true to the story's origin. Unfortunately, such faithful adherence to the legend is very rare in Goethe's play and for this great fault I can scarcely find language strong enough to censure him! The Devil has most cause for complaint on this account, for the poet's Mephistopheles bears not the slightest resemblance to the fallen angel of the chapbooks. This fact alone lends strength to my suspicion that Goethe had not read these works when he wrote his play.[73]

That is to say that, in spite of the undeniable connection with the puppet theatre that certainly functioned as one of his sources of inspiration, Goethe was not aware, according to Heine, of the much older tradition from whence the street entertainers derived their materials. Heine, on the contrary, assures us of his complete and intimate knowledge of it, and he is not afraid to show it off in the learned introduction to his dance poem, as well as in the richness and variety of themes he is capable of weaving together.

Going back to Goethe's work, if we keep Heine's observations in mind, we will be able to better appreciate the experimental dimension of the play: after all, it is a "container" in which have been collected various elements, forming a whole that is extremely critical of the scenic space it will occupy during the performance. Such a structure was bound to attract the attention of the Gruppo 63 writers, who were trying to renew traditional Italian literature. In the case of Pagliarani and Celli, there is an additional reason that makes the use of *Faust* almost inevitable: the connection that the plot composed by Goethe entertains with the history and the methodologies of the natural sciences and physics.

The famous scene in the study,[74] where Faust lists all the disciplines he has learned and laments their uselessness, shows this character as a modern hero, making him the symbol of the human passion for the accumulation of knowledge and the bearer of the paralysing doubt that everything might be, after all, useless to life. Even worse, perhaps it might be detrimental, for it prevents the creation of a balance with nature and the surrounding environment. This double uneasiness, the drive to knowledge and the suspicion that such a quest may take one away from happiness, makes Faust an excellent surrogate for contemporary man. Thus, given the familiarity of Celli and Pagliarani with the methodology and the evolution of scientific disciplines,[75] the reworking of Faust's vicissitudes must have seemed almost mandatory.

Their attitude is the opposite of the one assumed by Bertolt Brecht, who, in his *Life of Galileo*, transforms the Pisan physicist into a hero of free thought and a rebel against the oppression and obscurantism of the

Holy See. Although some of the details change with the different versions of the play penned by the author, the relationship between science and society remains constant: the scientist is the bearer of a disruptive truth that, through its technological innovations (the telescope, in this case), changes reality, altering the power structure within the social tissue. In spite of the numerous ambiguities that can be found in the persona and the vicissitudes described in *Life of Galileo*, Brecht displays an unshakable faith in the human capacity of knowing the world, a utopic belief in the possibility of bending it to the categories of the intellect, and an optimism that leads him to celebrate the scientific revolution, casting it as the first true materialistic revolution against the oppression of organized religion.

Celli and Pagliarani, instead, who belonged to a younger generation, were much more pessimistic regarding the prospects of science as the liberator of human consciences. As we will see in a few pages, although they both considered the scientific paradigm as a valid ally in questioning our preconceived notions of the world and reality, they were also concerned about the systematic control and manipulation exercised by the established political power over scientific research.

One of the most insidious and effective ways in which this control is exercised leverages the presumed neutrality of scientific inquiry, which is portrayed as essentially apolitical; in much the same way, scientists are presented as almost amoral beings, who spend their lives attempting to provide new and better opportunities for truth to manifest itself, ever more clearly and ever more directly. Naturally, it will be enough to question any scientist actively engaged in research to discover how far these expectations are from reality. Not only are the methods of science (as well as those who practise them) not neutral or impartial, but the very idea of an empirical truth that is always true, under every circumstance, is a rather problematic concept. Both Celli and Pagliarani focus on this precise issue in their *Faust*s, as well as in other plays, including some of their more theoretical reflections.

We have already made similar observations when discussing Pagliarani and his *Lezione di fisica* ("Physics Lesson"), in chapter 4, where we also mentioned Heisenberg and his uncertainty principle.[76] According to it, reality, even for the natural sciences (or, perhaps, better yet, especially for the sciences) is not a given, static entity, but rather a field of endlessly shifting possibilities. For both, Pagliarani and Celli, the scientific paradigm provides additional confirmation of their vision of the world and the effectiveness of their stylistic choices in describing it. This outlook is particularly relevant when analysing their renditions of *Faust*, on whose structure they project all their uneasiness (on the historical, sociological, and linguistic level) caused by the current events of world politics and the scientific discoveries of the *Novecento*.

In fact, the conviction that it is impossible to directly access and communicate the world is shared by almost all the authors of Gruppo 63, who, conversely, were all very suspicious of (if not openly hostile to) a mimetic brand of realism that led to a portrayal of reality as aproblematic, almost an open window through which one could see the world as it "really" is. A kind of literature that would adopt such an approach would carry serious political and ideological implications, effectively encouraging escapism and a consolatory, reactionary world view. Instead, in order to foster political and social change, one must deploy a critical approach in addressing not only the subject matter that is treated (the "contenuti," to use the terms of the contemporary debate), but also the actual categories that frame the discussion, among which language occupies a primary role.[77]

Returning to our *Faust*s, if it is true that the prejudices in favour of a supposed neutrality of language are stronger whenever science and its methods are involved, then, by demonstrating that precisely in the realm of scientific discovery such neutrality (of language, politics, morals) does not exist, one would prove that all manifestations of human thought, all linguistic utterances, are liable to display the same kind of distortions, obstacles, and imprecisions. And this can help us explain the convergence of Celli and Pagliarani on the rewriting of *Faust*: the negation of that neutrality that is at the core of their interests becomes apparent at the level of language, at the level of plot, and at the level of the theatrical conventions that are used to express both. Let us examine the texts.

Celli starts working on his *Le tentazioni del professor Faust* at the beginning of the 1970s, and stages it for the first time in 1975; that same year, he wins the Premio Pirandello. The protagonist of his play is a chemistry professor: we encounter him for the first time on the occasion of his fiftieth birthday. Faust had publicly criticized HT, an insecticide that caused horrible collateral effects on the human population (including genetic mutations). The CEO of Supernova, the "unlimited responsibility public company" that created and produces HT, a diabolical character whom Celli designates as "Praxeologo Massimo," charges Mefis, one of his trusted employees, with the task of silencing Faust. Praxeologo (his title also communicates the brute pseudo-positivism at the character's core) suggests a "silent death," but Mefis does not agree:

> Mefis: Solo gli ideali, le utopie, i sogni muoiono in un grande silenzio. Ogni uomo li ha veduti morire, in sé, a poco a poco. E, dopo, è uscito sulla

piazza, e si è sentito, ad un tratto, uguale a tutti gli altri. E ha scoperto – come tornato da un lungo esilio – la gioia del … consenso. Se deve morire – perché non diventi ciò che non è, una figura menzognera ed esemplare – deve prima abiurare e consentire.

Praxeologo massimo: Sì, deve, prima, riconoscersi in noi. Come farai?

Mefis: Con una lobotomia … spirituale…

Praxeologo massimo: Usando il bisturi d'acciaio della logica.

Mefis: … il rasoio assiderato della dialettica …

Praxeologo massimo: La parola è un'arma discreta …

Mefis: Discreta e micidiale: le sue vittime non imbrattano, con il sangue, i tappeti. Perdono quota a poco a poco, senza neppure accorgersene, finché nell'abisso trovano la loro personale … verità.[78]

[Mefis: Only the ideals, utopias, dreams die in a great silence. Every man has seen them die within himself, little by little. And, afterwards, he went outside and suddenly felt equal to all the others. And discovered – as if having returned from a long exile – the joys of … consensus. If he has to die – to avoid becoming what he is not, an exemplary liar – he must first renounce and accept.

Praxeologo massimo: Yes, first he must recognize he is like us. How will you proceed?

Mefis: With a spiritual … lobotomy …

Praxeologo massimo: Using the steel scalpel of logic?

Mefis: … the frozen razor of dialectics …

Praxeologo massimo: Words are discrete weapons …

Mefis: Discrete and deadly: their victims don't soil the carpet with their blood. They descend, little by little, without even realizing it, into the abyss, all the way down, until they find their own personal … truth.]

It is a matter of convincing Prof. Faust that, in spite of appearances, he and Supernova work toward the same goal, and thus belong to the same human and anthropological category. From this very first exchange we can observe one of the key features of the text: the punctuation is obsessively parsing the characters' words, as if the author were trying to exercise a continuous and direct control over the spoken language and diction of the actors, fragmenting them as much as possible.[79]

Gretchen's role, although radically revised, is here entrusted to Elena. At first, Mefis decides to tempt the professor by exploiting his loneliness and the woman's attractiveness, but this attempt fails. In the following passage, Elena, in order to better seduce Faust, asks him to meet her in his laboratory. There we find him, engaging in an idealized description of his work as a scientist:

Faust: … Quando sono qui e prevedo, verifico, deduco, inferisco, sperimento, non sono più solo. Tutti gli uomini che amano la verità sono con me. Una invisibile rete di simpatia e di collaborazione trasforma le cellule isolate dei laboratori del mondo in un unico, grande, palpitante organismo.
Elena: Non ti credo. Gli scienziati si odiano, come tutti gli uomini. Si battono a colpi di equazioni e di esperienze. Braccano i tuoi errori come una muta di lupi, che ti abbaia, dietro, nelle riviste scientifiche, instancabile. Tu non hai amici. Se mai: solo complici. Come lui. (*Indica Mefis*).[80]

[Faust: … When I am here I foresee, verify, deduce, infer, experiment, I am never alone. All the men that love truth are with me. An invisible network of sympathy and collaboration transforms the isolated cells of the world's laboratories into a sole, great, pulsating organism.
Elena: I don't believe you. Scientists hate one another, just like all men. They fight using equations and experiments. They tirelessly hunt your mistakes like a pack of wolves, barking after you, from scientific journals. You have no friends. If anything, you have accomplices. Like him. (*She points to Mefis*).]

The supposed neutrality and amorality of scientific research is here clearly denounced as a mere illusion. Not only that, but the very idea of truth is rendered problematic. In this regard, here is another exchange between Faust and Mefis, in which Celli highlights the professor's hypocrisy:

Elena (*con la voce dolce e un po' falsa di chi si rivolga a un bambino*): Hai detto delle bugie, Faust.
Faust: No, no. Perché non volete capire? Non mentivo.
Mefis: La verità ha molte facce, lo so.
Elena: Devi sempre dire la verità, ricordatelo, Faust.
Faust: Ma io … io la dicevo. Era solo un modo …
Mefis: Dialettico?
Faust: Si, un modo … dialettico di vedere le cose. A e B, tesi e antitesi, attraverso la loro opposizione, dalla loro mutua mobilitazione, scaturisce un nuovo valore, che li comprende, che li trascende. (*Disperato*) Non è così?[81]

[Elena (*with a sweet voice, a bit fake, like someone who is addressing a child*): You lied, Faust.
Faust: No, no. Why don't you want to understand? I wasn't lying.
Mefis: The truth has many sides, I know.

Elena: You always have to tell the truth, remember that, Faust.
Faust: But I ... I did tell the truth. It was just a way to ...
Mefis: A dialectic way?
Faust: Yes, a way ... a dialectic way to see things. A and B, thesis and antithesis, through their opposition, through their mutual mobilization, a new value is generated, one that comprises them, and transcends them. (*Desperate*) Isn't that right?]

It is important to notice the ironic use Celli makes of a certain lexicon and certain concepts (like "dialectics," for instance) that were so common in the 1960s and early 1970s, especially in the realm of politics and literary criticism. At this stage of the plot, Elena turns into a surrogate for the mother and evokes in Faust a childhood memory, an attempt he had made to poison the mice that were infesting his house but that had resulted in the death of the house cat. The scene takes place in the garden of memory, an oneiric space in which Elena and Mefis try to trap the professor, having him regress to an infantile state of mental and spiritual development.

In the meantime, however, Faust remembers he had been bitten by one of the mice he had first poisoned and then tried to nurse back to health. In the dreamlike dimension of his memories, that mouse becomes the symbol of an event that had been repressed, and that bite (a first emergence of the repressed) startles him back to reality, making him aware of the psychological manipulation to which Mefis and Elena have been subjecting him. Faust, having regained his senses, chases the two inopportune visitors away.

Mefis is then summoned by Praxeologo Massimo, and has to justify his failures; he is given one last chance to circumvent Faust. The new plan, in his own words, consists of switching from "psychology, from ... occult persuasion, to ideology."

Mefis: Gli uomini più puri, spesso, nascondono strane, imprevedibili latitudini. Vanno al di là dei loro rimorsi con una insospettata leggerezza. Il loro senso di colpa – perché sempre, sempre, la purezza è impura – che avresti giudicato così ... ipertrofico, così tirannico, è un paravento di carta attraverso cui passano facilmente, per tornare a sorridere nel mondo.
Praxeologo massimo: Sento che hai un piano.
Mefis: Sì.
Praxeologo massimo: Quante probabilità di riuscita?
Mefis: Tutte.
Praxeologo massimo: Che cosa farai?
Mefis: Passerò dalla psicologia, dalla ... persuasione occulta, alla ... ideologia.
Praxeologo massimo: Lo avrò?

Mefis: Non avevo capito una cosa.
Praxeologo massimo: E cioè?
Mefis: È sempre stato tuo. Lo è anche ora, che ti rinnega. Deve solo prenderne coscienza.[82]

[Mefis: The purest men often hide strange, unforeseen latitudes. They get past their regrets with unsuspected lightness. Their sense of guilt – for purity is always, always impure – which you would imagine as … hypertrophic, tyrannical, is just a thin facade they can easily pierce, and return to the world with a smile on their face.
Praxeologo massimo: I can sense you have a plan.
Mefis: Yes.
Praxeologo massimo: What are the chances of success?
Mefis: Almost certain.
Praxeologo massimo: What will you do?
Mefis: I will switch from psychology, from … occult persuasion, to … ideology.
Praxeologo massimo: Will he be mine?
Mefis: Until now, there was something I didn't understand.
Praxeologi massimo: What's that?
Mefis: He has been yours all along. Even now, as he is renouncing you. He only needs to become aware of it.]

Celli seems to imply that there is no such thing as a fundamentally good man. One must constantly check oneself, both in thoughts and actions. Additionally, he makes a strong argument against absolutist ideological positions: whenever someone (like Faust, for instance) is convinced an absolute truth exists, then all they need to do is believe that their actions are serving that truth, and any horrendous behaviour can be easily justified in pursuit of this greater purpose. Contrarily, when someone doubts the existence of a "natural" truth, any morally repugnant actions can only be seen as that: the opposite of good, no matter the rationalizations put forth to explain and excuse them.

Continuing with our play, Mefis announces the end of Faust, prophesying his suicide: the sight of blood, he tells us, repulses him; additionally, he doesn't want Faust to resent him:

Mefis (*la fissa a lungo, poi mormora*): Gli voglio bene, sai? Scivolerà nel buio dolcemente. Desidero che tutto gli sembri, in questo chiuso universo di geometrie e di belve, armonioso, organico, perfetto. Il suo ultimo sorriso mi assolverà. Elena, ascolta.
Elena: Sì.
Mefis: Solo chi persuade vince.[83]

[Mefis (*stares at her a while, then whispers*): I love him, you know? He will slide into the dark, softly. I want him to see this narrow universe of geometries and beasts as harmonious, organic, perfect. His last smile will absolve me. Elena, listen.
Elena: Yes.
Mefis: Only those who persuade, win.]

The method chosen by Mefis to eliminate Faust is not inconsequential: an instigation to suicide by means of ideological manipulation. This is an extreme illustration of how the neo-liberalist system works, preferring assimilation and neutralization to direct confrontation and open struggle. It is always best if people interiorize control (and the drive to consume), so that no open violence need be deployed by the state (or by the supra-national entities that control commerce and capital). This way, as if under the spell of a Stockholm syndrome that envelops the whole planet, one will fall in love with the jailers and their restricting chains. Given these circumstances, a capital sentence will appear as the impersonal pronouncement of justice, or even as a sort of liberation one has actively pursued throughout one's life.

This is a thread that runs through many of Celli's plays, an issue that is often at the centre of his reflections, especially when it applies to the role science and research play in furthering this social "order." This is how Claudio Beghelli frames the discussion:

C'è un ultimo aspetto della riflessione di Celli in merito al potere sul quale vorrei – brevemente – soffermarmi. L'Autore mostra a più riprese in alcuni dei suoi più importanti lavori teatrali (ne cito uno per tutti: *Le tentazioni del professor Faust*) come gli uomini di scienza, pur continuando ad affermare la propria neutralità, tendano, spesso (gli avvenimenti del ventesimo secolo lo testimoniano), a farsi "conniventi e complici" – in maniera più o meno diretta – di quella forza "oggettiva, impersonale, autonoma" (la quale travolge e supera, nei suoi effetti, le stesse volontà soggettive e particolari da cui viene innescata) che è il moderno potere tecnico economico. Tale potere egemone e invisibile, personificato – con brillante intuizione di Celli – nel praxeologo massimo ("demiurgo della produzione e degli scambi, del profitto e delle perdite, dei dividendi e dei pacchetti azionari, che è ormai l'unico vero dio dell'Occidente") fa avvelenare l'albero della conoscenza e si impadronisce della verità scientifica, distorcendola a proprio vantaggio: così l'opinione pubblica viene a sapere che l'HT è un insetticida utile a debellare l'insetto vettore della malaria e può contribuire allo sviluppo del terzo mondo, ma resta all'oscuro del fatto che, questa stessa sostanza, ha effetti secondari che potrebbero rivelarsi disastrosi per la salute dell'uomo e per la vita animale e vegetale del pianeta.[84]

> [There is one last aspect of Celli's meditations on power on which I would like to, briefly, pause. The author shows repeatedly in some of his most important plays (above all, *Le tentazioni del professor Faust*) how men of science, while continuing to stress their neutrality, often act, more or less explicitly, in a "conniving and complicit" way, supporting that "objective, impersonal, autonomous" force wielded by the modern technical and economic power, capable of trampling and replacing even the individual and subjective wills that set it in motion. Such hegemonic and invisible power, personified (thanks to one of Celli's brilliant intuitions) by Praxeologo Massimo ("that demiurge of production and exchange, of profits and losses, of dividends and shares, that is now the only true god of the West"), poisons the tree of knowledge and holds scientific truth hostage, forcing it to his own advantage: this way public opinion learns that HT is a useful insecticide, crucial in eradicating the bug that spreads malaria and thus beneficial to the well-being of developing countries. At the same time, however, the fact that this same substance has side effects detrimental to the health of humans, animals, and plants is kept secret.]

Returning to the plot, at this point in the play the events take a rather unexpected turn. In a scene titled "The Great Temptation," Mefis lets Faust believe that HT has the ultimate goal of reducing the birth rate not only within the insect population but also actually among humans. Furthermore, the mutations triggered by the chemical serve a eugenic program aiming at the "purification" of the human race. Those who are not deemed worthy of being part of the "new world," for they carry physical, moral, behavioural, or ideological "defects," are killed by HT. Faust, after an initial, weak resistance, reveals himself to be in agreement with the ultimate goal pursued by Mefis and Supernova, and is finally convinced by a vague promise of being considered for the Nobel Prize. In one of the last scenes, in order to symbolically seal their reconciliation, Faust and Praxeologo Massimo dance the waltz, while Mefis plays the piano.

The plot ends in a garden of memory (which, at this point, closely resembles a garden of Eden), where Faust dies after eating an apple into which he had injected a dose of HT. Given that Mefis had assured him that the pure and deserving were immune from the side effects of the insecticide, his death becomes the incontrovertible proof he was not worthy of inhabiting that new world he had helped to build. Right before the curtain is drawn, a radio announces that Prof. Faust had been awarded the Nobel Prize. The performance ends with Mefis, Elena, and Praxeologo Massimo spelling out the moral of the story by reciting a poem that sounds like a nursery rhyme, during a "quadro" that is entitled "Paradise's Music Hall."

Even from this brief synopsis of the play, it is easy to see how coherently and relentlessly Celli criticizes the idea that sciences are neutral, amoral, and apolitical. As mentioned earlier, researchers have an inescapable moral responsibility and are asked to make momentous choices regarding their discoveries and the ways in which they will be employed by society. This criticism, carried out through the plot, is intensified by the attention Celli dedicates to the language scientists and public relations experts use to conceal the less appealing consequences of their activities and promote the dubious benefits they bring. Finally, a third kind of criticism is levelled at those elements of the language of theatre belonging to the "bourgeois drama" that make the performance appear a natural, neutral, aproblematic sequence of events.

Let us begin with language: we have already noted the peculiar punctuation, and how the sentence is continuously interrupted and manipulated by the author. The general progression of the dialogue, however, seems to remain quite "natural": there aren't any strong caesurae or unconventional lexical choices, or any expressionistic distortions and exaggerations. This studiously spontaneous language is, actually, the result of the author's refined skills: he tries to achieve a tone that is a weighted average, a "newly found" directness, as he writes in the brief note that introduces *La zattera di Vesalio e altri drammi*, the volume that collects all his plays:

> Il teatro è un luogo dove gli uomini si sfidano a parole, e dove le peripezie dell'intelligenza si fanno, nella loquacità, trasparenti, con tutto il loro carico di implicita violenza. Perché l'uso intenzionale della parola, l'esercizio impudente della dialettica, la conversazione che si ponga al servizio del potere, evocano quella idea di teatro della crudeltà di Artaud, a cui devo molte delle prospettive di fondo dei miei testi. Ma se il teatro è parola, non è parola da strada o da osteria, due uomini che litigano al mercato fanno teatro solo a patto che il loro linguaggio sia passato attraverso quella sublimazione che lo trasporta al di sopra del grado zero della comunicazione. La scrittura teatrale esige, difatti, una naturalezza alla seconda potenza, non *data* ma *ritrovata*, e le parole, come diceva Mallarmé, devono assolvere a un processo di purificazione del linguaggio della tribù. Perché il teatro non è la vita, ma un'altra vita possibile, che si rispecchia nella prima attraverso l'infedeltà dei sogni, le prospettive della cultura e della storia, la necessità di passare dal quotidiano al sublime. Come ha detto Marianne Moore della poesia, il teatro è un giardino immaginario con rospi veri dentro.[85]
>
> [Theatre is the place where men challenge each other through words, and there the vicissitudes of intelligence become, through loquacity, transparent, with all their baggage of implicit violence. For the deliberate

use of words, the impudent exercise of dialectics, and the conversation that puts itself at the service of the ruling power evoke Artaud's idea of the theatre of cruelty, to which I owe many of the perspectives underpinning my texts. But if theatre is made of words, they do not belong to the street or the bar: two men arguing in a market are doing theatre only as long as their language is filtered through that same sublimation that pushes it above the zero degree of communication. In fact, theatrical writing demands a directness to the second power that is not *given* but *newly found*, and words, as Mallarmé wrote, must adhere to a process of the purification of the tribe's language. As Marianne Moore said about poetry, theatre is an imaginary garden containing real toads.]

This artfully built directness is then corrected, problematized, and rendered less transparent by the constant insertion of terms taken from the realm of the sciences. This is a stylistic trait that goes beyond the needs dictated by the plot and becomes a technique to prevent the audience from passively identifying with the plot. Here we can quote a passage by Celli himself, in which he explains why he resorts so often to scientific terms. In this essay, he was reflecting on his artistic journey, on the occasion of the fortieth anniversary of the founding of Gruppo 63:

> La scrittura che avevo adottato era stata intenzionalmente e massicciamente contaminata da parole pescate nel lessico scientifico, non usate, però, come semplici fonemi, ma come inneschi cognitivi, per un loro trasferimento di metafore, che tenessero conto delle nozioni d'origine, sempre trasparenti nella filigrana del verso.[86]
>
> [The writing style I adopted initially was massively contaminated by words fished from the scientific lexicon; however, they were not used as pure phonemes, but as cognitive triggers, as a way to transfer metaphors, while still keeping in mind their original meaning, which remained in the line, as if seen through a filigree.]

In addition to this subtle linguistic estrangement, Celli deploys an "irregular" staging of his plays in order to question even further the immediacy of traditional theatrical representations. This can be seen in at least three separate moments: the scenes set in the garden of memory, the intermission in which Praxeologo Massimo and Faust dance while Mefis plays the piano, and the final scene, where the moral of the story is couched in a nursery rhyme sung at the "Paradise Music Hall."

Particularly interesting is the first of these three breaches with the illusion of mimetic realism, for it introduces with great emphasis the reflection on the border (and the permeability of this border) between individual consciousness and the world. The result is a sort of wild-eyed realism which denounces the absurdity of a reality that science and technology have changed to such a radical degree that it has become uninhabitable. For a better insight into this issue, it might be useful to reread the following passage of a review that Celli wrote for Adriano Spatola's *L'ebreo negro* (*The Nigger Jew*), published in the *Quaderno 1* of *Malebolge*:

> Oggi è divenuto sempre più difficile discriminare se un evento sia pertinente al sogno o alla veglia, al funzionamento normale o anormale del pensiero, allorché tale discriminazione si fondi sul concetto di probabilità, nel senso che il sogno o l'idea coatta descriverebbero eventi e concatenazioni casuali estremamente improbabili a livello dell'esperienza. L'Apocalisse, il totale e improvviso annullamento planetario del genere umano, o del mondo biologico, dalla psicosi collettiva del Mille fino ad Alamogordo, si è configurata come un evento altamente improbabile, un'idea coatta confinabile a livello paranoico. In un mondo, però, dove esiste la bomba H e la possibilità di un conflitto nucleare, come convincere, osserva giustamente Franco Fornari, il malato di mente ossessionato dal terrore di un avvenimento escatologico che tale avvenimento è illusorio o che, per lo meno, possiede la massima impossibilità di avverarsi? … Non è più il sonno della ragione, è la ragione stessa che genera dei mostri.[87]

> [Today it has become more and more difficult to decide if an event belongs to the dreaming or the waking state, to the normal or abnormal functioning of thought, especially if we make that call basing it on the concept of probability, where a dream or a fixation would describe a scenario or a chain of events that is extremely unlikely and improbable to occur at the level of experience. The Apocalypse, the complete and sudden annihilation of human kind on this planet, or of the biological kingdom, moving from the collective psychosis of the year 1000 until the experiments of Alamogordo, had been a fixation limited to a high degree of paranoia. However, in a world that has built the H bomb and where a nuclear conflict is possible, how can one convince, as Franco Fornari rightly points out, someone with a mental illness, who is obsessed with the occurrence of an eschatological event, that such a circumstance is illusory or that, at the very least, it is highly unlikely that it will ever come to pass? … It is no longer the slumber of reason, but reason itself that generates monsters.]

Thus, the inclusion of the character's inner world within the theatrical representation shouldn't be interpreted as an escape into introspection. On the contrary, it is a criticism of a reality that, as a result of the absurdity of human choices, has become a waking nightmare. Another important feature of this passage is the interest in an apocalypse caused by humanity through technological means. It is an idea that we find in poems by Celli and Spatola, as well as the two versions of *Faust* we are here analysing.

In order to complete our quick overview of the play's anti-mimetic stylistic choices, we will pause one last time on the conclusion. As mentioned, the actors who have played the roles of Mefis, Elena, and Praxeologo Massimo (thus, in a sense, the plot's antagonists) are those entrusted with spelling out the moral of the story. Here is a passage from that scene:

Praxeologo massimo: Le differenze tra gli uomini
Sono apparenti
chi non ha unghie ha denti.
Mefis: Quando due uomini parlano
cercando la verità
uno dei due morirà.
Elena: La scienza è una bella ragazza
che si dà la notte a chi vuole
ma poi nella luce del sole
diventa una vecchia pazza.
Praxeologo massimo: All'ospedale di Hiroshima
si moriva in grande allegria
imbottiti di penicillina.
Mefis: Nel tribunale della storia
i fisici si dichiarano innocenti
hanno perduto la memoria.[88]

[Praxeologo massimo: The differences among men
are only apparent
if they have claws or fangs
Mefis: When two men talk
in search of the truth
one of them will end up kaput.
Elena: Science is a beautiful gal
at night she lies with who she wants
but then in the light of day
she turns into a crazy hag.
Praxeologo massimo: At the hospital of Hiroshima
they died in good spirits
all high on penicillin.
Mefis: In the tribunal of history
physicists claim their innocence
they must've lost their memory.]

Instead of closing the play with the end of Faust's vicissitudes, Celli adds this intermediate space, which lies outside the stage fiction and is contiguous to the reality inhabited by the spectators. It is a space used to make absolutely explicit the connection to current events, as if this were a chorus commenting on the action that had just ended. Finally, in this passage, the author adds the nuclear apocalypse to the concerns already expressed, that is, the biological and chemical manipulation of animals and plants and the scientists' lack of a strong moral fibre in dealing with their colleagues and their responsibilities toward society.

Pagliarani's *Faust di Copenaghen* is built precisely around this set of concerns: the nightmare of a nuclear war and the carelessness with which physicists have led all of us down this terrible path. In his case the approach to Goethe was mediated by the discovery of another *Faust of Copenhagen*, published by George Gamow in 1966. Gamow was a Russian physicist, a direct witness of that great season of scientific discoveries that run from the 1930s to the end of the Second World War. In his book, which Pagliarani read in its Italian translation, he relates many anecdotes regarding the protagonists of those years, along with the script of the *Faust di Copenaghen*, a farcical rendition of Goethe's *Faust* performed by students, and intended to parody the discoveries that were currently being presented at the most prestigious conferences in physics, especially regarding the theories surrounding the existence of a new subatomic particle, the neutrino. It is precisely the insistence on the idea of the neutrality (or, rather, the presumed neutrality) of the sciences that Pagliarani finds so appealing. He expresses it clearly on the occasion of the first performance of his *Faust*, in 1984, in an interview with Franco Pecori:

> Con la scusa del neutrone e del neutrino, loro mettevano le mani avanti; non c'era ancora il problema dell'atomica, ma capivano che stavano toccando delle cose da matti. Sicché, la parodia del Faust finiva con una specie di inno alla neutralità (neutrino, neutralità).[89]

> [With the excuse of the neutron and neutrino, they were trying to send a warning; there was no talk of an atomic bomb yet, but they all understood they were dealing with crazy things. Thus, their parody of *Faust* ended in a sort of celebration of neutrality (neutrino, neutrality).]

Later on in the same interview, we read more regarding the genesis of the play:

> Racconta Pagliarani: "Il testo originale, molto breve, l'ho letto nel '71, in un libricino del russo Gamow, edito da Cappelli nel '66, *I trent'anni che*

> *sconvolsero il mondo*, che parlava della fisica tra il '20 e il '50. Ho pensato subito di farne uno spettacolo. Mi ricordo che ero eccitatissimo, per due anni non mi sono occupato di altro. Tanto più che, contemporaneamente, successe che alcuni dei poemetti della mia *Lezione di fisica* furono tradotti da Fausta Segrè, la figlia del premio Nobel, per la rivista americana *New Directions*."[90]
>
> [Pagliarani recounts: "I read the original text, a very short one, in 1971, inside a little book by the Russian Gamow, published by Cappelli in 1966: *The Thirty Years That Upset the World*, which dealt with the innovations in physics between the 1920s and 1950s. I thought immediately of turning it into a show. I remember I was very excited and, for the following two years, I devoted myself exclusively to this project. Especially since, in the meantime, some of the poems included in my *Physics Lesson* were being translated into English by Fausta Segrè, the daughter of the Nobel prize winner, for the American journal *New Directions*."]

Pagliarani described the end of the play in the following terms:

> Ho scritto un finale, che ha due o tre possibili sviluppi, da scegliere. Ho messo insieme brani che mi sembravano profetici, misteriosi, apocalittici; una sorta di antologia sull'atomica.[91]
>
> [I wrote a finale that can have two or three different developments from which one can choose. I put together passages that seemed prophetic, mysterious, apocalyptic; a sort of anthology on the atomic bomb.]

And then, in one of his characteristic rhetorical jumps, he returns to the beginning:

> Ma prima del finale parliamo del prologo. "La struttura," dice Pagliarani "è molto banal-pirandelliana. Gli attori stanno provando, il regista spiega le parti, raccontando problemi e aneddoti sui personaggi. Rispetto al Faust di Copenaghen, l'unica figura inventata è Fausta (femminile di Faust). È il personaggio più reale di tutti, perché è Fausta Segrè e racconta la verità su di sé; mentre gli altri discutono, lei arriva e dice: so che Elio mi cercava per aiutarlo a tradurre la parte centrale ... dov'è Elio? ... mah, si vede che ho sbagliato. E si presenta: sono Fausta Segrè, sono nata nel '43 a Casella Postale Militare no. 1663. Era la casella di Los Alamos, quando non esisteva nemmeno sulle carte. Praticamente, una creatura nata accanto alla bomba atomica."[92]

> [But before discussing the finale we talked about the prologue: "The structure," Pagliarani says, "is very much trivial-Pirandellian. The actors are rehearsing, the director explains the roles, recounting anecdotes and issues of the various characters. When we look at the *Faust of Copenhagen*, the only new persona is Fausta (a feminine version of Faust). She is the most real of all the characters, since she is Fausta Segrè, and she tells us the truth about herself; while everyone else is there discussing their parts, she comes in and says: I know Elio was looking for me to help him translate the main role … where is Elio? … well, I must have gotten the day wrong. And she introduces herself: my name is Fausta Segrè, I was born in 1943, Military Mail Box no. 1663. It was the mail box of Los Alamos, when it was still just an unmarked point on the map. Basically, she was born right next to the atomic bomb."]

Thus, Pagliarani introduced an additional duplication for the character of Faust. If in the "original" *Faust of Copenhagen* (Gamow's) we see an overlap between Faust and Ehrenfest, Pagliarani's version is complicated even further by the ambiguity brought by Fausta, a female Faust. It is not easy to explain satisfactorily the reasons behind this addition, but I am strongly tempted to link this character with Carla, another protagonist of Pagliarani's novels in verse. If Carla was a daughter of post-Second World War Milan, Fausta "was born right next to the atomic bomb."

In spite of the many additions and interpolations, from here on out the events of *Il Faust di Copenaghen* closely follow the version published by Gamow: during an "apotheosis of the true neutron" Faust dies and is carried away by four spirits; an (ironic) eulogy of neutrality follows. The show, however, does not stop with the end of the narrated vicissitudes but continues with a poetry reading that includes passages from Goethe's own version of *Walpurgis Night* (a translation by Fortini), poems by William Carlos Williams, and Gregory Corso's "Bomb."

At this point, in spite of all the indications that we have drawn from Pagliarani's own words, the reader might still be a bit confused as to the dramatis personae of the various renditions of *Faust* we have mentioned, from the original to the its latest incarnations. Here is a brief recapitulation of the different layers: 1) there was a *Faust of Copenhagen*, whose author is as yet unknown, which was performed in 1932, in Copenhagen, during the annual physics conference; in this version, Goethe's characters are paired up with the most notable nuclear physicists of the time, while the actors were, in all likelihood, young graduate students; 2) the first rewriting of *Il Faust di Copenaghen* by Pagliarani: the angle used by the poet in this re-elaboration is defined, in his own words, as "banal-pirandelliano" (that is, "trivial-pirandellian") and follows the formula of *Six Characters in Search of an Author*. The initial discussion among the actors regarding the distribution of roles allows for the telling of several anecdotes about the scientists at the forefront of quantum physics at the beginning of the 1930s, often mixed with information the audience can use in appreciating the implications of those recent discoveries; 3) the second rewriting of *Faust* for the performance directed by Luigi Gozzi: in this version the didactic elements are balanced by a ludic dimension that reminds many critics and commentators of the historical avant-gardes, and especially futurism and Dadaism. Video and musical elements were also added, giving a multimedia dimension to the performance and facilitating the more immediate involvement of the audience.

The superimposition of various characters that are assigned to a single actor reminds one of a complicated set of nesting dolls. Let us take, for example, Mephistopheles, the devil charged with tempting the protagonist. In the first *Faust of Copenhagen*, the parodic school play staged in 1932, the spectator was asked to believe that the part was actually performed by Wolfgang Pauli, the discoverer of neutrinos. In the first rewriting by Pagliarani, the "trivial-pirandellian" framing added another meta-theatrical element by introducing the actor who played the part of Pauli (who, in turn, played Mephistopheles). The second rewriting by Pagliarani increased the space assigned to the meta-theatrical elements, highlighting the distance separating the actors from the double role they were assigned. The whole situation is further complicated by the fact that, as mentioned earlier, during that first performance of 1932, the actors were young physics students playing the parts of their professors (one of whom was Pauli) playing the part of Goethe's characters (in our example, Mephistopheles). Here is a passage in which Pagliarani's Gretchen (who is, "in reality," Fausta Segrè) tries to bring a little order:

> Gretchen: – È vero, è vero. Voi dovreste
> capire che si tratta di una rappresentazione
> convenzionale; Pauli che fa Mefistofele,
> Bohr che fa Dio, Ehrenfest eccetera.
> Perché poi niente è vero, cioè
> nessuno di questi che ho detto – illustri fisici
> fece la sua parte. Nella rappresentazione che ci fu,
> le parti di Bohr, Ehrenfest eccetera furono sicuramente
> interpretate dagli allievi più giovani.
> Adesso poi ci sono gli attori che fanno la parte
> degli allievi che facevano la parte dei maestri
> che a loro volta avrebbero dovuto fare la parte
> dei personaggi del Faust di Goethe.[93]

[Gretchen: – It's true, it's true. You need to
understand this is a conventional
performance; Pauli plays Mephistopheles,
Bohr plays God, Ehrenfest etc.
But then again nothing is real, that is
none of these illustrious physicists I mentioned actually
played their roles. In the performance that took place,
Bohr, Ehrenfest etc. were certainly
played by the younger students.
Now we have actors who play the part
of the students who played the part of their professors
who were supposed to play the parts
of the characters in Goethe's Faust.]

It is enough to make one's head spin. Clearly, Pagliarani is not interested in soliciting a passive participation in the unfolding of the play; on the contrary, the audience is continuously forced to face the artificial and arbitrary conventions followed by the actors performing on stage. The reality investigated by these pioneers of modern physics is strange, unfamiliar, and often regulated by counter-intuitive mechanisms. It leads one to question the very fabric of our cosmos, those rules and truths we have always taken for granted and thought of as immutable.

In much the same way, the stories of their lives and discoveries (and the consequences of their research) are told in a convoluted, layered narrative that makes everyone acutely aware of the linguistic and theatrical conventions we often assume as "natural" and therefore invisible and transparent. This parallelism between the means and language of scientific research and artistic research is made even more explicit by the playbill:

L'affinità tra le nuove procedure teoretico-scientifiche e quelle artistico-progettuali è tanto paradossale quanto significativa ed evidenzia un complessivo spostamento culturale. Elio Pagliarani, critico e scrittore da tempo impegnato in una rilettura di questi processi conoscitivi (*La lezione di fisica*, 1968), ha riscoperto, tradotto e curato il testo del Faust di Copenaghen riproducendolo come un frammento importante della nostra storia culturale. L'allestimento di Luigi Gozzi è invece occasione per rileggere le avanguardie teatrali nei loro impianti concettuali e formali, in particolare la convenzionalità della rappresentazione e l'uso multimediale del palcoscenico.[94]

[The affinity between the new theoretical and scientific procedures and the artistic and programmatic ones is paradoxical and extremely meaningful, for it highlights a general cultural shift. Elio Pagliarani, a critic and writer who has been engaging for a long time with a reinterpretation of these modes of knowledge (*Physics Lesson*, 1968), has rediscovered, translated, and edited this script for the *Faust of Copenhagen*, presenting it as an important fragment of our cultural history. Luigi Gozzi's production, instead, is an opportunity to reread the theatrical avant-gardes according to their conceptual and formal structures, with a particular attention to the conventionality of the performance and the use of multimedia on stage.]

But we can also look at a text that is crucial in shaping our understanding of Pagliarani's poetics, "Per una definizione dell'avanguardia" ("For a Definition of the Avant-garde"), in which he tried to settle the issue on a theoretical level, beyond the contingent details of individual works. In addressing the relation between science and the avant-garde, he writes,

> Ecco anche perché le avanguardie sono più direttamente coinvolte di altri movimenti artistico-letterari, lo sono istituzionalmente direi con altre manifestazioni socioculturali, dalla attività politica alla ricerca scientifica: anche perché l'indagine della funzione dell'operatore e del rapporto operatore-consumatore è prevalentemente scientifica (di qui il peso e la rispondenza particolari, nella nostra avanguardia, degli scritti e degli orientamenti di quanti storici della cultura operano a chiarire i rapporti tra arti e scienza, fra arti e società) e le proposte e il comportamento risultano prevalentemente etico-politici, e in maniera immediata, come non può non essere – almeno quanto a immediatezza – nell'opera d'arte.[95]
>
> [This is why, when compared to other artistic and literary movements, the avant-gardes are more directly involved (in an institutional manner, I would say) with the other socio-cultural manifestations, from political activism to scientific research. This is also because the investigation of the function of the operator and the relation operator-consumer is overwhelmingly scientific (hence the weight and the peculiar relevance, in our avant-garde, of the writings and interests of those historians of culture who work at clarifying the relation between the arts and sciences, between the arts and society) and its unfolding and recommendations take predominantly an ethical and political bent, especially when observed in the immediacy of the work of art.]

Pagliarani and Gozzi, in their show, manage to reconcile avant-garde and science in an intuitive and immediate way, exploiting the opportunities offered by variety shows, mimes, and circuses: these are all tools that had already been employed for the same purpose by the historical avant-gardes. For instance, here is a brief quotation from the opening – the actors make their way on stage while dramatizing a scientific experiment, a pantomime-demonstration of Heisenberg's principle of uncertainty:

(*entra la palla-dio che viene spinta da alcuni attori*)
C: – Heisenberg criticò nel millenovecentoventisette
la teoria classica della traiettoria di un corpo materiale in movimento
F: – Prendiamo un corpo di dimensioni limitate
(*gli attori manovrano la palla-dio*)
e facciamolo avanzare nello spazio
anche senz'aria. È infatti un esperimento ideale. (*respirazione affannosa*)
Poiché stiamo eseguendo un esperimento ideale (*migliore respirazione*)
dobbiamo tener conto di ogni effetto capace di disturbare
il moto delle particelle.
G: – Eccone uno!
A: – Sì, eccone uno, nonostante sia eliminata l'aria (*respirazione affannosa*)
— siamo in un esperimento ideale
— la luce proveniente
dalla lampadina esercita sulla particella (*tutti guardano la lampadina*)
una certa pressione che può deviare la particella medesima
dalla traiettoria parabolica classicamente provata. (*sbandamenti etc.*)
...
F: – Abbassiamo la luce e ripetiamo le osservazioni (*buio: nel buio la palla si sposta notevolmente*)
G: – Per quanto osserviamo
C: – per quanto riduciamo la luce
I: – non possiamo evitare di perturbare
la traiettoria di almeno un Σ (*luce: la palla è fuori posto, lite*)
che equivale alla più piccola lunghezza d'onda della luce
(*buio improvviso*)
G: – Dimostrazione: ogni osservazione ricorrendo
C: – almeno per poco
A: – anche per pochissimo
G: – alla luce, comporta una piccola anche
piccolissima deformazione a causa della piccola
C: – anche piccolissima
G: – quantità di luce usata (*luce normale; la palla-dio è al suo posto*)
A: – Heisenberg, mettendo da parte le geometrie lineari classiche
osservò che nella realtà i quanti di luce
modificano del tutto la procedura del nostro esperimento.[96]

[(*the god-ball enters, pushed by some of the actors*)
C: – In nineteen twenty-seven Heisenberg criticized
classic theory on the trajectory of a moving body
F: – Let us take a body of limited dimensions
(*the actors move the god-ball*)
and let us push it forward in space
removing the air. This is, after all, a thought experiment. (*panting visibly*)
Since we are conducting a thought experiment (*breathing improves*)
we have to keep in mind all factors capable of disturbing
the particle's movements.
G: There's one!
A: Yes, here is another one, in spite of the removal of air (*panting visibly*)
— we are performing a thought experiment
— the light emanating
from the bulb exercises on the particles (*all look at the light bulb*)
a certain pressure, capable of modifying its path
no longer the classically proven parable. (*swerving, etc.*)
...
F: – Let us dim the lights and repeat the observations (*dark: in the dark the ball moves noticeably*)
G: – No matter how many observations
C: – no matter how little light
I: – we can't help but distort
the trajectory by a factor of Σ (*light: the ball has been moved, a fight ensues*)
which equals the smallest wave length of the light
(*sudden darkness*)
G: – Demonstration: since each observation resorts
C: – at least briefly
A: – even just for an instant
G: – to light, it implies a small or even
minuscule perturbation caused by a small
C: – or even minuscule
G: – amount of light (*regular lighting; the god-ball is back in place*)
A: – Heisenberg, putting aside the classic linear geometries
observed that in reality quanta of light
modify completely the outcome of our experiment.]

The illustration of Heisenberg's uncertainty principle is transformed into an opportunity to indulge in physical slapstick comedy, and to introduce objects with abstract geometrical shapes: these are all elements typical of the theatre of the historical avant-gardes (one could think, for instance, of *Anihccam del 3000*, the mechanized futurist ballet that Fortunato Depero staged in 1924). Noteworthy also is the crumbling of the lines, parsed among the various actors; an observation that brings us back to what we said regarding Celli: in his case, punctuation was used to achieve this same effect, although in a less intrusive manner, and with less anti-mimetic results.

After this introduction, with experiments and pantomimes that communicate the importance of the discoveries and their profound implications for everyday life, the play moves on to the prologue to the *Faust of Copenhagen*, which is taken directly from Gamow's text, with the addition of a few clarifications indispensable for understanding the original context. One of these interpolations is exploited to offer an explicit comment on the issue of science's presumed neutrality. As we have seen, the discovery of the neutrino and its lack of an electric charge is at the centre of the plot, but Pagliarani wants to make sure the audience doesn't miss the connection with the moral implications raised by nuclear power:

> Drammaturgo: Sì, e in fondo *Il Faust di Copenaghen* può anche significare una gara fra il neutrino e il neutrone, e la prevalenza di quest'ultimo, che alla fine Pauli-Mefistofele saluta così: "Buona fortuna a te Ersatz, peso massimo, ti diamo con piacere il benvenuto; ma la passione fila sempre le nostre trame e Gretchen è il mio tesoro!"
> Attore 2: Neutrino o neutrone, il "Coro Mistico" degli scienziati atomici conclude *Il Faust di Copenaghen* con l'alibi della Neutralità!
> Drammaturgo: In realtà, sia il neutrino che il neutrone sono neutri, cioè non hanno carica elettrica, né positiva né negativa ...
> Gretchen: Ma la carica gliel'hanno data eccome ... ci bombardano il nucleo, coi neutroni ...[97]

> [Dramaturg: Yes, after all the *Faust of Copenhagen* can also be taken as a contest between the neutrino and the neutron, and the prevailing of the latter, which Pauli-Mephistopheles salutes in the following terms: "Good luck to you, Ersatz, heavyweight, we gladly welcome you; but passion is always inspiring our plotting, and Gretchen is my treasure!"
> Actor 2: The neutrino and neutron, the "Mystic Choir" of atomic scientists, concludes the *Faust of Copenhagen* with the alibi of Neutrality!
> Dramaturg: Actually, both the neutrino and neutron are neutral, that is they lack an electric charge, positive or negative ...
> Gretchen: But they surely received one ... they use neutrons to bombard the nucleus ...]

The play, then, returns to the plot of Gamow's text, where we find a parody of the famous scene in Faust's study. It continues following that version, with the addition of Fausta Segrè as Fausta, whom we have already mentioned.[98] The next scene is set in the "Basement of Mrs Ann Arbour," where a number of scientists attend a sort of conference to discuss the merits of the newly minted particle, the neutrino. And this concludes the first act.

At the opening of the second act we find the same incursions into the theatrical modules of the historical avant-gardes. This time they are used to illustrate the structure and the inner workings of the atom. From here on out, the subject becomes increasingly more technical while Pagliarani grows stingier with his didactic explanations. In fact, the events take a rather surreal turn, with a number of complicated theories and concepts piling up rapidly, one on top of the other, to the utter confusion of the average spectator who is not versed in the latest developments of quantum physics. This version of the *Walpurgis Night* is a Dadaist pandemonium populated by donkeys, Dirac holes, dragons of groups, and Gauge's invariances (all of which are technical terms belonging to the contemporary debate around quantum physics):

Maestro: – Osservate il segno falso: è perplesso e scocciato.
Ferito nel suo amor proprio. Ce l'ha fatta con Dirac,
ma Darwin è un osso duro, Darwin non lo si può manovrare,
Darwin è come un uccellino in cielo, non più di uno spicchio
di luce nell'occhio di un fisico
(*solleva un cartello con la scritta:*
RELAZIONE DI SCAMBIO PQ - QP = h/2 π i)
Guardate qui! Darwin si è trasformato in P. (*Entra Fowler*)
Ed ecco Fowler (lui è una Q). Come vedete,
per spiegare la Relazione scritta sul cartello,
saltano alla cavallina per tutto il palcoscenico.
(*salti; a ogni salto lampeggia la scritta "h/2 π i"; dal fondo un generico coro*)
Così P e Q si scambiano fra loro,
continuando a scambiarsi, continuando a scambiarsi,
eppure brilla sempre h/2 π i, h/2 π i!
Non avranno mai pace
finché resteranno qui impalati come oche
finché resteranno qui impalati come oche
eppure brilla sempre h/2 π i!
Attenzione! Attenzione! Stanno trasformandosi …

(*P e Q subiscono ora la dolorosa trasformazione in Elettroni Asinelli, e cadono in uno dei Buchi di Dirac*)
… in Elettroni Asinelli. Osservate: barcollano e cadono,
sbadatamente in uno di quei buchi
disseminati dappertutto come trappole
poveri cocchi!
(*passa lo Spin del Fotone, rapidamente*)
Attenzione! Sfreccia ora lo Spin del Fotone
vestito di un sari indiano e di una giacca.[99]

[Master of ceremonies: – Observe the false sign: it is perplexed and annoyed.
Wounded in its self-esteem. It succeeded with Dirac,
but Darwin is a tough nut to crack, Darwin cannot be outmanoeuvred,
Darwin is like a little bird in the sky, no more than a slice
of light in the eye of a physicist
(*raises a sign that reads:*
EXCHANGE RELATION PQ - QP = h/2 π i)
Look here! Darwin has been transformed into P. (*Fowler enters*)
And here is Fowler (he is a Q). As you can see,
in order to explain the Relation written on the sign,
they are jumping and skipping all over the stage.
(*jumps; at each jump the writing "h/2 π i" lights up; in the background we see a generic chorus*)
This way P and Q turn into one another,
they keep exchanging roles, they keep exchanging roles,
and yet it keeps flashing: h/2 π i, h/2 π i!
They'll never get peace
as long as they stay here, sitting like ducks
as long as they stay here, sitting like ducks
and yet it keeps flashing: h/2 π i!
Watch out! Watch out! They are turning …
(*P and Q now undergo a painful transformation into Donkey-Electrons, and they fall into one of Dirac's Holes*)
into Donkey-Electrons. Observe: they stumble and fall,
absentmindedly in one of those holes
scattered everywhere like traps
poor sweeties!
(*the Photon Spin walks by, quickly*)
Watch out! The Photon Spin is zipping by
dressed in an Indian sari and a jacket.]

The second act ends with the "Apotheosis of the True Neutron," which is also the conclusion of Gamow's *Faust*: the issue of neutrality has been sorted out and the new particle, the neutrino, which does not possess mass or charge, is added to the structure of the atom, alongside the neutron, which, while lacking a charge, has mass.

Finale – Apoteosi del vero neutrone
(*Wagner impersonifica lo sperimentatore ideale, tiene in equilibrio sul dito un palloncino nero.*)
Wagner: È nato, è nato il Neutrone
con la sua brava Massa,
e senza impicci di Carica.
Sei d'accordo, Pauli?
Mefistofele: Anche se la teoria non c'è
il frutto dell'esperienza
ha sempre qualche valore sicuro
ha sempre presa nella mente e nel cuore.
Buona fortuna a te, Succedaneo Pesante:
ti diamo con piacere il benvenuto!
Ma Gretchen-Neutrino
resta sempre il mio tesoro!
Coro mistico: Finalmente realtà
ciò che era visione.
Che classicità
grazia e precisione!
Accolta con cordialità
onorata nei cantici,
Eterna Neutralità, portaci con te![100]

[Finale – Apotheosis of the true neutron
(*Wagner impersonates the ideal experimenter, balancing a black air balloon on his finger*)
Wagner: It's born, the Neutron is born
with its good old Mass,
and without the hindrance of a Charge.
Do you agree, Pauli?
Mephistopheles: Even if the theory lags behind
the fruit of experience
always has a certain value
always has a hold on the hearts and minds.
Good luck to you, Heavy Substitute:

we gladly welcome you!
But Gretchen-Neutrino
remains my dear treasure!
Mystical Chorus: Finally it's reality
what was just a vision.
What classic
grace and precision!
Embraced with cordiality
honoured in songs,
Eternal Neutrality, take us with you!]

Given all the references to the atomic bomb that Pagliarani included throughout the play, this hymn to neutrality is charged with strong irony. His criticism is made even more explicit in the third and final act. Here are the indications provided by the author in a note to the text:

Terza e ultima parte

(Collage di poesie riducibili e/o orchestrabili, manipolabili a seconda delle esigenze della regia.)

(Arrivano in scena diverse persone come a formare un corteo, alcune recano cartelli, che al loro arrivo ostenteranno al pubblico. Portano scritto: "LE LIVRE ARBITRE DES ATOMES"; "Nel regno delle molecole e degli atomi (Visioni dilettevoli della Natura)"; "L'ESSENZA SPIRITUALE DELL'ATOMO"; "ATOMI IN AZIONE – IL MONDO DELLA FISICA CREATIVA"; "LA GENESI E L'ETERNA EVOLUZIONE PERIODICA DELLA MATERIA".)

(Ultimi Faust e Mefistofele, e poi un Fuoco Fatuo e Cori e Streghe, verosimilmente interpretati dai dimostranti dell'inizio, che declamano i seguenti brani della Notte di Valpurga, *nella traduzione di Fortini.)* [101]

[Third and Final Part

(A collage of poems that can be reduced and/or orchestrated, manipulated according to the needs of the director)

(A number of people walk on stage, almost like a protest march, some of them holding up signs, which they will show to the audience. The signs read: "LE LIVRE ARBITRE DES ATOMES"; "In the realm of molecules and atoms (Pleasant views of Nature)"; "THE SPIRITUAL ESSENCE OF THE ATOM"; "ATOMS IN ACTION – THE WORLD OF CREATIVE PHYSICS"; "THE GENESIS AND THE ETERNAL PERIODICAL EVOLUTION OF MATTER")

(Last come Faust and Mephistopheles, and then a Will-o'-the-Wisp, Chorus, and

Witches, in all likelihood interpreted by the same protesters at the beginning, and they will declaim the following passages from the Walpurgis Night, *Fortini's translation.)*]

This is an example of a textual strategy on which we have already remarked (see the previous chapter), and which is rather common in Pagliarani's poetry: what Ballerini calls "river delta."[102] From a comparison with Celli, we can derive the additional observation that this stylistic choice is not limited just to Pagliarani, at least in regard to the theatre. Both Pagliarani and Celli end their plays with a poetry reading that occupies the liminal space separating the performance and reality: poetry is used to connect the fiction that exists exclusively on stage to the real world outside the theatre. Thus, the implication seems to be that poetry is capable of mediating between art and politics, provided that it is read out loud, at the theatre, or at least before a live audience.

This is the last of the many parallelisms between the two authors. In their plays, language is anti-mimetic and fragmented, although to a different degree (more in Pagliarani, less in Celli). They both rely on the experiments of the historical avant-gardes: in their shows there is no room for the illusions of a naturalistic realism; on the contrary, the scenic space is constantly proven to be artificial and fictitious by a careful orchestration of the actors' roles, their movements, and their games. In addition, there are often oneiric inserts, and a ludic and Dadaist streak runs through them.

On the level of the themes, both writers strongly criticize the idea of neutrality, exploiting the opportunities offered by the relevance of science to their plots and the role played by its language in our society, coupled with the concrete risks of a (purportedly) amoral and apolitical implementation of its discoveries.

In addition to Celli's and Pagliarani's different degrees of experimentalism, the main distinction between the two can be traced to the way they criticize the language and the conventions of bourgeois theatre. Celli dissolves them from the inside, pushing to the breaking point their potential for communication, and then taking a step beyond, until they crumble and fall. The plot follows a clear line of development, in spite of the many suspensions and interruptions. The conclusion is a moment when the world of scenic representation and that of "real" action are forced to interact directly, even if just for a moment. Pagliarani deploys a more direct, more violent strategy, and is thus closer to the tradition of the historical avant-gardes: he transforms his *Faust* into a container in which provocations and extravagant stage directions coexist with pantomimes and poetic readings.

The most impressive point is the convergence of these two authors, in spite of their different styles, on a set of common traits. We have already mentioned how disagreement, according to Eco, had become the "statutory sport" of Gruppo 63,[103] and yet, looking at the two *Fausts* here discussed, one might think that there are many more commonalities than disagreements. After all, as we have already stated many times, using the theatre as a key element in the strategy to reform contemporary literature was something almost every member of Gruppo 63 agreed on.

5.13 Conclusions

Over the years, as I was researching this project, I often felt a bit of nostalgia for a time when a large group of artists, writers, and intellectuals was still dreaming of influencing the world directly, changing society and, together, pushing for more progressive, more inclusive models of organizing our *res publica*, resisting and counteracting the overwhelming forces of capitalism and the organized, undying greed of the modern, multinational corporation.

To be fair, writers still try to do just that. The difference between then and now is twofold: on the one hand, the number of different voices involved in the project and the degree of coordination among them. On the other hand, at the time of the Neoavanguardia, there seemed to be a more concrete hope for tangible results; it was as if the goal was just beyond reach: if only poetry would stretch a bit further it surely would be able, it seemed, to seize its objective. Hence the experiments with the theatre, the utopic space where revolutions such as this one could be tried out and modelled, and where poets and citizens could meet to envision, program, and sketch out the process through which these dreams could be implemented.

The great intuition of the Neoavanguardia was, I think, that of focusing its efforts on the linguistic and rhetorical manifestations of injustice, the unbearable pressure on language of those hegemonic institutions that pushed for the commodification and thus the neutralization of all forms of dissent and thwarted any attempt at radical reform by instantly absorbing any antagonistic, discordant elements within the current, dominant economy of the sign. As a consequence, the achievements they attained are still useful today, even if the material and historical conditions are radically different. The value they carry is in their exemplary nature: they outline a number of strategies that, mutatis mutandis, are still viable today. Positive proof of this statement can be found in the discussions that animated the meetings of Gruppo 93, as well as in the pages of journals such as *Quaderni di critica*, *Baldus*, and *Allegoria*, where the work done by the neo-avant-garde has served as the starting point for more sophisticated insights, more nuanced artistic projects.

It is also important to acknowledge that the Neoavanguardia has been criticized at every turn by many contemporary intellectuals, the most common accusation being that of producing too much in the way of theories and programmatic essays and too few actual works that would exemplify their poetics. This volume contributes, I hope, to disprove this accusation, showing these writers' sustained effort to experiment in the most practical way with their colleagues in the theatre, searching for possible solutions to their aesthetic problems in the practice of performance.

Throughout this volume we have been painstakingly reconstructing a part of the history of the Neoavanguardia that had been systematically excluded and almost forgotten. Among the other products of the Novissimi first, and Gruppo 63 later, with its periodic meetings, its readings of works in progress, and its public debates, theatre was always seen, from the very beginning, as an important venue where the ideas elaborated in poetry and in prose could be put to the test. Even more importantly, theatre was seen as the one place where direct contact with an audience could still be achieved, and therefore it was an invaluable tool to be deployed in the search for a new, reformed, national language.

Furthermore, we have shown how the push that around 1963 had brought theatre and poetry together was not limited to Italy, and was not a trend that had appeared overnight: through the concept of "corpo-voce" devised by Gasparini, we traced back this resurgence of voice and orality to the very beginning of modernism. The separation that has taken place within criticism between the history of theatrical performances and that of poetry is an unfortunate one that has damaged our understanding of both art forms.

This book begins to bridge that gap and to show how much we can learn when we see verse from the point of view of the stage, and theatre through the eyes of the poets. The other great obstacle this book has had to face is the difficulty of accessing the texts, the works, the interviews, the criticism. I hope that this situation will progressively improve, as some positive signs are already visible through a renewed interest among a new generation of critics.

In addition to clarifying the poetics of some of the better known poets of Neoavanguardia, this volume has also illuminated the path followed by highly original writers such as Antonio Porta and Giuliano Scabia; it has highlighted the great variety of techniques, opinions, and approaches surrounding the relationship between verse and stage. A comprehensive, comparative treatment of this issue across the various individual writers, such as the one we have attempted here, can reveal invaluable insights into their creative process and their poetics. See for instance, how we were able to draw comparisons and distinctions between and among the works of Sanguineti and those of Giuliani or Pagliarani. Finally, a close analysis of a number of texts shows in a very concrete way the connections between poetry and theatre, and the debt that the former has contracted with the latter.

Needless to say, this is just a first step in the direction of a more inclusive history of those crucial decades, but I think it demonstrates on the one hand that such a project is achievable even without access to a whole team of researchers; and on the other hand, it gives a first glimpse of all the benefits that can be gained if such a line of enquiry is finally pursued with the necessary dedication

Interview with Valentina Valentini, Rome, 25 March 2017

A professor in the Department of History of Art and Performing Arts at the Università La Sapienza in Rome, **Valentina Valentini** has published extensively on theoretical and historical issues relating to twentieth-century theatre, as well as the intersection between theatre, arts, and new media. Her most recent publications include a groundbreaking history of the neo-avant-garde theatre entitled *Nuovo Teatro Made in Italy. 1963–2013* (Bulzoni, 2015) translated into English as *New Theatre in Italy. 1963–2013* (trans. T. Haskell Simpson, Routledge, 2018); and *Worlds, Bodies, Matters: Theatre of the Late Twentieth Century* (Performance Research Books, 2014), a reassessment of the status of contemporary theatre within a larger cultural context, originally issued as *Drammaturgie sonore: Teatri del secondo novecento* (Mondadori, 2007). She has also published a two-volume study on the interaction between theatre and video: *Le pratiche del video* ("The Practices of Video," Bulzoni, 2003), a collection of interviews with renowned video artists; and *Le storie del video* ("The Stories of Video," Bulzoni, 2003), a group of essays written by herself and other international scholars in the field. For the publisher Rubbettino, Professor Valentini has edited a book series, Teatro contemporaneo d'autore, dedicated to contemporary performance and drama. She has also served as the artistic director of the international video art festival, Rassegna Internazionale del Video d'Autore at Taormina Arte, from 1986 to 1995, and has curated a number of exhibitions and screenings dedicated to video art, including: *Tempo Incerto* (Avellino, 2003); *Zero Visibility* (Genazzano, Castello Colonna, 2003); and *Le tribù dell'arte* (Galleria Comunale d'arte Moderna e Contemporanea di Roma, 2001). Her essays have been published in many scholarly journals, both national and international, including *The Drama Review, Close Up, Biblioteca Teatrale, Ariel, Drammaturgia, Performance Arts Journal*, and *Performance Research*.

Rizzo: I've been investigating the reasons why poets have turned to theatre in order to solve the problems they had in poetry – that is, reaching a wider audience, reconciling a certain need for realism with a certain linguistic experimentalism and a certain political engagement. Poets saw the theatre as a place where they could find solutions, given direct contact with the audience, given that the actor could take on part of the work that was necessary, and so on ... What I am interested in discussing now is the point of view of those who were active within the theatre world – What did they see in these poets? What was the advantage they saw in collaborating with them?

Valentini: Gabriele D'Annunzio, too, turned to theatre as a writer, exactly because he wanted to acquire political influence, establish a direct contact with the "beast" – that is, the common people – that, between the end of the 1800s and the beginning of the twentieth century, crowded the theatres where Eleonora Duse performed. His objective was to disseminate the word of the national "bard," promote the rebirth of Italy and theatre through a Mediterranean and modern form of tragedy. Theatre exercises a great appeal as a living means of communication, especially for those writers who feel compelled to have a direct impact on reality.

Looking at this relationship in the second half of the twentieth century, the directors and actors of the Nuovo Teatro in Italy did not have a particular affinity for the poetic and theatrical works of the Gruppo 63 writers, with the few exceptions of Ronconi, Sanguineti, Quartucci, and Gozzi. In these cases, the writer was a presence inside the working team, that is to say the ensemble, the collective in which collaborated, without a rigid hierarchy, director, actors, playwright, set designer, and all those who shared a common idea of theatre. Whenever the writer was inside this circle, along with the actors and the director, the collaboration was successful, and the distance between literature and theatre was bridged. In fact, when Gozzi was touring with Quartucci's *Camion*, he was one of the characters in his *Scarichi di Camion* ("Camion Unloadings"), alongside the actors Carla Tatò and Luigi Mezzanotte, and the occasional guests they encountered during their wanderings. In those cases, the collaboration worked because the writer was integrated into the group that planned and produced theatre. But when the writer demanded that the director stage a text he had written outside of this lively context within which theatre was made, the collaboration was less successful. Certainly, some spectacles were born when directors of the Nuovo Teatro "took charge" of the texts written by authors and poets of Gruppo 63. We could mention *Illuminazione* ("Illumination") by Nanni

Balestrini with Mario Ricci; *Iperipotesi* ("Hyperhypothesis") by Giorgio Manganelli; *Povera Juliet* ("Poor Juliet") by Alfredo Giuliani; *Gioco con la scimmia* ("Game with Monkey") by Enrico Filippini. Collaborating with the Gruppo 63 writers meant being immersed in a circuit of musical, literary, and poetic experimentation which they perceived as contiguous to their own, and yet belonging to a different world. In short, literature has always failed on stage whenever it strayed from live creation, from collaboration, from improvisation. Whenever, instead, the writer has challenged himself and worked alongside the director (like Sanguineti did, for instance), then it was successful, since the distance between the stage and the page was bridged. I am convinced of that. Just consider that among the signatories of the Ivrea Manifesto there is no one from Gruppo 63 … while other artists extraneous to the theatre were there: Cathy Berberian, Silvano Bussotti, Liliana Cavani, Marco Bellocchio …

Rizzo: And thus, whenever the Nuovo Teatro agreed to stage texts written by Gruppo 63, it was a matter of being good neighbours … "since we are all involved in an experimental approach to art, since we all do avant-garde research, let us stage our friends' works …"

Valentini: At the beginning of the 1960s there weren't many plays written by Italian writers, with the exception of Edoardo De Filippo. If you read the debates in the specialized magazines and journals of the time (such as *Sipario*), they lamented the absence of playwrights; they expressed hope for the emergence of a new Pirandello, which was long overdue … The inquiry published by *Sipario*[1] asked Italian *literati* (Quasimodo, Calvino, Eco, Montale, Arpino, Cassola, and many others) about their relationship with the theatre; the answer they gave showed an unbridgeable distance, similar to the one that characterized the previous generation (Verga and Capuana, for instance, interviewed by Ugo Ojetti in 1893). Writers considered the literary text sacred, so they could not conceive the possibility that the director could manipulate it so as to make it match the other languages of the stage; they did not even like to be judged by a theatre audience. The directors of the Nuovo Teatro resorted to texts by dead authors; take Carmelo Bene's shows as an example. Quartucci started exploring Beckett, as early as the 1950s. For the most part, the theatre relied on texts by foreign writers.

Rizzo: That way they were able to radically transform the plays …

Valentini: The idea at the core of the Nuovo Teatro, one they supported with great energy and which subverted the dramaturgic conventions of staging a text, was that the literary script was just raw material; directors would deploy the procedures of collage, a collection of texts by various authors, taken from different sources, through which something new would be created. Collage becomes a key word between the mid-1960s and the late 1960s …

Rizzo: What you say reminds me of Balestrini, who is one of the writers who has been very successful in these kinds of collaborations, especially because of his way of writing, which relied heavily on collage …

Valentini: His *Illuminazione* ("Illumination"), directed by Mario Ricci, combined the stage directions from Chekhov's *Cherry Orchard* with a physical exercise booklet. The director and the artist in charge of the visual design, Umberto Bignardi, built a show independent of the written text.[2]

Rizzo: The question, then, becomes: if such was the case, if there was such a deep and fundamental misunderstanding about the value to be ascribed to a text, how do we explain the fact that there has been a convergence between poetry and theatre, at least for a brief time, between 1962 and 1963? Especially if we remember that the theatre professionals, people like Bartolucci and Gozzi, thought of poetry as a model of experimentalism that could be followed. I think Gozzi had an article in the first issue of *Marcatre*, in which, when speaking of the first Gruppo 63 meeting in Palermo, he was comparing the advanced state of music and poetry to the backwardness of theatre.

Valentini: Yes, this is absolutely true. My reconstruction of those years in the monograph *Nuovo Teatro Made in Italy* begins in 1963 exactly because I acknowledge the driving force that Gruppo 63 exercised on the Italian theatre of the time: they pushed the experimenters, the few that were around at the time, to go beyond the disciplinary boundaries and think about theatre in a radically different way. They have been a catalysing force, bringing a heightened awareness that added to what Carlo Quartucci, Mario Ricci, Claudio Remondi, and Carmelo Bene were already doing. Gruppo 63 was a source of inspiration for the Nuovo Teatro, even though the relationship did not lead to stable collaborations. For instance, Elio Pagliarani's plays were not staged by them, with the exception of *Merce esclusa* ("Excluded Merchandise"), which was performed at the Teatro Parioli in 1965, along with the one-act plays by Falzoni, Balestrini, and Giuliani.

Rizzo: Yes, and even those few cases were limited engagements, running two or three evenings, or included within a theatre festival …

Valentini: The Gruppo 63 plays did not circulate as texts of a new Italian dramaturgy, for the historians and theoreticians of literature considered theatre a lesser art. At the same time, the historians of theatre never included them in their research, either. It was very difficult, until a few years ago, even to access these texts: libraries did not have them, not even the SIAE[3] kept any copies. Things changed recently, after the celebrations for the fiftieth anniversary of the founding of Gruppo 63. This marginalization can be explained, on the one hand, by this prejudice the *literati* had against the theatre; on the other hand, the directors of the Nuovo Teatro had little respect for the written text, for they valued a kind of stage writing that saw the script as raw material that had to be reshaped to fit within the distinctive, multi-code language of the theatre. Naturally, the Gruppo 63 authors did not ask for a traditional staging of their works. This situation exemplifies an inevitable conflict within the theatre: whenever we are faced with a work that possesses literary value, two authors clash – the director and the writer. Heiner Müller would solve this contradiction by saying that the two texts had to run parallel to one another …

Rizzo: Which is an elegant way of not addressing the issue at hand …

Valentini: Absolutely!

Rizzo: I am very relieved to hear your reconstruction of those years is similar to my own: there was an initial convergence, and then the path of the two experiments diverged. When did this split begin? Was there a point when poets and directors realized they were no longer working toward compatible goals?

Valentini: I don't think there was: the directors that were close to Gruppo 63 were very few, even Scabia, who was a member of Gruppo 63, and yet, he would write his own texts, so he didn't face this problem directly. If anything, Scabia had the problem of considering himself a writer and poet whereas the rest of the world saw him as a *teatrante*. Bene never had this problem; I don't think he ever read a text by a Gruppo 63 writer.

Rizzo: No, absolutely …

Valentini: Exactly. Pasolini was ferociously against Gruppo 63. On the other hand, the Nuovo Teatro did not exactly love Pasolini. Not even close: Pasolini was strongly rejected by the Nuovo Teatro, both his manifesto and his plays, which were staged only years after his death.

Rizzo: I would like to talk about this for a moment. Reading today Pasolini's *Manifesto per un nuovo teatro* ("Manifesto for a New Theatre"), with its idea of a *Teatro di Parola* ("Theatre of the Word"), one wonders: who was its intended audience? Who is the interlocutor Pasolini imagined? It couldn't be the poets of the neo-avant-garde, since he was clearly attacking them; it couldn't be those who were carrying out experiments derived from Brecht or Artaud … What do you think he had in mind? What did he want for his new theatre?

Valentini: In 1967 a number of different manifestos were published in Italy: one by Giovanni Testori entitled *Il ventre del teatro* ("The Theatre's Belly"), one by Pasolini, and one by the Ivrea collective. After writing his tragedies, and after an attempt to stage them with Laura Betti, Pasolini abandoned the theatre. There is a book by Stefano Casi, which is very well researched, which explains this strong relationship Pasolini had with the theatre at one point in his life, before he turned to cinema.[4] His drastic change of heart reminds one of the crisis that visited Eisenstein, who decided that he could not work in the theatre, and that his goals could be achieved only through cinema. Pasolini had a similar realization, although for different reasons. His *Manifesto per un nuovo teatro* was published before that of Ivrea, at a time when he had just opened a new theatre in Rome, with Alberto Moravia, Ennio Flaiano, and other writers who did not get along with Gruppo 63; then, he felt the need to plan and refine the aesthetic tools he needed to operate in that context … we must not forget this other group also existed and was part of this attempt to mediate between theatre and literature …

Rizzo: Right, the Teatro del Porcospino: Moravia, Maraini – they were intellectuals who wanted to work with the theatre, but in a much more traditional way.

Valentini: Yes, much more traditional, although they would also host the band Le Stelle, with whom the painter Mario Schifano often collaborated. In the 1960s there was a convergence toward the theatre: on the one hand, you had the big names of literature, whom Gruppo 63 rightly saw as more conservative, belonging to the bourgeoisie; then you have Gruppo 63 and the Nuovo Teatro, which didn't have the resources nor the notoriety of people like Pasolini, Moravia, Flaiano, Volponi, Sciascia. If that is the case, then for whom was Pasolini writing his manifesto? Who was he in dialogue with? First of all, he was talking to himself: it was a way of clarifying matters for his own sake. At a certain point he had realized that he could not have continued writing for the theatre, for that would have required a constant, daily effort. He had tried his hand at it with *Orgia* ("Orgy"), a play performed in Torino, which seems to have been the only positive experiment of staging one of his texts. So, I think, it was a clarification he wanted to have principally with himself. He did not have any real interlocutors, with the exception of Laura Betti, with whom he collaborated. And, perhaps, he wrote it also for his *literati* friends, as a way of helping them imagine the theatre they were trying to create. However, when his manifesto came out, all of the Nuovo Teatro dismissed it as conservative.

Rizzo: It is conservative in many ways …

Valentini: All the experimenters of the Nuovo Teatro, for a long time, have considered Pasolini as a conservative who despised the Living Theatre, despised the theatre of the body, preferring the theatre of the Word. Now that so much time has passed, I realize we misread that manifesto, when it came out: it is not as conservative as it looked at first, but it was immediately dismissed, rejected.

Rizzo: Right, if one rereads it, what it had to say about the oral dimension of Italian is still very relevant. The fact that, at that point in time, there wasn't yet a serviceable oral language available, an everyday language that could be used for the stage …

Valentini: Yes, absolutely!

Rizzo: … but then again, if one looks at Pasolini's plays …

Valentini: Certainly! But that is another, beautiful contradiction …

Rizzo: … in reading them one finds acrostics … in the middle of a scene! It really seems out of touch.

Valentini: This is another contradiction I examine in my essay "Il teatro come rito e come foro" ("Theatre as Ritual and Forum").[5] What was his ideal? He wanted the action on the stage to have a specific community as a point of reference, and that community was made up of intellectuals, not factory workers! And the theatrical event was meant to be a forum – in this sense he was a Brechtian —, it was supposed to be relevant to current events, and thus also in the political arena. In that manifesto, although sometimes he contradicts himself, Pasolini does not disparage the other linguistic codes of the theatre in order to praise the word. The actor is important, although not the main component. The manifesto has been rejected because of the environment from which it came; it couldn't have been received well, at that moment. It was too far removed from the concerns and issues that had been discussed in Ivrea: the laboratory, stage writing, the attention to the body, the search for a new audience, a new circuit … The two manifestos could not engage in a dialogue.

Rizzo: This is why I often wondered who was the audience Pasolini had in mind. Sometimes, it is as if he came from outside of the country, as if he were completely disconnected from the context of the Italian theatre.

Valentini: Yes, this is something we could look into; I've never done it, but we could look at what kind of comments Pasolini's *Manifesto* elicited when it first appeared in *Nuovi Argomenti* … I don't think there were any …

Rizzo: There is also another element, one that I think is Pasolini's most interesting contribution. He was a very gifted polemicist, he had a knack for getting important conversations started: in matters of linguistics (the "seconda questione della lingua" or "second issue of language," as they then called it), in matters of the stage, with this "Manifesto," in matters of semiotics, as it applies to the study of cinema. Some of his positions may leave one a bit perplexed, but it is undeniable that he was able to focus the attention and ignite the debate on all the most pressing problems. And this has had a crucial impact on Italian culture.

Valentini: Undoubtedly. However, his plays weren't performed until the 1990s. They had a revival in the 1990s, also due to the anniversary celebrations, that brought them to the attention of the public … before then, however, his plays were not read or performed; there weren't even any editions available. They were not known, and they didn't circulate, especially if we compare them to the rest of Pasolini's literary output. And then there is his cinema, which monopolized everyone's attention.

Rizzo: We've mentioned Sanguineti a few times, someone who had a long relationship with the theatre, throughout his long career, and we've also mentioned the tension between author and director, both of them competing for artistic control of the final "product." And if one thinks of Sanguineti's plays, his style, it's not exactly like Balestrini's, whose fragmented scripts allowed actors and directors greater freedom. Sanguineti's plays are written in a rather conventional way. How can we explain, then, Sanguineti's long and successful output for the theatre? How was he different?

Valentini: Sanguineti worked as a *dramaturg* rather than a playwright. He was successful when he adapted texts that already existed, rather than writing his own; we have very few performances of his own plays. He was, instead, an excellent dramaturg, a writer who collaborates with a director and accepts to be on his side. For a writer, the condition of dramaturg is a demotion; take Marco Praga, for instance: he wasn't considered a *letterato*, but a scribbler … This prejudice was still very much alive among Italian intellectuals. Sanguineti, instead, decided to work as dramaturg. If we look at the performances produced by the Nuovo Teatro between the end of the 1960s up until 1987 – when Franco Quadri made the famous pronouncement that it was time to return to the text, with its characters, a story, etcetera – you would be hard pressed to find shows that had been written by Italian authors. In part because everyone was unreasonably internationalist, in part because there was no real need for a proper play … a novel would have done just as well. I am thinking, for instance, of Gaia Scienza or Giorgio Barberio Corsetti … they would take inspiration from Tanizaki, Kafka … but I don't see many Italian writers.

Rizzo: And since there was no opportunity to practice, this kind of collaboration died, for that entire generation.

Valentini: The Italian tradition is that of the actor-author, for instance Dario Fo, Edoardo De Filippo, Enzo Moscato, Franco Scaldati: the same person writes, directs, and acts.

Rizzo: And the theatre company is built around them …

Valentini: Yes. On the one hand there is this tradition that, roughly, goes from Ruzzante to Edoardo De Filippo; an archipelago of "islands of tradition," if you will, because we cannot really talk about one national tradition; rather, there are several, regional ones. Among them, the Neapolitan tradition is the only one that went uninterrupted, for there is continuity between Scarpetta, Viviani, Edoardo De Filippo, and then Enzo Moscato. Here we could include the recent experiments of stage writing by the Nuovo Teatro, who also were actors-authors, working with all the elements of the language of theatre. That being said, I still can't shake a thought … almost a ghost, really: D'Annunzio. He was the first Italian author who insisted he wasn't a second-rate scribbler – like Praga, Capuana, etcetera – and wanted to create an artistically relevant theatre, and thus re-evaluate the status of the playwright. D'Annunzio had very little success (critically speaking) as a theatre writer: some of his shows were terrible flops, while some of his plays are just unreadable – see *La Nave* ("The Ship"), for instance. Both Pasolini and D'Annunzio used theatre for their own ideological and rhetorical purposes; as a consequence, the texts they wrote are difficult to read and to stage. Perhaps, there is a line of research that could focus on this path within the Italian theatre, starting with D'Annunzio and arriving at Pasolini.

Rizzo: A sort of theatre of poetry, although it is understood differently, depending on the historical moment …

Valentini: Yes.

Rizzo: Manganelli is another name that comes to mind in this context, someone who definitely displayed an exuberant language and who wrote a lot for the theatre …

Valentini: I wouldn't call it "theatre of poetry," though; it is too ambiguous a definition. Maybe Mariangela Gualtieri's is a theatre of poetry, since she brings poetry to the stage, but D'Annunzio's or Pasolini's, I wouldn't call them theatre of poetry.

Rizzo: We mentioned briefly Pagliarani. He was someone who played both sides, so to speak: he rearranged poems he had already published, and shaped them into plays, which he gave to actors and directors as material for them to use freely – for instance, the 1963 show in Palermo, or the *Tassista clandestino* ("Illegal Cabbie"), a reworking of *Ballata di Rudi* ("Rudi's Ballad"). On the other hand, he also wrote more conventional plays, with characters, plot, etcetera. What kind of impact do you think he had on the Roman scene? Also, considering that he was the theatre critic for *Paese Sera*, he was at every show. How did the *teatranti* see him?

Valentini: I met him because I was part of a circle of writers; there was also Amelia Rosselli, whom I met several times. Pagliarani was considered mainly a poet, and his work for the theatre was never really discussed. He was a poet.

Rizzo: Therefore, it was impossible to see him and interpret his work in any other way, even when he was writing for the theatre.

Valentini: I think so, yes. His work as a critic for *Paese Sera* was a way to earn a living, so it didn't really matter in the reception of his output. The same goes for Angelo Maria Ripellino, whose reviews were known only by those who read *l'Espresso* and who were interested in the theatre, in spite of the fact that he was an avid theatregoer and very effective in reviewing the shows.

Rizzo: Therefore, their plays did not leave an impression among their contemporaries …

Valentini: Their works were published in journals; they had a very limited circulation. It was an invisible theatre, from many points of view, including the staging and the dramaturgy (the histories of theatre don't mention the dramaturgy of Gruppo 63). I never met an actor or a director interested in the plays of Gruppo 63 among the members of the Nuovo Teatro I know. I don't know if we will have any posthumous interest in them, as for Pasolini, after the publication of their plays. At the end of the 1960s, when they were being written, nobody in Italy, with the exception of Carmelo Bene, was equipped to carry out research around poetry as a *corpo-voce* ("sound-body"), or the word as a "sound-body"; therefore, all the shows were devoid of words, and they were received as images, movement, choreography. A proper training – besides Carmelo Bene or Leo de Berardinis (whose talents we could consider readaptations of the Italian tradition of the great actor) – would start only in the 1990s.

Rizzo: I am reminded of other experiments, like projective verse, poetry recitation, the Festival Internazionale dei Poeti at Castelporziano ... or even Spatola, who was recording sound poetry on cassettes, for his audio journal *Baobab*. These were all isolated experiences, but I wonder if the world of the theatre was aware of them ...

Valentini: Certainly! Simone Carella worked at Beat 72, and there he was in charge of the programming for music – he hosted the contemporary experimental group Nuova Consonanza – and also for poetry. Castelporziano was his idea, together with Cordelli and Manacorda. But, according to Simone, poetry was something different from the theatre. Also, when he would direct plays, he would turn to Peter Handke more than the Gruppo 63 writers ... We should check if there were Gruppo 63 poets at Castelporziano. I don't think they were included in that international event.

Rizzo: These issues are not very well researched: we need to pull all these threads together, and make all the connections. I think that is a very important job.

Valentini: I loved Alfredo Giuliani's work, out of all these poets, because I frequented this circle of writers, and we all read the Novissimi ... but I never thought of Alfredo Giuliani as someone who wrote plays, too.

Rizzo: And yet, if we read their theoretical essays on poetry, poetics, and aesthetics, there are always references to the theatre ... Barba spoke of "leaving behind the shell of the theatre," in order to go beyond it; they were trying to leave behind the shell of written, linear verse ...

Valentini: Absolutely. The fact that theatre did not engage with their work doesn't devalue their plays at all. They had a better relation with visual poetry, with Giuseppe Chiari, for instance, who was a musician but also a visual artist and a performer. There was a separation ... For instance, I am not sure what Cordelli's opinion of Gruppo 63 was at that point. This is another issue worth investigating further.

Rizzo: From my point of view, I can clearly see what can be gained by studying these plays written by poets. Yet, as we were just saying, since the world of the theatre has largely ignored them, is there something that the specialists in that field can learn from these texts?

Valentini: The most immediate advantage is that you reconstruct a landscape, a cultural context, adding a missing tile to the mosaic. Franco Scaldati's works, for instance, are almost completely unpublished, and have never been staged, but we gain from publishing them because he is a great writer and we discover a whole world we knew nothing about through those texts. It works the same in this case: from the theatre's point of view, the research of Gruppo 63 is interesting because their lack of a plot, their attention to the materiality of language are traits they shared with the Nuovo Teatro, and thus there was a continuity in their experiments. It is crucial, necessary, and urgent that we reconstruct this landscape populated by writers that contributed to the theatre and that the world of theatre doesn't know about. Therefore, it is important to carry on a program of publications, critical analysis, and so on. I am sorry to see that the scholars of theatre are not contributing …

Rizzo: I also wanted to talk about the influence of Brecht and Artaud on the theatre of those years, which was extraordinary, especially if we look at it from our vantage point. You have Brecht, who basically dominates the theoretical reflection on theatre for almost a decade, even before his works were completely translated; then, two or three years after the publication of his collected plays in Italian, you have what they called "*sazietà brechtiana*" ("Brechtian satiety"). And then there is Artaud, whose ideas are used in all sorts of ways. And finally, you get to a point where people try to combine the two: Sanguineti writes an essay dedicated to the "literature of cruelty," in which he tries to reconcile Artaud with Brecht … and I am not really sure I understand how that is possible. In part, I suppose, it is because of Sanguineti's writing style, with all those incidentals …

Valentini: Where did he publish that essay? I am not sure I have read it … in *Quindici*?

Rizzo: Yes, and then it was included in the volume *Critica e Teoria*, which is an anthology of theoretical essays by the most prominent Gruppo 63 members. I can see someone like Antonio Porta talking about Artaud, and using him in his poems, especially since he had read the originals in French. But he never tried to combine it with Brecht …

Valentini: You must remember that, in Italy, in 1964, the Living Theatre had arrived, and it was like a bomb had exploded, even before the translation of [Artaud's] *The Theater and Its Double*. Gruppo 63 wrote about it … The Living Theatre put together Artaud and Brecht, this was their contribution, the novelty they brought. Judith Malina had been a student of Erwin Piscator. The Living Theatre reconciled polarities that in Italy, from a certain point on, had become antithetical. In Italy, until 1967, there was a situation in which research, experimentation, and the political dimension went hand in hand. Then, after Ivrea, they took two different paths: on the one hand you have the political theatre – which split into *Terzo Teatro* (Third Theatre) and the *Circoli Arci* (Dario Fo, La Comune, La Palazzina Liberty …) –, on the other hand you have the Nuovo Teatro. After 1968, Brecht was not really a part of the debate any longer; he wasn't mentioned by Dario Fo, nor by the *Terzo Teatro* groups. Strehler was the one who introduced Brecht in Italy with the creation of the Piccolo Teatro in Milan.

Rizzo: So, Brecht had simply become synonymous with political engagement.

Valentini: Yes! And therefore there was Strehler, on the one hand, who did very rigorous work on Brecht and the didactic theatre, which culminated with his *Galileo*. Then, there were directors like Missiroli, Guicciardini, who later became the directors of the *teatri stabili*, which built Brechtism, a theatre understood as public service, something to educate the audience using plot, characters, the resources of the spectacle. In 1968, the political theatre did not think of Brecht anymore; they had all moved beyond that. Take Dario Fo, for instance, who was one of the most prominent members of our political theatre; he wasn't Brechtian at all …

Rizzo: Where did this idea of reconciling Artaud and Brecht come from, then?

Valentini: It was the Living Theatre that had brought it to Italy. They worked a lot on the body, the voice, the screams, the collective dimension of the plays; they had this aspiration of turning the spectacle into a ritual and communal moment, something cathartic, a vehicle for transformation and liberation. Thus, in *Paradise Now*, they closed by preaching directly to the audience: "Follow us, grab a bag of rice and join our tribe." They advocated a very strong, pragmatic approach; they wanted to change the individual and the world; they pursued these goals with the tools of Artaud, not Brecht. And thus, they exploited non-verbal communication, they smoked marijuana together, let us get naked, let us celebrate the body, eroticism, the sexual revolution. They were Reichians.

Rizzo: So, Brechtism had simply become a form of political engagement? What about all the work of distancing oneself from the character, all the denunciation of the ideological superstructure?

Valentini: They turned all of that into moralism! The people at Ivrea were against Brechtian moralism, which was associated with the *teatri stabili*. They were the enemy because they were the bourgeois, official art of the establishment.

Rizzo: And thus Artaud became an antidote to the evils of Brechtism, but they remained politically engaged …

Valentini: Exactly! And the Living Theatre represented this synthesis, and it was important for the Nuovo Teatro because it was proof that a reconciliation between these two polarities was possible.

Rizzo: And then intellectuals like Sanguineti or Porta tried to translate this into literature …

Valentini: Yes, I remember an essay … published in *Quindici*, on Artaud and the literature of cruelty, but it wasn't by Sanguineti, it was by Antonio Porta.[6]

Rizzo: There were a few replies to Sanguineti's essay; maybe it was one of those. This is another point on which things began converging again. Theatre and poetry had taken separate paths after 1963, but then tried to reconnect again over Artaud, through a re-evaluation of the body of the poet, his voice, his presence …

Valentini: I like this idea …

Rizzo: And then it continues with Gruppo 93. Someone like Lello Voce, for instance, comes straight from this tradition, those attempts to resurrect orality, only they called it "oratura" … but it was not unlike what Pagliarani did when he read *La ragazza Carla* at the cafes, while he was still writing it.

Valentini: I saw they recently performed *La ragazza Carla* at the Teatro Argentina. I think the Gruppo 63 theatre will make a comeback.

Interview with Pippo Di Marca, Rome, 25 March 2017

Together with Nanni, Perlini, Vasilicò, Cecchi, and Carella, **Pippo Di Marca** belongs to the second generation of the Italian theatrical avant-garde. In Rome, in 1969, he made his debut as an actor in Giancarlo Nanni's company at the Teatro La Fede, with a performance of *L'imperatore della Cina* ("The Emperor of China"), a play by the Dadaist writer Georges Ribemont-Dessaignes. In 1970, while still a member of Nanni's company, he acted in *A come Alice* ("A as in Alice"), a dramatic interpretation of Carroll's *Alice's Adventures in Wonderland*. In 1971, he founded his own theatre, which he called Meta-Teatro, and directed his first show, entitled *Evento-Collage no. 1* ("Event-Collage No. 1"). Over the course of his career, he was friends and collaborated with the most prominent members of Nuovo Teatro, including Leo de Berardinis and Carmelo Bene. He created more than sixty shows, and participated in the most important avant-garde and independent theatre festivals, both in Italy and abroad, including Chieri, Salerno, Bologna, Milan, Nancy, Avignon, Paris-Saint Denis, Caracas, Mexico City, Oslo, New York, and Philadelphia. In spite of its international reach, Di Marca's theatre felt particularly at home in the Roman *cantina*, a place that Franco Quadri dubbed his "dark, alchemic lair." Over the decades, his Meta-Teatro moved to five different locations, all within Rome, creating a space where different artists, actors, and writers could come together and experiment on language and theatre. The last incarnation of this *cantina*, called Atelier Meta-Teatro, closed in 2013. In addition to his work as an actor and director, Di Marca has also become a point of reference for the history of the Nuovo Teatro. On this subject he published the remarkable *Sotto la tenda dell'avanguardia* ("Under the Tent of the Avant-garde," Titivillus, 2013), a vivid recollection of the protagonists, places, events, and plays that animated the Roman scene of the *cantine* and independent theatres from the 1960s to the present.

Rizzo: I have been working on a book that tries to reconstruct the connection between neo-avant-garde poetry and theatre, an exchange that has been very productive, especially here in Rome …

Di Marca: A correspondence between theatre as a form of the avant-garde, and poetry as a form of the avant-garde can be identified in the development of a deliberate will for renewal. If poetry and the visual arts felt the need for this renewal as early as the late 1950s, the theatre was lagging behind. We were still in a figurative phase, if you will. The literary and poetic avant-garde offered a stimulus to everyone, especially as a model for organization, or, to put it better, as a movement, which is a rather different thing. It was the first time we got together, we formed a group, and we tried to change things.

Rizzo: It wasn't a formalized group; there wasn't a manifesto that defined it. Rather, it seems to me, there was a set of shared problems, and the desire to solve them together.

Di Marca: The fact that there was no manifesto was a typical Italian thing. The Germans of *Gruppo 47* got together and produced a manifesto. In more recent years, the Danes published Dogma. Then, after four years, they threw it out, but they did it. As for Italy, after all, it is as if they actually did produce it. Still, there were huge differences between the various artists. For instance, there was Umberto Eco, who then became an intellectual of the establishment, and thus regressed. But others, like Nanni Balestrini, were standard bearers of a new attitude. Balestrini was the incarnation of that moment, especially because of his writing style, which has never been adequately appreciated. He also practised visual poetry, a field that many explored in those years. And visual poetry contains much theatricality. Take, for instance, Lamberto Pignotti: he was someone who came up in that environment. And if there are experiences that are close to the theatre, those are them. As for the theatre, like I said, it was stimulated by literature, so much so that Ivrea was born four years after Palermo, and it wouldn't have started, or, perhaps, it would have come much later, if it weren't for literature. In Ivrea we tried to write a manifesto, because there was a greater awareness, and a more homogeneous group, everyone being from the theatre: artists, performers, and critics.

Rizzo: Absolutely. Returning for a moment to what you were saying about the avant-garde, we could point out that, on the one hand, these writers were avant-garde because of their style. On the other hand, they were professors, editors in prominent publishing houses, they worked for RAI television… it wasn't exactly a bohemian environment, the one that usually produces avant-garde movements; they weren't exactly trying to redeem life through art …

Di Marca: Yes, this is a fair point, from an anthropological perspective. There were no such "bohemians" in literature. In the theatre, instead, there were many artists who were self-taught. Many of us were self-taught. I, for one, had to change my mind on many positions I thought were set in stone. I wanted to write for the theatre; I didn't want to actually do it. Then I realized it made no sense, and I had to get my hands dirty, and I started with the basics. Memè Perlini's case was the same, and so was Giancarlo Nanni's. They started from a dimension of ignorance: either actual ignorance, or with the determination to create a tabula rasa. There was no such attitude among the Italian poets. And at this point we should also question the terms we use to describe these experiences. Starting with the label of "neo-avant-garde": it was the first time that the prefix "neo" was being used to indicate the beginning of a new path, but it wasn't an avant-garde environment in the sense that we usually remember. There was a bit of rage and intensity, especially if you talk with Gaetano Testa, the only one left of the three of the *Scuola di Palermo*: he is still a force of nature. You can get an idea of the climate there was in Palermo in those days from the temperament of a few of them. It was equivalent to the tension and euphoria that we were going to experience inside the student movement during 1969, 1970, 1971 … even the attitude was the same. Take, for instance, Alberto Arbasino, who, with his lifestyle, was openly challenging contemporary bourgeois society. He was also someone who fought a lot for the theatre. He wrote a beautiful book, *Grazie per le magnifiche rose* ("Thank You for the Wonderful Roses"), published by Feltrinelli, which collects his theatre reviews. I highly recommend it, if you don't know it already. He was also a director in his own right … Giuliano Scabia was another artist who got his start at that time. Others preferred the path of visual poetry. But that is also a theatrical gesture. Then you have Castelporziano,[1] which was organized by Beat 72, Franco Cordelli, Simone Carella, and that whole group; it took place over a decade later, but it was immediately considered an epochal event, an out-of-control emanation of the theatrical post-avant-garde. Then we saw even stronger energies, take Raffaello Sanzio,[2] which brought about an extraordinary wave of innovation. This is also a way of saying that the avant-garde is born whenever it needs to be; it is not a matter of following dates. Around the mid-1970s we felt the need to escape the rhetorical idea of the avant-garde, with its modes of stage writing that fatally repeated themselves. Thus, many of us left the theatres and took our experiments elsewhere, outside, to different environments. Many started with literature and ended up in the theatre, but it was almost an organic evolution.

Rizzo: Right, and it seems to me that within the theatre there has been a coherent and sustained movement toward stage writing, as you just called it, using Bartolucci's famous expression. In poetry, I think, there was a similar movement toward orality …

Di Marca: Yes, this is why I made the connection with Castelporziano. I think we agree completely. Gozzi's show, the one he directed in Palermo, proves this convergence from the very beginning. Even though we don't have many documents from those years. There have been many experiments of which we have no traces. The only one who was a good archivist of himself was Michele Perriera, but he is dead, so he cannot help us.

Rizzo: Don't you think it is also part of the spirit of those events, the fact that no tangible traces were left behind? The moment I try to leave theatre behind, to abandon scripts and written texts, I also give up the possibility of preserving any document …

Di Marca: Absolutely. There was a whole group of writers and actors (Dacia Maraini, Paolo Bonacelli, Corrado Augias, Alberto Moravia) who had banded together as the Porcospino, at the theatre on Via Belsiana: they viewed theatre from a dramaturg's perspective, based on writing, on the written text. This attitude was radically different from ours, mine, and those who had come before me: we arrived at the theatre with the desire to participate physically, so to speak, we wanted to intervene on that set of tools, take them apart and put them back together, perhaps even arbitrarily. Instead, as far as the *literati* were concerned, they looked at the theatre because they wanted to write differently. And this ultimately resulted in shows and other initiatives. For instance, many turned to the authors of the theatre of the absurd; I would also take into consideration the work of the visual poets, and check how many of them were in Palermo … this is another connection worth investigating.

Rizzo: I would like to talk about the phenomenon of the cantine, here in Rome. What is your memory of that time and that environment? What was the atmosphere like?

Di Marca: In those years, we were living what was later going to be called the "economic boom." But even back then, at the end of the 1950s, the most sensitive of us were realizing that it was all a terrible scam. Therefore, it was inevitable that artists developed an antagonistic attitude, a political environment which can help explain the impulse that generated the literary neo-avant-garde: another reason that should be added to other ideal, cultural, ideological, and aesthetic considerations. This is also why most of the *teatranti* were bohemians. Carmelo Bene was not poor, but there was no place, no structure within which he could have expressed himself. That's why he had to create it on his own. The others were students, people who didn't have the appropriate cultural credentials, but who felt the need to express themselves, breaking free from the establishment. There was an antagonist, even rebellious will, so to speak. There were also influences coming from the United States, from the hippie and beatnik environment, through the protests against the Vietnam War. And then, bringing it closer to home, there was Paris: in those years many went there to see what was new. Mario Ricci, before he started his own theatre, which was really an anti-theatre based on marionettes, lived a couple of years in Paris. Speaking of Ricci, and speaking of the relationship between theatre and the literary avant-gardes, we should point out how he was one of the first to have direct ties with Gruppo 63; in particular, I would mention *Pelle d'Asino* ("Donkeyskin") by Elio Pagliarani and Alfredo Giuliani – performed in 1965 at the Orsoline 15 – and *Illuminazione* ("Illumination") by Nanni Balestrini – in 1967 at the Teatro La Ringhiera.[3] Naturally, Ricci did not stage plays in a traditional sense; however, the scripts were the dramaturgic basis for his visual elaborations. All these elements became the earth from which the theatrical avant-garde of the 1960s grew. At the beginning, in Rome, there were very few of them … about ten or so. But, little by little, an interesting environment took shape; Twombly, just to mention a name, moved there, and even Duchamp, for a short but intense period, set his residence in the city. It was a very lively environment. Carmelo Bene, together with Ricci, was the first to create these alternative spaces, in very small locations, but where there was complete autonomy and freedom. Then many, many others followed, but this story is rather well known. That was the original spirit: find a hole somewhere, perhaps a stinky den, something dirt cheap, where you might have to fight against dampness and humidity. I had this place, the Meta-Teatro, where I would draw ten to twenty litres of water from the air every day. I had one of those first dehumidifiers; I'd turn it on in the morning, and empty it every night. I spent a decade there. Then there were other places, like La Fede, Beat 72, and a number of "meta-teatri." There was a need and a desire, then as much as now, for creativity. And this is a tradition that is still alive in the gestures, in the attitude, in the attempts to turn the institutional narrative upside down.

Rizzo: I want to return to Carmelo Bene. In your book *Sotto la tenda dell'avanguardia* ("Under the Tent of the Avant-garde")[4] you start with him as the first pioneer. What were his relations with the poets? I am thinking of that famous episode at the Ivrea conference, where he had a confrontation with Bajini because he had made fun of Marinetti. I have always considered it as one of the many examples that show Bene's lucidity in understanding the relative aesthetic positions of the various factions within the neo-avant-garde. Although many among the *teatranti* resented the historical avant-gardes …

Di Marca: The relationship between the avant-garde that followed the Second World War and that first avant-garde that flourished earlier, around the First World War, is not entirely clear. In my company I had for a while one of the last surrealist painters; that is how he defined himself. And he would build very original sets … We're talking about the early 1970s; there were many of them around. We were nostalgically bringing back something that was connected with our own personal stories. I understood this only later on, after my "encounter" with Duchamp, toward the end of the 1960s. The historical avant-garde can be traced back to the advent of Impressionism; then, little by little, you have Jarry, etcetera. And then you reach the point of reinventing language: this is the crucial aspect, both for visual language and for poetry. The first poet to curse poetry was Rimbaud! To him it was a matter of critical awareness. There was the need to revive the discourse, raze it to the ground, and rebuild from there. The historical relevance of this step cannot be questioned by anyone. It is not by chance that one of the first plays I staged with Giancarlo Nanni was *L'imperatore della Cina* ("The Emperor of China"), a text by Ribemont-Dessaignes considered by the Dadaists themselves as a cornerstone of their theatre. And this play, among other things, was a stern condemnation of war. We might not remember it, but the First World War was an enormous shock. It had never happened that millions of people died all at once. Recently, I brought it back to the stage, with significant results. From the point of view of the theatre, however, there aren't many other texts that can adequately document the high level of that cultural season … Take *Locus Solus*, or *Impression d'Afrique*, by Roussel: they are beautiful, but if you compare them to their contemporary works of literature, they are really not the same; at that time Joyce was planning his *Ulysses* and Proust was working on his masterpiece. The same thing could be said about Marinetti.

Yet, Carmelo knew how to make these distinctions; he had realized Marinetti should have been appreciated like Montale, Leopardi, or Campana, who was his favourite, because of his dimension of madness, his suffering … Once he went to Recanati, where every year they hold a festival to honour Leopardi. They had asked him to perform there, inside the palace of the Leopardi family. It was the 1980s, and he got to Recanati, and everyone wanted to talk to him. The performance was scheduled at eight in the evening, but he didn't want to talk to anyone, not even Leopardi's heirs and descendants. He loved Leopardi, as much as he loved Mayakovski, and the same for Marinetti. So he gets there, locks himself up in Leopardi's library at two p.m., and then comes out only at seven-thirty … he didn't want to be disturbed. Imagine what he must have thought … so much for mystic meditations! And this really tells you who Carmelo was. Someone who, behaving like a fool, which was the attitude of the first avant-gardes, inhabited, in reality, a realm of great depth.

Rizzo: In Bene I seem to recognize an idea of the avant-garde as something that must be lived on your own skin … linguistic and stylistic innovations are the consequences of existential changes, of the work he performed on himself. On the other hand, artists like Sanguineti, Pagliarani, or Balestrini were looking at it more as an intellectual problem … they had a certain detachment. Bene, instead, tried to actively reduce the distance; he was exploring the issue as an incarnated problem.

Di Marca: Absolutely. Carmelo took straight from Marinetti the idea of gesture, a gesture that shattered the discourse. Like with the polemic against the moonlight: it had become unbearable. But not everyone had access to this insight. In general, however, everyone at the time looked back to the avant-gardes, although everyone followed different paths. Carmelo Bene, like all great artists, insisted on the originality of his own research; he always said, "I was born and I'll die all by myself." He was very egocentric and he couldn't stand the idea that he might have copied anything from someone who had come before him …

Rizzo: And he tried to leave no legacy at all …

Di Marca: Lately, I have been thinking about Carmelo Bene and Leo de Berardinis, and I want to write something on their experiences, since both of them died with the awareness of a sort of *damnatio* to which they were already destined. Carmelo used to say that he was dying while unrecognized. When Leo died, they had kicked him out of Bologna. His company did not exist any longer. The last show he put on was an extraordinary monologue that started with the last words of *Finnegans Wake* and ended with Molly Bloom's monologue. In between, he added a number of poems by poets he loved particularly, and Leopardi was one of them. Afterwards, he wanted to do a show that was going to be titled *Farsa nera* ("Black Farce") … you can get an idea of his state of mind. Nothing came of it. In Leo, we can see the influence of the historical avant-garde, but he often mentioned jazz and Schoenberg. He thought of many of the things he did in terms of music, and went beyond theatre and toward music. He spoke of a vocality that could be modified from one show to the next; his voice was an instrument. And all of this could be traced back to Schoenberg. Carmelo also saw music as fundamental, but he was an opera lover. For instance, he wanted to "redo" *Carmen*, based on his enthusiastic veneration for Bizet, but he never got around to it … So, a few seasons later, a bit as a joke, a bit as a friendly "provocation," I did it myself! This is one of the most interesting modes to work: when you redo a text, it is as if you are creating something completely new. The alternative, that is, reading a text on stage in a conventional and repetitive way, is absolutely untenable, since you add a deadly fiction to a work that is already dead. Instead, if you take a text, you filter it according to your own sensibility, then you get a text "according to Carmelo Bene," or "according to Di Marca," etcetera; that is the right way to do it: taking it apart and making it into something vital and lively. For instance, before I fell in love with Duchamp, I was in love with Lautréamont, who, in a way, is his opposite. But then I understood that Duchamp was one of the first to say that the work of art is there, and we can look at it. However, we'll never see the artist; yet, if the work of art is right, the artist is somewhere in there. The artist is the work of art!

Rizzo: And we are back to talking about Carmelo Bene …

Di Marca: Yes … actually, I was talking about Duchamp, but it is true also for Carmelo, for Leo, and for many others. Think about when Duchamp makes himself up, dresses like a woman, takes his pictures, multiplies his image, sits down around a table and plays cards, or chess, against himself. Here you can see how much of body art was born from a theoretical and practical basis that was already there. It had precedents. Think, for instance, of Abramović … even though, in all this, there is a bit of "calculation," it is inevitable … Where can you go with painting after Manet, Monet, Matisse, Picasso? The first paintings by Duchamp were in that vein, up until 1914–15. Then he decided he could not continue in that direction, tried to figure out how to move forward, and realized that the artist's gesture was the key to everything. Toward the end of his life, he simply kept playing chess, even though he left us with a posthumous work, the *Étant donnés*, which is an extraordinary trivialization of the sublime. I did a performance in front of the *Great Glass*, at the Philadelphia Museum of Art, and a few feet away there is a room with the *Étant donnés*, two "images" of the same thing: a woman, femininity, "laid bare." There is a door, rather rough, and a keyhole. You put your eye there, turning into a voyeur, and you see this thing: the origin of the world. And you get goose bumps, because you understand the two opposites: the confidence in yourself, and the triviality that surrounds even the most sublime of things. It is like saying that it is the artist that guarantees the efficacy of the work. It is a profound reflection on art's spirituality, and it applies especially to those artists that say they are not spiritual at all.

Rizzo: I would like, if we could, to return to talking about Rome, and how it was an important place for theatrical experimentations. Elio Pagliarani was someone who lived in Rome, was an important poet of the neo-avant-garde, and was in constant contact with the theatre; he also collaborated with Simone Carella, who staged two of his plays …

Di Marca: I staged several readings of *La ragazza Carla* ("The Girl Carla"), even recently …

Rizzo: That side of Pagliarani has been left in the shadows, at least until the book I edited, which collected his plays, published in 2013.[5] I am interested to know, from someone like you, who is active in the Roman scene, what Pagliarani's presence was like … Did people know about his theatre, and about what he wrote on the theatre?

Di Marca: When they organized poetry readings at Beat 72, Pagliarani was not included. There were Magrelli, Zeichen, Bellezza … they chose the younger generation. The Pagliarani from the 1960s, the one who wrote plays, later turned into a critic, and from that moment on he was perceived as such. *Paese Sera* was an important paper, and while there Pagliarani exercised his criticism for many years. Cordelli was his deputy, so to speak … Pagliarani reviewed the more important shows, while Cordelli, with Bartolucci, Quadri, Moscato, had become the chronicler of our theatre. In fact, there were some misunderstandings between our theatre and Pagliarani. Not too long ago Andrea Cortellessa called me, because he was working on a book that collects Pagliarani's reviews, and he told me he had found one on a show of mine; I did not remember it at all. Instead, I remember very well the ones written by Cordelli, who was the same age as me, and he had become the leader of this cohort of madmen … there is an anecdote I find very telling, although no one speaks of it anymore. Pagliarani had gone to see a show by Perlini, *Pirandello chi?* ("Pirandello Who?"),[6] his first one, if we don't count those he had done with Nanni at Teatro La Fede. The cast included Rossella Or, who was the daughter of Orecchio, a journalist at *Paese Sera*, I think his first name was Alfredo; Rossella was twenty at the time, and the show was at Beat 72. I can't recall all the details now, if Pagliarani had already published a bad review of the show, or maybe he wasn't following with enough attention, perhaps he was talking during the performance ... in any case, Rossella stopped in the middle of the show and yelled at him, telling him to get out, or something like that. This is just one incident, something very few remember at this point, but something that can help you glean the atmosphere, how there wasn't much love between avant-garde theatre and Pagliarani (as a critic). He was a great poet, a modern one, if you consider the poetry being published at the time, but he never quite got our strange antics, our more or less deliberate stuttering, the gratuitous, original, arbitrary choices at the core of our theatre, especially in those early years. The job of the critic is an uncomfortable one, at least in some cases and in certain circumstances, when it comes to some artists. For instance, even Cordelli, who had an education close to our own, since he was very young, who came from a literary background, and who was close to Pagliarani, and then Moravia, Siciliano, etcetera, could never really stomach Carmelo Bene. This is to say that even a great intellectual, close to the avant-garde, or to certain manifestations of the neo-avant-garde, can be out of sync, so to speak. There was the suspicion that underneath Bene's attitude and egocentrism there was no meaningful foundation; a critic must find some sort of meaning, even if only at the level of the signifier. One of the greatest friends, mentors, commentators, and connoisseurs of Bene's work was Maurizio Grande, a friend of Cordelli's, someone whom he often talked with; even he could not bring him to appreciate Bene. The same thing, in the opposite direction, happened between Pagliarani and the so-called avant-garde; it is as if there was no chemistry. Some of us had writers we looked up to, poets and critics. I have always done everything on my own, and in the end I was completely independent. And, speaking of misunderstandings, just to show you how funny these things can be ... Cordelli never really understood Bene; the same thing happened between Leo and Carmelo: he didn't even want to hear about Leo. Once they staged *Don Quixote* together, but they never collaborated again after that. Leo had many reservations regarding Carmelo and his sincerity ... he wouldn't have put it like this, but that was the gist of it.

Rizzo: That suspicion toward Bene is quite common; many wonder whether underneath it all there is nothing. Paradoxically, that is exactly Bene's message, but if you don't want to consider it as an option, then it is impossible to even engage in a dialogue.

Di Marca: Yes, you can see it in a number of ways. Returning to the relation between him and de Berardinis, the historical truth, the one we can glean from their stage life, is that they were two giants of the Italian (and European) theatre. If we lived in a country that was more culturally advanced and less hypocritical, there would be monuments to them. Their memory would be preserved, promoted, passed down as a national treasure. Instead, we keep trying to forget them. They were very different. Leo was a positive artist, he loved Charlie Parker, and he was a sentimental man, a true, great poet of the stage. Bene, instead, was an anti-poet; to him emotions were something that came from the outside, provided they were necessary. Yet, he was the one who taught us how to say no. To all of us!

Rizzo: What do you mean?

Di Marca: Throughout his life he refused to act within a structure he considered catatonic; rather, he did his best to create something new, something that was born in the moment. So much so that, for instance, he rehearsed very little; exactly for this reason, he relied on inspiration. And this is a completely different approach: you are not seeking beauty or harmony, but "liberation." He needed that. And he went after it by using, even more so than Leo, all the tools of the tradition in order to get rid of it. Paradoxically, he is an actor from the *Ottocento* that was capable of becoming an actor of the 2050s!

Rizzo: The event instead of the performance …

Di Marca: Exactly. He was someone who said, "I have the tragedy; tragedy is the impossibility of the tragic; at the theatre, you cannot represent the tragic." Others had expressed this same idea in other disciplines. For instance, going back to philosophy, Nietzsche said the same thing. Bene loved Nietzsche. But he was the first one to articulate this thought in theatrical terms. As a consequence, he opted for comedy, parody, employing the modes of the great actor.

Interview with Nanni Balestrini, Milan, 4 April 2017

One of the main protagonists of Italian literary life of the last five decades, **Nanni Balestrini** was a writer (poet, novelist, essayist, and playwright), visual artist, and cultural impresario. He collaborated with some of the most prominent artists of his time (fellow writers, musicians, painters, sculptors) and has been a fixture of the intellectual life of the nation. His first poems were published by Gillo Dorfles in his magazine *Mac Espace*. Balestrini's first book of verse was titled *Come si agisce* ("How to Act," 1957). In 1961 he contributed to the anthology *I* Novissimi (edited by Alfredo Giuliani) the poem "Tape Mark I," which he composed using an IBM computer, programmed to manipulate a set of pre-existing text fragments. The following year, he published *Un istante con figure* ("A Moment with Figures," 1962), which was the result of a sound poetry project funded by RAI's Institute of Phonology, in Milan. He collaborated with Luigi Nono on *Novae de infinito laudes* and *Contrappunto dialettico alla mente* ("Dialectical Counterpoint to the Mind"). He helped organize and also participated in Gruppo 63 meetings, and edited many of the anthologies and collective volumes that ensued from those conferences. In 1966, he published *Tristano* ("Tristan"), an experimental novel characterized by a complex structure that combines passages taken from the most disparate sources. At the end of the 1970s, he co-founded the journal *Alfabeta*. During the 1960s and 1970s he was very active in the political scene, supporting the students' and workers' movements. In 1979, because of the tense political situation in Italy, he was forced to move outside the country; he relocated to Paris, where he collaborated with Gallimard and edited the journal *Change International*. Over the ensuing decades, he has published numerous collections of verse and novels, including: *Vogliamo tutto* ("We Want It All," 1971); *Ballate della signorina Richmond* ("Miss Richmond's Ballads," 1975); *Blackout* (1980); *Gli invisibili* ("The

Invisibles," 1987); *L'editore* ("The Publisher," 1989); *I furiosi* ("The Furious," 1994); *Sfinimondo* (2001). In 2004, in collaboration with Roberto Saviano, Balestrini published *Sandokan: Storia di camorra* ("Sandokan: A Mob Story"). In 2015 he collected his poems from 1954 to 1969 in a volume titled *Come si agisce e altri procedimenti: Poesie complete volume I* ("How to Act and Other Procedures: Collected Poems, Volume I").

Rizzo: Why theatre? What can theatre offer poetry?

Balestrini: In antiquity, theatre was always in verse. Its language was based on the rhythm and the sound of verse. It has been like that for many centuries, and only recently has dialogue been made into prose. Thus, for a long time, the language of theatre was made of poetry. Now poetry is content with appearing on stage for public readings. For me, theatre has always been an episodic thing; even recently, there have been performances based on some of my works, both in prose – like *L'editore* ("The Publisher") and *I furiosi* ("The Furious") – and in verse – like *Blackout*. However, I was not involved in the adaptations, so I don't think of myself as the playwright for those shows. I did write some plays for a particular occasion, that first meeting of Gruppo 63, in Palermo in 1963.

Rizzo: From your point of view, what did poetry see in theatre, what could be gained by getting close to the theatre? This is something that all the authors of Gruppo 63 seem to do, especially those who were also Novissimi, they tend to direct their research toward the theatre …

Balestrini: In addition to the meetings, where we discussed our works, and the conferences and debates, we organized a show with the performance of one-act plays that had been commissioned for that occasion. Not only poets like me, Sanguineti, and Giuliani, but novelists like Malerba and Manganelli also took part in it; overall, there were eleven plays, directed by Luigi Gozzi and the American Ken Dewey. With the exception of Michele Perriera, none of us had ever written for the theatre before then. After that, the following year, Toti Scialoja and Piero Panza staged, in Berlin, texts by Sanguineti and Giuliani, and then in Rome, works by Balestrini, Falzoni, and Pagliarani; in 1965, once again in Palermo, Carlo Quartucci directed plays by Lombardi, Filippini, and Testa. A collective effort that was beautifully analysed by Giuseppe Bartolucci. These were works that extended the horizon of research for a number of Gruppo 63 authors, who were essentially poets and novelists. The interest of Gruppo 63 in the theatre derives also from the fact that in those years, the 1960s, the stage was undergoing a period of dazzling activity thanks to Carmelo Bene, whose explosive and isolated experiments influenced the entire theatre of the time. Rome saw the creation of something like a network, the theatre of *cantine*, as we called it, a number of small performing spaces, with an attentive and loyal audience. This was a whole little world that later disappeared. For the majority of Gruppo 63 authors, as for myself, writing for the stage was a short-lived experience, although a rather satisfying one. Only a few carried on over the years: Lombardi, Filippini, and Pagliarani, who was also a theatre critic for a newspaper.

Rizzo: What happened? Why did theatre and poetry part ways for you?

Balestrini: For me it was an experiment, the idea of expanding the space of poetry, both on a visual and on an oral level, which also led to a way of directly engaging the audience, beyond the traditional, dramaturgic forms of theatre. Although it has always been a matter of occasional performances. Historically, there are few cases of poets and novelists that have written regularly for the theatre. And for those who frequent it only episodically, it is difficult to find room in a system dominated by professional playwrights.

Rizzo: But there was the Compagnia dei Novissimi, at the Teatro Parioli in Rome, with Scialoja ...

Balestrini: Who was a painter in addition to being a poet. But it didn't last long. Back then, in the 1960s, there was also something else, something quite beautiful: writers, painters, musicians, and people from the theatre and cinema cultivated very close and lasting relationships, we all saw each other all the time; we lived closely together. With Scialoja, at the Teatro Parioli, I presented *Improvvisazione* ("Improvisation"), where the actors' lines were the stage directions of Chekhov's *The Seagull*. In 1967, at the Teatro della Ringhiera, the director Mario Ricci staged one of my plays, *Illuminazione* ("Illumination"), in collaboration with the artist Umberto Bignardi.[1]

Rizzo: On the one hand, as you were saying, there was a continued relationship between artists, which made collaboration almost natural ... yet, it seems to me, looking at it from a distance, there was also a constant effort to take the verse outside of the page, and have it become something else. Thus one has visual poems, sound poems, and, then, the theatre ...

Balestrini: Actually, in this play, *Illuminazione*, I think these procedures have been taken to their extreme consequences. We used stroboscopic lights, film footage, moving scenography, and a fragmentation of the verbal text that reduced it to pure sound. In those years we saw the coronation of what we called theatre *"di regia,"* a spectacle that was essentially visual, where the text was a mere pretext. It included a few authors, extraordinary directors like Quartucci and Ricci, and also Memè Perlini, as well as younger ones like Giancarlo Nanni with Manuela Kunsterman and Valentino Orfeo. But then, after the 1970s, everything died out.

Rizzo: Why did it die? What happened?

Balestrini: Little by little, all these small theatres disappeared. It's a phenomenon that can be explained from a number of perspectives. One of them is certainly the exhaustion of a creative impulse that had been taken to its extreme. But there is also the end of that great time of protest and social, political, and cultural revolt that had begun in 1968, for which the literary and artistic avant-gardes of the 1960s had served as precursors and incubators. At the same time, theatre ceased to be at the centre of Italian cultural life. From that point on, we witnessed its constant decline; so much so that, today, save for a few exceptions, it is just mere repertory theatre.

Rizzo: We were talking about those, among Gruppo 63, who had a long relationship with the theatre: Pagliarani, who was also a critic in addition to being a playwright, and Sanguineti, who has also written for teatri stabili, and was involved in big productions …

Balestrini: Sanguineti did, with Ronconi, that wonderful and groundbreaking show, the *Orlando furioso,* in 1969. He collaborated with Luciano Berio's musical theatre. All of the Novissimi had collaborated with the most important musicians; I worked with Nono in *Contrappunto dialettico alla mente* ("Dialectic Counterpoint to the Mind") and with Vittorio Fellegara for the ballet *Mutazioni* ("Mutations"), performed in 1964, at the Teatro della Scala in Milan, with magnificent scenography by Achille Perilli.

Rizzo: One of the things that, looking at the texts, comes across with great clarity is the use of theatre as the place where poetry can encounter its audience in a personal, physical way, thus providing the solution to the problem of political engagement, but without sacrificing experimentalism. That is to say, the moment we come together, and the poetic communication happens in person, through the mediation of an actor, many possibilities open up, from the point of view of linguistic experimentation.

Balestrini: Yes, certainly, and just last month, in Milan, there was a performance of a long poem of mine, *Blackout*, involving twelve quite young actors, a very physical show, based on the body and movement. The theme was the 1970s, presented through the physical emotions of the time, rather than a narrative. It used the body, vitality, energy, and action.

Rizzo: And focusing on the body, the movement, the energy, also implies a political message …

Balestrini: Yes, absolutely.

Rizzo: The other path I wanted to discuss with you, and we mentioned it earlier, is that of Scabia, who undertook the journey of the theatre in a much more serious, systematic way, and who made of that his career. He was telling me: "Pagliarani was a bit worried, and he'd say, 'You have to write poems, don't do theatre stuff, you have to focus on the poems!'" I am interested in those instances when poetry pressures the theatre to do certain things, to reach a certain audience. Scabia's case, instead, is different, for his relation with theatre was more systematic, all-encompassing.

Balestrini: Scabia came a bit later, with Gruppo 63, and he focused on street theatre; he did extraordinary things in the spirit of 1968, diving into a number of collective situations, like, for instance, Basaglia's mental hospital. The relation an audience has to poetry is a very peculiar, variable one. It certainly depends on the kind of poetry that the times produce. In the 1980s and 1990s, there was an explosion of oral poetry, many poets started to declaim in public and to write texts precisely with this kind of reception in mind. At the same time, in many different places, a number of poetry festivals had been created, based on exactly such readings and performances. They enjoyed a remarkable popular success, but lately, because of the economic downturn, the public funds that sustained them were cut. And so, nowadays, oral poetry is practised far less; also because there are fewer places hosting it than before. There still remains a bit of nostalgia for those times, as well as for the preceding decades, when poetry had found a space in the theatre. But those forms and possibilities have not disappeared; they still exist, but they are now individual cases and not collective phenomena.

Rizzo: For me this is a way of better understanding poetry. The lens of the theatre can be used to focus on a few issues that were prominent at the time. For instance, the urgency to escape the written page is one of the most relevant aspects of those years …

Balestrini: In a reading or declamation, poetry becomes essentially an oral event; but when it must also become a visual, theatrical spectacle, it enters another dimension, one that poets are usually unequipped to face. That is why collaborations are necessary, and one must often assume a subordinate role when dealing with directors, artists, scenographers, musicians, with all the adjustments that are necessary. The poet's voice is not autonomous any longer.

Rizzo: The path taken by visual poetry stems from this same problem – the poem that wants to leave the written page – or is it something else altogether?

Balestrini: It is the direction first initiated by Mallarmé and Apollinaire, which then exploded with the futurists, and continued through the entire century, in a diffused, disseminated way, across the continents, following various modalities. In Italy, the largest phenomenon has been that of visual poetry, centred around a Florentine group, which displayed a particular strategy, generally based on the relation (often ironic) between a photographic image and a slogan. In my opinion, however, the most interesting results are those by Arrigo Lora Totino and Adriano Spatola. Poetry's escape from the typographical cage is something I have pursued since the beginning of my activity. In search of a form of reading that could break free from the linear unidirectionality of verse, I used bi-dimensional surfaces on which I could spread textual fragments, opening the possibility for multiple, multi-directional readings.

Rizzo: One of the other central protagonists of those years, Spatola, whom you just mentioned, tried to pursue every possible direction outside of the written page, resorting even, with his journal Baobab, to cassettes. How do you see his experience, his attempts to move toward a poetry that has more presence?

Balestrini: According to his own definition, Spatola acted in pursuit of a "total poetry." The visual aspect, relating to space, the sound aspect, relating to time, offer, within poetry, endless possibilities for manipulation and hybridization; they provide the poet with continuous stimuli for the creation of ever new shapes, following one's sensibility and predispositions. This is the message Spatola has left us.

Rizzo: I was reading an essay by Bartolucci, collected in his book entitled *La scrittura scenica* ("Stage Writing"), in which he was discussing the theatre of Gruppo 63, especially Pagliarani's, Balestrini's, and Giuliani's. He grouped Balestrini and Giuliani together, saying that they both treated verbal materials in a deliberately arbitrary way, fragmenting the lines and assigning them in an almost random way to the actors. Now that many years have passed, do you think this is still a reasonable way of looking at those works?

Balestrini: It is, for it develops the process at the core of this kind of poetry: the collage, the assemblage of different elements. In this perspective, it makes sense to assign text fragments to different voices and different characters. Without creating a continuous, discursive thread, but on the contrary, breaking it at every turn.

Rizzo: Fragmentation is also a way of opening the text to involve the reader in the process of signification, so that we are all invited to attribute meaning to this broken discourse …

Balestrini: I think it's more about emotions than meaning, when it comes to such texts, which are actually fragments of meaning. The final result that they try to achieve is that of a mental emotion that contrasts with the portrayed reality, as if through an electric charge. Without providing any coherent meaning, discourse, or argument, but rather opposing the entirety of that … at least, this is what I have always tried to do.

Rizzo: Thus a way of freeing the linguistic materials from any determination of meaning?

Balestrini: Yes, a way of disrupting meaning. I think that poetry has always been a fight against meaning. The very use of an articulated syntax in addition to rhythmical metre and verbal sounds, something that has always been the norm in poetry, Dante included, results in transmitting emotions rather than concepts. Leopardi's verse "*dolce e chiara è la notte e senza vento*" (sweet and clear is the night, and without wind) is not a meteorological observation; rather, through the sound and rhythm of the words, it creates an atmosphere, it communicates a strong mental emotion. This is what poetry does, and has always done, along with every other form of art. To communicate concepts we have other forms of writing; poetry is not the right tool for that.

Interview with Giuliano Scabia, Florence, 1 April 2017

Poet, dramaturg, storyteller, actor, director, and social activist, **Giuliano Scabia** is one of the most original artists and intellectuals of the second half of the twentieth century. In 1964, he collaborated with Luigi Nono on *La fabbrica illuminata* ("The Illuminated Factory"), an electronic composition for which he wrote the libretto. That same year, he participated in the second meeting of Gruppo 63. In 1965, he published his first collection of verse, *Padrone e servo* ("Master and Servant"); at the end of the summer, his play, fantastically titled *Zip Lap Lip Vap Mam Cre Scap Plip Trip Scrap & la grande Mam*, debuted at the Venice Biennale (director: Carlo Quartucci; scenes by Emanuele Luzzati; among the actors were Leo de Berardinis, Claudio Remondi, and Rino Sudano). It was an epochal event that marked the introduction of the Nuovo Teatro to the national debate around theatre. The play strove to build an "acentric" space within which the traditional roles and hierarchies were replaced by a collective effort to build an event rather than a spectacle. Between 1968 and 1971, Scabia inaugurated his distinctive brand of theatre, based on a collaboration with the people who resided at the outskirts of the big Italian cities, or in rural and remote areas, traditionally cut off from the cultural life of the nation. Scabia travelled to these marginal places and organized laboratories that provided moments and places for the community to gather, interact, and engage in storytelling and performances. Out of these first experiences came his *Teatro nello spazio degli scontri* ("Theatre in the Space of Conflict," 1973). In 1972, he joined the newly created Dipartimento di Arte, Musica e Spettacolo (Department of Art, Music, and Theatre), DAMS in brief, at the Università di Bologna. In 1973, together with Franco Basaglia, he initiated a theatre laboratory within the psychiatric hospital of Trieste. This groundbreaking experience is documented in the volume *Marco Cavallo. Una esperienza di animazione in un ospedale psichiatrico* ("Marco Cavallo. A Theatre

Laboratory inside a Psychiatric Hospital," 1976). In 1974, with some of his DAMS students, he staged the *Gorilla quadrumàno* ("Four-Handed Gorilla"), a play that was part of a series of performances dubbed "*teatro di stalla*" (barn theatre), with which he toured the Apennine mountains around Reggio Emilia, and later participated in the Festival Mondial du Théâtre di Nancy. Between the 1980s and 2000s, while continuing his teaching in Bologna and the performance of his texts, Scabia intensified his activity as a writer, publishing his first novel, *In capo al mondo* ("At the End of the World," 1990), and the *Nane Oca* trilogy: *Nane Oca* (1992), *Le foreste sorelle* ("The Sister Forests," 2005), and *Nane Oca rivelato* ("Nane Oca Revealed," 2009). His books of verse include *Il tremito. Che cos'è la poesia?* ("Tremble. What Is Poetry?," 2006), and *Canti del guardare lontano* ("Songs about Looking Far Away," 2012).

Rizzo: For many years now I have been writing about those poets of the Neo-avant-garde who looked at the theatre as a solution to the problems they encountered while writing poetry: the relation with the audience, going beyond the page, the reconciliation of political engagement with the necessities of realism, understood not as an adherence to party directives, but rather as a critical approach to the linguistic materials that were being used, something that should undergo a critical analysis that could reveal the bias and distortions they contained. To them, theatre became the place where they could get together…

Scabia: To them?! … to us!

Rizzo: Absolutely, to you.

Scabia: I was the one who blazed that trail …

Rizzo: And that is why I came to you, to talk about it …

Scabia: Pagliarani lectured me about it. He had great faith in me when I published my first poems. He would say: "You have to focus only on poetry." And I would say: "But, Elio, *Cavallo*[1] is a poem written by twelve hundred of us …" but they didn't understand.

Rizzo: This is exactly what I would like to talk about. There were a great number of experiments, all centred on the same nucleus, but there wasn't much communication – people didn't understand one another, even less so between *teatranti* and *literati*. Their two paths ran parallel until 1965, 1966, and then something happened; a difference suddenly appeared. I wanted to ask you what you thought about this: why did the two paths diverge? Some started doing theatre, and only that, others only poetry. This is the book I am writing now. This story has never been told, especially in English, and from the point of view of poetry. The few accounts that exist are from the vantage point of the theatre.

Scabia: In the *Canti brevi* ("Short Songs") there is a garland of dedications to Quartucci, Nono, the Gorilla Quadrumàno, and my papier-mâché Cavallo. For me it has always been about this game: poetry's deep path has always been based on action … at a certain point the tree-poet appears. Where does it come from? I had built my Teatro Albero (Tree-Theatre); I'll show it to you later. And where does *Opera della notte* ("Night Opera") come from? It is from when, with *Teatro con bosco e animali* ("Theatre with Woods and Beasts"), I walked through the night. The experiences that come from action, that's it. This is something that poetry has lost, for the most part, although Italian poetry had embraced it in the 1200s. The action, the presence of the body in metre, in the song, is very important … where should one look for it? In the inaccessible places, not in academia, but in those places where people can't talk, where they are beginning to speak. This is why I went to the margins, to face the disaster and beauty of the new language. What Pasolini had deemed a disaster was in reality a group of people speaking different languages, many different dialects, which were meeting for the first time and had to try to understand each other. This is what interested me – the issue of language, our issue of language, which is still going on, make no mistake; it's not over yet. It is an immense wealth we all possess, this plurilingualism, and no one else has it. And this is what fed us and is still feeding us. Take, for instance, the forms of Venetian painting: they are closely tied to the presence of water, to the horizontality of the lagoon rather than the stereotyped image of Venice: look at Tancredi, Vedova, but also Nono … we all hated Commedia dell'Arte. Although Ruzzante has been crucial for my growth, especially his *Letters to the Cardinal*, to Alvarotto. Venice's waters entered Nono's music, from a certain point on. The same with the ancient *pavano* [Padua's dialect], which is an archetypical form, as well as a concrete point of reference. It is a metaphor for the earthly paradise … and it is not a matter of localism. Rather, I start from this heart, this matrix, as our master Dante put it, and from there I built the world of *Nane Oca*, which is a very realistic and, at the same time, very fantastical place, endlessly metaphorical, which leads to an image of paradise … not the heraldic one, but an ironic, detached, mediated one. I ran into the theatre by chance, and I got involved with it through music, the great discussion over musical theatre, a wonderful experience, with Clementi, Manzoni … he was the first to write opera, with *La sentenza* ("The Sentence"), *Atomtod* … and then *Intolleranza* was a crucial encounter for me, something that the official historiography has always neglected. De Marinis talked about it, but after I pointed it out to him. I was there for *Intolleranza,* and I know what it means to run into Svodoba, into Maderna as a director, into Nono's writing, an exceptional group of singers, Prague's Magic Lantern – all their realism had been radically altered by the genius of Vedova, who took away the photographs of workers with their raised fists and replaced them with abstract images.[2]

Rizzo: This type of realism was completely unheard of, in these forms, around those years.

Scabia: We were at war with realism. We fought so many battles, with Pestalozza, Nono, especially because these people, Trombadori, Salinari, they were for the kind of realism promulgated by the Soviet Union. We also fought against Guttuso. He was a great painter, but I had it in for him, even though I like many of his paintings. He owned the PCI; he owned the official cultural politics … But we were talking about action, actions; this was all that mattered. Then, little by little, I felt the metrical power of the body. Even though, when I first read *Zip* in front of the actors, who were each one better than the next … Leo de Berardinis, Cosimo Cinieri, Claudio Remondi: they weren't avant-garde actors yet, this happened before everything else they would have done in their careers. I had to fight with them; for instance, Leo didn't want me to project images on him. He would say: "I am the main actor …"

Rizzo: He took it as a lack of respect …

Scabia: He would say: "Aeschylus is theatre," and I would say, "Yes, I know, but then there's also us, come on! Aeschylus is an absolute master, but …" A constant battle. Quartucci, instead, was unstoppable … a wonderful run. And from that dialogue *Zip* was born. How did it happen? I went to Rome; we lived together with the company, we had a small theatre … I read them the text, but back then I didn't really know how to read. I gave a horrible reading! And those actors were looking at me as if … in the end Quartucci told me, "You read so horribly that it will take me a whole month to restore their faith in your play." From that moment on I started to understand that writing texts is not enough: you must give them breath. The same goes for poetry. And I decided I would work on this, little by little. Why did I do a hundred "azioni di strada" (street actions), in the most incredible, inaccessible places? Because I wanted to find today's epos – that is, the writing that is within the voice. And I found it, or at least, I think I found it, for the first time with *Nane Oca*. I had written down a few chapters, here and there. They were materials I had since I was in my twenties. I had notes

… but I couldn't find a beginning. I had written five or six of them, each one worse than the last … they were too rhetorical. I had found the right way for other chapters; sometimes everything starts with the last scene, and then the whole thing comes together. I was all alone, in the cold, in an isolated house, one night, at Christmas, all alone, at peace, and suddenly I hear … I come up with this sentence: "what a dark blue night." From there I could hear the beginning of the music, and then the first page came, and finally everything fell in line. "What a dark blue night" is the theme … since then I have performed this chapter many times, and it suits me. I was looking for this kind of poetry with my other texts as well. In general, whenever I write something, I read it to my friends to check if it resonates with them. If it doesn't, I rewrite it, or I throw it away.

Rizzo: There is always an oral dimension…

Scabia: There is epos … *In capo al mondo* ("At the End of the World"), for instance, it is the same. All of *Opera della notte* ("Night Opera") is like that. I write, and then I take out what doesn't fit the voice. Is it any good? I don't know. I think it is … This is something I find very hard to explain to my Italianist friends … I don't seem to be able to make them understand it. Now they are teaching a class on the *Trilogia di Nane Oca* ("Nane Oca Trilogy"), at Bicocca University; Angela Borghesi is leading that class … she came to visit me, and she is young, she understands. But even the great critics, who were absolute masters, people like Segre, Maria Corti, people who studied the *Chanson de Roland* according to these same criteria, could not see the connection … the other day Antonietta Grignani came to hear me at the University of Pavia: she wrote a wonderful essay on *L'azione perfetta* ("The Perfect Action"), which she published in *Autografo*. But the issue remains the same: "You are good if you write poetry, or prose, but if you write for the theatre, you are looked down upon." Folena didn't understand this, either. Only Marisa Milani realized it, in the end, because we had known each other for so many years, we were together at Folena's first lecture in Padova. She understood, and wrote about it; she dedicated her edition of the *Antiche rime venete* ("Ancient Venetian Rhymes") to me, and I dedicated the *Foreste gemelle* ("Twin Forests") to her. This issue of action, the pragma Euripides talks about, it isn't something you can do on the side … it is not something you can prep at home. Aeschylus acted, gentlemen! He sang! And the Provençal poets sang too, and all the Greek poets sang. Now, I am not saying that we all need to sing, but without a resounding body … you take away from poetry something like the wind of the soul, the soul of the wind. The song. Why are they called songs? I call these latest texts songs … it is a reference to Ariosto, Dante, to the *cantari*, and also to those friends of mine who sing the *ottava rima* when I go to visit them. Actually, most of them are dead now, and the younger generation doesn't sing anymore.

Rizzo: There is a different appreciation for the corporeal dimension of poetry. I think that nowadays a lot more people get it …

Scabia: Yes, yes: the poets, the younger generation understand.

Rizzo: Might it also be a result of the new mass media, with their unprecedented degree of diffusion and capillary penetration within society?

Scabia: Yes, it is also that … Although I always wanted my path to be an oral path, so to speak. Those media are phenomenal. And we have also studied the "sacred" texts … Zumthor, for instance. A corporeal action of poetry at the theatre is quite unique. Don't get me wrong; I have over sixty video documentaries, each one more beautiful than the next. Actually, I would like to show you some, if you are interested.

Rizzo: I would love to see them … but you were saying, the physical proximity makes a world of difference …

Scabia: It becomes a whole other writing; it turns into singing! I can see it when the actors perform my texts; they feel them differently, because they have music in them.

Rizzo: So it is a quality of the writing before it is a performance quality.

Scabia: Often the writing comes after the event. I often rewrite my texts after I perform them, many, many times. It is because I need to tune them to the deep chord of my breath. The metre is in the breath.

Rizzo: The importance of the breath, of breathing, has come up a couple of times already. I am reminded also of one of the people you mentioned at the very beginning, Pagliarani …

Scabia: Elio published the *Fiato dello spettatore* ("Breath of the Spectator"). He was a master of it! When he declaimed *La ragazza Carla* … boy! One of my *Canti brevi* ("Short Songs") is dedicated to him.

Rizzo: What was your relation with him like?

Scabia: He was rough: he never liked anything … I was afraid of Elio! He scared me! With Nanni Balestrini it was different; he was like a manager. With Antonio Porta I had a wonderful rapport … With Giuliani I had an academic relation; we talked often, but I found him a little fussy, and I wasn't very interested in what he was doing. Porta did wonderful things. And then Sanguineti was a teacher; he knew everything. I was scared of Sanguineti, too. Although another great teacher for me was Cucù, the madman. When I worked on *Marco Cavallo* there was one patient that would come every day to draw his wedges. He would make two hundred of them, and then he would leave. One day I remembered the visual music notations of my friends of Nuova Musica … Cucù did not speak; he only drew these signs. So I called him: "Cucù come here," and I started to modulate my voice following the inflections of the signs, "ohhoooh, hooohho," and so on, and he was so happy! From then on we started singing his sheet music: that was his voice. Those were his poems. He would write fifty, we would pick one, we would declaim it, and that made him so happy. How far can poetry extend? It can also stretch this far … but I spoke about this in the *Tremito* ("Tremble"), in those poems. This is how I extended this epos. But I am still studying it; I am still trying to understand.

Rizzo: From this point of view, your path is exemplary. You tried to use the theatre to pursue the goals of poetry, and, on stage, poetry becomes something else …

Scabia: Yes, but there is also storytelling. The key to this can be found in that short story, or maybe it is a monologue, or perhaps a prose poem, the "Teatro notturno" ("Night Theatre"), collected in *Teatro con bosco e animali* ("Theatre with Woods and Beasts"). There, at the core, is "Teatro notturno" … That book has a very distinctive structure. For instance, there are the "Lettere a un lupo" ("Letters to a Wolf"). Those were the first ones, then I wrote more … but I didn't know whether I should put them there, or somewhere else … then there is "Teatro notturno," where I describe a real action, in an imaginary way: those singers in the woods were not actually wood creatures, but my friends *maggerini* [folk singers], and they sang the *maggio* of Tancredi and Clorinda, that is *Jerusalem Delivered*. Celeste is an imaginary character but inspired by Domenico Notari, who was a stone mason, and who had participated in two *maggi* in his life, in Marmoreto. I met him in 1974, when I was doing *Gorilla*: they had us over for dinner once, all eighteen of us, and they sang their *ottave*, they showed us the *quartine*; that suddenly explained the whole history of *cantari*. They sang Ariosto, and Tasso, and Dante's tercets … not only the Notari, but other families too, and Scandiano was not too far away. As soon as you brought up the chivalric novels, people started to dream. These people, who in their everyday lives are woodsmen, stone masons, where did they learn all that? Often from the priests. Notari, for instance, was in the seminary up until he was sixteen, so he had time to read. And they kept these poems in their homes. The same goes for the Cervi … I went to their home several times, to talk with the grandchildren, and they had their little library, with the *Promessi sposi* ("Betrothed"), the treatises on agriculture, the poems, the *Reali di Francia* ("The Royal House of France"); the tradition of the *ottava rima* explains the history of those poems.

Rizzo: Therefore, it was a model of what could be achieved: *ottava rima* could explain the past but also illuminate the future.

Scabia: Yes. I have been going there for forty-two years now, and every year I create a new song. I will give you the latest, the *Canto della vita indistruttibile* ("Song of the Indestructible Life"). *Ottava rima* is something that harks back to the origins of poetry, to ancient Greece, an uninterrupted passing down of the song, which can also be channelled through the latest technologies. I don't have anything against them.

Rizzo: This brings us to another issue: this kind of orality also possesses a political dimension; it carries a very strong political message.

Scabia: How do you mean?

Rizzo: The choice not to rely on the press and the publishing houses to produce and distribute one's work, the physical presence in the same space of author and audience, the idea that a community must come together and gather around this orality …

Scabia: Well, when I first started, I stumbled on the theatre, so to speak. I wanted to be a poet. Then I wondered: can I do it? Who knows how you become a poet … I was trying to understand. At a certain point I felt the need to go out, to the outskirts of Milano, for instance, and that's where I did my first "azione di strada," the materials that were later collected in *Teatro nello spazio degli scontri*. I was in Sesto San Giovanni, Milano, and then Torino: this was a very intense and very tiring experience. What did I want to achieve? I wanted to build, together with common people, texts that we could share. It was the idea of creating a community, although it didn't really work too well. I managed to get it going, but my method clashed with what the institutions were asking of me. And, in the end, they dismissed me. They wanted me to finish the shows, but I had explained to them, I wrote them, together we can build a form of communication, we can follow certain threads, and we can come up with a set of shared stories, but that's all we can do. What brings a small town together? A common, shared set of stories. What will you find on top of Athens's Acropolis? A set of stories: all stuff that might have been stolen from Thebes, but they are there. There are gods, olive trees gifted by Athena, a series of stories, and that's what bound them together. This is not true anymore, in general, because people have moved out of the little towns, or new people have moved in; but the old communities were kept together by stories. In these neighbourhoods, in the cities, there were people coming from all over the place. We tried to get together, outside of the gates of FIAT, we tried to talk about the fact that we were trying to come together, and the next day we would tell each other that yesterday we got together, and so on. But if the end goal is putting on a show, and that's it, then it's a whole different thing. It may be that we will find the need to communicate what we are doing; we will set up a series of meetings to inform people what we are up to. This is something that worked very well in Trieste. That really came out nice. The *Cavallo* had been born. And then we didn't really build a show around the *Cavallo*; rather, we were invited to a party. The city had engaged in the right way, they participated in our game, and everything worked perfectly. If we had done a little show with the *Cavallo*, it would have all ended up there.

Rizzo: It would have been a way to neutralize the experiment.

Scabia: Exactly.

Rizzo: Therefore, there is this political element I just talked about …

Scabia: Political, in the sense just explained.

Rizzo: Right, not aligned with a political party … and then there is the linguistic element, which runs parallel to it. In order to get together, to gather as a small town and tell our stories, we need to agree on a common language. Some writers have followed a more avant-garde line, maintaining it was necessary to work on language in order to sharpen it, and make it more efficient. Others adopted a more reformist approach, unwilling to sacrifice accessibility and transparency, although they agreed on the general principle. How does this problem, the tension between these two approaches, overlap with the need to come together and tell stories?

Scabia: It is a matter of finding the right form. For instance, when I did *Un nome così grande* ("A Name So Big"), I overdid it, and it came out a tragedy. Instead, *600.000* is much more open: there I listened to all the voices, and then they were there, as if present: it was an assembly, with a few points of emersion. The *33 ore* ("33 Hours") performance was incredible.[3] Those young men and women were phenomenal. At a certain point the madmen from Collegno joined us. That was the first time I encountered madness, with Gamna and Pascal, two psychiatrists.

Collegno was a semi-open hospital. The patients participated in the show, and their contributions were the best ones. That is when I started seeing them as people: I no longer had any problem with them; they were just people, like the rest of us; some of them had been in some trouble, but there was no difference. What they said was always right. So, you see, it wasn't a matter of choosing a language: I was trying to connect all those languages, all those emersions …

Rizzo: It was a matter of listening, then.

Scabia: Exactly. Rosina, for instance … I have a few recordings of her, while she is searching for the melody to go along with the words of the storyteller: "I want to have fun and run." She does the same thing Brahms did when he was looking for a motif. She has a musical nature, and is a great storyteller. She got stuck on something when she was little, she had been committed to the hospital for a while, but every day at three she came out and wanted to sing. How did the storyteller come to be? Someone would say a sentence, another said something else, we would try to steer things a bit … we would ask, "What's Marco Cavallo up to now?" or: "What's Marco Cavallo saying?" and someone would contribute a sentence, and that's how the first stanza was born. "I want to have fun and run on the grass, with dirty and neat laundry …" I would have never come up with a sentence like that, "dirty and neat," it is beautiful. And the song? Someone would try, then someone else; nothing would work. Then Rosina would give it a try, and I have this remarkable recording … she tried a bit [sings]: "I want to have fun and run" … there it was, she found it! So, where's the right form?

Rizzo: It seems like a way of putting together a collage in a more organic manner …

Scabia: The laboratory is open; it is not a place to do something structured in a predetermined way, but a place where you can look for things. In Trieste, at the laboratory, anyone who wanted to could come. If they didn't feel like it, they didn't have to. If you wanted to smoke a cigarette, you could smoke a cigarette. If they didn't want to do anything, we would hang out, and chat. There were many opportunities to build something together. We would ask, "Do you want to do this or that?" and they'd say, "But how do you do it?" and we would tell them, we would share our knowledge. The only thing we kept doing every day was the *Cavallo*, but Vittorio Basaglia and Stefano Stradiotto were the ones who took care of it. The madmen did not make it. It had to be a marvellous thing; something done with all the techniques of master papier-mâché artists, and one of them was a student of Marino Marini!

The *Cavallo* was a masterpiece. The one we have today is a copy. The real *Cavallo* was burned at the slaughterhouse, and now there are six or seven horses around. This openness was the final objective of these experiments. I never liked saying, "The *Cavallo* was mine." Yes, I led the work, but the *Cavallo* belongs to everyone, to the whole world. It belongs to those who are not well, and to those who are fine. It is a blue horse that came out of an asylum for the first time in the world! It is a unique experience: it belongs to the world, and not to Giuliano Scabia! The same with the *Iliad* … it is Homer's, but how many Homers are there? Three thousand!

Rizzo: And we get to another issue I wanted to discuss: the "reduction of the I" in poetry … you achieve it in a very original way, something centred on the community. The others had the opposite problem …

Scabia: I count myself as one of them; I was very good friends with Spatola, for instance, with the Palermo group, and then with Porta, Nanni Balestrini, although I didn't like the fact that they were so deep inside literature …

Rizzo: The more institutional side of literature …

Scabia: The more formal side, let's say; there was an excess of formalism I didn't quite understand. That is why, at a certain point, I said "I'll go outside." There was that quote from Gombrowicz, "those who sing with you will change your song." I have been loyal to this principle to this day. The experiences I have had over the years changed me. The same happened with the adventure at the university. I had no plans of becoming a university professor. While I was fighting the dragon … I don't know if you know this story. It was 1972, I was in Massa d'Albe, on Monte Velino, dressed like a knight, and I was performing *Forse un drago nascerà* ("Perhaps a Dragon Will Be Born"). That day it had worked out, the dragon had come out, and I was fighting it. The dragon was the mouth of this little theatre, and the marionettes were its teeth, and all the children were underneath, carrying it around town. At a certain point a clerk from city hall approached me and told me, "There is a phone call for you at city hall." I said: "Let me finish this duel, and then we'll see who it is," and the clerk said, "A Squarzina." "I wonder what this is about." Squarzina had helped me debut with *Zip*. I finished up and went to city hall; they had left a phone number to call back. "Luigi, what's up?" and he said, "Would you like to teach at DAMS?" "And what is it?" It had just been created. I went to Bologna with my collaborators, and once there, in Strada maggiore, on a side street, we did the *azione* we usually started off with. There were a number of young people, some of the smartest and brightest active at that time: Massimo Marino, Eugenia Casini-Ropa, Paola Quarenghi, Dario Borzacchini, Aldo Sisillo, each one more talented than the next, although I didn't know them yet. They were enthusiastic about my theatre: I brought out the *Grande Pupazzo* ("Great Puppet) and then the Masks, and the banner with "Let's found a city together." Marzullo got closer and asked me, "Why don't you keep doing these things here with us?" I was a little afraid of the university; I feared I wasn't up to the challenge. I thought about it for three months, and then, having seen the other fellows that were joining, I accepted: there was Umberto Eco, Gianni Celati, Cruciani, Clementi, Bortolotto, who left immediately after, and then Manganelli was supposed to come, too, but he got scared and didn't come, and Nanni Loi, and Giuliani. It was a great group. And then also Cervellati, Maldonado. So I went, and I started a dialogue with Camporesi, Celati. It was a wonderful experience. What did I do? I continued with these experiments. And all of them are documented in the archive. Those are not reading packets; each of them is a different experiment. Some wrote that it was "Giuliano Scabia's *teatro stabile*." Every year I would do one or two experiments, starting with a basic structure. Why did I do the hot air balloons? I had first seen them in South America, during a tour. Then one of my collaborators told me people built them in his home town. So we travelled around Italy, and we learned how to make them. We could reproduce any shape, and we would send them up into the sky: they were like marionettes floating in the sky. That was the whole *azione*. In Bologna, around the time when they had killed Francesco Lorusso, and death was in the air, the university had been occupied, a lot of students had been arrested, we decided to release those hot air balloons all over the city: for days we would run after them, performing brief texts. That was theatre in the sky, with a narrative. One of the most beautiful *azioni* was written by Enrico Palandri, who graduated with me, and it was about a fish: beautiful. The university was a wonderful place; there is nothing better than being with young people and reading poetry. While I was there, we read all the best poets: Goethe, Euripides, Shakespeare, Garcia Lorca ... Speaking of Lorca, I have always felt he was like a brother to me. I went to his house, I sat at his piano, and I saw what was outside his window: the Sierra, capped with snow, and that Granada air ... although now they really spoiled it. At one point, in the *Poema del Cante Jondo*, you can feel the presence of the theatre. The third to the last text, and the one before the last, are theatrical and are made of quatrains. That's where Lorca was born as a man of theatre. I tried it out on my students: we sat down and we read the whole *Cante Jondo*; the whole thing takes forty to forty-five minutes. Little by little you get to these texts where you can feel the third dimension setting in: I never felt such a strong voice in any other poet's verse. It is because he sang along with the gypsies, he had the *duende*! Italians don't have it: it is a kind of magic, and if you have it, even if you don't have a good singing voice, you don't need anything else. He talks about it in his essay on the *duende*. He, Mayakovski, Dylan Thomas, they understood this, and practised it in their poetry.

Rizzo: If we look to the poets of your generation, we mentioned Gruppo 63, but someone who always used his voice, his physical presence, was Adriano Spatola …

Scabia: Bravo! That "Aviation, aviateur" of his … what a performance! Adriano was a force of nature!

Rizzo: Although it doesn't seem his line of research was continued by anybody …

Scabia: It never took off … I am part of Gruppo 63; I am not setting myself apart. We got together in Venice for one of those celebrations, but I don't like those. And after a certain point, I didn't care anymore; I was happier with the madmen than I had ever been with the *literati* …

Rizzo: We were saying that there has been a separation between the two paths …

Scabia: Yet, when we were in Venice, Nanni Balestrini told me, "You were the only one who really took theatre seriously," and I think I did. I have created ninety-six plays now … but they wouldn't understand what I was doing. They would even give me funny looks. They never tried to stage their own texts. I learned a lot from my experiences with actors, and when I started acting. Then I directed a play for the first time when I did *Commedia armoniosa del cielo e dell'inferno* ("Harmonious Comedy of Heaven and Hell") for the radio. I had excellent actors: Satta Flores, Tedeschi, Castri, Laura Panti. I had set aside for myself the part of Angelus Novus, the angel that closes the play. I was really nervous, but a lot had happened since that first reading of *Zip*; I had done story telling in the streets many, many times … I remember that Satta Flores complimented me. I relistened to it, and I would change many things: the breaths were not right, but all in all it wasn't too bad. Then, one time I was in Cagliari, I retold the story of my *Commedia*, and I saw people's eyes light up. From the pedestal of *Cavallo*, every once in a while, I would improvise short narratives: I would explain what had happened, a way to keep the game going. One day a nurse tells me,

"You know, we come here to listen to you tell us stories"; that's when I told myself, "I ought to think about this." And from then on I started to perform my own texts, not just as a director, but I would rather impersonate them. At one point I wanted to attempt a great test as an actor: the performance of the *Devil and His Angel*, something I took everywhere, even on top of the Eiffel Tower! I have a movie of it! I mention it because De Monticelli did not believe me when I came back: not even Molière did anything like this! Across the *banlieues* and to the Eiffel Tower: the pope did it fifty years later. I was there in 1968! New York University had gathered there, in Paris, for three days, a number of theatre people: Peter Brook, Cantor, John Arden, Ariane Mnouchkine, Bernard Dort, and I was the representative for Italy. For three days we told each other about our experiments on "teatro a partecipazione" [theatre of participation]. It was wonderful. I had just finished the *Cavallo*, and was doing the *Gorilla Quadrumàno*. I think that at that moment I was ahead of everyone: there was so much curiosity about my work; it was received as something truly new. Peter had crossed Africa with his group, and it had been an extraordinary experience. Ariane was part of the old theatre: she had rebuilt the Commedia dell'Arte in a different way from Strehler's. She heard about my magnificent journey, and she put it into her film on Molière. Ariane and I crossed Paris on foot, to go from a laboratory to a theatre, and while we were walking I told her all about my experiences with the *Gorilla* … she did Molière just like my *Gorilla*!

Rizzo: And so, if there was indifference or misunderstanding from the Italian poets, how did other *teatranti* see your work?

Scabia: There was the old controversy about the *teatro di parola* (theatre of the word). I had a good rapport with Roversi; I would often visit him. He understood what I did, although his approach was completely different than mine. I have beautiful letters from him. I also got along well with Zanzotto, from a certain moment forward. And with Rigoni Stern, too. Although I don't think Zanzotto really liked what I did; he liked what I wrote, so much so that he mentions me in a verse of his last book … "and Scabia, who knows ancient *pavano* …" He liked my *Nane Oca*. Franco Loi and I found each other after many years: once he came on a night walk with me, but he got scared … he thought I'd lead him into the abyss. I liked doing night crossings: every now and then I would go out for the sake of listening to the birds, and a poem or a story. For the last twenty years or so I had a good relation with Gianni d'Elia, who came from a very different background, but is a great reader. He is a follower of Baudelaire, and he comes from a very painful political past, he was in Lotta Continua. On top of that, he has this veneration for Pasolini, which I don't share, although I published one of his poems in Friuli dialect in my little journal, when I was in high school. I always read his things.

Rizzo: We should discuss Pasolini's theatrical experiments: I always found them rather perplexing.

Scabia: I never loved his theatre. I read it all, though. *Bestia da stile* ("Beast of Style") is a great text; it belongs to philology, filled with Dionysian apparitions. There are self-revelations, too: it is a heart-wrenching text. But I always thought his texts were unactable. Then some friends of mine staged them: they are difficult, but powerful. For instance, Federico Tiezzi and Sandro Lombardini presented *Porcile* ("Pigsty") …

Rizzo: But if we look at his "Manifesto …"

Scabia: The "Manifesto …" was terrible. It was aimed against us … terrible.

Rizzo: A few things were reasonable: for instance, the importance given to orality, to the voice. However, the idea that theatre should be addressed to intellectuals is the antithesis of what you were doing …

Scabia: The antithesis. I always thought Pasolini was a great poet. I think his screenplays are the best work he had ever done. And I always read him. Then I reread all of his stuff because I was invited to present at Casarsa, for an event. I was living in Milan back then, and Raboni called me. Now, Raboni is someone I always got along with; he understood me, and he wrote great things about my theatre. He was a great listener. He called me, on Pasolini's recommendation, to present *Calderón*; there were Musatti, Spinella, Petruccioli, and he, Pasolini… I didn't know him back then; I had never visited him. While we were there, he told me, with a grim face, "Do you still roll around in the dirt?" I told him "Well, I write plays, and then someone might roll around in the dirt, but we are up to all sorts of things …" From that I realized he knew nothing about what we were doing. Maybe he got scared because of the "Manifesto" we wrote in 1967 … maybe he was angry because we didn't include him … but Fadini, Bartolucci, Quadri, and that group were in charge of it …

Rizzo: The "Manifesto" that came out of Ivrea, it seems to me, was quite reasonable and focused on the right issues …

Scabia: Of course! And it brought together a number of different voices: a sentence is mine, another is Carmelo [Bene]'s … it is an amalgamation of many voices. We could have included his voice, too. Maybe we should have reached out to him, but he was already very famous, and it is as if he came from a different place …

Rizzo: He wasn't a team player …

Scabia: No, no. I didn't really think of including him … in any case, I didn't like his "Manifesto." But then I saw *Calderón* staged by Tiezzi … it came out great. Before it looked so flat … almost *adramatic*.

Rizzo: Literary in the worst sense of the word …

Scabia: Yes, yes … and he admitted it himself. When he staged *Orgia* ("Orgy"), in Turin, it was a disaster. Luca Ronconi saw it, and we talked about it: he said it was a disaster. However, Pier Paolo was honest and said, "I cannot continue with theatre, it is something I cannot do and I'll quit."

Rizzo: Right … he had the lucidity to see it clearly. I wanted to ask one last question about Ivrea, an epochal moment in the historiography of those years. It was, at the same time, a beginning and an end: a beginning, because it was the first attempt to organize as a group, and an end, because everyone realized the enormous differences separating each experiment. Beyond a set of common problems, and a set of adversaries, there was no possibility for unity. But I would like to hear your thoughts…

Scabia: Each of us had his or her own path. Quartucci and I were still close; then, who knows why, we grew apart… it was also because of the *teatro stabile*, which didn't let us do our show, the *Don Quixote*, and forced Quartucci to do *La Fantesca*. This led to the disbandment of the group, because no one wanted to do that show. We all went our separate ways. I would hear from Barba regularly. He wanted me to go on to the Odin Theatre and offered me a laboratory, but I never went. I wrote an *azione* for them. It is now published in *Culture teatrali*.[4] Eugenio wrote [to] me, "If you had come, our story would have been different." It was a beautiful *azione*: it was *Genesis*, and I had prepared seven days of creation. Each actor would build their own image, out of clay. I always talked with Ronconi, even though his path is completely different than mine, but we always respected each other. One of the last things he did, *Commedia di matti assassini* ("Comedy of Mad Assassins"), was a text of mine. I had reached out to him to ask if he thought that that play held up. He said, "Come by and we'll give it a try." He was very kind. I have always had a good rapport with Franco Quadri, and with Cathy Berberian: there was a moment when we got close, but we all lived in our own worlds. There was *Zip*, which was a real phenomenon. With Luzzati and Quartucci we published a manifesto of ten items in Quadri's *Sipario*. It was a reaction to the press *Zip* had gotten: it had been vilified by the old critics, and defended by the young ones. Augias, who still liked me at the time, although we had a fight later on, wrote a wonderful article about *Zip*, and published it in *Avanti*. Augias, Fadini, Bartolucci, Capriolo, they had all realized there was something moving in Rome: there was Ricci, and an incredible atmosphere. It would make your head spin: it was the beginning of 1968, there were international laboratories, Bozzolato had published Barba's book, *Alla ricerca del teatro perduto* ("In Search of the Lost Theatre") ... but then we all followed our own paths. And yet, I think, we achieved all those things we had set out to do in our Manifesto. The other day I reread it, as I was preparing for an event in Rome, and I told myself, "We've done all of this! Before these things didn't exist, now they do." It is unbelievable, but we did it all, in different ways: it went much better this way. We made a theatrical revolution, each of us in our own way! I like it better this way ...

Notes

Introduction

1 Pagliarani, *Tutto il teatro*, ed. Rizzo.
2 Pagliarani, *Pro-memoria a Liarosa (1979–2009).*
3 I found only echoes of it in Pagliarani's memoir, *Pro-memoria a Liarosa*: at page 118, where he talks about long, poetry-filled night walks that he and Bemporad took on the beach in Viserba, and at page 180, where he talks about a trip to Padua by car, when he was trying to enrol in the university.
4 Lucio Vetri, *Letteratura e caos*, vi–vii.

1 Why the Theatre? The Role of the Stage

1 In this chapter I included – after revisions, updates, and reworkings – ideas, quotations, and sometimes entire paragraphs I had previously published in the following articles and book chapters: "'*Proviamo ancora col corpo*': The Theatrical Dimension of Elio Pagliarani's Poetry," in Federica Santini and Giovanna Summerfield, eds, *The Politics of Poetics: Poetry and Social Activism in Early-Modern through Contemporary Italy* (Newcastle upon Tyne: Cambridge Scholars Publishing, 2013), 121–48; "'Se si vuole sapere se A è causa dell'effetto B': Scienza e realismo nelle sperimentazioni poetiche della neo-avanguardia," in *Studi Novecenteschi*, XLIV, no. 93 (2017): 79–101; "Il Faust della Neoavanguardia: Celli, Pagliarani e le riscritture di Goethe," in Gianluca Rizzo, ed., *On the Fringe of the Neoavantgarde / Ai confini della neoavanguardia, Proceedings of the Conference / Atti del congresso, Los Angeles, 17–19 Ottobre 2013* (New York: Agincourt Press, 2016), 189–217.
2 I would like to take this opportunity to thank the staff of the Centro Manoscritti for their support over the years: the president, Prof. Maria

Antonietta Grignani; the *direttrice tecnica*, Dr Nicoletta Trotta; and the librarian, Michela Tamburnotti.

3 From *Successo* (November 1963). As mentioned, the clipping found at the Centro Manoscritti di Pavia does not include the author's name, page number, or any additional information regarding the magazine.

4 Ibid.

5 Ibid.

6 See Alfredo Giuliani, Introduction to Di Marco, Testa, and Perriera, *La scuola di Palermo*. This same article was published in *Il Verri*, no. 7 (February 1963): 27–36. We quote from page 35 of the journal:

> Quale sia il comune impegno dei nostri tre palermitani abbiamo cercato di dire in principio; le differenze e i difetti si coglieranno nella lettura diretta dei loro testi. Qualcuno preferirà l'uno o l'altro, qualcuno proverà interesse a confrontare i loro risultati e trarne un'immagine d'insieme. Noi pensiamo che sia un'immagine, tutto considerato, sorprendente, nuova e intensa. Senza questi tre ragazzi Palermo esisterebbe un po' meno, e la piazza dello Spasimo non prometterebbe di diventare quello che è apparsa a un viaggiatore occasionale, un pomeriggio d'inverno del 1963: un luogo "figurale," una maceria da cui ci si solleva per vivere in uno spazio mentale diverso dall'antico.

> [We have already mentioned the common engagement shared by these three writers from Palermo; the differences and the faults of each one can be deduced by a direct reading of their texts. Some will prefer one or the other; some will find it interesting to compare the individual results and compile an overall image. We think that it would be, all in all, a surprising, new, and intense image. Without these three young men, Palermo would exist a little less, and Piazza Spasimo could not aspire to become what an occasional traveller observed on a winter afternoon in 1963: a "figural" place, a ruin from which one can rise to live in a mental space different from the ancient ones.]

7 One may be tempted to see in these six dissidents the first core of what would later become the "Anti gruppo Palermo gruppo anti," which would produce a few issues (at least six) of a journal that shared the same name and was subtitled "Rivista di anti testi di letteratura polemica." The thin, square booklets were printed (at the expense of the contributors) starting in 1974 and until 1975. Among the authors were: Nicola Di Maio, Nat Scammacca, Flavio Ermini, Nino Coci, Pietro Terminelli, Ignazio Apolloni, Giorgio Bellini, Giuseppe Zagarrio, Leandro Piantini, Eugenio Miccini, and Attilio Lolini. There is at least a decade between this group and the

foundation of Gruppo 63, which makes the identification rather dubious. However, the fact that one issue of this journal can be found among the papers of Corrado Costa, preserved at the Panizzi Library in Reggio Emilia, makes a connection between the two groups at least possible.

8 *Successo* (November 1963).

9 Ibid.

10 Picchione, *The New Avant-Garde in Italy*, 193. See also Picchione's essay "The Poetry of the *Neoavanguardia* and the Materiality of Language."

11 In addition to the two volumes already quoted, see at least the following anthologies: Balestrini and Giuliani, eds, *Gruppo 63: La Nuova Letteratura;* Balestrini, Giuliani, Barilli, and Guglielmi, eds, *Gruppo 63: L'antologia – Critica e teoria;* Barilli, Curi, and Lorenzini, eds, *Il gruppo 63 quarant'anni dopo;* Balestrini, ed., *Quindici;* and Balestrini and Cortellessa, eds, *Gruppo 63: Il romanzo sperimentale*. See also the following monographs: Barilli, *La neoavanguardia italiana;* Bello Minciacchi, *La distruzione da vicino;* Cavatorta, *Scrivere contro;* Chirumbolo, *Tra coscienza e autocoscienza;* Esposito, *Ideologie della neo avanguardia;* Gambaro, *Invito a conoscere la Neoavanguardia;* Luti and Verbaro, *Dal Neorealismo alla Neoavanguardia (1945–1969);* Muzzioli, *Teoria e critica della letteratura nelle avanguardie italiane degli anni sessanta;* Muzzioli, *Il Gruppo '63: Istruzioni per la lettura;* Santini, *Io era una bella figura una volta;* and Vetri, *Letteratura e caos*.

12 Such a reflection would come only later on, with the *Convegno di Ivrea*, in 1967 (see the next chapter for a full discussion of this). There are, however, four exceptions that must be noted: the monographic issues of *Il Verri*, no. 4 (1961) and no. 25 (1967); the monographic issue of *Nuova Corrente*, nos 39–40 (1966), devoted to "Teatro e linguaggio"; *Grammatica*, no. 2 (January 1967); and the many articles published in various issues of *Marcatrè*.

13 For a more in-depth discussion of the status of poetic texts and theatrical scripts within the Neoavanguardia, see chapter 3, in particular 181–93.

14 Balestrini, Giuliani, Barilli, and Guglielmi, eds, *Gruppo 63: L'antologia –Critica e teoria*, 35. The first anthology published by Gruppo 63 was Balestrini and Giuliani, eds, *Gruppo 63: La Nuova Letteratura;* another anthology was issued many years later: Balestrini and Giuliani, eds, *Gruppo 63: L'antologia*, first published by Testo & Immagine, Turin, 2002, then reissued by Bompiani in an edition that included also the older *Gruppo 63: Critica e teoria*, ed. Renato Barilli and Angelo Guglielmi (Milan: Feltrinelli, 1976).

15 Picchione, *The New Avant-Garde in Italy*, viii. A more in-depth discussion of the theoretical and aesthetic differences between modernist and postmodernist can be found at pages 59–60, where Picchione summarizes the differences between Edoardo Sanguineti (one of the key components of the modernist bloc) and Angelo Guglielmi, who belonged to the postmodern wing of the Neoavanguardia.

16 Giuliani, "Prefazione 1965," xvii.
17 Pagliarani, "Per una definizione di avanguardia," in Balestrini, Giuliani, Barilli, and Guglielmi, eds, *Gruppo 63: L'antologia – Critica e teoria*, 880.
18 Picchione, "The Poetry of the *Neoavanguardia* and the Materiality of Language," 149–50.
19 Picchione, *The New Avant-Garde in Italy*, 15.
20 While Giuliani called it a "reduction of the I," Pagliarani referred to it as the "tyranny of the I." See Pagliarani, "Cronistoria minima," 464.
21 For a more detailed discussion of the debate surrounding neorealism and the "experimental" approach to literature, see Part I of Ballerini and Cavatorta, eds, *Those Who from Afar Look Like Flies*, 55–157. This section, entitled "Windmills of Realism: A Querelle," focuses on the controversy surrounding the name and characteristics of the nascent new poetic sensibility that opposed neorealism and came from two distinct groups of intellectuals: Pasolini and the journal *Officina* on the one hand; Sanguineti and the poets of *Il Verri*, on the other.
22 Gozzi, "Gruppo '63 a Palermo," 13.
23 Here are all the details on that show: "La sera del 3 [ottobre], sempre alla Sala Scarlatti, è andato in scena uno spettacolo intitolato *Teatro Gruppo '63* a cura del Centro Teatrale di Bologna (regista: Luigi Gozzi; attori: Giuliano Colla, Piera Degli Esposti, Aldo Biagini, Roberto de Mattia) e dall'ACT di Roma (regista: Ken Dewey; attori: Carmen Scarpitta, Ciro Formichella, Amina Nosei, Robert R. Pellemberg). La scenografia dello spettacolo era di Achille Perilli. Lo spettacolo si articolava in tre parti: la prima, regista Luigi Gozzi, presentava: *Qualcosa di grave*, di Luigi Malerba; *La prosopopea*, di Francesco Leonetti; *Iperipotesi*, di Giorgio Manganelli; *Quartetto su un motivo padovano*, di Germano Lombardi; la seconda, regista Ken Dewey, presentava: *Serata in famiglia*, di Giordano Falzoni; *Lo scivolo*, di Michele Perriera; *Lezione di fisica*, di Elio Pagliarani; *Povera Juliet*, di Alfredo Giuliani; la terza parte, regista ancora Luigi Gozzi, presentava: *Imitazione*, di Nanni Balestrini; *Mister Corallo XIII*, di Alberto Gozzi; *K*, di Edoardo Sanguineti." From Balestrini, Giuliani, Barilli, and Guglielmi, eds, *Gruppo 63: L'antologia*, 907–8. [The evening of (October) 3rd, in the Sala Scarlatti, a show entitled *Teatro Gruppo '63* was staged by the Centro Teatrale of Bologna (director: Luigi Gozzi; actors: Giuliano Colla, Piera Degli Esposti, Aldo Biagini, Roberto de Mattia) and by the ACT of Rome (director: Ken Dewey; actors: Carmen Scarpitta, Ciro Formichella, Amina Nosei, Robert R. Pellemberg). The scenes were by Achille Perilli. The show was divided in three parts: the first, directed by Luigi Gozzi, presented: *Qualcosa di grave* [Something Serious], by Luigi Malerba; *La prosopopea* [The Prosopopoeia], by Francesco Leonetti; *Iperipotesi* [Hyperhypothesis], by Giorgio Manganelli; *Quartetto su un motivo padovano* [Quartet on a Paduan motif], by Germano Lombardi; the second, directed by Ken Dewey,

presented: *Serata in famiglia* [An Evening with the Family], by Giordano Falzoni; *Lo scivolo* [The Slide], by Michele Perriera; *Lezione di fisica* [Physics Lesson], by Elio Pagliarani; *Povera Juliet* [Poor Juliet], by Alfredo Giuliani; the third part, also directed by Luigi Gozzi, presented: *Imitazione* [Imitation], by Nanni Balestrini; *Mister Corallo XIII*, by Alberto Gozzi; *K*, by Edoardo Sanguineti.]

24 Gozzi, "Gruppo '63 a Palermo," 14.

25 Barilli, Curi, and Lorenzini, *Il gruppo 63 quarant'anni dopo*, 145.

26 Ibid., 146.

27 Ibid.

28 See Bartolucci's distinction between *scrittura drammaturgica* (theatrical writing) and *scrittura scenica* (stage writing) explained in the next chapter, 121–2. The main reason for the relatively small role played by Sanguineti in this volume is that the bulk of his plays (with, perhaps, the exception of earlier works such as *K* or *Traumdeutung*) display a more traditional *scrittura drammaturgica*. That is to say that Sanguineti acted as a dramaturge for the theatrical troupes with which he collaborated, a playwright in the traditional division of work within the theatre. We will return to this distinction later on in this very chapter.

29 A clipping of this article can also be found among the papers of Germano Lombardi, held at the Centro Manoscritti di Pavia. Pandolfi, "Il Gruppo '63 e la scena."

30 The article was, in all probability, published in the 6 October 1963 issue, but the clipping, which is in Lombardi's archive at the Centro Manoscritti in Pavia, is not dated. Its title is: "Una serata a teatro giocata in scena e a colpi di dadi. La quarta settimana palermitana di 'Musica Nuova.' Una serie di atti unici presentati dal Centro teatrale di Bologna e dalla Compagnia A.C.T. – *Povera Juliet* di Giuliani ha ottenuto il maggior successo" [An evening at the theatre spent on stage with a throw of dice. The fourth week of "New Music" in Palermo. A series of one-act plays presented by the Centro Teatrale of Bologna and the Compagnia A.C.T. – *Poor Juliet* by Giuliani had the greatest success.]

31 Dallamano, "Una serata a teatro giocata in scena e a colpi di dadi," 13.

32 Balestrini, Giuliani, Barilli, and Guglielmi, eds, *Gruppo 63: L'antologia*, 430.

33 On this issue, see Alessandra Briganti's "Preface" to Pagliarani's *Poesie da recita*, 12.

> Il punto di forza di questa poesia è rappresentato dalla sua intrinseca natura spettacolare che allude, a sua volta, a due fondamentali principi ispiratori dell'avanguardia, costituiti, per un verso, dalla manipolazione dei generi tradizionali e, per un altro, dall'intersezione dei diversi linguaggi artistici. La recita determina una conversione, verso esiti 'drammatici' e/o narrativi, della perdurante nostalgia lirica, mentre l'identificazione del gesto col

linguaggio (o viceversa) apre la strada ad una esecuzione che è recita, canto, ballo, dinamismo in ogni modo. Il gesto, che rappresenta una componente essenziale dell'esecuzione di Pagliarani, almeno quanto la modulazione della voce, denuncia un rapporto, una filiazione o una matrice culturale che sembra essere sfuggita finora all'attenzione dei lettori.

[The strength of this poetry is its intrinsic spectacular nature which, in turn, alludes to two different basic principles of the avant-garde: on the one hand the manipulation of traditional genres, and on the other hand the interpolation of different artistic languages. The performance causes a conversion, toward "dramatic" and/or narrative results, of the persisting lyric nostalgia, while the identification of the gesture with language (or vice versa) opens to the possibility of an execution that becomes an act, a song, a dance, a relentless dynamism. The gesture, that in Pagliarani's execution plays a crucial role, at least as crucial as the modulations of his voice, highlights a relationship, a parentage, a cultural matrix that, so far, seems to have escaped the attention of the readers.]

For a more in-depth analysis of this quotation, see chapter 4, 219–20. See also Barba's idea regarding "going beyond the shell of theatre," in chapter 3, 188.

34 Calvino, "Il midollo del leone," 18.
35 Ibid., 19. "Abbiamo detto che un rapporto affettivo con la realtà non ci interessa; non ci interessa la commozione, la nostalgia, l'idillio, schermi pietosi, soluzioni ingannevoli per la difficoltà dell'oggi ..."
36 Ibid., 20.
37 Giuliani, Introduction to Balestrini and Giuliani, eds, *I Novissimi. Poesie per gli anni '60*, reprinted in Luti and Verbaro, *Dal Neorealismo alla Neoavanguardia*, 158–62.
38 It is important to stress that, in spite of this point of contact between Giuliani and Calvino, the two adopted strikingly different objectives and literary practices in their works. Calvino, in fact, would go on to write three more essays, published in *Menabò*, where he further elaborates on these issues: "Il mare dell'oggettività" (1960); "La sfida del labirinto" (1962); and "L'antitesi operaia" (1964). His path would progressively diverge from that of the Neoavanguardia, leading him to a very personal reconciliation of the two needs for artistic research and *impegno*.
39 Giuliani, Introduction to Balestrini and Giuliani, *I Novissimi*, 159.
40 Ibid., 160.
41 Guglielmi and Pagliarani, Introduction to *Manuale di poesia sperimentale*, 23.
42 Elio Pagliarani, "Per una definizione di avanguardia," in Barilli and Guglielmi, eds, *Gruppo 63: Critica e Teoria* (1976), 312–17; and in Balestrini, Giuliani, Barilli, and Guglielmi, eds, *Gruppo 63: L'antologia*, 880.

43 Giuliani, Introduction to Balestrini and Giuliani, *I novissimi*, 160.
44 Pagliarani, "Per una definizione di avanguardia" (1976), 314.
45 Luperini et al., "'Officina' e il neosperimentalismo di Pasolini," 1003.
46 Pasolini, "La fine dell'avanguardia" (1999), 1416.
47 The Italian word "abatino" implies frailty and daintiness. An "abatino" is, or used to be, a cadet son of a prestigious noble family who, for reasons of politics and convenience, would undertake a religious career and would be active in the world of letters and culture. Thus, the word might also imply a degree of hypocrisy, sterility, unnecessary pomp and ceremony, and perhaps a reactionary outlook on society. The "journalist, imitator of Contini" mentioned by Pasolini is Gianni Brera (1919– 1992), whose fanciful and witty vocabulary revitalized the world of sports broadcasting.
48 Pasolini, "La fine dell'avanguardia," 1416.
49 For additional comments on this, and a more detailed analysis of this article by Pasolini, see Picchione, *The New Avant-Garde in Italy*, 76–9.
50 Pasolini, "La fine dell'avanguardia," 1417.
51 For more on Pasolini, cinema, and representation, see also Picchione, *The New Avant-Garde in Italy*, 74–80.
52 Camon, "Edoardo Sanguineti." 218.
53 Ibid., 219.
54 Ibid., 221.
55 Testa, introduction to *Dopo la lirica*, x.
56 Pagliarani, introduction to *Il fiato dello spettatore*, 12. This volume collects part of the reviews Pagliarani wrote for the newspaper *Paese Sera*, where he worked as a theatre critic. The introduction from which we quote is entitled "Teatro come verifica," and is a reworking of essays Pagliarani had written and published earlier. We were able to identify two of them: Pagliarani, "Dell'eroe linguistico" (1966), and "Artaud e la contestazione fisica del Living Theatre" (1967).
57 Pagliarani, "Sintassi e generi,"in Pagliarani, *Tutte le poesie*, ed. Cortellessa, 459–60.
58 See also chapter 4, 221–4, notes 10 and 12.
59 See the already quoted volume published by Marsilio, comprising Pagliarani's writings for the stage. Also, we mustn't forget Pagliarani's long collaboration with *Paese Sera*, a newspaper for which he served as a theatre critic.
60 It would be fascinating to analyse this same aspect of Pagliarani's poetry by using Ong's idea of orality and oral culture. In particular, it seems that his reflections on the formulaic style, on additive rather than subordinative syntax, and the agonistic tone, typical of oral texts, could also be applied to the kind of literature produced by Pagliarani. The reader can consult Ong, *Orality and Literacy: Technologizing of the Word*, 34,

37, 43–5. For the formulaic style one can't help but think of some of the *Detti conviviali di Martin Lutero*; the additive syntax and the agonistic tone are very common in the *romanzi in versi*, especially in *La ballata di Rudi*.

61 Testa, introduction to *Dopo la lirica*, vi–vii.
62 Ibid., vii.
63 Ballerini, "Prosimetro per la Ballata di Rudi," 68.
64 See, for instance, the pervasiveness of aposiopesis, a device that is systematically used in the *Ballata di Rudi* to postpone the conclusion of the *poemetto*. In this regard, see also Ballerini's previously quoted essay, where he talks about a "foce a delta" to describe the narrative structure of some of Pagliarani's works.
65 Giuliani, Introduction to *I novissimi*, 161.
66 Testa, Introduction to *Dopo la lirica*, viii.
67 Curi, "Poema come dialogo e gesto,"26.
68 Ibid., 27.
69 Ibid.
70 For more on this see the article by Edoardo Sanguineti, "Per una letteratura della crudeltà"; see also the reply by Tagliaferri, "La superstizione della crudeltà"; and their analysis in Muzzioli, *Teoria e critica della letteratura nelle avanguardie italiane degli anni sessanta*, 212–21. For a brief account of the introduction and diffusion of Artaud's ideas in Italy, see chapter 2, 145–7.
71 For more on the relations between visual poetry and poetry on stage see chapter 3, 178. A more systematic investigation of this relationship would be very interesting and useful to our research but, unfortunately, falls beyond the scope of this volume and, thus, must be postponed to a different occasion.
72 See Stefanelli, ed., *Il Gruppo 70 tra parola e immagine*; Cerritelli and Gazzotti, eds, *La poesia visiva 1963–2013: Omaggio al gruppo 70*.
73 Curi, "Poema come dialogo e gesto," 27.
74 First published in 1960 in *Menabò*, and then included in the 1961 Novissimi anthology, this *poemetto* relates the story of Carla, a young woman who grows up on the outskirts of Milan and gets a job as a secretary in a Milanese import-export company, experiencing the toll that the economic miracle was exacting on all Italians, especially when it came to their own personal relationships and sexuality. Carla's story is told from a variety of perspectives, and through a combination of styles and languages, using a collage technique that recalls film editing. In fact, the first incarnation of the plot was as a treatment for a film Pagliarani wanted to submit to De Sica (see chapter 4, 220).
75 Pagliarani, *La ragazza Carla*, in *Tutte le poesie*, 133. The translation is Patrick Rumble's, from Pagliarani, *The Girl Carla and Other Poems*, 47.

76 The second of the *romanzi in versi*, after *La ragazza Carla*, *La ballata di Rudi*, published in fragments from 1977 and then finally collected in a volume in 1995, tells the story of Rudi, a tourist entertainer from the Rimini Riviera, as well as a number of other more or less unsavoury characters who populated the world of summer tourism in the Romagna region. The stories of these characters are told in a variety of voices and from multiple perspectives, as was the case for *La ragazza Carla*. In *Rudi*, the juxtaposition between different segments feels even more discordant. Pagliarani also inserted a number of passages that explore issues of politics and poetics, thus reflecting the cultural climate of the time.

77 Pagliarani, "La ballata di Rudi," in *Tutte le poesie*, 282.

78 Ibid., 153; Rumble's translation, *The Girl Carla and Other Poems*, 83.

79 Ibid., 347; Rumble's translation, ibid, 184.

80 Baudelaire, *Les fleurs du mal*, 37. "Tu le connais, lecteur, ce monstre délicat, / – Hypocrite lecteur, – mon semblable, – mon frère!"

81 Note to *Epigrammi* reprinted in Pagliarani, *Tutte le poesie*, 368.

82 Bernardini, "Da Savonarola all'avanguardia."

83 By overinterpretation I mean that paranoid attitude toward reading against which Umberto Eco warns us in his *Interpretation and Overinterpretation*, in particular in chapter 2, 45–66. In this case, however, we could argue that such a paranoid point of view is encouraged by the author and the very fabric of the text, and would therefore constitute a proper reading rather than an appropriation or use.

84 The *pasquinata* is a short satirical text or an epigram characterized by demotic, bawdy humour and a populist, at times reactionary, at times revolutionary, political outlook. The name comes from the statue of Pasquino, a marble torso that decorates one corner of the Braschi palace in Rome, to which traditionally (and to this very day) such satirical texts are pinned for everyone to read. While Rome was ruled by the popes, Pasquino's voice was often the only real opposition to have any significant audience, and thus any relevance, within the city and the states of the church.

85 See Pagliarani, "Teatro come verifica," 9. On the same page we read: "A teatro è il fiato dello spettatore che dà fiato all'attore. Lo so per via che ogni tanto recito versi: io vario e essi variano, in funzione di chi ascolta, e *viceversa*. (E posso anche diventare bellissimo)." [At the theatre it is the audience's breath that gives a voice to the actors. I know that because every now and then I declaim verses: I change and they change depending on who is listening, and vice versa. (And sometimes I may even look beautiful).]

86 Pagliarani, "Cronistoria minima," 466.

87 Marin, *On Representation*, especially the chapter titled "Figures of Reception in Modern Representation in Painting," 320–36.

88 Ibid., 332.
89 Ibid., 326.
90 Ibid., 331:

> The King's Entry to Dunkirk thus constructs a structure of its own reception through these three figures, in a complex figure or metafigure, at once deictics and gaze, articulating the level of the narrative utterance and that of the narrational enunciation and its diverse modalities, a gaze-figure positioning the viewer as viewer, as witness-gaze, and a figure that, even as it is a narrative figure of the story ... is also, in the story itself, the figurative projection of the reading that the viewer (already positioned in this role) has to or is supposed to make of it, or, more precisely still, the representative delegation of the emotional expressive modality of the reading that the viewer is to make of it ...

91 Ibid., 330.
92 Pagliarani, *Tutte le poesie*, 125; Rumble's translation, *The Girl Carla and Other Poems*, 33.
93 Pagliarani, *Tutto il teatro*, 295.
94 Pagliarani, *Tutte le poesie*, 205; Rumble's translation, *The Girl Carla and Other Poems*, 129.
95 Ibid., 322. For a precise account of the different forms this text took over the years, see Cortellessa's informative note on page 62 of the same volume. Rumble's translation, *The Girl Carla and Other Poems*, 157.
96 This last experiment by Pagliarani reminds us of Adriano Spatola's sound poetry, in particular the series of "Aviation, aviateur," and "Seduction, seducteur." Most of that poetry is on the tapes that constitute the issues of *Baobab*, by now practically impossible to find. However, a video of one of Spatola's performances from *Videor*, the video-magazine of poetry edited by (among others) Pagliarani himself, can be found on YouTube: http://www.youtube.com/watch?v=8jVhUsEqPxc&feature=relmfu (last visited on 18 May 2018).
97 Pagliarani, *Pro-memoria a Liarosa*, 272–3.
98 We will have an opportunity to expand on this idea of theatre as the (ideal and actual) place where poetry routinely undergoes a process of verification in chapter 4.
99 The other exception is Giuliano Scabia, but his investment in theatre, which dates to the very beginning of his career, makes him unique among the other Gruppo 63 members.
100 For a thorough discussion of the issues connected with Sanguineti and his rewriting of literary classics for the stage, we refer the reader to the large bibliography already available, and, in particular, to: Chirumbolo

and Picchione, eds, *Edoardo Sanguineti: Literature, Ideology and the Avant-Garde*, and especially the essay from this volume by Moroni, "The Linguistic Gesture: Edoardo Sanguineti's Theatre"; Grignani, "Parola indigente e spazio claustrofobico"; Policastro, *Sanguineti*; Venturo, *Parola e travestimento nella poetica teatrale di Edoardo Sanguineti*; and Weber, *Usando gli utensili di utopia: Traduzione, parodia e riscrittura in Edoardo Sanguineti*.

101 Di Pesce, "Intervista ad Edoardo Sanguineti": http://www.parol.it/articles/sanguineti1.htm.

102 Ibid.

103 Vazzoller, "La scena, il corpo, il travestimento: Conversazione con Edoardo Sanguineti," 187.

104 For an in-depth discussion of *K* and *Traumdeutung*, see Venturo, *Parola e travestimento nella poetica teatrale di Edoardo Sanguineti*, 20–40; Moroni, "The Linguistic Gesture," 158–68.

105 See Pestalozza's interview with Sanguineti in the already mentioned monograph by Edoardo Sanguineti, *Per Musica*, 9–24.

106 Sanguineti, *Teatro*, 52, quoted in Moroni, "The Linguistic Gesture." The translation is Moroni's.

107 Ibid.

108 Di Pesce, "Intervista ad Edoardo Sanguineti."

109 See Sanguineti, "Per una letteratura della crudeltà."

110 Pagliarani, *Tutto il teatro*.

111 Giordano Falzoni published a great number of short texts intended for the stage in many of the journals of the Neoavanguardia (*Marcatrè*, *Grammatica*, *Il Caffè*, *Il Verri*, *Nuova Corrente*, to name just a few). His work was often presented alongside that of other Gruppo 63 members and was accorded equal attention by critics from the world of theatre as well as literature. Not many read or study his works anymore.

112 Falzoni, *Teatro da camera*. Here is the entire note in the original Italian:

Giordano Falzoni è nato a Zagabria nel 1925, mentre i genitori entrambi violinisti erano in tournée. Dopo aver studiato a Firenze e a Parigi, si è trasferito a Roma dove attualmente vive. Nel 1947 cominciò a collaborare con l'esposizione di alcune sue minuscole pitture all'attività della *Compagnie de l'Art Brut*. Nel 1948 esce sulla rivista parigina "Les Cahiers de la Pleiade" il suo saggio *La vie comme aventure*. Nell'anno successivo, sulla rivista surrealista 'Neon' esce il suo *Manifeste de la gaie Typographie*. La sua prima personale di pittura, alla Galleria dell'Obelisco di Roma, nel 1951, è presentata da André Breton. Ed è il gruppo surrealista di Breton ad organizzare la sua prima personale a Parigi, nel 1954. Nella primavera del 1963, dal suo incontro con il regista Americano Ken Dewey e con un gruppo di attori tra cui Carmen Scarpitta e John Coe, nasceva il Gruppo ACT di Roma: una piccola compagnia sperimentale che dava spettacoli semiclandestini nel teatrino del Maestro Nascimbene, subito salutata da un articolo di Pandolfi (*Nasce l'avanguardia a Roma*, "Il Punto," giugno 1963) come l'indizio che una nuova ondata innovatrice stava avvicinandosi per il teatro a Roma. La profezia fu confermata dai fatti. L'appello lanciato dal Gruppo ACT ai Novissimi di Roma, perché collaborassero con testi anche non nati per il teatro alla attività sperimentale della nuova compagnia fu subito raccolto da Alfredo Giuliani ed Elio Pagliarani. A Palermo, nell'autunno successivo, il Gruppo ACT era una delle due compagnie che con i loro spettacoli affiancavano i lavori del Gruppo '63: con testi di Falzoni, Pagliarani e Giuliani.

And here is the translation:

[Giordano Falzoni was born in Zagabria in 1925, while his parents, both violin players, were on tour. After studying in Florence and Paris, he moved to Rome, where he currently lives. In 1947 he participated, with a few minuscule paintings, in the exhibition of *Compagnie de l'Art Brut*. In 1948 the Parisian journal *Les Cahiers de la Pleiade* published his essay entitled "La vie comme aventure." The following year the surrealist magazine *Neon* published his "Manifeste de la gaie Typographie." His first solo exhibition at the Galleria dell'Obelisco in Rome, in 1951, was presented by André Breton. And it was the surrealist group of Breton that organized his first solo show in Paris, in 1954. In the spring of 1963, after his encounter with the American director Ken Dewey, and a group of actors which included Carmen Scarpitta and John Coe, the Gruppo ACT of Rome was born: a small experimental company that presented semi-clandestine shows at the theatre of Maestro Nascimbene, immediately hailed by Pandolfi ("Nasce l'avanguardia a Roma" in *Il Punto*, June 1963) as a sign that a new wave of innovation was about to impact Rome's theatres. That prophecy soon turned into reality. The Gruppo ACT reached out to Rome's Novissimi, inviting them to collaborate by providing scripts and texts (not necessarily meant for the stage) for the experiments that were being carried out by the new company; Alfredo Giuliani and Elio Pagliarani answered immediately. In Palermo, the next fall, the Gruppo ACT was one of the two companies that presented a show at the first meeting of Gruppo '63: the scripts were by Falzoni, Pagliarani, and Giuliani.]

113 I published it in its entirety as an appendix to the following article: Rizzo, "La verifica della poesia: Il teatro secondo I Novissimi, Pagliarani (e T.S. Eliot)."

114 Ibid., 134.

115 In this regard, see the work done by Francesco Muzzioli, Filippo Bettini, Aldo Mastropasqua, Marcello Carlino, and Giorgio Patrizi in their journal *Quaderni di critica*. In particular, the essays later collected in Bettini, and Muzzioli, eds, *Gruppo '93: La recente avventura del dibattito teorico letterario in Italia*. In this volume, as they try to define the salient traits of Gruppo 93 and how they relate to the experiments of Gruppo 63, the various contributors help illuminate the importance of Walter Benjamin and his ideas on allegory for the experiences of the second wave of the Italian avant-garde.

116 Here are Eliot's verses: "I feel like one who smiles, and turning shall remark / Suddenly, his expression in a glass. / My self-possession gutters; we are really in the dark."

117 Rizzo, "La verifica della poesia," 136.

118 Ibid.

119 The bibliography on Peirce and his approach to signs is rather vast. For an introduction, see the entry "Peirce's Theory of Signs" in the *Stanford Encyclopedia of Philosophy*, accessed 18 May 2018 at https://plato.stanford.edu/entries/peirce-semiotics/. I say index because I have in mind Peirce's classical example for this category of signs: smoke as an index for fire. The relationship that ties poetry and theatre, words and gestures, is similar to the relatonship binding smoke and fire.

120 Rizzo, "La verifica della poesia," 137.

121 Ibid.

122 Ibid.

123 Olson, "Il verso proiettivo."

124 Rizzo, "La verifica della poesia," 135.

125 Ibid., 135–6.

126 See Giuliani, "La forma del verso," in *I Novissimi: Poesie per gli anni '60*, 185.

127 Pound, *The ABC of Reading*, 36.

128 See Fenollosa, *The Chinese Character as a Medium for Poetry*.

129 Rizzo, "La verifica della poesia," 135.

130 I owe this intuition to a conversation with Mimmo Cangiano.

131 The other one-act plays presented were *L'occhio*, by Giordano Falzoni (with Sabina De Guida, Claudio Previtera; scenes and costumes by Toti Scialoja); *La merce esclusa*, by Elio Pagliarani (with Sabina De Guida, Franco Marchesani, Paola Megas, Valentino Orfeo, Piero Panza, Claudio Previtera, Grazia Volpi; scenes and costumes by Carlo Battaglia); and *Povera Juliet*, by Alfredo Giuliani (with Antonio Campanelli, Sabina De Guida, James Demby, Deborah Hayes, Franco Marchesani, Paola Megas, Valentino Orfeo, Piero Panza, Wilma Piergentili, Claudio Previtera, Grazia Volpi; scenes and costumes by Achille Perilli).

132 Balestrini, "Imitazione – Improvvisazione – Invocazione."

133 Balestrini, "Linguaggio e opposizione," 165.
134 As mentioned earlier, the playbill we have analysed also contained a short text by Pagliarani, which we will discuss in chapter 4, where we will look at Pagliarani's theatre in more detail.
135 Alfredo Giuliani's "Il teatro dei Novissimi" can be found in Giuliani's papers at the Archivio Manoscritti of the Università di Pavia. The two typed pages are in a folder named "Unità archivistica 207," in the section "Materiali letterari."
136 For more details, and from the point of view of someone who witnessed and participated in the shows, see Gozzi, "Lo spettacolo di Palermo."
137 Sanguineti, *Teatro: K, Passaggio, Traumdeutung, Protocolli*, 11.
138 Giuliani, *Povera Juliet*, 61.
139 Balestrini, "Imitazione – Improvvisazione – Invocazione," 7.
140 Giuliani, *Povera Juliet*, 61.
141 An invaluable analysis of Giuliani's and Balestrini's approach to the theatre, as well as that of a wider set of the Neoavanguardia authors who wrote for the theatre (Giorgio Manganelli, Enrico Filippini, Antonio Porta, Alberto Gozzi, Giordano Falzoni, Gaetano Testa, Manlio Marinelli, Gianni Novak), can be found in Giuseppe Bartolucci, "Di un teatro cinetico visivo."
142 See chapter 2, 146.
143 Giuliani, "La poesia a teatro," 74.
144 Ibid., 75.
145 Ibid.
146 Ibid., 76.
147 Ibid., 75.
148 Ibid., 77.
149 I am referring to the dissertation in *Letteratura italiana contemporanea*, which was recently submitted (Anno accademico 2016–17, appello primo) to the Università di Bologna by Margherita Carlotti, entitled "'Fibra dopo fibra, goccia dopo goccia, respiro dopo respiro': Influenze artaudiane nel teatro di Antonio Porta (1967–1989)."
150 Porta, "Poche osservazioni intorno allo spazio della poesia," 83.
151 For a more detailed account of Porta's ideas on this issue, see the already quoted essay by Bartolucci, "Di un teatro cinetico visivo."
152 Porta, "Poche osservazioni intorno allo spazio della poesia," 83.
153 See chapter 2, 115.

2 The Italian Stage in the 1960s

1 Mango, "L'invenzione del nuovo," 10. Here, as everywhere else in this chapter, unless otherwise stated, the translations are my own.

2 Ettore Capriolo, interviewed by Alfredo Tradardi and Roberto Pellerey, in Associazione Itàca, ed., *Ricerca sul Convegno per un Nuovo Teatro, Ivrea-Torino 9–12 giugno 1967*, quoted in Visone, *La nascita del nuovo teatro in Italia*, 248–9.

3 Visone, *La nascita del nuovo teatro in Italia*, 249.

4 See De Marinis, *Il nuovo teatro: 1947–1970*, 151–2.

5 Quadri, "Domanda al cittadino italiano," 1.

6 "Carosello" and "Campanile sera" were the names of two very popular shows in the early days of Italian television. "Carosello" (which aired from 1957 to 1977) collected a number of long commercials that united the promotion of consumer goods with a very sophisticated style of storytelling. "Campanile sera" (on the air from 1959 to 1962) was a quiz show that allowed the audience to participate from the comfort of their homes.

7 De Filippo's works display a long list of aesthetic merits that go far beyond his use of Neapolitan dialect.

8 To the many remarkable works that we will introduce shortly, all of which attest to Bene's importance as an actor, director, writer, dramaturge, and theoretician, we ought to add a brief but dense article, which we will not be able to discuss, but that directly addresses the relationship between poetry and theatre: "Della poesia a teatro," included in Bene, *Opere: Con l'Autobiografia di un ritratto*, 1157–9. I will transcribe just a quick, striking, aphorism: "'Imagismi' contemporanei a parte, dice Zenone cinico in un frammento: 'La voce è la dialettica del pensiero.' Guarda, guarda, che colpo alla macedone" (1157–8). That is to say: "Setting aside all contemporary 'imagism,' as Zeno the Cynic says in a fragment: 'The voice is the dialectic of thought.' Here, here: what a nice Macedonian coup." For a more in-depth discussion of the importance of the voice for the theatre and poetry of the 1960s and 1970s, see chapter 3.

9 Here I paraphrase the description of Bene's theatre sketched by De Marinis in his already-quoted *Il nuovo teatro*, 155.

10 In the Italian theatre the tradition of "grande attore" (great actor) denotes a specific way of organizing the shows and the theatre company around a well-known and well-loved actor, who would often participate in the writing of the play and in its direction, and would actively promote the shows, becoming a taste-setter in all matters of popular culture. This system began in the Ottocento (nineteenth century), and continued in the twentieth century when, at least in part, it extended to cinema, although in that context we would speak of "divismo."

11 Visone, *La nascita del nuovo teatro in Italia*, 102.

12 Bene also made a couple of feature films around Hamlet's story: *Un Amleto di meno* (One Hamlet Less) (1973) and *Un Amleto di meno, da W.*

Shakespeare a J. Laforgue (One Hamlet Less, after W. Shakespeare and J. Laforgue) (1974). The latter was produced for TV and is available on YouTube, accessed 31 May 2018, at https://www.youtube.com/watch?v=glAyhTHgzeo.

13 See, for instance, Gilles Deleuze, "Une manifeste de moines," in Bene and Deleuze, eds, *Sovrapposizioni*, and Deleuze, *Cinema 2: L'immagine tempo*.

14 The annual meeting of AATI, held in Cagliari in June 2018, offered hope for a renewal of interest in Bene: there I heard a very intelligent presentation and insightful discussion by a group of young critics and scholars active in Italy and in France.

15 Ricci, "Teatro-Rito e Teatro-Gioco," 219.

16 Ibid.

17 See De Marinis, *Il nuovo teatro*, 159. See also the materials, accessed 31 May 2018, at www.nuovoteatromadeinitaly.com/mario-ricci/, the companion site to Valentini, *Nuovo Teatro Made in Italy: 1963–2013*. In particular, see Ricci, "Il Teatro-Immagine. Spettacoli 1962–1973" (at www.nuovoteatromadeinitaly.com/mario-ricci/), a short memoir in which Ricci describes his early works. Speaking of this first show he notes, on page 1,

> Il breve lavoro è stato rappresentato per la prima volta in casa dello storico e critico d'arte Nello Ponente la notte del capodanno 1962/63 alla presenza di diversi artisti dell'avanguardia romana e quella di alcuni esponenti e di lì a poco fondatori del Gruppo '63 determinando, oltre che una scelta estetico-culturale, la possibilità di future collaborazioni con artisti poeti e scrittori rappresentanti di quella che allora in qualche modo rappresentava le istanze più avanzate della letteratura italiana.
>
> [The short piece was first performed in the house of art historian and critic Nello Ponente on New Year's Eve 1962/63; many artists of the Roman avant-garde were in attendance, as well as some of the intellectuals who would later create Gruppo 63. In addition to marking a cultural and aesthetic choice, this beginning also led to a number of collaborations with artists, poets, and writers belonging to the more advanced sector of the Italian literary scene.]

18 Ricci, "Teatro-Rito e Teatro-Gioco," 221.

19 Bartolucci, *La scrittura scenica*, 46.

20 That is to say, in the 1950s and 1960s, in the minds of all Italian intellectuals, futurism was closely identified with the fascist regime, and thus tainted beyond any hope of redemption. As Bartolucci puts it (ibid., 46) "this whole area of research [was] unquotable, experimentally and critically impossible to pursue." Only in the late 1970s and 1980s were the first

serious attempts made to separate its aesthetic innovations (which could still be useful and bear artistic fruit) from its hideous ethical and political complicity with one of the most horrid pages in our national history.

21 Ricci, "Teatro-Rito e Teatro-Gioco," 221.

22 The Nuovo Teatro attempted to free theatre from at least three different expectations: 1) presenting a conventional mimesis of the world; 2) within which a recognizable story takes place; 3) including a relatable set of characters. Out of these three expectations, the one that a play be "about something" – that, in other words, it present a story – is perhaps the most difficult to break. As De Marinis notes in his *Il nuovo teatro*, 158, Ricci tries to introduce "nuove *tecniche materiali* che chiarissero fin dal principio, in maniera inequivocabile, l'opzione anitimimetica, anticontenutistica e antipsicologica" [new *material techniques* capable of clarifying, from the very first moment, and without any doubt, an anti-mimetic, anti-contents, and anti-psychological option].

23 For more on this, see Visone, *La nascita del nuovo teatro in Italia*, 98–9.

24 See ibid., 125.

25 See Ricci quoted in Visone, *La nascita del nuovo teatro in Italia*, 126.

26 Ricci, "Collage per una automitobiografia," in Quadri, ed., *L'avanguardia teatrale in Italia: Materiali (1960–1976)*, 215.

27 Ibid., 216.

28 See also Visone, *La nascita del nuovo teatro in Italia*, 126.

29 Ibid., 127.

30 Ricci, "L'uso del cinema," in Quadri, ed., *L'avanguardia teatrale in Italia: Materiali (1960–1976)*, 237.

31 Ibid., 239.

32 Ricci's quotations and the details regarding *Illuminazione* come from Ricci, "Il Teatro-Immagine: Spettacoli 1962–1973," 6, accessed 31 May 2018, at www.nuovoteatromadeinitaly.com/mario-ricci/.

33 Sinisi, *Dalla parte dell'occhio: Esperienze teatrali in Italia 1972–1982*, 84–5.

34 Ricci, "Il Teatro-Immagine," 2.

35 See chapter 5, 261–9.

36 A consistent exception is Bene, but we have already pointed out how his personal approach to theatre cannot be generalized or turned into a system that others can use.

37 Fagiolo, "Con le marionette di Mario Ricci torna il teatro a passo ridotto." A slightly extended quotation follows:

> questa opera rientra (anche se il testo è corrosivo, la recitazione scattante, le musiche ben assortite) in un repertorio più abituale. Qui le marionette sono marionette nel senso tradizionale, e mimano gli atti dell'uomo, mentre nelle altre azioni sceniche Ricci ha trovato un ritmo nuovo, autonomo, funzionale.

[this work (although the text is corrosive, the acting energetic, the music well-chosen) belongs to a more conventional repertory. Here the puppets are puppets in a traditional way, and they simulate the actions of humans, whereas in his other stage actions, Ricci had found a new, autonomous, functional rhythm.]

38 De Marinis, *Il nuovo teatro*, 156.
39 Visone, *La nascita del nuovo teatro in Italia*, 42. "Gli esponenti della nascente avanguardia teatrale, Quartucci, Bene e Ricci, partono da presupposti retorici e sperimentali diversi, ma la loro ricerca va nella stessa direzione. Tutti e tre, infatti, intendono azzerare il linguaggio tradizionale del teatro e inventare una nuova grammatica composta da segni concreti e specifici della scena."
40 See De Marinis, *Il nuovo teatro*, 156–7.

Quartucci si rivolge alla drammaturgia e ai personaggi ... beckettiani come ai 'materiali' teatrali ideali per tentare di elaborare ... uno stile recitativo astratto, geometrizzante e freddamente formalizzato sia nelle emissioni foniche che nella gestualità ... Ciò che interessa insomma Quartucci, in quei primi anni, è sperimentare le possibilità – a teatro – d'un uso non-psicologico, non-narrativo e non-realistico, di parola, gesto e scenografia, intesi come mezzi espressivo-comunicativi autonomi.

41 Such treatment of Beckett's plays might sound arbitrary, even disrespectful according to today's standards. Yet, it is important to remember that, for the directors of the Nuovo Teatro, the script was just one of the many materials to be manipulated in the performance. It would be interesting to investigate whether the Irish playwright was aware of these experiments, and what he thought of them. For a general view of Beckett's reception in Italy, see Caselli, "Thinking of a 'Rhyme for Euganean.'"
42 Visone, *La nascita del nuovo teatro in Italia*, 42–3:

Alcuni critici considerano la drammaturgia di Beckett come la strada nuova da seguire per azzerare il linguaggio teatrale tradizionale e cercare nuove forme drammaturgiche e sceniche. Bartolucci, invece, mette in evidenza l'aspetto problematico di questa nuova prospettiva che si sta delineando.

[Some critics consider Beckett's dramaturgy as the right path toward erasing the traditional theatrical language and finding new dramatic forms for the stage. Bartolucci, instead, highlights the more problematic aspect of this new, emerging trend.]

43 Bartolucci, *La scrittura scenica*, 30.
44 Quoted in Visone, *La nascita del nuovo teatro in Italia*, 45–6.
45 Quartucci, "Sette anni di esperienze," 161.
46 Ibid., 152–5, quoted in De Marinis, *Il nuovo teatro*, 157.
47 For the description of the performance, see Visone, *La nascita del nuovo teatro in Italia*, 69–70; Quartucci's quotation comes from his already mentioned "Sette anni di esperienze."
48 Perrini, "Non abbiamo sbagliato aspettando Quartucci," 30.
49 For a more in-depth analysis of this opera and its ties to the neo-avant-garde, see Duran, "Operatic Neo-Avant-Gardism in Luigi Nono's *Intolleranza 1960.*"
50 The full text is available, in electronic form, at the already mentioned website, accessed on 31 May 2018: http://www.nuovoteatromadeinitaly.com/wp-content/uploads/2014/08/zip.pdf. In addition to the full script, there are also very interesting author notes.
51 These are all traits that would later come to full fruition with *Zip*, his first collaboration with Quartucci.
52 Scabia, *All'improvviso & Zip*, 47; electronic format, accessed 31 May 2018, at http://www.nuovoteatromadeinitaly.com/wp-content/uploads/2014/08/zip.pdf.
53 Scabia, "Nello spazio del teatro," 41, quoted in De Marinis, *Il nuovo teatro*, 165.
54 Scabia is not the only one to think about theatre as the place where the author's writing is verified, exposed to the repeated shock of directly encountering the audience. Similar considerations are at the core of Pagliarani's understanding of theatre. See chapter 4, 221–31.
55 Scabia quoted in Visone, *La nascita del nuovo teatro in Italia*, 79.
56 Ibid., 79–80.
57 See Visone, *La nascita del nuovo teatro in Italia*, 89.
58 See Scabia, quoted in Visone, *La nascita del nuovo teatro in Italia*, 80.
59 See De Marinis, *Il nuovo teatro*, 167.
60 See Visone, *La nascita del nuovo teatro in Italia*, 83–91.
61 Quartucci and Scabia, "Per un'avanguardia italiana," 11.
62 Ibid.
63 Ibid.
64 In this last section we summarize some of De Marinis's observations, expressed in De Marinis, *Il nuovo teatro*, 163.
65 For a thorough discussion of the people, places, and shows that made this Roman scene so lively and influential, see Visone, *La nascita del nuovo teatro in Italia*, 145–68.
66 See above, 115.
67 Bartolucci, *La scrittura scenica*, 40.

68 See Vice, "Prima del falò."
69 Mango, "La maschera e il volto."
70 See Pascutti, "Si affacciano alla 'Ringhiera' importanti attori di punta"; Tian, "Concerto Grosso per Brugh."
71 Visone, *La nascita del nuovo teatro in Italia*, 159.
72 Valentini, "Il dibattito sul nuovo teatro in Italia," 15.
73 Peter Brook (born 1925) is a key figure of twentieth-century avant-garde theatre. His productions of Shakespeare, Jean Cocteau, Sartre, and Weiss (among others) are particularly well-known and brought him international fame and recognition. Jerzy Grotowski (1933–1999) is another protagonist of the experimental theatre of the last century. In the 1960s he directed the Polish Laboratory Theatre of Wrocław; his acting method was based on a rigorous physical and mental discipline, which resulted in emotionally charged, sometimes shocking performances. The show *The Constant Prince* (1965) gave him world fame, and his ideas on theatre and acting were published as *Toward a Poor Theatre* (1968). The Living Theatre was an experimental troupe founded by Julian Beck and Judith Malina, characterized by an antagonistic and confrontational stance in regard to tradition, authority, and power. In 1964 the company left New York and moved to Europe, where it toured several performances that were received enthusiastically by critics. All of these theatre personalities (Brook, Grotowski, Beck, Malina) were influenced by the writings of Antonin Artaud on the theatre of cruelty (for more on Artaud, see section 2.8). They all exercised an important influence in the evolution of Italian theatre. A first introduction to their ideas and their contributions to the Italian stage can be found in Franco Perrelli, *I maestri della ricerca teatrale: Il Living, Grotowski, Barba e Brook* .
74 Bartolucci, "Per un diverso linguaggio critico," in Bartolucci, *La scrittura scenica*, 152.
75 See Visone, *La nascita del nuovo teatro in Italia*, 119, n417.
76 See Scabia, *Teatro nello spazio degli scontri*, 197.
77 See Valentini, *Nuovo Teatro Made in Italy*, 67.
78 Essentially the same issues with which, as we saw, the Italian literary neo-avant-garde was contending in the early 1960s.
79 Barthes, "Mutter Courage," 94, quoted in Visone, *La nascita del nuovo teatro in Italia*, 199.
80 Barthes was, in fact, one of the founding editors. For an overview of the history of this influential journal, see Consolini, "'Théâtre Populaire': Breve storia di una rivista teatrale."
81 On this issue, see in particular Dort, "Brecht ou l'anti-Racine."
82 Brecht, *Scritti teatrali*; Bronnen, *Giorni con Bertolt Brecht*; Brecht, *Teatro*.

83 See Squarzina, "Di Planchon, di Dort, di altri, di noi altri"; Bartolucci, "L'area formale brechtiana e le tecniche teatrali d'oggi"; and Bartolucci, "Preistoria e punti di riferimento per un rinnovamento del teatro italiano."

84 See Agostino, "Nelle mani del questore," 76:

> Nel caso di Brecht, alle tirannie mercantili dell'agente, si sono aggiunte per anni le pretese formali della vedova dello scrittore, Helene Weigel, che non si limitava ad imporre lo stile delle messinscene e a escludere tassativamente i tagli, ma si era eletta in Italia il suo regista (Giorgio Strehler) e il suo teatro (Piccolo Teatro di Milano), creando un autentico regime di monopolio.
>
> [In Brecht's case, to the mercantile tyrannies of the agent, one must add the formal demands of the writer's widow, Helene Weigel, who, for a number of years, not only imposed the general style of the performances and categorically prohibited any editing of the script, but had also chosen in Italy her favourite director (Giorgio Strehler) and theatre (Piccolo Teatro in Milan), thus effectively creating a monopoly.]

85 Paradoxically, these shows would be seen through the lens of Strehler's interpretation of Brecht (which had been the only one available in Italy in previous years), and were found to lack any radical originality. See Bartolucci, "Situazione brechtiana '66," 5; Schacherl, "Il Berliner Ensemble finalmente a Venezia."

86 Bartolucci, "L'area formale brechtiana e le tecniche teatrali d'oggi."

87 For an interesting and highly original analysis of the critical reception of Strehler's *Galileo*, see Cuomo, "Berliner Ensemble 1957 – Piccolo Teatro 1963." Many contemporary commentators were surprised by the amount of resources invested in this show, so much so that Carlo Terron, in an article in the *Corriere Lombardo,* titled "Il Galileo di Brecht è diventato capitalista," that is, "Brecht's Galileo has turned capitalist," reported that 120 million liras had been spent in preparation of the debut. This article, along with many others, is available on the *Piccolo* website, accessed 31 May 2018.

88 For a contemporary review, see Pandolfi, "Off-Broadway in Italia," 57: "Una maturità e un'esperienza espressive nuove, singolari, e al tempo stesso compiute, alleate finalmente ad opere di carattere eccezionale, dove il fine rilievo ironico si fonde allo spirito di un mondo che sembra autentico." [A maturity and an expressive experience that are new, singular, and at the same time complete, finally joined with exceptional scripts, in which fine ironic observations are melded with the spirit of a

world that seems truly authentic.] See also Jacobbi, "L'altra faccia della luna"; and Ottieri, "Colazione con Judith Malina."

89 For more information on this, see Visone, *La nascita del nuovo teatro in Italia*, 57, n155; one of the more interesting articles appeared in *Sipario*: Leigh, "Il 'Teatro della crudeltà' da Artaud a Peter Brook"; the same issue of *Sipario* contains an interview with Peter Brook and Charles Marowitz.

90 See Bassano, "Tempo di Frankenstein," quoted in Visone, *La nascita del nuovo teatro in Italia*, 59, note 162.

91 Bartolucci, "L'esempio del Living Theatre, teatro=vita," 58.

92 *Sipario*, no. 230 (June 1965); in addition to the materials already mentioned, the issue also included an exceptional essay by Giuseppe Bartolucci, "Il teatro di Genet come provocazione e illusione," and a number of pieces on the theatre of cruelty's influence outside of Italy, with a particular focus on England, as well as on the work of the Living Theatre.

93 *Sipario*, nos 232–3 (August–September 1965); the anthology included excerpts from *Le baccanti* (Euripides' *Bacchae*), *Il Tieste* (Seneca's *Thyestes*), White's *Arden of Feversham*, and *Peccato che sia una sguarldrina* (John Ford's *'Tis Pity She's a Whore*).

94 The proceedings of the conference were published by the journal *Teatro Festival*, nos 2–3 (February–March 1967). For the first time, the festival also featured performances of professional theatre troupes. Among those included, Mario Ricci and his Teatro Club Orsoline 15 and Charles Marowitz and his Experimental Group In-Stage are noteworthy. For a review of the shows, see Bartolucci, "Positivo bilancio del Festival Universitario: In luce a Parma gruppi italiani."

95 Derrida, "Prefazione." Incidentally, this is the first inclusive translation of Artaud's works to be published in Italy. Before the Einaudi volume, the only works by Artaud available in Italian were the ones published by *Sipario*, as well as an anthology of minor works: Antonin Artaud, *Nel paese dei Tarahumara e altri scritti*.

96 Derrida, "Prefazione," XXVI.

97 See Visone, *La nascita del nuovo teatro in Italia*, 60. See also Acca, "'La crudeltà non fa per me': Pasolini, Artaud e il teatro del 'quasi,'" 49; and Quadri, *Il rito perduto: Luca Ronconi*, 36, quoted in Visone, *La nascita del nuovo teatro in Italia*, 64.

98 Not everyone agrees with the relevance of this conference. De Marinis, for instance, wonders whether the importance of this event has been exaggerated. See De Marinis, *Il nuovo teatro*, 168:

Ma cosa rappresentò in realtà questo convegno? La consacrazione ufficiale della neoavanguardia ... o soltanto – come sostiene Quadri

… – la sua "prima codificazione tardiva?" Fu il tentativo di costituire un altro gruppo di potere o quello di dare vita a un nuovo movimento artistico? Oppure nulla di tutto questo, ma soltanto – come vorrebbe appunto qualcuno – l'incontro di poche individualità eminenti?

[What did this conference actually mean? Was it the official consecration of the neo-avant-garde … or simply – as Quadri maintains … – its "first late codification"? Was it an attempt to build another centre of power or rather a new artistic movement? Or, perhaps, none of the above, but merely – as some say – the encounter of a few eminent personalities?]

99 The "manifesto," entitled "Per un convegno sul nuovo teatro" was published for the first time in *Sipario*, no. 247 (November 1966): 2–3; then it was reprinted in Quadri, *L'avanguardia teatrale in Italia*, 135–7. It is also available online at: http://www.ateatro.it/olivieropdp/ateatro108.htm#108and6 (last accessed on 31 May 2018).
100 Ibid., 2.
101 Ibid.
102 See De Marinis, *Il nuovo teatro*, 171.
103 "Per un convegno sul nuovo teatro," 2.
104 Ibid; "Il teatro deve poter arrivare alla contestazione assoluta e totale."
105 De Marinis, *Il nuovo teatro*, 171: "un 'cartello' di teatranti il cui solo elemento unificante sta nel fatto di avere lo stesso nemico."
106 Bartolucci, Capriolo, Fadini, and Quadri, "Elementi di discussione del Convegno per un Nuovo Teatro."
107 Ibid., 139.
108 Ibid., 141.
109 Ibid., 146.
110 Visone, *La nascita del nuovo teatro in Italia*, 227–55.
111 See Francesco Bono, "Dossier Ivrea 1967: Il programma e la cronaca: Con il documento scritto da Bartolucci, Capriolo, Fadini e Quadri," http://www.ateatro.it/olivieropdp/ateatro108.htm#108and6:

Ben pochi dei punti originali del programma furono rispettati: quasi tutte le conferenze-spettacolo, ad eccezione di quella del Teatrogruppo di Quartucci, non furono presentate in questi termini, ma si trasformarono in semplici conferenze-discussione; gli interventi durante i dibattiti divagarono subito fuori dai confini dei temi proposti, per andare a trattare parallelamente e mescolare tutti gli argomenti "caldi" e le problematiche del rinnovamento teatrale. Ma era in effetti inevitabile che un convegno che trattava di avanguardia, innovazione e rifiuto delle regole non accettasse le imposizioni di uno schema rigido e prestabilito.

[Only a few of the program's original points were actually addressed: almost all the conferences-performances, with the exception of Quartucci's Teatrogruppo, were not approached as such, and turned into mere conferences-discussions; from the start, people's speeches wandered off the pre-determined issues and simultaneously addressed, mixing them together, the various "hot" topics and the problems of the theatre's renewal. In retrospect, it was inevitable that at a conference on the avant-garde, innovation, and the rejection of rules, people would not accept the imposition of a rigid and pre-determined agenda.]

112 See Boursier, "A convegno il teatro di domani," 5: "con tematiche popolari nelle quali il rapporto con la realtà è posto in termini problematici e non di atteggiamento moralistico … vale a dire con una presa di coscienza dei momenti decisivi della contemporaneità che stimoli alla messa in causa del sistèma politico e sociale." See also Visone, *La nascita del nuovo teatro in Italia*, 231.
113 Quoted in Visone, *La nascita del nuovo teatro in Italia*, 239. The interview quoted by Visone was originally published in Mario Ricci, "Intervista a cura di Lorenzo Mango," in *Ricerca sul Convegno per un Nuovo Teatro, Ivrea–Torino 9–12 giugno 1967*, a cura dell'Associazione Itàca di Milano (20 September 1986).
114 Quoted in Visone, *La nascita del nuovo teatro in Italia*, 239. Originally published in Leo de Berardinis, "Intervista a cura di Roberto Pellerey," in *Ricerca sul Convegno per un Nuovo Teatro, Ivrea–Torino 9–12 giugno 1967*, a cura dell'Associazione Itàca di Milano (20 September 1986).
115 The letter, addressed to Franco Quadri, is by Eugenio Barba, Hostelboro 17 September 1987, in Archivio "Orsa," Turin, also quoted in Visone, *La nascita del nuovo teatro in Italia*, 240. More regarding the conference of Ivrea can be found in Fadini, "Ivrea la bella, vent'anni dopo":

la solidarietà, il rispetto reciproco, l'affetto [avrebbero potuto] andare d'accordo con l'intransigenza [dal momento che questa è alla base del] problema dei rapporti fra uomini che seguono strade diverse, che a volte non si incontreranno mai, e che pure non possono restare soli in un ambiente che è ostile, malgrado l'accettazione o il successo di cui, di tanto in tanto, possono godere i teatri diversi.

116 See the beginning of this chapter.
117 Bajini, "Trascrizione del Convegno di Ivrea del 1967," 45, quoted in Visone, *La nascita del nuovo teatro in Italia*, 242–3.
118 See Visone, *La nascita del nuovo teatro in Italia*, 250: "ferm[o] alla centralità dei contenuti politici del teatro."

119 Giuseppe Bartolucci, in Bono, "Convegno per un Nuovo Teatro, Ivrea 1967,"104, quoted in Visone, *La nascita del nuovo teatro in Italia*, 251–2.

120 See also De Marinis, *Il nuovo teatro*, 242–3.

121 For a more in-depth treatment, see Rizzo, "Pasolini, Fo and the Issue of Language"; Valentini, "Il dibattito sul Nuovo Teatro in Italia"; Casi, *I teatri di Pasolini*; and Ottai, ed., *Pasolini Teatro Cinema*, the monographic double issue of *Biblioteca Teatrale*.

122 See Valentini, "Il dibattito sul nuovo teatro in Italia," 20:

> Il "Manifesto" elaborato da Pasolini si distanzia radicalmente da quello del nuovo teatro presentato a Ivrea e, senza discussione alcuna, venne rifiutato e rimosso sia dai fautori del nuovo che dai rappresentanti dell'establishment teatrale. La radicalità del "Manifesto" nei confronti del teatro dell'epoca fu bollata con il marchio di reazionarismo da parte dell'avanguardia e di rigorismo da oratorio dal versante della 'chiacchiera' e ignorata dal teatro politico che in quegli anni diventava un "genere."

> [The "Manifesto" written by Pasolini is radically different from the one presented in Ivrea by the New Theatre; without any real discussion, it was rejected and removed by both the supporters of the new, and the representatives of the theatrical establishment. The radical position of the "Manifesto" regarding the contemporary theatre was dubbed reactionary by the avant-garde, and considered as provincial rigorousness by the "chit-chat" theatre, while the political theatre that in those years was becoming a whole "genre" of its own simply ignored it.]

123 Pasolini, *Teatro*, 1156.

124 Valentini, "Il dibattito sul nuovo teatro in Italia," 22: "In realtà la 'vocazione teatrale' di Pasolini non corrisponde a una posizione teoricamente chiara e definibile, anzi è proprio il suo contraddirsi che segna il suo pensiero sul teatro." On that same page, in a note, Valentini quotes Ronconi, who focuses on this contradiction as a point of critique:

> Per parlare di Pasolini uomo di teatro, credo che si debba partire dalla contraddizione fra la lettura oggettiva delle sue opere e la lettura del suo "Manifesto per un nuovo teatro," due testi che secondo me fanno a cazzotti e si danneggiano vicendevolmente, perché leggere il teatro di Pasolini attraverso il suo manifesto, significa indubbiamente mortificarlo, cioè renderlo morto, cioè esattamente quello che lui ha fatto quando lo ha messo in scena.

[In speaking of Pasolini as a man of the theatre, I believe, one must begin with the contradiction between an objective reading of his works and that of his "Manifesto for a New Theatre," two texts that, in my opinion, are at odds with each other and are mutually damaging; in order to read Pasolini's theatre through his manifesto one must inevitably mortify it, that is, one must kill it, which is exactly what he did when he performed it on stage.]

Luca Ronconi, "Introduzione," in Casi, *I teatri di Pasolini*, 11.

125 See also Valentini, "Il dibattito sul nuovo teatro in Italia," 21.
126 See Pagliarani, "Teatro come verifica," 9; already quoted in chapter 1, note 85.

3 A Few Theoretical Notes on Breath and Text

1 The task, as will quickly become clear, is rather daunting, and exceeds what is possible to achieve within a single chapter. The knowledge and expertise that would be necessary in order to accomplish a satisfactory description and explanation of the long-term phenomenon we are investigating here would require a team of researchers. Not having access to such an *équipe* of colleagues (as mentioned in the introduction to the volume), I turned to a number of excellent monographs on this subject, or, rather, on subjects that are closely related to this one. The result is a collection of notes and intuitions that still needs to be harmonized in an overarching, coherent system. I have endeavoured to highlight the connections already existing between these different accounts of what happened, and I built a few new ones. Much of the work, however, has been left to the intelligence of the reader.
2 Valentini, *Nuovo Teatro Made in Italy*, 19.
3 Visone, *La nascita del nuovo teatro in Italia*, 41.
4 See also Mango, "L'invenzione del nuovo," 13:

la nozione letteraria di avanguardia sembrava a molti dei teatranti viziata di un eccesso di formalismo (in sintonia con obiezioni che al Gruppo 63 venivano fatte anche nell'ambiente letterario) ma soprattutto perché non era chiaro, ancora, cosa il termine avanguardia stesse a significare (poteva apparire oltre che un gioco troppo autoreferenziale sul linguaggio anche un appiattirsi sulla memoria del primo Novecento) e mancavano le condizioni – operative direi – perché ci si potesse riconoscere in qualcosa che aveva i tratti, nella sua configurazione "ortodossa," del movimento artistico.

[The notion of a literary avant-garde seemed, to many theatre professionals, as too formalist (in accordance with the objections that many in the literary environment had raised against Gruppo 63) but most of all because it wasn't clear, at that stage, what the term avant-garde meant (it appeared, to some, as a self-referential game on the level of language, or even a return to the practices of the first *Novecento*); also, there weren't the conditions – the operational conditions, I would say – to form something that had the "orthodox" configuration of an artistic movement.]

5 Giuliani, "Il teatro dei Novissimi," found in Giuliani's papers at the Archivio Manoscritti of the Università di Pavia. The two typed pages are in a folder named "Unità archivistica 207," in the section "Materiali letterari." Already quoted in chapter 1, 77–8.
6 In fact, he would later rework this central part of the essay into that brief text he included in the playbill for the show of "Teatro dei Novissimi," which we spoke of in chapter 1, 83.
7 Giuliani, "Teatro nudo," 34–5.
8 Barilli, *La neoavanguardia italiana*, 215.
9 See Rusconi, "Gli scrittori e il teatro," 4: "La sola idea che un eventuale copione debba venire esaminato, e possa subire le osservazioni di uno dei nostri attori, o d'uno dei nostri registi, basta a riempire l'animo di un raccapriccio così profondo da indurre decisioni disperate: non uscire mai dalla narrativa e dalla saggistica."
10 Valentini, *Nuovo Teatro Made in Italy*, 32: "L'ostilità è da imputare a un attrito insanabile fra scena e testo che gli scrittori italiani – non solo quelli ufficiali – non sono disposti a risolvere, aprendo il testo scritto all'oralità dello spazio scenico, all'attore, alla visione del regista."
11 De Marinis, *Visioni della scena*, 115–16.
12 Gasparini, *Poesia come corpo-voce*, 18.
13 Zumthor, *La presenza della voce*, 9.
14 Gasparini, *Poesia come corpo-voce*, 27.
15 Ibid., 24. In this passage, Gasparini is quoting from Antonin Artaud, "Il teatro della crudeltà (Primo manifesto)," 204.
16 Zumthor, *La presenza della voce*, 171.
17 Gasparini, *Poesia come corpo-voce*, 37.
18 For more on the relationship between Pound and the neo-avant-garde, see also chapter 1, 93–5.
19 Pound, *The ABC of Reading*, 14.
20 It is worth mentioning, in passing, that Alfredo Giuliani refers to the very passage we just quoted in his "La forma del verso" essay, which he appended to the Novissimi anthology. See Giuliani, "La forma del verso."
21 Pagliarani, "Dittico della merce: II. Certificato di sopravvivenza," 59. In this section of the diptych, Pagliarani addresses his friend and colleague Toti Scialoja, to whom the poem is dedicated, and in an oblique and

fragmented way discusses issues of poetics and its relation with politics, a very popular topic at the time, at the forefront of most intellectuals' minds.

22 Ballerini, "Elio Pagliarani: Poesia come respiro (e come continuo saltare)," in Ballerini, *4 per Pagliarani*, 106.
23 Ibid., 113.
24 Ibid., 109.
25 On the "gestural" dimension of poetry, and Giuliani's poetry in particular, see Picchione, *The New Avant-Garde in Italy*, 89–90:

> These experiments with collage led to *Chi l'avrebbe detto* (Who Would Have Said It) (Turin: Einaudi, 1973), a collection of poems written between 1952 and 1966 and described by Giuliani as "theatre of poetry" ("poesia di teatro"). In texts such as "Io ho una bella pera, e tu cos'hai?" (I Have a Beautiful Pear, and What Do You Have?) and "Povera Juliet" (Poor Juliet), Giuliani wants to abolish the representational dimension of theatre in order to reduce the linguistic sign to pure movement, action, gestural invention – not the arbitrary entity that represents, as a double or as a mirror, objective reality.

26 Gasparini, *Poesia come corpo-voce*, 60.
27 Olson, "Il verso proiettivo."
28 Giuliani, "La forma del verso," 190–1. For more on the relationship between Olson and the neo-avant-garde, see also Picchione, *The New Avant-Garde in Italy*, 18.
29 Olson, "Projective Verse," 53.
30 Ibid., 54.
31 Olson, "Notes on Language and Theater," 75.
32 Ibid., 76–7.
33 Gasparini, *Poesia come corpo-voce*, 61.
34 Olson, "Projective Verse," 57–8.
35 A good starting point would be: Spatola, *Verso la poesia totale*, translated into English as *Toward Total Poetry*; Ballerini, *La piramide capovolta*.
36 See chapters 1 and 2, especially 33–48, 114–35.
37 Zumthor, *La presenza della voce*, 287.
38 Gasparini, *Poesia come corpo-voce*, 68.
39 Barthes, *Elements of Semiology*, 9.
40 Picchione, *The New Avant-Garde in Italy*, 33–4.
41 Barthes, *Mythologies*.
42 Bradley, *Derrida's* Of Grammatology, 5–6.
43 Ibid., 6.
44 Ibid., 7–8:

According to the etymology of the term, "logocentrism" signifies the philosophical attempt to find what the ancient Greeks called the *logos*: a term which can be literally translated as "word" but also carries within it the larger sense of "logic," "reason," or "meaning." Yet, what characterizes this particular metaphysical attempt to establish a present ground, essence, or foundation, Derrida argues, is that it does so through the means of *speech*. To pave the way for another key move in his argument, Derrida contends that logocentrism prioritizes speech (*phone*) over writing (*gramme*) as the original or privileged means by which the presence of the *logos* is expressed.

45 See Sanguineti, "Sopra l'avanguardia," 63–81; see also Picchione, *The New Avant-Garde in Italy*, 60–5.
46 Pagliarani, "Per una definizione di avanguardia."
47 His *Theory of the Avant-Garde* was first published in Italy in 1962, then in the United States in 1968: Poggioli, *The Theory of the Avant-Garde*, see especially 30–6.
48 I am here referring to Umberto Eco, "Prolusione," 41–2. There we can find a brief summary of this dichotomy. See especially the following passage:

Ora c'è una differenza sostanziale tra movimenti di avanguardia e letteratura sperimentale … Renato Poggioli nella sua *Teoria dell'arte d'avanguardia* aveva bene fissato le caratteristiche di questi movimenti. Erano: *attivismo …, antagonismo …, nichilismo …, culto della giovinezza …, ludicità …, prevalenza della poetica sull'opera, autopropaganda …, rivoluzionarismo e terrorismo* … e infine *agonismo* … Invece lo sperimentalismo è devozione all'opera singola. L'avanguardia agita una poetica, rinunciando per amor suo alle opere, e produce piuttosto manifesti, mentre lo sperimentalismo produce l'opera e solo da essa estrae o permette poi che si estragga una poetica. Lo sperimentalismo tende a una provocazione interna al circuito dell'intertestualità, l'avanguardia a una provocazione esterna, nel corpo sociale … Ora nel Gruppo 63 sono convissute le due anime, ed è ovvio che l'anima avanguardistica abbia prevalso nel creare la sua immagine massmediatica.

[Now, there is a substantial difference between avant-garde movements and experimental literature … Renato Poggioli, in his *Theory of the Avant-Garde*, had clearly defined the characteristics of these movements. They were: *activism …, antagonism …, nihilism …, cult of youth …, a ludic dimension …, preference given to poetics over the individual work …, revolutionarism and terrorism …*, and finally *agonism* … Instead, experimentalism is devotion to the individual work. The avant-garde promotes a poetics and for its sake it renounces the works, producing, instead, manifestos; experimentalism, on the other hand, creates works and only from them it allows a poetics to be extracted. Experimentalism prefers a form of provocation that is internal to the intertextual circuit; the avant-garde elects an external one, which acts on the social body ... Now, in Gruppo 63, both tendencies coexisted, and clearly the avant-garde one was prominent in the mass-media depiction of the group.]

49 See the already quoted essay by De Marinis, "Teatro e poesia del Novecento: Alcune riflessioni," 119. Naturally, the discussion on the status of the dramatic text and the role of the script is a key component of the theoretical debate surrounding theatre, especially when it comes to the Italian stage of the 1960s and 1970s. An excellent overview of this issue is provided by De Marinis in his "Il testo drammatico: Un riesame."

50 Gasparini, *Poesia come corpo-voce*, 21.

51 Acca, "'La crudeltà non fa per me': Pasolini, Artaud e il teatro del 'quasi,'" 49; accessed 1 June 2018 at:https://antropologiaeteatro.unibo.it/article/view/2506.

52 Ibid., 50.

53 Another event, dating to August 1967, which could be taken as an end point of this first phase of the relationship between poetry and theatre is the festival *Parole sui muri*, held at Fiumalbo. For all the details, see the excellent monograph by Eugenio Gazzola, *Parole sui muri: L'estate delle avanguardie a Fiumalbo*.

54 Balestrini and Giuliani, eds, *L'antologia – Critica e teoria*, 35.

55 See Eco, "Prolusione," 42–3:

> Il momento in cui il Gruppo 63 ha scelto definitivamente la via dell'avanguardia è stato paradossalmente quello in cui ritornava, dallo sperimentalismo sul linguaggio, all'impegno pubblico e politico. È stata la stagione di Quindici, che ha visto drammatiche conversioni all'utopia sessantottesca, o sofferte resistenze, e alla fine ha portato la rivista (e indirettamente, con essa, il Gruppo) a un deliberato suicidio – proprio nel senso dell'agonismo di Poggioli. Nella catastrofe stoicamente voluta di Quindici sono venute ovviamente allo scoperto divisioni che esistevano sin dall'inizio, ma che erano state superate grazie alla scelta del dialogo reciproco. Confrontandosi con le tensioni immediate di un periodo storico tra i più contradditori e animati, il Gruppo ha deciso che non poteva continuare a fingere un'unità che non c'era all'inizio. Ma questa assenza di unità che aveva fatto la sua forza interna, e la sua energia di provocazione all'esterno, ora ne sanciva il giusto suicidio.

> [The moment Gruppo 63 definitively chose the avant-garde was, paradoxically, the moment it went back, from a linguistic

experimentalism, to political and public engagement. It was the phase of *Quindici*, which was marked by dramatic conversions to the utopia of 1968 or tormented resistances, and which finally led the journal (and, indirectly, the Gruppo) to a deliberate suicide – precisely in the sense of agonism, as defined by Poggioli. In the catastrophe, stoically sought by *Quindici*, the divisions that existed from the very beginning – but that had been bridged, thanks to a deliberate and sustained dialogue – came to the forefront. Facing the immediate tensions of an extremely contradictory and animated historical period, the Gruppo decided it could no longer pretend it possessed a unity that hadn't been there since the very beginning. This absence of unity, which had been its greatest strength, and the source of its energy of provocation, brought about its rightful suicide.]

56 Carella, "Dietro lo specchio di Castelporziano," 5.
57 Barba was referring to the experiments carried out in the 1970s in Franco Quadri, "Colloquio con Eugenio Barba," 72. Marco De Marinis, in his *Il Nuovo Teatro*, discusses this notion within the entire artistic output of Eugenio Barba; see in particular 181–7, 200–4.
58 Stomeo, *Intrecci: Teatro-Educazione-New Media*, 80: "liberare sia l'attore che lo spettatore dalla logica della rappresentazione / interpretazione."
59 This conceptual confusion and the lack of appropriate critical tools are also in part to blame for the absence of a systematic investigation of these issues, and help explain why, after over half a century, so much work remains to be done.
60 See, in particular, De Marinis, "Scrittura teatrale e partecipazione."
61 De Marinis, "Scrittura teatrale e partecipazione," 25.
62 Scabia, "Appunti per una discussione sul 'Teatro nello spazio degli scontri,'" in *Teatro nello spazio degli scontri*, XVIII.
63 De Marinis, "Scrittura teatrale e partecipazione," 29.
64 Scabia, *Nane Oca*. For more on the "oral" origin of this novel, see the interview at the end of this volume.
65 Gasparini, *Poesia come corpo-voce*, 32.
66 Scabia, "Il tremito," in *Il tremito*, 29.
67 We will see in more detail at the end of this chapter how voice, body, poetry, and hunger are connected when we describe the "battle of Castelporziano" and its poetic minestrone.
68 Porta, *Nel fare poesia*, 6–7.
69 Porta, "Prefazione," 8: "Ogni poeta, o scrittore, o critico [...] è un 'mangiatore di linguaggi.' Io sono onnivoro non solo per quel che riguarda i cibi ma anche per i linguaggi, da quello sportivo a quello dei comici, da quello della scienza a quello della poesia."

70 Porta, "Dialogo con Herz," in Giuliani, ed., *I Novissimi: Poesie per gli anni '60*, 152–3. The English translation is by Vangelisti, in Ballerini and Cavatorta, eds, *Those Who from Afar Look Like Flies*, 411–13.
71 Lorenzini, "Corporalità e crudeltà nella poesia degli anni sessanta," 3: "Scrive dunque Porta, quasi traducendo: 'è certo che adesso la letteratura si giustifica nella misura in cui si mette al servizio di "idee che hanno la stessa urgenza della fame."'"
72 Agosti, "Porta e la scena della crudeltà," 153–4.
73 Here is how Porta describes the origins of "La scelta della voce," in his auto-anthology *Nel fare poesia*, 87:

> Una richiesta di Tomaso Kemeny ha messo in moto il meccanismo di una mia reazione a un Amleto, con la nuova traduzione di Alessandro Serpieri e la regia e interpretazione di Gabriele Lavia con Ottavia Piccolo nella parte di Ofelia. Sono andato a teatro e la mattina dopo stavo scrivendo questa sequenza (che confluirà, poco dopo, in un'altra sequenza, *La scelta della voce*, per la recitazione di Paolo Bessegato e Valeria Falcinelli all'Out Off di Milano).
>
> [A request from Tomaso Kemeny started the mechanism of my reaction to a Hamlet newly translated by Alessandro Serpieri, directed and performed by Gabriele Lavia with Ottavia Piccolo playing the role of Ophelia. I went to the theatre and the next morning I was writing this sequence (which would later turn into another sequence, *La scelta della voce*, staged by Paolo Bessegato and Valeria Falcinelli at the Out Off in Milan).]

74 An in-depth analysis of how pervasive this phenomenon is, especially in regard to the early collections of verse, can be found in Margherita Carlotti's already mentioned dissertation (see chapter 1, n148): "'Fibra dopo fibra, goccia dopo goccia, respiro dopo respiro': Influenze artaudiane nel teatro di Antonio Porta (1967–1989)," especially 51–79.
75 We will investigate in more detail the connection between Jarry and the theatre of the neo-avant-garde in chapter 5, when we talk about Alfredo Giuliani and his *Nostro padre Ubu*.
76 For more on *Pelle d'Asino*, see chapter 5, 261–9. For more on Sanguineti and the differences between his theatre and that of the other members of Neoavanguardia, see chapter 5, 291.
77 It is worth mentioning that Jarry had designated with that same title (*The Poles*) a version of the Ubu play intended for the puppet theatre.
78 Bartolucci, "Di un teatro cinetico visivo," 50; see also his *La scrittura scenica*, 79.
79 Gozzi, "Di Jarry e del personaggio."
80 For more on this and other essays by Giuliani on Alfred Jarry, see chapter 5.

81 Porta, "Stark," 15: "gli attori scambieranno tra loro oggetti e prodotti indispensabili alla vita … L'azione non deve rappresentare soltanto una situazione economica di fondo ma deve cercare di 'totalizzarla,' dal cibo quotidiano a una metafisica dei valori possibili e continuamente distrutta."

82 Ibid., 15: "Le ombre ripeteranno i movimenti dello scambio, e dovrà avvenire in piena luce, un po' dappertutto, con oggetti molto evidenti: banane, ferri da stiro, pere, scarpe, ecc."

83 Naturally, it could also be a very Italian plural of "merda!," but I suspect the French origin to be more likely because of the literary references it implies, but also because, as an interjection or exclamation to express surprise, discontent, and so on, the word in Italian is usually given in the singular.

84 Picchione, *Introduzione a Antonio Porta*, 129. Porta is not the only one to be influenced by Jarry; as we will see later on, especially in chapter 5, Alfredo Giuliani was also a receptive reader of the Ubu plays. See Picchione, *The New Avant-Garde in Italy*, 83: "[Giuliani] is also attracted to the unconventional traits of a writer such as Alfred Jarry, whose farcical and grotesque theatrical language undoubtedly played a role in stimulating a search for new poetic solutions."

85 Porta, "Si tratta di larve," 63: "Al centro della scena un divano e due o tre poltrone; un tavolino con un servizio da tè. Naturalmente non ci sono altri oggetti in scena."

86 Ibid., 69.

87 Porro, "Il poeta Antonio Porta e il teatro artigiano," 46.

88 For more on this characterization of Ubu and his attributes, see Giuliani, "Prefazione," in Jarry, ed., *Ubu*, 7. Also quoted in chapter 5, 272, where we discuss the ties between Giuliani and Jarry.

89 See Giuliani, ibid., 6, also quoted in chapter 5, 279.

90 Benjamin's radical reinvention of the concept of allegory in the realm of criticism looks at the fragment and the detail as a window into the "exemplary" dimension of an artistic phenomenon (provided it is given an objective interpretation through its insertion in what Benjamin calls a "constellation" of other fragments and details. For a first introduction to this issue, see for instance Cowan, "Walter Benjamin's Theory of Allegory."

91 Here is Picchione's definition of "abject" in this same article:

> From a general perspective, in the poetry of the neoavant-garde the abject can be identified with the abnormal and the profane, trash and the repulsive, the schizomorphous and the alienated, indeed with all that has been banished from the social discourse of our daily existence. The everyday enters into the aesthetic space inasmuch as the practice of the abject turns linguistic refuse into art. In this respect, the abject clearly embodies a transgressive and subversive orientation that is in synchrony with avant-garde objectives.

> In fact, in this poetic context the abject embodies verbal disruption and disorder and, consequently, it cannot but declare the impossibility of the sublime or of the lyrical tradition. (Picchione, "Poetry and the Abject," 267)

92 Ibid.
93 See Klieger Stillman, *Alfred Jarry*, also quoted in chapter 5, 275–80.
94 Picchione, "Poetry and the Abject," 277.
95 Jarry, *The Ubu Plays*, 23.
96 Ibid., 39.
97 Ibid., 43.
98 Ibid., 24.
99 Antonio Porta, "La scelta della voce," in his *Tutte le poesie (1956–1989)*, 305. The English translation is by Pasquale Verdicchio in Porta, *Piercing the Page*, 193.
100 It is worth pointing out that *Stark* and *Si tratta di larve* also insist on the darkness of the space in which the actions and words of the characters take place.
101 Porta, "La scelta della voce," in *Tutte le poesie (1956–1989)*, 305. The English translation is by Pasquale Verdicchio in Porta, *Piercing the Page*, 193.
102 Ibid., 306; translation ibid., 194.
103 Ibid., 308; translation ibid., 199.
104 In Act 2, Scene 6 of *Ubu Roi*, the souls of Wenceslas, Boleslas, Landislas, and Rosamund appear to young Boggerls, the son of the King of Poland, whom Ubu had just betrayed and slain, clamouring for the young prince to exact revenge on the traitor Ubu. This has been traditionally recognized by critics as a nod to Shakespeare's *Hamlet*. Porta's "La scelta della voce" includes Hamlet and Ophelia among its characters. Both Jarry and Porta reused materials and plot devices taken from Shakespeare's masterpiece, often modifying them radically and unceremoniously, and thus displaying the same cannibalistic lust they show in the treatment of the characters' bodies as well as the verses and sentences of the plays.
105 Porta, "La scelta della voce," 317. The translation is mine.
106 Once again, we come across an extremely interesting issue that we cannot engage here: a thorough discussion must be postponed to another time. In the meantime, however, the reader can refer to Petrella, *Gruppo 93: L'antologia poetica*, especially 28–30; Petrella, "Avanguardia, postmoderno e allegoria: Teoria e poesia nell'esperienza del Gruppo '93," at http://www.cepollaro.it/poesiaitaliana/PetrelAvanTes.pdf – see in particular, 137–41; and Pianigiani, "Ong, l'oralità e la poesia dei giovani."
107 Carella, Febbraro, and Barberini, eds, *Il romanzo di Castel Porziano: Tre giorni di pace, amore e poesia*.
108 Pagliarani, "Funzione del pubblico e mezze ciliege," 4.

109 Pagliarani, "Un'attrice in tutù racconta Ripellino," 318.
110 On this point, see chapter 4, 225, note 17, where another passage in which Pagliarani makes this claim is quoted.
111 In 1980, Andrea Andermann released a documentary film about the festival entitled *Castelporziano, Ostia dei poeti*, accessed on 1 June 2018, at https://www.youtube.com/watch?v=QfMuy7bf-ik&t=4720s.
112 Cordelli, *Proprietà peduta*, 47. For more on the "Ragazza cioè," see also 40.
113 Carella, Febbraro, and Barberini, eds, *Il romanzo di Castel Porziano*, 85.
114 Gasparini, *Poesia come corpo-voce*, 27.
115 Carella, Febbraro, and Barberini, eds, *Il romanzo di Castel Porziano*, 51–2.
116 Cordelli, *Proprietà peduta*, 16.
117 Ibid., 22–3.

4 An Introduction to Pagliarani's Theatre

1 Briganti, "Preface," 5–6.
2 See in particular Ballerini, "Documenti per una preistoria della Ragazza Carla."
3 Transcript of an interview with Pagliarani dating back to the times of *Videor*, accessed February 2013: http://www.youtube.com/videorlab?gl=IT$hl=it#p/u/213/xQrzc1e68jI.
4 In addition to the already-cited Ballerini and Briganti, see also Muzzioli, "Montaggio e straniamento: La modernità radicale di Elio Pagliarani"; and Ottonieri, "Il romanzo del *focus*."
5 Naturally, there are a few notable exceptions; see, for instance, Guido Guglielmi, "In forma di recitativo."
6 Pagliarani, *Pro-memoria a Liarosa*, 295–6.
7 In 2013, I had the privilege of editing a volume of his complete plays, which are now available to study. See Elio Pagliarani, *Tutto il teatro*, ed. Gianluca Rizzo (Venezia: Marsilio, 2013). The introduction I wrote for that volume (translated and updated) constitutes the backbone of this chapter; naturally, I integrated its contents to reflect the changes that have intervened over the years, as well as my increased knowledge and understanding of Pagliarani and, in general, the Neoavanguardia theatre.
8 See chapter 1, 76.
9 This "*manifesto minimo*" by Pagliarani, along with the other theoretical texts contained in the playbill, have been published as an appendix to Rizzo, "La verifica della poesia: Il teatro secondo I Novissimi, Pagliarani (e T.S. Eliot)."
10 See Eliot, "The Possibility of a Poetic Drama" and "Rhetoric and Poetic Drama," in *The Sacred Wood*; "A Dialogue in Dramatic Poetry," in *Selected Essays*; "Poetry and Drama," in *Selected Prose of T.S. Eliot*; and especially *The*

Use of Poetry and the Use of Criticism, which collects the lectures he delivered at Harvard in 1932–3 when he was Charles Eliot Norton Professor of Poetry. At page 153, we read: "The ideal medium of poetry, to my mind, and the most direct means of social 'usefulness' for poetry, is the theatre."

11 Eliot, "Poetry and Drama," 138.

12 Eliot – and his writings on theatre and poetry – had a major influence on Pagliarani's entire career. In particular, the essay "The Three Voices of Poetry" (originally written as a speech, delivered in 1953, then collected in *On Poetry and Poets*, published in 1957, and translated by Giuliani into Italian as *Sulla poesia e sui poeti*, for Bompiani, in 1960) could be used as a blueprint for interpreting Pagliarani's journey from *Inventario privato* all the way to *Epigrammi*. See Eliot, "The Three Voices of Poetry," in *On Poetry and Poets*, 103–4.

13 Pagliarani, "Per una definizione dell'avanguardia," in Balestrini, Giuliani, Barilli, and Guglielmi, eds, *Gruppo 63. L'antologia. Critica e teoria*, 875.

14 Pagliarani, *Il fiato dello spettatore*. A new edition of this volume, which includes a larger selection of Paglarani's theatrical reviews as well as three additional theoretical texts, was recently published by the Roman publishing house L'Orma: Elio Pagliarani, *Il fiato dello spettatore e altri scritti sul teatro (1966–1984)*, ed. Marianna Marrucci (Rome: L'Orma, 2017).

15 I am quoting here from the last version of the essay, entitled "Teatro come verifica," published as the introduction to the first edition of *Il fiato dello spettatore* , 9–32. Previous versions appeared as Elio Pagliarani, "Dell'eroe linguistico," *Nuova Corrente*, nos 39–40 (December 1966): 281–4; and Elio Pagliarani, "Artaud e la contestazione fisica del Living Theatre," *Quindici*, no. 1 (1967): 87–92.

16 Elio Pagliarani, "Teatro come verifica," 9. See also chapter 1, 64, note 85, and chapter 2, 129, note 54.

17 Those lucky enough to have witnessed it agree on Pagliarani's skills as a reader of his own (and his friends') verse. In fact, the highest compliment he could pay a fellow poet would be to offer to read their compositions: "I'll come by to read your poems," he would say; that is, "*Vengo a leggerti le tue poesie.*" An idea of his abilities can be gleaned from the following video: YouTube, https://www.youtube.com/watch?v=Qtt12Yq4ECI. YouTube also has a channel entitled "Videor," which is the name of the video journal of poetry edited by Pagliarani between 1988 and 1991; all issues of the video journal are available at: https://www.youtube.com/watch?v=GYitmHoE-W0&list=PLE1E11A737881A1C4&index=1.

18 Pagliarani, "Rafael Alberti alla ribalta," 212.

19 See chapter 2, 121.

20 Elio Pagliarani, "Aspettava soltanto che lo mettessero in scena," in *Il fiato dello spettatore e altri scritti sul teatro (1966–1984)*, 207–8.

21 Pagliarani, "Teatro come verifica," 10–11.

22 Elio Pagliarani, "Intervento al convegno del Gruppo 63," 108: "Mantenere in efficienza, per tutti, il linguaggio."

23 "La merce esclusa" was performed for the first time at the Teatro Parioli, in Rome, on 3 June 1965; that same evening, as has already been mentioned several times, marked the debut of the Compagnia Teatro dei Novissimi. "Col semaforo rosso" dates to the same period, as it was published by the periodical *Terzo programma: Quaderni trimestrali* (Rome: ERI, 1965), 374. From this information, we can deduce that it had been aired on the radio in the previous months, either at the end of 1964, or at the beginning of 1965.

24 The most intricate examples of this technique can be found in the *Faust of Copenhagen* (see chapter 5, 307–9).

25 A more in-depth comparison between the poetic and the theatrical versions of this text must be postponed, unfortunately, to another time and another essay.

26 See chapter 3, 189.

27 Casi, *600.000 e altre azioni teatrali per Giuliano Scabia*, 56. The quotation in Casi's text is from Scabia, "Nuovo spazio, nuovo teatro, nuova cultura."

28 De Marinis, "Scrittura teatrale e partecipazione," 28.

29 Compare Pagliarani's position on this issue with Scabia's, summarized in chapter 3, 191, and in the interview at the end of this volume (365–6).

30 In order to provide further context to this truly unusual play, we transcribe here a few excerpts from the brochure distributed to the audience during the performance, staged by Luigi Gozzi at the Teatro Stabile di Roma, at the end of September 1984:

> I primi decenni del secolo videro lo sviluppo della teoria quantistica dell'atomo mentre le strade dei teorici di tutto il mondo portavano a Copenaghen da Niels Bohr il fisico che formulò l'esatto modello dell'atomo. All'Istituto di Fisica Teorica di Bohr ... si prese l'abitudine durante il consueto convegno primaverile di eseguire una rappresentazione satirica che alludesse agli sviluppi della fisica. Il convegno del 1932 seguiva a breve distanza la scoperta del fisico inglese James Chadwick di una nuova particella che lo scopritore chiamò neutrone. Due anni prima Wolfgang Pauli aveva utilizzato lo stesso termine per indicare l'esistenza ipotetica di un'altra particella, ben presto oggetto di accese discussioni tra i fisici. Per distinguere le due entità Enrico Fermi propose di denominare la particella di Pauli neutrino, cioè piccolo neutrone ... Nel 1932 all'Istituto Bohr venne allestito dagli allievi più giovani una parodia del Faust di Goethe, rimasta poi leggendaria come il "Faust di Copenaghen." Qui il personaggio

di Gretchen, Margherita diviene il misterioso neutrino mentre i fisici Ehrenfest, Pauli e Chadwick diventano rispettivamente Faust, Mefistofele e Wagner. Il Faust di Copenaghen è uno stravagante documento della storia della scienza, ma anche un prezioso indizio culturale: in quello stesso arco di tempo il teatro europeo sperimentava una dimensione non riproduttiva della scena, vista ora come luogo di ipotesi da confrontare con una realtà in gran parte sconosciuta e travolgendo le precedenti pratiche sceniche di tipo naturalistico. L'affinità tra le nuove procedure teoretico-scientifiche e quelle artistico-progettuali è tanto paradossale quanto significativa ed evidenzia un complessivo spostamento culturale.

[The first few decades of the century saw the development of quantum theory; the path of all theoretical physicists led to Copenhagen, to Niels Bohr's lab, the scientist who had first provided an accurate description of the atom. At Bohr's Institute for Theoretical Physics …, during the annual spring conference, a tradition was started: there would be a performance that satirized the most recent developments in the world of physics. The 1932 conference came right after the English physicist James Chadwick discovered a new particle, which he named neutron. Two years earlier, Wolfgang Pauli had used that same term to indicate the existence of another hypothetical particle, which became soon a topic of dispute among scientists. To distinguish these two particles, Enrico Fermi suggested that Pauli's be called neutrino, that is little neutron … In 1932, at the Bohr Institute, the younger participants to the conference staged a parody of Goethe's Faust entitled "The Faust of Copenhagen," which has since become legendary. The character of Gretchen became the mysterious particle, the neutrino, while physicists Ehrenfest, Pauli, and Chadwick became respectively Faust, Mephistopheles, and Wagner. The Faust of Copenhagen is an extravagant document of the history of science, but also a precious cultural artifact: at that same time, the European theatre was experimenting with a non-realistic use of the stage, which was seen as a place where a number of different hypotheses could be contrasted with a reality that was largely unknown, while overthrowing the previous dramatic conventions of a more naturalistic kind.]

See also Pagliarani, *Tutto il teatro*, 131–44.

31 For a detailed discussion of the relationship between Alexander, the character in Pagliarani's plays, and the historical Alexander Blok, see Serafini, "La parola tornerà ai poeti … 'La Bestia di Porpora o Poema di Alessandro.'" This play, incorporating directly Blok's own verse, loosely retells the biography of the poet, obliquely relating it to current Italian

events. In a note that accompanied the first publication of the play, Pagliarani explains:

Prima di tutto mi è doveroso chiarire che tutte le citazioni di versi di Alessandro Blok sono nella traduzione di Angelo Maria Ripellino (e, anzi l'idea stessa di questo mio testo la devo alle non molte righe che Ripellino dedica a Blok, nell'introduzione alla sua antologia della *Poesia russa nel Novecento* – ben più ampia e ricca dell'introduzione al volume dedicato alle *Poesie* nella collana di Lerici). ... Blok ... aspira all'impossibile e lo raggiunge, dopo di che lo capovolge in un altro impossibile e raggiunge anche quest'altro (un progetto di titolo era anche "La giacca rovesciata due volte," scartato poi perché troppo frusto) ... il Blok lo terminai nella tarda primavera non ricordo se del '68 o del '69. Ero rimasto bloccato sul finale, per un paio d'anni: mi mancava soltanto quella che poi risultò la scena unica del terzo e ultimo atto; mi pare che ciò significhi che l'intuizione di parlare di tutt'altro, anzi, meglio, di rovesciare il discorso, mi venne soltanto dopo una ventina o trentina di spettacoli teatrali visti e recensiti nella mia, freschissima allora, professione di critico teatrale per un quotidiano ... Io fui e sono tuttora soddisfatto di aver trovato quel finale, dal quale però si possono derivare alcune conclusioni: per esempio gridare come fece mia moglie Cetta una decina d'anni fa, quando, in occasione di un trasloco, si ritrovò in mano il dattiloscritto di questo Blok ed esclamò: "ma tu avevi previsto il crollo dell'Unione Sovietica!" Io avevo soltanto capito che il mio teatro, il mio Blok, per la tensione con cui era stato concepito non aveva più niente da dire, dopo il trionfo di quella rivoluzione, ma sapevo anche che quel trionfo non era la conclusione del dramma di Blok.

[First of all, I must clarify that all the quotations of Alexander Blok's verses are from Angelo Maria Ripellino's translation (and, actually, the idea for this play came from the few lines that Ripellino dedicates to Blok in his introduction to the anthology *Twentieth Century Russian Poetry* ... Blok aspires to reach the impossible, and he succeeds, then he turns that goal upside down, striving for another kind of impossible, and he achieves it once again (in fact, another title for the project was "The Twice-Turned Coat," which I then discarded, because it was too trite) ... I finished my Blok in the spring of 1968 or 1969, I don't remember. I had been stuck on the ending for a couple of years: I was missing only what turned out to be the one scene of the third and last act: this means that the intuition of changing the subject or, rather, of turning to the complete opposite of what had been said before, came to me only after I had reviewed twenty or thirty shows, as a consequence of my then newly found profession of theatre critic for a daily newspaper ... I was and still am satisfied with that ending, from which we can derive a few conclusions: for instance, one could say, like my wife Cetta did ten years ago when, as we were moving out of an apartment, she found the manuscript and, after reading it, exclaimed: "You had foreseen the fall of the USSR!" Actually, I had only realized that my theatre, my Blok, given the tension with which it had been created, after the triumph of that revolution had nothing more to say; but I also knew that that triumph was not the end of Blok's drama.]

Pagliarani's note to *La bestia di porpora* is reproduced in its entirety in Pagliarani, *Tutto il teatro*, 201–3.

32 The play opens with the dream of one of the main characters, Didio Giuliano, a senator of Rome who would later buy his way to the title of emperor and be killed by the very soldiers he had bribed. The dream is a pastiche of recipes from Apicius's *De Re Coquinaria* and excerpts from the banquet chapters in Petronius's *Satyricon*. The connection between power, food, money, and sex is explored throughout the play, as Didio's extended family uses the senator's greed and insecurities to encourage his imperial ambitions. In spite of all the accurate historical facts woven into the plot, Ancient Rome is a very transparent allegory for Italian current events (especially in the sphere of political economy).

33 This is a libretto for an opera; music by Angelo Paccagnini, directed by Bindo Missiroli, and presented at the 1959 Festival delle Novità of Bergamo. Pierrot, Colombina, Arlecchino, the Doctor, and other traditional characters of Commedia dell'Arte are presented in a very modern and very bourgeois environment, discussing medications, insurance claims, and rising rent.

34 In this play Pagliarani retells the famous fable by Perrault from a slanted perspective, focusing on the sleep of the protagonist and equating it to the lethargy of contemporary Italian society in facing the most pressing political issues of the day. Simone Carella, who directed the first staging, offered this note as a way of introducing the performance:

Questo componimento poetico procede per sostituzioni di immagini rispetto alla nota favola di Perrault, con la creazione cioè di figure poetiche che raccontano un'altra storia: l'attesa di un "evento rivoluzionario"; il sorgere e il trasformarsi dei vari tentativi di realizzarlo rappresentati dalla "sfilata" dei diversi principi aspiranti al bacio che ridarà vita alla Bella Addormentata caduta in un malvagio sonno. Durante questo lungo sonno attraverso la presentazione di altre poesie del poeta vengono suggerite varie e diverse emozioni e "questioni" affrontate e vissute da Pagliarani. La messa in scena vuole sperimentare tutta la modernità e l'attualità di questo linguaggio poetico-teatrale valorizzandone le possibilità ritmico-ironico-liriche e soprattutto provocatoriamente gioiose. Ripercorrendo il lavoro di scrittura di Elio Pagliarani lo spettacolo non è che la "recita" di un poemetto, materia per un'allegoria …

[When compared to the famous fable by Perrault, this poetic text proceeds through substitutions of images; that is to say, it creates poetic figures that tell a different story: the wait for a "revolutionary event"; the beginnings and unravelling of different attempts to bring it to fruition through the parade of the various princes who aspired to kiss Sleeping Beauty and wake her from her evil slumber. During this long dream, through the introduction of other poems by Pagliarani, various emotions are evoked and different "issues" are faced and lived. The staging intends to stress the modernity and relevance of this poetic-theatrical language, highlighting its rhythmic-ironic-lyric and, more importantly, joyfully provocative potential. Retracing Pagliarani's writing, the show is nothing but the "performance" of a *poemetto,* matter for an allegory …]

First published in Elio Pagliarani, *La bella addormentata nel bosco* (Milano: Copro 10, 1987), then in Pagliarani, *Tutto il teatro*, 115.

35 These poems are given in the wonderful Italian translation by Angelo Maria Ripellino: Blok, *Poesie.*

36 Adriano Spatola, review of Elio Pagliarani, *Lezione di fisica*, 98–9.

37 *Lezione di fisica,* directed by Ken Dewey, presented in Palermo, at the Sala Scarlatti del Conservatorio, on 3 October 1963. For more details, see chapter 1, 14–18.

38 Giuliani, "La poesia a teatro," in *Il Verri*, 74, and in Giuliani, *Le droghe di Marsiglia*, 349.

39 Ballerini, "Della violenta fiducia," in *4 per Pagliarani*, 69.

40 For more on each author, see pages 71–2 and 75 for Sanguineti, pages 55–6 for Curi, pages 82–3 for Giuliani, and pages 79–80 for Panza and Scialoja. See, also, in this chapter, the passage on "Teatro come verifica" quoted in note 50.

41 This is one of those areas in which a lucky archival discovery could quickly modify and deepen our understanding of the times and their protagonists.

42 See especially the "videorivista" *Videor*, which Pagliarani directed. All nine issues, published between May of 1988 and November of 1991, are available on the internet, at http://videor.it (in addition to the YouTube channel mentioned earlier).

43 See *Videor* 3, available on YouTube at: https://www.youtube.com/watch?v=gEyRjbMjILg&index=3&list=PLE1E11A737881A1C4.

44 It would be interesting to systematically compare the different definitions of "gesto linguistico" given, in those years, by the various members of the Neoavanguardia, in an attempt to create a sort of general theory.

Also related to this issue is the one of "letteratura della crudeltà," as discussed by Sanguineti and Tagliaferri in the following two crucial essays: Sanguineti, "Per una letteratura della crudeltà," and Tagliaferri, "La superstizione della crudeltà." See also Porta, "Tre ipotesi contro la normalizzazione dello scrittore," mentioned by Valentina Valentini in the interview at the end of this volume, page 336. Sanguineti, in the essay mentioned, argues for a "cruelty" that would function as a "justification" of literature. In his opinion, cruelty could be considered as a condition under which it would be possible to continue writing, for the author would face with the requisite "violent cynicism" the traditional, ideological linguistic conventions that prevented a direct access to reality. The fresher connection the writer could establish through this kind of cruelty would provide the necessary margins for a more impactful literature, capable of influencing society (and politics) in a more effective way. Tagliaferri, in his reply, expresses scepticism about this understanding of "cruelty," especially if it is considered a way of pursuing political goals through literary works. In his opinion, real and permanent political change can be achieved only through the tools of politics.

45 For a more systematic discussion of the legacy of medieval performers in the theatre of the *Novecento*, see my essay on Dario Fo and Pasolini: Rizzo, "Pasolini, Fo and the Issue of Language."

46 For a survey of the different positions held in this regard, see the excellent monograph by Oronzo Parlangeli, *La nuova questione della lingua*.

47 Elio Pagliarani, "La Bestia di Porpora o Poema di Alessandro," first published in *L'Illuminista: Rivista di cultura contemporanea* 2–3, no. 1 (2000), and then in Pagliarani, *Tutto il teatro*, 205–36. For more information on the genesis of the play, see Pagliarani's note, reprinted in *Tutto il teatro*, 201–3.

48 Fo, *Mistero buffo*, 27.

49 Pagliarani, *Tutte le poesie (1946–2005)*, 153; the translation is by Patrick Rumble, in Ballerini and Cavatorta, eds, *Those Who from Afar Look Like Flies*, 397.

50 Pagliarani, "Teatro come verifica," 12. In this quotation, we find another reference to gesture, which should be compared to the other ones scattered throughout Pagliarani's theoretical essays on theatre, as well as with the other definitions of gesture provided by his fellow Neoavanguardisti.

51 The reader of Pagliarani's poetry knows all too well that he doesn't appreciate metaphysical speculations, or any other suggestion of a transcendent dimension. In the poem "La ballata di Rudi," he writes: "mistica lingua del rosso mistica lingua del corpo mistica lingua del

cazzo / (se è mistica è del privato, Nandi non sa che farsene, / se nel codice è già incastrata, Nandi ti abbiamo fregato)," in Pagliarani, *Tutte le poesie (1946–2005)*, 322. That is: "mysticism language of the red mysticism language of the body mysticism language my ass / (if it's mysticism it's private, Nandi has no use for it, / if it is already embedded in the code, Nandi we screwed you)."

52 Heisenberg first formulated this idea in a paper entitled "Ueber den anschaulichen Inhalt der quantentheoretischen Kinematik und Mechanik," *Zeitschrift für Physik*, no. 43 (1927): 172–98. An English translation is available in Wheeler and Zurek, eds, *Quantum Theory and Measurement*, 62–84:

> At the instant of time when the position is determined, that is, at the instant when the photon is scattered by the electron, the electron undergoes a discontinuous change in momentum. This change is the greater the smaller the wavelength of the light employed, i.e., the more exact the determination of the position. At the instant at which the position of the electron is known, its momentum therefore can be known only up to magnitudes which correspond to that discontinuous change; thus, the more precisely the position is determined, the less precisely the momentum is known, and conversely. (64)

53 Pagliarani, *Tutte le poesie*, 176; the translation is by Rumble, in Ballerini and Cavatorta, eds, *Those Who from Afar Look Like Flies*, 1543.

54 Pagliarani, "Teatro come verifica," 12, emphasis in the original.

55 Ibid., 15.

56 Pagliarani, *Tutte le poesie*, 178. The translation is by Rumble, in Ballerini and Cavatorta, eds, *Those Who from Afar Look Like Flies*, 1545.

57 Pagliarani, "La bestia di porpora o Poema di Alessandro," in *Tutto il teatro*, 232.

58 Pagliarani, "A proposito del mio Blok," 73.

59 Pagliarani, "La bella addormentata nel bosco," in *Tutto il teatro*, 113.

60 Pagliarani, "Ballata di Rudi," in *Tutte le poesie*, 336.

61 Ballerini, "'Prosimetro' per Pagliarani," 21.

62 Guglielmi, "In forma di recitativo," 23.

63 Pedullà, "Elio Pagliarani," 193.

64 Pedullà, "Le sentenze finali di Elio Pagliarani," 179.

5 Collaborations and Convergences

1 Early versions of this chapter have been published in Gianluca Rizzo, "Il Faust della Neoavanguardia: Celli, Pagliarani e le riscritture del Goethe,"

in Gianluca Rizzo, ed., *On the Fringe of the Neoavantgarde: Ai confini della neoavanguardia: Palermo 1963–Los Angeles 2013* (New York: Agincourt Press, 2017), 189–217; and in Gianluca Rizzo, "Il guaio dell'asino morto è che ci vuole l'interpretazione. Giuliani, Pagliarani e le riscritture di Perrault," *Autografo*, no. 50 (anno XXI, 2013): 141–63.

2 I want to take this opportunity to thank Federico Milone, who first made this discovery and was kind enough to alert me to it.

3 I suspect it may have been printed in some ephemeral program or playbill, to be distributed before a performance, a copy of which may or may not have been preserved among the papers of the Neoavanguardisti, and will, we hope, resurface at some point in the future.

4 See chapter 1, 76.

5 From the Fondo Giuliani, held at the Fondo Manoscritti of the Centro di ricerca sulla tradizione manoscritta di autori moderni e contemporanei at the University of Pavia. Within the folder labelled Materiale Letterario, 206–9, sub-folder 207.

6 Giuliani, "La poesia a teatro," 74. See also chapter 1, 93.

7 From the Fondo Giuliani, Materiale Letterario, 206–9, sub-folder 207.

8 Ibid.

9 Giuliani, "La poesia a teatro," 74.

10 See chapter 1, 94.

11 Balestrini, "Improvvisazione," in *Grammatica*, no. 2 (gennaio 1967): 7. This is a very interesting issue of *Grammatica* that collects a number of useful plays and critical texts. Two other early plays by Balestrini are also published here: *Imitazione*, 5; *Invocazione*, 8.

12 Sanguineti, *Teatro. K, Passaggio, Traumdeutung, Protocolli*, 52.

13 From the Fondo Giuliani, Materiale Letterario, Folder 206–9, sub-folder 207.

14 Giuliani and Pagliarani, *Pelle d'Asino.*

15 Giuliani, "Lettera a Elio," 21.

16 From the Fondo Giuliani, the folder labeled Materiale Letterario, 202, two typed sheets.

17 Pagliarani, "La ragazza Carla," in *Tutte le poesie (1946–2005)*, 125–6; translation that follows is by Patrick Rumble, in Ballerini and Cavatorta, eds, *Those Who from Afar Look Like Flies*, 362.

18 Montale, *Ossi di seppia*, 39. "This is all we can tell you today / what we are not, what we do not want."

19 Pagliarani, "La ragazza Carla," 125; translation by Rumble, in Ballerini and Cavatorta, eds, *Those Who from Afar Look Like Flies*, 363.

20 Perrault, *Peau d'Âne*, 194. What follows is a very rough translation.

21 Of the many monographs one could quote on this issue, I will limit myself to the relatively recent one by Jacques Le Goff, *Money and the*

Middle Ages. In its Italian translation, the title of the book makes the connection explicit by using St Basil's famous condemnation of coins as "the devil's dung": Le Goff, *Lo sterco del diavolo: Il denaro nel Medioevo*. The original French is titled, more simply, *Le Moyen Âge et l'argent*.

22 See chapter 3, 204.
23 Picchione, "Poetry and the Abject," 272.
24 Ibid., 272.
25 Ibid., 273.
26 Giuliani and Pagliarani, *Pelle d'Asino*, now in Pagliarani, *Tutto il teatro*, 92.
27 Ibid., 100.
28 This, like the previous quotations from Giuliani, come from his papers, which are held at the Fondo Manoscritti in Pavia.
29 The original Italian reads, "Lei parla per sé – ma qui è l'opposto. Non è che un tipo di parodossia sessuale fomentata dall'organizzazione commerciale." "Ah conosco gli spasimi di un sistema nervoso corrotto dalla società. L'asino è un simbolo, lo so."
30 "Il guaio dell'asino morto è che ci vuole l'interpretazione."
31 Giuliani, "Il teatro d'azione di Ken Dewey," 429.
32 Ibid., 431.
33 Alfredo Giuliani, *Povera Juliet*, in Balestrini and Giuliani, eds, *Gruppo 63. L'antologia*, 244.
34 *Romeo and Juliet*, Act V, Scene 3.
35 Giuliani, *Povera Juliet*, 246–7.
36 Giuliani, *Nostro padre Ubu, inTre recite su commissione.*
37 The original French titles for these works, variously translated into English, are *Ubu Roi*, *Ubu Cocu*, and *Ubu Enchaîné*, respectively.
38 Giuliani, *Tre recite su commissione*, 63.
39 Giuliani, "Prefazione," in Jarry, *Ubu*, 7.
40 Ibid., 8.
41 Klieger Stillman, *Alfred Jarry*, 43.
42 Giuliani, "Prefazione," in Jarry, *Ubu*, 6.
43 Klieger Stillman, *Alfred Jarry*, 46–7.
44 Ibid., 47.
45 Giuliani, "Prefazione," in *Ubu*, 6.
46 Klieger Stillman, *Alfred Jarry*, 50–1.
47 Giuliani, "Prefazione," in *Ubu*, 9.
48 Gozzi, "Di Jarry e del personaggio," 28.
49 Ibid., 27.
50 Bogliolo, "I nipotini di Jarry."
51 I say "the general public," but, in fact, it is not quite clear on whose behalf Bogliolo is voicing this complaint.

52 Bogliolo, "I nipotini di Jarry": "che escludono come sacrilegio qualunque disinteressato processo di revisione critica." Just before this quick jab, Bogliolo had noted,

> Sembra insomma che la forza di provocazione che ha animato e condizionato tutta la vicenda letteraria ed umana di Jarry continui ad essere la sola responsabile di una fortuna postuma che ha corso soltanto tra le élites intellettuali e si esaurisce il più delle volte in una parola d'ordine di modernità e di anticonformismo: si è stabilito una volta per tutte che Jarry è un "grande precursore" e, in luogo di analisi e di verifiche, si è adottato nei suoi confronti il metodo delle celebrazioni e delle deliberazioni.

> [It seems that the power of provocation that animated and determined Jarry's entire literary and personal journey, more often than not, boils down to a mere slogan in support of modernity and anti-conformism: it has been decided once and for all that Jarry is a "great forerunner" and, rather than analysis and verifications, this statement has been met with celebrations and deliberations.]

Once again, it would seem, according to Bogliolo, the snobbish intellectual elites conspire to force on the unsuspecting public the knowledge of a writer who, at best, might have been a good provocateur, but lacks substance, and is not worth the attention of good, discerning men and women like himself. It might seem that I am dedicating a disproportionate amount of attention to a minor critical voice such as Bogliolo's; however, I always find it uncanny how persistent and predictable cultural journalism can be; across time and space, oblivious to the rise and fall of empires and regimes, it keeps rehashing the same old scripts. This seems a good opportunity to fight back, for what it is worth.

53 Ibid.

54 Ibid. "quando si tireranno le somme del nostro secolo ci si accorgerà che il Padre Ubu avrà avuto una schiera di nipotini ancora più fitta e ingombrante del vituperatissimo padre Bresciani."

55 Bresciani was also famous as a model of Jesuitical literary mediocrity, according to Antonio Gramsci, who coined the expression "Bresciani's nephews" in his *Quaderni del carcere*.

56 De Sanctis, "L'ebreo di Verona del padre Bresciani," 79. "Il padre Bresciani è un uomo di poco ingegno e di volgare carattere, senza fiele, senza spirito, uno di quegli uomini tagliati così alla grossa, di cui si dice con benevolo compatimento: – gli è un buon uomo!"

57 Cattabiani, "Nel riso dell'obeso re Ubu la fine del secolo diciannovesimo," 16.

58 Ibid.
59 Ibid. "Jarry non è stato infatti solo il grande ispiratore e fondatore del teatro grottesco e surrealista contemporaneo, ma anche il fratello maggiore, anzi lo zio mitico del Grande Gioco del Travestimento, rivisitato dalle generazioni succedute al '68."
60 See chapter 1, 73.
61 See especially his *Epigrammi ferraresi* and *Esercizi platonici*, collected in *Tutto il teatro*, 231–58 and 341–97. In chapter 1, 54, we discussed in more detail the role of masks in Pagliarani's poetry.
62 Giuliani, *Tre recite su commissione*.
63 Giuliani, "Un dibattito mai avvenuto: Nerone e Seneca," in *Tre recite su commissione*, 65.
64 Ibid., 75–6.
65 Giuliani, *L'ultimo colloquio dell'Agrimensore K.*, in *Tre recite su commissione*, 89.
66 Ibid., 90. "Ora vai, e copriti bene, sta nevicando. Addio!"
67 Giuliani, *Nostro padre Ubu*, in *Tre recite su commissione*, 39–40.
68 Jarry, *Exploits & Opinions of Dr. Faustroll, Pataphysician*, 115.
69 Celli, *Le tentazioni del professor Faust*. This play received the Pirandello prize in 1975. It was later reprinted in Giorgio Celli, *La zattera di Vesalio e altri drammi* (Mantova: Tre lune edizioni, 2007). Pagliarani, "Il Faust di Copenaghen," in *Tutto il teatro*. As we will see shortly, Pagliarani's *Faust* has a rather complicated history, but was first performed in 1984. An earlier version of the remarks that follow has been published as Gianluca Rizzo, "Il Faust della Neo-avanguardia," in Rizzo, ed., *On the Fringe of the Neoavantgarde*, 189–217.
70 Sanguineti, *Faust*.
71 Lorenzini, *Sanguineti e il teatro della scrittura*, 28. The chapter from which this long paragraph is taken is entitled "La parola all'inferno: Faust," and is based on the "Introduzione" Lorenzini had written for Edoardo Sanguineti, *Faust. Un travestimento* (Roma: Carrocci, 2003).
72 I read this small masterpiece in its English translation: Heine, *Doktor Faust: A Dance Poem*, 11.
73 Ibid., 28–9.
74 This is one of the few scenes that have been reused, almost without alterations, by all three authors: Celli, Pagliarani, and Sanguineti.
75 Regarding Pagliarani, Celli, and their relationship with science and its paradigms, see Rizzo, "Se si vuole sapere se A è causa dell'effetto B."
76 See chapter 4, 242, note 52.
77 For a more systematic discussion of this issue, see chapter 1, 36–44.
78 Celli, "Le tentazioni del professor Faust," in *La zattera di Vesalio e altri drammi*, 29.

79 Pagliarani, as we will note later, will adopt a similar strategy in pursuing the same objectives, although in his case actors and directors have more freedom to intervene.
80 Celli, "Le tentazioni del professor Faust," 42.
81 Ibid., 47.
82 Ibid., 60.
83 Ibid., 63.
84 Claudio Beghelli, "Meccanismi del potere," in Celli, *La zattera di Vesalio e altri drammi*, 802–3. The quotations within the passage are from Celli, *Da Borgia a Faust. Le tentazioni del potere*, 83 and 84, respectively.
85 Celli, "Qualche parola di introduzione," in *La zattera di Vesalio e altri drammi*, 11–12.
86 Celli, "Giorgio Celli presenta Adriano Spatola, Corrado Costa e se stesso," 69.
87 Celli, "L'ebreo negro di Adriano Spatola," 53. This issue of *Malebolge*, along with all the others ever published, has been collected and reprinted by Eugenio Gazzola in *"Malebolge. L'altra rivista delle avanguardie."*
88 Celli, *La zattera di Vesalio e altri drammi*, 82.
89 Pecorino's interview was titled "L''anima gemella' del superuomo è il neutrino e non Margherita. Elio Pagliarani ci racconta il suo *Faust di Copenaghen*" (Superman's Soul Mate Is the Neutrino and Not Margherita. Elio Pagliarani Tells Us about His *Faust of Copenhagen*), and was published in *Paese Sera* (Thursday, 31 May 1984). It is now in Pagliarani, *Tutto il teatro*, 134–6.
90 Ibid., 135.
91 Ibid.
92 Ibid.
93 Pagliarani, *Tutto il teatro*, 172.
94 The playbill has been republished in Pagliarani, *Tutto il teatro*, 133–4.
95 The essay "Per una definizione dell'avanguardia" (For a Definition of the Avant-garde) was first presented by Pagliarani at the conference COMES (Comunità europea degli scrittori) devoted to the avant-garde, which took place in Rome in October of 1965. It was later published in Barilli and Guglielmi, eds, *Gruppo 63. Critica e teoria*, printed for the first time by Feltrinelli in 1976. It has since been republished by Bompiani in Balestrini, Giuliani, Barilli, and Guglielmi, eds, *Gruppo 63: L'antologia – Critica e teoria*, 878–9.
96 Pagliarani, *Tutto il teatro*, 163–4.
97 Ibid., 157.
98 In the already quoted interview with Franco Pecori, we read, "The character of Fausta does not have much space, in the prologue, she just

makes a brief appearance, a minimal presence but … 'She possesses a frightening electric charge, to pull it off we'll need an actress with great stage presence, the kind of presence that, even if there are 5 other people in the scene, everyone just looks at her. Like with Eduardo [De Filippo], for instance. For Fausta I'd recommend someone like Lina Sastri, who is a real dynamo,'" "L''anima gemella' del superuomo è il neutrino e non Margherita. Elio Pagliarani ci racconta il suo *Faust di Copenaghen*" (Superman's Soul Mate Is the Neutrino and Not Margherita. Elio Pagliarani Tells Us about His *Faust of Copenhagen*), now in Pagliarani, *Tutto il teatro*, 134–6. "Il personaggio di Fausta non ha molto spazio, nel prologo, appare appena, una presenza minima, ma … 'Una carica elettrica paurosa, per farlo ci vuole un'attrice con un grande peso scenico, quel peso per cui, se sono 5 persone in palcosce-nico tutti ne guardano una sola. Eduardo per esempio. Per Fausta penserei a una Lina Sa-stri, che è una vera pila elettri-ca.'"

99 Pagliarani, *Tutto il teatro*, 184–5.
100 Ibid., 186.
101 Ibid., 187.
102 See chapter 4, 247.
103 See chapter 1, 20.

Interview with Valentina Valentini

1 Rusconi, ed., "Gli scrittori e il teatro."
2 See the materials (photographs, reviews, etc.) on this performance available at https://nuovoteatromadeinitaly.sciami.com/mario-ricci-illuminazione-1967/.
3 Società Italiana Autori ed Editori (Italian Society of Authors and Publishers), the agency in charge of overseeing copyright in Italy.
4 Casi, *Pasolini. Un'idea di teatro.*
5 Valentini, "La vocazione teatrale di Pierpaolo Pasolini."
6 Porta, "Tre ipotesi contro la normalizzazione dello scrittore."

Interview with Pippo Di Marca

1 The Festival Internazionale dei Poeti, organized by Simone Carella, Franco Cordelli, and Ulisse Benedetti, was held on the beach at Ostia, just outside of Rome, in 1979.
2 For more on the Societas Raffaello Sanzio, see https://nuovoteatromadeinitaly.sciami.com/societas-raffaello-sanzio/.
3 Both plays are discussed in this volume. For more on *Illuminazione*, see the interview with Balestrini, 350, chapter 2, 118–19, and the online

resources at: https://nuovoteatromadeinitaly.sciami.com/mario-ricci-illuminazione-1967/. For more on *Pelle d'Asino*, see chapter 5, 261–9.
4 Di Marca, *Sotto la tenda dell'avanguardia*.
5 Pagliarani, *Tutto il teatro*, ed. Rizzo.
6 For more on Perlini's play, see https://nuovoteatromadeinitaly.sciami.com/meme-perlini-pirandello-chi-1973/.

Interview with Nanni Balestrini

1 The stage directions from Chekhov's *The Seagull* are used by Balestrini in both plays. In *Illuminazione*, they are interpolated with instructions from a physical exercise booklet. For more details, see chapter 2, 118–19, and the online resources located here: https://nuovoteatromadeinitaly.sciami.com/mario-ricci-illuminazione-1967/.

Interview with Giuliano Scabia

1 Scabia is referring to his laboratory with the patients of Trieste's mental hospital as directed by Franco Basaglia. For more details on this extraordinary experience, see the already quoted Giuliano Scabia, *Una esperienza di animazione in un ospedale psichatrico* (Turin: Einaudi, 1976). See also the material available online at https://nuovoteatromadeinitaly.sciami.com/giuliano-scabia-marco-cavallo-1973/.
2 For more on Luigi Nono's *Intolleranza 1960*, see Duran, "Operatic Neo-Avant-Gardism in Luigi Nono's *Intolleranza 1960*."
3 Scabia is referring to the "azione" entitled *Sistema di reparto chiuso: Visita ad un'istituzione repressiva* ("System of a Closed Ward: Visit to a Repressive Institution"), a non-stop theatrical happening that lasted thirty-three hours, from three p.m. on Saturday, 7 February, to midnight of Sunday, 8 February 1970. Among the non-professional actors involved were Ronchetta, Salza, Vagliani, Vacchetto, Sacchi, and Ravera.
4 See Scabia, "Genesi/La creazione. Schema vuoto per l'Odin Teatret di Hostelboro (due stesure)," in *Culture Teatrali*, no. 12 (Spring 2005): 75–86. This issue, edited by Francesca Gasparini and Massimo Marino, is entirely dedicated to Scabia and is entitled: "'Della Poesia nel teatro il tremito.' Per Giuliano Scabia." It is also available online at https://www.culturateatrali.org/files/annuari_ct/CT12.pdf.

Works Cited

AA.VV. "Monographic Issue on Brecht and Theatre." *Il Verri*, no. 4 (August 1961).

– "Per un convegno sul nuovo teatro." First in *Sipario*, no. 247 (November 1966): 2–3; repr. in Quadri, ed., *L'avanguardia teatrale in Italia (Materiali 1960–1976)*, 135–7. Turin: Einaudi, 1977. Accessed 31 May 2018. http://www.ateatro.it/olivieropdp/ateatro108.htm#108and6.

– "Monographic Issue on 'Teatro e linguaggio.'" *Nuova Corrente*, nos 39–40 (1966).

– "Monographic Issue on Theatre." *Grammatica*, no. 2 (January 1967).

– "Monographic Issue on 'Teatro come evento.'" *Il Verri*, no. 25 (December 1967).

Acca, Fabio. "'La crudeltà non fa per me.' Pasolini, Artaud e il teatro del 'quasi.'" *Antropologia e Teatro*, no. 3 (2012): 42–59.

Agosti, Stefano. "Porta e la scena della crudeltà." In *Poesia italiana contemporanea*, 153–65. Milan: Bompiani, 1995.

Agostino, Roberto. "Nelle mani del questore." In Quadri, ed., *Il teatro del regime*, 60–81. Milan: Cremonesi, 1976.

Andermann, Andrea. *Castelporziano, Ostia dei poeti*. Documentary film accessed on 1 June 2018, at https://www.youtube.com/watch?v=QfMuy7bf-ik&t=4720s.

Arbasino, Alberto. *Grazie per le magnifiche rose*. Milan: Feltrinelli, 1965.

– *La maleducazione teatrale*. Milan: Feltrinelli, 1966.

Artaud, Antonin. *Nel paese dei Tarahumara e altri scritti*. Ed. H.J. Maxwell and Claudio Rugafiori. Milan: Adelphi, 1966.

– *Il teatro e il suo doppio*. Turin: Einaudi, 1968.

– "Il teatro della crudeltà (Primo manifesto)." In *Il teatro e il suo doppio*, 204–15.

Associazione Itàca, ed. *Ricerca sul Convegno per un Nuovo Teatro, Ivrea–Torino 9–12 giugno 1967*. Milan: Associazione Itàca, 1986.

Bajini, Sandro. "Trascrizione del Convegno di Ivrea del 1967." Ad opera dell'Associazione culturale Itàca, archivio privato di Alfredo Tradardi, 45. Quoted in Visone, *La nascita del nuovo teatro in Italia*, 242–3.

Balestrini, Nanni. "Imitazione – Improvvisazione – Invocazione." *Grammatica*, no. 2 (January 1967): 5–10.

– "Linguaggio e opposizione." In Alfredo Giuliani, ed., *I Novissimi: Poesie per gli anni '60*, 164–6. Turin: Einaudi, 2003.

Balestrini, Nanni, ed. *Quindici: Una rivista e il Sessantotto*. Milan: Feltrinelli, 2008.

Balestrini, Nanni, and Andrea Cortellessa, eds. *Gruppo 63: Il romanzo sperimentale: Palermo 1965: Col senno di poi*. Rome: L'Orma, 2013.

Balestrini, Nanni, and Alfredo Giuliani, eds. *I novissimi. Poesie per gli anni '60*. Milan: Rusconi e Paolazzi, 1961.

– *Gruppo 63: La Nuova Letteratura: 34 scrittori: Palermo ottobre 1963*. Milan: Feltrinelli, 1964.

– *Gruppo 63: L'antologia*. Turin: Testo & Immagine, Turin, 2002.

Balestrini, Nanni, Alfredo Giuliani, Renato Barilli, and Angelo Guglielmi, eds. *Gruppo 63: L'antologia – Critica e teoria*. Milan: Bompiani, 2013.

Ballerini, Luigi. "Elio Pagliarani: Poesia come respiro (e come continuo saltare)." In *Studi Novecenteschi*, 2, no. 4 (March 1973): 101–21. Repr. in Ballerini, *4 per Pagliarani*, 89–113.

– *La piramide capovolta*. Venice: Marsilio, 1975.

– "Della violenta fiducia." First in *Carte Italiane*, 2, no. 1 (February 2005). Repr. in Ballerini, *4 per Pagliarani*, 45–72.

– "Documenti per una preistoria della Ragazza Carla." First in *L'Illuminista*, VII, nos 20–21 (September–December 2007): 121–38. Repr. in Ballerini, *4 per Pagliarani*, 13–44.

– *4 per Pagliarani*. Piacenza: Scritture, 2008.

– "'Prosimetro' per Pagliarani." *L'immaginazione*, no. 254 (April–May 2010): 20–2.

– "Prosimetro per la Ballata di Rudi: Dal verso 'a fisarmonica spalancata' alla 'prosa in prosa' con sberleffo." *L'Ulisse*, no. 13 (2014): 68–72.

Ballerini, Luigi, and Beppe Cavatorta, eds. *Those Who from Afar Look Like Flies: An Anthology of Italian Poetry from Pasolini to the Present, Vol. I, 1956–1975*. Toronto, Buffalo, London: University of Toronto Press, 2017.

Barilli, Renato. *La neoavanguardia italiana: Dalla nascita del "Verri" alla fine del "Quindici."* Lecce: Manni, 2007.

Barilli, Renato, Fausto Curi, and Niva Lorenzini, eds. *Il gruppo 63 quarant'anni dopo: Bologna 8–11 maggio 2003: Atti del convegno*. Bologna: Pendragon, 2005.

Barilli, Renato, and Angelo Guglielmi, eds. *Gruppo 63: Critica e teoria*. Milan: Feltrinelli, 1976.

Barthes, Roland. "Mutter Courage." *Théâtre Populaire*, no. 8 (July–August 1954): 94–7.
– *Elements of Semiology*. Trans. Annette Lavers and Colin Smith. London: Jonathan Cape, 1967.
– *The Pleasure of the Text*. Trans. Richard Miller. New York: Hill and Wang, 1975.
– *Mythologies*. Trans. Annette Lavers. New York: Hill and Wang, 1995.
Bartolucci, Giuseppe. "L'area formale brechtiana e le tecniche teatrali d'oggi." *Sipario*, no. 219 (July 1964): 25–7.
– "Il teatro di Genet come provocazione e illusione." *Sipario*, no. 230 (June 1965): 29–34.
– "L'esempio del Living Theatre, teatro=vita." *Sipario*, nos. 232–3 (August–September 1965): 50–74.
– "Per un diverso linguaggio critico." First in *Nuova Corrente* (1966). Repr. in Bartolucci, *La scrittura scenica*, 152–7.
– "Positivo bilancio del Festival Universitario. In luce a Parma gruppi italiani." *Paese Sera* (8 April 1966).
– "Situazione brechtiana '66." *Sipario*, no. 245 (October 1966): 4–12.
– "Preistoria e punti di riferimento per un rinnovamento del teatro italiano." *Teatro*, II, no. 2 (Autumn–Winter 1967): 91–123.
– "Di un teatro cinetico visivo." In Bartolucci, ed., *La scrittura scenica*, 74–86.
– *Testi critici. 1964–1987*. Ed. Valentina Valentini. Rome: Bulzoni, 2007.
Bartolucci, Giuseppe, ed. *La scrittura scenica*. Rome: Marcalibri/Lerici Editore, 1968.
Bartolucci, Giuseppe, Ettore Capriolo, Edoardo Fadini, and Franco Quadri. "Elementi di discussione del Convegno per un Nuovo Teatro." In Quadri, ed., *L'avanguardia teatrale in Italia (Materiali 1960–1976)*, 137–48. Turin: Einaudi, 1977.
Bassano, Enrico. "Tempo di Frankenstein." *Il Dramma*, no. 349 (October 1965): 63.
Baudelaire, Charles. *Les fleurs du mal*. Fresno, CA: Academy Library Guild, 1954.
Beghelli, Claudio. "Meccanismi del potere." In Celli, *La zattera di Vesalio e altri drammi*, 795–803. Mantua: Tre lune edizioni, 2007.
Bello Minciacchi, Cecilia. *La distruzione da vicino: Forme e figure delle avanguardie del secondo Novecento*. Naples: Oèdipus, 2012.
Bene, Carmelo. *Opere. Con l'autobiografia di un ritratto*. Milan: Bompiani, 2008.
Bene, Carmelo, and Gilles Deleuze. *Sovrapposizioni*. Milan: Milano, 1978.
Bernardini, Francesca. "Da Savonarola all'avanguardia." *Avanguardia*, no. 9 (1998): 17–23.
Bettini, Filippo, and Francesco Muzzioli, eds. *Gruppo '93: La recente avventura del dibattito teorico letterario in Italia*. Lecce: Manni, 1990.

Blok, Aleksandr. *Poesie*. Trans. Angelo Maria Ripellino. Milan: Lerici, 1960.

Bogliolo, Giovanni. "I nipotini di Jarry. Possiamo parlarne senza celebrazioni?" *La Stampa* (3 June 1978).

Bono, Francesco. "Dossier Ivrea 1967: Il programma e la cronaca. Con il documento scritto da Bartolucci, Capriolo, Fadini e Quadri." http://www.ateatro.it/olivieropdp/ateatro108.htm#108and6.

– "Convegno per un Nuovo Teatro, Ivrea 1967: Rivoluzioni dimenticate e utopie realizzate." PhD diss. Libera Università di Lingue e Comunicazione di Milano, a.a. 2003–2004. Quoted in Visone, *La nascita del nuovo teatro in Italia*, 251–2.

Boursier, Guido. "A convegno il teatro di domani." *Sipario*, no. 255 (July 1967): 5–7.

Bradley, Arthur. *Derrida's* Of Grammatology. Bloomington: Indiana University Press, 2008.

Brecht, Bertolt. *Scritti teatrali*. Trans. Emilio Castellani, Roberto Fertonani, and Renata Mertens. Turin: Einaudi, 1962.

– *Teatro*. Ed. Emilio Castellani. Turin: Einaudi, 1963.

Briganti, Alessandra, ed. "Preface." In Pagliarani, *Poesie da recita*, 5. Rome: Bulzoni, 1985.

Bronnen, Arnolt. *Giorni con Bertolt Brecht*. Milan: Rizzoli, 1962.

Calvino, Italo. "Il midollo del leone." *Paragone*, no. 66 (June 1955): 17–31.

Camon, Ferdinando. "Edoardo Sanguineti." In *Il mestiere di poeta*, 215–39. Milan: Lerici, 1965.

Caproni, Giorgio. *Congedo del viaggiatore cerimonioso e altre prosopopee*. Milan: Garzanti, 1965.

Carella, Simone. "Dietro lo specchio di Castelporziano." In Carella, Febbraro, and Barberini, eds, *Il romanzo di Castel Porziano: Tre giorni di pace, amore e poesia*, 5–6.

Carella, Simone, Paola Febbraro, and Simona Barberini, eds. *Il romanzo di Castel Porziano: Tre giorni di pace, amore e poesia*. Viterbo: Stampa Alternativa, 2015.

Carlotti, Margherita. "'Fibra dopo fibra, goccia dopo goccia, respiro dopo respiro': Influenze artaudiane nel teatro di Antonio Porta (1967–1989)." PhD diss. *Letteratura italiana contemporanea*, submitted for Anno accademico 2016–17, appello primo, to the Università di Bologna.

Caselli, Daniela. "Thinking of a 'Rhyme for Euganean': Beckett in Italy." In Mark Nixon and Matthew Feldman, eds, *The International Reception of Samuel Beckett*, 209–33. London: Continuum, 2009.

Casi, Stefano. *Pasolini. Un'idea di teatro*. Udine: Campanotto, 1990.

– *I teatri di Pasolini*. Milan: Ubulibri, 2005.

– *600.000 e altre azioni teatrali per Giuliano Scabia*. Pisa: Edizioni ETS, 2012.

Cattabiani, Alfredo. "Nel riso dell'obeso re Ubu la fine del secolo diciannovesimo." *Il Tempo* (10 February 1978): 16.

Cavatorta, Beppe. *Scrivere contro: Viaggio nella narrative sperimentale italiana del XX Secolo.* Piacenza: Scritture, 2010.
Celli, Giorgio. "L'ebreo negro di Adriano Spatola." *Malebolge, Quaderno* no. 1 (Spring–Summer 1967): 53–6.
– *Il pesce gotico.* Bologna: Geiger, 1968.
– "L'operazione poetica." In *Il pesce gotico*, np. Bologna: Geiger, 1968.
– *Le tentazioni del professor Faust.* Milan: Feltrinelli, 1976.
– *Da Borgia a Faust. Le tentazioni del potere.* Bologna: Aspasia, 1997.
– "Giorgio Celli presenta Adriano Spatola, Corrado Costa e se stesso." In Barilli, Curi, and Lorenzini, eds, *Il Gruppo 63 quarant'anni dopo*, 69–74. Bologna: Pendragon, 2005.
– "Qualche parola di introduzione." In *La zattera di Vesalio e altri drammi*, 11–12.
– *La zattera di Vesalio e altri drammi.* Mantua: Tre lune edizioni, 2007.
Cerritelli, Claudio, and Melania Gazzotti, eds. *La poesia visiva 1963–2013: Omaggio al gruppo 70.* Mantua: Tre Lune, 2013.
Chirumbolo, Paolo. *Tra coscienza e autocoscienza: Saggi sulla narrative degli anni Sessanta: Volponi–Calvino–Sanguineti.* Soveria Mannelli: Rubbettino, 2009.
Chirumbolo, Paolo, Mario Moroni, and Luca Somigli, eds. *Neoavanguardia: Italian Experimental Literature and Arts in the 1960s.* Toronto: University of Toronto Press, 2010.
Chirumbolo, Paolo, and John Picchione, eds. *Edoardo Sanguineti: Literature, Ideology and the Avant-Garde.* London: Legenda, 2013.
Consolini, Marco. "'Théâtre Populaire': Breve storia di una rivista teatrale." *Culture teatrali*, no. 4 (Spring 2001): 51–86.
Cordelli, Franco. *Proprietà peduta.* Rome: L'Orma, 2016.
Cowan, Bainard. "Walter Benjamin's Theory of Allegory." *New German Critique*, no. 22 (Winter, 1981): 109–22.
Cuomo, Francesco. "Berliner Ensemble 1957 – Piccolo Teatro 1963. La scienza nella ricezione del *Galileo* di Brecht dalle rassegne stampa delle due rappresentazioni." *Journal of Science Communication*, no. 5 (March 2006). Accessed 31 May 2018: https://jcom.sissa.it/archive/05/01/A050101.
Curi, Fausto. "Poema come dialogo e gesto." *Quindici*, no. 13 (November 1968): 26–8.
Dallamano, Piero. "Una serata a teatro giocata in scena e a colpi di dadi." *Paese Sera* (6 October 1963): 13.
de Berardinis, Leo. "Intervista a cura di Roberto Pellerey." In *Ricerca sul Convegno per un Nuovo Teatro, Ivrea–Torino 9–12 giugno 1967*, a cura dell'Associazione Itàca di Milano (20 September 1986). Quoted in Visone, *La nascita del nuovo teatro in Italia*, 239.
de Berardinis, Leo, and Franco Molè. "Il lavoro su *Amleto*." First in *Teatro*, no. 2 (Autumn–Winter 1967–8): 65–77. Repr. in Quadri, ed., *L'avanguardia teatrale in Italia (Materiali 1960–1976)*, 243–55. Turin: Einaudi, 1977.

Deleuze, Gilles. *Cinema 2: L'immagine tempo*. Rome: Ubulibri, 1989.
De Marinis, Marco. *Il nuovo teatro: 1947–1970*. Milan: Bompiani, 1987.
– *Visioni della scena*. Bari: Laterza, 2004.
– "Il testo drammatico: Un riesame." In *Visioni della scena*, 95–114.
– "Teatro e poesia del Novecento: Alcune riflessioni." In *Visioni della scena*, 115–22.
– *Al limite del teatro: Utopie, progetti e aporie nella ricercar teatrale degli anni Sessanta e Settanta*. Bologna: Cue Press, 2016.
– "Scrittura teatrale e partecipazione: L'itinerario di Giuliano Scabia (1965–75)." In *Al limite del teatro*, 25–52.
Derrida, Jacques. "Prefazione." In Artaud, ed., *Il teatro e il suo doppio*, XXV–XXVII. Turin: Einaudi, 1968.
De Sanctis, Francesco. "L'ebreo di Verona del padre Bresciani." In *Saggi critici*, vol. I, 44–79. Bari: Laterza, 1965.
Di Marca, Pippo. *Sotto la tenda dell'avanguardia*. Corazzano: Titivillus, 2013.
Di Marco, Roberto, Gaetano Testa, and Michele Perriera. *La scuola di Palermo*. Milan: Feltrinelli, 1963.
Di Pesce, Maria Dolores. "Intervista ad Edoardo Sanguineti." In *Parol. Quaderni d'arte e di epistemologia*. Accessed 18 May 2018: http://www.parol.it/articles/sanguineti1.htm.
Dort, Bernard. "Brecht ou l'anti-Racine." *Théâtre Populaire*, no. 11 (January–February 1955): 27–36.
Duran, Adrian. "Operatic Neo-Avant-Gardism in Luigi Nono's *Intolleranza 1960*." In Rizzo, ed., *On the Fringe of the Neoavantgarde / Ai confini della neoavanguardia. Palermo 1963, Los Angeles 2013*, 37–50. New York: Agincourt Press, 2017.
Eco, Umberto. *Interpretation and Overinterpretation*. Cambridge: Cambridge University Press, 1992.
– "Prolusione." In Barilli, Curi, and Lorenzini, eds, *Il Gruppo 63 quarant'anni dopo. Bologna, 8–11 maggio 2003. Atti del convegno*, 20–43. Bologna: Pendragon, 2005.
Eliot, T.S. *The Use of Poetry and the Use of Criticism*. London: Faber and Faber, 1964.
– "The Three Voices of Poetry." In T.S. Eliot, *On Poetry and Poets*, 96–112. New York: The Noonday Press, 1967.
– "A Dialogue in Dramatic Poetry." In T.S. Eliot, *Selected Essays*, 31–45. London: Faber and Faber, 1972.
– "The Possibility of a Poetic Drama." In T.S. Eliot, *The Sacred Wood: Essays on Poetry and Criticism*, 54–63. London and New York: Methuen, 1972.
– "Rhetoric and Poetic Drama." In T.S. Eliot, *The Sacred Wood: Essays on Poetry and Criticism*, 71–7. London and New York: Methuen, 1972.
– "Poetry and Drama." In *Selected Prose of T.S. Eliot*, ed. Frank Kermode, 132–47. New York: Harcourt Brace Jovanovich; Farrar, Straus, and Giroux, 1975.

Esposito, Roberto. *Ideologie della neo avanguardia*. Naples: Liguori, 1976.
Fadini, Edoardo. "Ivrea la bella, vent'anni dopo." *Il castello di Elsinore*, I, no. 1 (1988): 97–106.
Fagiolo, Maurizio. "Con le marionette di Mario Ricci torna il teatro a passo ridotto." *L'Avanti* (6 March 1965).
Falzoni, Giordano. *Teatro da camera*. Milan: Rizzoli, 1965.
Fenollosa, Ernest. *The Chinese Character as a Medium for Poetry*. San Francisco: City Lights Publishers, 2001.
Fo, Dario. *Mistero buffo: Giullarata popolare*. Ed. Franca Rame. Turin: Einaudi, 1997.
Gadda, Carlo Emilio. *Quer pasticciaccio brutto de via Merulana*. Milan: Garzanti, 1987.
Gambaro, Fabio. *Invito a conoscere la Neoavanguardia*. Milan: Mursia, 1993.
Gasparini, Francesca. *Poesia come corpo-voce: Ipotesi teoriche e esempi novecenteschi (Yeats, Lorca, Artaud, Bene)*. Rome: Bulzoni, 2009.
Gazzola, Eugenio. *Parole sui muri. L'estate delle avanguardie a Fiumalbo*. Reggio Emilia: Diabasis, 2003.
Gazzola, Eugenio, ed. *"Malebolge. L'altra rivista delle avanguardie."* Reggio Emilia: Diabasis, 2011.
Giuliani, Alfredo. Introduction. In di Marco, Testa, and Perriera, eds, *La scuola di Palermo*,11–37 . Milan: Feltrinelli, 1963.
– "La scuola di Palermo." *Il Verri*, no. 7 (February 1963): 27–36.
– "Teatro nudo." *Marcatrè*, no. 3 (February 1964): 34–5.
– "Il teatro d'azione di Ken Dewey." In Balestrini, and Giuliani, eds, *Gruppo 63. La nuova letteratura. 34 scrittori. Palermo 1963*, 426–31. Milan: Feltrinelli, 1964.
– "La poesia a teatro." First in *Il Verri*, no. 25 (December 1967): 74–7. Repr. in Alfredo Giuliani, *Le droghe di Marsiglia*, 346–50. Milan: Adelphi, 1977.
– *Nostro padre Ubu*. Rome: Cooperativa scrittori, 1977. Repr. in *Tre recite su commissione*, 9-63.
– "Prefazione." In Alfred Jarry, *Ubu: Ubu Re, Ubu Cornuto, Ubu incatenato, Ubu sulla Collina*, trans. Bianca Candian, 7–10. Milan: Adelphi, 1977.
– *L'ultimo colloquio dell'Agrimensore K*. First in *Il Verri*, no. 9 (1978). Repr. in *Tre recite su commissione*, 81–90.
– *Povera Juliet*. In *Versi e nonversi*, 61–7. Milan: Feltrinelli, 1986.
– "Un dibattito mai avvenuto: Nerone e Seneca." In *Tre recite su commissione* , 65–79.
– *Tre recite su commissione*. Bergamo: Pierluigi Lubrina Editore, 1990.
– "Lettera a Elio." *L'immaginazione*, no. 190 (August–September 2002): 21.
– "Prefazione 1965." In Alfredo Giuliani, ed., *I Novissimi: Poesie per gli anni '60*, x–xix. Turin: Einaudi, 2003.
– "La forma del verso." In Alfredo Giuliani, ed., *I Novissimi: Poesie per gli anni '60*, 183–91. Turin: Einaudi, 2003.
Giuliani, Alfredo, and Elio Pagliarani. *Pelle d'Asino: Grottesco per musica*. Disegni di Gastone Novelli. Milan: Scheiwiller, 1964.

Goldmann, Lucien. *Method in the Sociology of Literature.* Oxford: Basil Blackwell, 1981.

Gozzi, Luigi. "Gruppo '63 a Palermo." *Marcatrè: Notiziario di cultura contemporanea*, no. 1 (November 1963): 13–16.

– "Lo spettacolo di Palermo." In Balestrini, and Giuliani, eds, *Gruppo 63: La Nuova Letteratura: 34 scrittori: Palermo ottobre 1963*, 417–25. Milan: Feltrinelli, 1964.

– "Di Jarry e del personaggio." *Il Verri*, no. 25 (December 1967): 14–33.

Grignani, Maria Antonietta. "Parola indigente e spazio claustrofobico: Sul teatro di Sanguineti." *Moderna*, 1, no. 9 (2007): 85–99.

Guglielmi, Angelo, and Elio Pagliarani. Introduction to *Manuale di poesia sperimentale*, 5–29. Milan: Mursia, 1966.

Guglielmi, Guido. "In forma di recitativo." *L'immaginazione*, no. 190 (August–September 2002): 23.

Heine, Heinrich. *Doktor Faust: A Dance Poem.* Trans. Basil Ashmore. Intro. J.C. Trewin. London and New York: Peter Nevill, 1952.

Jacobbi, Ruggero. "L'altra faccia della luna." *Sipario*, no. 183 (July 1961): 18.

Jarry, Alfred. *Œuvres complètes d'Alfred Jarry.* Lausanne: Éditions du livre, Monte-Carlo et Henri Kaeser, 1948.

– *The Ubu Plays.* Trans., ed., and intro. Simon Watson Taylor. New York: Grove Weidenfeld, 1968.

– *Ubu: Ubu Re, Ubu Cornuto, Ubu incatenato, Ubu sulla Collina.* Trans. Bianca Candian. Milan: Adelphi, 1977.

– *Exploits & Opinions of Dr. Faustroll, Pataphysician.* Ed. and trans. Simon Watson Taylor. Boston: Exact Change, 1996.

Klieger Stillman, Linda. *Alfred Jarry.* Boston: Twayne Publishers, 1983.

Le Goff, Jacques. *Le Moyen Âge et l'argent.* Paris: Perrin, 2010. English edition: *Money and the Middle Ages.* Malden: Polity Press, 2012; Italian edition: *Lo sterco del diavolo: Il denaro nel Medioevo.* Bari: Laterza, 2012.

Leigh, Elisabeth. "Il 'Teatro della crudeltà' da Artaud a Peter Brook." *Sipario*, no. 215 (March 1964): 2–16.

Lorenzini, Niva. "Corporalità e crudeltà nella poesia degli anni sessanta." In John Butcher and Mario Moroni, eds, *From Eugenio Montale to Amelia Rosselli. Italian Poetry in the Sixties and Seventies*, 1–11. Leicester: Troubador, 2004.

– *Sanguineti e il teatro della scrittura. La pratica del travestimento da Dante a Dürer.* Milan: Franco Angeli, 2011.

Luperini, Romano, et al. "'Officina' e il neosperimentalismo di Pasolini; 'Il Menabò' di Vittorini e Calvino e la discussione su letteratura e industria." In *La scrittura e l'interpretazione*, 1003–6. Palermo: Palumbo, 1999.

Luti, Giorgio, and Caterina Verbaro. *Dal Neorealismo alla Neoavanguardia (1945–1969).* Florence: Le Lettere, 1995.

Luzi, Mario. *Nel magma.* Milan: Garzanti, 1966.

Manganelli, Giorgio. *Tragedie da leggere.* Milan: Bompiani, 2008.
Mango, Achille. "La maschera e il volto." *Mondo Nuovo* (20 January 1966): 37.
Mango, Lorenzo. "L'invenzione del nuovo." In Visone, *La nascita del nuovo teatro in Italia*, 9–18.
Margiotta, Salvatore. *Il nuovo teatro in Italia: 1968–1975.* Pisa: Titivillus, 2013.
Marin, Louis. *On Representation.* Stanford, CA: Stanford University Press, 2001.
Martines, Lauro. *An Italian Renaissance Sextet: Six Tales in Historical Context.* New York: Marsilio Publishers, 1994.
Molinari, Cesare. *Teatro e antiteatro dal dopoguerra a oggi.* Rome, Bari: Laterza, 2007.
Montale, Eugenio. *Ossi di seppia.* Milan: Mondadori, 1948.
Moroni, Mario. "The Linguistic Gesture: Edoardo Sanguineti's Theatre." In Chirumbolo and Picchione, eds, *Edoardo Sanguineti: Literature, Ideology and the Avant-Garde*, 158–68. London: Legenda, 2013.
Muzzioli, Francesco. *Teoria e critica della letteratura nelle avanguardie italiane degli anni sessanta.* Rome: Istituto della Enciclopedia Italiana fondata da Giovanni Treccani, 1982.
– "Montaggio e straniamento: La modernità radicale di Elio Pagliarani." *L'illuminista*, nos 8–9 (2003): 83–102.
– *Il Gruppo '63: Istruzioni per la lettura.* Rome: Odradek, 2013.
Olson, Charles. "Il verso proiettivo." Trans. Aldo Tagliaferri. *Il Verri*, no. 1 (February 1961): 9–23.
– *Human Universe and Other Essays.* San Francisco: The Auerhahn Society, 1965.
– "Notes on Language and Theater." In Olson, *Human Universe and Other Essays*, 73–8.
– "Projective Verse." In Olson, *Human Universe and Other Essays*, 51–62.
Ong, Walter J. *Orality and Literacy: Technologizing of the Word.* London and New York: Routledge, 2002.
Ottai, Antonella, ed. *Pasolini Teatro Cinema. Biblioteca Teatrale*, nos 35–6 (July–December 1995).
Ottieri, Silvana. "Colazione con Judith Malina." *Sipario*, no. 183 (July 1961): 21.
Ottonieri, Tommaso. "Il romanzo del *focus*." *L'illuminista*, VII, nos 20–1 (September/December 2007): 167–71.
Pagliarani, Elio. "Sintassi e generi." First in *Nuova Corrente*, no. 16 (1959). Repr. in the anthology *Novissimi* (1960); and in Pagliarani, *Tutte le poesie (1946–2005)*, ed. Andrea Cortellessa, 459–60.
– "Col semaforo rosso." In *Terzo programma: Quaderni trimestrali*, 374–82. Rome: ERI, 1965.
– "Per una definizione di avanguardia." First in *Nuova Corrente*, no. 37 (1966). Repr. in Barilli and Guglielmi, eds, *Gruppo 63: Critica e teoria*, 312–17, Milan:

Feltrinelli, 1976. 2nd repr. Turin: Testo & Immagine, 2003. 3rd repr. in Balestrini, Giuliani, Barilli, and Guglielmi, eds, *Gruppo 63: L'antologia – Critica e teoria*, 875–81, Milan: Bompiani, 2013.
– "Intervento al convegno del Gruppo 63." In Balestrini, ed., *Gruppo 63. Il romanzo sperimentale. Palermo 1965*, 104–15. Milan: Feltrinelli, 1966.
– "Dell'eroe linguistico." *Nuova Corrente*, nos 39–40 (December 1966): 281–4.
– "Artaud e la contestazione fisica del Living Theatre." *Quindici*, no. 1 (1967): 87–92.
– "Funzione del pubblico e mezze ciliege." *Quindici*, no. 5 (15 October–15 November 1967): 4.
– "Dittico della merce: II. Certificato di sopravvivenza." *Lezione di fisica e Fecaloro*, 59–62. Milan: Feltrinelli, 1968.
– "Rafael Alberti alla ribalta." *Paese Sera*, XIX, no. 85 (27 March 1968). Repr. as "La poesia in teatro," in *Il fiato dello spettatore e altri scritti sul teatro (1966–1984)*, ed., Marucci, 211–13.
– "Le faccende italiane del teatro." First in *Quindici*, no. 13 (November 1968). Repr. in *Il fiato dello spettatore e altri scritti sul teatro (1966–1984)*, ed. Marucci, 203–7.
– "Aspettava soltanto che lo mettessero in scena." First in *Sipario*, no. 299 (March–April 1971). Repr. in *Il fiato dello spettatore e altri scritti sul teatro (1966–1984)*, ed. Marucci, 207–8.
– *Il fiato dello spettatore*. Padua: Marsilio, 1972.
– "Teatro come verifica." In Pagliarani, *Il fiato dello spettatore*, 9–32.
– "Un'attrice in tutù racconta Ripellino." First in *Paese Sera*, XXX, no. 144 (2 June 1979). Repr. as "Poesia in pubblico," in *Il fiato dello spettatore e altri scritti sul teatro (1966–1984)*, ed. Marucci, 318–19..
– *Poesie da recita*. Rome: Bulzoni, 1985.
– "La bestia di porpora o poema di Alessandro." First in *L'Illuminista: Rivista di cultura contemporanea*, 2–3, no. 1 (2000). Repr. in Pagliarani, *Tutto il teatro*, ed. Rizzo, 205–36.
– "A proposito del mio Blok." *L'Illuminista*, nos. 4–5 (anno II, 2001): 73–6.
– *Tutte le poesie (1946–2005)*. Ed. Andrea Cortellessa. Milan: Garzanti, 2006.
– "Cronistoria minima." In Pagliarani, *Tutte le poesie*, ed. Cortellessa, 464–70.
– *The Girl Carla and Other Poems*. Ed. and trans. Patrick Rumble. New York: Agincourt, 2009.
– *Pro-memoria a Liarosa*. Venice: Marsilio, 2011.
– "Il Faust di Copenaghen." In Pagliarani, *Tutto il teatro*, ed. Rizzo, 129–95.
– "La bella addormentata nel bosco." In Pagliarani, *Tutto il teatro*, ed. Rizzo, 101–27
– *Tutto il teatro*. Ed. Gianluca Rizzo. Venice: Marsilio, 2013.
– *Il fiato dello spettatore e altri scritti sul teatro (1966–1984)*. Ed. Marianna Marrucci. Rome: L'Orma, 2017.

Pandolfi, Vito. "Off-Broadway in Italia." *Il Dramma*, no. 298 (July 1961): 56–9.
– "Il Gruppo '63 e la scena." *Il punto* (26 December 1964).
Parlangeli, Oronzo. *La nuova questione della lingua*. Florence: Paideia, 1971.
Pascutti, Luigi. "Si affacciano alla 'Ringhiera' importanti attori di punta." *Telesera* (11 January 1967).
Pasolini, Pier Paolo. *Le ceneri di Gramsci*. Milan: Garzanti, 1957.
– "La fine dell'avanguardia (appunti per una frase di Goldmann, per due versi di un testo d'avanguardia, e per un'intervista di Barthes)." First in *Nuovi Argomenti*, n.s., nos 3–4 (July–December 1966). Repr. in Pier Paolo Pasolini, *Empirismo eretico. Saggi sulla letteratura e sull'arte*, Vol. I: 1405–28. Milan: Mondadori, 1999.
– *Teatro*. Ed. Walter Siti. Milan: Mondadori, 2001.
Pecori, Franco. "L''anima gemella' del superuomo è il neutrino e non Margherita. Elio Pagliarani ci racconta il suo *Faust di Copenaghen*." First in *Paese Sera* (Thursday, 31 May 1984). Repr. in Pagliarani, *Tutto il teatro*, ed. Rizzo, 134–6. Venice: Marsilio, 2013.
Pedullà, Walter. "Elio Pagliarani." In Nino Borsellino and Walter Pedullà, eds, *Storia generale della letteratura italiana*, vol. XII, *Sperimentalismo e tradizione del nuovo*, 182–99. Milan: Federico Motta, 1999.
– "Le sentenze finali di Elio Pagliarani." *L'Illuminista*, VII, nos 20–1 (September/December 2007): 173–86.
Perrault, Charles. *Peau d'Âne*. In *Œuvres choisies de Charles Perrault*, ed. Collin de Plancy, 175–94. Paris: Peytieux, 1826.
Perrelli, Franco. *I maestri della ricerca teatrale: Il Living, Grotowski, Barba e Brook*. Rome, Bari: Laterza, 2007.
Perrini, Alberto. "Non abbiamo sbagliato aspettando Quartucci." *Lo Specchio* (22 August 1963): 30.
Pestalozza, Luigi. "Intervista a Sanguineti." In Sanguineti, *Per Musica*, ed. Pestalozza, 9–24. Milan and Modena: Ricordi-Mucchi, 1993.
Petrella, Angelo. "Avanguardia, postmoderno e allegoria: Teoria e poesia nell'esperienza del Gruppo '93." PhD diss., Università La Sapienza di Roma, 2002–3. Accessed 1 June 2018: http://www.cepollaro.it/poesiaitaliana/PetrelAvanTes.pdf.
Petrella, Angelo, ed. *Gruppo 93: L'antologia poetica*. Civitella in Val di Chiana: Zona, 2010.
Pianigiani, Guglielmo. "Ong, l'oralità e la poesia dei giovani." *Allegoria*, no. 15 (1993): 107–14.
Picchione, John. *Introduzione a Antonio Porta*. Bari: Laterza, 1995.
– *The New Avant-Garde in Italy: Theoretical Debate and Poetic Practices*. Toronto: University of Toronto Press, 2004.
– "Poetry and the Abject: The Case of the Italian New Avant-Garde." In Leslie Boldt-Irons, Corrado Federici, and Ernesto Virgulti, eds, *Beauty and the*

Abject. Interdisciplinary Perspectives, 267–80. New York and Oxford: Peter Lang, 2007.
– "The Poetry of the *Neoavanguardia* and the Materiality of Language." In Chirumbolo, Moroni, and Somigli, eds, *Neoavanguardia: Italian Experimental Literature and Arts in the 1960s*, 149–70. Toronto: University of Toronto Press, 2010.
Poggioli, Renato. *The Theory of the Avant-garde.* Cambridge, MA, and London: The Belknap Press of Harvard University Press, 1968.
Policastro, Gilda. *Sanguineti.* Palermo: Palumbo, 2009.
Porro, Sergio. "Il poeta Antonio Porta e il teatro artigiano." *Canturium*, no. 25 (July 2010): 42–9.
Porta, Antonio. "Stark." *Grammatica*, no. 2 (January 1967): 15–22.
– "Tre ipotesi contro la normalizzazione dello scrittore." *Quindici*, no. 1 (1 June 1967): 2.
– "Poche osservazioni intorno allo spazio della poesia." *Il Verri*, no. 25 (December 1967): 82–3.
– "Si tratta di larve." *Il Caffè*, no. 3 (June 1968): 63–72.
– *Nel fare poesia.* Florence: Sansoni, 1985.
– "Prefazione." In Tito Maccio Plauto, ed., *La stangata persiana*, 6–14. Milan: Corpo 10, 1985.
– *Tutte le poesie (1956–1989).* Ed. Niva Lorenzini. Milan: Garzanti, 2009.
– *Piercing the Page. Selected Poems (1958–1989).* Ed. Gian Maria Annovi. Los Angeles: Otis Books/Seismicity Editions, 2011.
Pound, Ezra. *The ABC of Reading.* London, Boston: Faber and Faber, 1991.
Puppa, Paolo. *Teatro e spettacolo nel secondo Novecento.* Rome, Bari: Laterza, 1990.
Quadri, Franco. "Domanda al cittadino italiano." *Sipario*, no. 199 (November 1962): 1–6.
– *Il rito perduto: Luca Ronconi.* Turin: Einaudi, 1973.
– "Colloquio con Eugenio Barba." In Franco Quadri, ed., *Il teatro degli anni Settanta: Invenzione di un teatro diverso*, 70–82. Turin: Einaudi, 1984.
Quadri, Franco, ed. *Il teatro del regime.* Milan: Cremonese, 1976.
– *L'avanguardia teatrale in Italia: Materiali (1960–1976).* Turin: Einaudi, 1977.
Quartucci, Carlo. "Sette anni di esperienze." In Quadri, ed., *L'avanguardia teatrale in Italia: Materiali (1960–1976)*, 151–64. Turin: Einaudi, 1977.
Quartucci, Carlo, and Giuliano Scabia. "Per un'avanguardia italiana." *Sipario*, no. 235 (1965): 11–12.
Ricci, Mario. "Teatro-Rito e Teatro-Gioco." In Bartolucci, ed., *La scrittura scenica*, 219–24. Rome: Marcalibri/Lerici Editore, 1968.
– "Collage per una automitobiografia." Ed. Germano Celant. In Quadri, ed., *L'avanguardia teatrale in Italia: Materiali (1960–1976)*, 212–21. Turin: Einaudi, 1977.
– "L'uso del cinema." In Quadri, ed., *L'avanguardia teatrale in Italia: Materiali (1960–1976)*, 237–9. Turin: Einaudi, 1977.

– "Intervista a cura di Lorenzo Mango." In *Ricerca sul Convegno per un Nuovo Teatro, Ivrea–Torino 9–12 giugno 1967*. A cura dell'Associazione Itàca di Milano (20 September 1986). Quoted in Visone, *La nascita del nuovo teatro in Italia*, 239.

– "Il Teatro-Immagine. Spettacoli 1962–1973." Accessed 31 May 2018: www.nuovoteatromadeinitaly.com/mario-ricci/.

Rizzo, Gianluca. "Pasolini, Fo, and the Issue of Language." *L'anello che non tiene. Journal of Modern Italian Literature*, 18–19, nos 1–2 (Spring–Fall 2006–7): 95–109.

– "'*Proviamo ancora col corpo*.'" In Federica Santini and Giovanna Summerfield, eds, *The Politics of Poetics: Poetry and Social Activism in Early-Modern through Contemporary Italy*, 93–120. Newcastle upon Tyne: Cambridge Scholars Publishing, 2013.

– "Il guaio dell'asino morto è che ci vuole l'interpretazione. Giuliani, Pagliarani e le riscritture di Perrault." *Autografo*, no. 50 (anno XXI, 2013): 141–63.

– "La verifica della poesia: Il teatro secondo I Novissimi, Pagliarani (e T.S. Eliot)." *Autografo*, no. 50 (anno XXI, 2013): 133–7.

– "Se si vuole sapere se A è causa dell'effetto B: Scienza e realismo nelle sperimentazioni poetiche della neo-avanguardia." *Studi Novecenteschi*, XLIV, no. 93 (2017): 79–101.

– "Il Faust della Neoavanguardia: Celli, Pagliarani e le riscritture del Goethe." In Rizzo, ed., *On the Fringe of the Neoavantgarde*, 189–217.

Rizzo, Gianluca, ed. *On the Fringe of the Neoavantgarde / Ai confini della neoavanguardia. Proceedings of the Conference / Atti del congresso, Los Angeles, 17–19 Ottobre 2013*. New York: Agincourt Press, 2017.

Rusconi, Marisa. "Gli scrittori e il teatro." *Sipario*, no. 229 (May 1965): 2–14.

Sanguineti, Edoardo. *Laborintus*. Varese: Editori Magenta, 1956.

– *Opus metricum*. Milan: Rusconi e Paolazzi, 1960.

– *Triperuno*. Milan: Feltrinelli, 1964.

– "Per una letteratura della crudeltà." First in *Quindici*, no. 1 (1967). Repr. in Edoardo Sanguineti, *Ideologia e linguaggio*, Milan: Feltrinelli, 1970. And repr. in Balestrini, Giuliani, Barilli, and Guglielmi, eds, *Gruppo 63. L'antologia. Critica e teoria*, 895–8, Milan: Bompiani, 2013.

– *Teatro*. Milan: Feltrinelli, 1969.

– *Teatro. K, Passaggio, Traumdeutung, Protocolli*. Milan: Feltrinelli, 1969.

– "Sopra l'avanguardia." In *Ideologia e linguaggio*, 63–81. Milan: Feltrinelli, 1970.

– *Faust. Un travestimento*. Genoa: Costa and Nolan, 1985.

– *Per Musica*. Ed. Luigi Pestalozza. Milan and Modena: Ricordi-Mucchi, 1993.

Santini, Federica. *Io era una bella figura una volta: Viaggio nella poesia di ricerca del secondo Novecento*. Piacenza: Scritture, 2013.

Scabia, Giuliano. *All'improvviso & Zip*. Turin: Einaudi, 1967.

– "Nello spazio del teatro." *Teatro*, II, no. 2 (1967–8): 33–3
– "Nuovo spazio, nuovo teatro, nuova cultura." *Sipario*, no. 291 (July 1970): 72–5.
– "Appunti per una discussione sul 'Teatro nello spazio degli scontri.'" In Scabia, *Teatro nello spazio degli scontri*, XI–XXIII.
– *Teatro nello spazio degli scontri*. Rome: Bulzoni, 1973.
– *Una esperienza di animazione in un ospedale psichiatrico*. Turin: Einaudi, 1976.
– *Nane Oca*. Turin: Einaudi, 1992.
– "Genesi / La creazione. Schema vuoto per l'Odin Teatret di Hostelboro (due stesure)." *Culture Teatrali*, no. 12 (Spring 2005): 75–86.
– *Il tremito: Che cos'è la poesia?* Casagrande: Bellinzona, 2006.
Schacherl, Bruno. "Il Berliner Ensemble finalmente a Venezia." In Schacherl, *Il critico errante*, 96–01.
– *Il critico errante*. Florence: Le lettere, 2005.
Serafini, Carlo. "La parola tornerà ai poeti … 'La Bestia di Porpora o Poema di Alessandro.'" *L'illuminista*, nos 20–1 (September–December 2007): 209–18.
Sereni, Vittorio. *Gli strumenti umani*. Turin: Einaudi, 1965.
Sinisi, Silvana. *Dalla parte dell'occhio: Esperienze teatrali in Italia 1972–1982*. Rome: Edizioni Kappa, 1983.
Spatola, Adriano. Review of Elio Pagliarani's *Lezione di fisica*. *Il Verri*, no. 20 (February 1966): 98–9.
– *Verso la poesia totale*. Turin: Paravia, 1978. Translated into English as *Toward Total Poetry*. Trans. Brendan W. Hennessey and Guy Bennett. Afterword Guy Bennett. Los Angeles: Otis Books/Seismicity Editions, 2008.
Squarzina, Luigi. "Di Planchon, di Dort, di altri, di noi altri." *Sipario*, no. 217 (May 1964): 10.
Stefanelli, Stefania, ed. *Il Gruppo 70 tra parola e immagine*. Florence: Società editrice fiorentina, 2004.
Stomeo, Anna. *Intrecci: Teatro–Educazione–New Media*. Melpignano: Amaltea, 2006.
Tagliaferri, Aldo. "La superstizione della crudeltà." First in *Quindici*, no. 8 (15 February–15 March 1968): 3. Repr. in Balestrini, Giuliani, Barilli, and Guglielmi, eds, *Gruppo 63. L'antologia. Critica e teoria*, 899–904. Milan: Bompiani, 2013.
Terron, Carlo. "Il Galileo di Brecht è diventato capitalista." *Corriere Lombardo* (24 April 1963). Available on the *Piccolo* website. Accessed 31 May 2018: http://archivio.piccoloteatro.org/eurolab/index.php?tipo=9&ID=7295&imm=1&contatore=2&real=0.
Testa, Enrico. *Dopo la lirica. Poeti italiani 1960–2000*. Turin: Einaudi, 2005.
Tian, Renzo. "Concerto Grosso per Brugh." *Il Messaggero* (12 January 1967).
Valentini, Valentina. "Il dibattito sul Nuovo Teatro in Italia." In Giuseppe Bartolucci, *Testi Critici: 1964–1987*, ed. Valentini, 9–39 Rome: Bulzoni, 2007.
– "La vocazione teatrale di Pierpaolo Pasolini." In Alessandro Canadé, ed., *Corpus Pasolini*, 207–39. Cosenza: Pellegrini, 2008.

– *Worlds, Bodies, Matters: Theatre of the Late Twentieth Century.* Trans. Thomas Haskell Simpson. Aberystwyth: Performance Research Books, 2014.
– *Nuovo Teatro Made in Italy: 1963–2013.* Rome: Bulzoni, 2015.
– *New Theatre in Italy: 1963–2013.* Trans. T. Haskell Simpson. London and New York: Routledge, 2018.

Valentino, Mimma. *Il nuovo teatro in Italia: 1976–1985.* Pisa: Titivillus, 2015.

Vazzoller, Franco. "La scena, il corpo, il travestimento. Conversazione con Edoardo Sanguineti." In Sanguineti, *Per Musica*, ed. Pestalozza, 183–211. Milan and Modena: Ricordi-Mucchi, 1993.

Venturo, Mariafrancesca. *Parola e travestimento nella poetica teatrale di Edoardo Sanguineti.* Rome: Fermenti, 2007.

Vetri, Lucio. *Letteratura e caos: Poetiche della "neo-avanguardia" italiana degli anni sessanta.* Mantua: Edizioni del Verri, 1984.

Vice. "Prima del falò." *L'Unità* (27 September 1966).

Visone, Daniela. *La nascita del nuovo teatro in Italia: 1959–1967.* Pisa: Titivillus, 2010.

Weber, Luigi. *Usando gli utensili di utopia: Traduzione, parodia e riscrittura in Edoardo Sanguineti.* Bologna: Gedit, 2004.

Wheeler, J.A., and W.H. Zurek, eds. *Quantum Theory and Measurement.* Princeton, NJ: Princeton University Press, 1983.

Zumthor, Paul. *La presenza della voce: Introduzione alla poesia orale.* Bologna: Società editrice il Mulino, 1984.

Index

www.ingramcontent.com/pod-product-compliance
Lightning Source LLC
LaVergne TN
LVHW090145080826
844660LV00013B/678/J
* 9 7 8 1 4 8 7 5 0 6 6 6 7 *